PRINCIPLES AND PRACTICE OF MANAGEMENT AND BUSINESS COMMUNICATION

Written in accordance with the New Syllabus of Three-year BCom (General) and BCom (Honours) course of Calcutta University introduced from the academic session 2010-11

PRINCIPLES AND PRACTICE OF MANAGEMENT AND BUSINESS COMMUNICATION

For three year BCom (General and Honours) students

Dr Tapan Kumar Pan

Ex-Reader, Commerce Department and
Ex-Teacher-in-Charge, Nabagram Hiralal Paul College
Nabagram, Hooghly
Ex-Part-time Lecturer, Commerce Department
Khidirpur College, Kolkata
S. N. Girls' College, Bhadrakali, Hooghly, Kharagpur College
Kharagpur, Midnapore

Madan Mohan Karmakar

Associate Professor, Commerce Department
Nabagram Hiralal Paul College, Nabagram, Hooghly
Guest Lecturer, Department of Business Administration
Burdwan Raj College
Ex-Part-time Lecturer, Commerce Department
Burdwan Raj College (Evening Unit)

New Central Book Agency (P) Ltd

LONDON

HYDERABAD ERNAKULAM BHUBANESWAR

DELHI KOLKATA PUNE GUWAHATI

NCBA

REGD OFFICE

8/1 Chintamoni Das Lane, Kolkata 700 009, India
ncbapvtltd@eth.net

OVERSEAS

NCBA (UK) Ltd, 149 Park Avenue North, Northampton, NN3 2HY, UK
ncbauk@yahoo.com

EXPORT

NCBA Exports Pvt. Ltd, 212 Shahpur Jat, New Delhi 110 049
ncbaexports@ncbaindia.com

BRANCHES

208B Peacock Lane, Shahpur Jat
New Delhi 110 049
ncbadel@ncbapvtltd.com

Shop Nos. 3 & 4, Vinayak Towers
681/B Budhwar Peth, Appa Balwant Chowk
Pune 411 002
ncbapune@ncbapvtltd.com

Shop No. 15, Bharati Towers, Ground Floor
Forest Park, **Bhubaneswar** 751 001
ncbabub@ncbapvtltd.com

House No. 3-1-315, 1st Floor
Nimboliadda, Kachiguda, **Hyderabad** 500 027
ncbahydb@ncbapvtltd.com

GSS Shopping Complex, 1st Floor
Opposite College Post Office, Convent Road
Ernakulam 682 035
ncbaernk@ncbapvtltd.com

Radhamayee Complex (Second Floor)
Opp. SBI, Panbazar, Jaswanta Road
Guwahati 781 001
ncbaguwahati@ncbapvtltd.com

PRINCIPLES AND PRACTICE OF MANAGEMENT
AND BUSINESS COMMUNICATION • Tapan Kumar Pan, Madan Mohan Karmakar

First Published: July 2012

PUBLISHER & TYPESETTER
New Central Book Agency (P) Ltd
8/1 Chintamoni Das Lane, Kolkata 700 009

PRINTER
New Central Book Agency (P) Ltd
Web-Offset Division, Dhulagarh, Sankrail, Howrah

COVER DESIGNER
Soumen Paul

COVER PRINTER
Liba Graphics, Kolkata

PROOF CHECKING
Subas Maitra

PROJECT TEAM
Joydeep Ghosh, Pradyot Majumder, Pradip Baidya, Piyasa Dutta, and Prabhat Jas

ISBN 978 81 7381 783 0

Price ₹ 215.00

Main Characteristics of the Book

- Written strictly in accordance with the New Syllabus of the Calcutta University.
- Use of easy, simple and clear language.
- Introduction of primary idea about the subject-matter at the beginning of each chapter.
- Description with the help of Diagram wherever needed.
- Discussion based on the questions of thirty years of BCom Examination of the Calcutta University.
- Provision for Essay-type and Short Answer-type Questions with Answer-hints in the Exercise.
- Inclusion of Model Questions of the New Syllabus.
- Addition of answers of the Important Short Questions.
- New and exceptional composition compared to the existing Text-books.

CONTENTS

MODULE I

PRINCIPLES AND PRACTICE OF MANAGEMENT

MODULE II

BUSINESS COMMUNICATION

PREFACE

In view of the introduction of three year degree course in the universities of West Bengal, Calcutta University has revised its syllabus on BCom (General and Honours) Course from the academic session 2010-2011. In the New Syllabus the subject **'Principles and Practice of Management and Business Communication'** (Paper 1.4) has been introduced. We wrote two books on the subject, 'Entrepreneurship Development and Business Communication' and 'Business Management' in 2003 in Bengali for the Bengali-medium students. These books were widely appreciated by the teachers and students of various colleges. We have been encouraged by the tremendous response we received. Some teachers of English medium colleges requested us to write an English version of these two books for the benefit of English-medium students. It is in response to their request that the present book on 'Principles and Practice of Management and Business Communication' has been written. It should be noted that this book is not a mere translation of the Bengali book. Rather, it is a new book based on our Bengali books.

The main purpose of introducing the subject 'Principles and Practice of Management and Business Communication' is to help the students acquire the necessary knowledge and skill so that they can set up their own ventures and can become self-employed. Instead of looking for government jobs, the commerce graduates can take up the profession of becoming 'Managers' or 'Managing Directors' of business enterprises. For this, they should know the various principles, procedures and techniques of management and various aspects of communication. They should also know how to manage an enterprise. All these ideas have been introduced in this subject. Hence the study of this subject will be socially useful.

The main feature of this book is that it has been written strictly according to the New Syllabus of Calcutta University. All the topics included in the syllabus have been covered in the book. It has been written in a simple language and in a lucid manner. Exercises have been given at the end of each chapter. Exercises include long as well as short answer type of questions. The answers to some important short questions have been given in the Appendix for the benefit of the students.

The book is meant primarily for the students. The authors will feel that their labours are amply rewarded if the book becomes really useful to the students. Any suggestion for improvement of this book will be gratefully acknowledged. In this connection we like to thank Mr. Amitabha Sen and the employees of New Central Book Agency (P) Ltd, Kolkata, for their cooperation in bringing out the book quickly.

14 April 2012

Dr. Tapan Kumar Pan
259 Joy Krishna Street
Uttarpara, Hooghly
Madan Mohan Karmakar
81 Meghnad Saha Pally
Krishnapur Road, Burdwan

SYLLABUS

Common Paper for BCom Honours and General

Paper 1.4 Chg : PRINCIPLES AND PRACTICE OF MANAGEMENT AND BUSINESS COMMUNICATION

Module I

PRINCIPLES AND PRACTICE OF MANAGEMENT

Marks 50

Unit 1. Introduction to Management : Management—definition; importance; functions; Nature—as profession; science and art; universality of management; Levels of management; managerial tasks and skills. [5 lectures/4 marks]

Unit 2. Different Schools of Management Thought : Classical School—contributions of Taylor and Fayol; Neo-classical School—Human Relations approach and Behavioural Science approach; Modern School—Systems approach and Contingency approach. [12 lectures/8 marks]

Unit 3. Planning : Concept, importance, types, steps, premises, barriers to effective planning and remedial measures; Strategic Planning—concept; Forecasting—concept, techniques. [12 lectures/8 marks]

Unit 4. Organizing : Concept, importance, principles, different organization models—Line and Staff, Functional; Departmentation—need, basis, principles; Delegation of Authority—elements, steps, barriers; Centralisation and Decentralisation of Authority; Span of Management—concept and determining factors. [10 lectures/8 marks]

Unit 5. Motivation : Concept, importance, contributions of McGregor, Maslow, and Herzberg. [8 lectures/8 marks]

Unit 6. Leadership : Concept, importance, types, leadership traits; Tannenbaum and Schmidt's Model and Blake and Mouton's Model. [8 lectures/8 marks]

Unit 7. Co-ordination : Concept, significance, principles, techniques. [2 lectures/2 marks]

Unit 8. Control : Concept, steps, tools. [4 lectures/4 marks]

Module II

BUSINESS COMMUNICATION

Marks 50

Unit 1. Introduction—Definition, objectives, importance, elements, process, forms, models; Levels of analysis of business communication; Principles of effective communication, barriers to communication and remedial measures, role of communication in conflict resolution. [10 lectures/10 marks]

Unit 2. Types of Communication—Formal and informal communication; Grapevine; Characteristics of Corporate Communication; Communication network. [10 lectures/10 marks]

Unit 3. Tools of Communication—Emergence of communication technology; Modern forms of communication—Fax, E-mail, Video Conferencing. [10 lectures/10 marks]

Unit 4. Drafting—Notice, circular, resolution, minutes, report; CV writing, business letter writing—offer letter, quotation, status enquiry, confirmation, execution, refusal and cancellation of order, recommendation, credit collection, claim, bank loan. [20 lectures/20 marks]

DISTRIBUTION OF MARKS IN THE NEW SYLLABUS

Module I

Principles and Practice of Management

(50 Marks)

Group A :	2 Marks × 5 Questions (Out of 8 Questions)	= 10
Group B :	4 Marks × 4 Questions (Out of 6 Questions)	= 16
Group C :	8 Marks × 3 Questions (Out of 5 Questions)	= 24
Total :		50

Module II

Business Communication

(50 Marks)

Group A :	2 Marks × 5 Questions (Out of 8 Questions)	= 10
Group B :	4 Marks × 5 Questions (Out of 8 Questions)	= 20
Group C :	10 Marks × 2 Questions (Out of 3 Questions)	= 20
Total :		50

Module I

PRINCIPLES AND PRACTICE OF MANAGEMENT

CHAPTER

1

Introduction to Management

"The conventional definition of management is getting work done through people, but real management is developing people through work."
—Agha Hasan Abedi

TOPICS

Subject-matter of the Chapter : *Effective and efficient management is the key to success of any type of enterprise—trading or non-trading. The process of getting the works done by the working groups of employees engaged in an enterprise is called 'Management'. It becomes easily possible to achieve the goals of an enterprise, if this process is conducted in an effective way and with efficiency. In the business sector it is management that arranges for producing and supplying the necessary commodities and rendering essential services for the people of the society and creating employment opportunities for many persons. The economic, social and cultural development of any country depend on efficient management. Particularly, for the economic development of the developing and under-developed countries, the role of management is very important. Management is a universal process. Its basic principles and various theories are applicable to all kinds of enterprises. In the present chapter the concept, meaning, nature, objectives, functions, importance and levels of management will be discussed. Besides professional management, universality of management, role of a manager, managerial skills and the differences among organisation, administration and management etc. will also be described.*

1.1 Definition and Meaning of Management

Ordinarily, **'Management' is an activity for getting the objectives of any enterprise accomplished through the efforts of its personnel.** For getting the work of an enterprise completed through the efforts of its people in grouped activities, it becomes necessary to guide, direct and unify human efforts towards the fulfilment of certain common goals. Management represents that skill or activity which directs, regulates and integrates human efforts in the discharge of all operations required for running an enterprise. Strictly speaking, management is a functional concept and it is so comprehensive and covers so many aspects that it is very difficult to give an exact definition of management.

Management, being a new discipline, has drawn concepts and principles from economics, sociology, psychology, anthropology, history and other subjects. The result is that each group of writers and thinkers has treated management differently. For example, the economists consider management as one of the factors of production; the sociologists see it as a class or group of persons; while the practitioners of management regard it as a process. There are others to whom management is a technique of leadership or a means of co-ordination. Naturally, all these divergent groups view the nature and scope of management from their own angles. Taking all these points of view together, it is not so simple to define management in a precise and comprehensive way. Moreover, management is concerned with human beings whose behaviour is unpredictable.

However, to provide a background of the meaning of management, a few of its definitions as given by the renowned writers on the subject are stated below :

Henry Fayol, the famous French Management expert, defined 'Management' in a manner that gives us a better understanding of the nature of management. His definition runs as follows :

"To manage is to forecast and plan, to organise, to command, to co-ordinate and to control." This functional definition of management gives us an idea as to what a manager has to do.

F. W. Taylor, the Father of Scientific Management, defined 'Management' as an art of "knowing what you want men to do and then seeing that it is done in the best and cheapest way." This definition is productivity-oriented.

Joseph L. Massie, an eminent Management author, observed 'Management' as a "process by which a co-operative group directs action towards common goals."

Lawrence Appley, once the President of the American Management Association, gave a very acceptable definition—"Management is the accomplishment of results through the efforts of other people,"

Harold Koontz and Cyril O'Donnell defined 'Management' as the "creation and maintenance of an internal environment in an enterprise where individuals working together in groups can perform effectively and efficiently towards the attainment of group goals."

The American Society of Mechanical Engineers has stated "Management is an art and science of organising and directing human efforts applied to control the forces and to utilise the materials of nature for the benefit of man."

According to D. S. Kimball "Management embraces all duties and functions that pertain to the initiation of an enterprise, its financing, the establishment of major policies, the provision of all necessary equipment, outlining the general form of organisation under which the enterprise is to operate, and the selection of the principal officers."

In the light of the above discussion a comprehensive definition of 'Management' may be given as follows :

Management is the sum total of those activities which lay down plans, policies, procedures and programmes; secure men, money, materials and machinery required for the realisation of these purposes; put all of them into operation; co-ordinate various actions; supervise and check the performance of the men engaged for the execution of these desired operations and provide them material incentive and mental satisfaction. The concept of management is universal in the sense that it is concerned with the government of industrial and commercial enterprises and any other organisation.

1.2 Features of Management

Management is an executive function of getting things done through and with the help of other people according to the pre-arranged plans and policies. It covers a comprehensive and all-pervading field. In fact, the process of management is composed of various factors.

The features or characteristics of management include the following :

1. Organised Activities : Management is a process of organised activities. Without organised activities, groups of people cannot be involved in the performance of work. Where a group of people are involved in working towards a common objective, management comes into existence. The organised activities may take a variety of forms. But all organisations have one thing in common; they want to progress efficiently towards the achievement of their objectives through the co-ordinated efforts of people. This is done by management process.

2. Existence of Objectives : An objective or a set of objectives must exist towards which the organised group activities are directed. Without objectives, it becomes difficult to define the direction to which the organised group activities would lead. Management is necessary for the better accomplishment of operating work of any enterprise. The realisation of objectives is sought through the co-ordinated efforts of the people constituting an organisation.

3. Relationship with Resources : The essence of management lies in integration of various organisational resources to achieve common goals. Resources include men, money, materials and machines. All these resources are made available to those who manage. They apply knowledge, experience, principles etc. for getting deserved results. However, since people of operative level do the things by the use of various physical and other resources, it is more important for the managers to take care of integration of human resources. Thus management is concerned with the proper utilisation of human resources which, in turn, utilise other resources.

4. Co-existence of Superior-Subordinate Employees : Management involves working with people and getting organisational objectives achieved through them. For getting the work done by others, the managers must have a number of subordinates to assist them. The managers usually divide the work into groups and sections, and allocate them to the subordinates. Through the process of assignment and re-assignment of activities, the actual work is performed by the people at the operative level.

5. Productivity : Managerial work holds the key to greater productivity by way of utilising the rare faculties of human beings. But the contributions of material resources to productivity are insignificant. As material resources are subject to the laws of mechanics, they cannot have any greater output than the value of their input.

6. Decision Making : Managerial work involves mental efforts for decision-making at various levels while operating work calls for physical efforts on the part of non-managerial personnel. Decision-making basically involves selecting the most appropriate alternative out of the several. The quality of the alternative which a manager selects determines the organisation's performance, and the entire future of the organisation depends on the degree to which the right decisions are made by the managers. Therefore, the success or failure of the managers can be judged by the quality of decisions made by them.

7. Leadership : Another important feature of the management process is the exercise of leadership over the followers. Leadership consists in influencing, guiding and directing the behaviour of the subordinates towards certain objectives. If a manager is required to get things done through others in the exercise of the managerial functions, he must have the capacity and capability to win their trust and confidence, and to guide and direct them towards the accomplishment of organisational objectives.

8. Differences in Work : Management is composed of some basic functions like planning, organising, staffing, directing and controlling. The co-ordinated performance of these functions leads to the realisation of organisational objectives. But the contents of operating work vary from institution to institution. For a business institution, operating work is constituted by production, sale, purchase, financing, etc, whereas, for educational institutions or hospitals, operating work, is constituted in a different way.

9. Authority : Existence of a manager depends on the managerial authority. For performing the basic functions of management, plans are to be made, organisation is to be built up, personnel are to be appointed, directives are to be given and activities are to be controlled. For all these functions, receiving and application of administrative authority become necessary. If the manager has no authority, management becomes unworkable.

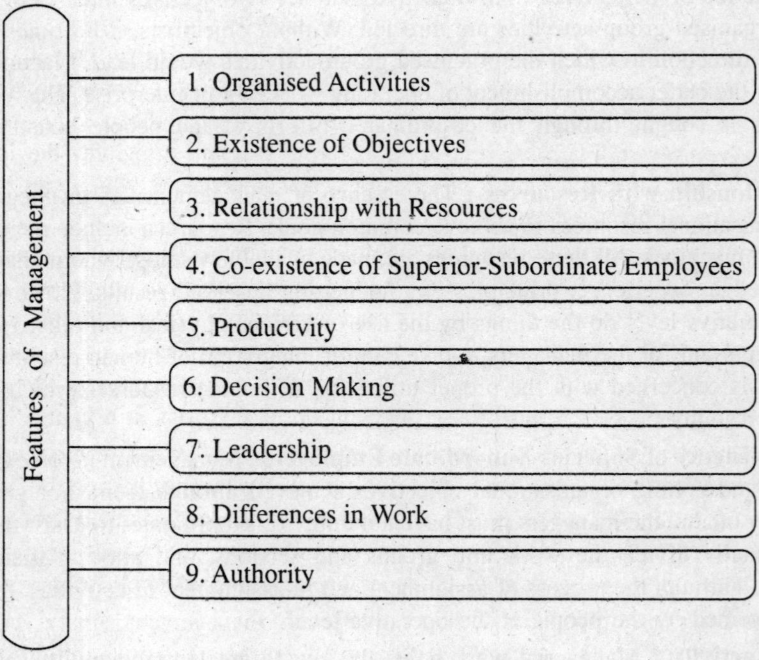

Fig. 1.1: Features of Management.

1.3 Nature of Management

The nature of management can be described as follows :

1. Work Process : Management consists of the basic and inter-related functions and activities which constitute a process known as 'Management Process'. It is the function of guiding, directing and unifying human efforts and activities for the accomplishment of the given tasks. It is, in other words, principally the task of planning, organising, directing, motivating, co-ordinating and controlling the efforts of others towards the attainment of specific objectives. Management mainly functions to utilise properly and effectively all the factors of production and its productive units for achieving the goal of an enterprise.

2. Co-ordination of Different Elements : The different elements essential for proper running of an enterprise are to be integrated. These elements are man-power, money, materials, machinery, methods, market and motivation. The managers co-ordinate these elements by scientific application of the principles of management, give life to the producing organisation and thus try to achieve the desired objectives.

3. Means of Accomplishing Objectives : Management links and puts together many things and many human faculties into one complete whole, creates an organisation with the allocation of authority, responsibility and exerts necessary leadership and control over the activities . It thus directs the active operations within the enterprise and combines the work of the employees with the available resources and equipment for the realisation of its pre-determined objectives.

4. Supervisory Activities : Management is responsible for accomplishment of work through the efforts of other people. So, there is a distinction between those who have to work to perform the assigned tasks and those who have to take steps to see that this other category works effectively and fulfils the objectives set for them. The former category consists of 'workers or non-managers', while the latter comprises 'managers' who have to guide, direct and co-ordinate the efforts of others towards certain specific objectives.

5. Multi-disciplinary : Management is basically multi-disciplinary. This implies that, although management has been developed as a separate discipline, it draws knowledge and concepts from various disciplines such as psychology, sociology, anthropology, economics, ecology, operation research, statistics, history, etc. Management integrates the ideas and concepts taken from these disciplines and presents newer concepts which can be put in practice for managing the organisations.

6. Harmonisation of Diversity : Various types of interested groups are found in the organisations. The owners of an organisation expect more profit, the employees claim for higher pay and bonus, the suppliers claim for ready settlement of dues, the buyers expect to get quality goods at a fair price, the surrounding society expects a usual contribution towards social development and the Government demands for more taxes, etc. The managers try to harmonise the expectations of these different interest groups in a planned way.

7. Universality : The universal character of management is evident from the fact that, its basic principles and techniques are applicable not only to business concerns, but also to non-business institutions like social, political, cultural, religious etc. situated in any country. In spite of differences in the activities of the organisations, the nature and pattern of management are similar. As such, managerial work has universal application.

8. Dynamism : One of the most significant features of management is that it is dynamic. The principles of management are flexible in nature and these are to be modified according to the needs and situation.

9. Continuity : Maintaining continuity is a fundamental nature of management. It continually goes on with the going of an organisation. So long business exists, the functions of management continues. Thus, it is the nature of management to go on performing the functions uninterruptedly.

10. Management as a Class : One of the important concepts of management is to regard it as a class. It signifies that the managers are given the full responsibility of management. **Peter Drucker** points out : manager manages the business, manages the

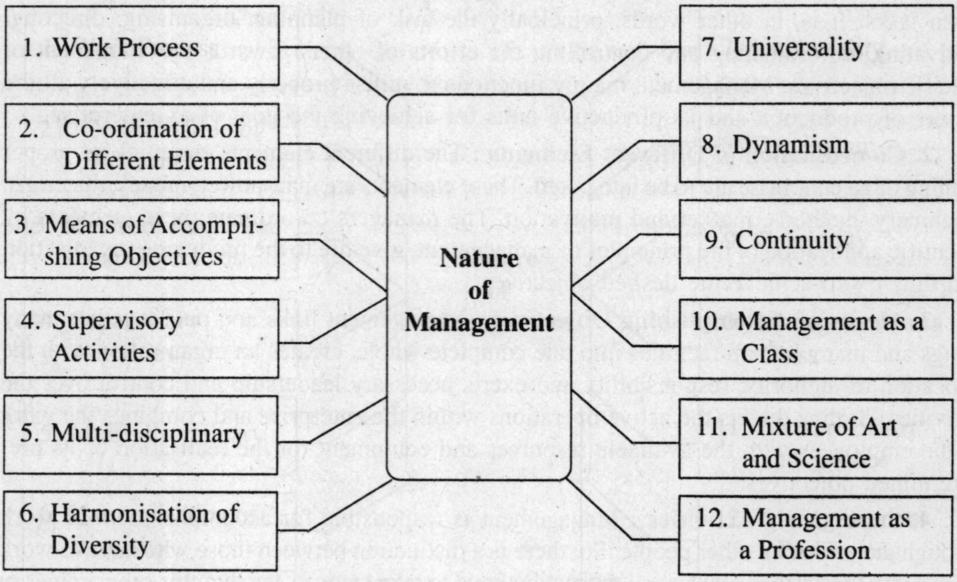

Fig. 1.2: Nature of Management.

managers, workers, and the work. In a big enterprise management is classified into three levels—top, middle, and lower levels of management. The responsibility and decision-making power are delegated step by step from the top to the middle, and from the middle to the lower level of management. These three levels are separated from the ordinary workers and they are called management authority.

11. Mixture of Art and Science : On the basis of modern outlook, management is considered to be a combination of art and science. Management is an 'art' since it is a process or method or knowledge or technique, which can be acquired by learning, which are applicable and applied to manage the affairs of an enterprise. Management is also a science as it is a particular knowledge guided by causes and effects, the basis of which is experiment or research, which are applicable to manage the affairs of all enterprises. It is obvious, then, that management is a mixture of art and science. Managers are management scientists and artists as well.

12. Management as a Profession : Management is regarded as a profession by many, although it does not possess all the essential features of a profession. Those who practice the art of management have to function as members of a profession.

1.4 Objectives of Management

The objectives of management may be classified into three categories as follows :

1. Organisational Objectives : The fundamental goals of any type of enterprise are survival and growth. It is management that acts as a tool for achieving these goals. In order to maintain the existence and for development of any enterprise the managers have to perform the following tasks.

(i) Ensuring maximum output with minimum costs;

(ii) Preventing the wastage and misuse of the natural, financial and human resources of the enterprise.

(iii) Optimum utilisation of the capital and giving certainty about the expected return on investment;

(iv) Arranging for progress and expansion of the enterprise; and

(v) Increasing goodwill and prosperity of the enterprise.

2. Individual Objectives : The owners and the employees have separate individual objectives. It is the responsibility of the managers to make balance between the objectives of these two groups. For this purpose, the managers should :

(i) Ensure sufficient amount of dividend for the owners of the enterprise;

(ii) Arrange for adequate remuneration of the employees and security of their jobs;

(iii) Create good work environment; and

(iv) Arrange for proper training for the development of the employees.

3. Social Objectives : The business enterprises are important part of the society and these are established for meeting the social needs. In order to fulfil the common goals of the enterprise and individual objectives of the owners and employees, the managers have to perform the following social functions :

(i) To supply goods and render services of proper quality to the customers at fair price;

(ii) To pay the Government tax and dues to the local authority in right time;

(iii) To arrange for preservation of natural resources and environment;

(iv) To establish and maintain good relationship with the competitors and other concerned parties or institutions;

(v) To maintain and increase the ethical values of the managers themselves in thier day to day work.

1.5 Importance of Management

Management occupies a prominent position in every organisation. In every enterprise and in every work where joint effort is required, management is necessary :

1. Providing Vitality to Organisation : Just as the mind directs the body of a man to fulfil its desires, so management is a vitalising factor that energises, directs and controls the organisational activities to reach its desired goal. It is a comprehensive and pervasive activity linking many units into one cohesive whole, welding many human faculties into one powerful instrument. It is management that animates productive forces and vibrates the organisation with activity.

2. Topmost Activating Element : A business is constituted by several elements viz. men, money, materials, machines, methods, markets and management. Of these seven 'M's the most vital and strategic factor is management. It is the capacity of the managers that accounts for the ultimate success or failure of the concern.

3. Key to Productivity : Success and progress of an enterprise depend much on its productivity which in turn depends on managerial efficiency. That is, management is instrumental for greater productivity and holds the key to it. **Urwick Breach** has rightly observed : "no ideology, no ism, no political theory can win a greater output with less effort from a given complex of human and material resources except sound management."

4. Achievement of Goals : Efficient management is necessary for the fulfilment of the objectives of the enterprise. Proper management arranges for the production of socially desirable and essential goods and services by utilising the resources of the country fruitfully and effectively. It is through the managers' endeavour that an organisation realises its objectives and serves the society. In the words of **John F. Mee** "Management is the art of securing maximum results with a minimum effort so as to secure maximum prosperity and happiness for both employer and employee and give the public the best possible service."

5. Better Performance : Efficient management creates in the minds of all working personnel a desire to act together as a team to perform their work smoothly. They feel oneness under an able and efficient management authority and strive hard to give their best services for the achievement of goals of the enterprise.

6. Creativity : Good management provides creativity to an enterprise infusing day to day in it fresh imagination, thoughts, ideas, and knowledge to make it dynamic and to lead the enterprise to its success and survival.

7. Co-ordination of Various Interests : The manager tries to harmonise the different interests existing in the organisation. A business enterprise has diverse group of interested parties and the interest of one group often collides with the other. The manager tries to co-ordinate all the divergent interests. As **P. F. Drucker** says, " To manage a business is to balance a variety of needs and goals."

8. Proper Utilisation of National Resources : A good management ensures proper and maximum utilisation of human and natural resources and prevents the misuse and loss of national wealth. One of the causes of sickness of industries in our country today is the management of these enterprises by inefficient managerial personnel through unscientific management process.

9. Driving Force of Motivation : Management acts as the motivating force by way of creating a favourable working environment, co-ordinating the disorganised parts of production and leads them to achieve the desired goals of the organisation. As a driving force, management inspires people, knits them into one entity, and creates conditions for the optimum use of resources.

10. Introduction of Moderanisation and Innovations : Being faced with stiff competition, the managers have to foresee the future and to devise ways and means for encountering such competition. By looking into the future, they introduce necessary modernisation and new innovations in different spheres of work. Innovation of new varieties of products, application of new management technique, use of new machinery, production technique and technology help to make the business dynamic for achieving success in the long run.

11. Proper Tackling of Business Problems : A successful manager serves as a 'friend, philosopher and guide' in tackling business problems. Good managers take right decisions on all matters of an enterprise and run the business on the right track. They are able to solve various intricate problems of an enterprise with their practical outlook and skill of performance.

12. Good Standard of Living : Management, being very much powerful and purposeful in the creation of utilities, can help people to lead meaningful lives and make a significant social contribution. A sound management develops and strengthens the national economy and enhances peoples' standard of living. It improves the standard of living of the workers by increasing their productivity and earning. It improves also the standard of living of the consumers by producing new varieties of commodities and creating new tastes and fashions.

13. Establishment of Industrial Peace : Peace in industry can be maintained by good management. Selection and appointment of right and efficient personnel, placing them in right positions after proper training, making provisions for their promotion, paying adequate and reasonable remuneration to them and encouraging them by human behaviour, are possible through proper management.

14. Economic Development : Government can expedite the economic development of the country and remove the poverty of the masses by formulating proper plans and policies with the help of management. In the developing and under-developed countries, the national resources cannot be utilised properly and economy cannot be developed quickly for want of efficient management.

15. Wealth Creating Organ : The social impact of good management is also very significant. Business is a wealth-creating organ of the society. It is good management that maintains its wealth-creating resources intact. In the words of **Marshall E. Dimock** : "Management...is the power to determine what shall happen to the personalities and happiness of entire people, the power to shape the destiny of a nation and the nations which make up the world."

From the above discussion it is clear that sound management is a must for all organisations, whether they are business enterprises or educational, religious, charitable or governmental institutions.

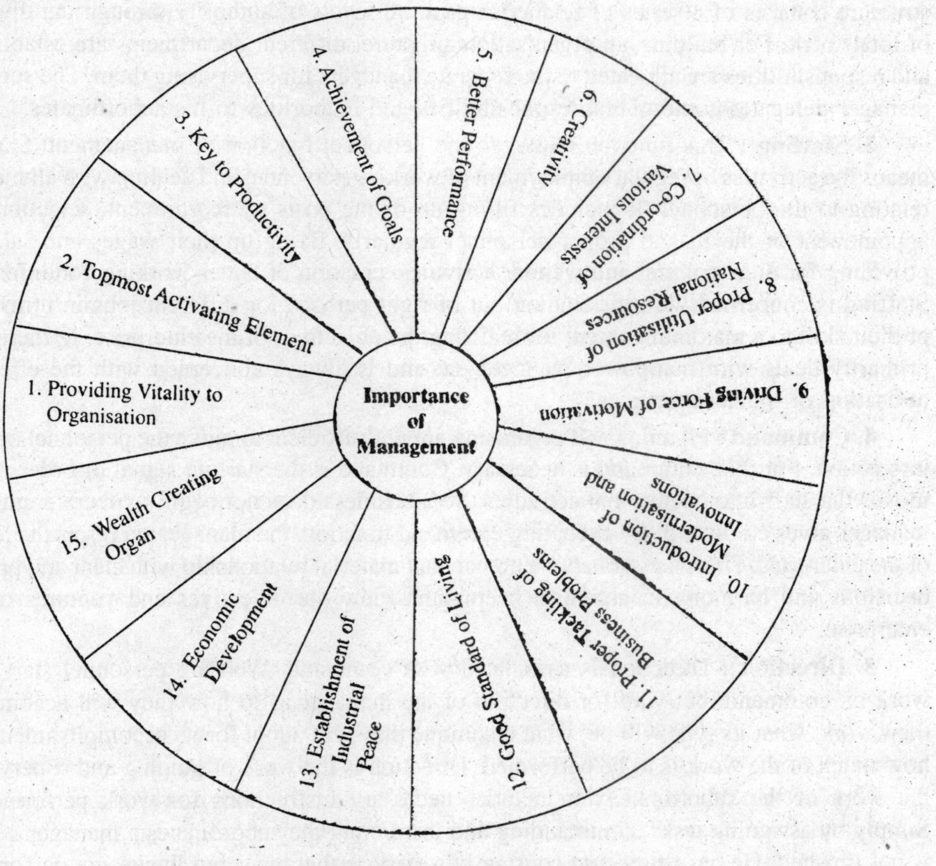

Fig. 1.3: Importance of Management.

1.6 Functions of Management

Management is what a manager does. A manager gets things done by working with people and other resources in order to achieve an objective. He co-ordinates the activities of others. The functions of management are inter-related and inter-dependent. The sum total of managerial functions is known as the management process. The principal functions of management in most of the business and non-business enterprises may be described as follows :

1. Planning : The first function of management is planning. Planning is deciding in advance what is to be done and the method of doing it in an orderly way. It is the determination of a course of action to achieve a desired result. It clarifies the objectives and evolves a complete set of policies, programmes and procedures. The aim of planning is, of course, the establishment of objectives and finding out the way of realisation of these objectives through the optimum use of available resources. Planning includes some amount of forecasting and decision-making. Forecasting is the process of assessing the future and providing for expansion and development in future. Decision-making will diagnose the problem, find out several alternatives, estimate the feasibility and profitability of the different alternatives, and select the best course of action.

2. Organising : After planning, the next function of management is to establish an organisation. Organising means the creation of a structure of functions and duties to be performed by a group of people to attain the goals of the enterprise. The organisation structure consists of a series of relationships at all levels of authority through the division of total work. For building up organisation structure, different departments are established and responsibilities are allocated to the separate managers for supervising them. The superior manager delegates some of his responsibilities and authorities to his subordinates.

3. Staffing : This function relates to the personnel function of management. Staffing means the activities of regular employment of working personnel and dealing with all matters relating to the personnel. It includes filling up of the posts by recruitment, selection and appointment of the fit and proper personnel regularly, fixing up their wages and salaries, providing for their training and welfare activities, creation of better working condition etc. Staffing is concerned with the finding out of right persons for different jobs in utilisation of their skill to a maximum extent for realising the objectives of the enterprise. It, therefore, primarily deals with manpower management and is always concerned with the effective utilisation of human resources.

4. Command : Planning and organising are not sufficient to move the personnel or staff into action. For this, command is necessary. Command is the starting signal or order which moves the staff into operational activities. So a business does not begin to operate until the manager gives command. By executing command function, the manager serves as the leader of the enterprise. Thus, it establishes a human and material relationship with clear and precise decisions and harmony in activities keeping in view the objectives and ventures of the enterprise.

5. Direction : Direction is associated with command. Working personnel start their work on command, but wait for direction of the manager as to how they will accomplish their work, what its type will be, what technique they will adopt for its accomplishment and how much of the work is to be performed. Direction is the work of guiding and supervising the work of the subordinates. It includes necessary instructions for work performance. Simply by assigning tasks, commanding and instructing the subordinates a manager's work is not finished. He has to see and constantly supervise that his subordinates are performing their allocated duties properly. For the success of the business, direction should be precise, clear and acceptable. It must be thoroughly understood, received and respected.

6. Motivation : Motivation may be regarded as the most vital element in the process of management. It is the act of stimulating someone to get a desired course of action. It creates willingness in the personnel to work and co-operate for the accomplishment of common purposes. It is the actuating force that inspires a man to put his best for the fulfilment of his assigned task. Motivation is a powerful tool in the hands of the managers to develop and intensify a desire in every member of the organisation to work effectively for achieving the established goals. Direction or command will lose much of its significance and effectiveness unless the workers are motivated to their jobs. The manager's duty is to study carefully the needs for which the subordinates are striving and to see that these needs are fulfilled.

7. Co-ordination : Co-ordination involves unification and integration of group efforts. The aforesaid functions will not give the desired result unless the operation of different parts of the organisation are carefully blended and harmonised. And this is the task of co-ordination. Co-ordination is the orderly arrangement of group efforts to provide unity of action in the pursuit of a common purpose. Co-ordination maintains a balance among different activities of an enterprise and helps running it smoothly.

8. Control : Control is to see that the performances of the organisation are matched with the plans. As **Henry Fayol** observed : "control consists in verifying whether everything occurs in conformity with the plan adopted, the instructions issued and principles established." Its object is to point out weakness and errors in order to rectify them and prevent their recurrence. A manager is to see that everything is being done according to the policies laid down and the instructions given and that actual performance corresponds with the planned course of action. Control is the ultimate weapon in the hands of the managerial force to remove mistakes or faults, to modify defective plans, and to effect co-ordination of diverse elements where it is lacking. Setting standards for measuring the desired works, evaluation of performances and taking corrective actions are the steps involved in controlling. The controlling function of a manager may be compared to the control of flying a kite by its owner.

The above-noted functions are regarded as the basic functions of management. But there are also some ancilliary functions that come along with executing those functions. These are mentioned below :

Fig. 1.4: Control of Management.

(i) Innovation : Innovation is an important function of management. For growth and expansion, the managers should promote innovations. Managerial innovation includes the introduction and application of new or modern techniques of management and introduction of new means of success. Keeping an eye to the present changes and future demands is a must for innovation. Innovation is essential to cater to the needs of modernisation of production to survive in cut throat competition.

(ii) Reporting and Budgeting : To ensure effective control management requires reporting and budgeting. The details of execution and progress of work is conveyed to the concerned authority through submission of reports. Budgeting enables control over financial aspect through allocation of resources in the form of income and expenditure. This reduces the chances of waste.

(iii) Communication : Communication refers to convey and exchange of facts, information, instructions, orders, advice etc. with the people within and outside the organisation. It is an essential part of management and the key to its functioning. The leader and the higher executives of an organisation can establish their authority over their subordinates through a good system of communication. The managers are required to explain the principles of the enterprise to the employees working at different levels and report to the higher authority about the compliance of the principles by the employees. The managers order the employees to finish their alloted work timely, on the one hand and collect information regarding their

Table 1.1: Functions of Management

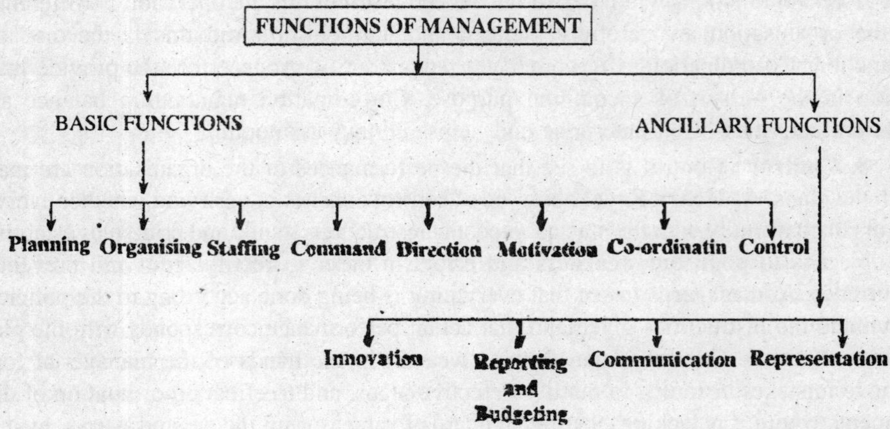

wants and grievances on the other. Misunderstanding among the employees is the main problem on the way to co-ordination. This can be avoided if there is a scope for mutual discussion. All these activities are within the purview of communication. Therefore, the manager cannot perform his duties efficiently without establishing a proper communication system in an organisation where a large number of employees are at work.

(iv) Representation : This is also considered to be one of the important functions of management. It involves representing the organisation in dealing with the external world. The act of representation is to explain the principles and methods of activities of the enterprise to the customers, workers' union, suppliers of materials, financial institutions, government officials and the public in general, and to maintain contact with them.

1.7 Principles of Management

Principles of management are meant to be the guidelines to the managers for their thinking and action to take decisions. Since the time of **F. W. Taylor** and **Henry Fayol**, the principles of management are on the road to a progressive development. Many managers and scholars have been motivated for research and analysis for formulating certain principles to improve managerial efficiency.

Henry Fayol, the pioneer in the field of management science, has introduced fourteen principles of management. Modern management experts like **L. F. Urwick, Harold Koontz, E. Dale** and others have added a few other principles in the list. These various principles are enumerated below :

1. Division of Work : This is nothing but the principles of specialisation needed for proper and efficient work performance in all spheres of activity, both technical and managerial. The overall work of an enterprise are divided into several divisions. The work of each division is entrusted to a particular worker or a group of workers to perform. This improves efficiency.

2. Authority and Responsibility : "Authority is the right to give orders and the power to exact obedience." Whenever a manager is allocated tasks, he should be given requisite authority so that the particular manager can exercise his own skill and initiative for performing the entrusted tasks. Delegation of authority to managers necessarily signifies that they have responsibility for the delegated tasks. "Responsibility is the corollary of authority, it is its natural consequences and essential counterpart." In order to discharge responsibility properly, authority must be commensurate with responsibility. If there is no parity between the two, there will be either wastage or misuse of authority.

3. Discipline : Discipline is absolutely essential for smooth running of business. Discipline must be maintained in all its levels for successful management. **Fayol** points out that for the maintenance of discipline, efficient and good managers are needed at the top level and there should be clear agreement between the employer and the employees. Discipline is of paramount importance for the smooth running of production.

4. Unity of Command : This principle makes it clear that an employee should receive orders from one superior only. One person will command one worker or each group of workers. If several commands come from different masters to the workers, the latter may be bewildered as to what is to be done or whose order should be followed.

5. Unity of Direction : According to this principle, direction to work must come to the workers of each department or section from one authority. In other words; each group of activity with the same objective must have one head and one plan. Unity of direction is different from unity of command in the sense that the former is concerned with functioning of the organisation in respect of its grouping of activities or planning, while the latter is concerned with functioning of the personnel at all levels in the organisation.

6. Subordination of individual Interest to General Interest : This principle demands that in management the common interest is considered to be over and above the individual interest. When there is any conflict between the two, the manager should reconcile them.

7. Remuneration of Personnel : Remuneration of personnel is the price of services rendered by them. This principle requires that the remuneration payable to the staff must be fair and reasonable and it should bring maximum possible satisfaction for both the employees and the employers. The remuneration factor must not cause any grievance for either party.

8. Centralisation : In management, 'centralisation' means the centralised authority or leadership of an organisation and 'decentralisation' signifies the dispersal of such authority or leadership to different levels of an organisation. The principle of centralisation calls for that a balanced system of centralisation must be introduced to produce the best results taking into consideration the individual circumstances. The objective to pursue is the optimum utilisation of all faculties of the personnel. So the question of centralisation and decentralisation is a matter of proportion. In small firms, there is absolute centralisation, but in large concerns, there are a series of intermediaries between the top and bottom level and, as such, decentralisation of authority is essential. So the principle to be followed in this respect is to maintain a proper balance between the two.

9. Scalar Chain : It is the chain of superiors running from the highest authority to the lowest level for the purpose of communication. The highest level of the organisation must be linked with its different levels by a line of direct authority. It implies that each communication going up or coming down must flow through each position in the line of authority.

10. Order : This principle refers to the arrangement of persons and things required in any organisation. Order is divided into material order and social order. In material order, there should be a "place for everything and everything in its place", so that wastage of materials can be avoided. Similarly, in social order, there should be a "place for everyone and everyone in his place" that is the placement of "right man in right job." This kind of order demands precise knowledge of the human requirements and resources of the organisation and a constant balance between these requirements and resources.

11. Equity : This principle calls for the maintenance of an attitude of justice and generosity towards the working personnel and treating them equally and sympathetically. This is necessary to secure devotion and loyalty of the subordinates for good performance.

12. Stability of Tenure of Personnel : Stability of tenure of service is essential to get an employee accustomed to new work and succeeding in doing it perfectly and well. For this purpose, as far as possible, frequent and unnecessary labour turnover should be avoided because instability is both the cause and effect of bad management.

13. Initiative : Initiative is the power of thinking out and execution of a plan. It is one of the powerful stimulants of human endeavour. So to create zeal and energy, the managers should permit the employees to exercise as much initiative as possible.

14. Esprit de Corps : It means the unity of spirit or, in other words, team-spirit. This unity of spirit is the moving force which ensures maximum of co-ordinated efficiency in

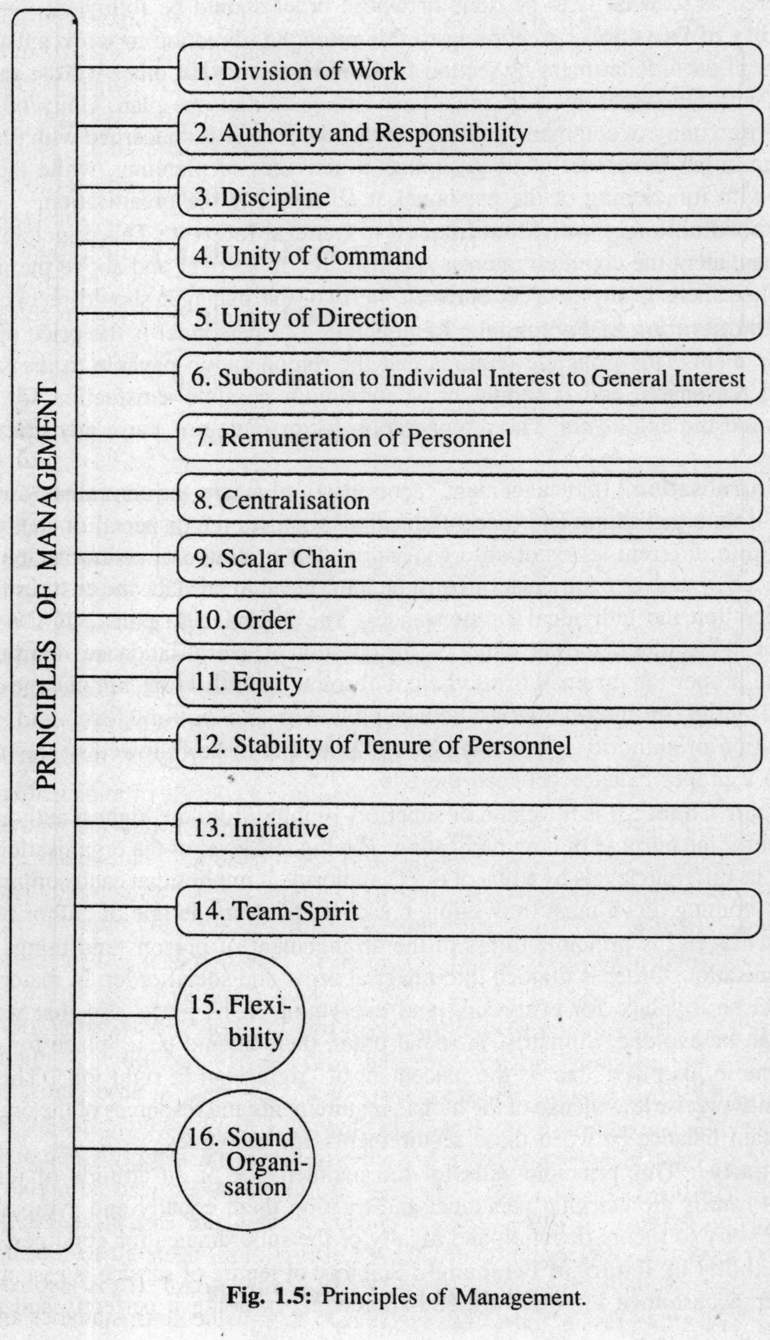

Fig. 1.5: Principles of Management.

any undertaking. Collective effort is essential for the success of any enterprise. So the managers should create a mentality of co-operation and team spirit among all the working personnel of the enterprise, so that they work as a team for its success.

Besides these principles as enunciated by **Henry Fayol,** in modern management science a few more principles have been introduced. These are as follows :

(i) Flexibility : Management should be flexible in nature. Its activities should be so planned, organised, directed and controlled that it can adjust with the changed time and circumstances. Market conditions are subject to constant changes. Price of commodities, tastes and fashions, demand for the products are also changing. New machinery and equipment are being found out, newer varieties of products are now manufactured. All these changes and technological advancements require supporting changes in the technique of production and business policies. Therefore, it becomes imperative that the management technique should be as flexible as possible to adjust with these changing conditions.

(ii) Sound Organisation : Organisation is the framework of management. For effective management of the different affairs of the business, a sound organisation is to be built up. The type of organisation depends on the nature of business, the nature of product and the technique of production. In the cases of diversification of products and the production of standardised products in different places administrative authority is to be decentralised to a great extent. In the case of others, particularly production of a single item, centralised leadership is preferred.

1.8 Levels of Management

The number of levels of management in an organisation depends on its size, technology used and the degree of diversity in its range of production. A large concern needs a number of levels of management so that the activities at different points are properly planned, organised, directed and controlled. Similarly, a concern using a complex technology of manufacture i.e., a technique where a product passes through several stages to become the final output, also needs to set up several levels of management. And of course, a concern manufacturing a large number of diverse products needs several layers of management.

A business enterprise may have different levels of management—(i) Top level to include the directors and senior executives, (ii) Middle level to include departmental heads and superintendents, and (iii) Lower level to include foremen, supervisors, overseers etc.

In order to ensure greater efficiency and productivity, the levels of management should be kept to the minimum. Thoughtless increase in the number of levels will increase costs and create problems of communication between the various levels—thus making effective co-ordination and control a difficult task. Lack of communication between the management employees and operative staff may also cause misunderstanding and bitterness.

The functions of different levels of management may be discussed in the following manner :

(A) Top Level Management : Top managers refer to those who occupy the top most positions in the organisation and are entrusted with the responsibility of planning and executing broad policy decisions. Thus top level of management in an organisation like a public limited company comprises the Board of Directors, Chief Executive like the Managing Director or General Manager and the senior executive like the Deputy General Manager. The Board of Directors lays down the objectives and policies. He who is in charge of the execution of these objectives and policies is known as the Chief Executive. He is assisted by the senior executives. He issues instructions for execution, takes all necessary steps to put into effect the objectives and policies laid down by the Board. He is also responsible to the Board for the progress of the company. He is to submit accounts, statistics and reports from time to time to the Board for evaluation of his performance. He is also the chief liaison officer who maintains a link between the Board and the rest of the personnel of the organisation. He is to see that all functions are properly exercised for the business. On the whole, top level management is more creative than operative.

Top level of management generally performs the following important functions :

(i) Determining the general objectives and policies of the business;

(ii) Laying down the guidelines for the departmental heads;

(iii) Organising the business into various sections and departments for the efficient accomplishment of the enterprise goals; and

(iv) Reviewing the work of the executives at different levels and ensuring that their performance is in accordance with the pre-determined plans.

(B) Middle Level Management : The heads of different departments such as Purchase Officer, Production Manager, Sales Manager, Personnel Manager, Chief Engineer, Secretary, Chief Accountant, Research and Development Officer, Public Relations Officer and such other personnel of similar rank constitute the middle level of management.

They lie between the top management personnel above and the supervisory staff below. They have to take instructions from the chief executive and direct and guide the supervisors under their charge. The primary function of middle level of management is to maintain co-ordination between different departments. Middle level management assists the top level management to understand the problems of different departments. This level is, thus, less creative but more co-ordinative. The important functions of the middle level of management may be stated as follows :

(i) To determine the short-term goals of their departments;

(ii) To prepare plans including programmes, work schedule etc.;

(iii) To provide link between the top level management and lower level management by explaining the policies and directions of the former to the latter and conveying the feelings and grievances of the latter to the former;

(iv) To train, direct and guide the subordinates; and

(v) To keep close control over their activities and check their performances regularly.

(C) Lower Level Management : The lower management level consists of Foremen, Supervisors, Office Superintendents, Section-in-charges, Sales Executives, Inspectors etc. Being placed at the bottom of the hierarchy of management they are directly in touch with the operating workers. They are more concerned with getting the work done by the staff under their control. They instruct, guide, encourage and order the workers to do particular tasks. The grievances of the workers are represented by them to the higher levels of management. They have to establish high morale in their subordinates. The most important part of their job is to see that the work is properly carried into effect by the workers according to order and instructions issued. The lower management personnel are the real working managers, because they are required to deal with the actual work to be accomplished, the people who are to do the work and the environment in which they will have to work. By getting the work done by the workers, they represent the workers before the middle level of management to whom they look forward for their own security and promotion as well as for decisions, orders, help and guidance. These personnel also represent the higher management authority to the workers. The lower level management is, thus, mainly operative and is concerned with the workers, works and equipment directly.

The functions of lower management are as follows :

(a) To plan and organise the work of their respective units or sections;

(b) To maintain records of performance;

(c) To train up the workers;

(d) To ensure their safety and good working environment;

(e) To take care of the machinery and equipment;

(f) To build up morale of the workers and improve productivity; and

(g) To give effect to the directives of the middle level of management etc.

The relationship between these levels is that the top level management directs the middle level. Middle level managers get the instructions from the top level, direct the lower level managers and control them. They are responsible and accountable to the top level. Lower level managers are to submit an account of their performances to the middle level management.

Managers at Different Levels

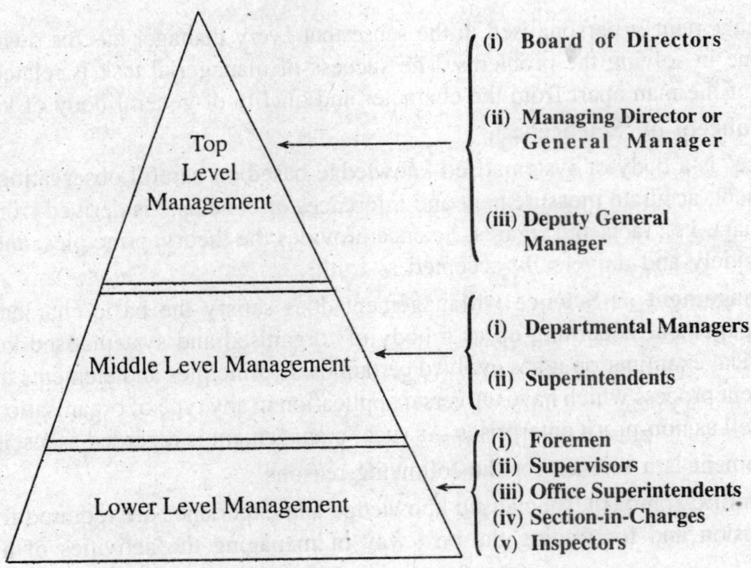

Fig. 1.6: Levels of Management.

1.9 Is Management an 'ART' or a 'SCIENCE'?

There is a controversy whether management is an 'art' or a 'science'. However, management is both an art and a science. This aspect is explained below :

(A) Concept of 'Art' :

An 'Art' is a practical skill for the effective accomplishment of some concrete results. It is acquired by learning and is related to application of intellect and techniques. Art is thus concerned with the understanding of how a particular work can be performed. It is a blend of imagination, skill and experience to do something. Painting of a picture is an art, since a picture is painted by imagination with skill and experience of an artist. As an art is concerned with the creation of objects or events it is called creative.

● **Management as an Art :** According to some experts, management is an art. They advance the following reasons in support of their claim :

1. The process of management does involve the use of know-how and skills like any other art such as music, painting, sculpture etc. A person is able to manage well if he has the social skills necessary for the exercise of leadership and the technical skills and knowledge required for correct decision-making on various aspects of the work of an organisation.

2. The process of management is directed to achieve certain concrete results as other fields of art do. Projects have to be completed, production levels have to be attained, sales target are to be hit, a proper rate of return on investment is to be secured, the distribution of product has to be arranged for different territories, and peace and harmony have to be maintained in relations with the workers. These are some concrete ends for the accomplishment of which management has to strive.

3. Good management is effective management. Unless the exercise of management results in effective realisation of organisational goals, it is not considered successful.

4. Management is creative like any other art. It creates new situations for further improvement.

5. Management is personalised in the sense that every manager has his own approach and technique in solving the problems. The success of managerial task is related with the personality of the man apart from the character and quality of general body of knowledge.

(B) Concept of 'Science' :

'Science' is a body of systematised knowledge based on careful observation, research and experiment, accurate measurement and inferences or conclusions derived from detailed analysis of data, i.e., facts and figures. Science provides the theory, principles, and the laws which are widely and universally accepted as truth.

- **Management as Science :** Management does satisfy the basic characteristics of science. Management is coming up as a body of organised and systematised knowledge. Through critical examination it has evolved certain basic principles and elements in the form of management process which have universal application in any type of organisation—profit-making as well as non-profit enterprises. As such, management is regarded as a science also.

Management is a science for the following reasons :

1. Scientific approach, specialised knowledge and experience are required for making the best decision and for finding the best way of managing the activities of a business enterprise.

2. According to **Taylor,** management is a science-based method, which is based on the truth or reality of facts and experiences of successful managers.

3. Management is a scientific method, which is applied to avoid errors of omissions or commissions of the managers.

4. Specialisation is essential in management as in science. For example, special knowledge, skill and efficiency are required for solving the intricate problems of accounting and forecasting.

Management, however, is not comparable to exact Pure Sciences like Physics, Chemistry and Mathematics. Management is basically concerned with the direction of human effort and accomplishment of work and, as such, deserves to be placed in the category of Social Sciences like Economics, Psychology, Sociology etc. It is quite obvious that the principles of management are not fundamental truths and their application may not yield the desired results always. Human behaviour is ever-changing and unpredictable. It is not governed by the laws of mechanics. Hence, management dealing with complex human beings is bound to be an inexact science.

(C) Management : Both Science and Art :

Management may be regarded as both an art and a science. The science of management provides certain general principles which can guide the managers in their professional efforts. The art of management consists in tackling every problem in an effective manner. Thus, to be a successful manager, a person requires the knowledge of management principles and also the skills of how that knowledge can be applied. Absence of either will result into inefficiency.

As a scientist, the manager relies on the existing theory and philosophy of management and develops new knowledge, new principles and new schools of management thought. As an artist, he has to depend on his own experience and judgment while making a decision on any managerial problem and taking action on the decisions to realise the objectives. Scientific attitude and scientific method shall be applied in problem-solving approach, e.g., marketing research, business research etc. In reality, theoretical base of knowledge is essential for developing sound practice. Theory must be supplemented by practical knowledge continuously. Science and art are complementary and each supplements the other. For example, theoretical teaching of medicine and engineering is invariably accompanied by practical work in a hospital or workshop.

We need artistic managerial ability to perform a managerial job. The art of management is fully reflected in the decision-making capacity of a manager. Management and managerial success depend upon the skilful art of application of scientific theories and principles of management. So it is obvious that management is both an 'art' and a science'.

1.10 Management as a Profession

Management is regarded as profession by many, although it does not possess all the requisite features of a profession. Therefore, it is desirable to find out whether management is a profession.

'Profession' is an occupation in which one to be specially educated and trained in a particular subject, for rendering his services to people of the society with their specialised knowledge, skill and proficiency. The professionals like lawyers, doctors, chartered accountants etc. help people to solve their problems by the application of their expert knowledge. All professions are occupations in the sense that they provide means of livelihood. However, all occupations are not professions because some of them lack certain characteristics of a profession.

The following are the fundamental characteristics of a profession :

1. Existence of an organised and systematised body of knowledge : Profession emerges from the establishment of the fact that there is a body of knowledge which has to be studied for being a successful professional. This is true for all professions.

2. Formal method of acquisition of knowledge : One has to acquire the specialised knowledge and skills through formal training from a recognised institution in order to take up a profession as his occupation. After passing the prescribed examination of the recognised educational institution, one becomes a professional in his discipline.

3. Existence of Professional Association : Members of a particular profession form themselves into an association that works as an authoritative body of that profession. The professionals have to obtain a licence and a certificate of practice from this body.

4. Formulation of Ethical Codes : For every profession, some ethical standards are formulated by the controlling authoritative body and every individual of the profession is expected to maintain conformity with these standards.

5. Service motive : While ethical code provides the behavioural pattern for professionals, service motive concept suggests that the professionals should keep social interest in their mind while charging fees for their professional services.

Management has been developed as a distinct body of knowledge. The development of knowledge in management field has been due to the need for managing complex and large organisations in a better way. Thus, management satisfies the requirement of a profession in the form of existence of a specialised knowledge.

In India and in many countries in the West, almost all the aforesaid characteristics are present in management. However, the receiving of specialised education and training by the managers and management consultants and obtaining licences and certificates by them have not yet been made compulsory by the authority. Therefore, management cannot be termed as a true profession, though it is emerging as a profession and the move is towards management as profession. Management may not be a profession similar to the medical or legal profession but none can deny that it possesses some important and basic elements of a profession. As such **George S. Claude** says : "Management is not outright a profession, but is taking giant steps in that direction."

1.10.1 Professionalisation of Management in India

The basic characteristics of management as a profession are found in Indian management in varying degrees. Facilities of formal education in management, establishment of All India Management Association, growing divorce of ownership and management in the public companies, and formulation of code of conduct by All India Management Association suggest that management is now professionalised in India. However, this is not the total picture of Indian management.

Indian industry is under-developed, partly because its management is unscientific, inefficient and inactive; and mainly because it is managed mostly on family basis, under the control of big business houses. Management of joint stock companies, since its inception in India, has been in the hands of members, friends or relatives of those families. The positions of top level executives of the family business are held by them. They are privileged to be the directors, executives, managers etc, even though they might have limited or no academic or professional qualification, knowledge, efficiency, experience and training in management.

The features of an enterprise managed on family basis are : (i) its management and control remain confined to the members of a family or their friends and relatives; (ii) its objective is to maximise profit, even at the cost and interest of the shareholders, society, state and the nation; (iii) it is not managed almost in all cases strictly in accordance with the widely accepted scientific theories, norms and principles of modern management.

In India, big business and industrial enterprises have tremendous prospects and potentialities before them. There is probably only one impediment to their success, and it is the absence of professionalisation in their management. For successful, fruitful and effective management that is most vital for attaining the desired objectives of an enterprise— its management should be divested from its ownership.

It should be placed under the control and responsibility of the professionally qualified and trained managerial personnel. In this context, **P. L. Tandon**, an eminent management expert, observes : "In a family business, you have professional engineers, accountants and marketers, but all decision-making is centralised at the top, with the head of the family, who has no professionalism, but perhaps only experience and intuition, the decisions are not likely to be as good as that of a modern professional Board."

Professionalisation in management, thus, is not adequately introduced by the entrepreneurs in management of private sector enterprises in India and so, in professional management, India has not yet been able to improve her position.

In public sector enterprises, in the role of entrepreneur, the state aims not only at earning profit, but also at discharging its duties and responsibilities to society, country and the nation.

In reality, in many public sector organisations, the situation is not at all better. It implies that the government—while running the public sector enterprises as entrepreneur—does not seem to be fully aware of the need of managing the enterprises according to the modern theories, norms and principles of management by professional managerial personnel in all levels. Mainly the personnel of administrative services are appointed at the top or middle level management of the public sector enterprises. However, in recent past, trend to employ qualified and trained managers in these enterprises has been noticed, but that is not sufficient to claim that management in this sector has been able to gain the professional status.

The above discussion suggests that management in India is slowly marching towards professionalisation, though a large part of it is still following the traditional pattern of management. However, in the time to come, the process of professionalisation of management is likely to be faster because of the increasing complexity of managing business, growing awareness of the need for professionalisation, and more and more availability of professionally trained managers.

Finally, it can be said that, unless acquisition of professional qualification and training by the managers are made compulsory, adequate number of professional institutions are set up for imparting education and training on management principles and practice and unless it is fully conceived that the qualified and professional managers are not only needed for multinational concerns but also for institutions of all size and nature, professionalisation of management in India would remain a far cry.

1.11 Universality of Management

Management as a process is universal for it is found in all organised activities, irrespective of country, culture, or size. Its principles are widely applicable to all concerns, where a collective effort is made towards attainment of certain common objectives. The various elements of management process i.e., planning, organising, staffing, directing and controlling—are universal for all organisations and a manager must perform these functions. Only the intensity of a particular element may differ depending on the variables affecting management practices. This is the principle of universality of management. It implies that any theory or principle about a particular managerial function will be applicable to all managers—irrespective of their levels in the organisation.

In every social institution like school, college, university, temple, church, hospital, club, municipality etc. the same process of management is required. The secretary of a club, the head priest of a temple, the bishop of a church, the chairman of a municipality, the head of an educational institution and even the prime minister of a country has to perform the same managerial job as the manager of a business enterprise does. So management is a function applicable not only to the business enterprises but to other social organisations also.

F. W. Taylor believes in the universality of management. He points out : "The fundamental principles of scientific management are applicable to all human activities from our simplest individual acts to the work of our great corporation." According to **Henry Fayol,** the general principles of management are applicable to enterprises of any nature, kind and size. **Koontz** and **O'Donnell** says : "Management's fundamental theory and principles have universal application to every kind of enterprise and at its every level."

Another concept of universality of management is that the managerial knowledge and experience can be transferred from one person to another person, from one firm to another firm in the same country and from one country to another country. Since the basic function is the same, the experience a manager has gained in one enterprise or department or performing any activity, he can use it in another enterprise, or department or activity. The technical task may be different in different enterprises or activities but the managerial task is the same. **Dalton E. Mcfarland** observes : "Management skill is an exportable commodity and indeed, it is one of the important exports of the multinational or international firms." He means that, management is universal, as its principles and knowledge are transferable from one institution to another or even from one country to another country.

However, some persons like **Gonzalez, Macmillan** and **Robert Simon** do not agree about the universal nature of management. For, **Gonzalez** and **Macmillan** say : "Management philosophy is culture bound implying thereby that external environmental forces influence the management philosophy." To them management is entirely situational and there is nothing like universal principles of management. The application of the principles of management depends upon culture and environmental conditions of the organisations. These principles and methods are not universally applicable.

But it is evident from the observations of majority of the authorities that the concept of universality of the methods and principles of management are widely accepted. Where there is a need of a collective effort for reaching the common goal, the necessity and universality of the methods and principles of management cannot be denied.

1.12 Role or Tasks of a Manager

The job of a modern manager is very complex and multi-dimensional. The managerial activity may be divided into three groups—(i) those which involve primarily in inter-personal relationships, (ii) those which deal basically with transfer of information, and (iii) those which essentially relate to decision-making. On the basis of these groups, a manager's role or work has three phases—(a) inter-personal, (b) informational, and (c) decisional. A brief description of these phases of managerial role is given below :

1. Inter-personal Role : This role is concerned with the manager's contacts and dealings with other people. Formal authority of a manager gives him a special position of status in the organisation. Because of this, he performs the role of a **'figurehead'** that is the head of a particular unit. In this role a manager executes symbolic duties required by the status of his office. Making speeches, welcoming official visitors, bestowing honours, distributing gifts to retiring employees are a few examples of such ceremonial and social duties.

Secondly, the manager has to represent his organisation in all formal matters. This is called **'liaison-maker's** role. It relates to a manager's relationships with the outsiders. A manager maintains mutually beneficial relations with other organisations, governments, industrial groups etc.

Thirdly, the manager has to communicate with his own subordinates. He motivates them and activates them to work in pursuit of the desired objectives and thus performs the role of a **'leader'**.

2. Informational Role : Because of his inter-personal role, the manager is in a unique position to get information. He becomes a kind of nerve centre of organisational information. In this role a manager has to receive and collect information so that he can develop a thorough understanding of his organisation. This may be called the role of a **'recipient'** or a **'monitor'**.

Secondly, he functions as a **'disseminator'**. In this aspect he transmits special information and judgements to the members of his organisation. This information is gathered by him from internal operations and external environments.

Thirdly, he performs the role of a **'spokesman'** . In this role, a manager speaks for his organisation and defends his enterprising activities. A manager addressing the trade union is an example of such role.

3. Decisional Role : There are four decisional roles that a manager has to perform :

Firstly, he has to perform the role of an **'entrepreneur'** by initiating change and undertaking the risks involved in introducing change.

Secondly, he has to assume the role of a **'disturbance handler'**. This refers to taking charge when the organisation faces problems or crisis. A manager handles conflicts, complaints and competitive actions.

Thirdly, he performs the role of an **'allocator of resources'**. In this role a manager approves budgets, sets priorities, and distributes resources.

Fourthly, he performs the role of a **'negotiator'** in which he deals with those situations where he has to enter into negotiations on behalf of the organisation. As a negotiator, a manager bargains with the suppliers, dealers, trade unions, agents etc.

Table 1.2: Role of a Manager

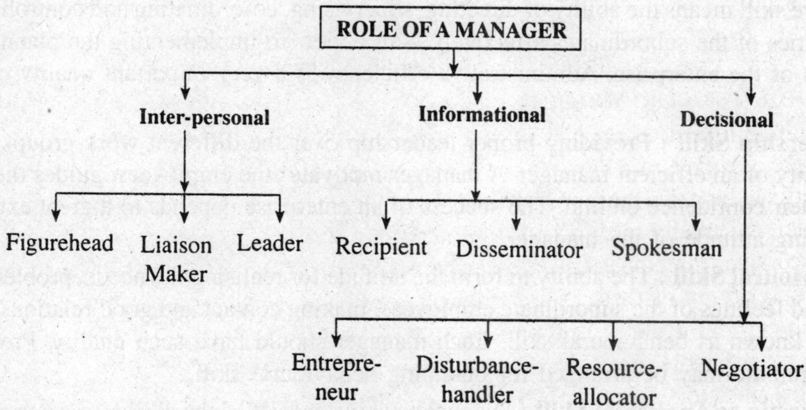

1.13 Managerial Skills

The job of a manager has become very critical and complex. Several skills are, therefore, required in order to be a successful manager. The skills of an effective manager may be grouped into the following nine categories :

1. Organisational Skill : For the success and prosperity of the enterprise, the manager must have organisational skill. In spite of procurement of required materials, proper land, efficient workers and adequate amount of capital, the business of the enterprise will not be fruitful if the manager lacks organising capacity. In order to utilise fully and advantageously the different factors of production the manager has to determine proper organising method.

2. Technical Skill : Technical skills include the ability and knowledge in using the techniques, procedures and equipment involved in performing specific tasks. These skills require specalised knowledge and proficiency in a particular mechanical job. For instance, ability in programming and operating computer is a technical skill. A manager should understand two things about technical skills. Firstly, he must know which skills should be employed in his enterprise. And secondly, he must understand both the role of each skill and the inter-relationships among the skills.

3. Conceptual Skill : Conceptual skills refer to the ability to see the entire picture of the whole organisation and the inter-relationships among its parts. Such skills help the manager to conceptualise the environment to analyse the forces working in a situation and to take a broad view of the organisation. Conceptual skills also include the competence to understand a problem in all its aspects and to apply original thinking in solving it. Such competence is necessary for rational decision-making.

4. Human Skill : Human skill means the ability to work effectively with other people —both as an individual and as a member of a group. These are required to win co-operation of others and to build effective work teams. Such skills require a sense of feeling for others and capacity to see things from others' point of view. Human skills are reflected in the way a manager perceives his superiors, subordinates, and peers. While technical skills involve mastery of 'things', human skills are concerned with understanding of 'people'.

5. Decision-making Skill : Decision-making is, in fact, the main function of a manager. The managers have to make decisions in various matters such as collection of fund, purchasing, production, sales, etc. They are to take quick decisions in changed situations. They have to decide the best method for the solution of different problems. So, it is essential that every manager should posses the skill for taking right decision in proper time.

6. Administrative Skill : A successful manager must have administrative skill. Administrative skill means the ability of directing, supervising, co-ordinating and controlling various activities of the subordinates effectively with a view to implementing the planning and decisions of the enterprise. Administrative efficiency is a very important quality of a manager.

7. Leadership Skill : Providing proper leadership over the different work-groups is a special quality of an efficient manager. A manager motivates the employees, guides them, and creates their confidence on him. The success of an enterprise depends to a great extent on right leading attitude of the manager.

8. Behavioural Skill : The ability to form the attitude for realising the needs, problems, grievances and feelings of the subordinate employees, making contact and good relationship with them is known as behavioural skill. Each manager should have such quality. Proper training programme may be arranged for obtaining behavioural skill.

9. Diagnostic or Analytical Skill : Diagnostic skills consist of the ability to determine the nature and circumstances of a particular situation by analysis and examination. It is the capacity to cut through unimportant aspects and quickly identify the heart of the problem. Diagnostic skills are probably the most difficult skills because these require logical thinking, analytical ability, intelligence, and creativity to be effective.

Technical skills are the most important at the supervisory or operating level of management where a thorough understanding of job techniques is required to guide the workers. As one moves to the higher levels of management, technical skills become less important. The higher level managers deal with the subordinate managers and specialised technical knowledge is comparatively less important for them. Conceptual skills are important for top managers in preparing long-term plans, formulating broad policy decisions, and relating the enterprise to its industry and economy. Human skills and all others are, however, equally important at all levels of management.

1.14 Administration and Management

The process of determining the objectives and policies of an enterprise by the top level authority is known as 'Administration'. The persons of this level of authority determine the goals of the enterprise and accordingly formulate the required policies. The owner in sole proprietorship, the partners in the partnership business and the directors in a joint stock company accomplish the functions of administration. According to **Oliver Sheldon,** "Administration is the function in the industry concerned with .the determination of the corporate policy, the co-ordination of finance, production and distribution, the settlement of the compass (structure of the organisation) under the ultimate control of the executive."

On the other hand, he opines that, "Management is the function in industry concerned in the execution of policy within the limits set up by administration, and the employment of the organisation for the particular objects before it."

1.14.1 Distinction between Administration and Management

Points of Difference	Administration	Management
1. Nature of Work :	1. Administration is the process of determining the objectives and policies of an enterprise.	1. Management is the process of implementing those objectives and policies.
2. Actual Activity :	2. Administration formulates the rules and regulations for execution of the goals of the enterprise.	2. The function of management is to execute the rules and regulations set up by the administration.
3. Area of Function :	3. Administration includes planning, decision-making and establishing organisation structure.	3. Command, directing, motivating, co-ordinating and controlling are the tasks of management.
4. Nature of Process :	4. Administration is a thinking and determinative process.	4. Management is an executive process.
5. Level of Authority :	5. The managers of the top level perform the administrative activities.	5. The managers of the middle level and lower level operate the managerial functions.
6. Limit of Performance :	6. Administration sets up the organisation structure within which the functions of management are performed. The operations of the employees are not directed by administration.	6. Management directs the workers to get the work done by them. It supervises the performance of the subordinate employees.
7. Responsibility :	7. Generally, the employees engaged in the highest level of authority are responsible for administrative work of the enterprise. They act as the representative of the proprietors of the enterpise.	7. Usually, the salaried employees of the middle and lower level of authority undertake the responsibility of the managerial activities.
8. Dependability :	8. Administration does not depend upon management.	8. Management has to depend on administration.

1.15 Distinction between Organisation and Management

'Organisation' is the second basic function of 'Management'. Organisation is a structure by which a harmonious inter-relation is set up among the various employees and their work and the activities are performed effectively for the execution of the pre-determined objectives of the enterprise.

On the other hand, 'Managerment' is a specific process consisting of several successive functions which are performed through proper supervision of the works of the operative employees in order to implement the planned goals of the enterprise effectively and efficiently. The various functions of management are—planning, organising, command, directing, motivating, co-ordinating and controlling.

Organisation structure of an enterprise is established through the process of organising. In fact, the setting up of organisation structure is a very important function of management upon which the success of its other functions depends to a great extent. Organisation acts as a tool of management for achieving the pre-determined goals of the enterprise.

The differences between 'Organisation' and 'Management' are pointed out below :

Points of Distinction	Organisation	Management
1. Meaning :	1. 'Organisation' is the structure by which a harmonious inter-relation is established between the workers and their work.	1. 'Management' is the executive process of getting works accomplished by the subordinate employees.
2. Nature of Work :	2. Through organisation authority and responsibility are delegated. These are organisational activities.	2. The functions of management are administrative activities.
3. Area of Function :	3. Organisation is one of the various functions of management. As a part of management, organisation helps it to execute its other functions.	3. Management is the sum total of several activities—making plan, setting up organisation, giving command and direction, motivating the employees, co-ordinating and controlling various functions of the enterprise.
4. Accomplishment of Function :	4. Organisation acts as a tool in the hands of the managers.	4. With the help of organisation the managers perform their duties and responsibilities.
5. Aim :	5. Organisation aims at performing the planned activities through creating proper work environment.	5. The objective of management is to supervise the accomplishment of work of the subordinate employees and to give necessary direction for getting the desired result for achieving the pre-determined target.
6. Dependability :	6. The setting up of effective organisation structure depends on efficient management.	6. Efficient management largely depends on strong organisation.
7. Comparison :	7. Organisation may be regarded as the hands of human body.	7. Management may be compared to the whole human body.

1.16 Distinction among Organisation, Administration and Management

The major differences among Organisation, Administration and Management are mentioned in the following chart :

Organisation	Administration	Management
1. The function of organisation is to set up a harmonious inter-relation between the employees and their work by delegating authority and responsibility among them.	1. The task of administration is to determine the objectives and policies of the enterprise.	1. The activity of management is to get the various work done by the operative employees to fulfil those objectives according to the policies determined by administration.
2. Establishment of organisation is one of the basic functions of management.	2. Administration includes formulation of plan and determination of organisation structure.	2. Planning, setting up organisation structure, giving command and direction, motivating the subordinate employees, co-ordinating and controlling the various functions performed by them etc. are the activities of management.
3. Organisation is the work-centre of the employees of all levels of the enterprise.	3. Administration is the centre of the employees of higher level.	3. Management is the work-field of the employees of middle and lower level.
4. Organisation is the foundation of managerial work.	4. Administration determines the structure by which the functions of management are directed.	4. The managers supervise and control the work of the subordinate employees according to plan.
5. Through the process of creating organisation structure authority and responsibility are delegated. So, the nature of this process is organisational.	5. The work of administration is to determine rules, regulations and principles. Therefore, it is determinative in nature.	5. Management implements those rules, regulations and principles. So, it is an executive function.
6. The nature of organisation is reflected through the performance of work.	6. The nature of administration is reflected in fixation of objectives, determination of policies and decision-making.	6. The nature of management is disclosed by the performance of work and application of the rules and principles.
7. Organisation may be compared to the hands of a human body; because it helps directly in performance of work.	7. Administration my be compared to the brain of the human body; because its activities relate to thinking process like fixation of target, decision making etc.	7. Management may be regarded as the eyes of a human being; as it observes whether the work is being performed according to the rules and policies to achieve the desired result.

EXERCISES

[A] Essay-Type Questions

1. Define 'Management'. Discuss the nature of Management.
[**Ans.** Sections 1.1. and 1.3]

2. Discuss the functions of management. [C.U. B.Com. 1986]
[**Ans.** Section 1.6]

3. Discuss the major principles of management. [C.U. B.Com. 1994, 1996, 1998]
[**Ans.** Section 1.7]

4. Is management a science or an art ? Discuss.
[**Ans.** Section 1.9]

5. Is management a profession? Give reasons for your answer.
[**Ans.** Section 1.10.1]

6. Discuss the importance of management.
[**Ans.** Section 1.5]

7. Discuss the various features of management.
[**Ans.** Section 1.2]

8. Explain the different levels of Management. How far they are practised in Indian Business? [C.U. B.Com. 1988]
[**Ans.** Section 1.8]

9. Discuss the different levels of management. Do you think that such levels are necessary in all cases? [C.U. B.Com. 1980, 1983]
[**Ans.** Section 1.9]

10. "Management is not a profession but is making great steps in that direction."—Discuss.
[**Ans.** Section 1.10.1]

11. (a) Mention the different levels of management.
(b) Discuss the nature and functions of the different levels of management. [C.U. B.Com. 1985]
[**Ans.** Section 1.8]

12. "Management is both a science and an art."—Comment. [C.U. B.Com. 1994, 1998]
[**Ans.** Section 1.9]

13. Explain the process of management. [C.U. B.Com. 1995]
[**Ans.** Section 1.6]

14. What is Management? Discuss the principles of management. [C.U. B.Com. 1996]
[**Ans.** Section 1.1 & 1.7]

15. Explain the levels of Management. Enumerate the functions of each of them. [C.U. B.Com. 1999]
[**Ans.** Section 1.7]

16. Explain the nature and scope of management. [C.U. B.Com. 1999]
[**Ans.** Section 1.3]

17. Give the meaning and definition of management. Discuss the nature of management. [C.U. B.Com. 1999]
[**Ans.** Sections 1.1 and 1.3]
18. Discuss briefly the major functions of management. [C.U. B.Com. 2006]
[**Ans.** Section 1.6]
19. "Management is a process."—Discuss [C.U. B.Com. 2006]
[**Ans.** Section 1.6]
20. Explain why management has become so important for modern business. [C.U. B.Com. 2009]
[**Ans.** Section 1.5]
21. Define 'Management'. Explain the main features of management. [C.U. B.Com. 2010]
[**Ans.** Section 1.1 and 1.2]
22. Describe the objectves of 'management'.
[**Ans.** Section 1.4]
23. Distinguish between 'Organisation' and 'Management'.
[**Ans.** Section 1.15]
24. Explain the distinctions between 'Administration' and 'Management.'
[**Ans.** Section 1.14.1]
25. Describe the different roles or tasks of a manager.
[**Ans.** Section 1.12]
26. Narrate the various managerial skills.
[**Ans.** Section 1.13]

[B] Short Answer-Type Questions

1. Explain the following terms:
(i) Management [C.U. B.Com. 1988]
[**Ans.** Section 1.1]
(ii) Organisation
[**Ans.** Section 1.7]
(iii) Co-ordination
[**Ans.** Section 1.7]
(iv) Motivation
[**Ans.** Section 1.7]
(v) Planning
[**Ans.** Section 1.7]
(vi) Control
[**Ans.** Section 1.7]

2. Write short notes on the following:
(i) Nature and scope of Management [C.U. B.Com. 1996]
[**Ans.** Section 1.3]
(ii) Management as a Profession [**Ans.** Section 1.10]
(iii) Management as an Art [**Ans.** Section 1.9]
(iv) Universality of Management [**Ans.** Section 1.11]
(v) Management as a Science. [**Ans.** Section 1.9]

3. Answer briefly the following questions:

(i) Mention the different levels of management. [C.U. B.Com. 1987]
[**Ans.** Section 1.8]

(ii) Is Management a profession? [C.U. B.Com. 1995, 1998]
[**Ans.** Section 1.9]

(iii) What do you understand by 'universality of management'? [C.U. B.Com. 1996]
[**Ans.** Section 1.11]

(iv) Is management a science? [C.U. B.Com. 1996]
[**Ans.** Section 1.9]

(v) What is Management? [C.U. B.Com. 1997]
[**Ans.** Section 1.1]

(vi) Is management a profession? [C.U. B.Com. 2000, 2008]
[**Ans.** Section 1.10.1]

(vii) Mention any four functions of management. [C.U. B.Com. 2001]
[**Ans.** Section 1.6]

(viii) Is management an art or a science? [C.U. B.Com. 2001, 2005, 2006]
[**Ans.** Section 1.9]

(ix) What do you mean by universality of management? [C.U. B.Com. 2002, 2004, 2010]
[**Ans.** Section 1.11]

(x) Define the term 'Management'. [C.U. B.Com. 2006, 2011]
[**Ans.** Section 1.1]

(xi) Is management universal? [C.U. B.Com. 2006]
[**Ans.** Section 1.11]

(xii) Mention the functions of management. [C.U. B.Com. 2006]
[**Ans.** Section 1.6]

(xiii) Why management is important to an organisation? [C.U. B.Com. 2007]
[**Ans.** Section 1.5]

(xiv) Why management is universal? [C.U. B.Com. 2008]
[**Ans.** Section 1.11]

(xv) Define 'Management'. [C.U. B.Com. 2011 (Old and New Syllabus)]
[**Ans.** Section 1.1]

(xvi) Mention levels of management with a diagram.
[**Ans.** Section 1.8] [C.U. B.Com. 2011 (New Syllabus)]

(xvii) State two managerial tasks. [C.U. B.Com. 2011 (New Syllabus)]
[**Ans.** Section 1.12]

CHAPTER 2

Different Schools of Management Thought

"The goal of management is to remove obstacles." —Paul Orfalea

TOPICS

2.1 Development of Modern Management Thought ◆ 2.2 Different Schools of Management Thought ◆ 2.3 Scientific Management ◆ 2.4 Basic Principles and Features of Scientific Management Thought ◆ 2.5 Benefits of Scientific Management ◆ 2.6 Taylor's Contribution to Management Science ◆ 2.7 Criticism of Scientific Management ◆ 2.8 Fayol's Contribution to Modern Management Theory ◆ 2.8.1 Comparison of Taylor's and Fayol's Approach to Management ◆ 2.9 Human Relations Approach to Management ◆ 2.10 Contribution of Elton Mayo to Management Thought ◆ 2.11 Human Behavioural Approach to Management ◆ 2.12 Follet's Contribution to Management Thought ◆ 2.13 System Approach to Management ◆ 2.14 Contingency or Situational Approach to Management ◆ 2.15 Bureaucratic Management.

Subject-matter of the Chapter : *The form of management thought which is seen today was not built in a day. Modern management has evolved through different stages with the change of time and gradual evolution of civilisation. It is the outcome of a time-long evolution of thoughts. Sometimes management thought developed slowly and sometimes it grew fast. But Scientific Management has evolved fast in the last two centuries. The growth of modern management as a storehouse of deciplined knowledge is a grand success of the twentieth century. Management has been recognised as one of the elements of production and universal process in the very twentieth century. Management thoughts are well-known as arts from ancient times but the growth of management as science is a recent phenomenon. Management is a large canvas. Different theories have been built up centring round the thoughts, concepts, approaches and opinions expressed at different times by various management thinkers, social scientists, psychologists and researchers. Most of the theories have emphasised on some special aspect of management.*

A detail discussion on different schools of management thought has been accomodated in this chapter.

2.1 Development of Modern Management Thought

Management practice is as old as human civilisation when people started living together in groups, In the ancient civilisations, there are instances of the application of the principles of management. Administrative problems received attention even in ancient Mesopotamia, Greece, China, and India also. During this period management generally took the form of personal leadership. This leadership was found reflected in almost all homes and families, clubs, games, churches, military forces and many other social and political organisations. But this was much used in the business world so long as the structure of industry was simple and there had been no development of managerial tools of analysis until the expiry of the Dark Ages (5th-15th century).

With the onset of the Industrial Revolution, from about 1760, however, the position went under a radical change. The structure of industry became extremly complex. The expanding size of industry and commerce and the complexities of human relationship offered a serious challenge for entrepreneurs in the task of management. The need for expansion further added to the worries of the business leaders. They started thinking of a solution to the problem of how the limited resources could be applied in a better way. The growth and subsequent development of corporate form of business in the Western World introduced a distinction between the functions of the owners and functions of the managers. The distinction paved the way for the study of management as a separate and distinct field of knowledge. Diversification of industries, growing competition and complexity of managing large business demanded efficiency in management process which could be attained only by developing and applying systematic management concept and principles.

At this stage, the development of a formal theory of management—both of work and the workers—became absolutely necessary. Obviously, this situation led the theorists to make a thorough analysis of the business problems and to find out a sound theory of management for efficient, easy and speedy work performance.

It was against this background that the pioneers of modern management thought laid the foundation of modern management theory and practice. Management theory was evolved by tireless efforts of a few eminent management experts and industrialists. F. W. Taylor, Henry Fayol, Oliver Sheldon, Lyndall Urwick, Mary Parker Follet, Peter F. Drucker, Charles Babbage and Robert Owen are some of the modern thinkers of and contibutors to the subject.

The real development of management thought started with the scientific management approach given by Taylor, though some of the concepts were developed by early thinkers mostly in the field of public administration and technical aspects of business. The contribution of these thinkers were limited mostly to the field of developing concepts to make resources more effective at the shop floor levels. These contributions were made bit by bit and in haphazard manner and had failed to stimulate management as a distinct discipline for further study. However, their ideas created an awareness about managerial problems. By the end of the nineteenth century, the stage was set for making systematic study of management and the beginning was made by Taylor in the early part of the twentieth century. During the last five decades, there has been enormous development of thoughts in management.

2.2 Different Schools of Management Thought

Some pioneers and outstanding contributors in the field of management have evolved different schools of management thought by means of a comprehensive thinking on different aspects of management. These contributions have different backgrounds and they created a diversity in management thought by adopting divergent approaches.

The process of the development of management thought can be studied chiefly under three broad heads or stages, such as—(a) Taylor's scientific approach, (b) Henry Fayol's functional approach, and (c) the modern human relations approach or, the behavioural science approach.

Different schools of management thought and the contributions made by the pioneers in the respective field are discussed below :

1. Scientific Management School : This school envisages management to be a scientific management. It means that, scientific methods and scientific principles are to be followed and applied in managing the affairs of an enterprise. **Frederick Winslow Taylor** (1856-1915), popularly known as the 'Father of Scientific Management Movement', was the first to recognise and emphasise the need for adopting a systematic scientific approach to the task of managing an enterprise. Taylor joined the Midvale Steel Company in the USA, as a worker and later on rose to the position of chief engineer. Subsequently he joined the Bethelehem Works where he experimented with his ideas and made his contribution to management theory for which he is so well-known. He studied the causes of low efficiency in industry and came to the conclusion that much of the waste and inefficiency is due to the lack of order and system in the methods of management. He observed that the managers were usually ignorant of the amount of work that could be done by a worker in a day and had no clear notion of the best method of doing the work. It was his realisation that there was lack of efficient work standard, absence of clear-cut division of works between the managers and workers, lack of incentive of the workers, unscientific selection and placement of workers. He, therefore, suggested that the managers should follow a 'scientific approach' in their work and apply scientific methods for achieving higher efficiency. With a view to improving management practice, he conducted a series of experiments. On the basis of these experiments he developed his concepts and techniques into a philosophy which is known as 'Scientific Management'. He published many papers and books and all his contributions were compiled in his book '*The Principles of Scientific Management*'.

Taylor's ideas on scientific management were greatly expanded by H. S. Person, Henry L. Gantt, and Lillian Gilbreth, Harrington Emerson and M. L. Cooke.

2. Management Process School : This school builds up the idea that management is a process of getting things done through and with other people operating in organised groups. It analyses the management process by describing its functions like planning, organising, directing, co-ordinating and controlling. The executives perform this process. In this approach importance is given to the activities of the managers, the general principles and rules which they should follow.

Henry Fayol is considered to be the 'Founder of Management Process School'. He points out that management is a functional concept which is universal and applicable to any type of enterprise, be it a business enterprise or otherwise. Other persons who worked to develop this approach are J. D. Mooney, A. C. Reiley, Lyndall Urwick, Harold Koontz and O'Donnell, Newman, Luther Gullick, George Terry, E. F. L. Brech, Mcfarland, etc.

3. Human Relations School : In scientific management, importance is given to its technical side to increase the efficiency of the organisations. On the other hand, 'Human Relations School' believes in the importance of human resources in the management. This approach focusses attention on the relationship between the management authority and the working personnel. The importance of working personnel in management is immense. If their mentality, aspirations, desires, wants and needs are properly looked into and satisfied by the managers, their activities become effective and meaningful. The main aspect of this approach is to treat the workers as human beings.

This school highlights the importance of informal social groups in the organisation, good human relations, the need for managerial motivation, greater recognition, participation, better communication and good leadership. According to this school, an organisation is not merely a formal arrangement of men and functions, more than that, it is a social system, and the human factor is the most important element within it.

In the early twentieth century **Elton Mayo**, professor at the Harvard University, could realise the importance of this thought by experiments and observations in the factory of the Western Electric Company at Hawthorne city in Chicago. These experiments and observations of Prof. Elton Mayo are known as 'Hawthorne Experiment'. These experiments revealed that physical and environmental factors do not materially influence the workers' performance and attitude to work. Mayo realised first the necessity to consider and solve the problems of the workers with human relation approach. He thought that the productivity of workers depends upon human relationship. Other important propagators of this school of management thought are—Roethlis Berger, William J. Dickson, Mary Parker Follet and A. F. Maslow.

4 Human Behavioural School : The behavioural approach to management relates to the application of the methods and findings of psychology and sociology to the organisational behaviour. This school emphasises the actions and reactions of the human beings in group activity. Mental reactions like emotions, feelings, aims, instincts, hopes and desires regulate a man's behaviour or conduct. 'Human Behavioural School' believes that, unless these mental reactions of the workers are considered, and their problems are either solved or at least attempts are made to fulfil their needs and demands by the managers, effective and meaningful management is not possible. Thus, according to this school, performance of managerial activities in consideration of the conduct or behaviour of working personnel is an effective and decent management.

As a result of the experiments, observations and researches of many psychologists and sociologists, and after the Hawthorne Experiment, 'Human Behaviour Management Thought' was evolved out. In this respect, the contribution of **Mary Parker Follet,** a member of Human Behaviour School, is particularly mentionable. Other notable propagators of this school are A. F. Maslow. F. H. Herzberg, McGregor, Keith Davis and Chrris Argrys.

The following other schools of management thought are also important in modern management :

5. System Approach School : According to this school, management is a 'system' of co-ordination of some different factors forming the parts of an overall management process, which are inter-related or inter-dependent. If the activities related to production of an enterprise are performed, giving much importance to one of its factors or parts, without considering its relationship and dependence on other factors, the desired result cannot be obtained. For example, men, machine, money and raw materials are the factors of production in management. These elements are not isolated, rather they are correlated and inter-dependent on one another. A perfect assemblage of these factors results in production. Efficient workers cannot perform their activities well with bad machines. Good work cannot be expected of inefficient workers working with good machines. So, management is a system to assemble the different correlated and inter-dependent factors that are parts of the overall system. It must be viewed in the context of total environment, and the managers should take into account the various characteristics and changes therein in managing the organisation.

The major contributors to this school are Kenneth, Boulding, Johnson, F. E. Kast, J. E. Rosenzwig, Katz and Kahn, Forester and C. W. Churchman.

6. Decision Theory School : The essence of management lies in decision-making. Whatever a manager does is the outcome of a decision made by him from several alternatives available to him. The 'Decision Theory School' of management thought concentrates its attention on decision-making and treats the various aspects of decision-making as constituting the scope of the study of management. Advocates of this school opine that decision-making is the most critical function of management and any study of management should focus directly on the decision-making process. Rational approach to decision-making is the basis of this school.

To perform the managerial functions properly and effectively, one has to learn the procedures, techniques, causes and effects of taking decisions. Top level management authority has to take decisions at the stage of planning and the managers in charge of execution of plans have to take decisions at the stage of its implementation. It becomes proper, meaningful and effective only if decisions are taken through a reasonable procedure.

Among the proponents of this theory, the names of Herbert Simon, Stephen Robins and Chester Barnard are especially mentionable.

7. Mathematical or Quantitative School : This school views Management as a system of mathematical models and process. The exponents of this school of thought believe that effective solution of the intricate problems of management of an enterprise can be achieved through organising mathematical or quantitative model. Management or organisation, planning or decision-making, as a logical process, can be expressed in terms of mathematical symbols and relationships, The contributors to this school of thought have been using mathematical and quantitative techniques in developing the models of various kinds of decision and problems involved in managing the organisations with a view to understanding them and also for finding out solutions to them. This theory uses the techniques of Operation Research, Games Theory, Linear Programming, Queing Theory and Model Building. As proponents of this theory the names of L. Ackoff, C. W Churchman, Newman, Hicks and Joel Dean may be mentioned.

8. Contingency Approach School of Management : According to this approach, management is a subject that is situational by nature. It has no hard and fast principle and theory. In one way, this is an extension of the system approach. The basic idea of the contingency approach is that there cannot be a particular management action which will be suitable for all situations. Study of management, according to this approach, lies in identifying the important variables in the situation. An appropriate management action is one that is designed on the basis of external environment and interal states and needs. Management may be effective and fruitful, if its principles and procedures are appropriately followed and its techniques are intelligently applied according to the circumstances. Contingency theorists suggest that the systems approach does not adequately spell out the precise relationship between the organisation and its environment. Contingency approach tries to fill this gap by suggesting what should be done in response to an event in the environment. The supporters of this theory are mainly, Lorsch and Lawrence, John Woodward, Fiedler and H. M. Carlisle.

2.3 Scientific Management

(A) Meaning : In a fundamental sense, Scientific Management is an attitude and a philosophy which discards its traditional hit-or-miss and rule-of-thumb method of managing the works and workers. It means the application of the method of scientific investigation for the solution of the problems of industrial management. Taylor defined 'Scientific Management' as "the art of knowing exactly what you want men to do, and then seeing that they do it in the best and cheapest way." Management, according to him, is a science based on clearly defined laws and principles which are applicable to all forms of human activity. To develop each man to his greatest efficiency and to maximise prosperity for both the employer and the employee should be the objective of management.

By eliminating wastage and inefficiency, production and productivity can be improved and, to do that, management should have a scientific approach to managerial problems. In other words, Scientific Management may be regarded as a set of scientific techniques that are meant to increase the efficiency of the plant or any other functional organ of an organisation. According to it, the workers in a plant can increase their productivity if the managers set before them a standard task. The standard task has to be set through scientific investigations, research and experimentation. The managers will analyse the operation involved in each job to eliminate wasteful movements of body and to determine the best method of doing the job. To ensure that the standard task is performed by the use of suggested methods, the managers will also take steps to train the workers, standardise the tools and equipment, and improve the work environment. It will also systematise the procedure of selection and placement of workers to eliminate wastage and inefficiency caused by misfits in the undertaking. This programme of action leading to scientific management presupposes the presence of perfect cordiality between the workers and managers. In the absence of mutual understanding and good faith, it will loose its point.

(B) Nature, Objective and Importance of Scientific Management : The main contents of Scientific Management is the substitution of 'rule-of-thumb' method or quack system of production by adopting scientific principles for maximisation of production, avoidance of disputes or differences, and establishment of unity of relationship between the workers and managers. Scientific Management stresses upon the mutual co-operartive efforts in the performance of activities and rendering equal scope or opportunity to each worker to show his maximum efficiency in order to develop his overall capacity.

The main objectives of Scientific Management are promotion and maximum improvement of the standard of management, and the efficiency and standard of performances of the workers. Such improvement is expected to bring a revolution in management process and in workers' performance. With the improvement of the standard of management and the efficiency of workers to the maximum level with the help of Scientific Management, the output is bound to be optimum.

If the principles and procedures of Scientific Management are followed and applied, it can prevent the wastage of time and labour in industry, reduce cost of production, increase efficiency of the workers and improve the relationship between the managers and workers. Herein lies the importance of Scientific Management.

(C) Tools of Scientific Management : Taylor and his associates and followers have brought perfection to the efficiency techniques through which the principles of Scientific Management could be implemented. The main techniques are the following :

(i) **Work Study :** It involves work measurement and work improvement through scientifically conducted time, motion, method and fatigue studies.

  (a) **Time Study :** It involves the careful measurement of the time required to do each detailed part of an industrial operation. The basic purpose of time study is to determine the proper time for performing the operation.

  (b) **Motion Study :** It is study of the movements of an operator (or even of a machine) in performing an operation for eliminating useless motions. The purpose of such a study is to find out the best method of job performance which every worker will be expected to follow.

  (c) **Method Study :** It involves the determination of the standard task to be performed by the workers.

(d) **Fatigue Study :** The purpose of such study is to provide for measures to eliminate or minimise fatiguê of the workers at jobs. It is necessary to regulate the working hours and provide for rest to the workers at scientifically determined intervals. This would provide the workers an opportunity to restore the energy lost in continuous work.

(ii) **Introduction of Functional Organisation :** It is done by separating the functions of planning and implementation between two sets of foremen.

(iii) **Differential Piece Plan of Wage Payment :** Under this system, the workers performing the standard task within the prescribed time are paid a much higher rate than those who are not able to come up to the standard set.

(iv) **Standardisation of Tools and Equipments** for workers, machine speeds, materials and working conditions.

(v) **Scientific Selection, Placement and Training** of the workers by a centralised personnel department.

(vi) **Mental Revolution on the part of the Employers and the Workers** in regard to the mutual co-operation for increased productivity.

2.4 Basic Principles and Features of Scientific Management

The features and basic principles of Scientific Management are enumerated below :

1. **Develpment of Science for each Element of a Man's Work :** Taylor has emphasised that, in scientific management, organised knowledge should be applied which will replace the rule-of-thumb policy. Each man's work will be determined on the basis of scientific principles instead of traditional method.

2. **Scientific Selection and Training of Workmen :** To increase the workers' efficiency and loyalty, Taylor has suggested that they should be selected on scientific basis taking into account their education, work experience, aptitude, ability, etc. A worker should be given the work for which he is physically and technically most suitable. Apart from that, proper emphasis should be given on the training of the workers that makes them more efficient and effective. The duty of the managers should be to determine by experiment and observation the nature of each activity and responsibility involved in its performance.

3. **Separation of Planning from Doing :** Taylor emphasised the separation of planning aspect from actual doing of the work. Those who plan must not be allowed to execute anything, and those who execute plans are not to be allowed to make plans. Planning function is to be allocated to the managers and doing function to the workers.

4. **Job Analysis :** The best way of doing a job is one which requires the least movements, consequently less time and cost. This can be determined by taking up time, motion and fatigue studies. Time study involves the determination of time required to complete the standard task. Motion study is the study of movements in parts which are involved in doing a job and thereby eliminating the unnecessary movements. Fatigue study shows the amount and frequency of rest required to complete the work. After certain period of time, the workers feel fatigue and cannot work with full energy and capacity. Therefore, they require rest. When the rest is allowed, they start working with full capacity. Thus job analysis, as given by Taylor, suggests the fair amount of a day's work requiring certain movements and rest periods to complete it.

5. Standardisation : As far as possible, standardisation should be maintained in respect of equipment, materials, tools, time required, amount of work, working conditions, cost of production, etc. These things should be fixed in advance on the basis of job analysis and various elements of costs in performing a work.

6. Friendly Co-operation between the Managers and Workers : Scientific Management is based on mutual co-operation between the managers and the workers. For success of a business, active co-operation and cordial relationship between them should be established. For this, change of thoughts and attitude of the managers and workers is essential, which indicates a mental revolution of both of them. The workers must keep in their minds that they have to do their work smoothly, efficiently and effectively. The manager has also to realise that the workers are not only the tools in his hands and under his command and control, rather, they are human beings with sentiments and aspirations. They should be adequately appreciated and rewarded for their performances.

7. Harmony in Group Action : Taylor has pointed out that attempts should be made to obtain harmony in group action rather than discord. Group harmony suggests that there should be mutual give-and-take situation and proper understanding so that the group as a whole contributes to the maximum.

8. System of Functional Foremanship : In Scientific Management, the introduction of leadership, on the basis of function, is an important aspect. For this purpose, Taylor evolved the concept of functional foremanship based on specialisation of functions. He recommended the employment of eight expert leaders or foremen namely,—(i) Gang boss, (ii) Speed boss, (iii) Repair boss, (iv) Inspector, (iv) Route clerk, (iv) Instruction card clerk, (vii) Time and cost clerk, and (viii) Shop disciplinarian. Each of such foremen is an expert in his own area and he is allotted absolute power and authority to discharge his duties and to direct his workers.

9. Development of Workers : In Scientific Management, all workers should be developed to the fullest extent possible for their own sake and for the highest prosperity of the organisation. Development of workers requires their scientific selection and providing them with training at the work place. Training should be provided to the workers in order to keep them fully fit according to the requirement of new methods of working.

10. Economy : While applying Scientific Management, not only scientific and technical aspects should be considered, but adequate consideration should be given to economy and profit. For this purpose, techniques of cost estimates and control should be adopted. The economy and profit can be conceived by making the resources more productive as well as by eliminating the wastage.

11. Financial Incentives : Financial incentives can motivate the workers to put in their maximum efforts. If provision exists to earn higher wages by putting in an extra effort, the workers will be motivated to earn more. Taylor himself applied the concept of differential piece rate system of wage payment which was highly motivating. According to this scheme, a worker who completes the normal work gets wages at higher rate per piece and one who does not complete it gets at lower rate.

12. Maximum Output : Scientific Management involves continuous increase in production and productivity instead of restricted production either by the managers or the workers. Taylor hated inefficiency and deliberate curtailment of production. Therefore, he advised the managers and workers to "turn their attention towards increasing the size of the surplus."

2.5 Benefits of Scientific Management

Following the principles of Scientific Management, if planning of the entire work of the organisation is done on the basis of proper investigation, and by ensuring that every one does his work in the given time and according to the instructions, all types of wastage and losses are avoided, output is maximised and costs are lowered.

The following are the merits or advantages of Scientific Management :

(a) It removes traditional practices by developing and introducing scientific principles and procedures at every stage of operating activity.

(b) In it, working personnel are selected, trained and employed on the basis of scientific principles. As a result efficiency, skill, and loyalty of the workers are increased.

(c) By avoiding guesswork and encouraging scientific analysis and observations for plans and procedures, it increases productivity to a great extent and eliminates wastage and losses.

(d) In it, right men are employed and placed in right jobs and it combines machinery, materials and man-power in such a manner as to maximise output.

(e) In it, instead of conservative attitude, the managers are guided by progressive outlook, and, as such, a mentality of co-operation instead of conflict is created in the minds of the workers and managers.

(f) As a result of time study, motion study and fatigue study, unnecessary physical and mental labour of the workers are dispensed with. For this reason, production at increased rate can be effected by them.

(g) Incentive wages are paid to the workers in Scientific Management. As the employees are adequately remunerated for their work, production of goods sharply increases.

2.6 Taylor's Contribution to Management Science

F. W. Taylor occupies a unique position among the thinkers on management. The development of management thought may be said to begin with him (1856-1915). He was the first to introduce scientific methods, observation and experiment to the problems of industrial management. He is well-known for his famous work '*The Principles of Scientific Management*' published in 1911. Scientific Management, as founded by him, has been approved and adopted in modern management. As Taylor has first evolved the philosophy of scientific management on the basis of scientific principles obtained through several researches, experiments and observations, he is called the 'Father of Scientific Management'.

F. W. Taylor

He stated that "the best management is a true science resting upon clearly defined laws, rules and principles as foundation." The scientific method consists of observation, measurement, experimentation and inference. Taylor advocated the classification by the management of all knowledge concerning work and its formulation into rules, laws and formulas. The managers should also fix the standards of work to be followed by the trained workers.

To achieve these ends, Taylor advocated the separation of planning functions from doing functions; the managers performing the planning, thinking or supervisory functions; and the workers doing their work as detailed in the instructions provided.

The manager has new functions in the form of setting principles, namely—

(i) Following scientific methods in place of rule-of-thumb methods;

(ii) Scientific selection, placement and training of the workmen;

(iii) Co-operation of the managers and workers, resulting in harmony;

(iv) Maximum output through the application of scientific methods;

(v) Development of each worker to achieve maximum efficiency and prosperity;

(vi) Equitable division of work and responsibility between the managers and workers.

Taylor's insistence on the application of scientific methods to managerial problems and his analytical search for the best methods of doing jobs are his principal contributions to management theory. He was concerned with the efficiency of the workers and the job of the managers in the production of goods. Besides other principles, he developed time and motion study which is regarded as the 'corner-stone of scientific management'.

The significance of Taylor's work really lies in the emphasis on the use of the scientific method and the scientific approach for the solution of the problems of business management. He laid the true foundation for the development of modern management science.

2.7 Criticisms of Scientific Management

It must be admitted that Scientific Management offered a new approach to the management of men at work. It has helped in the best utilisation of men, machine and materials. Both the employer and the employees are benefited in a number of ways by the application of its principles. But it has not become universally popular; and has been criticised by various sections of the society on several grounds.

Scientific Management is subject to the following criticisms :

1. Production Management only : Although Taylor's principles of scientific management were intended for broad application, the actual emphasis was not on the general management of the enterprise but management at the shop level. The application of the principles of Scientific Management is found to be combined with the activities in relation to production. No principle in respect of marketing management, financial management, sales management etc. is found in Scientific Management. These are as important as production management. It speaks of skill of the workers, increase in production and problems related to production management. Thus, it tends to be more of industrial engineering than a general theory of management.

2. Objections of the Employers : The employers oppose Scientific Management on the ground that the introduction of it involves huge expenditure. Overhauling of the existing plant, making time and motion studies—all these involve too much expenditure. The employers also argue that scientific management disorganises the production pattern and the existing plant and machinery become obsolete entailing huge loss. The creation of the planning section under scientific management is also criticised by the employers on the ground of expenditure involved in organising such a section.

3. Unsuitable for Small-Scale Firm : There are some methods or arrangements in Scientific Management—such as the establishment of a separate personnel department, conducting of time, motion and fatigue studies, introduction of cost accounting—which are too expensive. On account of the introduction of functional foremanship, there arises the necessity of employing high-salaried experts. This also results in an increase in the cost of production. As such, Scientific Management is possible only in large organisations. Its introduction may not be possible within the capacity of small enterprises.

4. Dissatisfaction of the Workers : Taylor's Scientific Management is opposed by the workers. This is because it treats them like machines and provides for exessive supervision over their performance of work. These measures may go against the workers' interest and cause loss of their health. Specialisation spoken of in Scientific Management may cause monotony of their activities. It divides the workers into efficient and inefficient classes and results in their exploitation as all the gains of increased productivity are not passed on to them. Introduction of modern machinery may cause unemployment of the workers. and the loss of influence and power of the Trade Unions. For all these reasons, the workers refuse to accept the method of Scientific Management.

5. Objection of the Managers : The managers oppose it on the ground that the system of Scientific Management imposes heavy burden of duties and responsibilities over the managers but it has not recommended additional remuneration for them.

6. Impractical : It is unrealistic to suggest, as Taylor did, that the two functions—planning and doing—should be performed by different sets of people who do not come in direct contact with each other. Planning divorced from doing will be impractical and doing separated from planning is mechanical. As **P. F. Drucker** ably points out : "it will be very much like suggesting that the function of eating and digesting should be performed by two separate bodies."

7. Misconception about 'One Best Way' : The psychologists point out that there is no 'one best method of job performance'. A worker may find out a distinct and effective way of doing work, which may be suitable to his own ability and propensity. So individual differences among the workers must be taken into account while selecting the workers and assigning work to them.

8. Undemocratic : Taylor's 'Differential Piece Rate' system of wage payment is undemocratic, discriminatory, and unreasonable. So this method of wage payment has not been universally accepted.

9. Mechanical Approach : The psychologists' objection to Scientific Management is in regard to its mechanical approach towards the workers undermining the human element in industry. The workers are virtually reduced to the level of 'automations' and are expected to work like cogs in a huge machine rather than as active and inspired members of a group of human beings. Industrial psychologists point out that the workers are human beings and they cannot be standardised in the same way as machines and materials and, therefore, they urge that the managers should adopt a human approach to the management of workers.

10. Other Defects :

(i) Taylor's thought speaks of mental revolution of both the managers and the workers and revolutionary change of the methods of production. These ideas seem to be idealistic in nature but unrealistic in practice.

(ii) Introduction of Taylor's 'functional foremanship' may cause indiscipline and changes in work performance.

(iii) In Scientific Management new methods and techniques of production are evolved through continuous experiments, researches and utilisation of new modern machinery. This may result in frequent changes in the process of activities related to production and such changes may cause break of continuity of production.

2.8 Fayol's Contribution to Modern Management Theory

Henry Fayol

Almost simultaneously with Taylor, **Henry Fayol** (1841-1925), a French industrialist and manager, developed his theory of management. He is regarded as the 'Father of Modern Management Theory', for he was the first to suggest the functions of management which are recognised as the essential part of a manager's work by the modern authorities on management.

He was a mining engineer of a large coal mining company and subsequently became its managing director. When he joined the company, it was almost bankrupt. When he retired after 30 years, the company was among the most successful enterprises with a long history of handsome profits and dividends. During his successful career he searched for sound management principles. In 1916 he published his famous work, '*General and Industrial Management*.'

Fayol's work is concerned with the higher level of the organisation. He identified the following six activities which, he believed, had to be accomplished in all industrial undertakings :

(i) Technical (relating to production and manufacturing);
(ii) Commercial (buying, selling and exchange);
(iii) Financial (search for capital and its optimum use) ;
(iv) Security (protection of property and persons);
(v) Accounting (record keeping, preparation of balance sheet, costing and statistics);
(vi) Managerial (functions of planning, organising, commanding, co-ordinating, controlling etc.).

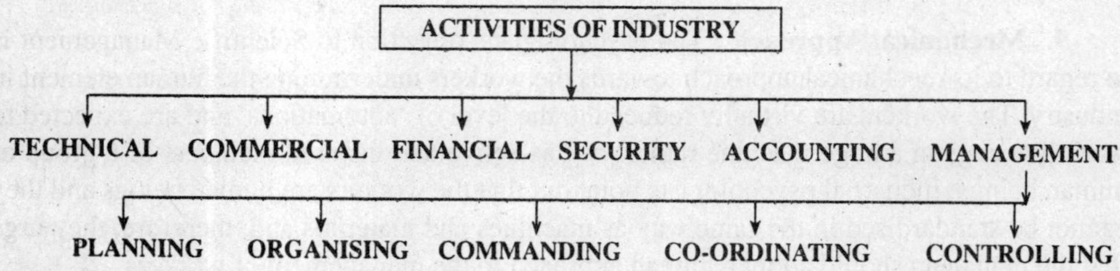

Fig. 2.1: Division of the Activities of Industrial Organisations

Pointing out that the first five activities are well-known and found in all organisations, Fayol devoted most of his discussion to the analysis of managerial activities. He divided his approach of studying management into three parts : (a) Managerial qualities and training, (b) General principles of management, and (c) Elements of management.

(A) Managerial Qualities and Training : Fayol was the first person to identify the qualities required in a manager. According to him, there are six types of qualities that a manager requires. These are as follows :

(i) Physical (health, vigour);
(ii) Mental (ability to understand and learn, judgement, mental vigour and adaptability);
(iii) Moral (energy, firmness, initiative, loyalty, tact, and dignity);

(iv) Educational (general acquaintance with the matters not belonging exclusively to the function performed);

(v) Technical (peculiar to the function being performed); and

(vi) Experience (arising from the work).

Fayol observed that the most important ability for a worker is technical and the relative importance of managerial ability increases as one goes up the scalar chain. He recognised a widespread need for the principles of management and managerial teaching. He held that managerial ability should be acquired first in school and later in the workshop.

In order to acquire managerial knowledge, he developed the principles of management to be taught in academic institutions.

(B) General Principles of Management : Fayol laid down some basic principles of management. He believed in the flexibility of these principles. According to him, the light of principles, like that of light-houses guides, only those who know the way into port. He listed and described fourteen principles of management. These principles have been discussed in detail in Section 1.7. However, a brief summary of them is given below for quick reference :

(i) Division of Work—Fayol has advocated it to take the advantages of specialisation. This principle can be applied at all levels of the organisation for higher productivity.

(ii) Authority and Responsibility—Responsibility is the corollary of authority and arises from it.

(iii) Discipline—Discipline is essential for successful management and, to ensure it, Fayol suggested good supervision at all levels, agreements with the employees as clear and fair as possible, and judicious imposition of penalties.

(iv) Unity of Command—It means that an employee should get orders from only one superior. Fayol has considered unity of command as an important aspect in managing an organisation. He suggested firmness and goodness on the part of the superiors, fair agreements with the workers and constant supervision by the managers to ensure good management.

(v) Unity of Direction—Each group of activities having the same objectives must have one head and one plan.

(vi) Subordination of Individual Interest to Group Interest—This principle reveals that the interest of the group should always prevail over the individual interest.

(vii) Remuneration of Personnel—Remuneration and methods of payment should be just and fair so that maximum satisfaction can be attained by both the employers and the employees.

(viii) Centralisation—"Everything which goes to increase the importance of the subordinates' role is decentralisation, everything which goes to reduce it is centralisation." The degree of centralisation of authority should vary according to the needs of the situation.

(ix) Scalar Chain—It is the chain of the superiors from the ultimate authority to the lowest rank. A subordinate should follow the line of authority.

(x) Order—According to Fayol, order means "a place for everything and everything in its place" and "a place for everyone and everyone in his place"; i.e., the right man in the right job.

(xi) Equity—Equity is a combination of justice and kindliness. The managers should exercise kindliness and justice in dealing with the subordinates. This will create loyalty and devotion among the employees.

(xii) Stability of Tenure of Personnel—It is a big factor for the success of an organisation. Fayol pointed out that instability in tenure of service is both the cause and effect of bad management.

(xiii) Initiative—Managers should permit the subordinates to take some initiative in thinking out and executing plans to keep up their zeal and energy.

(xiv) Esprit de Corps—This is the principle of 'Union is Strength'. Team-work and proper communication among the members of the group are important for the success of an organisation. Fayol wanted the managers to encourage cohesiveness and esprit de corps among their subordinates.

(C) Elements of Management : Fayol opines that management should be viewed as a process consisting of five elements. He has regarded these elements as the functions of management. These are planning, organisation, command, co-ordination and control. According to him, 'planning is the most important managerial function. Creation of 'organisation structure' and execution of commanding function are necessary to implement plans. 'Co-ordination' is necessary to make sure that everyone is working together, and 'control' ensures that everything is proceeding according to the plan. Fayol holds the view that these functions are required at all levels of management and in all types of organisations.

The contribution of Fayol have made the real beginning of the development of management as a separate field of study. It is true that, as a practical man, Fayol only set down the principles that he had observed and practised; yet his observations are admirably fit for the currently developing theory of or approach to management.

Fayol was thus the first man to develop a comprehensive theory of management capable of universal application. His concepts and principles are generally accepted even today. He is, therefore, 'the real founder of modern management'.

● **Criticism :** The contribution of Henry Fayol in the field of management thought is very important. He was the first person who pointed out the functions of management separately. However, in spite of such importance, his theory of management is not beyond criticism.

The management theory of Henry Fayol is criticised in the following aspects :

1. Higher Level Management : The most important criticism regarding Fayol's concept is that he has analysed management mainly from the view point of the top level managers. He considers that the top level managers only plan vital role in making an enterprise successful. But, practically it is not true. He has not considered the role and significance of the lower level managers of the organisation. It should be remembered that the operative employees work under the supervision and control of the lower level managers who actually get things done through the group activities of their subordinate workers.

2. Less Emphasis on Human Aspect : Fayol has not given proper emphasis on the utilisation of human resource. In his management theory human relation aspect is neglected.

3. Negligence of Joint Management : There is no place for joint management in Fayol's concept of management. Modern age is the age of joint management. At present the workers also participate in management through their trade union leaders.

4. Controversial Universality of Management : Fayol opines that the elements, principles and methods of management indicated by him are applicable to all types of enterprises—trading or non-trading. But the principle of universality of management is very controversial. Because the principles of management depend on time, place, and situation of application and these are changed accordingly.

5. Ineffective in Culture-bound Management : In recent times there is a tendency to establish culture-oriented management. Henry Fayol states that his principles can be changed, extended and rectified according to need and situation. If it can be done, the general theory do not have its utility and effectiveness.

2.8.1 Comparision of Taylor's and Fayol's Approach to Management

The contribution of both F. W. Taylor and Henry Fayol is very significant in the development of management theory. Both of them are renowned in management world and believed in productivity approach. They both were managers in their professional life. So they explained their thoughts and concepts on management on the basis of their personal experience. Before becoming managers both of them made research work in their own areas. That is to say, they have introduced the theory of management in the light of their practical knowledge. Development of management and its universal and rational application are noticed in the thoughts of both of them. They both have emphasised on scientific principles for the solution of practical problems of an organisation. Both think that if the workers at various levels are utilised properly an enterprise is sure to achieve success through increase in productivity. They also think that the problem of personnel and its management at all levels is the main factor of industrial success.

In spite of having so much similarities in their thoughts and ideas, some basic differences are found in their approaches. The distinction between Taylor's and Fayol's approach to management may be drawn on the following points :

1. **Area of Discussion :** Taylor has analysed management in a methodical way and from mechanical point of view. He has given emphasis chiefly on Shop Management and Production Process. He has discussed how to increase the production of a factory and solve the problems of Production Management.

On the other hand, Fayol has given emphasis on the Functions and Principles of Management. He has discussed in detail on Administrative Management and introduced a general theory of management.

2. **Concept :** Taylor's approch is a revolutionary change in industrial management. He is the first man who applied scientific approach in production and indicated the means to increase industrial productivity.

On the other hand, Henry Fayol considers management as a process consisting of five elements, such as—planning organising, commanding, co-ordinating and controlling. He is the first person who innovated the wide principles of management in macro-level approach.

3. **Perspective :** Taylor's approach is mainly based on the principle of efficiency. He started his studies from the lower level of industrial management to the upper levels, where as Fayol worked from the highest level to the lower levels of management.

4. **Applicability :** Taylor's principles of Scientific Management are applicable to specialised situation. But Fayol's general principles of management are applicable universally.

5. **Increase in Productivity :** Taylor gives emphasis on the scientific methods for increasing productivity, while Fayol emphasises on the skills and efficiency of the personnel to increase productivity.

2.9 Human Relations Approach to Management

Management is the process of getting things done by people. Any organisation can be compared to a building that is made up of bricks of people. The relationships among these people are the cementing force that bind them together in the pursuit of common objectives.

According to Human Relations Approach, management is the study of behaviour of people at work. This approach had its origin in a series of experiments conducted by **Professor Elton Mayo** and his associates at the Harvard School of Business at the Western Electric

Company's Hawthorne Works, near Chicago. These studies brought out for the first time the important relationships between social factors and productivity. Before it, productivity of the employees was considered to be a function only of physical conditions of work and money wages paid to them. For the first time it was realised that productivity depended largely upon the satisfaction of the employees in work situations.

Following the Howthorne Experiments, a great deal of work has been carried on by behavioural scientists belonging to a variety of disciplines including Psychology, Sociology, Philosophy and Anthropology in studying the behaviour of people at work. Those who subscribe to the Human Relations School of Thought are of the view that the effectiveness of any organisation depends on the quality of relationships among the people working in the organisation. So, according to them, the managers must concern themselves with an analysis of organisational behaviour, that is, interaction of people with the organisation. The basic assumption of this school still remains that the goals of the organisation are achieved through and with the people. Apart from the study of formal organisation and techniques used by such organisations, this school studies the psychological processes in the organisations, informal organisations, conflict, change, motivation and relationships, and the various techniques of achieving organisational development by improving the relationships among the various groups of people constituting the organisation and its internal environment. Thus, it may be said that this school concentrates on people and their behaviour within the formal and informal organisations.

The main features of the Human Relations Approach to management are the following :

(a) Since management is getting things done through and with people, a manager must have a basic understanding of human behaviour in all respects—particularly in the context of work groups and organisations.

(b) The managers must study the inter-personal relations among the people at work.

(c) Larger production and higher motivation can be achieved only through good human relation.

(d) The study of management must draw the concepts and principles of various behavioural sciences like Psychology and Sociology.

2.10 Contribution of Elton Mayo to Management Thought

George Elton Mayo (1880-1949) was a professor at the Harvard Business School. He published the books—'*Human Problems of an Industrial Civilisation*' (1933), '*Social problems of an Industrial Civilisation*' (1945), '*Training for Human Relations*' (1949) etc. He conducted the famous 'Hawthorne Experiments' at the Hawthorne plant of the Western Electric Company in the USA during 1927-32 with his associates. These experiments are described below :

George Elton Mayo

1. Illumination Experiments : From these experiments, it was revealed that productivity could be increased not only by improving the working environment, but also through informal social relations among the members of the working group.

2. Relay Assembly Test Room Experiment : In this experiment a small homogeneous working group was constituted. Several new elements were introduced in the work environment such as—shorter working hours, proper rest periods, improved physical conditions, friendly supervision, free social interaction among the group members, and so on. During the period of the experiment, productivity and morale increased. Productivity and morale were maintained even if the improvements in the working conditions were withdrawn. The researchers concluded that socio-psychological factors such as the feelings of being important, recognition, participation, informal work group, non-directive supervision etc. held the key for higher productivity.

3. Mass Interviewing Programme : A large number of workers were interviewed to know their perceptions and orientation on the working life. The results again confirmed the importance of informal relation, social and psychological needs and their impact on the behaviour of the workers.

4. Bank Wiring Observation Room Experiment : A group of 14 workers was observed with regard to their work behaviour. The observation revealed the informal production norms set by the workers and the existence of informal relations in the group.

The conclusion of the Hawthorne Experiments are pointed out below :

(i) A factory is not only a techno-economic unit but a psycho-social organisation also.

(ii) The workers spontaneously form small informal groups. The norms and values of such groups have significant influence on the behaviour and performance of the workers.

(iii) Physical conditions of work have some influence on the workers' morale and productivity. But their inter-personal relations, attitude of the supervisors and other social and psychological factors have a far greater influence.

(iv) Usually, the workers act or re-act not as individuals but as the members of a group.

(v) The workers are not mere economic men motivated by money alone. They respond to the total work situation including recognition, participation etc.

(vi) The informal leaders play an important role in setting and enforcing group norms.

(vii) The managers must understand and recognise the inter-personal and group relations on the job.

Elton Mayo is known as the 'Father of Human Relations Movement'. The Hawthorne Experiments provided a landmark in the evolution of management thought. Many organisations initiated the measures to improve relations with the workers. The managers were supposed to assume a new role and to develop new concepts of authority, motivation and leadership.

However, the Hawthorne Experiments were criticised for lack of scientific analysis and research. It was alleged that the researchers had certain pre-conceived perceptions and orientations. The experiments were too narrow and small to provide generalisation.

The findings of Hawthorne Experiments are, however, accepted even today. Mayo's work was a turning point in the development of management thought. His work challenged the basic postulates of the classical approach. His studies revealed the over-whelming significance of human and social factors in industry. He is rightly called the 'Founder of the Human Relations Approach' to management.

2.11 Human Behavioural Approach to Management

Classical approach to management gives stress on the jobs, but the behavioural approach to management focuses on the people performing these jobs. Here attention is directed towards the human aspects of management. The neglect of human factor and over-emphasis on machines and materials in scientific management thought led to the development of human behavioural approach. Prof. Elton Mayo is considered to be the founder of the behavioural school of thought. He conducted the famous Hawthorne Experiments. These expriments revealed the overwhelming influence of social and psychological factors on employee morale and productivity. The findings had a significant impact on management thought. The job-holders became the central point of attention in place of the job. The managers began to understand the desires of the employees for better working condition, greater recognition, participation in decision-making—which directly affect them. A new movement, known as a human relations movement emerged.

The pioneers of human relation movement point out that management involves getting things done with and through people. So, the study of management should be based on inter-personal relations. They concentrated on the study of the individual and his socio-psychological motives. The human relations scientists neglected the behavioural pattern of human groups. This led to the development of 'Organisational Behaviour.' It involves the study of attitudes, behaviour and performance of individuals and groups in organisational setting. The behavioural pattern of groups in an organisation is analysed on the assumption that an enterprise is a social organism. Behavioural approach is multi-dimentional in nature. Under it the knowledge drawn from behavioural sciences (Psychology, Sociology, and Anthropology) is applied to explain and predict human behaviour. For this reason, this approach is also known as 'Behavioural Sciences Approach'.

The behavioural science approach is thus an improved and more modern version of the human relations approach. It focuses on human behaviour in an organisation and seeks to promote verifiable propositions for scientific understanding of human behaviour in organisations. This approach draws its concepts largely from Psychology and Sociology. Motivation, leadership, communication, various groups and participative management are the core elements of this approach.

The basic propositions of the behavioural approach to management are as follows :

(a) An organisation is a socio-technical system;

(b) A variety of factors influence the inter-personal and group behaviour of people in the organisation;

(c) There should be a fusion between organisational goals and human needs;

(d) Several differences in the attitudes, perceptions and values of the employees exist and influence their behaviour and performance;

(e) Some degree of conflict may be inevitable in an organisation.

Mary Parker Follet is the pioneer contributor to the behavioural approach of management.

2.12 Follet's Contribution to Management Thought

Mary Parker Follet

Mary Parker Follet (1868-1933) of Boston, USA, is another prominent authority who made significant contribution to the development of management thought. Her approach to the study of management was to apply psychological insights and findings of the social sciences to industry. She offered a new concept relating to the nature of management and human relationships within industrial groups. She was noted for her practical observations about the value of human relations for the basic principles of organisation. Her ideas about organisation were very much appreciated. Her analysis of human behaviour is very penetrating and stimulating. The contents and characteristics of her thoughts are mainly as follows :

1. Group : Workers—being social beings—create groups which may be different from their official group. The group determines the norm of behaviour of its members. It has a value which makes it useful to the community as a basis of human action. Thus, management should deal with the workers not as individuals but as the members of a work group subject to the influence of the group.

2. Authority : Authority generally carries the implication of somebody having the power to order to somebody else because of his/her official position. This notion, Follet contented, offends human vanity and creates resentment in the minds of subordinates. Therefore, authority in an organisation should be depersonalised so that the employer-employee relationship rests on functional co-operation rather than on status. Functional co-operation between the employers and employees should be secured so that both can make effective contribution to management.

3. Conflict : Three alternative remedies are available for removing conflict in any organisation—(i) domination, (ii) compromise, and (iii) integration. Follet rejected domination because it offends the feelings of the dominated, and compromise because it gives a feeling of loss and surrender of both sides. She was for the integration of the desires of both sides in a conflict. Both sides should feel that their desires have been fulfilled and neither has sacrificed his desires. This is obviously a more stable solution of the problem of conflict than the other two mentioned above.

4. Integration : Follet regarded a business organisation as a well-integrated entity. She wanted that the various parts of the organisation are to be so well-co-ordinated and closely knit that they work as a single entity. Follet was also concerned with the methods of integrating the interests of the workers, investors, and consumers.

5. Leadership : Follet revolted against the old dominating and aggressive type of leadership. She believed that "'the leader guides the group and at the same time is himself guided by the group." "The power of leadership," she maintained, "is the power of integrating. The leader stimulates what is best in a man; he unifies and concentrates what we feel only groupingly and scatteringly." A real leader's duty is to teach and train the workers and motivate them to give their best services.

2.13 System Approach to Management

The System Approach to Management was applied to organisations during 1950. Many pioneers such as Kenneth Boulding, F. E. Kast, R. A. Johnson and Chester Barnard have made significant contributions towards the development of the system approach to management. A system is a set of distinguishable but inter-dependent and inter-related parts operating in a logical manner in order to achieve a goal. Each part affects the others and the system as a whole. Every system operates within a wider system. A system is a goal-oriented and comprised of inter-related parts.

Business organisation is an open adaptive system. System approach is comparatively a new approach to management thought.

The basic features of the system approach to management are as follows :

1. An organisation is a system consisting of several sub-systems. In a business enterprise production, sales and other departments are the sub-systems. All these sub-systems are functionally inter-acting and inter-dependent.

2. Parts and sub-parts of a system are mutually related to each other—some more, some less, some directly, some indirectly. Any change in one part may affect other parts also.

3. An organisational system has a boundary which separates it from other systems. The boundary determines which parts are internal and which are external.

4. An organisation is a dynamic system because it is responsive or sensitive to its environment. It is vulnerable to changes in its environment.

The system approach represents a new thinking on organisation and management. It stresses that the managers should avoid analysing the problems in isolation and should develop the ability for integrated thinking. It provides a unified focus to organisational efforts. It stresses on the dynamic, multi-dimensional and adaptive nature of organisations. It provides a strong conceptual framework for meaningful analysis and understanding of the organisations. It recognises the inter-action and inter-dependence among the different variables of the environment.

The system approach is criticised as being too abstract and vague. It cannot directly be applied to practical problems. It does not offer specific tools and techniques for the practising executive. It fails to specify the nature of inter-actions and inter-dependences—particularly between an organisation and its external environment.

2. 14 Contingency or Situational Approach to Management

The 'Contingency Approach to Management' is relatively a new approach to management. It is an extension of the system approach. The basic idea of the contingency approach is that the organisation has to cope up with different situations in different ways. There is no single best way of managing applicable to all situations.

In order to be effective, the internal functioning of an organisation must be consistent with the demands of the external environment. The managers must keep the functioning of an organisation in harmony with the needs of its members and the external forces.

The main characteristics of the Contingency Approach to management are pointed out below :

1. Management is entirely situational. The application and effectiveness of any technique is contingent on the situation.

2. Management should match its approach to the requirements of the particular situation. To be effective, management policies and practices must respond to environmental changes. The organisation structure, the leadership style, the control system—all should be designed to fit the particular situation.

3. As management's success depends on its ability to cope with its environment, it should sharpen its diagnostic skills so as to anticipate and comprehend environmental changes.

4. The managers should understand that there is no one best way to manage.

5. Because of the specific organisation-environment relationship, no action can be universal. It varies from situation to situation.

Contingency approach is pragmatic in nature. It avoids vague judgements and widens the horizons of practising managers. It guides them to be alert and adaptive to environmental factors while choosing their techniques and styles. They get the opportunity of becoming innovative and creative. The contingency approach has a wide-ranging applicability and practical utility in organisation and management. It advocates comparative analysis of the organisations to bring about matching between the organisational structure and situational peculiarities. Hence, this approach is also known as 'Situational Approach to Management'.

The contingency approach focuses attention on specific situational factors that affect the management strategy. It requires the managers to develop skill in situational analysis. It combines the mechanistic and humanistic approaches to fit the particular situation. It is an improvement over the system approach as it not only examines the relationships between the sub-systems of an organisation but the relationship between the organisation and its environment too.

The contingency approach is the outcome mainly of the research studies conducted by Tom Burns and G. W. Stalker, Joan Woodward, Paul Lawrence and Jay Lorsch, James Thomson and others. These experts analysed the relationships between the structure of an organisation and environmental conditions.

2.15 Bureaucratic Management

(A) Meaning : 'Bureaucratic Management is a remarkable aspect in management theory and practice. **Max Weber** (1864-1920), a reputed German Sociologist firstly developed the theory of bureaucratic management. He has discussed it from two angles—structural and behavioural. According to structural point of view, bureaucratic management is an organised structure of human relationship. From behavioural view point it refers to hierarchy of division of work and authority. The functioning in such system of management is bound by rules. The bureaucratic managers set norms which are to be enforced in an enterprise. Specific rules and regulations are framed and orders are issued which must be obeyed for the smooth, efficient, and effective functioning of the organisation.

The aim of such type of management is to increase the efficiency of administration and management of an enterprise. According to the opinion of Weber, bureaucratic management is the best way of imposing control over the employees. It is applicable to all types of large and complex organisations like business enterprises, government offices, educational institutions, and other social organisations.

(B) Features : The characteristics or features of Bureaucratic Management as pointed out by Max Weber are as follows :

1. **System of Rules and Regulations :** In bureaucratic structure of management, some specific rules and regulations are framed and these are to be obeyed by the employees of the organisation. A set of formal rules is determined to ensure uniformity of group efforts. A well-established set of regulations provides stability and continuity of an enterprise.

2. **Hierarchy of Authority :** In such management process, the principle of hierarchy of scalar authority is followed. Each lower level is under the supervision and control of the top level, so that no level of management remains uncontrolled. It indicates that authority is delegated from the top level to middle level, and from the middle level to lower level of management. It sets up a scalar chain of authority.

3. **Systematic Division of Work and Specialisation :** Division of labour and specialisation are made in bureaucratic management structure. The functions of the enterprise are divided into smaller activities and the responsibility to perform the activity is given to the managers who are specialised in the accomplishment of a particular activity. Max Weber recognises that delegation of authority is essential to carry out allocated duties. Each manager is obligated to perform his functions.

4. **Superior-Subordinate Relationship :** A Superior-subordinate relationship is established in such type of management process. The senior managers command the subordinate managers and issue orders, instructions and directives to them.

5. **Official Relationship :** In bureaucratic management, managerial relationship is based on official or formal relations. Personal relationships among the managers of various levels or departments have no importance.

6. **Written Regulations :** Bureaucratic management is a system of management by rules. Here management refers to management by law. The manager of every level is bound to abide by the established rules and regulations. Weber gives emphasis on the necessity of maintaining a systematic explanation of the norms and enforcement of the rules which can be done only through written communications. The rules, regulations, and administrative decisions are formulated and recorded in writing.

7. **Negligence of Human Relation :** In bureaucratic pattern of management, human relation is ignored. No informal relation is recognised in such management system. Formal relationship is very strictly followed here.

Max Weber

8. No External Control : There is less possibility of outside control in bureaucratic management. Rules, regulations, procedures etc. are provided more emphasis. In such system of management, control means obedience to the rules and regulations.

9. Method of Promotion : In this management pattern, the promotion of the managers and other employees is based on seniority.

10. Suitability : The bureaucratic management structure is suitable for the large and complex enterprises such as business, governmental, educational and other social organisations.

(C) Evaluation : Bureaucratic management can be considered from the following three point of views :

1. Bureaucratic structure can be considered to be an organised form where works are divided and specialisation are made among the employees. Division of work and hierarchy of authority are the important aspects of an organisation.

2. Bureaucratic management can be considered from the view point of behavioural aspects. Weber states that if it develops in the fullest extent it takes a specific form which is cordially received by capitalism.

3. Bureaucratic system of management can be judged from the point of view of realisation of objectives. In this regard it is considered as a tool.

Bureaucratic management system is such type of management that brings maximum efficiency in administration of an enterprise. It is the most effective process of management for the modern large and complex organisations. It is suitable for decision-making and maintenance of stability, appropriateness, **dependence** and discipline.

(D) Criticism : Bureaucratic management is criticised from the following aspects :

1. Negligence of Human Consideration : It is a non-human or mechanical school of thought. It has not given proper importance on the personal or informal relation of the members of the organisation. It does not recognise personal growth and the development of natural personalities. Human approach is not given any importance.

2. Abstract Rules and Regulations : In such type of management less emphasis is given on the realisation of the enterprise objectives. Rules, regulations, methods or systems are very rigidly followed here.

3. Non-existence of Informal Relationship : It does not recognise the existence and importance of informal relationship among the employees. Mistakenly it believes that the rules, regulations and procedures are the instruments for the success of an enterprise.

4. Mechanical System : It neglects the psychological and social elements of the managers. It compels them to behave in a mechanical manner.

5. Lack of Initiative : Individual initiatives and participations are not encouraged in bureaucratic pattern of management. It turns the employees into dull persons.

6. Excessive Writing Work : Detailed recording of rules, regulations, procedures, decisions, and actions are needed to be written in bureaucratic management process. So the work of writing is excessively increased.

7. Absence of Flexibility : This system of management is not flexible to adapt readily to the dynamic nature of modern management. Its system of authority and control are hopelessly outdated.

8. Delay in Accomplishment of Work : In such management system, the problems of red-tapism are noticed. So the performance of normal activities are delayed for the complicated official rules and regulations. Any specific job is not completed in right time.

9. Lack of Creativity : Bureaucratic form of management is suitable for routine works, but it is not fit for creative activities.

EXERCISES

[A] Essay-Type Questions

1. Discuss F. W. Taylor's contribution to the history of management thought. Comment on the limitations of Taylor's ideas. [C.U. B.Com. 1989]
   [**Ans.** Section 2.6]
2. Assess Henry Fayol's contribution to management thought.
   [**Ans.** Section 2.8]
3. Explain the main characteristics of Scientific Management. What are its merits? [C.U. B.Com. 1981]
   [**Ans.** Sections 2.4 and 2.5]
4. Give a brief outline of Henry Fayol's contribution to the history of management thought. [C.U. B.Com. 1990]
   [**Ans.** Section 2.8]
5. Discuss the major contribution of F. W. Taylor to the development of modern management thought. State the limitations of Taylor's ideas. [C.U. B.Com. 1993]
   [**Ans.** Section 2.6]
6. Highlight the different aspects of the Behavioural Science Approach. [C.U. B.Com. New Syl. 2011]
   [**Ans.** Section 2.6]
7. Analyse the significance of behavioural approach to management thought.
   [**Ans.** Section 2.11]
8. Discuss the contribution of Follet in the field of management. [C.U. B.Com. 2000]
   [**Ans.** Section 2.12]
9. Write the significance of Scientific Management. Indicate its important criticisms. [C.U. B.Com. 2002]
   [**Ans.** Sections 2.5 and 2.7]
10. Discuss the contributions of Taylor towards the development of management thought. [C.U. B.Com. 2005]
    [**Ans.** Section 2.6]
11. Write a brief note on the contributions of Human Relation School of Management. [C.U. B.Com. 2006]
    [**Ans.** Section 2.9]
12. Why is F. W. Taylor called the Father of Scientific Management?
    [**Ans.** Section 2.6]

13. Discuss the contribution of Mary Parker Follet to the history of management thought.
[**Ans.** Section 2.12]

14. Give a brief outline of Henry Fayol's contribution to the history of management thought. [C.U. B.Com. 2006]
[**Ans.** Section 2.8]

15. Explain the major principles of Scientific Management. [C.U. B.Com. 2008]
[**Ans.** Section 2.4]

16. Discuss the general principles of management accordings to Henry Fayol. [C.U. B.Com. 2009]
[**Ans.** Section 2.8]

17. Discuss, in brief, fourteen Principles of Management as propounded by Henri Fayol. [C.U. B.Com. New Syl. 2011]
[**Ans.** Section 2.8]

18. What do you mean by the Human Relations Approach to management. Explain the principles of Human Relations Approach. [C.U. B.Com. 2010]
[**Ans.** Section 2.9]

19. What do you mean by 'Bureaucratic Management'. Explain its features.
[**Ans.** Section 2.15]

20. Evaluate Max Weber's Bureaucratic Structure of Management with criticism.
[**Ans.** Section 2.15]

21. Enumerate the contribution of Henry Fayol in the field of management thought. What are the criticisms in his approach to management?
[**Ans.** Section 2.8]

22. Distinguish between Taylor's Approach and Fayol's Approach to management.
[**Ans.** Section 2.8.1]

[B] Short Answer-Type Questions

1. Write short notes on the following:

(i) Contribution of H. Fayol. [C.U. B.Com. 1994]
[**Ans.** Section 2.8]

(ii) Behavioural Approach to management thought.
[**Ans.** Section 2.11]

(iii) Fundamental Principles of Scientific Management.
[**Ans.** Section 2.4]

(iv) System Approach to management thought.
[**Ans.** Section 2.13]

(v) Contingency Approach to management thought.
[**Ans.** Section 2.14]

2. Answer briefly the following questions:

(i) What is 'Scientific Management.'? [C.U. B.Com. 1984]
[**Ans.** Section 2.3]

(ii) What do you mean by 'Time Study'? [C.U. B.Com. 1987, 1990, 1993]

[**Ans.** Section 2.3(C)]

(iii) What is 'Motion Study'? [C.U. B.Com. 1994]

[**Ans.** Section 2.3(C)]

(iv) Who is called the Father of Scientific Management? [C.U. B.Com. 1987]

[**Ans.** F. W. Taylor]

(v) What are the contributions of H. Fayol? [C.U. B.Com. 1998]

[**Ans.** Section 2.8]

(vi) Define Scientific Management. [C.U. B.Com. 2000]

[**Ans.** Section 2.3]

(vii) Name any four Principles of Management as framed by Mr. Fayol. [C.U. B.Com. 2002]

[**Ans.** Section 2.8]

(viii) Write any two features of Scientific Management. [C.U. B.Com. 2002]

[**Ans.** Section 2.4]

(ix) What is Scientific Management? [C.U. B.Com. 2003, 2007, 2009, 2010]

[**Ans.** Section 2.3]

(x) What is meant by Bureaucratic Management?

[**Ans.** Section 2.15]

(xi) Who innovated the Bureaucratic Pattern of Management?

[**Ans.** Max Weber]

CHAPTER 3

Planning

"Planning is bringing the future into the present so that you can do something about it now."

—Alan Lakein

TOPICS

3.1 Definition and Meaning of Planning. ◆ 3.2 Nature and Characteristics of Planning. ◆ 3.3 Importance of Planning. ◆ 3.4 Elements of Planning. ◆ 3.5 Steps in Planning. ◆ 3.6 Basic Principles of Planning. ◆ 3.7 Types of Enterprise Plan. ◆ 3.8 Strategic Planning : Concept. ◆ 3.9 Forecasting. ◆ 3.10 Role of Forecasting. ◆ 3.11 Steps in Forecasting. ◆ 3.12 Planning and Forecasting. ◆ 3.13 Techniques of Forecasting. ◆ 3.14 Decision-making : Definition and Meaning. ◆ 3.15 Importance of Decision-making ◆ 3.16 Steps in Decision-making. ◆ 3.17 Principles of Decision-making. ◆ 3.18 Types of Decision.

Subject-matter of the Chapter : *Planning is one of the basic functions of management. It is the first step in the management process, and an essential factor in fulfilling the objectives of an enterprise. Future schedule of work and mode of performance are determined through planning.*

Planning originates from decision-making. To select the best course of action from among alternatives is the task of decesion-making. The managers forecast the possibility of future events, get ready to cope up with the future situation, and determine the mode of activity to attain the target through planning.

In this chapter, discussions have been made regarding the nature, elements, importance, principles and types of planning and the various steps involved in planning process. In this context the features, importance and different methods of forecasting, characteristics, role, principles and various types of decision-making and its different steps have also been described.

3.1 Definition and Meaning of Planning

Planning is a major and primary function of management. No organisation can operate properly without planning. Planning is a preparatory step for action. It means systematised pre-thinking for determining a course of action to achieve some desired result. Planning is essentially a process of deciding in advance what is to be done, when and where it is to be done, and how, it is to be done, and by whom. To plan is to look ahead and chalk out the future course of operations of an enterprise. Through planning, the manager fixes the objectives of the organisation as a whole and, in the light of this, the goals of its various departments. Then he proceeds to prepare a kind of 'blueprint' mapping out the ways of attaining these objectives. Therefore, planning may be defined as follows :

Planning is the process by which the managers of an organisation set objectives, make an overall assessment of the future, and chart the courses of action with a view to achieving the organisational goals. From this definition it follows that the planning process involves—(i) the determination of appropriate goals and objectives, (ii) the specification of the actions needed to reach the established objectives; and (iii) the optimum period of time for achieving them. Since planning is concerned with the identification of alternatives and selection of the most favourable alternative, it may rightly be described as "the most basic tool of management functions." Thus planning is a process of deciding the business targets and charting out a rational path of attaining those targets.

Some important definitions of planning, given by the eminent authors are stated below :

According to **Koontz and O'Donnell,** planning is "an intellectual process, the conscious determination of courses of action, the basing of decisions on purpose, facts and considered estimates."

George Terry writes : "by means of planning management members try to look ahead, anticipate eventualities, prepare for contingencies, map out activities and provide an orderly sequence for achieving the objective."

Henry Fayol views : "the plan of action is, at one and the same time, the result envisaged, the line of action to be followed, the stages to go through, and methods to use."

❐ **Planning and Decision Making :** Planning decides the future course of action and involves choosing it from alternatives. From this point of view, decision-making and planning move together and one depends on the other. Truly speaking, planning as a whole with its component parts is the outcome of decision-making. So decision-making has a pervasive influence upon planning and it is a part of the planning process. Thus, decision-making and planning have intimate relation with each other.

But, decision-making has a wider connotation than planning. By this we mean to say that the application of decision-making is extended beyond the horizon of planning and, in any business, almost every position is a decisional centre. Decision-making is required not only in planning, it is also necessary in other areas of management functions such as organising, direction, co-ordination, and control. Mention may be made here of varied operating orders and instructions which are outside of planning, but are subject to decision-making. Again, there are many managerial functions like motivating the employees, disapproving their work or discharging them form service which call for decision-making, but these functions cannot be included within planning from the point of view of analytical study of different management processes.

3.2 Nature and Characteristics of Planning

Planning is concerned with the establishment of objectives of an enterprise and finding out the way of realisation of those objectives. However, without setting the objectives there is nothing to organise, direct or control. Therefore, every organisation is required to specify what it wants to achieve. Planning is basically related with this aspect.

The nature and characteristics of planning may be stated as follows :

1. Intellectual Process : Planning is an intellectual and rational process. Planning is a mental exercise involving imagination, foresight and sound judgement. It requires a mental disposition of thinking before acting in the light of facts rather than guess. The quality of planning depends upon the abilities of the managers who are required to collect all relevant facts, analyse and interpret them in a correct way. How far into the future a manager can see and with how much clarity he will depend on his intellectual calibre, are chalked out through planning process. In thinking of objectives, alternative courses of action and, above all, in making decision for choosing certain alternatives, the planner goes through an intellectual process.

2. Goal-orientation : All planning is linked up with certain goals and objectives. It follows, therefore, that every plan must contribute in some positive way to the accomplishment of group objectives. Planning has no meaning without being related to goals and objectives. It must bridge the gap between where we are and where we want to go at the minimum cost.

3. Primary Function : Planning is said to be the most basic and primary function of management. It occupies first place and precedes all other functions of management which are designed to attain the goals set under planning. This is so because the manager decides upon the policies, procedures, programmes, projects, etc. before proceeding with the work. The other functions of management—organising, direction, co-ordination and control—can be performed only after the manager has formulated the necessary planning.

4. Pervasiveness : Planning pervades all managerial activities. It is the job of all managers in all types of organisation. It is undertaken at all segments and levels of the organisation—from the general manager to the foreman. Whatever be the nature of activity, management starts with planning. The character and breadth of planning will, of course, vary from one job to another—depending on the level of management.

5. Uniformity : There may be separate plans prepared in different levels in the organisation, but all the sub-plans must be united with the general plan so as to make up a comprehensive plan for operation at a time. So, uniformity must be there in all levels of planning to match the general plan.

6. Continuity : To keep the enterprise as a going concern without any break, it is essential that planning must be a continuous process. So, the first plan must follow the second plan and the second plan the third and so on in never-ending series in quick succession.

7. Flexibility : Plans should not be made rigid. It should be as flexible as possible to accommodate all possible changes in the enterprise with a view to coping with the changing conditions in the market. In fact, planning is a dynamic activity.

8. Simplicity : The language of the work schedule or programme in the planning should be simple so that each and every part of it may easily be understood by the employees at different levels, specially at the lower level.

9. Precision : Precision is the soul of planning. This gives the planning exact, definite, and accurate meaning in its scope and content. Any mistake or error in planning is sure to upset other functions of management and, thus, precision is of utmost importance in every kind of planning.

10. Feasibility : Planning is neither poetry nor philosophy. It is based on facts and experience, and thereby realistic in nature. It represents a programme which is possible to execute with more or less existing resources.

11. Choice among Alternative Courses : Planning involves selection of suitable course of action from several alternatives. If there is only one way of doing something there is no need of planning. Planning has to find out several alternatives, estimate the feasibility and profitability of the different alternatives, and to choose the best one out of them.

12. Efficiency : Planning is directed towards efficiency. A plan is a course of action that shows promise of optmising return at the minimum expense of inputs. In planning, the manager evaluates the alternatives on the basis of efficiency. A good plan should not only attain optimum relationship between output and input but should also bring the greatest satisfaction to those who are responsible for its implementation.

13. Inter-dependence : The different departments may formulate different plans and programmes for their integration in the overall planning. But sectional plans cannot but be inter-dependent. For example, production planning depends upon sales planning—and vice versa. Again, planning for purchase of raw materials, employment of labour, etc. cannot be an isolated act apart from sales planning and production planning. Planning is a structured process and different plans constitute a hierarchy. Different plans are inter-dependent and inter-related. Every lower-level plan serves as a means towards the end of higher plans.

14. Forecasting : Above all, no planning can proceed without forecasting—which means assessing the future and making provision for it. Planning is the synthesis of various forecasts—short-term or long-term, special or otherwise. They all merge into a single programme and act as a guide for the whole concern.

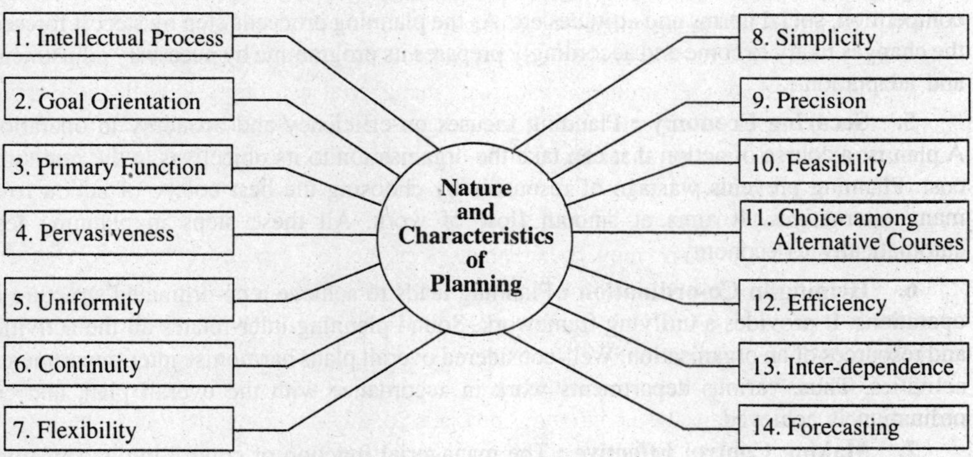

Fig. 3.1: Nature and Characteristics of Planning.

3.3 Importance of Planning

Planning is the key to success of an organisation. In fact, most of the company's achievements can be attributed to careful planning. Planning is a function of every manager at every level in an enterprise. Every manager is required to plan first for systematic and orderly performance of his assigned duties. It is within the planning function that goals are determined, decision-making takes place, forecasts are made and strategies are initiated.

Thus, planning has assumed great importance in all types of organisation—business or non-business, private or public sector, small or large.

As a managerial function, planning is important for the following reasons :

1. Providing Basis of Decision : The first and most important reason for planning lies in the fact that it provides a basis on which decisions are made. It is an immense need for the managers of an enterprise to fix up their minds as to what they want to accomplish and then plan the use of time, resources, and efforts towards the achievment of their objectives.

2. Focusing Attention on Objectives : Planning concentrates attention on the objectives of an enterprise. The first function of planning is to spell out its objectives. The objectives are defined in more concrete, precise and meaningful terms. As a result of such attention, it becomes possible for the planners to determine the policies, procedures, programmes and the rules for an orderly advance towards the ultimate goals desired to be achieved.

3. Minimising Uncertainty and Risk : The future is uncertain. Planning helps the managers in taking care of future uncertainties and thus minimises business risk. It anticipates future events and sets the course of action to control these events to one's advantage. With the help of planning, an enterprise can predict future events and make due provision for them. This, no doubt, eliminates or reduces the possibility or jumping into uncertainties.

4. Adapting with Changes : Business planning has become imperative due to the fact that an enterprise operates in a changing and dynamic environment. The aspects of this changing environment include changes in technology, government policies, the nature of competition, social norms and attitudes etc. As the planning proceeds step by step, it foresees the changes likely to come and accordingly prepares its programme by necessary adjustments and adaptation.

5. Securing Economy : Planning focuses on efficiency and economy in operation. A plan is a course of action that can take the organisation to its objectives at the minimum cost. Planning prevents wastage of resources by choosing the best course of action from many alternatives. It aims at smooth flow of work. All these steps in planning lead automatically to economy.

6. Helping in Co-ordination : Planning leads to achieve a co-ordinated structure of operations. It provides a unifying framework. Sound planning inter-relates all the activities and resources of an organisation. Well-considered overall plans harmonise inter-departmental activities. Thus, various departments work in accordance with the overall plan, and co-ordination is achieved.

7. Making Control Effective : The managerial function of controlling is concerned with a comparison between the planned performance and the actual performance of the subordinates and departments of the organisation. Thus, control is exercised in the context of planning action as the standards against which actual results are to be compared are set up through planning. So planning provides the basis for control. Thus, planning and control are inseparable.

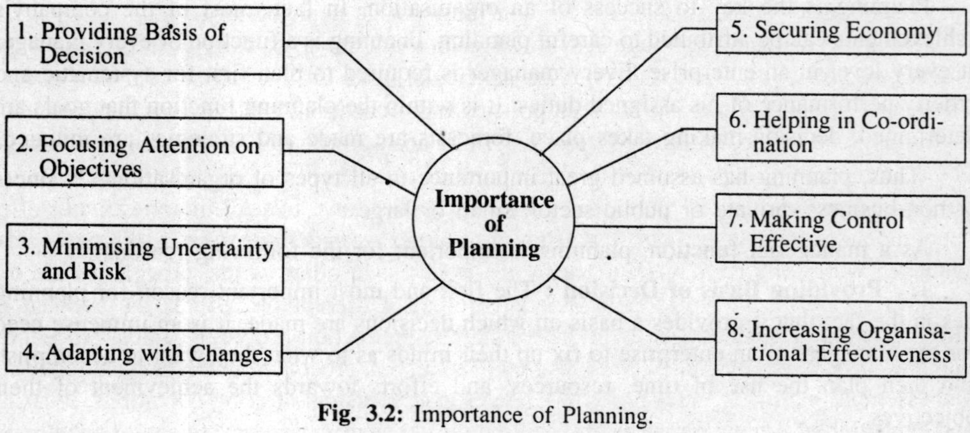

Fig. 3.2: Importance of Planning.

8. Increasing Organisational Effectiveness : Planning ensures organisational effectiveness in several ways. It states the objectives of the organisaton in the context of given resources; provides for proper utilisation of resources to the best advantage, gives necessary competitive strength for continuous growth and steady progress by foreseeing what the competitors are likely to do and evolving its strategies accordingly.

The process of planning generates the purposeful and orderly setting up of activities to be carried on. It defines the boundaries within which the business should operate. This enables the businessman to concentrate upon those matters which are actually relevant and vital to business success.

3.4 Elements of Planning

Planning as a managerial process consists of the following elements or components :

1. Objectives : The important task of planning is to determine the objectives of the enterprise. Objectives are the goals towards which all managerial activities are aimed at. All planning work must spell out in clear terms the objectives to be realised from the proposed business activities. When planning action is taken, these objectives are made more concrete and meaningful. For example, if the organisational objective is profit earning, planning activity will specify how much profit is to be earned looking into all facilitating and constraining factors.

2. Forecasting : It is the analysis and interpretation of future in relation to the activities and working of an enterprise. Business forecasting refers to analysing the statistical data and other economic, political and market information for the purpose of reducing the risks involved in making business decisions and long range plans. Forecasting provides a logical basis for anticipating the shape of the future business transactions and their requirements as to man and material.

3. Policies : Planning also requires laying down of policies for the easy realisation of the objectives of business. Policies are statements or principles that guide and direct different managers at various levels in making decisions. Policies provide the necessary basis for executive operation. They set forth overall boundaries within which the decision-makers are expected to operate while making decisions. Policies act as guidelines for taking administrative decisions.

In a big enterprise, various policies are formulated for guiding and directing the subordinates in different areas of management. They may be production policy, sales policy, financial policy, personnel policy etc. But these different policies are co-ordinated and integrated in such a way that they ensure easy realisation of the ultimate objectives of business. Policies should be consistent and must not be changed frequently.

4. Procedures : The manner in which each work has to be done is indicated by the procedures laid down. Procedures outline a series of tasks for a specified course of action. There may be some confusion between policies and procedures. Policies provide guidelines to thinking and action, but procedures are definite and specific steps to thinking and action. For example, the policy may be the recruitment of personnel from all parts of the country; but procedures may be to advertise and invite applications, to take interviews and offer appointment to the selected personnel. Thus, procedures mean definite steps in a chronological sequence within the area chalked out by the policies. In other words, procedures are the methods by means of which policies are enforced. Different procedures are adopted in different areas of business activities. There may be production procedure, sales procedure, purchase procedure, personnel procedure etc. Production procedure involves manufacturing and assembling of parts; sales procedure relates to advertising, offering quotations, securing and execution of orders; purchase procedure indicates inviting tenders, selecting quotations, placing orders, storing the goods in godown and supplying them against requisition to different departments and personnel procedure is the recruitment, selection and placement of workers to different jobs.

5. Rules : A rule specifies necessary course of action in a particular situation. It acts as a guide and is essentially in the nature of a decision made by the management authority. This decision signifies that a definite action must be taken in respect of a specific situation. The rules prescribe a definite and rigid course of action to be followed in different business activities without any scope for deviation or discretion. Any deviation of rule entails penalty. Rule is related to parts of a procedure. Thus, a rule may be incorporated in respect of purchase procedure that all purchases must be made after inviting tenders. Similarly, in respect of sales procedure, rule may be enforced that all orders should be confirmed the very next day.

6. Programmes : Programmes are precise plans of action followed in proper sequence in accordance with the objectives, policies and procedures. Programmes, thus, lead to a concrete course of inter-related actions for the accomplishment of a purpose. Thus, a company may have a programme for the establishment of schools, colleges and hospitals near about its premises along with its expanding business activities. Programmes must be closely integrated with the objectives. Programming involves dividing into steps the activities necessary to achieve the objectives, determining the sequence between different steps, fixing up performance responsibility for each step, determining the requirements of resources, time, finance etc. and assigning definite duties to each part.

7. Budgets : Budget means an estimate of men, money, materials and equipment in numerical terms required for implementation of plans and programmes. Thus, planning and budgeting are inter-linked. Budget indicates the size of the programme and involves income and outgo, input and output. It also serves as a very important control device by measuring the performance in relation to the set goals. There may be several departmental budgets which are again integrated into the master budget.

8. Projects : A project is a single-use plan which is a part of a general programme. It is part of the job that needs to be done in connection with the general programme. So a single step in a programme is set up as a project. Generally, in planning a project, a special task force is also envisaged. It is a scheme for investing resources which can be analysed and appraised reasonably and independently. A project involves basically the investment of funds, the benefits from which can be accrued in future. Examples of such investment may

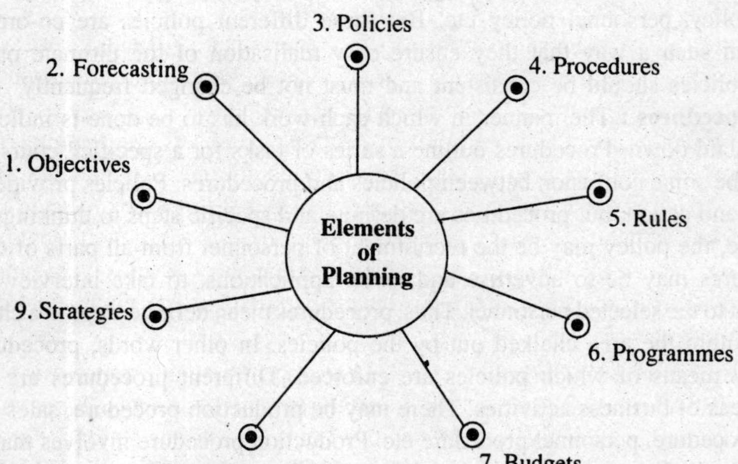

Fig. 3.3: Elements of Planning.

be outlays on land, building, machinery, research and development, etc. depending upon the situation.

9. Strategies : Strategies are the devices formulated and adopted from the competitive standpoint as well as from the point of view of the employees, customers, suppliers and government. Strategies thus may be internal and external. Whether internal or external, the success of the plans demands that it should be strategy-oriented. The best strategy of planning from the competitive standpoint is to be fully informed somehow about the planning 'secrets' of the competitors and to prepare its own plan accordingly. Strategies act as reserve forces to overcome resistances and reactions according to circumstances. They are applied as and when required.

3.5 Steps in Planning

A plan is essentially today's design for tomorrow's action and an outline of the steps to be taken in future. A good plan must be simple, balanced and flexible, and make utmost use of the existing resources. It must be based on clearly defined objectives. For preparation of such a plan, a definite process involving the following steps has to be followed :

1. Perception of the Opportunities : The manager must first identify the opportunity that calls for planning and action. This is very important for the planning process because it leads to formulation of plans by providing clue as to whether opportunities exist for taking up particular plans. Perception of opportunities includes a preliminary look at possible opportunities and the ability to see them clearly and completely, an understanding of why the organisation wants to solve the uncertainties, and a vision what it expects to gain. This provides an opportuntiy to set the objectives in real sense.

2. Establishment of the Objectives : The next step in the planning process lies in the setting up of objectives to be achieved by the enterprise in the clearest possible terms keeping in view its strength and limitation. Objectives specify the results expected in measurable terms and indicate the end points of what is to be done; where the primary emphasis is to be placed, and what is to be accomplished by various types of plans. Enterprises start with a general objective. From this are developed subordinate goals that contribute to the attainment of the general objective. These, in turn, are supported by the specific objectives for the departments. In this process a hierarchy of objectives is created. The plans at each level of the organisation are made for the attainment of the appropriate objectives in the hierachy. This hierarchy can be built up by co-ordinatng the plans of different departments.

3. Building the Planning Premises : After determination of the organisational goals, it is necessary to establish planning premises, that is, the conditions under which planning activities will be undertaken. This involves collection of facts and figures necessary for planning the future course of the enterprise. 'Planning Premises' are planning assumptions relating to the expected environmental and internal conditions. So, planning premises are of two types—external and internal. External premises include total factors in the environment like social, political, technological, competitors' plans and actions, government policies, etc. Internal factors include the organisation's policies, resources of various types, and the ability of the organisation to withstand the environmental pressure. The plans are formulated in the light of both external and internal factors.

4. Identifying the Alternatives : The next step in planning process is to search for various alternative courses of action based on the organisational objectives and planning premises. A particular objective can be achieved through various actions. For example, if an organisation has set its objective to grow further, it can be achieved in several ways like expanding the field of business or product line, joining with other organisations, or taking over another organisation, and so on. Within each category, there may be several alternatives. Since all alternatives cannot be considered for further analysis, it is necessary for the planner to reduce in preliminary examination the number of alternatives that do not meet the minimum preliminary criteria. Preliminary criteria can be defined in several ways—minimum investment required, matching with the present business of the organisation, control by the government, etc.

5. Evaluation of the Alternatives : Various alternative courses that are considered feasible in terms of preliminary criteria have to be taken for detailed evaluation. Alternative courses of action can be evaluated against the criteria of cost, risks, benefit and organisational facilities. The strong and weak points of every alternatives should be analysed carefully. Since there are so many complex variables connected with each goal and each possible plan, the process of comparative evaluation is extremely difficult. For example, one alternative may be the most profitable but requires heavy investment; another may be less profitable but also involves less risk. Moreover, there is no certainty about the outcome of any alternative course because it is related with future which is not certain. Ultimately, the choice will depend upon what is determined as the most critical factor from the point of view of the objectives of the enterprise.

6. Choice of the Course of Action : After the evaluation of various alternatives, the most appropriate one is selected as the plan. Sometimes evaluation shows that more than one alternatives are equally good. In such a case, the manager may choose more than one alternative at the same time. There is another reason for choosing more than one alternative. Alternative course of action may be required to be undertaken in future in changed situations. So, the planner must also be ready with alternative—normally known as contingency plan—that can help coping up with the changed situation.

7. Formulation of Supporting or Derivative Plans : After the best alternative is decided upon, the next step is to derive various plans for different departments or sections of the organisation to support the main plan. In an organisation, there can be various derivative plans like planning for buying raw materials, and equipment, developing new product, recruiting and training the personnel, etc. These derivative plans are formulated out of the main plan and so they support it. The break-down of the master plan into departmental and sectional plans provides a realistic picture of the actions to be taken in future.

8. Establishing the Sequence of Activities : After formulating the basic and derivative plans, the sequence of activities is determined so that the plans are put into action. Based on the plans at various levels, it can be decided who will do what and at what time. Budgets for various periods can be prepared to make plans more concrete for implementation.

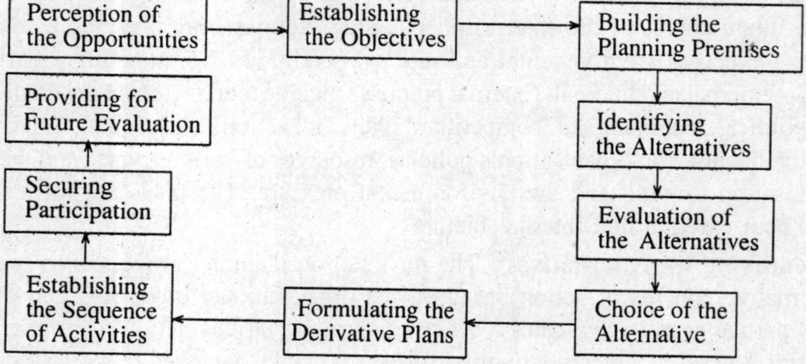

Fig. 3.4: Planning Process.

9. Securing Participation : Plans must be communicated in greater details to the subordinates to increase their understanding of the proposed action and for enlisting their co-operations in the execution of plans. It will, thus, add to the quality of planning through the knowledge of additional facts, new visions and revealing situations.

10. Providing for Future Evaluation : For ensuring that the selected plans are proceeding with the right lines, it is of paramount importance to devise a system of continuous evaluation and appraisal of the plan. It will help in detecting the shortcomings and pitfalls of the plans and taking remedial actions well in time.

All the steps in the process of planning must be linked and co-ordinated with each other. For successful implementation of a plan, it must be communicated to all levels of the organisation.

3.6 Basic Principles of Planning

Planning requires scientific thinking and it should spell out in clear terms the definition of the purpose, analyse the problem and make a careful and diligent search for all the facts bearing upon it. The task of planning will be well-accomplished if some fundamental principles are followed in the process. The important principles may be stated as follows :

1. Principle of Commitment : This means that certain resources must be committed or pledged for the purpose of planning. Planning is not an easy task. So, necessary help is to be taken from experts. The enterprise must be ready to exhaust the available resources for the achievement of a plan.

2. Principle of the Limiting Factor : A plan involves varied factors of different importance. This principle implies that more emphasis has to be put on that factor which is scarce or limited in supply or extremely costly. This will help in selecting the most favourable alternative.

3. Principle of Reflective Thinking : Planning, being an intellectual activity, is based on rational considerations. These involve reflective thinking which signifies problem-solving thought process—a process by which past experiences are superimposed on the facts of the present situation and possible future trends. None can be a planner whose mind is not active, who does not possess any deliberate power and whose sense of judgement is not strong.

4. Principle of Flexibility : Though a plan is prepared after reflective thinking, this does not mean that no departure can be made in the course of its operation. The plan should be so prepared that there is sufficient scope for changing it from time to time. Changes must necessarily be effected in the plan for taking into account new developments that may take place in the course of the operation of the plan.

5. Principle of Contribution to Enterprise Objectives : A major plan is prepared and it is supported by many derivative plans. But all plans must contribute in a positive way towards the achievement of the enterprise objectives.

6. Principle of Efficiency : A plan should be made efficient to attain the objectives of the enterprise at the minimum cost and least effort. It must also achieve better results with the minimum of unexpected happenings. Therefore, it is to be seen that what is expected is likely to be achieved.

7. Principle of Selection of Alternatives : Planning is basically a problem of choosing. The essence of planning is the choice among alternative courses of action. There is no need for planning if there is only one way for doing something. In choosing from alternatives, the best alternative will be that which contributes most efficiently and effecively to the accomplishment of a desired goal.

8. Principle of Planning Premises : A plan is prepared against some foundations or backgrounds known as 'Planning Premises'. There must be complete agreement among the managers in respect of planning premises over which the structure of plan is to be framed.

9. Principle of Timing and Sequence of Operations : Timing and sequence of operations determine the starting and finising time for each piece of work according to some definite schedule and give practical and concrete shape and form to work performance.

10. Principle of Securing Participation : To secure participation of the employees with whole-hearted co-operation in execution of the plan, it is necessary that the plan must be communicated and explained to them for their full understanding. This understanding provides the basis for additional knowledge about new facts and matters to the employees. This is needed for improvement in the quality of planning. It also ensures an obligation of the personnel of the enterprise to execute the plan by individual and joint participation.

11. Principle of Pervasiveness : Though major planning function is entrusted to the top management, it is not restricted to the top level only. It is a function of every manager at every level in the organisation.

12. Principle of Strategic Planning : Strategic planning is essential where there is competition. It is prepared in the light of what the competitors are intending to do. Planners must take into account the strategies of the rival organisations, otherwise the planning projection may land them in trouble.

13. Principle of Innovation : A good system of planning should be responsive to the opportunities for innovation. Innovation consists in creating something new for increasing satisfaction of the consumers. This may also be stated as an important strategy of business. Innovation is a necessity for its sustaining growth in this dynamic world. Innovation is achieved through research and development and planning is required to provide such scope.

14. Principle of Follow-up : In the course of execution of a plan, certain obstacles may crop up in midway and planning may require revision, alteration or correction. This is why there must be a follow-up system in the planning process itself. This allows timely changes in the planning and makes it more effective.

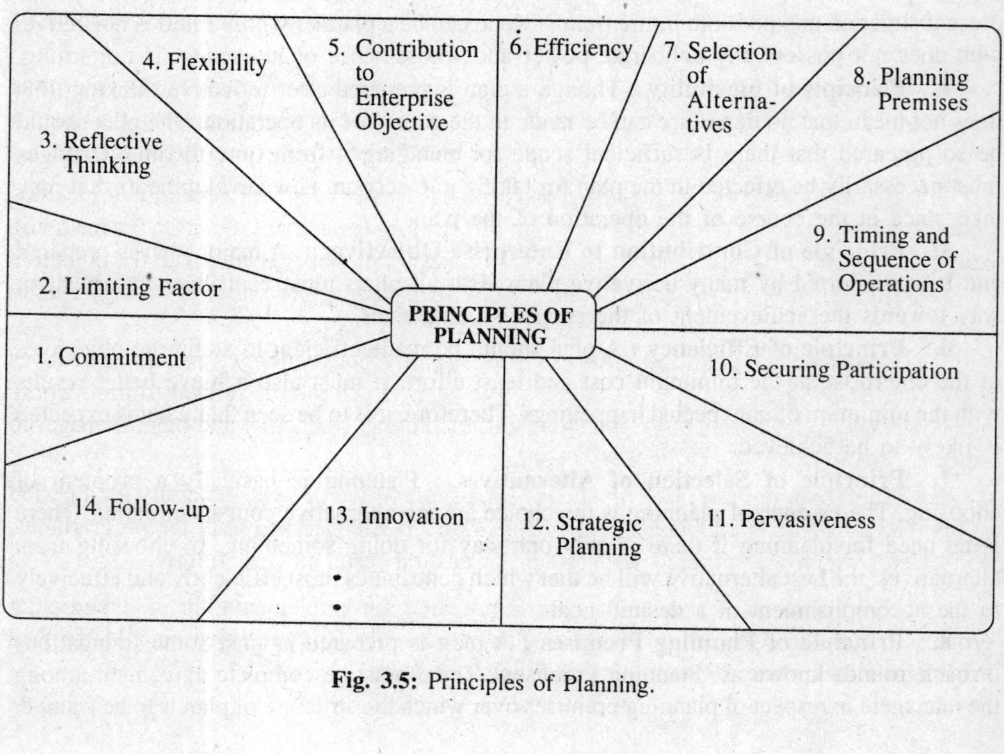

Fig. 3.5: Principles of Planning.

However, to plan any kind of work, the following facts demand utmost attention :

(i) The nature, quality and quantity of work to be done, the best way of doing it, the time available for its accomplishment, how to do it, when it is to be done and who are to do it.

(ii) Adequate knowledge about the capacity of the force available through observations and experiments and from established standards.

(iii) The priority to be given in succession for the accomplishment of different tasks through careful analysis.

3.7 Types of Enterprise Plans

The planning of a business enterprise may be of different types as follows :

1. **Primary or Basic Plan :** The plan which is prepared to determine the principal objectives of an enterprise and the means to achieve them is called 'Primary or Basic Plan'. All other functions of the managers are managed and controlled on the basis of such plan.

2. **Physical Plan :** The plan made for constructing the building, establishing the machinery or equipment, installing the furnitures, etc. is known as 'Physical Plan'.

3. **Master Plan :** 'Master Plan' is prepared for the performance of activities of the entire enterprise. This plan includes the objectives, policies, procedures, programmes, budget, time-schedule, strategies, etc. that are required for proper execution of management-activities.

4. **Derivative Plan :** The plans which are made in different departments of an enterprise are called 'Derivative Plans'. Such plans help in the implementation of the basic plan of the enterprise.

5. **Functional Plan :** When a plan is made for performing any one type or related functions, it is called 'Functional Plan'. Such a plan is concerned with a particular or several closely-related jobs. For performance of the routine work of the enterprise, this type of plan is prepared. 'Production Plan', 'Sales Plan', 'Financial Plan' etc. are the examples of functional plans.

6. **Comprehensive Plan :** In order to achieve the long-term objectives of an enterprise such type of plan is made. When a plan is prepared for the entire enterprise at a time, it is known as 'Comprehensive Plan'. It includes both physical plan and functional plan.

7. **Standing Plan :** This plan is needed for the activities of repetitive nature. It includes policies, procedures and rules. 'Standing Plan' determines the courses of action for recurring activities and frequently changing situations. This type of plan is prepared with the objective of maintaining the activities and conduct of the management personnel always similar in nature.

8. **Long-range Plan :** 'Long-range Plan' means the plan which is formulated to cover a long period of time—usually for three to five years. Such plan is related to production, manpower planning, research and development, marketing, financing, and other managerial aspects.

9. **Short-range Plan :** The plan made for a short period of time, generally for a period of one or two years, is known as 'Short-range Plan'. It is concerned with the programmes, budget etc. which are required for getting the desired result in near future.

10. **Single-use Plan :** When a plan is prepared for implementation of a particular project, it is called 'Single-use Plan'. The Third Hooghly Bridge Project and Metro Rail Project in Kolkata are the examples of Single-use Plan.

11. Strategic Plan : 'Strategic Plan' refers to the plan for determining the major objectives of an enterprise, adopting the courses of action and allocation of resources required to achieve those objectives. Such plan is the key to long-term success of an enterprise.

12. Operational Plan : 'Operational Plan' is the plan which is formulated to determine the utilisation of allocated resources and introduce controlling system for the achievement of the pre-determined objectives.

Such plan is concerned with the application of strategy and execution of the objectives. It gives emphasis on the performance of job and so it is called operational plan. The plans for purchasing raw materials, training of the employees, maintenance of tools and machinery, measurement of the qualitative standard of product, etc. are under the category of operational plans.

13. Temporary Technical Plan : Such type of plan is prepared for tackling temporary situation which calls for immediate action. For instance, if any competitor reduces the price of his product the counterpart of the competitor has to consider whether he will also decrease the price of his goods or develop its quality for the interest of the customers.

14. Developmental Plan : This plan is formulated for organisational development of the enterprise. It is made keeping in view long-term possibilities such as—diversification, research and development, etc.

15. Corporate Plan : 'Corporate Plan' refers to the plan which involves all the departments of a company in the context of anticipating the probability of development in the market condition. Corporate plan includes determination of company objectives, evaluation of the internal and external factors which will affect the execution of these objectives, and making comprehensive but flexible plans to ensure that the objectives of the company are really achieved.

The formulation of corporate plan depends on industry condition, competition, price of the products, input supply, market situation, technological development, government policy, etc.

16. Divisional Plans : Divisional plans are the separate plans for each of the divisions of the enterprise. These plans chalk out the programme of action for each of the divisions. Thus, if an enterprise has separate divisions for products like television sets, electronic calculators and spare parts, divisional plans have to be prepared for each one of these divisions separately. These plans require to be integrated with the overall master plan.

17. Geographical or Regional Plans : If an enterprise has regional divisions or zonal groups, it will have to prepare the plans for each one of these regions or zones. Such plans are, therefore, territorial plans.

3.8 Strategic Planning : Concept

Planning is related with future. A planning process involves different degrees of futurity. Some parts of the organisation require planning for many years into the future while others require planning over a short period only. For instance, capital expenditure is related to long-term period while budget for a year is of short-term nature. The former is called strategic planning or long-range planning.

'Strategic planning' may be defined as the process of determining the objectives of the organisation and the resources to be used to attain these objectives, as also the policies to govern the acquisition, utilisation and disposition of these resources.

Examples of strategic planning in an organisation are—diversification of business into new lines, planned growth rate in sales, type of products to be offered, etc. Strategic planning encompasses all the functional areas of business and is affected within the existing and long-term framework of economic, technological, social and political factors. It also involves the analysis of various environmental factors—particularly with regard to how an organisation relates to its environment. Generally, for most of the organisations, strategic planning period ranges between three to five years.

- **Strategic Planning Process**

The process of strategic planning consists of the following steps :

1. **Determination of Mission and Objectives :** Strategic planning starts with the determination of the mission for the organisation. The principal objectives for which the organisation has been set up should be clearly defined. Strategic planning is concerned with an organisation's long-term relationship to its external environment. So, the business mission should be fixed in terms of social impact of the organisation.

2. **Environmental Analysis :** In order to identify the opportunities and threats, the external environment of the organisation is analysed. A list of important factors likely to affect the organisation's activities is prepared.

3. **Self-appraisal :** In the next step, the strengths and weaknesses of the organisation are analysed. Such an analysis will enable the enterprise to capitalise on its strengths and to minimise its weaknesses. The enterprise can utilise the external opportunities by concentrating on its internal capacity. By matching its strengths with the environmental opportunities, an enterprise can face competition and achieve growth.

4. **Strategic Decision-making :** Strategic alternatives are then generated and evaluated. After that, a strategic choice is made to reduce the performance gap. The organisation must select the alternative that is best suited to its capabilities. For instance, in order to grow, an enterprise may enter into new markets or develop new products or sell more in the present markets.

Choice of strategy depends upon external environment, managerial perception, the managers' attitude towards risk, past strategies and managerial power and efficiency.

5. **Strategy Implementation and Control :** Once the strategy is determined, it must be translated into tactical operational plans. Programmes and budgets are developed for each function. Short term operational plans are prepared to use the resources. Control should be developed to evaluate performance as the the strategy is put into use. Wherever actual results are below the expectation, the strategy should be reviewed or reappraised. It must be modified and adapted to the changes in the external environment.

3.9 Forecasting

In preparing plans for the future, the management authority has to make some predictions about what is likely to happen in the future. It shows that the managers know something of future happenings even before things actually happen. Forecasting provides them this knowledge. Forecasting is the process of estimating the relevant events of future, based on the analysis of their past and present behaviour. The future cannot be probed unless one knows how the events have occurred in the past and how they are occurring presently. The past and present analysis of events provides the base helpful for collecting information about their future occurrence. Thus, **forecasting may be defined as the process of assessing the future normally using calculations and projections that take account of the past performance, current trends, and anticipated changes in the foreseeable period ahead.**

Whenever the managers plan business operations and organisational set-up for the years ahead, they have to take into account the past, the present and the prevailing economic, political and social conditions. Forecasting provides a logical basis for determining in advance the nature of future business operations and the basis for managerial decisions about the material, personnel and other requirements. It is, thus, the basis of planning. When a business enterprise makes an attempt to look into the future in a systematic and concentrated way, it may discover certain aspects of its operations requiring special attention. However, it must be recognised that the process of forecasting involves an element of guesswork and the managers cannot stay satisfied and relaxed after having prepared a forecast. The forecast will have to be constantly monitored and revised—particularly when it relates to a long-term period. The managers should try to reduce the element of guesswork in preparing forecasts by collecting the relevant data using the scientific techniques of analysis and inference.

On the basis of the definition, the following **features** of forecasting can be identified :

1. Forecasting relates to future events.
2. Forecasting is needed for planning process because it devises the future course of action.
3. It defines the probability of happening of future events. Therefore, the happening of future events can be precise only to a certain extent.
4. Forecasting is made by analysing the past and present factors which are relevant for the functioning of an organisation.
5. The analysis of various factors may require the use of statistical and mathematical tools and techniques.

3.10 Role of Forecasting

Since planning involves the future, no usable plan can be made unless the manager is able to take all possible future events into account. This explains why forecasting is a critical element in the planning process. In fact, every decision in the organisation is based on some sort of forecasting. It helps the managers in the following ways :

1. Basis of Planning : Forecasting is the key to planning. It generates the planning process. Planing decides the future course of action which are expected to take place in certain circumstances and conditions. Unless the managers know these conditions, they cannot go for effective planning. Forecasting provides the knowledge of planning premises within which the managers can analyse their strengths and weaknesses and can take appropriate actions in advance before actually they are put out of market. Forecasting provides the knowledge about the nature of future conditions.

2. Promotion of Organisation : The objectives of an organisation are achieved through the performance of certain activities. What activities should be performed depends on the expected outcome of these activities. Since expected outcome depends on future events and the way of performing various activities, forecasting of future events is of direct relevance in achieving an objective.

3. Facilitiating Co-ordination and Control : Forecasting indirectly provides the way for effective co-ordination and control. Forecasting requires information about various factors. Information is collected from various internal and external sources. Almost all units of the organisation are involved in this process. It provides interactive opportunities for better unity and co-ordination in the planning process. Similarly, forecasting can provide relevant information for exercising control. The managers can know their weaknesses in the forecasting process and they can take suitable action to overcome these.

4. Success in Organisation : All business enterprises are characterised by risk and have to work within the ups and downs of the industry. The risk depends on the future happenings and forecasting provides help to overcome the problem of uncertainties. Though forecasting cannot check the future happenings, it provides clues about those and indicates when the alternative actions should be taken. Managers can save their business and face the unfortunate happenings if they know in advance. what is going to happen.

3.11 Steps in Forecasting

The process of forecasting generally involves the following steps :

1. **Developing the Basis :** The future estimates of various business operations will have to be based on the results obtainable through systematic investigation of the economy, products and industry.

2. **Estimation of Future Operations :** On the basis of the data collected through systematic investigation into the economy and industry situation, the manager has to prepare quantitative estimates of the future scale of business operations. Here the managers will have to take into account the planning premises.

3. **Regulation of Forecasts :** It has already been indicated that the managers cannot take it easy after they have formulated a business forecast. They have to constantly compare the actual operations with the forecasts prepared in order to find out the reasons for any deviations from forecasts. This helps in making more realistic forecasts for future.

4. **Review of the Forecasting Process :** Having determined the deviations of the actual performances from the positions forecast by the managers, it will be necessary to examine the procedures adopted for the purpose so that improvements can be made in the method of forecasting.

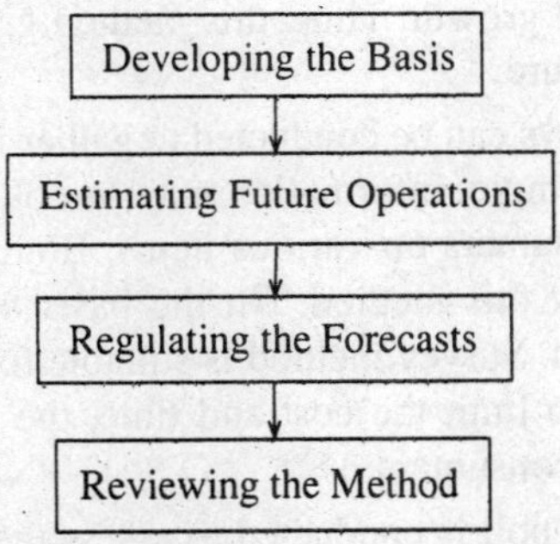

Fig. 3.6: The Forecasting Process.

3.12 Planning and Forecasting

Many persons equate planning and forecasting because both deal with future events. The 'Father of modern management', **Henry Fayol**, thought that the entire plan of an enterprise is made up of a series of separate plans called 'forecasts'. However, both are different, and clear-cut differences can be drawn between the two. The difference lies basically in the scope of the two processes. Planning is more comprehensive and includes many sub-processes and elements in order to arrive at decisions. Such decisions may be in terms of what is to be done, why is to do, where to be done, how to do, with which to do, when to be done, and who is to do.

Forecasting, on the other hand, involves the estimate of future events and provides parameters to the planning. Forecasting process may also involve many sub-processes and elements, but these are used to predict what will happen in future. This may not require any commitment of action, but may help in deciding the future course of action. In fact, forecasting is one of the major ingredients of planning, because planning is concerned with the determination of future course of action in the light of forecasts made.

There is another difference between planning and forecasting. Since planning involves making comprehensive decisions in the organisation, a large number of persons are involved in planning process, though major decisions are taken at the top level of management. On the other hand, forecasting is normally made at the middle or lower level. Forecasting does not involve decision-making but helps in decision-making by projecting what is likely to happen in future.

3.13 Techniques of Forecasting

There are vairous methods of forecasting. However, no method can be suggested as universally applicable. In fact, most of the forecasts are done by combining various methods. A brief discussion of the major forecasting methods are given below :

1. **Historical Analogy Method :** Under this method, forecast in regard to a particular situation is based on some analogous conditions elsewhere in the past. The economic situation of a country can be predicted by making comparison with the advanced countries at a particular stage through which the country is presently passing. Similarly, it has been observed that if anything is invented in some part of the world, this is adopted in other countries after a gap of a certain time. Thus, based on analogy, a general forecast can be made about the nature of events in the economic system of the country. It is often suggested that social analogies have helped in indicating the trends of changes in the norms of business behaviour in terms of life. Likewise, changes in the norms of business behaviour in terms of attitude of the workers against inequality, find similarities in various countries at various stages of the history of industrial growth. Thus, this method gives a broad indication about the future events of general nature.

2. **Survey Method :** Surveys can be conducted to gather information on the intentions of the concerned people. For example, information may be collected through surveys about the probable expenditure of consumers on various items. Both quantitative and qualitative information may be collected by this method. On the basis of such surveys, demand for various products can be projected. Survey method is suitable for forecasting demand—both of existing and new products. To limit the cost and time, the survey may be restricted to a sample from the prospective consumers.

3. **Opinion Poll :** Opinion poll is conducted to assess the opinion of the experienced persons and experts in the particular field whose views carry a lot of weight. For example, opinion polls are very popular to predict the outcome of elections in many countries including India. Similarly, an opinion poll of the sales representatives, wholesalers or marketing experts may be helpful in formulating demand projections. If opinion polls give widely divergent views, the experts may be called for discussion and explanation of why they are holding a particular view. They may be asked to comment on the views of the others, to revise their views in the context of the opposite views, and consensus may emerge. Then, it becomes the estimate of future events.

4. **Business Barometers :** A barometer is used to measure the atmospheric pressure. In the same way, index numbers are used to measure the state of an economy between two or more periods. These index numbers are the device to study the trends, seasonal fluctuations, cyclical movements, and irregular fluctuations. These index numbers, when used in combination with one another, provide indications as to the direction in which the economy is proceeding. Thus, with the business activity index numbers, it becomes easy to forecast the future course of action. However, it should be kept in mind that business barometers have their own limitations and they are not sure road to success. All types of business do not follow the general trend but different index numbers have to be prepared for different activities, etc.

5. Time Series Analysis : Time series analysis involves decomposition of historical series into its various components, viz. trend, seasonal variances, cyclical variations, and random variances. When the various components of a time series are separated, the variation of a particular situation, the subject under study, can be known over the period of time and projection can be made about the future. A trend can be known over the period of time which may be true for the future also. However, time series analysis should be used as a basis for forecasting when data are available for a long period of time and tendencies disclosed by the trend and seasonal factors are fairly clear and stable.

6. Regression Analysis : Regression analysis is meant to disclose the relative movements of two or more inter-related series. It is used to estimate the changes in one variable as a relult of specified changes in other variable or variables. In economic and business situations, a number of factors affect a business activity simultaneously. Regression analysis helps in isolating the effects of such factors to a great extent. For example, if we know that there is a positive relationship between advertising expenditure and volume of sales or between sales and profit, it is possible to have estimate of the sales on the basis of advertising, or of the profit on the basis of projected sales, provided other things remain the same.

7. Input-Output Analysis : According to this method, a forecast of output is based on given input if relationship between input and output is known. Similarly, input requirement can be forecast on the basis of final output with a given input-output relationship. The basis of this technique is that the various sectors of economy are inter-related and such inter-relationships are well-established. For example, coal requirement of the country can be predicted on the basis of its usage rate in various sectors like industry, transport, household, etc. and how the various sectors behave in future. This technique yields sector-wise forecasts and is extensively used in forecasting business events as the data required for its application are easily obtained.

3.14 Decision-Making : Definition and Meaning

Most writers on management think that managemement is basically a decision-making process. They argue that it is only through making decisions that an organisation can accomplish its short-term and long-term goals.

A decision is an act of selection or choice of one action from several alternatives. **Decision-making can be defined as the process of selecting a right and effective course of action from two or more alternatives for the purpose of achieving a desired result.**

Decision-making is the essence of management. According to **P. F. Drucker** : "Whatever a manager does, he does through making decisions." All matters relating to planning, organising, direction, co-ordination and control are settled by the managers through decisions which are executed into practice by the operators of the enterprise. Objectives, goals, strategies, policies and organisational designs are all to be decided upon in order to regulate the performance of the business. The entire managerial process is based on decisions. Decisions are needed both for tackling the problems as well as for taking maximum advantages of the opportunities available. Correct decisions reduce complexities, uncertainties and diversities of the organisational environments.

Geroge Terry defines decision-making "as the selection of one behaviour alternative from two or more possible alternatives."

In the words of **D. E. Mcfarland :** "A decision is an act of choice wherein an executive forms a conclusion about what must be done in a given situation. A decision represents behaviour chosen from a number of alternatives."

The definition of decision-making has three different but inter-related implications. These are as follows :

1. When the managers make decisions, they exercise choice. They decide what to do on the basis of some conscious and deliberate logic or judgement.

2. When making a decision the managers are faced with alternatives. An organisation does not take a wise manager to reach a decision when there are no other possible choices. It does require wisdom and experience to evaluate several alternatives and select the best one.

3. When taking a decision, the managers have a purpose. They propose and analyse the alternative courses of action and finally make a choice that is likely to move the organisation in the direction of its goals.

3.15 Importance of Decision-Making

Management is essentially a bundle of decision-making process. The managers of an enterprise are responsible for making decisions and ascertaining that the decisions made are carried out in accordance with defined objectives or goals.

Decision-making plays a vital role in management. Decision-making is perhaps the most important component of a manager's activities. It plays the most important role in the planning process. When the managers plan, they decide on many matters as what goals their organisation will pursue, what resources they will use, and who will perform each required task. When plans go wrong or out of track, the managers have to decide what to do to correct the deviation. In fact, the whole planning process involves the managers constantly in a series of decision-making situations. The quality of managerial decisions largely affect the effectiveness of the plans made by them. In organising process, the manager is to decide upon the structure, division of work, nature of responsibility and relationships, the procedure of establishing such responsibility and relationship and so on.

In co-ordination, decision-making is essential for providing unity of action. In control, it will have to decide how the standard is to be laid down, how the deviations from the standard are to be rectified, how the principles are to be established, how instructions are to be issued, and so on.

The ability to make good decisions is the key to successful managerial performance. The managers of most profit-seeking firms are always required to take a wide range of important decision in the areas of pricing, product choice, cost control, advertising, capital investments, dividend policy, personnel matters, etc. Similarly, the managers of non-profit seeking concerns and public enterprises also face the challenge of taking vital decisions on many important matters.

Decision-making is also a criterion to determine whether a person is in management or not. If he participates in decision-making, he is regarded as belonging to management staff. In the words of **George Terry** : "If there is one universal mark of a manager, it is decision-making." According to **P. F. Drucker** : "Whatever a manager does, he does through making decisions."

In any business, whether large or small, the conditions are never static, they are perceptively dynamic. The old order is always yielding place to new either in personnel or in unforeseen contingencies. Changes in conditions are the usual rule. Such a situation calls for actions that involve decision-making.

So, decision-making is deeply related with management functions and both are bound up together inseparably. When a manager plans or organises, orders or advises, approves or disapproves anything, he will have to move with the process of decision-making. In all managerial functions, decision-making is an indispensable accompaniment.

3.16 Steps in Decision-Making

Every decision is the outcome of a dynamic process. The process of decision-making involves the following stages or steps :

1. To diagnose the problem : The first step in decision-making is to understand the exact problem. Just as a disease cannot be cured without proper diagnosis, so also no decision-making is possible unless the problem is properly diagnosed or known. It is told that a disease is half cured if it is correctly diagnosed. Similarly, if the problem is correctly understood, its solution will be easier. For example, when a company is faced with declining profits, it shows the symptom and not the disease. The managers may decide to solve the problem through intensive sales effort. But if the real problem lies elsewhere which may need change or product lines, or reduction of price and improvement of quality, the intensified sales effort will not bring the desired result. So, correct assessment of the real problem is essential for decision-making. Diagnosing the real problem implies knowing the gap between what is and what ought to be, identifying the reasons for the gap, and understanding the problem in relation to higher objectives of the organisation.

2. To analyse the problem : After correct diagnosis of the problem, the next task is to analyse the problem. This means splitting up of the problem into its different elements based on collection of facts, data and relevant information. For instance, if there is a declining trend in sales, it should analyse its extent in regard to market, price, product line, etc. So, all possible facts and data relating to the situation must be gathered to find out the revealing circumstances that may help the decision-maker to gain an insight into the problem. The whole approach of analysis of the problem should be based around the limiting or critical factors within minimum possible time and efforts.

3. To search for alternative solutions : After ascertaining and analysing the problem, different possible alternatives are to be found out for its solution. A problem can be solved in several ways. However, all the ways cannot be equally satisfying. Further, if there is only one way of solving a problem, no question of decision-making arises. That particular way is to be accepted. Therefore, the decision-maker must try to find out the various alternatives available in order to get the most satisfactory result of a decision. However, it should be borne in mind that it may not be possible to consider all alternatives, because information about all alternatives may not be available, or some of the alternatives cannot be considered for selection due to the obvious limitation of the decision-maker. While determining alternatives, the concept of limiting factor should be applied. A limiting factor is one that stand in the way of accomplishing a desired objective. If these factors are identified, the managers will confine their search for alternatives to those which will overcome the limiting factors. For instance, if an enterprise has limitation in raising sizable finances, it cannot consider the projects involving high investment.

4. To evaluate the alternatives : After the vairous alternatives are identified, the decision-maker will go for evaluating them to find out how each alternative may contribute towards the objectives supposed to be achieved by implementing the decision. In evaluating an alternative both tangible and intangible factors have to be taken into account. Tangible

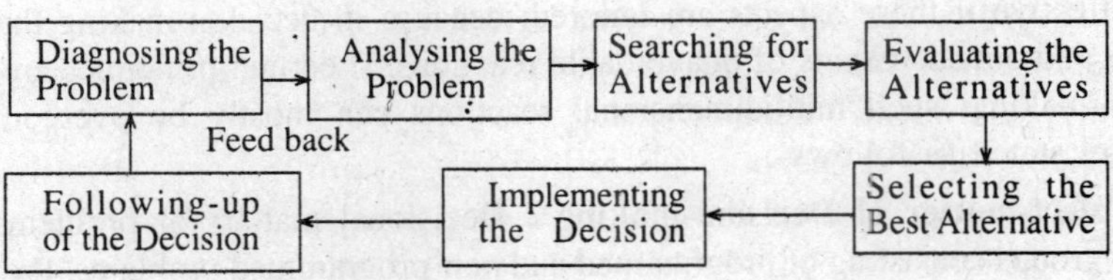

Fig. 3.7: The Decision-Making Process.

factors are those which can be quantified because they are quite obvious like the cost per unit, investment required, output to be received, etc. Such factors can be measured easily. As against these, intangible factors are mostly qualitative and cannot be measured in terms of quantity. For example, in a plant location, various non-economic factors like psychological problem arising out of displacement of persons from the plant site, ecological balance, etc. have to be considered which cannot be quantified.

5. To select the best alternative : The evaluation of various alternatives presents a clear picture as to how each one of them contributes to the objectives under question. A comparison is made among the likely outcomes of various alternatives and the best one is chosen. Choice aspect of decision-making is related to deciding the most acceptable alternative which gives the greatest number of wanted consequences to fit with the organisational objectives. A manager with sound knowledge, long experience and considerable ability may choose the best course of action easily. When there is any confusion, some criteria may be useful for picking up the best solution. These criteria are—(i) degree of risk against the expected gains; (ii) economy of effort; (iii) timing, and (iv) availability of resources.

6. To make the decision effective : Once the alternative is selected, it is put into action. Truly speaking, the actual process of decision-making ends with the choice of the best alternative through which the objectives can be achieved. However, decision-making, being a continuous and on-going process, must ensure that the objectives have been achieved by the chosen alternative. Unless this is done, the managers will never know what result their choice has contributed.

The decision, in order to be implemented must be communicated to the employees concerned in clear and simple language and their acceptance of the decision must be secured. All decisions affect the employees and their work. It is, therefore, necessary to secure their willing support and whole-hearted participation.

7. To follow-up the decision : When the decision is put into acton, it brings certain results. If a good decision is taken and implemented properly, its results should correspond with the objectives. So, results of the decision indicate whether decision-making and its implementation are proper. But all decisions cannot be said to be perfect and flawless. Decisions are not always based on facts, some guesswork may be necessary for this purpose. Moreover, there is the human limitation associated with each decision-making process. In order to provide safeguards against incorrect, bad and inappropriate decisions, it is desirable to introduce a system of follow-up in the light of feedback received from the results. This provides the scope of rectifying the wrong decisions and modifying similar future decisions to tune them up with environmental changes.

It is clear from the above discussion that decision-making is not a simple affair. Its formulation and effectiveness depend upon a number of factors stated above.

3.17 Principles of Decision Making

Effective decision involves two important aspects—the purpose for which it is intended, and the environmental situation in which it is taken. Even the best and correct decision may become ineffective if these aspects are ignored; because in decision-making there are so many inside and outside chains of unavoidable reactions. If certain principles are followed for decision-making, such multidimensional reactions can mostly be overcome. These principles are stated as follows :

1. Subject-matter of Decision-making : Decisional matters or problems may be divided into groups consisting of programmed and non-programmed problems. Programmed problems, being of routine nature, repetitive and well-founded, are easily definable and, as such, require simple and easy solution. Decision arrived in such programmed problems has, thus, a continuing effect. But in non-programmed problems, there is no continuing effect because they are non-repetitive, non-routined, and novel. Every event in such problems requires individual attention and analysis and its decision is to be arrived at according to its special features and circumstances.

2. Organisational Structure : The organisational structure, having an important bearing on decision-making, should be readily understood. If the organisational structure is rigid and highly centralised, decision-making authority will remain confined to the top management level. This may result in delayed and confused decision and create suspicion among the employees. On the contrary, if the organisational structure provides scope for adequate delegation and decentralisation of authority, decision-making will be flexible and the decision-making authority will be close to the operating centres. In such a situation, decision-making will be prompt and expected to be more effective and acceptable.

3. Analysis of the Objectives and Policies : Proper analysis of the objectives and policies is needed for decision-making. The clear definition of objectives and policies is the basis that guides the direction of decision-making. Without this basis, decision-making will be aimless and unproductive.

4. Analytical Study of the Alternatives : For decision-making, analytical study of all possible alternatives of a problem with their merits and demerits is essential. This is necessary to make out a correct selection of decision from among the alternatives.

5. Proper Communication System : Effective decision-making demands a machinery for proper communication of information to all responsibility centres in the organisation. Unless this structure is built up, ignorance of decision or ill-informed decision will result in misunderstanding and loose co-ordination.

6. Sufficient Time : Effective decision-making requires sufficient time. It is a matter of common experience that it is usually helpful to think over various ideas and possibilities of a problem for the purpose of identifying and evaluating it properly. But in no case a decision can be delayed for an indefinite period, rather it should be completed well in advance of the scheduled dates.

7. Study of the Impact of a Decision : Decision is intended to be carried out for the realisation of the objectives of the organisation. A decision in any particular area may react adversely in other areas of the organisation. As all business activities are inter-related and require co-ordination, it is necessary that a study and analysis of the impact of any decision should precede its application.

8. Participation of the Decision-maker : The decision-maker should not only be an observer while others will perform as per his decision. He should also participate in completing the work for which decision was taken by him. This experience will help him in decision-making in future. The principle of participation in work of the decision-maker will enable him to understand whether the decision taken is practical and also guide him in forthcoming decisional matters.

9. Flexibility of Mind : This is essential in decision-making, because decisions cannot satisfy everybody. Rigid mental set-up of the decision-maker may upset the decisions. The flexible mental disposition of the decision-maker enables him to change the decision and win over the co-operation of all the diverse groups.

10. Consideration of the Chain of Actions : There is a chain relationship in all the activities of any organisation. Different activities are tied up in a chain sequence. Any decision to change a particular work brings change in other related works also. Similarly, decision-making also proceeds following the chain of action in different activities. Therefore, before taking a decision one should consider the chain relationship among different activities.

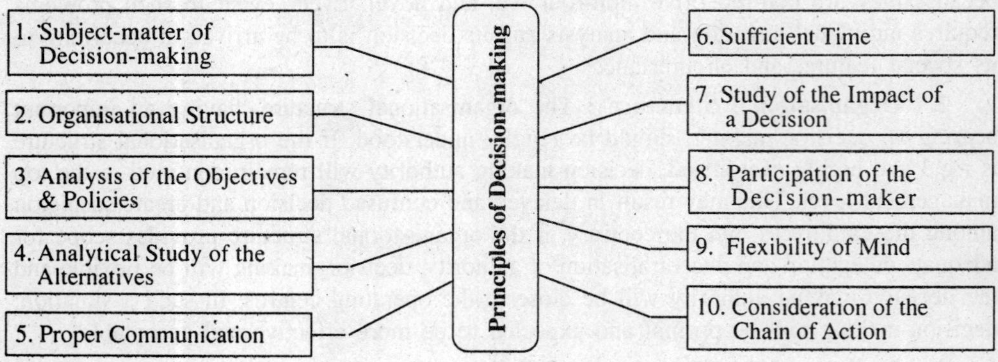

Fig. 3.8: Principles of Decision-making.

3.18 Types of Decision

Decisions may be of the following different types :

1. Routine Decisions : This type of decision is required to carry on the day to day activities of an enterprise. No special knowledge or skill is needed to arrive at routine decisions, because it moves along a fixed path with means and ends clearly defined to secure the final result. The lower level executives may make such type of decisions.

2. Strategic or Vital Decisions : A strategic decision has no fixed line or action, rather it brings about a change between the established means and ends. It is directly related to the achievement of organisational goals and affects the whole or major part of the organisation. So it calls for a thorough knowledge and extraordinary skill with reflecting analysis and thinking, Such decision-making is the task of the top ranking executives.

3. Programmed Decisions : Programmed decision means the routine and repetitive decision made within the framework of organisational policies and rules. Such decision-making process is applicable to the enterprises with sound organisational structure. The executives of the lower level management take these decisions.

4. Non-programmed Decisions : Such type of decisions are the decisions that are concerned with the solution of unusual problems in which different alternative courses of action cannot be determined in advance. Such decisions are required to be made for opening a new branch, closing an old branch, production of a new commodity, mechanisation of business activities, etc. Such decisions are usually taken by the executives of the top level management. The cost of such decision-making is very high and it has long-term consequences.

5. Basic or Policy Decisions : These decisions are very important and the success of an organisation depends much on them. Such decisions are taken at the top level management and remain effective for a longer period in comparision with the other types of decisions.

6. Special Decisions : Special decision is taken in respect of any important job. The executives of the top level management generally take such decisions.

7. Departmental, Inter-departmental and Enterprise Decisions : 'Departmental Decision' are taken by the managers of the respective departments. On the other hand, the decisions taken by the superior executive in collaboration with the departmental heads concerned are called 'Inter-departmental Decision'. And, the decisions, that cover the activities of the enterprise as a whole and are taken by the top-level executives are known as 'Enterprise Decisions'.

8. Tactical or Operational Decisions : There are temporary decisions relating to day to day operation of the organisation. Such decisions are short-term in nature and affect a narrow part of the organisation. Generally, the lower level managers make these decisions.

9. Group Decisions : Sometimes decisions are arrived at in a business enterprise not by a single manager but by many jointly. These are 'Group Decision'. Important and far reaching decisions are taken in the form of group decisions. The Board of Directors of a public company makes the group decisions. Moreover, in big companies Committees are formed in different areas of management such as—Production Committee, Sales Committee. Finance Committee and so on, and the business affairs are managed by means of group decisions of these committees.

10. Value Judgement Decisions : These types of decisions are concerned with non-economic factors like moral, ethical or human values. These are related to qualitative and intangible problems. Decisions regarding such problems demand a judicial mind and, as such, can only be taken by the top level executives.

11. Frequent and Rare Decisions : 'Frequent Decision' implies repeated routine decision with a minimum risk and uncertainty. Such a decision can be arrived at within the framework of the established policies and procedures and, as such can be an affair of the lower level executives.

On the other hand, 'Rare Decisions' are hardly covered by the established policies and procedures. These require searching and analysis of the core of the matter. Such decisions should be taken by the top level executives.

EXERCISES

[A] Essay-Type Questions

1. What is business planning? State the importance and characteristics of business planing.

   [**Ans.** Sections 3.1, 3.2 and 3.3]

2. What are the elements of planning? Discuss the basic principles to be observed in relation to good planning.

   [**Ans.** Sections 3.4 and 3.6]

3. Discuss the steps involved in the planning process.

   [**Ans.** Section 3.5]

4. What is meant by decision-making? Discuss its importance.

   [**Ans.** Sections 3.14 and 3.15]

5. Discuss the decision-making process.

   [**Ans.** Section 3.16]

6. Explain the basic principles of decision-making.

   [**Ans.** Section 3.17]

7. What do you understand by forecasting? How is it related with planning?

   [**Ans.** Sections 3.9 and 3.12]

8. Discuss the various techniques of forecasting.

   [**Ans.** Section 3.13]

9. Explain the steps involved in the process of forecasting.
[**Ans.** Section 3.11]

10. Discuss the role of planning as an element of management process.
[**Ans.** Section 3.3]

11. "Planning is an intellectual process, the conscious determination of courses of action, the basing of decisions on purpose, facts and considered estimates." Discuss the statement.
[**Ans.** Section 3.1]

12. "Decision-making is the primary task of the management." Discuss the statement and explain the process of decision-making.
[**Ans.** Sections 3.15 and 3.16]

13. Discuss the role of decision-making in business management.
[**Ans.** Section 3.15]

14. Discuss the different steps in planning. [C.U. B.Com. 1995]
[**Ans.** Section 3.5]

15. What is planning? Why is it important? Discuss the steps in planning. [C.U. B.Com. 1989]
[**Ans.** Sections 3.1, 3.3 and 3.5]

16. Discuss the major steps in planning. [C.U. B.Com. 1993, 1994]
[**Ans.** Section 3.5]

17. What do you mean by planning? Enumerate the principles of planning. [C.U. B.Com. 1997]
[**Ans.** Sections 3.1 and 3.6]

18. Discuss the nature and characteristics of planning.
[**Ans.** Section 3.2]

19. Discuss the different types of enterprise plans.
[**Ans.** Secton 3.7]

20. What is meant by planning? State the importance of planning in modern business. What are the universal steps involved in a planning process? [C. U. B.Com. 1999]
[**Ans.** Section 3.1, 3.3 and 3.5]

21. Explain the steps in forecasting. [C.U. B.Com. 2000]
[**Ans.** Section 3.5]

22. Discuss the characeristics of a sound plan. [C.U. B.Com. 2000, 2005]
[**Ans.** Section 3.2]

23. "Planning and forecasting are not synonymous"—Discuss. [C.U. B.Com. 2002]
[**Ans.** Section 3.12]

24. Discuss the steps in planning. [C.U. B.Com. 2003]
[**Ans.** Section 3.5]

25. Describe the different steps in decision-making. [C.U. B.Com. 2004]
[**Ans.** Section 3.16]

26. What do you mean by planning? Discuss the characteristics of a sound plan. [C.U. B.Com. 2005]
[**Ans.** Sections 3.1 and 3.2]

27. Describe the different steps in decision-making. [C.U. B.Com. 2006]
[**Ans.** Section 3.16]

28. Discuss the different steps in planning. [C.U. B.Com. 2006]
[**Ans.** Section 3.5]

29. State the planning process. [C.U. B.Com. 2007]
[**Ans.** Section 3.5]

30. Briefly discuss the different types of plan. [C.U. B.Com. 2008]
[**Ans.** Section 3.7]

31. Discuss the importance of planning in the modern business world. [C.U. B.Com. 2009]
[**Ans.** Section 3.3]

32. Define 'forecasting'. Explain the importance of forecasting. Write a note on the relation between planning and forecasting. [C.U. B.Com. 2009]
[**Ans.** Sections 3.9, 3.10. and 3.12]

33. Discuss the importance of decision-making in management. [C.U. B.Com. 2010]
[**Ans.** Section 3.15]

34. Explain the importance of planning in modern business world. [C.U. B.Com. 2011]
[**Ans.** Section 3.3]

35. What do you mean by planning in management? Discuss the universal steps involved in a planning process. [C.U. B.Com. 2011]
[**Ans.** Sections 3.1 and 3.5]

36. Describe the various types of decision.
[**Ans.** Section 3.18]

[B] Short Answer-Type Questions

1. Write short notes on the following:

(i) Steps in planning. [C.U. B.Com. 1994]
[**Ans.** Section 3.5]

(ii) Different steps in decision-making.
[**Ans.** Section 3.16]

(iii) Planning premises. [C.U. B.Com.]
[**Ans.** Section 3.5]

(iv) Importance of forecasting.
[**Ans.** Section 3.10]

(v) Planning and decision-making.
[**Ans.** Section 3.1]

(vi) Planning and forecasting.
[**Ans.** Section 3.12]

(vii) Elements of planning.
[**Ans.** Section 3.4]

(viii) Role of Decision-making.
[**Ans.** Section 3.15]

(ix) Importance of planning.
[**Ans.** Section 3.3]

2. Answer in brief the following questions:

(i) What is planning? [C.U. B.Com. 1995]
[**Ans.** Section 3.1]

(ii) What is decision-making? [C.U. B.Com. 1997]
[**Ans.** Section 3.14]

(iii) What are the principles of planning? [C.U. B.Com. 1998]
[**Ans.** Section 3.6]

(iv) Point out any four principles of decision-making.
[**Ans.** Section 3.17]

(v) What is forecasting?
[**Ans.** Section 3.9]

(vi) Mention the major elements of the planning process.
[**Ans.** Section 3.4]

(vii) What do you mean by planning premises?
[**Ans.** Section 3.5(3)]

(viii) Mention any two forecasting techniques. [C.U. B.Com. 2001]
[**Ans.** Section 3.13]

(ix) Name any two principles of planning. [C.U. B.Com. 2002]
[**Ans.** Section 3.6]

(x) State the different techniques of forecasting. [C.U. B.Com. 2003]
[**Ans.** Section 3.13]

(xi) Name the elements of planning. [C.U. B. Com. 2004]
[**Ans.** Section 3.4]

(xii) Mention the characteristics of decision-making. [C.U. B.Com. 2005]
[**Ans.** Section 3.14]

(xiii) What is planning? [C.U. B.Com. 2006]
[**Ans.** Section 3.1]

(xiv) What is meant by decision-making? [C.U. B.Com 2006]
[**Ans.** Section 3.14]

(xv) What do you mean by planning? [C.U. B.Com. 2007]
[**Ans.** Section 3.1]

(xvi) Define forecasting. [C.U. B.Com. 2007, 2010]
[**Ans.** Section 3.9]

(xvii) Mention two features of forecasting. [C.U. B.Com. 2008]
[**Ans.** Section 3.9]

(xviii) What is derivative plan? [C.U. B.Com. 2008]
[**Ans.** The plan which is formulated in order to implement the various parts of the basic plan is known as the 'derivative plan.']

(xix) What do you mean by planning in management? [C.U. B.Com. 2009]
[**Ans.** Section 3.1]

(xx) What is 'master planning'? [C.U. B.Com. 2011]
[**Ans.** Section 3.7]

(xxi) Briefly explain the importance of planning. [C.U. B.Com. 2011, New Syl.]
[**Ans.** Section 3.3]

(xxii) Give an idea of 'policy' as a plan. [C.U. B.Com. 2011, New Syl.]
[**Ans.** Section 3.4]

(xxiii) Define 'forecasting'. [C.U. B.Com. 2011, New Syl.]
[**Ans.** Section 3.9]

(xxiv) Give an idea of the 'planning premises'? [C.U. B.Com. 2011, New Syl.]
[**Ans.** Section 3.5]

(xxv) Mention the different types of decision.
[**Ans.** Section 3.18]

CHAPTER 4

Organising

"Organising is what you do before you do something, so that when you do it, it is not all mixed up."

—A. A. Milne

TOPICS

Subject-matter of the Chapter : *With the completion of planning activities in the process of management the various elements—money, material, machinery, manpower, etc. are required to convert the plan into action. All these elements build up the organisation of the business enterprise. There are two aspects of organisation—one is organisation of money and material, and the other is the organisation of human aspect or manpower. The organisation of human aspect is the most important as it is the human being who arranges for money, material, machinery and other requirements, In fact, organisation refers to management of human being. After planning the second step of management process is organising. The other activities of management are carried out through the organisation structure. As life is necessary to keep the body active, organisation is also essential to keep the business activities of an enterprise in progress and to make development and extension. The key to fulfil the objectives of an organisation is always in the hands of the employees. No organisation can be successful without their help. A detail discussion of the nature, importance and benefits of organisation and different aspects of organising is made in this chapter.*

4.1 Concept and Definition of Organising and Organisation

The term 'Organising' and 'Organisation' are given a variety of interpretations. In the first sense, 'organising' refers to a dynamic process and a managerial activity by which different elements or parts of an enterprise are brought together to obtain a desired result. This process places the enterprise into working order by defining and allocating the duties and responsibilities of different employees and provides it with everything useful to its functioning—raw material, tools, capital and personnel. It thus combines and co-ordinates their activities for commonness of purpose. So the term 'organising' implies co-ordination and arrangement of men and materials of an undertaking in order to achieve a certain purpose.

When used in the other sense, the term 'Organising' is understood as the creation of a structure of relationships among various positions and jobs for the realisation of the objectives and goals of the enterprise. In this sense, 'Organisation' is the vehicle through which goals are sought to be attained. The organisation structure is also viewed differently by various writers. Some of them regard it as a network of relatonships, a blueprint of how the managers will assign the various activities and connect them together. Some others look upon it as a social system, consisting of human relationships existing among the people performing different activities. To some other authors, an organisation is a system with inputs (men, materials, machines, etc. in the case of business), and processes through which these are converted into outputs (goods and services, profits, etc.)

Organising is a part of management activity devoted to establish a structural relationship of the resources of an undertaking and is a mechanism that enables the employees to work together. The work of organising in this way looks to the structural as well as functional aspects of business and correlates the different factors with their functions. All business enterprises, irrespective of their forms, require organisation for their economic operation and smooth running of business. The larger the size of a business, the more complicated and formal becomes the task of organising.

'Organisation' and 'Organising' have been defined by different authors in various ways. Some important definitions are given below :

G. E. Milward— "Organisation is the harmonious inter-relation of functions and staff."

Mooney and Reiley—"Organisation is the form of every human association for the attainment of common purpose."

Louis A. Allen— "Organisation is the process of identifying and grouping the works to be performed, defining and delegating responsibility and authority and establishing relationship for the purpose of enabling people to work more effectively together in accomplishing objectives."

Kimball and Kimball—"Organising embraces the duties of designating the departments and the personnel that are to carry on the work, defining their functions and specifying the relations that are to exist between the departments and individuals."

Theo Haimann—"Organising is the process of defining and grouping the activities of the enterprise and establishing the authority relationships among them. In performing the organising function, the manager defines, departmentalises and assigns the activities so that they can be effectively executed."

Thus, **'Organising is concerned with a well-planned division of the numerous functions of an enterprise, assignment of duties and responsibilities to the individual executive and subordinate employees supported by a strong system of supervision and co-ordinated control in order to ensure the effective execution of the plans as formulated by those in administrative authority.**

On the other hand, **'Organisation' is the structure in which harmonious inter-relationship of functions and personnel is created through the process of grouping the work to be performed, allocating duties and responsibilities, and delegating authority for the purpose of realising the objectives of the enterprise.**

4.2 Nature of Organisation

There are some common features of organisation through which a clear idea about its nature can be obtained. These are indicated below :

1. Process : Organisation is a process of defining, arranging and grouping the activities of an enterprise and establishing the authority relationships among the persons performing these activities. It is the framework within which people associate for the attainment of an objective. The framework provides the means for assigning activities to various parts and identifying the relative authorities and responsibilities of those parts. In simple term, organisation is the process by which the chief executive, as a leader, groups his men in order to get the work done.

2. Structure : The function of organising is the creation of a structural framework of duties and responsibilities to be performed by a group of people for the attainment of the objectives of the concern. The organisation structure consists of a series of relationships at all levels of authority. An organisation as a structure contains an "identifiable group of people contributing their efforts towards the attainment of goals." It is an important function of management to organise the enterprise by grouping the activities necessary to carry out the plans into administrative units, and defining the relationships among the executives and workers in such units.

3. Dividing and Grouping the Activities : Organising means the way in which the parts of an enterprise are put into working order. In doing such, it calls for the determination of parts and integration of one complete whole on the other. In fact, organisation is a process of divi-ding and combining the activities of an enterprise. Activities of an enterprise are required to be distributed between the departments, units or sections as well as between the persons for securing the benefits of division of labour and specialisation, and are to be integrated or combined for giving them a commonness of purpose. **L. Urwick** defines organisation as : 'determining what activities are necessary to any purpose and arranging them as groups which may be assigned to individual."

4. Accomplishment of Goals or Objectives : An organisation structure has no meaning or purpose unless it is built around certain clear-cut goals or objectives. In fact, an organisation structure is built-up precisely because it is the ideal way of making a rational pursuit of objectives. **Haney** defines organisation as : 'a harmonious adjustment of specialised parts for the accomplishment of some common purpose or purposes."

5. Authority-Responsibility Relationship : An organisation structure consists of various positions arranged in a hierarchy with a clear definition of the authority and responsibility associated with each of these. An enterprise cannot serve the specific purposes or goals unless some positions are placed above others and given authority to bind them by their decisions. In fact, organisation is quite often defined as a structure of authority-responsibility relationships.

6. Human and Material Aspects : Organisation deals with the human and material factors in business. Human element is the most important element in an organisation. To accomplish the task of building up a sound organisation, it is essential to prepare an outline of the organisation which is logical and simple. The manager should then try to fit in suitable men. **Henry Fayol** says in this connection : "see that human and material organisations are suitable" and "ensure material and human order".

From these features of organisation, it emerges that, **an organisation is essentially an administrative 'process' of determining what activities are necessary to be performed for the achievement of objectives of an enterprise, dividing and grouping the work into individual jobs and, a 'structure' of positions arranged in a hierarchy with defined relationships of authority and responsibility among the executives and workers performing these tasks for the most effective pursuit of common goals of the enterprise.**

4.3 Importance and Significance of Organisation

All business and non-business enterprises require sound organisation for their smooth, efficient and economical operation to achieve maximum results with minimum of cost and efforts. Evidently, when two or more people are engaged in an institution, the task of each person is required to be fixed through the division of total activities among them and they should have a concerted action. Each one's work must be directed in such a way that they can reach the commonness of purpose.

A sound organisation is a must for success in any line of business. This is necessitated by the magnitude and complexities of business enterprises. The entire work of such enterprises is beyond the capacity of a single person to manage. When there is specialisation and division of work into its logical component parts, it can attain economies of large-scale production. The speed of performance is ensured and the standard of work performed is improved by distributing the work constantly among a number of persons on the basis of their knowledge, experience and capacity.

Organisation sets the relationship between people, work, and resources. Whenever groups of people exist in a common effort, organisation must be employed to get productive results.

Organisation is a tool of efficient management. It is the mechanism through which the manager directs, co-ordinates and controls the business affairs. It is, indeed, the foundation of business and, as such, it provides a means by which human efforts are properly directed to more and more productive, effective and fruitful results.

Organisation is a means by which the problems of the enterprise connected with policies, operations, and administration can efficiently be solved. Sound organisation can contribute greatly to the success and continuity of the enterprise. The importance of sound organisation will be more clear if we remember what **Andrew Carnegie** once said : "Take away our factories, take away our trade, our avenues of transportation, our money, leave us nothing but our organisation, and in four years we shall have established ourselves."

So, no institution or enterprise—whether business, educational, cultural or governmental—can function properly and successfully without sound organisation. And herein lies the need for and significance of organisation.

4.4 Benefits of Sound Organisation

Organising of people and things is essential for co-ordinated work. Good organisation structure is an indispensable means for better business performance and better achievement of the objectives. A planned organisation outlines the required functions, relates those functions in a systematic manner and assigns requisite authorities and degrees of responsibility to the people performing those functions.

The benefits of sound organisation lies in its advantages. The principal advantages of organisation may be stated briefly as folows :

1. Efficient Administration : A properly designed organisation facilitates administration. Proper division of work with systematic and specific functionalisation of duties and consistent delegation of authority with well-defined inter-relationship will not only ensure better utilisation of the personnel and their abilities but also smooth the management of business activities. It avoids confusion and misunderstanding, eliminates delay and inefficiency in the performance of work; it removes all bottlenecks in the flow of work and facilitates quick and correct decisions. It secures optimum use of physical, mechanical and human resources.

2. Prompt Accomplishment : It adds definiteness to the activities to be accomplished by allocating the duties and responsibilities to the individual members of the enterprise. It, thus, secures certainty and promptness in accomplishment of the task.

3. Growth and Diversification : It promotes growth and facilitates diversification. Expansion of business and diversification of production process depend on sound organisation. Giant businesses are the outcome of organisational ability of the managers.

4. Optimum Use of Advanced Technology : Present technical development greatly influences the need for more adequate organisation structure and for understanding the proper form of organisation best designed to accommodate the new factors. The high cost of installation, operation and maintenance of new equipment call for proper organisation.

5. Stimulating Creativity : Good organisation stimulates independent creative thinking and initiative by providing well-defined areas of work with provision for development of new and improved ways of doing things. In short, the organisation structure demands creative result from creative people. By establishing clear-cut accountability it provides recognition for the professionals and the specialists in terms of their achievements.

4.5 Steps in Organisation Process

The management function of organising consists in making a rational division of work and integration of the activities into specific groups to achieve a well-co-ordinated and orderly structure for the accomplishment of work.

The various steps involved in this process are the following :

1. Determination of Activities : The first step in organising is to divide the total job of an enterprise into several essential activities such as—production, financing, purchasing, sales, personnel, and so on. Identification of work enables the managers to concentrate attention on important activities, to avoid duplication of work, and eliminate overlapping or wastage of effort.

2. Grouping or Classification of Activities : The various activities identified under the first step are then classified into appropriate departments, divisions, sections, sub-divisions etc. on the basis of functions, products, territories or customers. For example, the various activities connected with production may be grouped and classified as 'production department activities.' This will facilitate specialisation. Such grouping of activities is called 'Departmentation.'

3. Allocation or Assignment of Duties to Individuals : After the creation of departments or divisions, the next step will be to fix suitable and qualified persons into the activities of each department. Each person in the department will be given a speficic part of the job to do and will be made responsible for it. So, the task of management in this step is to appoint workers, foremen, supervisors, etc. and to define the responsibility of each one of them. While assigning duties, the requirements of the job and the competence of the individual should be properly matched together. Assignment of duties creates responsibility and ensures certainty of work performance.

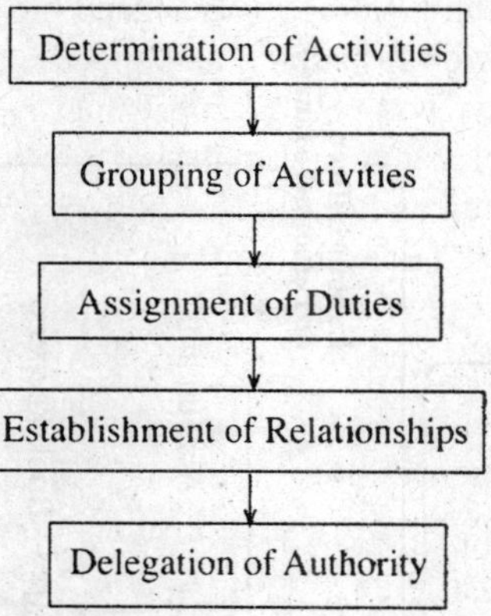

Fig. 4.1: The Organisation Process.

4. Establishment of Relationships : Through the assignment of tasks to individuals superior-subordinate relationships beween various positions are established in the enterprise. The superior manager commands his subordinates and the subordinate manager gives him the reports of his performances. Such relationships and channels of communication should be clearly defined. Each and every individual should know clearly from whom he is to take orders and to whom he is accountable for his performance.

5. Delegation of Authority : Appropriate amount of authority is delegated to people to enable them to perform the assigned duties with confidence. No one can discharge his responsibilities regarding a particular work in the absence of requisite authority to do the same. So the manager will have to pass on authority for completing the assigned work to the sectional managers and the sectional managers to others below them. Delegation of authority means conferring of operational decision-making power by the top manager to the subordinate manager.

Keeping this process of building up organisation structure in view, one will find enough reason to agree with this definition of organisation : "Organisation embraces the duties of designating the departments and the personnel that are to carry on the work, defining their functions and specifying the relations that are to exist between departments and individuals."

4.6 Organisation Structure

In simple term, 'structure' is the pattern in which various parts or components are inter-related or inter-connected. Thus, organisation structure is the framework that provides a set of relationships among various components or parts of the enterprise. This prescribes the relationships among various activities and positions. Since these positions are held by various persons, the structure is the pattern of relationships between and among individuals and groups in the enterprise. According to **Albert K. Wickesberg** : "the set of inter-personal relationships which operates in the context of position, procedure, process, technology and social environment comprises what is known as organisation structure."

Organising is a facilitating function and structure is its mechanism. The concept of organisation and its structure, and inter-personal relationships is extremely complex. So, it is desirable to build up a suitable organisation structure which will assist economical and effective attainment of objectives avoiding the complexities as far as possible.

Organisation is a means to an end. Organisation structure is an important means in this respect. Good structure is, therefore, indispensable. Unsound structural framework will seriously impair good business performance and may even destroy it. So, it should be the task of the managers to establish a structure best suited for the enterprise. The structure depends upon the needs of the enterprise.

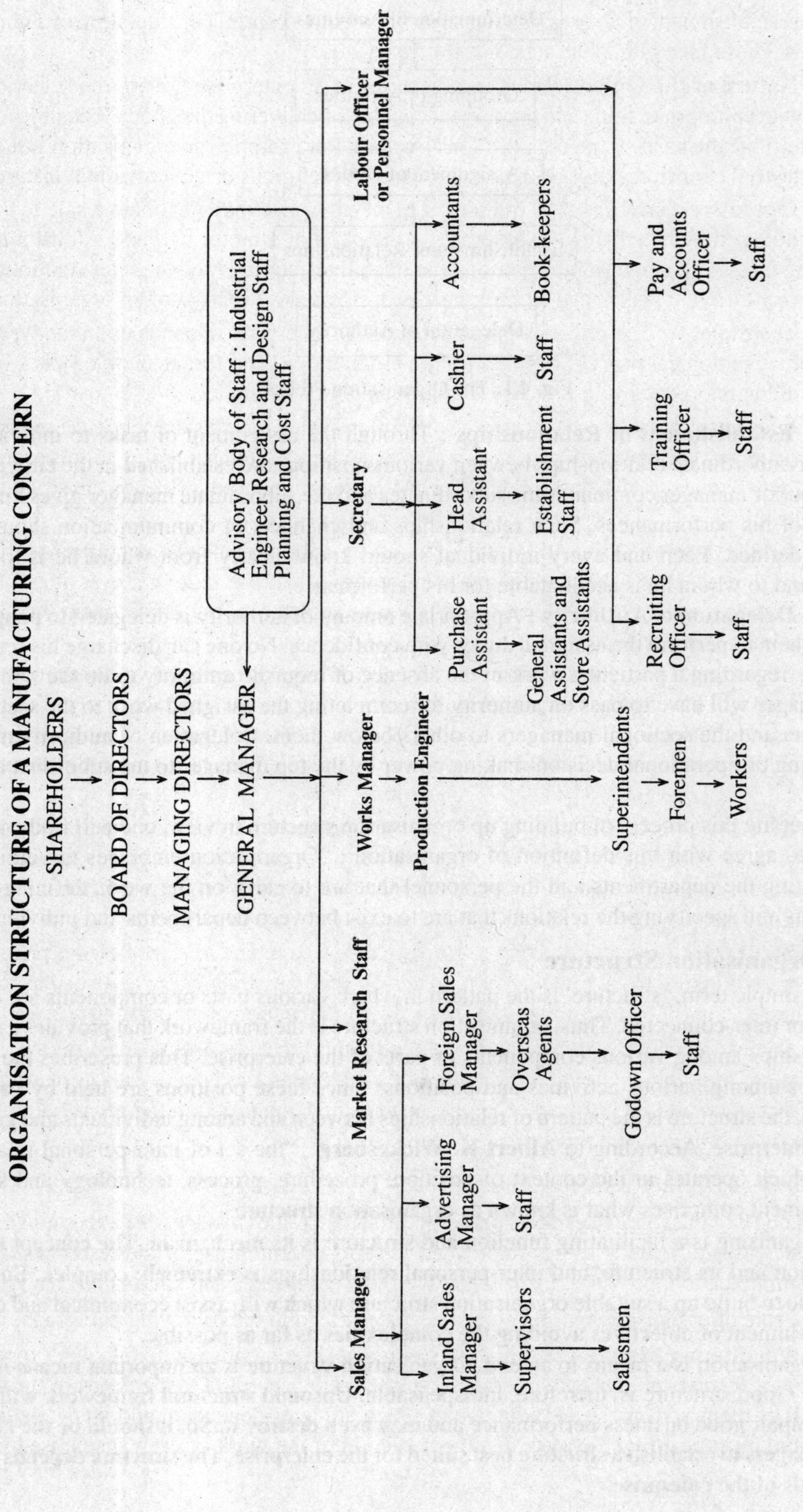

Fig. 4.2: A Sample of an Organisation Structure.

4.6.1 Determinants of Organisation Structure

The establishment of an organisation structure requires careful consideration of a number of factors. These factors may be stated as follows :

1. Nature of the Objectives : The objectives of an enterprise govern the selection of persons with appropriate skills and equipment capable of delivering the goods. The objectives, thus, determine the basis of the organisation structure. For example, an organisation structure of an industrial concern cannot be the same as that of a religious or governmental institution.

2. Operative Activities : An individual in an enterprise may negotiate a sale to a customer; another may be engaged in assembling the parts of a motor car; and a third may be collecting market data or cost information. The operative activities and the inter-relations that exist among different tasks have an important bearing on the structure of an organisation.

3. Technology : The organisation structure of an enterprise depends upon the type and nature of technological process adopted for the production. Therefore, technology is a factor for consideration in determining the structure of an organisation.

4. Sequence of Tasks : The nature of technology often dictates the sequence of tasks to be performed and human relationships are required to be adjusted according to this sequence of tasks. This sequence of tasks also acts as a major determinant to influence the structure of the organisation.

5. Limitations of Skill and Working Capacity : Individuals in an enterprise differ in their skills and abilities. These individual differences affect the tasks to be assigned to an individual and, as such, the structure is required to be adjusted taking into account the limitations of human skill and ability.

6. Managerial Functions : The managerial functions at one level or department may be different from that of other level or department. Therefore, the structure of organisation is to be devised to maximise effective inter-relationships at different management levels so that it can facilitate the attainment of objectives by the effective efforts of the subordinate employees.

7. Size and Scope : The smaller the firm, the more informal and loose become the interpersonal contacts and relationships. But they will be otherwise in the case of big concerns. So, the size of the enterprise and its scope of performance have an effective influence on the organisation structure.

8. Strategy : After considering the organisation structure of various enterprises the management thinkers have come to the conclusion that the strategy plays a special role in determining the outline of authority and flow of communication in an organisation.

9. Social Needs : The social needs of an individual such as—status, recognition, sense of belonging, opportunity for development of abilities or the satisfaction of ego need—require that they should be given due weight for their fulfilment within the organisation. The structure of an organisation cannot ignore these social needs.

4.6.2 Role of Organisation Structure

A good organisation structure of an enterprise helps the managers to accomplish their duties, increases efficiency of the employees, ensures optimum use of the resources, facilitates communication, provides job satisfaction to the employees and stimulates creativity.

The role of organisation structure has been described in the following paragraphs :

1. Facilitating Management Action : Where a large number of people work together, some sort of formal structuring is required to place them according to the needs of the enterprise. All of them perform various functions which are inter-dependent and inter-related. As such, there must be a plan for systematic completion of the work of each specialised job so that the total activities can accomplish the common objectives. Further, these activities should be completed in a co-ordinated way. Organisation structure is the mechanism through which a manager directs, co-ordinates, and controls the organisational activities. A properly designed organisation structure facilitates management operation. Management actions take place with certainty and continuity only if appropriate functional groups are provided to help the managers. The grouping and arrangement of activities directly affect the operating results. If the important activities are overlooked, the results would be detrimental to the organisation.

2. Encouraging Efficiency : Organisation is the framework within which an enterprise functions. In this functioning, efficiency is the major element. Therefore, the members of the organisation try to maximise the output of goods or services resulting from a given input of resources. It is necessary to develop some measures of systematic, orderly, rational, and co-ordinated effort, and to control waste and loss. In fact, various organisation structures try to achieve efficiency in organisational operations.

3. Optimum Use of Organisational Resources : Organisation structure provides for making optimum utilisation of organisational resources by ensuring their allocation to the points where these are needed. It gives higher place to the activities which are more important for the achievement of organisational objectives. Thus, placing the activities according to their importance, organisation structure provides guidelines for resource allocation. Optimum allocation of resources to various organisational units is essential for growth and vitality of an enterprise.

4. Helping Communication : Sound organisation structure provides the pathways for communication among the members of the organisation as well as between the organisation and its environment. In fact, when we say that organisation structure establishes relationships, we mean that it creates reporting relationships, that is, who will communicate with whom. Similarly, when the organisation interacts with its environment, a communication process is involved. Thus, organisation structure serves the purpose of communication. Within the organisational boundary, communication is necessary in horizontal, vertical and lateral directions— and the organisation, if designed properly, provides the lines of communication in all these directions.

5. Job Satisfaction : Since organisation structure provides relatedness among the tasks, responsibilities, and people, the members of the organisation sooner or later come to evaluate the nature of those relationships and of their own relationships to the organisation and their jobs. Organisation structure provides for each person a place of status among his fellows. This works as motivating factor to them. Most of the people spend a large part of their lives at work associated with the organisation. They expect their work to provide a reasonable degree of job satisfaction, and the framework for this is in the structure of the organisation itself.

6. Stimulating Creativity : A sound organisation structure based on specialisation stimulates creative thinking by providing well-defined area of work with the provision of development of new and improved ways of working. It tries to put people where they are required. When they work on a job for considerably long time, they are in a position to suggest something new. Many practitioners have contributed to the development of management thinking which show the results of their creativity that has come because of the organisation structure itself.

Organisation structure can facilitate to perform the above activities only when it is properly designed. Further, organisation structure should be viewed as a means towards specific ends. As such, it can be used as a tool, not as an end.

4.6.3 Features of a Good Organisation Structure

A good organisation structure is one that is designed in an appropriate manner to facilitate performance of the day-to-day activities of the organisation. The structure should be helpful in establishing co-ordination in joint efforts and accomplishing the work of planning, directing and controlling by the managers successfully. The features of a good organisation structure are :

1. Simplicity : An organisation structure should be basically simple. It implies that the structure should have the simplest possible framework which will fulfil the purposes intended with due emphasis on economical and effective means of accomplishing the objective of the enterprise. This will ensure economy of effort, minimise overhead costs, and reduce all possible difficulties that may arise out of poor communication due to the complexity of intricate structure. Every person in the organisation should be clear about with whom he has to consult in a particular matter. Too many levels, communication channels, and committees often cause more problems than solving them. Ideally speaking, their numbers and places in the organisation should be based on organisational needs.

2. Flexibility and Continuity : The organiser should build the structure not for today or tomorrow, but for the distant future. As such, continuity must be maintained in the organisation structure over the period of time. However, since organisation structure is based on circumstances and these are not fixed but change over the period of time, there is a need for incorporating the changes in the organisation structure also. Hence, the structure should be adaptable enough so that it provides the opportunity to accommodate the changes where these are needed.

3. Clear Line of Authority : Whatever the form of structure be adopted, there should be clear lines of authority running from top to bottom or in horizontal directions. It implies that one should be very clear about what he is expected to achieve or contribute and what relationships should be maintained by him at his official level. The failure to clarify the lines of authority results into frictions and inefficiencies. Often, in bureaucratic structure followed by the government organisations, the problem of jurisdiction of a department or division arises and the work suffers.

4. Application of Ultimate Authority : It suggests that, although a superior manager assigns some of the work to his subordinates, he is ultimately responsible for the accomplishment of the total work. Thus, he is responsible for his own work as well as for the work performed by his subordinates. If this concept is applied, it ensures that every person carries dual responsibility; responsibility for his own work and that for his subordinates' work. As a whole, a manager is responsible for the total work assigned to him by his superior.

5. Proper Delegation of Authority : The concept of ultimate authority will be effective only when there is proper delegation of authority at various levels of the organisation. Delegation of authority refers to authorisation of a manager to make certain decisions. A common problem in the organisational life is that the managers often fail to delegate adequate authority and suffer from various problems. Such problems may be in the form of decision bottlenecks, delay in implementation of decision, more pressure on the higher level managers for making decisons, etc. All these factors affect organisational efficiency adversely. These problems can be solved by appropriate delegation of authority.

6. Unity of Command and Direction : The principles of unity of command and direction should be followed. Unity of command suggests that one person should receive orders and instructions from one superior only. Unity of direction refers to the concept of 'one plan one man'. Every work in an organisation having the same objective must be assigned to a single person. Thus, the activities and functions of same type can be grouped together. This provides clarity in carrying out the activities.

7. Minimum Possible Managerial Levels : As far as possible, there should be minimum managerial levels. Greater the number of managerial levels, longer is the line of communication in the chain of command—creating problems of delay and distortion. Moreover, more managerial levels increase cost in the organisation. Though it may not be possible to suggest how many managerial levels should be there in an organisation, the principle of minimum levels can be followed.

8. Proper Emphasis on Staff : Line functions should be separated from staff functions and adequate emphasis should be placed on important staff activities. This is important particularly in large organisations. A line activity is that which serves the organisational objectives directly; for example, production activities in a manufacturing concern. On the other hand, contribution of staff activities are indirect, that is, they help in carrying out the line activities so as to realise the organisational goals. Staff activities may be personnel, accounting etc. Both of these activities should be clearly spelled out to run the organisation smoothly.

9. Provision for Top Management : In the company form of organisation, the shareholders are generally indifferent to the day-to-day affairs of the company. Similarly, the members of the board of directors also do not meet on regular basis. Therefore, a link should be provided between the regular management team and members of the board and shareholders. The organisation structure should clearly specify how these top management groups will participate in management of the company and exercise control over its functioning.

4.6.4 Types or Forms of Organisation Structure

Organisation structure is basically concerned with the allocation of duties and delegation of authority. There are different methods of division of work and distribution of authority. As a result, several types of organisation structures have been evolved.

Mainly there are seven types of organisation structures. Those are as follows :

(i) Line Organisation, (ii) Staff Organisation, (iii) Functional Organisation, (iv) Line and Staff Organisation, (v) Project Organisation, (vi) Matrix Organisation, and (vii) Committees.

Among these types of organisation structures, only the types which are included in the syllabus will be described in the following paragraphs :

(A) Line Organisation :

• **Meaning :** 'Line Organisation' is the oldest and simplest form of organisation structure. It is also known as 'Military Organisation', because it originated in the army. In line organisation, authority flows from the man at the top to the lowest man vertically. In other words, the directions are issued by the man-in-charge of the whole organisation and are directly conveyed to the persons responsible for the execution of the work. The business unit may be divided into departments headed by the departmental managers. A departmental head receives orders from the General Manager and passes them on to his immediate subordinates. The subordinates similarly communicate the orders to the workers. The various persons heading the different departments are perfectly independent of each other and enjoy equal status.

In case the manager of one department wishes to issue guidance or directions to a subordinate in another department, he will go up the line and convey the message to the top manager who will then pass it down the line in the other department. For instance, if the Finance Manager of an enterprise has to convey a message to a Superintendent in the production department, he will have to send the same upwards to the General Manager who will then pass it down to the Production Manager. And the Production Manager will further pass it down to the Superintendent concerned. Line organisation may be of two types—(i) Pure line organisation, and (ii) Departmental line organisation. In Pure line organisation, all individuals at a given level perform the same type of work and departments are created only to facilitate supervision and control. But in departmental line organisation, work performed in each department is of a different nature.

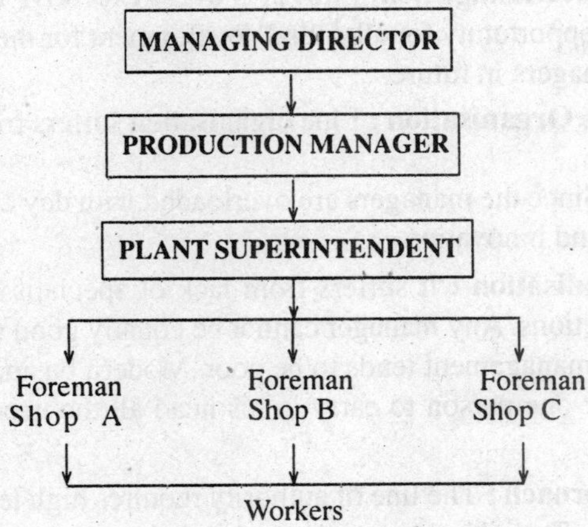

Fig. 4.3: Line Organisation.

• **Features of Line Organisation :** Line organisation has the following characteristics :

(i) Authority flows vertically from top to the bottom.

(ii) The command is given through a straight line.

(iii) Each subordinate receives orders from one superior and is responsible to him only.

• **Merits of Line Organisation :** The line organisation has the following important advantages not usually found in other types of organisation :

1. Simplicity : Line organisation is the easiest to establish and operate and simplest to explain to the employees. Lines of authority and responsibility are direct, simple and clear. Every individual understands to whom he is responsible. The authority and responsibility of every position is clearly defined.

2. Prompt Decision : Every manager can take decisions independently without consulting with others. He does not depend on others for advice, assistance or service. So, decision-making process is easier and quick in such type of organisation structure.

3. Strong Discipline : It ensures effective discipline. Each position is under the direct control of its immediate superior. Therefore, it is easy to maintain discipline among the people in the organisation.

4. Unified Control : Unity of command results in close personal contacts between the superiors and subordinates. Direct and close contacts facilitate effective supervision and control.

5. Fixed Responsibility : Everybody in this type of organisation knows to whom he is responsible and who are responsible to him.

6. Flexibility : Since each executive has sole responsibility in his own position, he can easily adjust the organisation to changes in the business situation.

7. Economical : Line organisation is quite economical because staff specialists are not required here.

8. Effective Co-ordination : Since all activities relating to one department are managed by one person, co-ordination can be effective.

9. Orderly Communication : Communication between the superiors and subordinates flows in a direct vertical line. Such communication is easy to maintain and it is orderly in nature.

10. Development of Management Skill : As every executive has to perform a variety of functions, there is an opportunity for all-round development for them. They will emerge as skilled and efficient managers in future.

● **Demerits of Line Organisation :** Line organisation suffers from the following weaknesses :

1. Over-loading : Since the managers are overloaded with day-to-day work, they do not find time for creativity and innovation.

2. Lack of Specialisation : It suffers from lack of specialisation. A manager has to perform a variety of functions. Any manager cannot be equally good in all the functions and, therefore, the quality of management tends to be poor. Modern business is so complex that it is extremely difficult for one person to carry in his head all the necessary details about his work in his department.

3. Autocratic Approach : The line of authority requires high level of obedience on the part of the subordinates. There is concentration of authority at the top. There is usually no communication upwards from the lower rank. The managers at the top may be devoid of the realities of the situation. As a result, decisions may be arbitrary or wrong. There is a scope for favouritism and autocracy.

4. Low Morale : The subordinates are to carry out the decisions taken by the superiors at the upper level. This leads to lack of initiative on the part of the subordinates. Their opinions and grievances are not properly communicated upwards.

5. Instability : The success and continuity of an organisation depend upon a few competent managers. Succesion problem is acute and there may be lack of continuity when the key executives retire.

● **Suitability of Line Organisation :** In the following cases line organisation is suitable :

(i) In small-scale business with a small number of subordinates,

(ii) Where the work is of routine nature,

(iii) In industries where continuous processes are followed, for example, sugar industry,

(iv) In industries where automatic machines are used requiring less expertise of the foremen.

(B) Staff Organisation :

● **Meaning :** 'Staff Organisation' means that type of organisation in which some experts are employed to execute the advisory functions. These experts act as the advisors of the organisation. The staff persons have no authority to command and provide directions. They only give advice to the line manager in various organisational aspects. The experts who are employed for such advice are known as 'Staff Officers', like Purchase Staff Officer, Production Staff Officer, Sales Staff Officer, Personnel Staff Officer. The staff officers advise the line managers as and when required, but they bear no liability or responsibility of executing or getting work done. The managers may follow their advice or may not follow them.

The staff organisation is auxiliary in nature. In such type of organisation structure, benefits of specialisation can be obtained. So the efficiency and effectiveness of the line managers are increased. However, it is an expensive process of organisation.

The structure of staff organisation is shown in the following diagram :

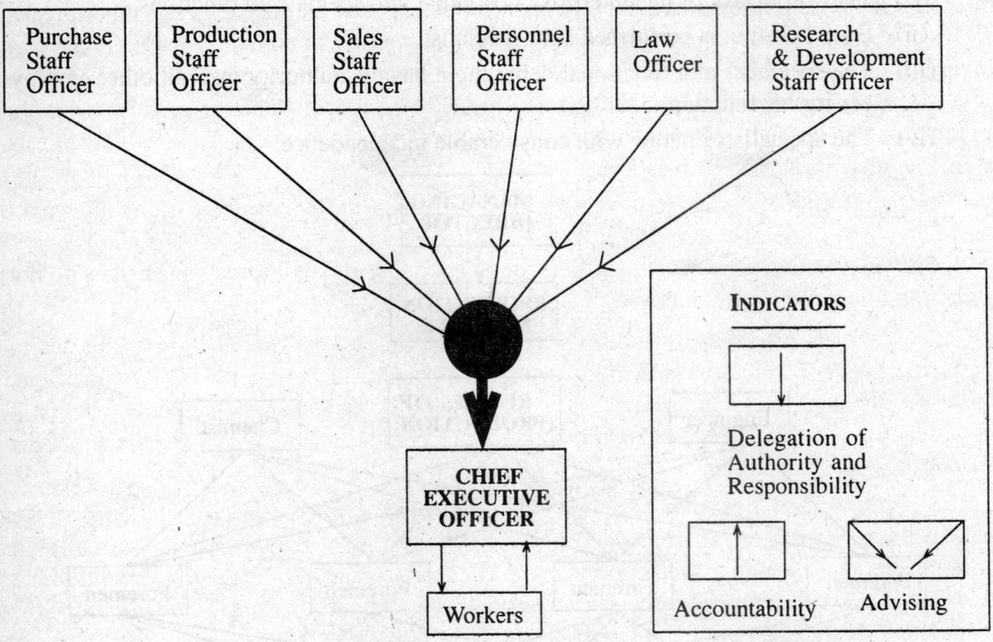

Fig. 4.4: Staff Organisation.

● **Features of Staff Organisation :** The basic characteristics of a staff organisation may be pointed out as under :

(i) The experts of the staff organisation gives specialised service to the line organisation.
(ii) The staff organisation is auxiliary in nature.
(iii) It is an advisory body consisting of some functional experts.
(iv) The staff people have no authority to command the line organisation, they can recommend only.

(C) Functional Organisation :

● **Meaning :** The 'Functional Organisations' are based on the concept of 'Functional Foremanship' suggested by **F. W. Taylor,** a pioneer in Scientific Management. In functional organisation, the organisation is divided into a number of functional areas. Each function is managed by a functional expert in that area. Every functional area serves all other areas. For example, the personnel department recruits employees, arranges for their training, and deals with the people required for all the other departments. The purchasing department handles purchases for the entire concern. Every functional manager enjoys functional authority over the subordinates in other departments. Within a functional department every operating executive receives orders from several functional specialists. For example, each foreman receives orders from the factory superintendent, chief engineer, chemist, etc.

While dividing the management functions into departments care should be taken that— (i) the entire work has been divided into various departments and no activity remains unallotted; (ii) there should not be any duplication in the sense that an activity should not be allotted to more than one department; and (iii) the work allotted to one department should consist of inter-related jobs.

● **Features of Functional Organisation :** The principal characteristics of functional organisation are stated below :

(i) The whole task of the enterprise is divided into specialised functions.

(ii) Each function is performed by a specialist.

(iii) The specialist of a functional department has the authority over all other employees for his function.

(iv) The specialists operate with considerable independence.

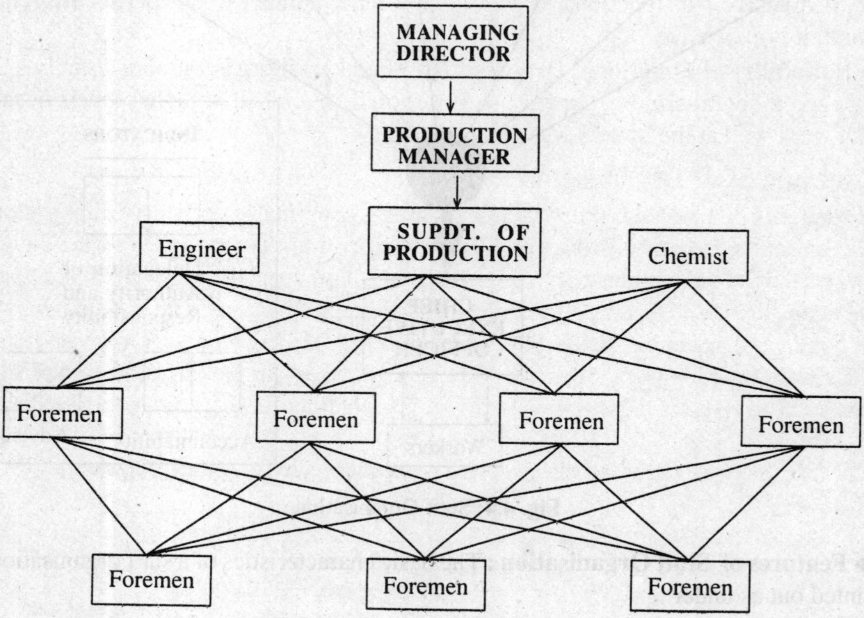

Fig. 4.5: Functional Organisation.

● **Merits of Functional Organisation :** The functional organisation enjoys the following advantages :

1. Specialisation : Functional organisation ensures a logical division of work. This results in specialisation of functions. Every functional manager is an expert in his area and all workers get the benefit of his expertise.

2. High Degree of Efficiency : Every employee in the organisation concentrates on one function only and receives the expert guidance from the specialists. As a result, efficiency of operation becomes high.

3. Scope for Expansion : It facilitates mass production through specialisation and standardisation. A change can be introduced in this type of organisation. There is scope for expansion.

4. Reduction of Work Load : Every functional head looks after one function only and, so, the work burden on the top executive is reduced. It ensures the separation of mental and manual functions.

5. Better Control : In functional organisation there is joint supervision of work. As a result, functional control becomes more effective in comparison with line or staff organisation.

● **Demerits of functional Organisation :** Functional organisation suffers from the following drawbacks :

1. Complexity : There are many cross-relationships which create confusion. A worker may receive conflicting orders.

2. Absence of Unity of Command : In such organisation a person is accountable to several superiors. As a result, responsibility for results cannot easily be fixed.

3. Lack of Co-ordination : It is too complicated in operation because it entails the division of functions into a number of sub-functions. This leads to lack of co-ordination among the workers and functions.

4. Delay in Decision-making : Arriving at a decision requires the involvement of several specialists. So, decision-making process in functional organisation is slow.

5. Expensive : In functional organisation a large number of specialists are required. Therefore, it is expensive.

● **Suitability of Functional Organisation :** Functional organisation is usually suitable for large and medium-sized enterprises. But it should be applied at higher levels because it does not work well at the lower levels.

(D) Line and Staff Organisation :

● **Meaning :** 'Line and Staff Organisation' is a combination of Line Organisation and Staff Organisation Structure. In such organisation, line authority flows in a vertical line in the same way as in the line organisation and, in addition, staff specialists are employed to advise the line managers for efficient performance of the special functions. The staff expert is advisory in nature and has only the authority to recommend. He has no power over the line positions. His main function lies in rendering advice, assistance and making provision of specialised service. Such type of organisation structure is more popular specially in large enterprises.

The line and staff organisation structure is shown in the following diagram :

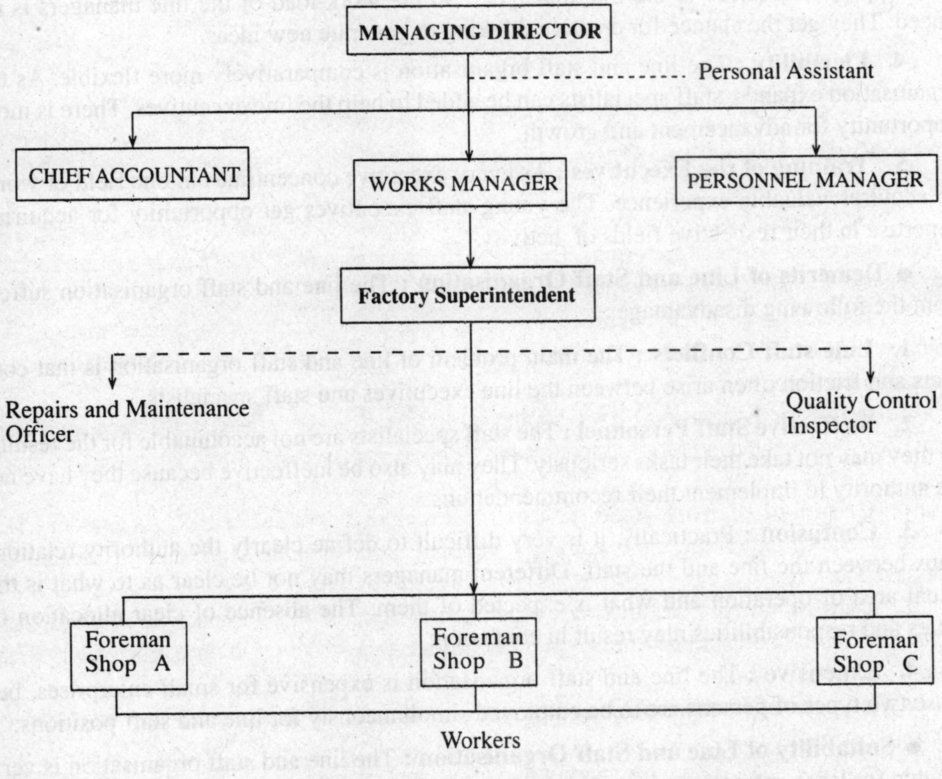

Fig. 4.6: Line and Staff Organisation.

● **Characteristics of Line and Staff Organisation :** The following are the main features of a line and staff organisation :

1. Two types of personnel exist in this form of structure—line personnel and staff experts. It adds functional specialists with the line organisation.

2. As compared to line organisation, the structure of line and staff is more complicated. Besides the line officers, the structure is equipped with specialists in different levels.

3. The staff members are only for giving assistance and specialised advice to the line officers. The line officers have no binding to accept their advice.

4. Such organisation structure is applicable specially in large enterprises.

5. The subordinate is answerable only to his immediate boss and not to his staff specialist. So line and staff organisation, besides following the principle of unity of command, also provides specialisation that leads to efficiency of work.

● **Merits of Line and Staff Organisation :** Line and staff organisation has the following advantages :

1. **Specialised Advice :** The line managers receive the benefit of expert advice and assistance from the staff specialists. The staff experts enable the line managers to discharge their responsibilities more efficiently.

2. **Better Decisions :** The staff specialists provide adequate information and expert advice. As a result, the line managers can take quality decisions.

3. **Reduction of Work-burden :** The staff specialists carry out detailed investigation and supply information to the line managers. So the work-load of the line managers is reduced. They get the chance for creative thinking to generate new ideas.

4. **Flexibility :** The line and staff organisation is comparatively more flexible. As the organisation expands, staff specialists can be added to help the line executives. There is more opportunity for advancement and growth.

5. **Training of the Executives :** As every executive concentrates in one field of work, he acquires valuable experience. The young staff executives get opportunity for acquiring expertise in their respective fields of activity.

● **Demerits of Line and Staff Organisation :** The line and staff organisation suffers from the following disadvantages :

1. **Line-staff Conflicts :** The main problem of line and staff organisation is that conflicts and friction often arise between the line executives and staff specialists.

2. **Ineffective Staff Personnel :** The staff specialists are not accountable for the results. So they may not take their tasks seriously. They may also be ineffective because they have not the authority to implement their recommendations.

3. **Confusion :** Practically, it is very difficult to define clearly the authority relationships between the line and the staff. Different managers may not be clear as to what is the actual area of operation and what is expected of them. The absence of clear allocation of duties and responsibilities may result in confusion.

4. **Expensive :** The line and staff organisation is expensive for small enterprises, because two types of persons are to be employed simultaneously for line and staff positions.

● **Suitability of Line and Staff Organisation :** The line and staff organisation is very suitable for large enterprises. It provides ample scope for specialisation without violating the unity of command.

4.6.5 Organisation Chart

(A) Meaning : 'Organisation Chart' is a diagrammatical presentation of the various positions in the enterprise and the formal relationships among them. It gives a picture of the relationships between different departments or divisions of an enterprise and the relationships between people of various levels.

The main characteristics of an organisation chart are as follows.

(i) It is a graphic presentation.

(ii) It shows at a glance the lines of authority and responsibility.

(iii) It serves as a blueprint of the structure of the organisation and helps to clarify the allocation of duties.

(iv) It represents the formal organisation structure.

(v) It shows clearly the various positions in the organisation and how they relate to one an other.

(vi) It indicates the channels of communication.

(B) Types of Organisation Chart : The organisation charts may be of the following three types :

1. Vertical Charts : It shows the lines of command flowing from top to bottom in vertical lines. The highest position is shown at the top and the next highest position is shown thereafter. This process proceeds up to the lowest position, which is placed at the bottom. This chart is also called 'Top-to-Down Chart'. It is the mostly used chart.

A specimen of vertical chart is given below :

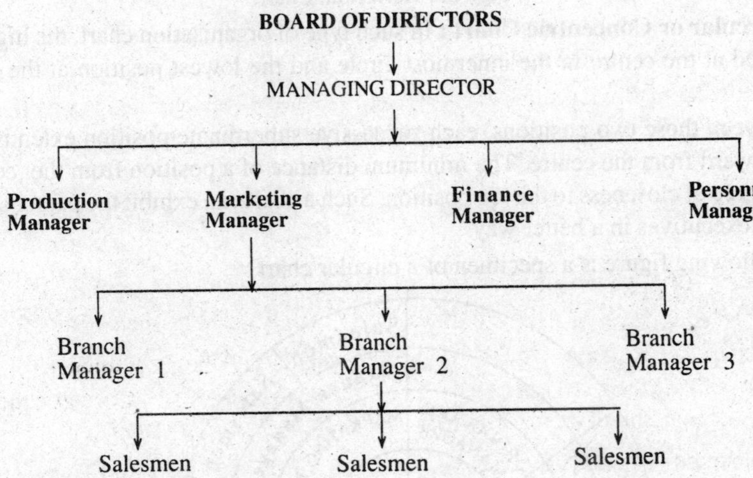

Fig. 4.7: Vertical Chart.

2. Horizontal Chart : In this type of organisation chart the highest position is placed horizontally at the extreme left and the lowest position is shown at the extreme right. In between the two, each successive subordinate position goes on from left to right. It is also known as 'Left-to-Right Chart'.

A specimen of horizontal chart is given in the following figure :

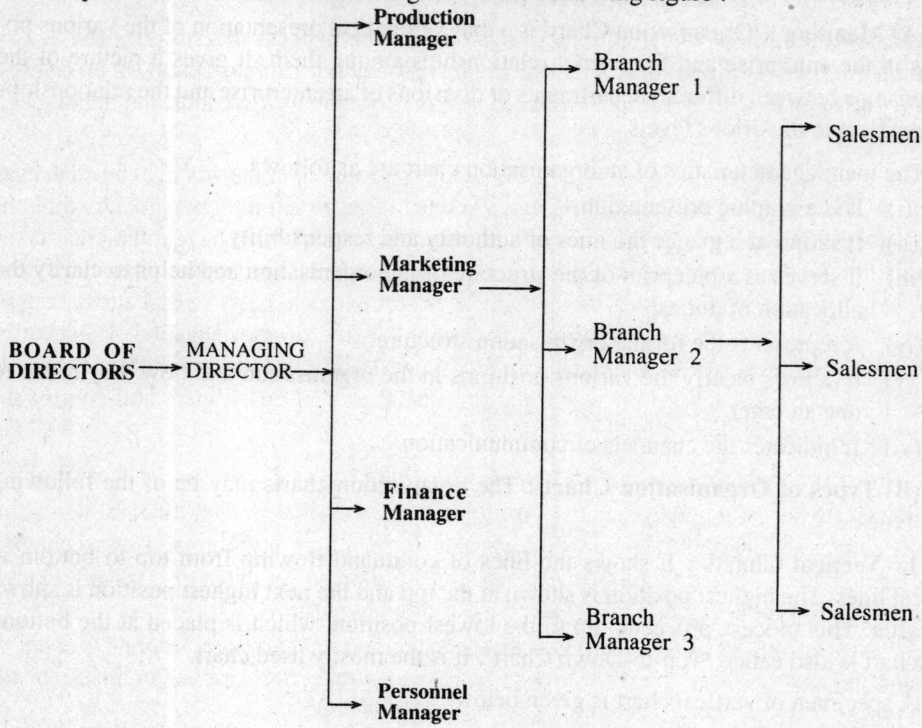

Fig. 4.8: Horizontal Chart.

3. Circular or Concentric Chart : In such type of organisation chart, the highest position is placed at the centre in the innermost circle and the lowest position at the outermost circle.

In between these two positions, each successive subordinate position extends in all directions outward from the centre. The minimum distance of a position from the centre indicates the degree of closeness to the top position. Such a chart can exhibit the personal relationships of the executives in a better way.

The following figure is a specimen of a circular chart :

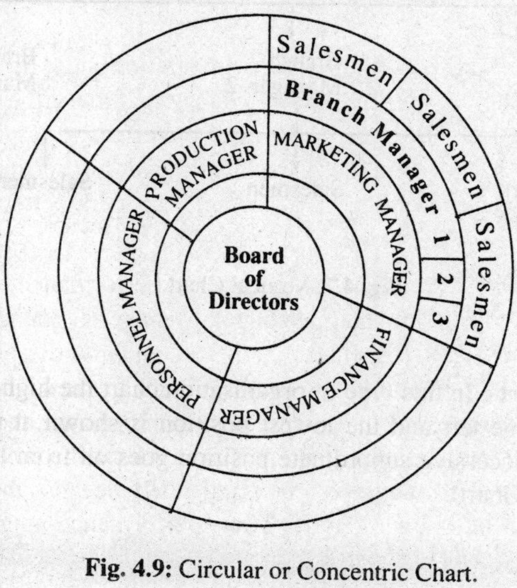

Fig. 4.9: Circular or Concentric Chart.

4.7 Departmentation : Definition and Meaning

'Departmentation' or 'Departmentalisation' is the process of grouping the activities of an enterprise into several units for the purpose of administration at all levels. The administrative units so created may be designated as departments, divisions, units, branches, sections, etc.

The process of organising consists of dividing and grouping of the works to be done in an enterprise and assigning different duties and responsibilities to different people. Dividing the work naturally means the identification of individual activities which have to be undertaken for the attainment of the organisational objectives. But once the various activities have been identified, it is necessary to group them together on some logical basis so that a team can be organised. Departmentation can provide a necessary degree of specialisation of executive activity for efficient performance. It can simplify the tasks of management within a workable span. It also provides a basis on which the top managers can co-ordinate and control the activities of the departmental units.

4.7.1 Need for and Importance of Departmentation

The basic need for departmentation is to make the size of each departmental unit manageable and secure the advantages of specialisation. Grouping of activities and, consequently, of personnel, into departments makes it possible to expand an enterprise to any extent. Departmentation is necessary on account of the following reasons :

1. **Advantages of Specialisation :** Departmentation enables an enterprise to avail of the benefits of specialisation. When every department looks after one major function, the enterprise is developed and efficiency of operations is increased.

2. **Feeling of Autonomy :** Normally departments are created in the enterprise with certain degree of autonomy and freedom. The manager in charge of a department can take independent decisions within the overall framework of the organisation. The feeling of autonomy provides job satisfaction and motivation which lead to higher efficiency of operations.

3. **Expansion :** One manager can supervise and direct only a few subordinates. Grouping of activities and personnel into departmentation makes it possible for the enterprise to expand and grow.

4. **Fixation of Responsibility** : Departmentation enables each person to know the specific role he is to play in the total organisation. The responsibility for results can be defined more clearly, precisely and accurately and an individual can be held accountable for the performance of his responsibility.

5. **Upliftment of Managerial Skill :** Departmentation helps in the development of managerial skill. Development is possible due to two factors. Firstly, the managers focus their attention on some specific problems which provide them effective on-the-job training. Secondly, managerial need for further training can be identified easily because the managers' role is prescribed and training can provide them opportunity to work better in their area of specialisation.

6. **Facility in Appraisal :** Appraisal of managerial performance becomes easier when specific tasks are assigned to departmental personnel. Managerial performance can be measured when the area of activities are specified and the standards of performance are fixed. Departmentation provides help in both these areas. When a broader function is divided into small segments and a particular segment is assigned to each manager, the area to be appraised is clearly known; and the factors affecting the performance can be pointed out more easily. Similarly, the standards for performance can be fixed easily because the factors influencing the work performance can be known clearly. Thus, performance appraisal becomes more effective.

7. Administrative Control : Departmentation is a means of dividing the large and complex organisation into small administrative units. Grouping of activities and personnel into managable units facilitates administrative control. Standards of performance for each and every department can be precisely determined.

4.7.2 Basis or Types of Departmentation

There are several bases of Departmentation. The more commonly used bases are—function, product, territory, process, customer, time etc. These are explained below :

(A) Departmentation by Functions : The enterprise may be divided into departments on the basis of functions like production, purchasing, sales, financing, personnel etc. This is the most popular basis of departmentation. If necessary, a major function may be divided into sub-functions. For example, the activities in the production department may be classified into quality control, processing of materials, and repairs and maintenance. The organisation chart based on functional departmentation is shown in Fig. 4.10 :

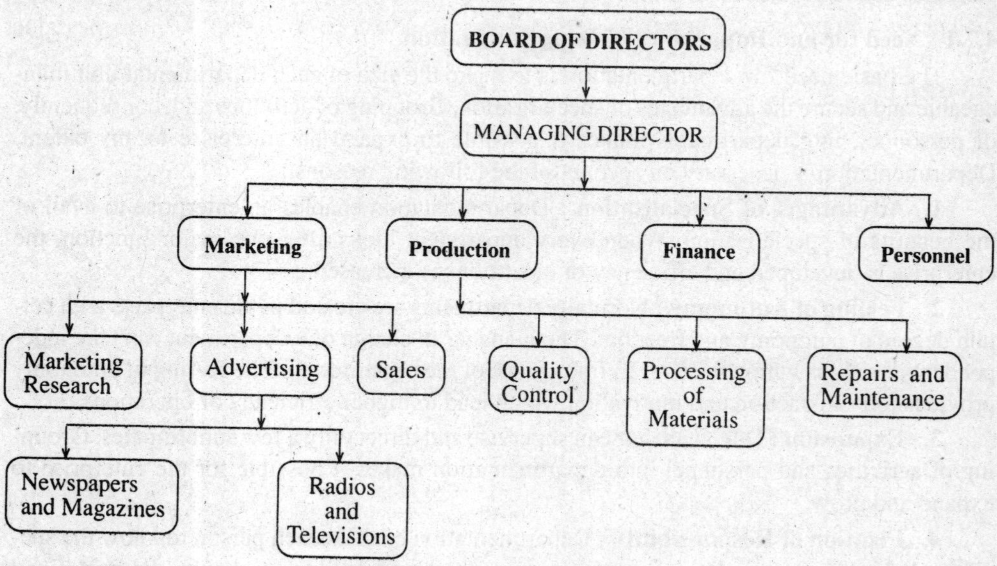

Fig. 4.10: Functional Departmentations.

- **Advantages :** The advantages of functional departmentation include the following :

(a) It is the most logical and natural form of departmentation.

(b) It ensures the performance of all activities necessary for achieving the organisational objectives.

(c) It provides occupational specialisation which makes optimum utilisation of man-power.

(d) It facilitates delegation of authority.

(e) It enables the top managers to exercise effective control over a limited number of functions.

(f) It eliminates duplication of activities.

(g) It simplifies training because the managers are to be experts only in a narrow range of skills.

- **Disadvantages :** There are some problems associated with functional departmentation. These are mentioned below :

(a) There may be conflicts between departments.

(b) The scope for management development is limited. Functional managers do not get training for top management positions. The responsibility for results cannot be fixed on any one functional head.

(c) There is too much emphasis on specialisation.

(d) There may be difficulties in co-ordinating the activities of different departments.

(e) There may be inflexibility and complexity of operations.

(B) Departmentation by Products : In product departmentation, every major product is organised as a separate department. Each department looks after the production, sales and financing of one product. Product departmentation is useful when the expansion, diversification, manufacturing and marketing characteristics of each product are primarily significant. It is generally used when the production line is complex and diverse requiring specialised knowledge and huge capital is required for plant, equipment and other facilities such as in automobile and electronic industries. In fact, many large companies are diversifying in different fields and they prefer product departmentation. For example, a big company with a diversified product line may have three product divisions, one each for plastics, chemicals, and metals. Each division may be sub-divided into production, sales, financing, and personnel activities.

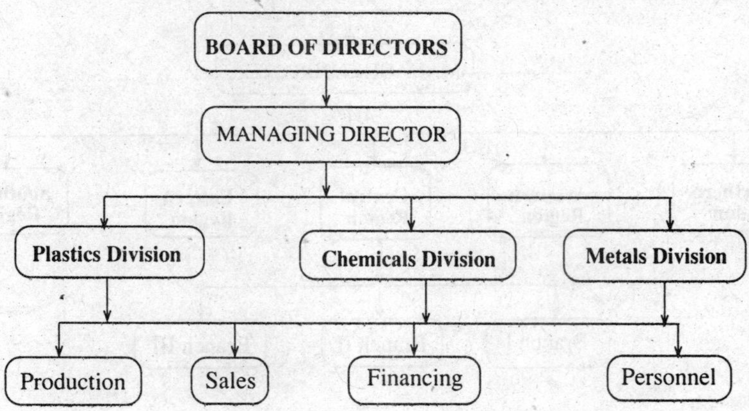

Fig. 4.11: Departmentation by Product.

• **Advantages :** Product departmentation provides several advantages which may be stated as follows :

(a) Product departmentation focuses individual attention to each product line which facilitates the expansion and diversification of the products.

(b) It ensures full use of specialised production facilities. Personal skill and specialised knowledge of the production managers can be fully utilised.

(c) The production managers can be held accountable for the profitability of each product. Each product division is semi-autonomous and contains different functions. So, product departmentation provides an excellent training facility for the top managers.

(d) The performance of each product division and its contribution to total results can be easily evaluated.

(e) It is more flexible and adaptable to change.

• **Disadvantages :** Product departmentation presents some problems as follows :

(a) It creates the problem of effective control over the product divisions by the top managers.

(b) Each production manager asserts his autonomy disregarding the interests of the organisation.

(c) The advantages of centralisation of certain activities like financing, and accounting are not available.

(d) There is duplication of physical facilities and functions. Each product division maintains its own specialised personnel due to which operating costs may be high.

(e) There may be under-utilisation of plant capacity when the demand for a particular product is not adequate.

(C) Departmentation by Territory : Territorial or geographical departmentation is specially useful to large-scale enterprises whose activities are widely dispersed. Banks, insurance companies, transport companies, distribution agencies etc. are some examples of such enterprises, where all the activities of a given area of operations are grouped into zones, branches, divisions etc. It is obviously not possible for one functional manager to manage efficiently such widely spread activities. This makes it necessery to appoint regional managers for different regions. The organisation chart of territorial departmentation may take the following form :

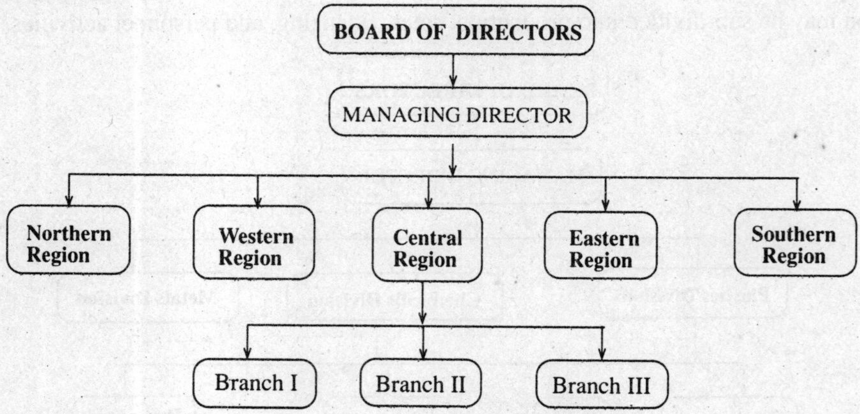

Fig. 4.12: Departmentation by Territory.

● **Advantages :** Territorial departmentation offers certain facilities in operation. These are pointed out below :

(a) Every regional manager can specialise himself in the peculiar problems of his region.

(b) It facilitates the expansion of business to various regions.

(c) It helps in achieving the benefits of local operations. The local managers are more familiar with the local customs, preferences, styles, fashion, etc. The enterprise can gain intimate knowledge of the conditions in the local markets.

(d) It results in savings in freight, rents, and labour costs. It also saves time.

(e) There is better co-ordination of activities in a locality through setting up regional divisions.

(f) It provides adequate autonomy to each regional manager and opportunity to train him as he looks after the entire operation of a unit.

● **Disadvantages :** Territorial departmentation have the following problems :

(a) There is the problem of communnication.

(b) It requires more managers with general managerial abilities. Such managers may not be always available.

(c) There may be conflict between the regional managers.

(d) Co-ordination and control of different branches from the head office become less effective.

(e) Owing to duplication of physical facilities, costs of operation is usually high.

(f) There is multiplication of personnel, accounting and other services at the regional level.

(D) Departmentation by Customers : In such method of departmentation, the activities are grouped according to the type of customers. For example, a large cloth store may be divided into wholesale, retail, and export divisions. This type of departmentation is useful for the enterprises which sell a product or service to a number of clearly defined customer groups. For instance, a large readymade garment store may have a separate department each for men, women, and children. A bank may have separate loan departments for large-scale and small-scale businessmen. The organisation chart of customer-oriented departmentation may appear as follows :

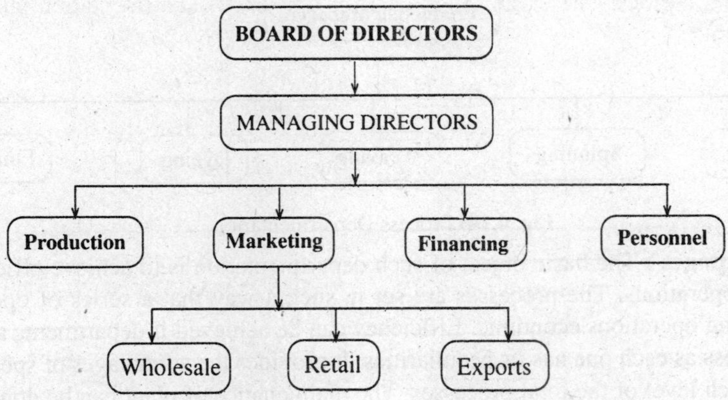

Fig. 4.13: Customer Departmentation.

● **Advantages :** The important advantages of customer departmentation are the following :

(a) Special attention can be given to the particular tastes and preferences of each type of customer.

(b) Different types of customers can be satisfied, easily through specialised staff. Customers' satisfaction enhances the goodwill and sale of the enterprise.

(c) The benefits of specialisation can be gained.

(d) The enterprise may acquire intimate knowledge of the needs of each category of customers.

● **Disadvantages :** This method of departmentation may have certain disadvantages, specially when it is followed very rigidly. These are as follows :

(a) Co-ordination between sales and other functions becomes difficult because this method can be followed only in marketing division.

(b) There may be under-utilisation of facilities and manpower in some departments, particularly during the period of low demand.

(c) It may lead to duplication of activities and heavy overheads.

(d) The managers of customer departments may put pressures for special benefits and facilities.

(E) Departmentation by Process or Equipment : In such type or departmentation the activities are grouped on the basis of production processes involved or equipment used. This is generally used in manufacturing and distribution enterprises and at lower levels of organisation. For instance, a textile mill may be organised into ginning, spinning, weaving, dyeing and finishing departments. Similarly, a printing press may have composing, proof reading, printing and binding departments. Such departmentation may also be employed in engineering and oil industries. The organisation chart of departmentation by process or equipment in the manufacturing department of a textile industry has been shown in Fig. 4.14 :

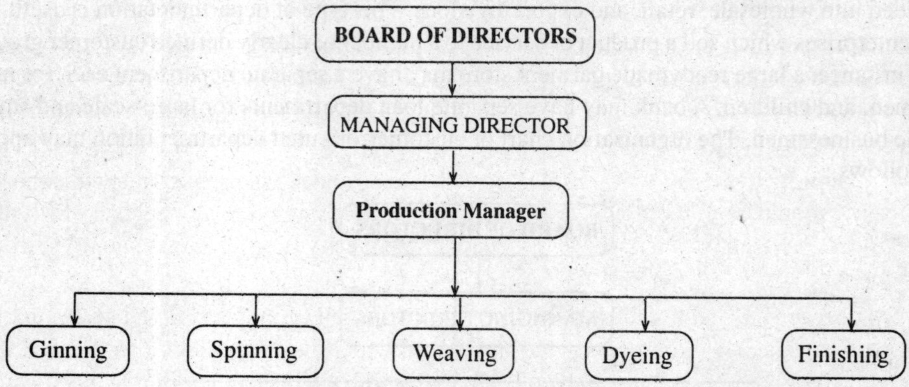

Fig. 4.14: Process Departmentation.

• **Advantages :** The basic object of such departmentation is to achieve efficiency and economy of operations. The processes are set in such a way that a series of operations is feasible making operations economic. Efficiency can be achieved if departments are created for each process as each one has its peculiarities. It provides the advantages of specialisation required at each level of the total processes. The maintenance of plant can be done in better way and manpower can be utilised effectively.

• **Disadvantages :** In such departmentation, there may be difficulty in co-ordinating the different process-departments, because the work of each process depends fully on the preceding process. So, there are chances of conflicts among the managers looking after the different processes. It cannot be used where manufacturing activity does not involve distinct processes.

(F) Departmentation by Time and Numbers : Under this method of departmentation the activities are grouped on the basis of the time of their performance. For instance, a factory operating 24 hours may have three departments for three shifts—one for the morning, the second for the day, and the third for the night.

In the case of departmentation by numbers, the activities are grouped on the basis of their performance by a certain number of persons. For instance, in the army, the soldiers are grouped into squads, companies, battalions, regiments and brigades on the basis of the number prescribed for each unit. Such type of departmentation is useful where the work is repetitive, manpower is an important factor, group efforts are more significant than individual efforts, and group performance can be measured. It is used at the lowest level of organisation.

4.7.3 Principles or Factors to be Considered in Departmentation Or, Choosing a Basis for Departmentation

A suitable basis of departmentation is one which facilitates the performance of organisational functions efficiently and effectively so that the objectives of the organisation are achieved. Since each basis is suitable to a particular type of organisation, often a combination of various basis is adopted. So, the determination of suitability of departmentation basis should be considered in the light of various principles or factors affecting the functioning of an organisation. These factors or principles are described below :

1. **Specialisation :** The activities of an organisation should be grouped in such a way that it leads to specialisation of work. Specialisation helps to improve efficiency and ensure economy of operations. It enables the personnel to become experts.

2. **Co-ordination :** Quite different activities may be grouped together under one executive because they need to be co-ordinated. So, the basis of departmentation should ensure that the dissimilar activities are put together in one department.

3. **Control :** Departmentation should be such that it facilitates the measurement of performance and adoption of timely corrective action. It should enable the managers to hold the employees accountable for results. Effective control helps to achieve organisational objectives economically and efficiently.

4. **Proper Attention :** All the activities which contribute to the achievement of subordinate results should be given adequate attention. This will ensure that all necessary activities are performed and there is no unnecessary duplication of activities. Key areas should be given special attention.

5. **Economy :** Creation of departments involves extra cost of additional space, equipment and personnel. So, the pattern and number of departments should be so decided that maximum possible economy is achieved in the utilisation of physical facilities and personnel.

6. **Local Condition :** While forming departments adequate attention to the local conditions should be given. This is more important to the organisation which operates in different geographical areas. Departmentation should be adjusted according to the available resources. It should aim at full utilisation of resources.

7. **Human Consideration :** Departmentation should also consider the human aspect in the organisation. So, along with the technical factors discussed above, departments should be created on the basis of availability of personnel, their attitude, aspiration and value systems, informal work groups, cultural patterns, etc. Due attention to the human factors will make departmentation more effective and more efficient.

4.8 Delegation of Authority : Definition and Meaning

Delegation of Authority is an important step in organising. It means granting of authority by the superior manager to his subordinates in order to accomplish particular assignments. When the work of an executive increases so much in volume that he cannot cope with it, he has to divide it among his subordinates. This process of dividing the work with others and giving them authority to do it is referred to as 'Delegation'. So, **Delegation may be defined as the process of entrusting some part of the work of operations or management to others; thus sharing one's responsibilities with others.** It involves granting the right to decision-making in certain defined areas and charging the subordinates with responsibility for carrying out the assigned tasks. In the words of **N. R. Spriegel** : "Delegation is the act of conferring authority by higher source of authority."

The process of dividing up the work of an enterprise among people creates a number of jobs or positions for both the managers and the operators. Organisation being a mechanism to provide for integrated and co-operative action, all managerial and operating jobs are to be tied together in a consistent manner. Delegation is the element that holds the jobs or positions together. The chief executive of an enterprise cannot personally manage all the activities. Obviously, for the individual departments, there must be departmental managers and, for the divided sections of a particular department, there should exist sectional managers. These departmental and sectional managers derive their authority from the chief executive. The chief executive delegates a part of his authority to different subordinates for enabling them to discharge the work responsibilities or duties in all areas of the business.

In delegating authority, the chief executive retains some reserved authority for his own performance as well as the power of demanding accountability from the subordinates for ensuring satisfactory performance on their part. This accountability can never be delegated by a manager to his subordinates. Thus, delegation is the means by which a manager can share his duties with his immediate subordinates who, in turn, delegate to their subordinates, and the process is continued until managerial work reaches the supervisors at the lowest level of management and operating work is assumed by the workers. By means of delegation, the manager extends his area of operation. Delegation enables the managers to distribute their load of work to others—thus leaving them free to concentrate on the other important functions of management. Besides, it influences the relationship between the subordinate and his superior and the performance of the subordinate.

4.8.1 Features of Delegation of Authority

Delegation of authority has the following features or characteristics :

1. Delegation is authorisation to a manager to act in a certain manner. The degree of delegation prescribes the limits within which a manager has to decide the things. Since the formal authority originates at the top level, it is distributed throughout the organisation through delegation and re-delegation.

2. Delegation has dual characteristics. As a result of delegation, a subordinate employee receives authority from his superior, but, at the same time, his superior still retains all his original authority. **George Terry** comments on this concept : "It is something like imparting knowledge. You share with others who then possess the knowledge, but you still retain the knowledge too." Delegation does not imply reduction in the authority of a manager.

3. Delegation does not mean a manager loses control and power. Authority once delegated can be enhanced, reduced or withdrawn depending on the situation or requirement. For example, change in the organisation structure, policy, procedure, methods etc. may require change in the degree of delegation of authority.

4. A manager delegates authority out of the authority vested in him. He cannot delegate which he himself does not possess. Moreover, he does not delegate his full authority to his subordinates, because if he delegates all his authority, he passes his position to the subordinates.

5. Delegation of authority is always made to the position created through the process of organising. The individual occupying a position may exercise the authority so long as he holds the position. Therefore, the authority is recovered fully from the individual when he moves from the particular position.

6. The extent of authority to be delegated depends upon several factors, like the ability and willingness of the executive to delegate, the ability of the subordinates to accept delegation, the confidence of the superior in his subordinates, the philosophy of management, etc.

7. Delegation of authority may be specific or general. It is specified when the courses of action for particular objectives are specified. It is general when these are not specified, though objectives may be specified.

4.8.2 Necessity of Delegation of Authority

Delegation of authority is the most essential requirement for successful management. It is the key to organisation and a cementing force for binding the formal organisation together. In a big concern, due to its complexities, delegation is a must. It is not possible and practicable for a chief executive to manage and control everything. In spite of the fact that the ultimate responsibilities rest on him, he delegates some of his activities and authority to many of his subordinates. The delegation of authority arises from the natural limitations of the human being. As the organisation grows up or becomes more complex, a point may be reached at which the single manager is no longer able to cope with the full load of responsibilities. He finds that neither time nor his own capacity and knowledge permits him to give adequate attention to the proper utilisation of human and material factors upon which effective management is based. This is the reason that gives rise to the need for delegation.

Apart from physical limitation the need for delegation arises in a big complex organisation for securing expert's services. It is also not practicable for a chief executive to give specialist's advice on every matter. He may have time and energy but he may not have the skill. A business has different kinds of jobs, some of which may require specialist persons for their accomplishment. The top executive delegates these responsibilities to the experts, viz, secretary, accountant, and legal adviser. Moreover, for a business with branches situated at different places, there is no alternative to delegation.

Delegation also ensures continuity in business because the managers at lower levels are enabled to acquire valuable experience in decision-making. They get an opportunity to develop their abilities and gain enough competence to fill higher positions in case of need.

4.8.3 Process or Elements of Delegation

The process of delegation involves the following three essential elements :

1. Assignment of Duties : As one manager cannot perform all the tasks, he must allocate a part of his work to the subordinates. The sharing of duties between a manager and his subordinates can only be done when the work is divided into parts. In delegating duties, the manager has to decide what part of the work he will keep for himself and what parts should be transferred to his subordinates. Defining the work of the subordinates by their superior manager is known as assignment of duties. It also covers defining of the results expected from the subordinates. The manager may assign various duties in terms of goals, functions or results. Duties may also be assigned in terms of job description. Expressing the duties in terms of goals will probably result in more effective delegation, because it provides mental satisfaction to the subordinates of being involved in fulfilling a mission through the performance of certain allotted activities. Duties should be allocated according to the qualification, experience and aptitude of the subordinates.

2. Granting of Authority : If the delegated duties are to be discharged by the subordinates, they must be granted requisite authority for enabling them to perform such duties. Assignment of duties is meaningless unless adequate authority is given to the subordinates. The same rights and powers as would have been necessary on the part of a manager for his self-performance are to be conferred upon his subordinates. In the process of delegating authority, the executive gives power or permission to the subordinate to use certain rights—such as the right to spend money, to direct the work of other people, to use raw materials and other property, or to represent the organisation to outsiders. Effective delegation, however, requires that the limits of authority should be made clear to each subordinate. The superior and the subordinate should clearly understand the subordinate's right to act, to request others to act, and to maintain discipline. The superior can delegate only that for which he has the authority and power to perform. He, however, does not give away the total authority; he only delegates a part of it, retaining the ultimate authority and responsibility to himself.

3. Creation of Obligation or Accountability for Performance : The last step in the process of delegation of authority is the creation of moral compulsion or obligation on the part of the subordinates for the satisfactory performance of their duties. The subordinates to whom authority is delegated must be made answerable for the proper performance of the assigned duties and for the exercise of delegated authority. The creation of obligation is—in real sense—assumption of responsibility by the subordinates. By accepting an assignment (i.e. a delegated task), a subordinate, in effect, gives his promises to do his best in carrying out his duties. His obligation to do the task assigned makes him accountable to the delegator for discharge of his duties. As the manager himself remains ever accountable to his superior for the satisfactory performance of the work, he has to exercise control over the performance of his subordinates. This control is exercised through demanding accountability from the subordinates. Duty and authority can be delegated by a manager to his subordinates, but accountability flows from subordinates to the superior in an upward direction.

The process of delegation is shown in the following diagram :

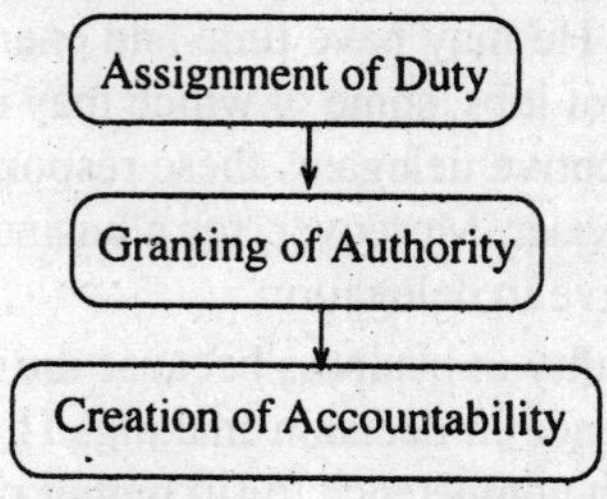

Fig. 4.15: The Process of Delegation.

4.8.4 Benefits of Delegation

Delegation provides the following advantages :

1. Basis of effective functioning : Delegation lays down the basis of effective functioning of an organisation. By establishing structural relationships throughout the organisation, delegation helps in securing co-ordination of various activities for accomplishing the enterprise objectives.

2. Reduction in work-burden of the chief executive : Delegation reduces the executive burden by way of relieving the superior of the need to attend to minor or routine duties. It, thus, enables him to devote greater attention and effort towards broader and more important responsibilities.

3. Benefits of specialised service : Delegation enables the manager to utilise the specialised knowledge and experience of the persons at lower levels.

4. Efficient running of branches : In the modern world, where a business rarely confines its activities to a single place, only delegation can provide the key to smooth and efficient running of the various branches of the business at places far and near.

5. Aid to expansion and diversification of business : As delegation provides the means of extending and multiplying the limited capacity of the superior, it is instrumental for encouraging expansion and diversification of the business.

6. Aid to employee development : Delegation permits the subordinates to enlarge their jobs, to develop their capacity and to broaden their understanding. By forcing the subordinates to assume greater responsibilities and to make important decisions, the superior insists on the development of subordinates' executive talents. Delegation improves the morale of the subordinates by way of raising their status and importance in the organisation.

4.8.5 Difficulties and Problems in Delegation

Delegation is apparently a simple process, but, in practice, certain difficulties and problems generally crop up to hamper this process. This is often partly on account of the superior manager's attitude towards delegating authority and partly due to the subordinate's hesitation in accepting delegation. These difficulties or obstacles in the way of proper delegation may be summarised as follows :

(A) Reluctance on the part of the Executives : A superior manager is likely to delegate less authority in the following situations :

1. Superiority complex : Some executives tend to feel that they can do the job better themselves, and, for this reason, they do not delegate their authority. They consider themselves indispensable—neither they respect the ideas of others nor do they give the subordinates a chance to prove their merit.

2. Maintenance of tight control : A manager does not delegate authority because he wants to maintain tight control over the operation assigned to him.

3. Lack of confidence in the subordinates : A manager may not delegate authority because he feels that his subordinates are not capable and reliable. He lacks confidence in his subordinates. If delegation is not made, the future manager has no opportunity to gain experience. Confidence is built up gradually and on the basis of success.

4. Lack of ability to direct : Many managers have difficulty in giving suitable directions to guide the efforts of the subordinates. Sometimes the boss may like to delegate authority but may not be able to do it effectively due to his inability to identify, interpret and communicate the essential features of his plans. So, an executive who lacks ability to direct cannot delegate.

5. Absence of control techniques that warn of coming troubles : In the cases where the executive in charge of operations has practically no means of knowing serious difficulties in the working of the organisation in advance, he may hesitate in delegating authority.

6. Conservative and cautious temperament : A conservative and over-cautious manager will never like to take any risk. Since delegation of the task to a subordinate involves some elements of chance or risk, the executive may hesitate to delegate anything to anyone.

7. Fear of exposure : A superior manager, specially an incompetent one, may not like to delegate simply because adequate delegation may reveal his weakness and shortcomings. This may happen specially when the superior has poor operating procedures, methods and practices. He feels that delegation may undermine his influence and prestige in the organisation. He keeps all the authority to himself for fear of being exposed.

8. Fear of the subordinates : A manager may not delegate adequate authority because of his fears of the subordinates. The fear of a subordinate's growth may be real. It can take two forms. First, the subordinate might show that he can perform the superior's work so well that he becomes entitled to the manager's position, status or prestige. Second, the subordinate's increasing ability might earn him a promotion to some other part of the organisation and the superior may lose his best subordinate. In this case, the superior may adopt a defensive behaviour. He simply fails to delegate the kind of authority that would have such a result.

9. Love for authority : A superior may not delegate his authority specially if he is an autocrat. Such a manager has intense desire to dominate others, to make his importance felt in the organisation, and to see that his subordinates come frequently for approval. He thinks that delegation will lead to reduction of his influence in the organisation.

(B) Reluctance on the part of the Subordinates : The subordinates may not always like to accept delegation and shoulder responsibility. A subordinate may shrink from accepting authority for the following reasons :

1. Dependence on the boss for decisions : If a subordinate finds it easier to depend upon his boss for taking decisions while tackling problems, he may avoid accepting authority even when his boss is ready to delegate it.

2. Fear of criticism : The subordinates sometimes fear criticism on the part of their superiors. This fear is often justified. In fact, some superiors tend to criticise any action taken by a subordinate and even a small genuine mistake. This discourages initiative, causes resentment, and destroys a subordinate's self-confidence.

3. Lack of information or resources : A subordinate will generally be unwilling to accept authority when adequate information, working facilities, and resources required for the proper performance of a task are not available.

4. Lack of self-confidence and fear of failure : A subordinate who does not possess self-confidence will generally try to shirk responsibility even though the executive is prepared to delegate. Such subordinates often feel that they will fail, and so, do not want additional responsibilities through delegation.

5. Inadequacy of positive incentive : A subordinate hesitates in accepting more work delegated to him by the boss if he does not get sufficient positive incentives in the form of recognition, credit, and other rewards.

6. Over-work : When the subordinates are already over-burdened with duties, they may avoid delegation because they feel that they will not be able to do an additional task along with those which they presently have been assigned, This may be a perfectly legitimate reason.

DIFFICULTIES IN DELEGATION

ON THE PART OF THE EXECUTIVES

1. Superiority complex
2. Maintenance of tight control
3. Lack of confidence in the subordinates
4. Lack of ability to direct
5. Absence of control techniques
6. Conservative and cautious temperament
7. Fear of exposure
8. Fear of the subordinates
9. Love of authority

ON THE PART OF THE SUBORDINATES

1. Dependence on the boss for decisions
2. Fear of criticism
3. Lack of information or resources
4. Lack of self-confidence
5. Inadequacy of positive incentive
6. Over-work

Fig. 4.16: Difficulties in Delegation.

4.8.6 Basic Principles of Delegation of Authority

Delegation, to be effective, must be governed by certain working rules or principles. The following rules or principles are fundamental in relation to delegation of authority :

1. Functional Definition : Before delegating authority, a manager should define clearly the functions to be performed by the subordinates. The objectives of each job, the activities involved in it, and its relationship with other jobs should be clearly defined.

2. Delegation by Result Expected : Authority should be delegated to a position according to the results expected from that position. Duties of the subordinates become clear to them only when they understand what activities they must undertake and what results they must show. By spelling out the duties in terms of goals or expected results, advance notice is to be given to the subordinates as to the criteria on which their performance will be judged.

3. Clarity of Lines of Authority : Each position in the organisation is linked with others through authority relationships, some directly through line authority, others indirectly. More clearly these lines of authority are defined, more effective is the delegation of authority. A clear understanding of the lines of authority is needed for smooth functioning of the organisation. Everyone must know from whom he gets authority and to whom his authority must be referred.

4. Level of Authority : It implies delegation of decision-making authority to the competent managers at some level. The superior is not expected to interfere with the decision-making process which is, by delegation, within the competence of the subordinate manager at the lower organisation levels concerned.

5. Absoluteness of Responsibility : Responsibility cannot be delegated. An executive cannot free himself from his own obligations to his superior by delegating duties. In fact, by delegating authority he increases his responsibility as he will be now accountable to his superior for the acts of his subordinates also. The ultimate responsibility for the accomplishment of the task is his, even though it has been assigned to his subordinates.

6. Parity of Authority and Responsibility : A subordinate should be given necessary authority to perform his assigned duties. Authority must correspond to perfom his responsibility. There must be a proper balance between authority and responsibility of a subordinate. It is unfair to hold a person responsible for something over which he has no authority. Responsibility without authority will make a subordinate ineffective as he cannot discharge his duties. Similarly, authority without responsibility will make the subordinate irresponsible. Therefore, authority and responsibility sould be co-extensive.

7. Motivation : It should be the policy of the managers to provide material and psychological incentives to the subordinates so that they spontaneously accept the delegated responsibility and duty and exercise the authority delegated to them. Higher wages, bonus, promotion to better positions, greater recognition and prestige etc. may have a stimulating effect for productive performance of duties.

4.9 Centralisation of Authority

Meaning : 'Centralisation of Authority' means the systematic and consistent reservation of authority at the central points within an organisation. Thus, centralisation of authority refers to the reservation of authority at the top level of an organisation. This results into a number of **benefits** in the organisation. These are pointed out below :

1. Centralisation of authority provides opportunity for personal leadership.
2. It makes communication and control easier in the organisation.
3. It facilitates integration of efforts.
4. It helps in reducing wastage of efforts by avoiding duplication of work.
5. Quick decisions are possible in this case.
6. There is uniformity in actions throughout the organisation and, thus, co-ordination can be achieved easily.

Centralisation of authority is quite suitable for smaller organisations which produce single or homogeneous products and operate in limited geographical areas.

4.10 Decentralisation of Authority : Definition and Meaning

'Decentralisation of Authority' refers to the dispersal of authority for decision-making in various levels of organisational operations throughout the organisation.

In the words of **Louis A. Allen** : "Decentralisation is the systematic effort to delegate to the lowest levels of authority except that which can be exercised at central points."

Decentralisation is actually an extension of the concept of delegation. Delegation can take place from one superior to one subordinate and is a complete process, but decentralisation takes place only when the fullest possible delegation or distribution of authority is made to all—or most of the people in the organisation—in respect of the specific function, activity or responsibility. It is, however, to be remembered that decentralisation does not necessarily mean distribution of authority in respect of all activities. One function may be decentralised and another stay centralised. For example, in an automobile manufacturing concern, the sales function may be distributed or decentralised to product division, while labour relations may remain centralised. The extent to which decentralisation exists in any organisation depends on the extent to which clear-cut decision-making authority is vested in levels below the top management level.

Therefore, when delegation is widespread and authority is delegated to lower levels of management, to all, or most of the people who are entrusted with responsibilities, decentralisation of authority takes place. On the other hand, when delegation is restricted to the top level of management, and the subordinates are simply to implement the decisions taken at the top level, the authority is said to be centralised to that extent.

Decentralisation is a question of degree. It is not what is delegated but how much is delegated. **Henry Fayol** pointed out "everything that goes to increase the importance of the subordinate's role is decentralisation, everything which goes to reduce it is centralisation." However, there cannot be any absolute centralisation or absolute decentralisation in an organisation. Absolute centralisation is possible if there is one person with absolute authority and there is no other subordinate manager under him that means there is no structured organisation. Similarly, there is no absolute decentralisation. Actually centralisation and decentralisation are inclinations, tendencies or bents towards reservation of authority in varied degrees. In an organisation, authority may be centralised, but some amount of decentralisation also becomes necessary.

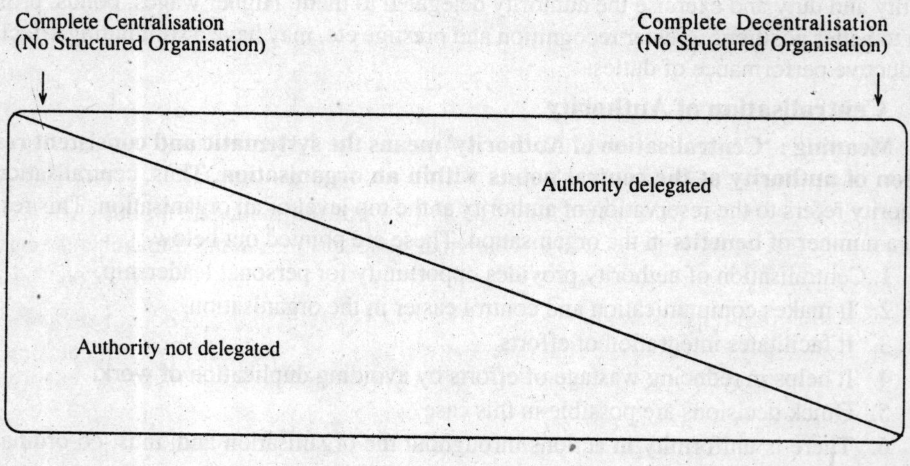

Fig. 4.17: Centralisation and Decentralisation.

4.10.1 Importance of Decentralisation of Authority

Decentralisation is useful basically to large organisations with multiple products or operating in different geographical locations. Decentralisation becomes inevitable in an industry with every growth in size. Its importance may be noted as follows :

1. Relief to the Top Executives : Diminishing the work-load of the senior executives who are already over-burdened, decentralisation helps to reduce the volume of their routine affairs. They can devote greater time and attention to important policy matters by decentralising authority for routine operational decisions.

2. Motivation of the Subordinates : Decentralisation motivates the lower level managers by increasing their chances of recognition, improving their status and offering them a feeling of accomplishment. The facility to make decision and function independently activates strong drives among the individuals and, thus, results in increased productivity.

3. Improvement of Work Performance : The operating decisions in a decentralised setting tends to be of higher quality. Decisions will be more appropriate, timely and quick because they are made nearest to the points of the problem, information and actions. Decisions will also be democratic and acceptable as these are made by the people who are responsible for implementing them.

4. Promotion of the Subordinate's Morale : Decentralisation tends to promote the subordinate's morale due to relative equalisation of power and authority at all levels of the organisation, scope for participating in problem identification, decision-making and implementation, increased job satisfaction, and reduced gap between problems and decisions, and also between decisions and actions.

5. Increasing Flexibility : Decentralisation is a structural strategy to manage organisational growth and diversification and to cope with the complexity, uncertainty and volatility of the external environment.

4.10.2 Advantages of Decentralisation

The advantages of decentralisation may be listed as follows :

1. Increasing Efficiency of Management : Decentralisation reduces the burden of the top executives, relieves them of the anxiety of details, allows them to concentrate on other important tasks of planning, co-ordination and controlling etc. and increases overall efficiency of the management.

2. Facilitating Diversification of Activities : Decentralisation facilitates the growth and diversification of product lines. As one single product or a group of related products is made the basis for creating divisions, all important features like present position, future prospects and comparative efficiency of each product can be readily ascertained.

3. Minimisation of Risk : Decentralisation not only spreads over decision-making authority among various executives of middle and lower level management but also facilitates the availability of the benefits of expert advice of the specialists and thus helps the business in minimising possibilities of loss.

4. Ensuring Quick Performance : The close contact and consequent greater understanding between the managers and the managed can cope successfully with constant business changes. Thus, it provides a dynamic character to the business and ensures quick decision and prompt action.

5. Developing Future Executives : When authority is decentralised, the subordinates get the opportunity of exercising their own judgement. They learn how to decide and develop managerial skills. Thus, decentralisation provides a better means of developing future managers and executives. This is probably the most important benefit, particularly in our country where shortage of competent managers is the major limiting factor of the rapid growth of our economy and principal industries.

6. Motivating the Subordinates for Better Performance : By consistent and adequate delegation of managerial work, the organisation structure promotes individual initiative and mutual understanding and motivates the subordinates for higher performance.

7. Improvement of Morale : Decentralisation stimulates the formation of small cohesive groups. Since local managers are given a large degree of authority, they weld their people into well-knit groups. With high degree of participation, constant effort to communicate, and continuous interest in the welfare of the members of the group, they are able to secure a high degree of morale among the subordinates.

4.10.3 Disadvantages of Decentralisation

Decentralisation offers marked benefits and no large organisation can hope to sustain without it. In spite of that, there are many disadvantages or limitations in decentralisation process. Some of the major problems of decentralisation are noted below :

1. **Problem of Co-ordination :** Decentralisation calls for a high degree of differentiation of functions and tasks. The top management authority may find it difficult to co-ordinate the diverse goals, functions and activities of different autonomous decision-making units or divisions. The executives may develop narrow outlook and sectional interests may overshadow the organisational goals. Therefore, maintaining co-ordination among the departments becomes more difficult.

2. **Lack of Uniformity :** Decentralisation may lead to inconsistencies in the organisation when uniform procedures are not followed by various departments. Each department may formulate its own policies and procedures.

3. **Costly and Uneconomical :** Decentralisation tends to increase the cost of operation of the enterprise. It involves duplication of procedure, equipment and services as there are autonomous and self-sufficient units or departments in terms of physical facilities and trained personnel.

4. **Delay in Decision-making :** Decentralisation becomes an important handicap in case of quick emergency decisions. Some executives do not like to share the responsibility of decision-making.

5. **Limitation of Scale :** To bring about decentralisation it is necessary to create departments and divisions. This is possible only when an enterprise is large enough and tends itself to departmentation and divisionalisation. Thus, small organisations do not have much scope for decentralisation.

4.10.4 Basic Principles of Decentralisation

The basic principles of decentralisation may be stated as follows :

1. **Proximity of Decision-making Points :** All schemes of decentralisation must aim at providing for the proximity of the decision-making points nearer to the place of action.

2. **Real Delegation of Authority :** Successful and proper decentralisation demands full and real delegation of authority. Reporting or checking of details before arriving at decisions by the subordinates will make decetralisation ineffective.

3. **Confidence in the Subordinates :** The superiors must place full confidence in the abilities of the subordinates in taking correct decisions at the right time wihout interfering in their day-to-day functioning.

4. **Conciliation between Line and Staff Personnel :** Staff Personnel, with their experience and talent, must advise and encourage the inexperienced Line Operators so that correct decisions may be taken by them.

5. **Parity of Responsibility and Authority :** In order to make decentralisation effective and successful, the subordinate must shoulder responsibility commensurate with the authority which is exercised by him.

6. **Conviction about the Superiority of Decentralised Decision :** The top managers must be convinced that the aggregate of many individuals' decision will always be better and superior in the general interest than the centrally planned and controlled decisions.

7. Result-oriented Personnel Policies : Result of personnel policies must be capable of being measured and compared with the standards already laid down. There should be arrangements for offering reward or inflicting penalty, respectively, in respect of the success or failure of these personnel policies.

4.10.5 Factors Determining the Degree of Decentralisation

The degree and nature of decentralisation are generally influenced by the following factors :

1. Size of the Organisation : Decentralisation depends on the size of the organisation. The larger the size of the concern, the greater shall be the number of decisions and the need for decentralisation of authority.

2. History of the Enterprise : Decentralisation of authority depends on the way the organisation has been built up over the period of time. Organisations built under the direction of the owner-founders are likely to show a marked tendency to minimise decentralisation. On the contrary, the enterprises created through combination, amalgamation or merger tend to be more decentralised.

3. Outlook of the Top Managers : The character and philosophy of the top level managers have considerable influence on the extent to which authority is decentralised. When the top executives believe in individual freedom, there will be a high degree of decentralisation. But if the top managers is conservative and prefers centralised control, there is likely to be centralisation of authority.

4. Availability of Competent Managers : Availability of qualified managers directly affects the degree of decentralisation, because the exercise of authority requires competence on the part of those who exercise authority. When the managers at lower levels are able and experienced there is more chance for decentralisation. Lack of trained executives restricts decentralisation.

5. Dispersal of Operations : Authority tends to be decentralised when the operations of the organisation are dispersed over different territories. Geographical dispersion of activities makes communication difficult under centralised decision-making. For example, the activities of banking, insurance and transport organisations have to be decentralised.

6. Uniformity of Policy : Decentralisation will tend to be limited in all those cases where uniformity of policy is of a critical importance to the business such as policy of fixation of wages or prices or public relations, etc.

7. Control Techniques : Poor control techniques or inefficient business systems tend to encourage centralisation. Effective techniques to control the work of the subordinates, well-established systems and procedures, improvement in accounting techniques enable greater decentralisation in bigger concerns.

8. Importance of Decision : Greater the impact of a decision on the success and survival of the enterprise, higher is the degree of centralisation. Vital and crucial decisions involving investment of huge capital funds are taken at the top level, because top officials are better trained and more experienced and, hence, the authority is not decentralised.

9. Rate of Change in the Organisation : The rate of change in the organisation also affects the degree to which authority may be decentralised. If the business is fast developing and it is facing problems of expansion, there is more chance that authority will be decentralised. As against this, in old and, well-established or slow-moving organisations, there is a natural tendency to centralise authority.

10. Environmental Influence : External factors like government policies, trade union activities, tax policies etc. also have significant influence on the degree of decentralisation. Many of the problems of industry such as labour disputes, price fixation, etc. are to be tackled at the top level of management, thus encouraging centralisation rather than decentralisation.

4.11 Delegation and Decentralisation

'Delegation' and 'Decentralisation' should not be confused. Though these terms are closely related, decentralisation is much more comprehensive than delegation. Delegation means transfer of authority from one individual to another, whereas decentralisation implies diffusion of decision-making authority throughout the organisation. Thus, both these terms should be used differently. In reality, there is considerable difference between the two. The two terms devote different degrees of authority at various levels and consequent managerial process.

The distinction between delegation and decentralisation may be pinpointed with reference to the following :

1. Decentralisation is an extension of the principle of delegation. The object of delegation may be confined to relieve the excessive burden of the top managerial personnel; but decentralisation carries a deeper meaning. Delegation can take place from a superior to his subordinate and be a complete process. But decentralisation is completed when the fullest possible delegation is made at all levels of the organisation.

2. Delegation merely devotes authorisation of the managers of various levels to make decisions. It is the process of entrusting a part of the work of management to the subordinates. Since decentralisation reflects the dispersal of authority to the ultimate level of the organisation, it can be said to be the result of a systematic delegation of authority. It is the end result of the policy of making delegation of authority widespread in the organisation. Therefore, delegation is a process of management, while decentralisation is the end result of delegation. Delegation of authority, hence, can take place without decentralisation but decentralisation without delegation is not possible.

3. Delegation creates authority-responsibility relationship between the superiors and the subordinates, while decentralisation creates autonomous decision-making centres.

4. Delegation is more or less necessary for management because no manager can have the ability to perform and look after all the aspects of business. On the other hand, decentralisation is optional. The managers may or may not adopt the policy of dispersal of authority.

5. Under delegation of authority, the delegator still has some directive responsibility in relation to his subordinates. But in the case of decentralised setting, direction is—to a large extent—substituted by control by the top managers.

6. Delegation is a technical and routine administrative activity, and it involves only the managers and the subordinates. Decentralisation, on the contrary, is a conscious and deliberate organisational action with strategic nature, to manage growth and expansion under conditions characterised by competitive and environmental pressures, challenges and opportunities.

4.12 Centralisation and Decentralisation

In management, 'Centralisation of Authority' refers to concentration or reservation of authority at the top level of the organisation. On the other hand, 'Decentralisation of Authority' indicates systematic dispersal or delegation of authority in the organisation. The concepts of centralisation and decentralisation are two extreme points in the matter of distribution of authority. However, there can neither be absolute centralisation nor can there be absolute decentralisation.

Centralisation of authority is beneficial to the smaller organisations. But when the organisation increases in size and diversify, the benefits of centralisation turn into limitations which affect the operational efficiency of the organisation. In such organisation, decision-making becomes quite complex; but, at the same time, faster decisions are required. This is not possible in centralisation. Therefore, its alternative—that is, decentralisation—is preferable.

Decentralisation is useful basically to large organisations with multiple products or operating in different geographical locations. Further, if the organisation grows rapidly and works in dynamic environment, then decentralisation is the best way to achieve positive results.

EXERCISES

[A] Essay-Type Questions

1. Discuss the need and significance of organisation in business.
   [**Ans.** Section 4.3.1]
2. Discuss the benefits of a sound organisation.
   [**Ans.** Section 4.4]
3. Discuss the meaning and importance of organising as a function of management. What steps have to be taken in designing an organisation?
   [**Ans.** Sections 4.1, 4.3 and 4.5]
4. What are the essential features of a good organisation structure?
   [**Ans.** Section 4.6.3]
5. What is Delegation? Discuss its advantages and limitations.
   [**Ans.** Sections 4.8., 4.8.4 and 4.8.5.]
6. Discuss the main elements of delegation. What are the difficulties in the process of delegation of authority?
   [**Ans.** Sections 4.8.3 and 4.8.5]
7. What is an Organisation Structure? Discuss its importance in administrative management. [C.U. B.Com. 1989]
   [**Ans.** Sections 4.6 and 4.6.2]
8. State the main principles of delegation of authority.
   [**Ans.** Section 4.8.6]
9. Explain the three aspects of delegation.
   [**Ans.** Section 4.8.3]
10. Explain the meaning of 'Decentralisation of Authority'. Discuss the merits and demerits of decentralisation.
    [**Ans.** Sections 4.10, 4.10.2, and 4.10.3]
11. Discuss the basic principles of decentralisation.
    [**Ans.** Section 4.10.4]
12. Enumerate the factors determining the degree of decentralisation.
    [**Ans.** Section 4.10.5]
13. Describe the role of organisation structure in business management.
    [**Ans.** Section 4.6.2]
14. Why is decentralisation necessary in business undertaking?
    [**Ans.** Section 4.10.1]

15. "No delegation is complete without a clear understanding of duties, authority and obligation."—Explain. What difficulties frequently arise in delegating authority in actual practice?
[**Ans.** Sections 4.8.3 and 4.8.5]

16. Explain the term 'Delegation of Authority'. Why is delegation necessary in business undertaking? [C.U. B.Com. 1985, 1988]
[**Ans.** Sections 4.8 and 4.8.2]

17. What do you mean by Managerial Function of Organising? Discuss the steps involved in organising. [C.U. B.Com. 1996]
[**Ans.** Sections 4.1 and 4.5]

18. What do you mean by Organisation? Explain the basic principles and elements of organisation.
[**Ans.** Sections 4.1, 4.5 and 4.6.3]

19. Describe the elements and basic principles of Delegation of Authority. [C.U. B.Com. 1997]
[**Ans.** Sections 4.8.3 and 4.8.6]

20. Explain the principal features of a sound organisation. [C.U. B.Com. 1999]
[**Ans.** Section 4.6.3]

21. What is Delegation of Authority? Explain its characteristics. [C.U. B.Com. 1999]
[**Ans.** Sections 4.8, 4.8.1]

22. Narrate the differences between delegation and decentralisation. [C.U. B.Com. 2002]
[**Ans.** Section 4.11]

23. Explain the features of a sound organisation in management. [C.U. B.Com. 2002]
[**Ans.** Section 4.6.3]

24. Explain the different steps of organising. [C.U. B.Com. 2003, 2005]
[**Ans.** Section 4.5]

25. Discuss briefly the basic principles of delegation of authority. [C.U. B.Com. 2004]
[**Ans.** Section 4.8.6.]

26. Distinguish between delegation of authority and decentralisation. [C.U. B.Com. 2004]
[**Ans.** Section 4.11]

27. Explain the process of delegation of authority. [C.U. B.Com. 2005]
[**Ans.** Section 4.8.3]

28. What are the advantages and drawbacks of decentralisation? [C.U. B.Com. 2006]
[**Ans.** Sections 4.10.2 and 4.10.3]

29. What is Line and Staff Organisation? Mention its merits and demerits. [C.U. B.Com. 2006]
[**Ans.** Section 4.6.4 (D)]

30. (a) "Organising is a process"—Discuss.
(b) State the advantages and limitations of line and staff organisation. [C.U. B.Com. 2007]
[**Ans.** Sections 4.1 and 4.6.4 (D)]

31. State the advantages and disadvantages of functional organisation structure. [C.U. B.Com. 2008]
[**Ans.** Section 4.6.4(B)]

32. "Just as authority is the key to the manager's job, delegation is the key to organisation"—Explain. [C.U. B.Com. 2008]
[**Ans.** Section 4.8]

33. Enumerate the features of line and staff organisation structure. [C.U. B.Com. 2008]
[**Ans.** Section 4.6.4(D)]

34. Explain the features of a healthy organisation. [C.U. B.Com. 2010]
[**Ans.** Section 4.6.3]

35. Define Organisation. What do you mean by Organisation Structure? Discuss the importance of organisation structure. [C.U. B.Com. 2010]
[**Ans.** Sections 4.1, 4.6 and 4.6.2.]

36. Discuss the features of a sound organisation. [C.U. B.Com. 2011]
[**Ans.** Section 4.6.3]

[B] Short Answer-Type Questions

1. Write short notes on the following:

(a) Organisation Structure.
[**Ans.** Section 4.6]

(b) Delegation of Authority.
[**Ans.** Section 4.8]

(c) Decentralisation.
[**Ans.** Section 4.10]

(d) Delegation and Decentralisation.
[**Ans.** Section 4.11]

(e) Nature of Organisation.
[**Ans.** Section 4.2]

(f) Steps in Organisation.
[**Ans.** Section 4.5]

(g) Benefits of Delegation.
[**Ans.** Section 4.8.4]

2. Answer the following questions briefly:

(i) What is 'Organisation'? [C.U. B.Com. 1983, 1986, 1991, 1998]
[**Ans.** Section 4.1]

(ii) What do you mean by 'Decentralisation'? [C.U. B.Com. 1983, 1994, 1996, 1999]
[**Ans.** Section 3.10]

(iii) What is 'Delegation of Authority'? [C.U. B.Com. 1987, 1993, 1996, 1997]
[**Ans.** Section 4.8]

(iv) What is meant by 'Organisation Structure'?
[**Ans.** Section 4.6]

(v) What is meant by a Line Organisation? [C.U. B.Com. 2001]
[**Ans.** Section 4.6.4(A)]

(vi) What is meant by Delegation of Authority? [C.U. B.Com. 2001]
[**Ans.** Section 4.8]

(vii) What do you mean by Delegation of Authority? [C.U. B.Com. 2003, 2007]
[**Ans.** Section 4.8]

(viii) What do you mean by 'Line Organisation'? [C.U. B.Com. 2003, 2005]
[**Ans.** Section 4.6.4 (A)]

(ix) What is decentralisation? [C.U. B.Com. 2003, 2005, 2008]
[**Ans.** Section 4.10]

(x) Describe the elements of Delegation of Authority. [C.U. B.Com. 2004]
[**Ans.** Section 4.8.3]

(xi) What is an Organisation Chart? [C.U. B.Com. 2005]
[**Ans.** Section 4.6.5]

(xii) What is Organisation? [C.U. B.Com. 2005]
[**Ans.** Section 4.1.]

(xiii) Can an Organisation work without Delegation of Authority? Give reasons for your answer. [C.U. B.Com. 2006]
[**Ans.** Section 4.8.2]

(xiv) What is Delegation of Authority? [C.U. B.Com 2006]
[**Ans.** Section 4.8]

(xv) What are the features of a good organisation? [C.U. B.Com. 2007]
[**Ans.** Section 4.6.3]

(xvi) Define Organising. [C.U. B.Com. 2008]
[**Ans.** Section 4.1]

(xvii) Explain the term 'Organisation Structure'. [C.U. B.Com. 2009]
[**Ans.** Section 4.8.3]

(xviii) Mention the elements in the process of Delegation of Authority.
[**Ans.** Section 4.8.3] [C.U. B.Com. 2009]

(xix) What do you mean by 'Decentralisation'? [C.U. B.Com. 2010]
[**Ans.** Section 4.10]

(xx) What do you mean by 'Line Organisation'? [C.U. B.Com. 2011]
[**Ans.** Section 4.6.4 (A)]

(xxi) Distinguish between 'Centralisation' and 'Decentralisation'. [C.U. B.Com. 2011]
[**Ans.** Section 4.12] [New Syllabus]

(xxii) Draw the relationship between 'Line' and 'Staff' with a diagram and examples. [C.U. B.Com 2011, New Syllabus]
[**Ans.** The Staff Persons in an organisation only give advice to the Line Managers—in various organisational aspects. They act as the advisors of the organisation. But they have no authority to command and provide direction. Staff service is auxiliary in nature. The line managers may or may not follow the advice of the staff personnel. [For diagram, see Fig. 4.6; and for examples, see the sections 4.6.4(A) and 4.6.4(B)]

CHAPTER 5

Motivation

"Motivation is the art of getting people to do what you want them to do because they want to do it."

—Dwight Eisenhower

TOPICS

Subject-matter of the Chapter : *The aim of Management is to utilise the physical and human factors of the enterprise so that the objectives of the enterprise are fulfilled effectively and efficiently. The effectiveness of materials, machines, equipment etc. depends on the quantitative and qualitative standard of performance of the employees. In order to make the factors of production effective, development of the employees' work accomplishment is very essential. For this purpose, it is necessary to inspire and encourage the employees of the enterprise so that they perform their assigned tasks willingly and enthusiastically. The managerial process of creating willingness in the subordinate employees to do work eagerly for the achievement of the goals of the enterprise is known as 'Motivating' or providing 'Motivation'. It is a special function of the managers. It arouses will force and morale in the workers—by providing them with financial and psychological satisfaction. The behaviour of a subordinate employee is greatly influenced by the motivating capacity of the manager. If the employees are properly motivated, productivity and profit of the enterprise obviously increase.*

In this chapter the meaning, characteristics, importance and various factors of motivation will be discussed. And, in this connection, the theories of motivation according to the syllabus will be analysed critically.

5.1 Motivation : Definition and Meaning

'Motivation' is the process of inspiring people in order to intensify their desire and willingness for executing their duties effectively and for co-operating to achieve the common objectives of an enterprise. In other words, it means to induce, instigate, incite or prompt someone to a particular course of action for getting the results expected from him. Motivation is the actuating force that stimulates a man to put his best in the accomplishment of a task. In the words of **E.F.L. Brech :** "Motivation is a general inspiration process which gets the members of the team pull their weight effectively to give their loyalty to the group, to carry out properly the tasks they have accepted and generally to play an effective part in the job that the group has undertaken."

In fact, motivation may be regarded as an integral part of the process of direction. In directing the subordinates, the manager has to try to create in them the willingness to pursue the goals of the organisation enthusiastically. In trying to do so, the manager may be said to concern himself with motivation. The term 'motivation' is derived from the word 'motive'. A motive is "an inner state that energises, activates or moves, and that directs or induces human behaviour towards goals." Motives are the expression of a person's needs and desires. In order to motivate individuals to work for the realisation of the goals and objectives of the organisation, the manager has to determine the motives or, in other words, the needs of the employees that call for their satisfaction. So, motivation may be described as the process whereby an individual is given the opportunity to satisfy his needs by pursuing certain objectives.

Motivation is a powerful tool in the hands of a manager for inducing his subordinates to act in the desired manner by satisfying their needs and desires. It is concerned with how behaviour gets started, is energised, initiated, sustained and directed. A successful manager knows that the issue of directions, however well-conceived, does not mean that they will be followed. He makes appropriate use of motivation to enthuse the personnel to work effectively for the attainment of the established goals.

5.1.1 Factors of or Aids to Motivation

Effective motivation depends upon several factors or aids. The motivation process is determined on the basis of the factors discussed below.

1. **Adequate Financial Incentive :** Provisions should be made for fair and adequate remuneration of the employees of the enterprise. Remuneration must be fixed in such a way that the employees are satisfied. If they are not well paid they will not be motivated to perform their work with sincere efforts. Therefore, proper arrangements are to be made for sufficient amount of wages and salaries, bonus, various allowances, etc. in order to encourage the employees.

2. **Congenial Work Environment :** Conducive work environment is needed for motivating the employees effectively. If favourable working conditions are not created, the process of motivation will not be fruitful. A suitable work environment means proper arrangements for ventilation and lighting, cleanliness and healthy atmosphere at the work place.

3. **Provision for Promotion :** The employees are motivated through their promotion in future. Arrangement for promotion should be based on seniority or efficiency of the employees.

4. **Non-monetary Facilities :** Besides financial incentives, some non-monetary facilities like the provisions for travelling, education, accommodation and medical treatment of the employees—free of cost—should be arranged for motivation.

5. Retirement Benefits : Retirement benefits of the employees should be satisfactory for influencing them to work more. Arrangement of the important retirement benefits like the provisions of provident fund, pension, gratuity, etc. are to be made.

6. Security of Job : The employees should be ensured about the stability of their employment. If they feel safe and secured in their jobs, they will be highly motivated.

7. Goodwill and Possibility of Development of the Enterprise : The employees will be well-motivated to perform their jobs more effectively if the enterprise in which they work has a good reputation in the market and there lies the possibility of expansion, growth and prosperity in near future.

8. Recognition of Good Work : The performance of good work by the employees should be recognised, accepted and praised by the upper level managers for creation of motivation among the employees.

9. Unity among the Employees : Through the establishment of unity among the employees, motivation can be created. For this purpose, cordial relationship should be made among them. Equal and impartial behaviour to the employees of all levels and improvement of working relation are also necessary.

10. Good Behaviour of the Higher Level Authority : Sweet behaviour of the higher authority and good relation between the employees and higher authority are needed for motivating the employees properly and adequately.

5.2 Characteristics of Motivation

The salient features or characteristics of motivation are as follows :

1. Human Aspect : Motivation is concerned exclusively with the human side of an enterprise. It means a process of stimulating human beings to make action for getting desired results. It creates will to work in the individuals. If a manager can enthuse, initiate and build up loyalty of the employees towards the achievement of the enterprise objectives with their willing co-operation, the sum total of all these will amount to motivation. Thus, motivation is a behavioural concept that directs human behaviour towards certain goals.

2. Psychological Concept : Motivation is a psychological concept which generates feelings of certain needs within an individual. Human needs are nothing but feelings in the mind of a person that he lacks certain things. Such internal feelings affect the behaviour of the person. The workers, even with extraordinary abilities, will not be able to perform as desired unless they are effectively motivated. Effective performance on the part of the workers can be said to be the end result of their abilities backed by proper motivation. Thus,

Performance = Motivation × Abilities.

3. Need-Satisfying Activity : Motivation is related to satisfying human needs. It can be effective only upon an accurate analysis of the workers' needs for the satisfaction of which they can be induced to work in the desired manner. A worker will perform the desired activity only so long as he sees his action as a means of continued fulfilment of his cherished needs. All motivated behaviour on the part of human beings are directed towards satisfaction or fulfilment of needs.

4. Motivation is Total, not Part : A worker cannot be motivated in parts. Each individual in the organisation is a self-contained and inseparable unit and all his needs are inter-related. These affect his behaviour in different ways. To be successful, motivation must take a worker as an indivisible unit and seek to appeal to all his urges and aspirations.

5. Financial and Non-financial : Motivation may assume several forms depending upon the needs, emotions, and sentiments of the workers. Broadly speaking, it can be classified as financial and non-financial. Financial motivation may be created by way of increasing wages, allowances, bonus, prizes, and other perquisites; while non-financial motivation may take the form of praise, recognition, providing greater responsibility or increased participation in decision-making, etc.

6. Constant Process : Human needs are infinite. As very aptly put by **Abraham H. Maslow,** "Man is a wanting animal—as soon as one of his needs is satisfied, another appears in its place. This process is unending..." This means motivation cannot be a time-bound process. It is continuous.

5.3 Role or Importance of Motivation

Motivation is one of the most important factors determining organisational efficiency and effectiveness. All organisational facilities will go waste in the lack of motivated people to utilise these facilities effectively. Every superior in the organisation must motivate his subordinates to create in them the will to work.

The role or importance and significance of motivation may be summed up as follows:

1. Removal of Apathy : It is the considered view that the workers as a rule do not exert adequate energy for the accomplishment of a task assigned to them. This is because they are somehow dissatisfied with work, work situation or with the management authority. Motivation removes this apathy of the workers for peak performance.

2. Combining 'Will to work' with 'Capacity for work' : The will to work differs from the capacity for work. A man may have the capacity for doing a work having physical strength, technical skill, sufficient intelligence and mental alertness; but he may not have the mentality to apply them in full to his work. Motivation removes this psychological barrier and combines the will to work with the capacity for work of the workers.

3. Securing Full Support and Energy of the Workers : The vital mark of a successful manager is his capacity to ensure full support and co-operation of the workers with their energy, ability and enthusiasm. "You can buy a man's time, you can buy a man's physical presence at a given place, but you cannot buy his enthusiasm, initiative or loyalty and his capacity, will and energy without motivation." The vital mark of a successful manager is, thus, associated with motivation.

4. Understanding the Employees' Needs : Motivation makes the managers understand and realise the needs of the employees and gives satisfaction to them accordingly. If there is this understanding, and motivation works behind it, the managers are sure to receive needed co-operation of the employees for the profitability of the enterprise.

5. Maximum Utilisation of the Resources : Motivation inspires the workers to make the best possible use of different factors of production. They work whole-heartedly to apply their abilities in minimising waste and cost. This will enable the enterprise to utilise its human, physical and financial resources to the maximum.

6. Increase in Efficiency and Output : Motivation is an effective instrument in the hands of the managers to maximise efficiency of operations and output of the enterprise. Motivated employees put higher performance as compared to other employees. A happy and contended work force ensures improved efficiency and higher output. Increase in labour productivity results in higher wages for the workers and increased profits for the enterprise. The high performance is a must for an organisation being successful and this performance comes through motivation.

7. Low Employee Turnover and Absenteeism : Motivated employees stay in the organisation and their absenteeism is quite low. High labour turnover and absenteeism create many problems in the organisation. Existence of attractive financial and non-financial incentives helps to retain the employees. They are not easily tempted away by offers from the competitiors. With reduced labour turnover, it becomes possible for the enterprise to plan its activities on a long-term basis.

8. Acceptance of Organisational Changes : Organisations are integral parts of the society. The changes taking place in the society, i.e. changes in technology, knowledge, value system, etc., require an organisation to incorporate those changes to cope up with the requirement of the time. When these changes are introduced in the organisation, there is a tendency to resist changes by the employees. However, if they are properly motivated, they will accept, introduce and implement these changes and keep the organisation on the right track of progress.

9. Better Industrial Relations : Existence of attractive motivational schemes promotes closer identification between the enterprise and its workers. They merge their individual interests with the organisational objectives. There arises a sense of belonging and mutual co-operation at all levels. Motivation will foster team spirit among the workers. This will reduce labour unrest and create better relations between the managers and workers.

10. Facilitating Other Functions of Management : The successful accomplishment of different functions such as planning, organising, directing, co-ordinating and controlling—all are inter-linked with motivation. Motivation is the right force that can make planning successful, organisation sound, direction forceful, co-ordination tight and control effective.

From the above discussion, it is clear that motivation is of great importance to business activities as it is a vital part of management process. No tangible result of best performance is possible without motivation.

5.4 Theories of Motivation

(A) Maslow's Theory of Need Hierarchy : The behaviour of an individual at a particular moment is usually determined by his strongest need. Psychologists claim that, as the basic needs are satisfied, an individual seeks to satisfy the higher level needs. If his basic needs are not met, efforts to satisfy higher level needs should be postponed.

A. H. Maslow

Abraham H. Maslow, a famous American Social Scientist, has developed a general theory of motivation, known as the 'Need Hierarchy Theory'. The essence of this theory is that motivation of an individual is based on a pre-determined hierarchy of needs. He has skilfully arranged the range of human needs in terms of a hierarchy with physiological needs at the bottom level and self-actualisation needs at the top level as shown in Fig. 5.1

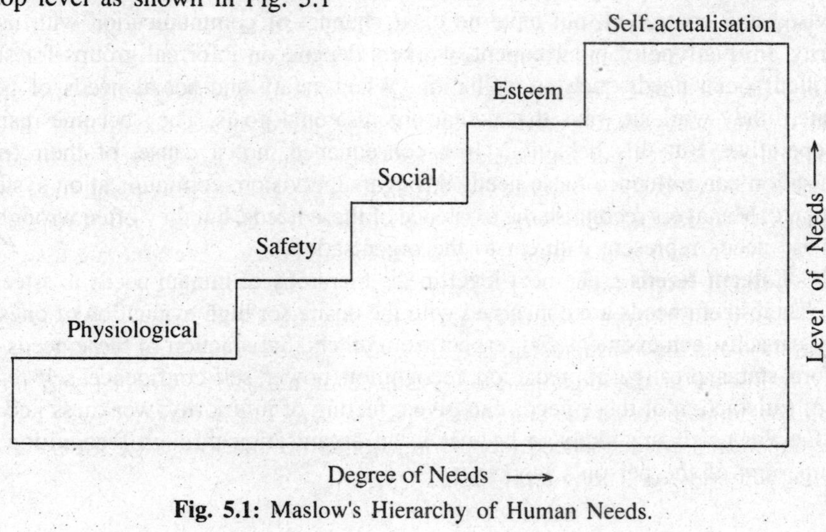

Fig. 5.1: Maslow's Hierarchy of Human Needs.

The basic human needs identified by Maslow in an ascending order of importance are as under :

1. Physiological Needs : The starting point of motivation is the physiological needs which stand at the lowest level of the need hierarchy. These needs are for food, water, air, clothing, shelter, sleep, etc. which are essential for the existence of life. Therefore, these needs are also known as 'Survival Needs'. Until these needs are satisfied to the degree needed for the efficient operation of the body, the majority of a person's activities will probably be at this level and the other levels will provide him with little motivation. "Man cannot live by bread alone", says the Bible, but hardly anything is more important when there is no bread. In most normal situations, our need for love, status, or recognition is inoperative when we are hungry for a while. But when we eat regularly and adequately we ignore hunger as an important motivator. The same is true of other physiological needs such as for air, water, rest, shelter, etc. The manager attempts to satisfy these needs in the work place primarily through proper salary and wages.

2. Safety Needs : When an individual's physiological needs are satisfied to a reasonable level, safety needs get the most important priority as motivator. Such needs refer to the protection that a man needs against accident, physical torture, unemployment, disability, old age, etc. A man seeks safety against what threatens his survival physically and economically, e.g. fear and danger of loss of job, life or limb, and property. Since most employees are in a dependent relationship in their work place, they often regard their safety needs as being very important. Arbitrary management actions, such as—favouritism or discrimination and unpredictable application of policies—often become powerful threats to the safety needs of any employee at any level.

Peter F. Drucker has suggested that one's attitude towards security is an important consideration in choosing a job. Organisation can influence these security needs either positively through pension schemes, insurance plans, etc.—or negatively by arousing fears of dismissal, demotion, etc.

3. Social Needs : As soon as the minimum safety needs are satisfied, social needs become important in the need hierarchy. Since man is a social being, he has a longing for belonging to a group or community and for being accepted and understood with love, affection, compassion, friendship, association, etc. When social needs become dominant, a person will strive for meaningful relations with others. If the opportunity for association with other people is reduced, men often take vigorous action against the obstacles. In the organisation, workers form informal group. Such groups develop where the work is routine-bound, tedious or over-simplified. This situation is made worse when the workers are closely supervised and controlled, but have no clear channel of communication with managerial authority. In this type of environment, workers depend on informal groups for support of unfulfilled social needs such as affiliation. When safety and social needs of people are frustrated, they work in ways that defeat organisatonal goals. They become resistant and unco-operative. But this behaviour is a consequence, not a cause, of their frustration. Organisation can influence these needs through supervision, communication system, work groups, etc. Managers recognise the existence of these needs, but they often wrongly assume that these needs represent a threat to the organisation.

4. Esteem Needs : The next level in the hierarchy of human needs is esteem or ego needs. The esteem needs are concerned with the desire for high evaluation of oneself based on real capacity, achievement and respect from others. Satisfaction of these needs embrace, therefore, status, prestige, appreciation, recognition, power, self-confidence, self-respect, etc. Lack of satisfaction of these needs can give a feeling of inferiority, weakness and helplessness. Esteem needs are likely to be met in an organisation through recognition by peers and superiors of the person's work.

However, these needs are rarely satisfied in full. It is because people seek to get more satisfaction of these needs once they have become important to them. The conventional method of organising work, particularly in mass production industries, gives hardly any consideration to these motivational aspects.

5. Self-actualisation Needs : Maslow's highest need level, self-actualisation or self-realisation relates to the desire for self-fulfilment, i.e. the need to develop one's abilities to the fullest extent, and to maximise the use of one's potentialities to accomplish something creative. If a man possesses a quality, he likes to actualise it. An artist likes to paint, a poet likes to compose verse, a player likes to show his skill in the game, etc. In other words, a man wishes to become what he is capable of becoming. A man with high intensity of achievement needs self-actualising will force. He will be restless unless he can attain what he intends to do. However, the quality of work environment in most organisations gives very little scope for fulfilling these needs. When other needs are not satisfied, the workers attempt to satisfy those lower-order needs, and the needs for self-fulfilment remain dormant.

All these observations in regard to motivation are based on the following propositions about human behaviour :

(a) Man, being a wanting creature, wants more and more. As soon as one want is satisfied, the next want appears on the scene. This process of need satisfaction continues from birth to death.

(b) When a particular need is satisfied, it can no longer act as a motivator of behaviour. At this stage, only unsatisfied needs can influence behaviour and motivate people.

(c) As soon as the person's needs are met on one level, he advances up to the next level of needs. He will focus on the first level need until it is satisfied at least at minimum level before moving to the next level.

(d) If satisfaction is not maintained for a once-satisfied need, it will become a priority need again. For instance, if a person has just satisfied security needs and has moved up to the social needs level, security will become a priority once again if the person is fired from his job.

Thus, in Maslow's theory, needs can be thought of as being ranked in a hierarchy in which one need is more important than others until it is satisfied. Once the most important need is satisfied, the next higher need becomes predominant and demands satisfaction. The theory implies that human beings are motivated by unsatisfied needs rather than satisfied needs.

Maslow has divided his five needs into two levels—lower order needs and higher order needs. The lower order needs comprise physiological, safety and social needs and the higher order needs include esteem and self-actualisation needs. According to Maslow, there is a prepotency of needs under which satisfaction of the higher order needs will have no effect until the lower order needs are satisfied.

- **Criticism :** Maslow's theory has gained reasonable support and extensive popularity for the hypothesis that human needs have some hierarchical order. The theory is based on the true assumption that man has endless wants. All his needs are never fully satisfied. As soon as one need is reasonably satisfied, another need comes out to replace it. Thus, at last, some needs remain unsatisfied which serve the man to strive to satisfy. It presents a very simple solution of managerial problems, that is, the managers can try to satisfy the needs of people in this particular order. It is compatible with the economic theory of demand. The theory helps to explain why a person behaves differently in two similar situations. It provides an insight into what is common to all. It extends to all areas of human life and is not limited to work situation only.

But the hierarchy of needs theory has been widely criticised in the following respects:

Firstly, Maslow has not specified the works related to satisfying the needs of employees. He looks upon the general needs of human beings in their work and home surroundings.

Secondly, there exists no definite prepotency of needs as suggested by Maslow. Subsequent studies show that there is no strict ordering of needs in which they are felt. For example, many people do not care for job security but care for social need. Similarly, there are certain persons for whom self-esteem needs are more important than social needs.

Thirdly, there is often a lack of direct cause-effect relationship between need and behaviour. Thus, a particular need may effect behaviour in different ways to different persons. Similarly, one particular behaviour may be the result of different needs. For example, if a person is thirsty, he may take water, or some soft drink, or some juice. Likewise, people may earn money to satisfy their several types of needs, not only physiological needs. So, need theory is not so simple as it seems to be.

Fourthly, the theory is concerned with the content of motivation rather than the process of motivation. It does not tell the way in which human behaviour and performance are influenced by the need of hierarchy.

Lastly, there is another problem in applying the theory into practice. A person tries for his higher level need when his lower order need is reasonably satisfied. What is this reasonable level is a question of subjective matter. Thus, the level of satisfaction for a particular need may differ from person to person.

So, there are some basic problems involved in the application of Maslow's need hierarchy theory. At every level it can be seen that the role of the individual is very important. Since individuals differ, it may not be quite possible to prescribe one standard action for solving the motivational problems of all persons. However, Maslow's theory should be regarded as a general guide to the managers, for it is a relative concept, not an absolute explanation of all human behaviour. It provides a convenient conceptual framework for the study of motivation.

(B) Herzberg's Two Factors or Motivation-Hygiene Theory : Frederick Herzberg of the Western Research University, Ohio, USA, and his associates made a valuable contribution to the development of a theory of motivation by indicating the way to the industry to better performance through increased job satisfaction.

F. Herzberg

Their study consisted of an intensive analysis of the experiences and feelings of 200 engineers and accountants in eleven different companies in Pittsburgh area, USA During the structured interview, they were asked to describe a few previous job experiences in which they felt 'exceptionally good' or 'exceptionally bad' about their job. From the replies received Herzberg discovered that there are some job conditions which operate primarily to dissatisfy the employees when the conditions are absent, but their presence does not motivate them in a strong way. Another set of job conditions operates primarily to build strong motivation and high job satisfaction, but their absence rarely proves strongly dissatisfying. The first set of job conditions were called by him 'Hygiene Factors' and the second set of job conditions 'Motivating Factors'.

(i) Hygiene Factors : These factors are related to the work environment. According to Herzberg the following factors are included in this category :

(i) Company policy and administration; (ii) quality of technical supervision; (iii) inter-personal relationship with the supervisors, subordinates and peers; (iv) salary; (v) job security; (vi) working condition; (vii) employee benefits; (viii) personal life; and (ix) job status. Hygiene factors do not produce any growth in the worker's output; they only prevent losses in the worker's performance due to work restrictions. For this reason, these factors are also called 'Maintenance Factors'. These factors are necessary to maintain a reasonable level of satisfaction in the employees. Any increase beyond this level will not provide any satisfaction to the employees; but, any cut below this level will dissatisfy them. As such, they are also called 'Dissatisfier'. Since any increase in these factors will not affect the employee's level of satisfaction, these are of no use for motivating them.

(ii) Motivating Factors : These factors have a positive power to satisfy and produce high performance. Herzberg included six factors that motivate the employees to work. These are : (a) achievement; (b) responsibility; (c) recognition; (d) advancement; (e) creative and challenging work; and (f) possibility of growth and development. Most of these factors are related to job contents. An increase in these factors will satisfy the employees. So these factors are also called 'Satisfiers'. However, any decrease in these factors will not affect their level of satisfaction. Since these factors increase the level of satisfaction in the employees, they can be used in motivating them for higher output.

From the point of view of management, the significance of Herzberg's theory lies in the warning that merely removing the causes of dissatisfaction will not make the workers do any better. More particularly, more pay cannot be the basis for long range satisfaction. Better performance can come only when positive motivation is built up through improvement in the job content by making it more interesting, challenging, responsible and worthwhile. The managers can work on both fronts by reducing the dissatisfaction arising out of hygiene factors and building up the motivators for bringing employees' satisfaction.

- **Criticism :** Herzberg's theory is based on the fact that most of the people are able to satisfy their lower order needs considerably. As such, they are not motivated by any further addition of satisfaction of these needs. This motion is true and it has been supported by many studies both in India and foreign countries. Herzberg's model has been applied in the industry and has given several new insights. One of them is job enrichment. This job enrichment applies to improvement of jobs in such a way that they have more motivators than before. Thus, Herzberg's theory has solved the problems of the managers who were wondering why their fancy personnel policies failed to motivate their employees adequately.

However, Herzberg's model is not applied in all conditions. It has the following weaknesses :

Firstly, according to this theory, it is assumed that there is a high correlation between the employees' satisfaction and productivity. Herzberg bothers too much about satisfaction of the workers. But although satisfaction creates good morale, it does not lead to increased productivity in all cases.

Secondly, there is considerable amount of mixing of maintenance and motivating factors. Therefore, various factors relating to jobs may not be classified into maintenance and motivating factors.

Thirdly, situational variables have been ignored here.

Fourthly, this theory does not attach much importance to pay, status or inter-personal relationships—which are held generally as important contents of satisfaction.

Douglas Mc Gregor

Lastly, Herzberg's model is 'method-bound', and a number of other methods used for similar study have shown different results not supporting his contentions. Thus, the theory has limitations in general acceptibility.

(C) Mc Gregor's Theory X and Theory Y : Douglas Mc Gregor has presented two opposite views of human behaviour in the organisation in the form of what he calls Theory 'X' and Theory 'Y'. Theory 'X' represents the traditional view of human nature and behaviour, and emphasises the need for control and direction over man. On the other hand, Theory 'Y' indicates the individual and organisation behaviour both and highlights the need for improving and utilising inner motivation.

The basic assumptions about human nature and behaviour in working according to both these theories are given below:

● **Theory 'X' :** According to the traditional view of human behaviour, the following assumptions hold good about the work behaviour of people :

1. The average individual has an inherent dislike of work and will avoid it if he can.
2. Most people must, therefore, be pressurised, controlled, directed, and threatened by punishment by their superiors to get them put forth adequate efforts towards organisational objectives.
3. The average human being prefers to be led, wishes to avoid responsibility, and has relatively little ambition.
4. The average person actually prefers to be directed to being led on his own.
5. Most people are by nature resistant to change and look for security above all.
6. An average human being is inherently self-centred, and indifferent to organisational goals.

The above assumptions are negative in nature. According to Mc Gregor, an organisation built upon Theory 'X' approach will be one in which there is close supervision and control of subordinates and high centralisation of authority. Leadership in such organisation will tend to be autocratic, and the workers will have very little say in decisions affecting them.

● **Theory 'Y' :** Mc Gregor recognised certain needs that Theory 'X' fails to take into account. These relate to self-fulfilment, ego satisfaction and the social needs of the individual workers. To meet these human needs in the organisation, Mc Gregor suggested a counter-approach to motivation in management called Theory 'Y'.

Theory 'Y' is based on the following assumptions :

1. People like to work. It is as natural as rest or play.
2. Man will exercise self-direction and self-control in the service of objectives to which he is committed. External control or threat of punishment is not the only means of motivating people to work and achieve organisational goals.
3. People commit themselves to those objectives which promise them the satisfactions they want.
4. The average human being learns, under proper conditions, not only to accept responsibility but also to seek it.
5. The capacity to exercise a relatively high degree of imagination, ingenuity and creativity in the solution of organisational problems is widely distributed in the population.

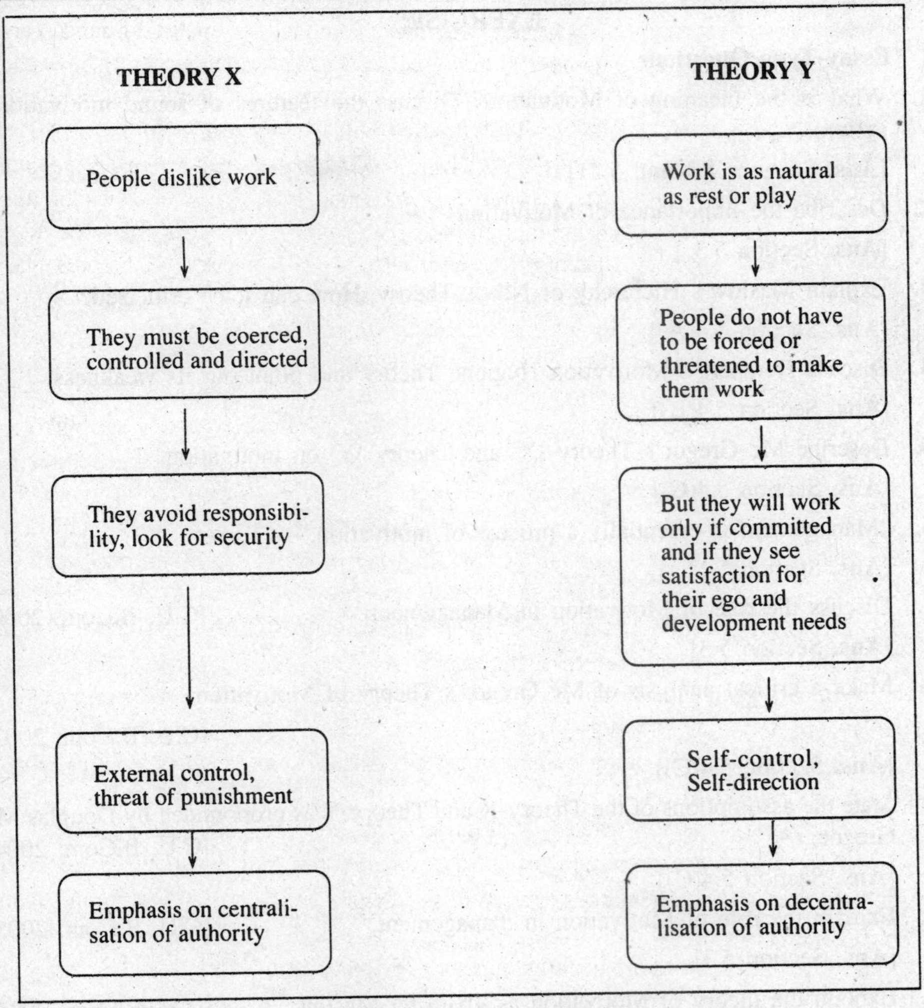

Fig. 5.2: Theory 'X' versus Theory 'Y'.

6. Under conditions of modern industrial life, the intellectual potentialities of people are only partially utilised. In reality, people have unlimited potential.

7. Since the other needs of most of the people in work organisations are pretty well-satisfied, the management authority can achieve better results through them by appealing to their ego and development needs.

Theory 'Y' represents a modern and dynamic nature of human beings. According to this theory, the manager is in charge of work, not people. So he delegates freedom rather than authority. An organisation designed on the basis of Theory 'Y' is characterised by decentralisation of authority, job enrichment, participative leadership and two-way communication system. The focus is on self-control and responsible jobs. Theory 'X' places exclusive reliance on external control of human behaviour, while Theory 'Y' relies on self-regulation.

If we relate Theory 'X' and Theory 'Y' to Maslow's hierarchy of needs theory, it may be said that Theory 'X' may be more applicable where a man is concerned with the lower level of needs. Once he has an adequate level of satisfaction of the basic physiological and safety needs, Theory 'Y' may be used for making an appeal to the higher level needs.

EXERCISES

[A] Essay-Type Questions

1. What is the meaning of Motivation? Discuss the features of sound motivational system.
   [**Ans.** Sections 5.1 and 5.21]
2. Describe the importance of Motivation.
   [**Ans.** Section 5.3]
3. Explain Maslow's Hierarchy of Needs Theory. How can it be criticised?
   [**Ans.** Section 5.4(A)]
4. Discuss Herzberg's Motivation Hygiene Theory and point out its weakness.
   [**Ans.** Section 5.4(B)]
5. Describe Mc Gregor's Theory 'X' and Theory 'Y' on motivation.
   [**Ans.** Section 5.4(C)]
6. "Management is essentially a process of motivation."—Discuss.
   [**Ans.** Section 5.1]
7. Discuss the role of Motivation in Management. [C.U. B.Com. 2000]
   [**Ans.** Section 5.3]
8. Make a critical analysis of Mc Gregor's Theory of Motivation.
   [C.U. B.Com. 2002]
   [**Ans.** Section 5.4(C)]
9. State the assumptions of the Theory-X and Theory-Y as propounded by Douglas Mc Gregor. [C.U. B.Com. 2004]
   [**Ans.** Section 5.4(C)]
10. Explain the role of Motivation in management. [C.U. B.Com. 2005]
    [**Ans.** Section 5.3]
11. Explain the theory of Motivation as given by Maslow. [C.U. B.Com. 2006]
    [**Ans.** Section 5.4(A)]
12. Critically analyse Mc Gregor's Theory of Motivation. [C.U. B.Com. 2006]
    [**Ans.** Section 5.4(C)]
13. State Mc Gregor's Theory of Motivation. What are the limitations of this theory?
    [C.U. B.Com. 2008]
    [**Ans.** Section 5.4(C)]
14. Explain the assumptions of Theory X and Theory Y as propounded by Mc Gregor.
    [C.U. B.Com. 2011]
    [**Ans.** Section 5.4(C)]
15. Elaborate the needs in Maslow's Hierarchy of Needs Theory.
    or
    Explain 'Dissatisfiers' and 'Motivators' in Herzberg's Theory of Motivation.
    [C.U. B.Com. 2011 (New Syllabus)]
    [**Ans.** Section 5.4(A) and 5.4(B)]

B] Short Answer-Type Questions

1. Write short notes on the following:

(i) Role of Motivation.
[**Ans.** Section 5.3]

(ii) Nature of Motivation.
[**Ans.** Section 5.2]

(iii) Maslow's Needs Theory on Motivation.
[**Ans.** Section 5.4(A)]

(iv) Mc Gregor's Theory Y.
[**Ans.** Section 5.4(C)]

(v) Herzberg's Theory on Motivation.
[**Ans.** Section 5.4(B)]

2. Answer briefly the following questions:

(i) What do you understand by Motivation? [C.U. B.Com. 1986, 1989]
[**Ans.** Section 5.1]

(ii) Mention the different categories of human needs as suggested by Abraham Maslow. [C.U. B.Com. 1984]
[**Ans.** Section 5.4(A)]

(iii) Name the five human needs referred to by Abraham Maslow. [C.U. B.Com. 1990]
[**Ans.** Section 5.4(A)]

(iv) What are the types of needs mentioned by Maslow? [C.U. B.Com. 2001]
[**Ans.** Section 5.4(A)]

(v) What is Motivation? [C.U. B.Com. 2004, 2009]
[**Ans.** Section 5.1]

(vi) Write two factors of Motivation. [C.U. B.Com. 2002]
[**Ans.** Section 5.1.1]

(vii) What is the significance of Motivation in Management? [C.U. B.Com. 2006]
[**Ans.** Section 5.3]

(viii) Mention two features of Motivation. [C.U. B.Com. 2007]
[**Ans.** Section 5.2]

(ix) Mention two factors of Motivation. [C.U. B.Com. 2008]
[**Ans.** Section 5.1.1]

(x) Mention the levels of the Hierarchy of Needs Theory of Maslow. [C.U. B.Com. 2010]
[**Ans.** Section 5.4(A)]

(xi) State two factors of Motivation. [C.U. B.Com. 2011]
[**Ans.** Section 5.1.1]

CHAPTER 6

Leadership

"If your actions inspire others to dream more, learn more, do more and become more, you are a leader."

—John Quincy Adams

TOPICS

Subject-matter of the Chapter : *Every manager of an enterprise should possess leadership quality. In Management, 'Leadership' means the ability of influencing the behaviour of the subordinates or followers through proper direction, supervision and communication so that they are motivated to perform their assigned tasks willingly and eagerly for the realisation of the goals of the enterprise. Leadership plays a vital role for the success of business activities. Effective and efficient leadership of a manager inspires the employees to accomplish their duties enthusiastically.*

The concept, features, importance, and functions of leadership, essential qualities of successful leadership, and different types or styles of leadership have been discussed in detail in this chapter. In connection with this the difference between 'management' and 'leadership' has also been pointed out.

6.1 Definition and Meaning of Leadership

In general terms, 'Leadership' is the ability to persuade others to seek defined objectives enthusiastically. It is the human factor that binds a group together and motivates it towards certain goal. Operationally, leadership is the process by which an executive or a manager directs, guides and influences the work of others for attaining the specified goals by mediating between the individual and the organisation in such a manner that both obtain maximum satisfaction. Conceptually, leadership is an inter-personal influence, exercised in a given situation and directed through communication process, towards the attainment of a specific goal.

'Leadership' may be defined as the ability, the art or process of influencing the behaviour of the subordinates (followers) so that they strive willingly towards the achievement of group goals with zeal and confidence in a given situation. Zeal reflects earnestness and intensity in the execution of work; confidence reflects experience and technical ability.

According to **George R. Terry** : "Leadership is the activity of influencing people to strive willingly for group objectives". In the words of **Koontz and O'Donnell**, leadership means "Influencing people to follow the achievement of a common goal. It is the ability to exert inter-personal influence by means of communication towards the ahievement of a goal."

A leader has the function of interpreting the objectives of the business, suggesting the course of actions and guiding the group efforts as a team towards realisation of these objectives. To lead is to guide, direct and precede. The leaders act to help a group in attaining the objectives with the maximum application of its capabilities. They do not stand behind a group to push and to prod; rather they place themselves before the group as the guiding force and inspire the group to accomplish the organisational goals. A pertinent example is that of the orchestra leader, whose function is to produce co-ordinated sound and correct tempo through the integrated efforts of the instrumentalists. Leadership process comprises three elements—the leader, the follower, and other variables.

6.2 Importance of Leadership

Leadership is an essential ingredient for successful organisation. Providing proper and effective leadership to his subordinates is an important responsibility of a manager or supervisor. In fact, whenever a group of people work for a common purpose, they are required to be imbued with the will force to accomplish the task and leadership should be there to provide these necessary impetus. Leadership shows the way the group should follow by providing the group with necessary guidance, assistance and motivation. "There is an active and guiding power in every group undertaking; this power is leadership." A good leader is a dynamo generating energy that charges and activises the whole group in such a way that the objectives may be achieved. The history of business is full of instances where good leaders led the business concerns to unprecedented peaks of success through their ability and wise policies. So, effective leadership has a significant role in business management.

The importance of good leadership may be discussed as follows :

(1) The first and foremost job of a leader is to guide and direct the group. He acts as the captain of his team and takes lead in all activities to win the confidence and co-operation of his followers. He convinces them about the goals and policies of the group. A leader secures their co-operation and ensures co-ordination by setting a good example through his own conduct.

(2) Leadership acts as a motive power or force to group efforts. Management is the process of getting things done by others. Group efforts and teamwork are fundamental factors for getting such things. In such circumstances, leadership provides the necessary spark to motivation by guiding, inspiring, assisting and directing the members of the group for the achievement of unity of actions, efforts and purposes. So, leadership pulls up the group for proper work performance.

(3) Authority alone is not enough to generate the initiative and resourcefulness of the subordinates necessary for work performance. It is the effective leadership that can aid authority to reach its goal, because effective leadership contains all the ingredients for proper exercise of authority and responsibility. If the subordinates are guided only by rules and

requirements enforced by managerial authority, they may work at about 60 or 65 percen of capacity—just enough to satisfy the requirements for holding their jobs. To raise efforts towards total capability, the manager must induce the subordinates by exercising proper leadership.

(4) Efficient leadership by providing the social skill transforms management into a social process. This social process is needed at all levels of management from top management downwards to supervisory level. Effective leadership works at all levels and persuades the employees to follow this social process with identity of interest, initiative and enthusiasm. So, leadership can only fulfil the objectives of the enterprise through high performance by creating a well-to-do environment among the workers.

(5) Fruitful leadership not only influences the subordinates, it is also influenced by their problems, feelings and aspirations. So, leadership by its conduct and behaviour realises properly their problems and feelings with due sympathy, careful listening and proper handling of the situation. In this way, it wins their confidence and earns a true spirit of co-operation from them.

(6) No organisation structure can provide for all kinds of relationship. That is why, one notices several informal groups operating within the framework of a formal organisation. If there is no formal and recognised leadership, informal leadership is the natural outcome. As a result of the growth of such informal leadership, the managers may fail to induce the workers for proper work performance. In such a situation, if a competent leadership is brought in, it will be in a position to integrate the formal and informal leadership for the benefit of the organisation and the achievement of its objectives.

(7) In a competitive economy, the role of leadership is wide and comprehensive. It initiates necessary measures with its own ideas and also the ideas of other employees for healthy and progressive development of the undertaking. In the face of technological, economic and social changes taking place in the world, an organisation having no effective leadership may find it difficult to maintain its existence for long.

(8) Those working in an enterprise come from different backgrounds. They have different interests, values, beliefs and intellectual and temperamental make up. So long as the attitudes and behaviour of these individual members are in conformity with the enterprise goals and objectives, there is no need to do anything about it. Problems arise when there is a conflict between the two. It is here that the need for competent leadership arises because it alone can resolve and reconcile such conflicts of interests.

(9) Good administrative work also depends upon effective and skillful leadership. It is to issue orders and see that human endeavours are directed to abide by the orders.

(10) Efficient leadership has the ability to arrive at prompt and correct decision. This quality enables it to take decisions in relation to its own work-situation and work-group so as to gain confidence of the subordinates.

So, effective leadership is essential for good management. It produces a good business by creating a vital, dynamic and life-giving force in the organisation.

6.3 Nature and Characteristics of Leadership

The nature and characteristics of good leadership may be described as follows :

1. Existence of Followers : Leadership presupposes the existence of followers. A man becomes a leader when he has some followers. There should first of all be the growth of followers and the leadership will come next when these followers, by common consent, agree to follow the lead of a person among them known as 'leader'. Leadership thus cannot exist in a vacuum. Leadership and followers are rather co-existent. A successful leader is one who has the unstinted loyalty, confidence, respect and obedience of his followers. In such a situation, the authority exercised over his group is willingly accepted by that group.

2. Process of Influencing Behaviour : Leadership is a continuous process of influencing the behaviour of individuals around the leader to fulfil certain pre-determined objectives. A leader tries to influence the individuals to behave in a particular way.

3. Interaction : An effective leader is one who not only secures desired behaviour from his subordinates, but also creates a sense of satisfaction among them. Again, leadership is exercised in a particular situation. The variables of situation also affect the effectiveness of leadership. Effective leadership is the outcome of the interaction among the leader, the subordinates, and the environment.

4. Leadership cannot be Imposed : A person may exercise authority over his subordinates, but that does not make him a true leader unless he wins their confidence. If the authority is imposed on the group without voluntary acceptance of its members, it will amount to command and domination. So, leadership cannot be imposed or conferred; it must be acquired. The implication of this characteristic of leadership is that it should be gained through obedience and confidence of the followers by virtue of its own merit.

5. Assumption of Responsibility : In the exercise of authority it is necessary for a leader to assume full responsibility for the deeds and happenings of his followers. This responsibility should work for redressing all grievances of the followers, providing protection to the weak and controlling the strong and preparing necessary ground for teamwork. This also demands that a leader should provide necessary stimulus and encouragement for the growth of their initiative and enthusiasm.

6. Clear Understanding of the Feelings and Problems of the Followers : A good leader tries to satisfy the personal and social needs of his followers, and acts as 'a friend, philosopher and guide' to meet their needs. For this, he is required to understand clearly and fully realise their feelings, difficulties and problems, and, accordingly, to take necessary steps to promote their well-being. In order to understand their problems and difficulties, it is necessary for the leader to keep close contact with them as far as possible, inform them of all developments and allow their participation in decision-making in important matters.

7. Community of Interests : Leadership is not an isolated factor. He cannot work for one purpose and his subordinates for another purpose. So, leadership denotes community of interest and mutuality of objectives. Though absolute community of interest and unity of purpose between a leader and his subordinates are very difficult to achieve, it should be the duty of a leader to reconcile the differences and evolve a workable formula for unity of action in all affairs.

8. Self-awareness and Exemplary Conduct : The actions and conduct of a leader have great influence on the behaviour pattern of his followers. So, a leader should be fully aware of his own preferences, weakness and the impression which his followers may develop on his personal traits. It should be his duty to set good example on his own behavioural pattern that may serve as an inspiring lesson among his followers. He should make his followers feel that he can do great deeds and should guide and stimulate them to do great deeds.

9. Common Objectivity : A leader should maintain a common objectivity throughout the organisation by fair play and absolute justice in all affairs. He should be impartial in all matters. This is to be shown in all decisions and actions, placement and transfer, promotion and demotion, communication and participation.

10. Dynamic Process : In the field of business, the situation or environment is never static. It is dynamic and ever-changing. A leader should take note of this and must have the adaptability to changing situations and must exercise his leadership accordingly. Moreover, education, training and experience of the subordinates shape the pattern of leadership. The emergence of new situations according to flexibility of operations of a business enterprise may have a significant influence in the role and skill of leadership. So, a leader will have to face different problems, situations and attitudes with variable effects. This interaction demands varied leadership qualities to meet the different situations.

11. Active Participation : A leader's position should be in the forefront. He should ask his men to follow him. Leadership means not to say, 'go on' but 'come on'. So, he should be an active participant and carry on his task with his subordinates along with him.

The above characterstics of leadership hold good in any organisation—whether be it a business, political, religious or any other organisation.

6.4 Functions of Leadership

Leadership is an important factor for making an organisation successful. Without a good leader, an organisation cannot function efficiently and effectively. Since the organisation is basically a deliberate creation of human beings for attaining certain specified objectives, the activities of its members need to be directed in a definite way. Direction of activities in the organisation is effected by leadership.

The following are the important functions to be performed by a successful leader :

1. Initiating Action : A leader is the person who takes the initative in all those matters and activities which are needed to put into effect the objectives and programmes of the organisation.

2. Fostering Conviction : The leader interpretes, explains and brings home to the subordinates all those objectives, policies and programmes. He convinces them of their utility and appropriateness and rouses the active interest of the subordinates in them.

3. Providing Direction : A leader directs his subordinates to work for the accomplishment of the enterprise goals and objectives. By issuing clear, concise and complete orders and instructions, he presents his followers with a challenge which they take pride in meeting effectively.

4. Maintaining Discipline : Discipline is the force that prompts individuals to observe rules, regulations and procedures which are necessary for the attainment of objectives. A leader depends more on consistency of behaviour and impartial treatment to enforce discipline. He makes less use of penalties for the violation of regulations and focuses more on self-discipline.

5. Giving Inspiration : One of the major functions of managerial leadership is to create and sustain enthusiasm in his subordinates for the implementation of organisational goals and activities. A leader has to enthuse and inspire his subordinates for getting their best performance. If the subordinates are properly induced and stimulated, they would themselves strive to the utmost for the accomplishment of the enterprise goals.

6. Motivating the Employees : Motivation is necessary for work performance. The higher the motivation, the better would be the performance. A good leader, by exercising his leadership, motivates the employees for higher performance. Good leadership in the organisation itself is a motivating factor for the individuals. The manager exercising leadership in motivating his subordinates towards organisational goals should, therefore, try to determine the conditions or factors in the organisational situation that prompt a subordinate to put in his best efforts.

7. Creating Confidence : A good leader may create confidence in his followers by directing them, giving them advice and getting through them good results in the organisation. Once an individual with the help of a leader puts in high efficiency, he tries to maintain it as he requires certain level of confidence towards his capacity. Sometimes, individuals fail to recognise their qualities and capabilities to work in the absence of good direction. The leader can also win and maintain his subordinate's confidence in him by establishing his superiority in knowledge and ability to provide psychological support when needed.

8. Building Morale : Morale is expressed as attitudes of the employees towards the organisation, management and offering voluntary co-operation to reach the goal of the enterprise. High morale leads to high productivity and organisational stability. Through providing good leadership in the organisation, employee's morale can be raised high ensuring higher productivity and greater stability in the organisation.

As stated by **Drucker :** "Leadership is the lifting of a man's vision to higher sights, the raising of man's performance to a higher standard, the building of a man's personality beyond its normal limitations."

9. Representing the Group : A leader is the true representative of his followers—both to those working for the group as well as the outside world. He serves as their spokesman and guardian.

10. Creation of Work Environment : In order to obtain full co-operation and voluntary efforts of the subordinate employees, a leader has to create suitable work environment in the enterprise. In good work environment they are inspired to perform their jobs satisfactorily. It is a very important task of a leader.

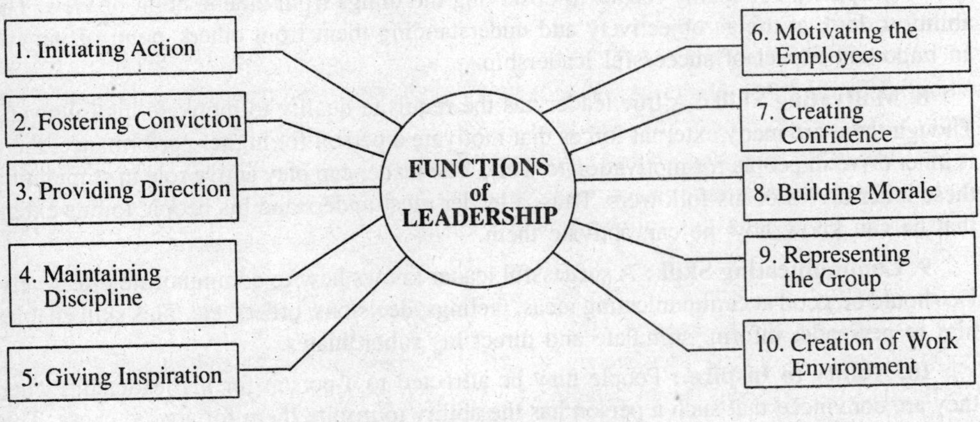

Fig. 6.1: Functions of Leadership.

A good leader has to perform the above funcions. Good leadership functions ensure success in the organisation, and unsatisfactory human performance in any organisation can be primarily attributed to poor leadership. In fact, there is no substitute for effective leadership.

6.5 Requisite Qualities of Good Leadership

Successful leadership calls for the highest physical, mental and emotional energy. The higher the position of the leader and greater his responsibility, the higher will be the expectation in terms of qualities of leadership. Generally, the following qualities are associated with the successful leaders :

1. Physical and Mental Strength : A leader has to put in hard physical and mental work. This requires tremendous physical stamina and mental energy to sustain long and irregular hours of work.

2. Intelligence : For leadership, higher level of intelligence is required. Intelligence is generally expressed in mental ability. The level of intelligence of a leader should be somewhat higher than prossessed by the followers.

3. Emotional Stability : A leader should have high level of emotional stability. He should not be unduly moved by emotion or sentiment. He should be able rationally to analyse the problems before him and reach a decision without any fear or favour. He should not lose his temper or show indecision even in the face of heavy odds. A good leader is self-confident and believes that he can meet most situations successfully.

4. Power of Judgement : A leader should be a master of human psychology. He should possess the skill of understanding human behaviour, emotions, sentiments, needs, motives, etc. This would enable him to anticipate the response to his decisions and actions.

5. Knowledge of Human Relations : A successful leader should have adequate knowledge of human relations, that is, how he should deal with human beings. Since an important part of a leader's job is to get the follower's voluntary co-operation for achieving work performance, he should have intimate knowledge of them and their relationship with each other.

6. Objectivity : Objectivity implies that what a leader does should be based on relevant facts and information. He must assess these without any bias or prejudice. The leader must base his relationship on this objectivity.

7. Empathy : Empathy relates to observing the things from others' point of view. The ability to look at things objectively and understanding them from others' point of view is an important aspect of successful leadership..

8. Motivating Skill : A true leader has the requisite quality to motivate his followers. Though there are many external forces that motivate a person for higher performance, there is inner drive in people for motivation to work. The leader can play active role in stimulating these inner drives of his followers. Thus, a leader must understand his people to this extent that he can know how he can activate them.

9. Communicating Skill : A successful leader knows how to communicate effectively. He should be good at communicating ideas, feelings, decisions, orders, etc. This skill enables him to persuade, inform, stimulate and direct his subordinates.

10. Ability to Inspire : People may be attracted to a person for his leadership when they are convinced that such a person has the ability to inspire them for a good cause. This confidence arises if they feel that he fully understands their problems, knows what to do to solve them, and is doing everything possible to help them and protect their interests.

11. Technical Competence : A leader should possess a thorough knowledge of the theory and practice of his jobs. The ability to plan, organise, delegate, analyse, make decisions, control and win co-operation requires the use of important qualities which constitute technical skill of leadership. The various technical competence of a leader may win support from the followers.

12. Sense of Responsibility : A leader should always be aware of his duties and responsibilities. When authority of performance is delegated to a leader it is his responsibility to get the works accomplished by his subordinates through exercising his authority over them. Consciousness about responsibility is an essential quality of a good leader.

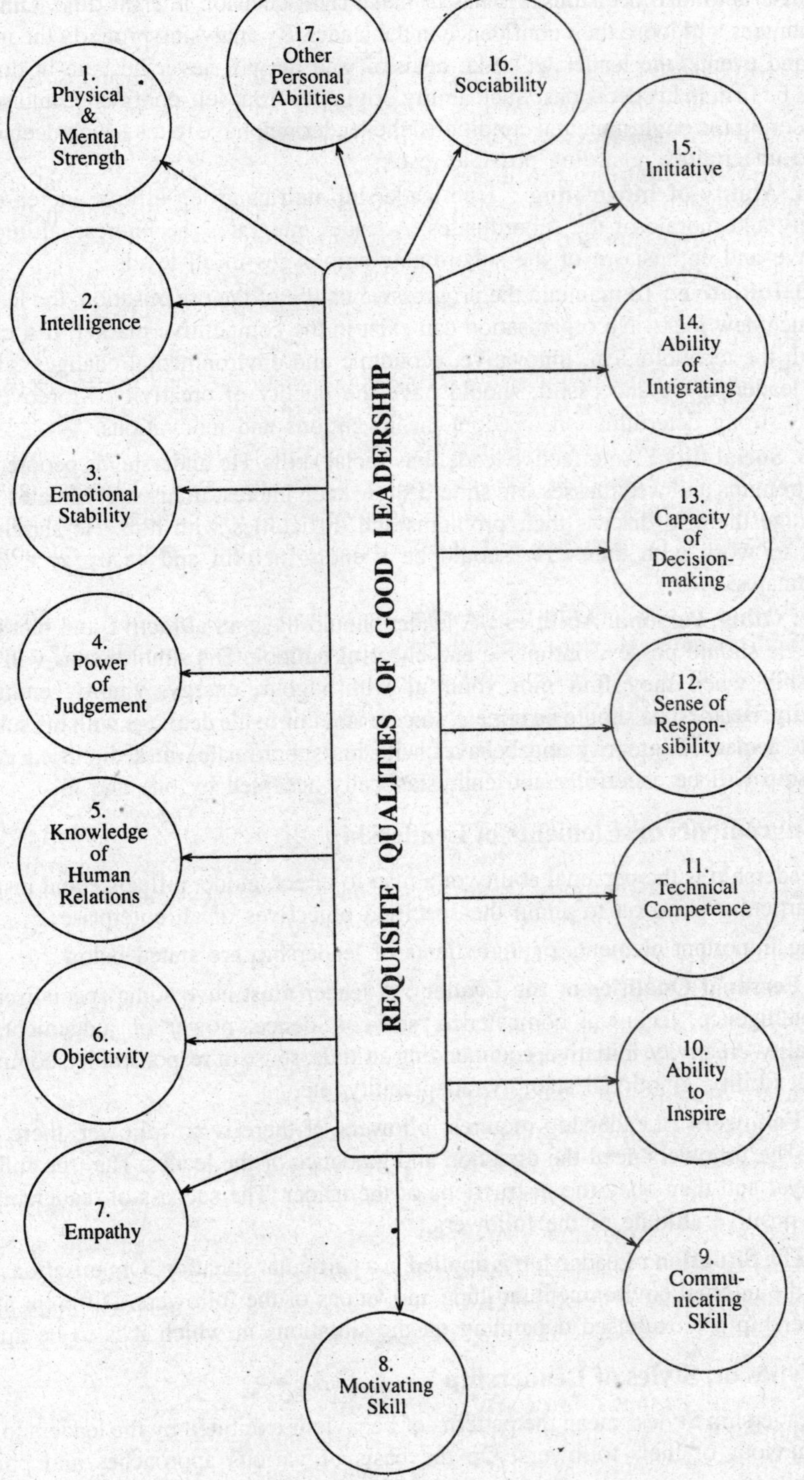

Fig. 6.2: Requisite Qualities of Good Leadership.

13. Capacity of Decision-making : The most important task of a leader in a business enterprise is to take decisions. He has to make right decision in right time. Otherwise, the subordinates will loose their confidence in the leader. By analysing properly the information facts and events, the leader will take decision and he will never hesitate in doing so. He should be firm in his decisions. Such ability originates from self-confidence and self-control Considering the environmental conditions, the leader will have to take such decision as there lies no uncertainty regarding possible results.

14. Ability of Integrating : True leadership unifies group efforts, increases working capacity and morale of the subordinates. A leader integrates the interest, attitude, motive initiative and enthusiasm of the subordinate employees in all levels.

15. Initiative : To maintain the progressive nature of the organisation, the leader should introduce new ideas. No organisation can exist in the competitive market, if it cannot cope up with the technological, innovative, economic and environmental changes taking place So, a leader, to be successful, should have the quality of creativity. Moreover, he must possess strong determination to adopt the inventions and innovations.

16. Sociability : An effective leader has social skills. He understands people and knows their strengths and weaknesses. He should show keen interest in his subordinates. He should encourage them to discuss their problems and difficulties with him. He should have the ability to work with them. He should be friendly, helpful and easily accessible to his subordinates.

17. Other Personal Abilities : A leader should have an attractive and pleasing personality. He should possess optimistic and cheerful outlook. His subordinates will accept his leadership when they find him youthful with vigour, energy, vitality, endurance and creativity. Besides, he should be honest, sincere and fair in his dealings with his subordinates. If he is a man of integrity and behaves with his subordinates in a dignified manner, his leadership will be cheerfully and enthusiastically accepted by one and all.

6.6 Ingredients or, Elements of Leadership

Leadership is the personal ability of a man to direct, guide, influence and inspire others in a particular situation to attain the specified objectives of an enterprise.

The important elements or ingredients of leadership are stated below :

1. Personal Qualities of the Leader : A leader must have some specialised qualities like intelligence, technical competence, self-confidence, power of judgement, dynamic personality, creativity, initiative, commanding attitude, sense of responsibility, communicating skill, flexibility, emotional stability, adaptability, etc.

2. Followers : Leadership requires followers. If there is no follower, there can be no leader. The followers need the direction and guidance of the leader. The true followers are very loyal and they obey the instructions of the leader. The success of leadership depends on the positive attitude of the followers.

3. The Situation : Leadership is applied in a particular situation. Organisational situation means the internal environment, attitude and values of the followers. Different approaches of leadership are exercised depending on the situations in which it is to be applied.

6.7 Types or, Styles of Leadership

'Leadership Styles' mean the patterns of behaviour exhibited by the leaders to influence the behaviour of their followers. On the basis of various approaches and philosophies followed towards the subordinates, leadership may be classified into different types as follows :

According to motivation, leadership is of two types—(i) Positive leadership, and, (ii) Negative leadership.

1. Positive Leadership : 'Positive Leadership' is the pattern of behaviour of a leader which motivates the subordinates by increasing their satisfaction. A positive leader does not only issue orders; he explains the orders, ensures that his subordinates have requisite skills and tools for performing their jobs, and delegates them authority to carry out his orders. He allocates a fair work-load to his followers, assigns them the jobs they can perform, and recognises the jobs which are well done. A positive leader exercises power through people instead of power over people. Under positive leadership the subordinate employees strive to work willingly and give the highest co-operation in order to achieve the objectives of the enterprise.

2. Negative Leadership : 'Negative Leadership' means the type of leadership followed by a leader to motivate his followers through fear and insecurity by threatening. A negative leader acts dominantly as superior to people. To get the work done, he threatens the followers about losing their jobs, demotion, transfer, etc. He exercises authority over the subordinate employees by thus frightening them. He acts as the 'boss', not the 'leader'.

However, both positive and negative leadership get results. The difference between the two is that the former achieves the result with satisfaction of the subordinates; but latter gets so with their dissatisfaction.

Based on the basic approaches used by the leaders towards their followers, leadership may be classified as under :

(i) Autocratic or Authoritarian Leadership;

(ii) Bureaucratic Leadership;

(iii) Democratic or Participative Leadership; and

(iv) Free-rein or Laissez-faire Leadership.

The above types of leadership will be described in the following sections.

6.7.1 Autocratic or, Authoritarian Leadership

In 'Autocratic or Authoritarian Leadership', a leader centralises authority in himself and takes all decisions without consulting with the subordinates. There is no participation of them in decision making. They have to simply do what they are asked to do. An autocratic leader exercises complete control over the subordinates, dominates and drives them through issuing orders. He expects that they will follow his orders unquestioningly. He uses rewards and holds the threat of penalities to direct the subordinates. The autocratic leaders are usually thought of 'Pushers', like military instructors.

(A) Characteristics : The features of Autocratic Leadership are pointed out below :

1. An autocratic leader holds the whole authority and never delegates it to his subordinates.

2. The subordinates have no right to express their opinions.

3. They are to obey the orders of the leader.

4. The leader takes all decisions and the subordinates have only to implement those decisions.

5. Full control over the subordinates is applied by the leader.

6. Downward communication is followed in such type of leadership.

(B) Advantages : The advantages of Autocratic Leadership are the following :

1. Quick decision-making is possible because the decisions are taken only by the leaders.

2. It provides strong motivation to the leader.

3. Less competent subordinates can perform the activities of the enterprise as the subordinates are not to participate in making plans, organising and taking decisions.

4. Effective control is possible in such leadership style.

5. Unity of command is maintained because commands come from the autocratic leader.

(C) Disadvantages : The Autocratic Style of Leadership suffers from the following disadvantages :

1. The subordinates are not motivated in such type of leadership. It leads to frustration, low morale and conflict among the subordinates.

2. They do not like this leadership style as strict control and discipline are maintained.

3. They are not encouraged to do more work and are apt to neglect their responsibilities.

4. Full potential of them and their creative ideas are not utilised.

5. There is every possibility of wrong decision-making as the decision is taken solely by the leader.

6. The subordinates are more dependent on the leader and they get no opportunity for their own development. So, no leadership is created in future and the organisational continuity is threatened in the absence of the leader.

7. As the leader does not delegate authority to his followers, the benefits of delegation of authority cannot be enjoyed.

(D) Suitability : The Style of Autocratic Leadership may be appropriate when the subordinates are uneducated and unskilled. Lack of proper knowledge and experience on the part of the subordinates makes it necessary that the leader takes decisions himself. This style may also be desirable when the enterprise imposes punishment, penalities and fear as accepted disciplinary techniques.

6.7.2 Bureaucratic Leadership

'Bureaucratic Leadership' is also known as 'Rule-centred Leadership'. This style depends on the rules which specify the responsibilities and obligations of the subordinates. The rules direct them to perform particular jobs in definite ways. They have no right of participation in decision-making. The rules provide a specification of minimum level of acceptable performance on the part of the subordinates. So, the process of management is reduced by the rules to a series of routine mechanical actions.

Such type of leadership leads to workers' apathy. The subordinate workers may remain indifferent to the work, because they know just how minimum they have to do and still remain secured. The rules specify performance without participation, lead to red-tapeism and too much paper work. Bureaucratic leadership is generally followed in the government organisations.

6.7.3 Democratic, or, Participative Leadership

In 'Democratic Style of Leadership' or 'Participative Leadership', the leader takes decisions in consultation and participation with the subordinates. Such style is also called 'Consultative Leadership' or 'Group-centred Leadership'. A democratic leader decentralises authority and allows the subordinates to share his power. He largely relies on the involvement of all members of the group in setting the basic objectives of the group, establishing the strategies, and determining job assignments. He does what the group wants and follows the majority opinion. He provides freedom of thinking and expression. He listens to the suggestions, grievances and opinions of his subordinates.

(A) Characteristics : The nature or characteristics of Democratic Leadership Style are as follows :

1. The democratic leaders consult with their followers in making the decisions.

2. The authority is decentralised to the subordinates.

3. Two-way communication is followed here.

4. Creativity is developed among the subordinates.

5. A good relationship is established between the leader and the subordinates.

6. Importance is given on thinking and opinion of the subordinates.

7. Control is not very strict in such type of leadership.

(B) Advantages : The advantages of Democratic Leadership are stated as follows :

1. Democratic leadership provides job satisfaction and improves the morale of the subordinates. It ensures organisational stability.

2. The opinions, suggestions and recommendations of the subordinates are listened to and received for making decisions. They are motivated to work more for the enterprise in order to implement the decisions in which they participated.

3. The quality of decision is improved.

4. The subordinates share the responsibility of doing the job and achieving the objectives with the leader.

5. The subordinate employees are self-controlled. No external control is imposed on them. So, labour absenteeism and labour turnover are reduced.

6. This type of leadership develops positive attitude and reduces resistance to change.

7. Creative leadership is developed, as the subordinate employees are allowed to participate in the leadership process.

(C) Disadvantages : There are some limitations in Democratic Leadership Style. These are as follows :

1. Democratic style of leadership is time-consuming and it may result in delays in decision-making.

2. It requires considerable communicating and persuasive skills on the part of the leader.

3. Such leadership style cannot be applied in a complex organisational structure.

4. Some subordinates may have the mentality only to work under others. So, they do not work unless directed and controlled by others.

5. A large number of employees are reluctant to participate in the process of leadership.

6. As responsibility is not given properly and specifically, the subordinates may try to avoid responsibility.

7. Over a period of time the subordinates may develop the habit of expecting to be consulted on every issue and they may feel frustrated when they are not consulted in certain matters.

8. Consultation may interpret as a sign of incompetence on the part of the leader to deal with the problems.

(D) Suitability : Democratic Leadership is considered to be more effective than Autocratic Leadership Style. Democratic Style is more compatible with the prevailing value system which requires freedom of expression and independent thinking. However, the choice of leadership style depends on the immediate goal of the enterprise and the needs of the subordinates. If the immediate goal of the enterprise is to increase in productivity, or the subordinates have low need for independence, autocratic leadership may be followed. But when the goal is to provide job satisfaction to the employees and they have a high need for independence, democratic style may be more fruitful and effective. Democratic leadership is also appropriate where the leader really wants to share the decision-making with the subordinates and the subordinates have accepted the goal of the enterprise.

6.7.4 Free-rein or, Laissez-faire Leadership

'Free-rein or Laissez-faire' Style of Leadersip means giving complete freedom to the subordinates in decision-making. Such style involves complete delegation of authority to the subordinates so that they themselves take decisions. The free-rein leader avoids power and allows his followers to do what they want to do. He serves only as a 'contactor' to bring the information and resources needed by the subordinates. He is more or less passive and initiative is with the subordinates. This type of leadership can produce effective results if the subordinates are highly educated and experienced persons making sincere efforts to work with responsibility.

(A) Characteristics : The characteristics of Free-rein or Laissez-faire Leadership are stated as under. :

(i) Under this style of leadership, the subordinates take most of the decisions.

(ii) There is full delegation of autohority in such leadership.

(iii) Control process is liberal here.

(iv) There is freedom of expression of opinions of the subordinates. They do their work freely.

(v) The leader plays the role of an advisor. He does not give direction to his followers.

(vi) Open communication system is followed in such leadership style.

(B) Advantages : Free-rein Leadership Style has the following advantages :

(i) There is positive effect on job satisfaction and morale of the subordinates.

(ii) A good relationship is set up between the subordinates and the leader.

(iii) Full ultilisation of production capacity of the subordinates is possible and, as a result, productivity of the enterprise increases.

(iv) There is maximum possibility for development of the subordinates.

(C) Disadvantages : The followings are the problems of Free-rein Leadership Skill :

(i) In such leadership style, the subordinates do not get the guidance of the leader. The leader has no significant role to play.

(ii) It ignores the leader's contribution.

(iii) The subordinates may move in different directions and may work at cross-purposes which may lead to chaos.

(iv) There may be lack of co-ordination.

(v) In such style, the unity among the subordinates cannot be established in all cases. So, team-spirit cannot be developed.

(vi) As the subordinates enjoy more freedom, proper management is not possible.

(D) Suitability : Free-rein leadership style becomes appropriate in the organisation where the subordinate employees are highly educated, self-motivated, well-trained and ready to perform work with responsibility.

6.8 Tannenbaum and Schmidt's Behaviour Model of Leadership

Robert Tannenbaum and **Warrren H. Schmidt** developed the concept of 'Leadership Continuum' in order to highlight the range of possible leadership styles. The continuum moves from autocratic or 'boss-centred' leadership behaviour at one end to democratic or 'subordinate-centred' leadership behaviour as shown in Fig. 6.1 on the next page.

At the left end of the continuum is the autocratic leadership style while at the right end is the democratic leadership. As one moves from the left extreme to the right extreme, the degree of control goes down and the freedom of the subordinates goes up. The diagram shows that leadership includes a variety of styles, ranging from highly boss-centred to highly subordinate-centred. It varies with degree of freedom allowed by a leader to the subordinates. According to the concept of leadership continuum, an appropriate style of leadership depends on personalities and situations.

Different points (1, 2, 3 ... 7) in the diagram indicate different forms or types of leadership as stated below :

1. Manager makes decisions and announces it : This is an extreme form of autocratic leadership in which the boss takes the decision and orders the subordinates to implement it.

2. Manager sells the decision : In this type of leadership, the boss alone takes the decision and persuades the subordinates to accept it.

3. Manager presents ideas and invites questions : Such style involves greater participation of the subordinates. The boss arrives at the time of decision making and asks the subordinates to express their opinions on it.

4. Manager presents tentative decision subject to change : In this style the boss takes a tentative decision and modifies it in the light of the views expressed by the subordinates.

5. Manager presents problems, gets suggestions and takes decisions : Here the boss takes decisions after listening to the suggestions from the subordinates.

6. Manager defines the limits and asks the group to make decision : In this case the boss gives freedom to the subordinates to take decisions subject to the pre-determined limits.

7. Manager permits the subordinates to function within the limits defined by him : Under this type of leadership, full participation of the subordinates is involved. The boss defines the overall limits. The subordinates are free to decide and act within these limits.

The concept of the continuum leadership approach provides a wide range of leadership behaviours. It identifies alternative behaviours available to a manager and highlights the dynamic nature of leadership. It also proposes that the leadership style should be adapted to the needs for the particular situation.

While choosing the appropriate style of leadership, a manager should have to consider the following factors :

1. Forces Operating in the Managers Personality : These include the manager's value system, his confidence in the subordinates, his inclinations towards leadership and feeling safe in uncertain conditions.

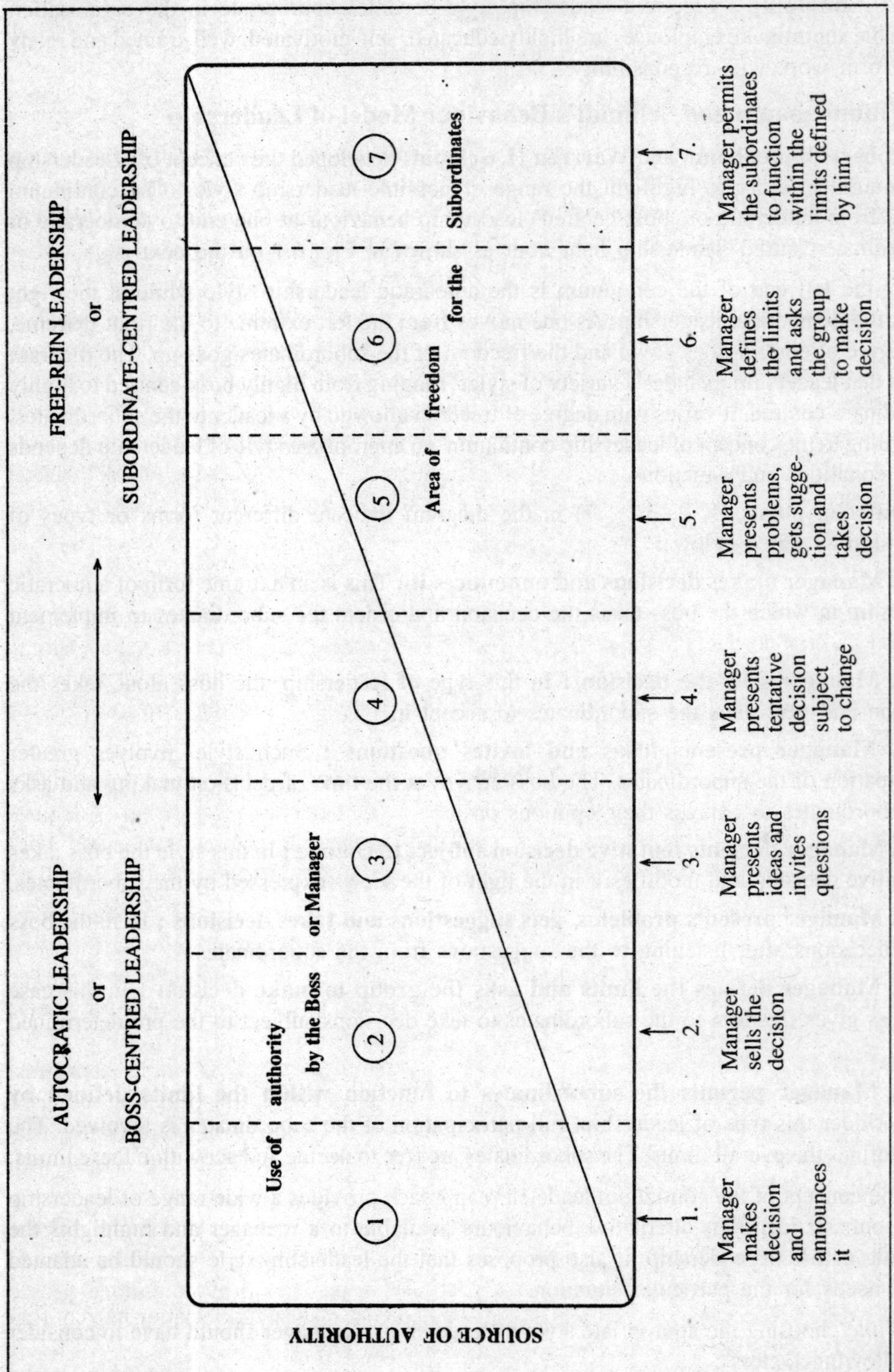

Fig. 6.3: Continuum Leadership Behaviour.

2. Forces Operating in the Subordinates : These forces are—the subordinates' need for freedom, their willingness to perform responsibility for decision-making, understanding of and interest in the problems, identification with and understanding of the organisational goals, and their experience with and expectations of leadership.

3. Forces in the Situation : These forces include the type of organisation, nature of the problems, effectiveness of the group, the pressure of time, etc.

6.9 Blake and Mouton's Managerial Grid

Blake and **Mouton** of the University of Texas developed a two-dimensional concept of leadership style called 'Managerial Grid'—built on the work of the Ohio State and Michigan Studies—to explain leadership behaviour. They pointed out that leadership style is a blend wherein task-oriented and relation-oriented behaviour are mixed in different degrees.

The two-dimensional model and five different types of leadership styles are shown in Fig. 6.4. on the next page. In the grid, the X-axis represents the 'concern for production' while the Y-axis represents the 'concern for people'. Concern for production means the managerial attitudes about the volume of output, procedures and efficiency of work, etc. And, concern for people refers to the degree of personal commitment, responsibility based on trust and satisfying inter-personal relations, self-esteem of the workers, etc. A manager is concerned with both the task and the people as he has to get things done through people.

The managerial grid identifies five combinations of these two factors. The five leadership styles are explained below :

1. Impoverished (1-1) Management Style : In this style, the manager shows less concern for both production and people. It implies the manager's less interest in the position. In this situation minimum effort is needed for getting the work done and sustaining organisation membership. The leader acts as an observer, avoiding controversy and confrontation.

2. Country Club (1-9) Management Style : Under this style the manager is highly concerned with the people. He tries to establish close personal relationship. Adequate attention to the needs of people leads to a comfortable organisation environment and work culture. The leader has maximum concern for people and minimum concern for production.

3. Middle of the Road (5-5) Management Style : In this case, the manager gives emphasis on both production and relationship with the people. Proper organisation performance is possible through balancing the necessity of getting work done through maintaining morale of the people at a satisfactory level. The leader balances tasks with concern for people through compromise.

4. Task (9-1) Management Style : In this situation, the manager is mainly concerned with production and has little concern for people. He gives emphasis on getting the tasks done to increase production. The task is well-planned and the authority is well-defined. This is the task-oriented, or autocratic style of leadership. The leader leads the people with instructions and discipline.

5. Team (9-9) Management Style : In this case, the manager has maximum concern for both production and people. This is the team leadership style in which the leader consults with his team and harmonise organisational goals. Work performed by committed people and inter-dependence through common organisational goals leads to the relationships of trust and respect. This style is considered to be the best leadership style.

Managerial grid approach helps the managers to identify their own leadership styles. It is a useful framework for assessing the styles of leadership. It has been used successfully in improving the attitudes and behaviour of people throughout an organisation. This approach is very popular among the managers. But it is highly controversial among the theorists who consider it to be only a tool, not a theory of leadership—because it lacks empiricical evidence. According to their opinion, it is an attitudinal and conceptual description of leadership. It does not point out the reason for failure of a manager in one part of the grid or the other.

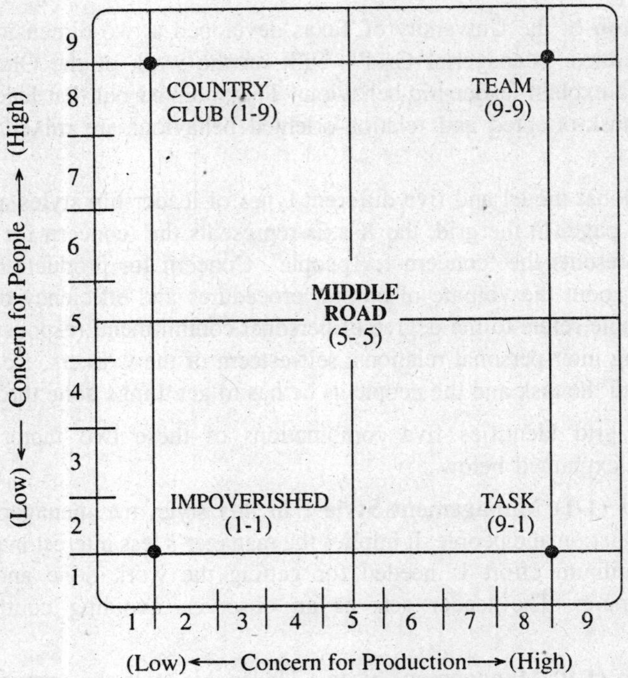

Fig. 6.4: The Managerial Grid Leadership Style.

6.10 Leadership and Management

'Leadership' is the process of directing, guiding and influencing the followers and establishing inter-personal relationship for achieving the objectives of an organisation. On the other hand, 'Management' is the process where some pre-determined goals are achieved to secure maximum output with minimum efforts and cost through planning, organising, directing, motivating, co-ordinating and controlling. In fact, there are several differences between Leadership and Management. These differences are described pointwise as follows :

1. Relationship : Management implies superior-subordinate relationship within a formal organisation. On the other hand, leadership can exist with or without formal organisation. The followers of a leader are not necessarily his juniors or subordinates. They may be the leader's peers, associates and even seniors.

2. Sources of Influence : A manager obtains authority from his position. He uses his formal authority to influence the behaviour of his subordinates. But, a leader derives his power from his followers who accept him as their leader. A leader utilises this power to influence the attitude and behaviour of his followers.

3. Accountability : A manager is accountable for his own behaviour as well as for the job behaviour of his subordinates. His accountability for performance is clearly defined. But there is no clear-cut accountability in leadership. A manager has to achieve the organisational goals, but, a leader is more concerned with the group goals and the satisfaction of the followers.

4. Basis of Following : Both the managers and the leaders have followers. But the people follow them for different reasons. People follow a manager because they are required to follow by the job description supported by a system of rewards and penalties. On the other hand, people follow a leader on voluntary basis. A manager may continue in office so long as his performance is considered to be satisfactory, whereas a leader can survive as long as the followers accept him.

5. Functions : A manager has to perform the functions of planning, organising, directing, motivating, co-ordinating and controlling. But the main job of a leader is to guide and inspire the effors of his followers. Leadership is one aspect of directing. All managers should have the quality of leadership, but leadership may exist without being a manager. The managers formulate broad policies to guide the operations of the enterprise. And, leadership initiates the actions for implementation of the objectives of the enterprise.

"A leader need not be a manager, but a manager must have many of the qualities of a good leader". This statement has two features. Firstly, a leader need not be appointed or elected. He can be successful if people accept his leadership whole-heartedly. Secondly, a manager can become more successful if he possesses the quality of leadership. With the help of his formal authority, he can obtain only average or ordinary performance from his employees. But with leadership qualities he can arouse co-operation and compliance beyond the level of normal duty. To secure outstanding work performance from his subordinates a manager requires his acceptance by his subordinates. Ability to lead is one of the requirements for becoming an effective manager. So, a manager must acquire leadership qualities.

EXERCISES

[A] Essay-Type Questions

1. Define 'Leadership'. Discuss the needs for leadership.
[**Ans.** Sections 6.1 and 6.2]

2. Explain the role of leadership in business. [C.U. B.Com. 1987]
[**Ans.** Section 6.2]

3. State the qualities of leadership.
[**Ans.** Section 6.5]

4. Describe the functions of leadership.
[**Ans.** Section 6.4.]

5. Discuss the features of leadership.
[**Ans.** Section 6.3]

6. Discuss the different ingredients of good leadership. [C.U. B.Com. 2002]
[**Ans.** Section 6.5]

7. Define leadership. Explain its imporance in management. [C.U. B.Com. 2003]
[**Ans.** Sections 6.1. and 6.2]

8. Discuss the elements of a good leadership. [C.U. B.Com. 2005]
[**Ans.** Section 6.5.]

9. (a) Explain briefly the concept of 'Leadership'. (b) Discuss the theory of leadership as propounded by Tannenbaum and Schmidt. [C.U. B.Com. 2005]
[**Ans.** Section 6.8]

10. Discuss the role of a Manager as a Leader. [C.U. B.Com. 2006]
[**Ans.** Section 6.10]

11. (a) What do you mean by 'Leadership Style'?
(b) Discuss the theory of 'Managerial Grid' as propounded by Blake and Mouton with suitable diagram. [C.U. B.Com. 2006]
[**Ans.** Sections 6.7 and 6.9]

12. What do you mean by qualities of leadership? Discuss different styles of leadership. [C.U. B.Com. 2008]
[**Ans.** Sections 6.5 and 6.7]

13. Explain the importance of leadership in management. [C.U. B.Com. 2009]
[**Ans.** Section 6.2]

14. Narrate the differences between 'Management' and 'Leadership'. Write a note on leadership styles. [C.U. B.Com. 2010]
[**Ans.** Sections 6.10 and 6.7]

15. How many types of Leadership may be there? Discuss the advantages and disadvantages of various types of Leadership. [C.U. B.Com. 2011]
[**Ans.** Sections 6.7, 6.7.1, 6.7.2, 6.7.3 and 6.7.4.]

16. Explain the Leadership Model of Tannenbaum and Schmidt. [C.U. B.Com. 2011]
[**Ans.** Section 6.8.]

17. Narrate, in detail, the importance and types of Leadership. [C.U. B.Com. 2011 New Syllabus]
[**Ans.** Sections 6.2. and 6.7.]

[B] Short Answer-Type Questions

1. **Write short notes on the following:**
(i) Leadership.
[**Ans.** Section 6.1]
(ii) Importance of leadership.
[**Ans.** Section 6.2]
(iii) Nature of leadership.
[**Ans.** Section 6.3]
(iv) Essential qualities of leadership.
[**Ans.** Section 6.5]

2. **Answer briefly the following questions:**
(i) What do you understand by 'Leadership' in management? [C.U. B.Com. 1992, 2006]
[**Ans.** Section 6.1]
(ii) Point out any four qualities of successful leadership.
[**Ans.** Section 6.5]
(iii) Briefly state the significance of leadership in management. [C.U. B.Com. 1984]
[**Ans.** Section 6.2]
(iv) Mention various styles of leadership. [C.U. B.Com. 1994]
[**Ans.** Section 6.7]

(v) What are the elements of leadership? [C.U. B.Com. 2007]
[**Ans.** Section 6.6]

(vi) What are the characteristics of democratic or participative leadership? [C.U. B.Com. 2008]
[**Ans.** Section 6.7.3]

(vii) Mention any four qualities of a good leadership. [C.U. B.Com. 2009]
[**Ans.** Section 6.5]

(viii) Is a manager always a leader? Justify your answer. [C.U. B.Com. 2006]
[**Ans.** Section 6.10]

(ix) Define 'Leading'. [C.U. B.Com. 2011]
[**Ans.** Section 6.1]

CHAPTER 7

Co-ordination

"Co-ordination is orderly arrangement of group efforts to provide unity of action in the pursuit of common goals." —Mooney and Reiley

TOPICS

Subject-matter of the Chapter : *Co-ordination is the managerial function of integrating all the group actions in an enterprise in order to attain its pre-determined common objectives. It is a process by which the managers achieve harmonious group efforts and unity of action through balancing the activities of all employees in different departments, divisions, sections, units etc.*

The effectiveness of co-ordination depends highly upon the co-operation of the employees. Co-operation refers to the collective efforts directed for the accomplishment of some work by a group of persons.

In this chapter the meaning and characteristics of co-ordination, its role in management, the principles and techniques of co-ordination and various aids to co-ordination have been discussed. In this respect the relation between co-ordination and co-operation has also been clearly explained.

7.1 Meaning of Co-ordination

Co-ordination is very essential in management. Business has various functions. These functions are performed by different individuals. Moreover, performance of these functions requires division of work and grouping of activities and making decisions at different levels. All these necessitate co-ordination for attaining the desired goals.

Co-ordination is concerned with synchronising, integrating or unifying all the group actions in an enterprise to achieve its objectives. It is a process by which the manager achieves harmonious group efforts and unity of actions through balancing the activities of different individuals and groups of individuals and reconciling their differences in interest or approach, for the attainment of common goals. In the words of **Mcfarland**, "Co-ordination is the process whereby an executive develops an orderly pattern of group efforts among his subordinates and secures unity of actions in the pursuit of a common purpose."

In an organisation, a number of persons work and every individual work is related with others. Since all persons in the organisation contribute to the same end result, their contributions should be maximum. Therefore, it is the task of the manager to put together all the group efforts of the enterprise, and harmonise them carefully so as to give them commonness of purpose. This managerial function is known as 'co-ordination'. He is to ensure that everybody in the organisation understands the main objectives of the enterprise and works towards their fulfilment in active co-operation with others. Co-ordination is like the team spirit of a football match or the harmonious symphony of an orchestra. In a football match, the individual players may be good at games and may put forth their best efforts to win the match. But unless there is team spirit and co-operative efforts, the game may not be won. Similarly, in an orchestra, everyone may be excellent instrumentalists, but their individual work may take the turn of a disorder, if they are allowed to play on their instruments independently. It is the duty of the captain of the team and the conductor of the orchestra group to maintain team spirit and unity of action for perfect harmony. So the function of co-ordination is also to maintain this unity of action among the workers in order to realise the business objectives. Co-ordination eliminates conflict between the head office and branches as well as between departments of an organisation and removes difficulty in communication. Instead of regarding co-ordination as a separate function of management, it must be considered as the essence of management.

7.2 Features of Co-ordination

The principal featuress of co-ordination may be stated as follows :

1. Co-ordination is concerned with the integration of group efforts and not individual effort. It involves the orderly arrangement of the activities of a group of people. However, individual performance is related to the group performance. Co-ordination makes the individual efforts integrated with the total process.

2. Co-ordination is the concerted efforts of requisite quality and quantity given at the proper time. In other words, co-ordination denotes co-operation i.e. collective efforts, plus time element and direction element. According to **Haimann** : "Co-ordination is the orderly synchronisation of efforts of the subordinates to provide the proper amount, timing and quality of execution so that their unified efforts lead to the stated objective, namely the common purpose of the enterprise."

3. Co-ordination is a continuous and dynamic process. It is a continuous concept in the sense that it is achieved through the performance of functions. And it is dynamic in nature because the functions themselves are dynamic and may change over the period of time.

4. Co-ordination has three important elements, namely, balancing, timing and integrating. Co-ordination of different activities becomes possible only when different duties are performed in the right time and in the right quantity. As for example, if the purchase department of an enterprise buys the required raw material in right time and in right quantity and supplies them to the production department, the production department produces the commodities in right time and in proper quantity; and the sales department of the enterprise can execute the order placed by a customer within the specified time.

5. The task of co-ordination and co-operation do not mean the same thing. Co-operation simply means that two or more persons are associated voluntarily in the performance of some work through collective efforts. But it has no bearing with time, amount and direction-dimensions in group efforts. In contrast, co-ordination implies application of requisite amount of group efforts in the right time at the right direction through deliberate executive action.

6. Co-ordination is the responsibility of every manager in the organisation, because he tries to synchronise the efforts of his subordinates with others.

7. Co-ordination, as a blending factor of all activities and efforts, is to be exercised both within and outside the enterprise. That is to say, **co-ordination may be internal and external.** Internal co-ordination means the co-ordination of activities between the employees, between the departments and managers at different levels inside the enterprise. Outside the enterprise, the work of co-ordination is extended to bring about a harmonious relationship with the activities of the competitors, suppliers and customers; the technological and technical advances of the time, the regulatory measures of the government, the national and inter-national inter-dependence as well as with the wishes and wants, likes and dislikes of the consumers, employees and owners.

8. Co-ordination may be horizontal and vertical. Horizontal co-ordination refers to co-ordination between the horizontal departments of the same level in the managerial hierarchy. For example, co-ordination is necessary between the sales manager, works manager, finance manager and the buyer, so that when the sales department is ready to sell the new product, the production department will be in a position to fill the orders; and the financial arrangements have been made so that the necessary funds are available to have the suitable raw material and other factors. Co-ordination of various functions between the independent managers calls for a greater ability on the part of the superior manager. He has to ensure greater understanding between the departmental managers so that they may co-operate.

On the other hand, vertical co-ordination takes place between the various links of the different levels of the organisation. For example, take the case of production department where we have the works manager, and under him the superintendent and then the foreman, and, lastly, the workmen. In this situation, the activities assigned to the different levels must be co-ordinated. This vertical co-ordination is secured by delegating authority, together with the means and manner of directing, supervising and controlling.

7.3 Importance or, Necessity of Co-ordination

Co-ordination is regarded nowadays as the essence of management function. Need for co-ordination arises out of the fact that different elements and efforts of an organisation are to be harmonised and unified to achieve the common objectives. Without proper co-ordination among all the members of a group, management cannot bring together the diverse elements into one harmonious whole. Its significance can be indicated by pointing out its importance or necessity in the following points :

1. Co-ordination is necessary to ensure harmonious and smooth working of an enterprise with its several departments, divisions or subdivisions. For example, to ensure harmonious functioning of an organisation, it is essential that the functions of purchasing, production and sales departments are co-ordinated. If the sales manager procures a huge order to be executed within a specified time, without reference to the production manager and the purchasing manager, it may turn out that the goods cannot be produced in quantities ordered within the specified time.

Therefore, the inter-relationship among the functioning of purchase department, production department and sales department demands the establishment of co-ordination. According to **Henry Fayol** : "to co-ordinate is to harmonise all the activities of a concern to facilitate its working and its success."

2. Co-ordination ensures unity in direction in the midst of diversified activities. By bringing together the different divisions and parts into oneness of the enterprise, co-ordination enables the management authority to see the enterprise as one unified whole from its different segments.

So, co-ordination is necessary to link the functions of different departments, divisions, sections and the like together and assure their contribution to total result.

3. Co-ordination removes the conflict between personal interest of the employees and general interest of the organisation. Individuals join the organisation to fulfil their needs. Many times, these needs may be different from the group needs and goals. In such situations, organisational and individual goals are not fully achieved. More the number of individuals in an organisation, the higher will be the degree of such incompatibility.

It is essential for the organisational efficiency that both these goals are brought to a level of conformity, and the managers tries to integrate the individual and group goals through co-ordination.

4. Co-ordination can produce something greater out of the collective efforts of the individuals. Properly co-ordinated group efforts achieve a greater result than what is possible from the isolated efforts of the individuals.

5. Co-ordination provides a balance between the people of different capacities and abilities. It compensates the shortcomings of one by the strength of the other.

6. Co-ordination reconciles the impact of internal and external forces in the organisation and ensures smooth running of affairs. Internally, it combines the various resources of the business—money, materials, machinery and methods—for the attainment of common goals of the organisation. Externally, the environment is made more favourable to the business by giving due consideration to customers, employees, financiers and the government. In this manner, co-ordination helps in producing better results and becomes the essence of management.

7. Besides simplification of the organisation process, **co-ordination harmonises and integrates the different programmes and policies of the business**. Well-planned methods of co-ordination not only strengthen supervision but ensures voluntary co-operation of the different members of the group.

8. Co-ordination is a basic element in all effective organisations and is said to be the first principle in organisation. It makes planning more purposeful, organisation more well-knit and control more regulated.

7.4 Principles of Co-ordination

For achieving effective co-ordination, the following fundamental principles are to be followed :

1. Direct Contact : Co-ordination should be attained by direct contact with the parties concerned. Direct personal communications bring about agreement on methods, actions and ultimate achievement. It also eliminates red-tapeism and ensures prompt action. Direct contact is an effective means of co-ordination.

2. Early Beginning : Co-ordination can be achieved more readily at the initial stages of planning and policy-making. Therefore, direct contact must begin in the very early stages of the process. If an order for the supply of a particular goods has been booked and the raw materials to produce them are not available, there will be trouble. Contact among the purchasing manager, production manager and sales manager at an early stage would have made it possible to know whether the order could be executed.

3. Continuity : Co-ordination must be maintained as a continuous process. It starts from planning and ends when the objective is accomplished. Whenever there is division and distribution of functions among the managers and departments, co-ordination is necessary. Every time a new situation arises, a fresh effort of co-ordination is needed. So, the manager must constantly work at it until the purpose is served.

4. Reciprocal Relationship : Co-ordination should be regarded as a reciprocal relating to all factors in a situation, viz. production, sales, finance, men, and management. For example, when 'P' works with 'Q' and 'Q', in turn, works with 'R' and 'S', each of the four finds himself influenced by the others.

5. Pervasiveness : Co-ordination is an all-embracing activity in every management function. It is required in all the activities at every level of the organisation. It is to be exercised both within and outside the organisation.

6. Leadership : Leadership is the most effective instrument of co-ordination. A leader in a group is the co-ordinator of the group activities. He harmonises all efforts of persons in the group. A manager does not himself produce anything nor does he sell anything in the market. He gets the commodities produced by the workers and gets them sold in the market by the salesmen. In fact, he provides leadership and co-ordinates various functions.

7. Timing : Timing is an important element of co-ordination. This principle points out that all functions in the enterprise are to be done at the same time and at the same speed. If the purchase department purchases and supplies materials timely to the production department, and if the production is done timely, then the sales department can deliver the commodities to the customers within the scheduled time.

8. Balancing : This principle refers to the quantitative element of co-ordination. It means that all works are to be done in right quantity. For instance, if a department produces half, another one-third and the third the full quantity, their activities cannot be balanced. They have to perform their job in right quantity for achieving co-ordination of their jobs.

9. Integrating : All activities, decisions and opinions are to be integrated to achieve the enterprise objective. For integration what is necessary is that all men and departments must perform their jobs at the right time. For example, if all the parts of a machine are manufactured by the different departments at the right time, they can be assembled within the specific time. Assembling the parts of the machine is a co-ordinating function.

7.5 Techniques of Effective Co-ordination

The following measures or techniques have to be adopted in practice as tools for securing better co-ordination in the working of an organisation :

1. Simplified Organisation : In large organisations, there is a tendency towards over-specialisation. The organisation gets divided into a whole series of units each one of which concentrates just on its own task. In fact, each unit tends to be bureaucratic and its activities become ends in themselves instead of being means to the overall ends of the organisation. This creates problems of co-ordination. The remedy for this lies in placing the closely-related functions and operations under the charge of an executive who functions as a co-ordinator. Re-arrangement of departments may also be considered to bring about a greater deal of harmony among the various wings of the organisation. Furthermore, clear-cut organisation structure and procedures that are well-known to all concerned will ensure co-ordination. Organisational procedures should cover all activities and each person must be given to understand what he is responsible for and how his work is related to that of other individuals.

2. Harmonised Programmes and Policies : The ideal time to bring about co-ordination is at the planning stage. The plans prepared by different individuals or divisions should be checked up to ensure that they all fit together into an integrated and balanced whole. The co-ordinating executive must ensure that all the plans add up to a unified programme. Moreover, co-ordinated activities must not only be consistent with each other, but also be performed at the proper time.

3. Well-designed Methods of Communication : Good communication brings about proper co-ordination and helps the members of a business organisation to work together. Flow of communication in all directions will facilitate co-ordination and smooth working of the enterprise. The use of formal tools like orders, reports and working papers, and informal devices like the grapevine will provide adequate information to all concerned. Continuous, clear and meaningful communication provides every member with a clear understanding of the nature and scope of his work as well as that of other persons whose responsibilities are related to him. This aids the executives in co-ordinating the efforts of the members of their teams.

4. Special Co-ordinators : Generally, in big organisations, special co-ordinators are appointed. They normally work in staff capacity to facilitate the working of the main managers. A co-ordination cell may also be created. The basic responsibility of the cell is to collect the relevant information and to send this to various heads of sections or departments so that inter-departmental work and relationship are co-ordinated.

5. Co-ordination by Committees : Co-ordination in management by committees is achieved through meetings and conferences. Sometimes different committees are appointed to look after different areas of management, namely, Purchase Committee, Production Committee, Sales Committee, Finance Committee, etc. These committees take the group decision by exchanging their views and ideas and so it has co-ordinating elements.

6. Group Discussion : Group discussion is the other tool for co-ordination. It provides opportunities for free and open exchange of views and inter-change of ideas, problems, proposals and solutions. Face-to-face communication enables the members to attain improved understanding of organisation-wide matters and leads to better co-ordination.

7. Voluntary Co-ordination : In ideal conditions, co-ordination should take place through voluntary co-operation of the members. The basic principle of voluntary co-ordination is the modification of functioning of a department in such a way that each department co-ordinates with other departments. Each department or section or individual affects others and is also affected by others. Therefore, if those departments, sections or individuals apply a method of working which facilitates others, voluntary co-ordination is achieved. This can be done by horizontal communication.

8. Co-ordination through Supervision : The supervising executives have an important part to play in co-ordinating the work of their subordinates. Where the work-load of an executive is so heavy that he cannot find adequate time for co-ordination, staff assistants may be employed. They may recommend to the senior official the action that he may take for ensuring co-ordination.

The cardinal principle involved in co-ordination is the balancing and keeping together the different activities for a well-knit aggregate function, and its effectiveness depends upon satisfactory delegation of authority, sharing of responsibilities and accountability, and proper supervision—keeping in view the oneness of the organisation.

7.6 Co-ordination and Co-operation

'Co-operation' and 'Co-ordination' are the two vital pillars of any form of business organisation. These two go hand in hand and one without the other is like a boat without a rudder. So, in business they should move together and one without the other is fatal. How they are inter-related and inter-linked will be clear from the following discussion :

'**Co-operation**' denotes collective efforts directed for the accomplishment of some work when two or more persons are engaged voluntarily to do that work. Collective efforts are needed and is of paramount importance when a particular job cannot be performed by the efforts of a single individual. Desired result is achieved through co-operation of all the members of the group.

On the other hand, '**Co-ordination**' is a process of arranging the activities in relation to time, place and effort that each will be taken care of according to the needs of the situation. It implies putting together all the efforts of the enterprise, carefully unified and blended so as to give them a commonness of purpose.

But co-ordination should not be confused with co-operation. Though there is much similarity in the two terms, they denote different meanings and one cannot be substituted for the other. The basic points of difference between the two may be identified as follows :

1. Co-operation is mere willingness of individuals to help each other. It is, mostly the result of voluntary attitudes on the part of the members in an organisation. Co-ordination, on the other hand, cannot voluntarily be produced by the co-operating persons. An example may be cited to illustrate this point. A boy intending to catch an early morning train sets his watch ahead by 15 minutes before going to bed. His father, knowing his son's desire went to his son's bedroom and turned the watch up by another 15 minutes so that his son may not be put in a hurry to catch the train. Likewise, his mother also repeated the same act. Consequently, the boy got up 45 minutes before and lost the much needed sleep by 30 minutes. In this case, there was co-operation among the son, father and mother but no co-ordination. So, in a given situation, co-opertaion may exist without co-ordination.

2. By means of co-ordinating process, the executive directs the efforts of the subordinates of the organisation in such a way that the total result is a co-ordinated result. For example, take the problem of five men trying to push a car out of mud. No matter how strong and active their desire to co-operate may be, only co-ordinated effort inspired by the leader's signal will move the car out of its position. Thus, co-operation is a valuable element in co-ordination but cannot be a substitute for it.

3. Co-ordination means integration and harmonisation of different activities. But co-operation does not refer to integration of activities and timing and balancing factors. Balancing, timing and combining are, therefore, essential and indispensable elements of co-ordination.

When two or more persons are engaged to do a particular job by collective efforts, they are said to be co-operating with each other. But it will not be called co-ordination unless the collective efforts of requisite quality and quantity are given at the right time and proper place according to the situation.

4. The basic principles of co-ordination consist of direct contact, early start, continuity of efforts, and reciprocal relations among the persons whose efforts are to be co-ordinated. On the other hand, the basic principles of co-operation include voluntary association, democratic process in performance of activities, common welfare and a spirit of dedication and service with absolute honesty.

In spite of the differences between the two, that they are inter-connected will be more evident and clear if their relation is analysed under the following points :

(i) Co-operation is the foundation on which the structure of co-ordination is built.

(ii) Co-ordination cannot be achieved unless there is co-operation.

(iii) Co-ordination rotates round the co-operation and gets necessary nourishment.

(iv) Co-operation among parts brings about co-ordination of the whole.

Thus, co-operation and co-ordination are essential accompaniments in sound management. Without co-operation there cannot be any co-ordination. They are inter-linked and inter-woven. So, in business, "co-operation without co-ordination, or vice versa, is fatal."

7.7 Aids to Co-ordination

In order to make the process of co-ordination effective, the various techniques and principles should be rightly applied. For proper implementation of those techniques and principles some assistance, convenience, infrastructure, favourable environment, or, in other words, aids are essential. These aids to co-ordination are pointed out below :

1. Unfolding of the Objectives : The blue print of the pre-determined objectives of the enterprise and the means of their realisation should be given to each employee. As a result, the employees can become aware of their duties and responsibilities and at the same time feel the importance of co-ordination.

2. Definite Policy and Procedure : If the policies and procedures are definite, the task of co-ordination becomes easy. Because, if all employees work in accordance with the definite policy and procedure there is less possibility of hampering co-ordination.

3. Sound Management Process : If the other functions of management—planning, organising, directing controlling, etc. are properly accomplished, the work of co-ordinating will proceed on naturally.

4. Proper Organisation Structure : The organisation structure of the enterprise should be strongly built up so that the activities and responsibilities of the different departmental heads become clear and definite and co-operative relationship among them is established. As a result, the task of co-ordination becomes easy and simple.

5. Good Communication : Prompt and direct communication system is a very important aid to effective co-ordination. In order to convey information relating to the problems of business, the means of their solution and the decision of the management authority in this respect to all employees in right time, easy and proper communication system is essential. Thus, good communication is the key to effective co-ordination.

6. Favourable Attitude of the Managers : The attitude of the managers of an enterprise towards the subordinate employees should be helpful for effective co-ordination. If the managers realise the importance of good relationship between them and the subordinates, and take initiative for creating proper environment accordingly, the work of co-ordination is sure to become easier.

7. Committee System : To make co-ordination fruitful the representative committee should be formed in various areas and levels of operation. If the responsibilities of formulating policies and supervision are delegated to these committees, it may become highly effective for proper co-ordination.

8. Regular Discussion : Regular discussion on various problems of the enterprise among the managers of different levels should be made through holding formal or informal meeting. This removes misunderstanding, disorderly condition and lack of uniformity.

9. Informal Personal Contact of the Manager : If the manager meets the subordinates to discuss informally their problems, wants, grievances, etc. and makes necessary arrangement to remove them, it helps the task of co-ordination.

10. Special Supervision : If special supervisor is employed to supervise the activities of an enterprise according to its nature and responsibility, co-ordination becomes more effective. Such supervisors observe the work of co-ordination in different departments and take remedial measures where there is any lack of co-ordination.

11. Checking and Inspection : There should be provision for adequate checking and inspection to know where the problem of co-ordination exists and what are the factors for such problems. Such provision assists in solving the problems of co-ordination.

EXERCISES

[A] Essay-Type Questions

1. Explain the meaning of co-ordination. Discuss the role of co-ordination in business management.
   [**Ans.** Sections 7.1 and 7.3]
2. Discuss the importance of co-ordination in business management.
   [**Ans.** Section 7.3]
3. Describe the principles of co-ordination.
   [**Ans.** Section 7.4]
4. Give an account of various techniques of co-ordination.
   [**Ans.** Section 7.5]
5. Discuss the features of co-ordination.
   [**Ans.** Section 7.2]
6. "In business, co-operation without co-ordination, or vice versa, is fatal"—Discuss the statement.
   [**Ans.** Section 7.6]
7. (a) What is co-ordination?
   (b) "Co-ordination is the essence of management."—Discuss.
   [C.U. B.Com. 1998, 2005]
   [**Ans.** Section 7.3]
8. What is co-ordination? Discuss its principles and techniques. [C.U. B.Com. 1996]
   [**Ans.** Sections 7.1, 7.4 and 7.5]
9. Explain the different techniques of co-ordination. [C.U. B.Com. 1994]
   [**Ans.** Section 7.5]
10. Define co-ordination. Discuss its importance. [C.U. B.Com. 1993]
    [**Ans.** Sections 7.1 and 7.3]
11. Define co-ordination. Discuss the major principles of co-ordination.
    [C.U. B.Com. 1993]
    [**Ans.** Sections 7.1 and 7.4]

12. Discuss briefly the principal techniques of co-ordination in management. [C.U. B.Com. 2000, 2002, 2003, 2005]

[**Ans.** Section 7.5]

13. What is meant by co-ordination in management? Briefly discuss its principles. [C.U. B.Com. 2004]

[**Ans.** Sections 7.1 and 7.4]

14. Discuss the basic principles for effective co-ordination in an organisation. [C.U. B.Com. 2006]

[**Ans.** Section 7.4]

15. State the importance of co-ordination. [C.U. B.Com. 2008]

[**Ans.** Section 7.3]

16. Explain, in brief, the various techniques of co-ordination. [C.U. B.Com. 2009]

[**Ans.** Section 7.5]

17. (a) "Co-ordination is the essence of management".—Discuss.

(b) Discuss the principles of effective co-ordination. [C.U. B.Com. 2010]

[**Ans.** Sections 7.1 and 7.5]

18. Discuss the various aids to co-ordination.

[**Ans.** Section 7.7]

[B] Short Answer-Type Questions

1. Write short notes on the following:

(i) Importance of co-ordination.

[**Ans.** Section 7.3]

(ii) Co-operation and co-ordination.

[**Ans.** Section 7.6]

2. Distinguish between co-ordination and co-operation.

[**Ans.** Section 7.6] [C.U. B.Com. 1988]

3. Explain the term 'co-ordination'.

[**Ans.** Section 7.1]

4. Answer the following questions briefly:

(i) What is meant by co-ordination in management? [C.U. B.Com. 1990, 1992]

[**Ans.** Section 7.1]

(ii) Mention any four principles of co-ordination. [C.U. B.Com. 2007, 2009]

[**Ans.** Section 7.4]

(iii) What is 'co-operation'?

[**Ans.** Section 7.6]

(iv) What is the distinction between co-ordination and co-operation?

[**Ans.** Section 7.6]

(v) Point out any four techniques of co-ordination.

[**Ans.** Section 7.5]

(vi) Mention any two features of co-ordination.

[**Ans.** Section 7.2]

(vii) Distinguish between co-ordination and co-operation?

[C.U. B.Com. 2001, 2004, 2006]

[**Ans.** Section 7.6]

(viii) Define co-ordination. [C.U. B.Com. 2005 2008, 2011]

[**Ans.** Section 7.1]

(ix) Enumerate four techniques of co-ordination. [C.U. B.Com. 2006]

[**Ans.** Section 7.5]

(x) Mention any four aids to co-ordination.

[**Ans.** Section 7.7]

(xi) Why is co-ordination treated as essence of management?

[C.U. B.Com. 2011, New Syllabus]

[**Ans.** Section 7.1]

(xii) State the principles of co-ordination. [C.U. B.Com. 2011, New Syllabus]

[**Ans.** Section 7.4]

CHAPTER

8

Control

"He who controls the present, controls the past. He who controls the past, controls the future."

—George Orwell

TOPICS

Subject-matter of the Chapter *Controlling is the last basic function of Management. The process of management starts with planning and ends by controlling. The success of a business enterprise depends mainly upon two aspects—(i) proper planning, and (ii) efficient controlling. The method of measuring the work performance of the subordinate employees, by comparing the actual result with the expected result in order to verify any deviation and taking corrective measures so that the performance of the employees conforms with the target is known as 'control'. The objectives of an enterprise are formulated through planning and it is control that brings the performance of the employees to the planned level in order to achieve those objectives. Plan becomes successful by effective controlling; and the pre-requisite of efficient control is proper planning.*

In this chapter the meaning, characteristics and importance of control, various steps in controlling process, essential factors of effective control, different types and techniques of controlling, etc. will be discussed in detail. And, in this respect the relationship between the planning and controlling process will also be described

8.1 Definition and Meaning of Control

Control is a fundamental function of management. In short, control means to see that everything is being done in accordance with the rules laid down and the instructions given and that actual performance corresponds with the planned course of action. It involves guiding and regulating the operations towards some pre-determined goals. According to **Henry Fayol** : "Control consists in verifying whether everything occurs in conformity with the plan adopted, the instructions issued and principles established. It has for its object to point out weaknesses and errors in order to rectify them and prevent recurrence." In the words of **Koontz and O'Donnell** : "The managerial function of controlling is the measurement and correction of the performance of the activities of subordinates in order to make sure that enterprise objectives and the plans devised to attain them are being accomplished." According to **Robert N. Anthony** : "Management control is the process by which managers assure that resources are obtained and used effectively and efficiently in accomplishment of an organisation's objectives."

However, **'Control' as a managerial function can be defined as the process of analysing whether the actions are being taken as planned and taking corrective measures to make these to conform to planning.** It is the continuous process of measuring the actual results of the operations of an organisation in relation to the planned results and of minimising the gap between the two. The process of control tries to find out deviations between planned performance and actual performance and to suggest corrective actions wherever needed.

After the plans are put into action, there can be several hurdles in the achievement of the goals. Direction may be faulty; environmental conditions may be changed, and results may fall short of targets. Therefore, the managers must find out what is going wrong, what changes in plans and directions are required and what must be done to set the things right. This is the function of control.

The activities of business need to be properly controlled. Actual results should be measured and compared with the plans, and then corrective action should be taken to bring the results more nearly in line with what is desired. Control not only provides a historical record of what has happened to the business as a whole, but pinpoints the reasons behind such happening and provides a data base that enables the chief executive or the departmental head to take corrective steps, if he finds that the things are going wrong. A manager controls the activities of his subordinates so that they can perform their functions effeciently and according to his plans to realise the enterprise objectives. When control exists in the organisation, the employees know what targets they are striving for, they know how they are doing in relation to the targets and they also know what changes, if any, are needed to keep their performance at a satisfactory level.

8.2 Nature of Control

The real nature of the controlling function of management is brought out by the following analysis of the control process :

1. Planning is the Basis of Control : Control can be exercised only with reference to and on the basis of plans. Unless the managers are able to fix the objectives of the organisation in clear terms and can chart out a clear and realistic course of action for their attainment, effective control is impossible. Whereas planning sets the course, control observes the deviations from the course and initiates action to return to the chosen course to an appropriately changed one. In practice, budgets are used as the standards of performance on the basis of which the actual performance is evaluated and controlled.

2. Action is the Essence of Control : Control means the measures to correct the deviation that is found between the standards and actual results. To control, a manager has to initiate action which will guide the operations within the sphere of plans. For this purpose, actions and further actions are necessary; each time there may be correction and change in the actions depending upon the information provided by control procedure. Thus, in a real sense, control means the action to correct a condition found to be in error or measures to prevent such a condition from arising and is never achieved without having the action as an essential step.

3. Delegation is the Key to Control : Control is exercised by taking action, and action may be taken within the authority delegated. An executive can perform the control function only if he enjoys the authority to take remedial action and is to be held accountable for results. That is why the managerial function of control calls for proper delegation of authority by the superiors to their subordinates.

4. Information is the Guide to Control : Control is exercised by a manager on the basis of the information and reports from those actually doing the job. Such information and reports may be called the 'feedback' from operations. Feedback enables the manager to determine how far the operations are proceeding in conformity with the plans and standards and where remedial action is called for. Every manager in the organisation must have adequate information about the performance, standards and actual contributions made by the employees working under his control. It is important to note that the information and reports relating to the operations must be timely communicated to the appropriate authority.

8.3 Characteristics of Control

The salient features or characteristics of control may be described as follows :

1. Control is the end function of management : Management functions start with planning. Then comes organising, command, direction, motivation and co-ordination. Control follows up these functions, sees and examines how these functions are going on with men, money, materials, machines, etc. for the accomplishment of the tasks according to the standards and schedules established.

2. Control has a forward-looking character : Control aims at the future because one can control future events and not the past. It is in the nature of control to follow-up other functions of management. It reviews and examines past events, gathers experience from them and suggests steps for future improvement and guidance. In these various ways, control tries to minimise loss, wastage, inefficiency and deviation.

3. Control is a continuous process : It is concerned with constant vigilance over the performance. As long as an organisation exists, some sort of control is required. Though managerial control enables the manager to exercise control at the point of action, it follows a definite pattern and timetable, month after month, and year after year on a continuous basis.

4. Control involves measurement : To control means to check the actual performance, to keep a watch on the activities. It requires measuring the results against pre-established targets and review of the outcome of the activities. Control not only involves checking current performance, it also suggests guidelines for future course of action. It helps to steer the events towards targets so as to make things happen. Measurement and evaluation are the main functions of control process.

5. Control is a co-ordinated and integrated system : Although data collected for one purpose may differ from those with another purpose, these data should be reconciled with one another. In fact, management control is a system consisting of certain inter-dependent elements, e.g. goal or standard, device to monitor the events, mechanism to detect and analyse the deviations, and adjustment or corrective actions.

6. Control is concerned with individuals : It measures the performance of the individuals who work behind the machinery and materials and make the machines go. Though control is not related with the machines, materials, methods or money, it is ultimately concerned with the human beings who are responsible for defects, shortcomings or financial lapses. Control is, in other words, the checking and correcting the operations of some people by other people for the welfare and well-being of the organisation.

7. Control is the correlation and sum-total of multitude operations : It is nourished upon the principle of feedback. The superior holds control over the subordinates, but it cannot be exercised effectively without relevant information from the subordinates in respect of their feelings, difficulties and reactions in work performance.

8. Control may be close or general : Control is said to be close when it is exercised by a superior over his immediate subordinates. It is also known as first-line control. But control is said to be general when it is exercised by the top authority through scalar chain. It is rather overall control. The employees prefer general control because this gives them freedom and initiative in work performance.

9. Control is exercised from the beginning : Although control is treated as the last function of management, it does not take place only for once after happening some events. It is concurrent and continuous with operations. The primary object of control is to bring to light the variations between the actual performance and standards as soon as they appear and then take steps to prevent such variations in future. Intended results are established through planning, and control aims at securing such results. So, after the completion of work, the actual results—whether good or bad—can never be improved or corrected. Accordingly, control is exercised from the commencement of the work.

10. Control is correlated with the other functions of management : Though control is considered as one of the functions of management, it cannot stand by itself. It is correlated with other functions and cannot proceed without them. As a fundamental managerial function, control follows other functions. It affects all other functions of management and is affected, in turn, by their influences.

11. Control process is universal : This process consists of the same element irrespective of the type of organisation or function to be controlled. It is the responsibility of every manager to regulate the ongoing activity and keep the operations focussed towards attainment of goals.

12. Control is flexible and dynamic : Control is not static and has no rigidity in it. It is to adjust itself to the changing circumstances.

8.4 Importance of Control

Control is an indispensable function of management. Without control the management process is incomplete. The control function essentially ensures that the planned performance is achieved with minimum of disorder and disruptions. It assures that the plans are carried out and the objectives are reached. Control is the ultimate weapon at the hands of the managerial force to remove mistakes, to modify defective plans, to check misdirection, and to effect co-ordination of diverse elements where it is lacking. A combination of well-planned objectives, strong organisation, capable direction, and efficient motivation have little probability of success unless there exists an adequate system of control.

The importance and significance of control may be stated as follows :

1. Guide to Operations : Like a traffic signal, control guides the organisation and keeps it on the right track. It measures progress towards the goal and brings to light the adjustments, if any, required in day-to-day operations. It is control that finds out whether plans are being observed and suitable progress towards the objectives is being made, and, if necessary, corrective action has been taken. A sound control system is needed to measure progress, to uncover deviations, and to indicate corrective measures.

2. Policy Verification : For organisational functioning, the managers formulate certain policies and other planning elements. In the process of control, the managers can verify the quality of various policies. It may reveal that the goals need to be modified. Control helps to review, revise and update the plans. Without feedback of an efficient control system, even the best plans may not work out as expected.

3. Managerial Responsibility : In every organisation, managerial responsibility is created through assignment of activities to various individuals. When a manager assigns some activities and delegates authority to his subordinates, he remains responsible for the ultimate performance of the same. It is quite natural that when a person is responsible for the performance of his subordinates, he must check up the performance of them to ensure that they are utilising the delegated authority in the desired manner. In this way, control enables the managers to discharge their responsibilities.

4. Better Performance : Control process puts a psychological pressure on the individuals for better performance. The performance of the individuals is evaluated in the light of targets set for them. A person is likely to put better performance if he is aware of that his performance will be evaluated. This is further complemented by the reward and punishment based on performance. Since the performance measurement is one of the basic elements of the control process, it ensures that every person in the organisation contributes to his maximum ability.

5. Co-ordination in Action : Control facilitates the work of co-ordination, one of the vital functions of management. It is ensured by keeping all the activities and efforts of the business within their fixed boundaries and schedules and making them move towards a rightful and desired direction.

Control systems are designed in such a way that they focus not only on the operating responsibility of a manager but also on his ultimate responsibility. This compels a manager to co-ordinate the activities of his subordinates in such a manner that each of them contributes positively towards the attainment of objectives of the superior.

6. Organisational Efficiency and Effectiveness : Proper control ensures efficiency and effectiveness of the organisation. It helps the process of delegation, permits individual freedom and initiative, and secures adequate work performance from the employees. Control eliminates the risk of non-conformity between the intended performance and the actual performance. Besides, it provides a check on other managerial functions and points out their weaknesses. In addition to the operational aspect, the financial aspect of business is thoroughly checked and regulated by control. In this process, it ensures the efficient working of the organisation. Since control focuses on the achievement of organisational objectives, it necessarily leads to organisational effectiveness.

8.5 Steps in Controlling Process

Controlling process involves the following steps in all situations :

1. Establishment of the Standards : Control is to see that everything is being done according to the standard established. So, the first step in controlling is to establish the standard of performance which is to be used for checking or measuring the performance. Standards represent the established criteria against which the actual results can be measured. In order to ascertain whether the performance is becoming better or worse, or remaining at the existing level, an yardstick of camparison is required to be evolved. So the standard established will act as the basis of such comparison. For setting the standards for control purposes, it is important to identify clearly and precisely the results which are desired. In the context of control, these refer to the enterprise goals, objectives, targets, etc. The actual performance of the enterprise is judged against them. So, the standards must be set and stated specifically in tangible terms, such as—in terms of quantity, quality, time, cost, revenue, profit, and investment. Standards can be set for many intangible items such as—the result to be expected from a training programme, or an advertisement campaign or employee morale, etc.

2. Measurement of the Performance : The second step in control process is to make arrangements for the measurement of performance. This involves measuring the performance in respect of a work in terms of the control standard established. This measurement may be undertaken in two ways : (a) Direct personal observation or inspection, and (b) Through regular reports—verbal or written. In the cases where the results of operations and the standards are tangible, it is not a difficult task to measure it. Examples of such activities are—volume of production, cost of production, number of persons employed, quality of materials used, quantity of sales effected. These measurable performances may be evaluated by direct personal observation or inspection or through reports submitted by the subordinates. But in the case of intangible performances, where measurement in concrete or numeral terms are difficult, direct personal observation is the usual procedure. Ideally, measurement should be such that the deviations may be detected in advance of occurrence and avoided by appropriate actions. It is often possible for an alert and forward-looking manager to predict probable deviations from the standard.

3. Comparing the Actual Performance with the Standard : The third step in the process of control is the comparison of actual with the standard performance. Such comparison will reveal the deviation between the actual and desired results. The manager should go deep into the matter and investigate into the causes or factors that stand behind such deviations. It involves two steps—(i) Finding out the extent of deviation, and (ii) Identifying the causes of such deviations. When adequate standards are developed and actual performance is measured accurately, any variation will be clearly revealed. The causes or factors that work behind the deviations are generally the consequences of defective materials, machinery, process, lethargic work approach, etc. But this comparing work should be done as close to the point of performance as possible. This assists in quick location of the defects and results in correction with minimum losses.

It should be remembered that in the initial stages of an enterprise or in a small concern, control may be exercised at all points and at all stages. But in a large concern having many points and stages, it is better to pay attention to some strategic and key points. Again, such evaluation should be a continuous affair when the work is in progress.

4. Correcting the Deviations by Remedial Action : This is the last step in the control process. It signifies that proper actions should be taken to maintain the desired degree of control in the system or operation. In implelentation of this step, the first three steps will act as the fact-finding steps. They will provide necessary information, facts and data, point out the need for action and indicate the directions in which corrective measures are to be undertaken. The aim of such corrective action is to improve the profitability of the business for its long-run survival and growth. Corrective actions may be directed to operational,

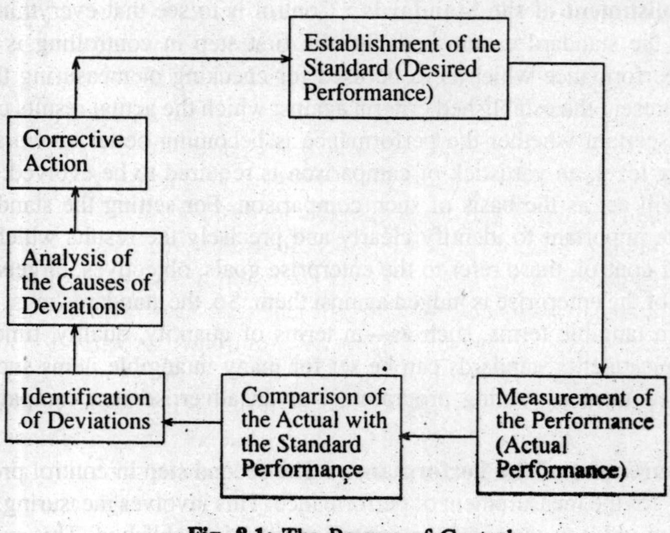

Fig. 8.1: The Process of Control.

financial and structural modifications. They may be remedial and preventive. But preventive measures are preferable to remedial measures. Remedial measures cannot be wiped out altogether from the business operations. These are necessary for solving the multiple problems of the dynamic world. Corrective actions—remedial or preventive—should be prompt with the identification of deviations or variances.

Before the above-mentioned steps in the process of control are executed, certain pre-requisites are required to be present in the organisation. These are—clear and consistent planning, complete understanding of the organisational objectives by the members, and sufficient authority in the exercise of control.

8.6 Limitations of Control

A control system may be faced with the following limitations :

1. External factors : Unlike the internal factors which can easily be controlled, it is sometimes very difficult to anticipate and control the external factors such as—government policy, technological changes, social changes, changes in the tastes and fashions of the consumers, etc.

2. Difficulty of measurement : Control needs establishment of standards. They are based on factual information. Control system loses its effectiveness when the standards of performance cannot be defined in quantitative terms. Standardisation of human behaviour—the most important element in business—is not possible. Certain things, such as—loyalty of a worker, and employee morale are unmeasurable in exact terms.

3. Difficulty in the fixation of individual responsibility : Control presupposes fixation of individual responsibility for negative deviations from the standard. Occasions arise where it may not be possible to fix up responsibility for any negative deviation on specific individuals.

4. Expensive : Control requires sufficient attention to observe the performance of the subordinates and careful investigation into the causes of variations from the standard established. These investigations may prove to be very expensive—both in terms of time and money.

8.7 Types of Control

Control may be of different types. These are mentioned below :

1. Physical and Financial : Physical control aims at quantitative and qualitative evaluation of the products. Quantitative control examines the volume of production, unit of production per machine or man-hour, etc. Qualitative control looks after hardness, durability, fastness, fineness, etc. The physical control can be exercised by direct checking, reporting, accounting and comparing the product against the agreed standard.

Financial control is exercised in monetary terms and involves the calculation of cost incurred or amount spent and the revenue or income earned. It thus signifies evaluation from the standpoint of cost standard and revenue standard. Financial statements are prepared to know the total investments and the return on investments. Every year Profit and Loss Account and Balance Sheet of the companies are prepared to show the net result of the working, the net worth of the business, and the liabilities to be paid for. The managers compare the financial statements of the different years and exercise necessary control. Another important financial control is budgetary control. After carefully studying the past experiences, budgets are prepared for estimating future earnings and expenditure. Budgets are the effective means of controlling the finances of the organisation. Different budgets, namely, cost budget, revenue budget, expenditure budget, etc. are prepared for effective control in different areas. Another important means of financial control is 'cost control'. Cost of production is controlled to increase profit. Different methods of costing are now employed for this purpose.

2. Control over the Actual and Anticipatory Performance : The physical and financial control as stated above are the examples of control over actual performances designed in terms of quantity, quality, cost and time. But the managers are also required to exercise some control over the future. It means that they will have to anticipate future performance and accordingly lay down budgets and keep check or control over them through budget. Budgets are based on anticipatory performance. Such budgets may be physical and financial.

3. Control over the Activity or Area of Operation : The above types of control cover overall performance. But control is also exercised over an activity or area of operation. This type of control extends its grasp over many aspects of the activities or areas of operation. Some of these are stated below :

(i) **Control over the Policies and Procedures :** The object of this control is to see whether the policies and procedures laid down are expected to serve the best interest of the enterprise and whether they are being followed properly in practice. Control over policies demands that they should be clearly stated, properly communicated, must be reviewed, improved and updated. Again, control over policies cannot be said to be complete unless their operations are checked and examined in terms of their results. Control over the procedures can be effectively exercised if they can be standardised. The object of such control is to look after their simplicity, speed and effective implementation, and to guard against excesses, obsolescences, duplication and inflexibility.

(ii) **Control over the Organisation :** Control over the organisation is necessary to see that the organisation is running smoothly according to the plan and purpose, and is in a position to adjust itself to the changing circumstances. Such control is exercised with the help of organisation charts, manuals, reports and interviews. The charts clarify the organisational relationships, and manuals reveal summary statements of duties assigned and authority delegated to every executive.

(iii) **Control over the Personnel :** Generally, the personnel manager or head of the personnel department keeps control over the personnel in the organisation. Such control is necessary to maintain the quality of the personnel for efficient work performance.

(iv) **Control over Wages and Salaries :** Control over the wages and salaries is done having programme of job evaluation and, wage and salary analysis. The functions are carried on by the personnel and industrial engineering departments. Often a 'wage and salary committee' is formed to provide help to these departments. This control is essential to see that the wages and salaries conform to the methods and policies followed by the similar concerns.

(v) **Control over Costs :** Control over costs is exercised through making comparision between standard costs and actual costs, Standard costs are set in respect of different elements of costs. Controller's department provides information for setting standard costs, calculating actual costs and pointing out differences between the two.

(vi) **Control over Production, Product and Product Line :** Production control is necessary to maintain the flow of production according to the plan. Its object is to guide and direct productive activities in such a way that required quantity of goods of desired quality is produced at the required time in the best and cheapest method. The techniques adopted for this purpose are planning, routing, scheduling, despatching, expediting, inspection and quality control.

Control over product is intended to analyse the ways of its improvement and that is carried out with proper check on research and development so that quality product may be produced with minimum expenditure and waste.

When an enterprise produces multiple products, instead of a single product, it becomes necessary to select the profitable lines of product. Control over product line is intended to secure the highest return on investment from the line chosen. Such control is exercised by a committee whose members are drawn from production department, sales department and research department. This committee controls through studies about market needs. Efforts are made to simplify and rationalise the line of products.

(vii) **Control over Inventory or Stocks :** Control over inventory is to see that the stocks in store are adequate to meet the requirements of production, and also to see that unnecessary stocks in large quantity are not kept, This is necessary to prevent wastage, minimise expenses and to maximise economical use of materials.

(viii) **Control over Quality :** It is a statistical method and goes by the name of Statistical Quality Control (S.Q.C.). It measures the deviations from a standard quality by means of sample tests and recording them on a chart. When manufacturing operations go on, this chart shows the deviations from previously approved limits. It is a corrective measure to prevent excessive errors and unnecessary scrap, and thus saves labour costs involved in re-work losses and material costs resulting in scrap losses.

(ix) **Control over Sales and Prices :** Sales budget or sales programme provides the basis of such control. The overall sales performance can be found out by means of ratio analysis. Sales control cannot leave aside control over prices, because, if prices are fixed too high, the customers will refuse to buy the product. If they are too low, the organisation will suffer losses. So, control over prices involves considerations in respect of consumer situation, cost considerations, competitive positions, promotional policies, etc.

(x) **Control over Capital Expenditure :** Control over capital expenditure is exercised through the system of evaluation of projects on the basis of their importance, generally on the basis of their earning capacity. For effective control over capital expenditure, there should be a plan to identify the realisation of benefits from capital expenditure and to make comparison with anticipated results. Such comparison is important in the sense that it serves as an important guide for future capital budgeting activities.

(xi) **Control over External Relation :** External relations are regulated by the public relation department. This department may prescribe certain measures to be followed by other departments while dealing with the external parties. External relations exert an important influence over the total performance of the enterprise and, as such, it is also necessary to have control over the external relations.

(xii) **Overall Control :** The different types of control as stated above are partial in nature, because each of them applies to a part of an enterprise and cannot measure total or overall performance. A comprehensive control on overall performance is necessary as overall planning is necessary for an enterprise. Control over each segment of the organisation contributes to overall organisational control. Some special measures are devised to exercise overall control. This is done through budgetary control, projecting profit and loss account and balance sheet. A master budget is prepared by integrating and co-ordinating the budgets prepared by each segment. This budget acts as an instrument for overall control. Profit and loss account and balance sheet are also used to measure the overall results.

8.8 Relation between Planning and Control

Control is a fundamental management function that ensures work accomplishment according to plans. Control is closely related with planning. In the planning stage, the managers decide how the resources of the enterprise would be utilised to achieve the organisational objectives; and, at the controlling stage, the managers try to visualise whether the resources are utilised in the same way as planned.

Control is concerned with checking the actual performance against the agreed standards of plans with a view to ensuring adequate progress of intended performances. The intended performance is indicated through planning in the shape of standards or targets; and control is to see that the performances tally with the plans. Desired results of both individual performance and organisational performance are established in planning, and control aims at securing such results. Control compels the events to conform with the plans. Planning and control go hand in hand. **H. G. Hicks** has rightly stated : "Planning is clearly a pre-requisite for controlling." Without planning there can be no control, and without control planning target cannot be achieved.

Planning is the basis of control. It provides the entire spectrum on which control function is based. Plan directs the behaviour and activities in the organisation, and it is control that measures these behaviour and activities, and suggests measures to remove deviations, if any. Control further implies the existence of goals and standards. These goals are provided by the planning process. Control is the result of particular plans, goals, or policies. Thus, planning offers and affects control.

On the other hand, the planning is also affected by control in the sense that many of the information provided by control is used for planning and replanning. Thus, there is a reciprocal relationship between planning and control as presented in Fig. 8.2. Various elements of planning provide what is intended or expected and the means by which the goals can be achieved. They provide a means for reporting back the progress made against the goals and a general framework for new decisions and actions in an integrated pattern. Properly-conceived plans become important elements for implementing effective control.

Thus, planning is meaningless without control; and control is aimless without planning. In fact, "Planning and control are the inseparable twins of management."

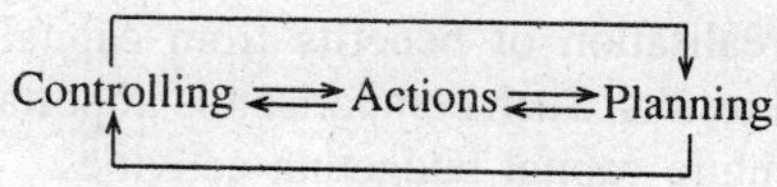

Fig. 8.2: Planning and Controlling Relationship.

8.9 Span of Control

'Span of Control' refers to the number of subordinates that a manager can supervise and control effectively. It is also known as 'Span of Supervision', or, 'Span of Management'. There is a limit to which a person can supervise others. The problem of span arises because an executive has limited time, attention and capacity. The principle of span implies that no executive should have more subordinates than he can effectively manage. If the span of control is narrow, there will be more organisational levels. Again, if the number of levels is reduced and the span of control widened, the supervisory load may become too great.

It is said that control is efficient when the number of subordinates reporting directly to the manager is small. But the number should be neither too large nor too small.

However, no hard and fast rule can be prescribed for this purpose. Opinion is divided on what should be the ideal span. **Hamilton** stated that the average human brain can handle three to six other brains. According to **Lyndall F. Urwick**, the ideal number of subordinates is four at higher levels and eight to twelve at lower levels. Again, most of the authorities prescribe a maximum of six for this. Such numerical limits are, however, meaningless as the underlying needs and capacity vary between individuals.

The span of control is affected by a number of factors which are as follows :

1. Nature of the Work : In the case of routine and repetitive operations, span can be wide as the subordinates do not need frequent guidance from the superior. As a result, the manager can supervise a large number of subordinates. On the other hand, in the case of specialised and frequently changing duties and those involving constant interaction, span of control has to be narrow.

2. Competence of the Superior : The executives possessing the qualities like leadership, decision-making and communication can control more subordinates than those who are less competent. Moreover, the attitude and personality of a manager also determine the span.

3. Calibre of the Subordinates : Trained and experienced subordinates may perform their jobs efficiently without much help from the manager. They need only broad guidelines. In such a case, less time is needed for supervising, and the span can be larger. New and inexperienced employees require more time of a supervisor than experienced and efficient employees. More qualified and experienced the subordinates, lesser will be the pressure on the superior, and wider can be the span.

4. Staff Assistance : An executive can handle more subordinates when advice and assistance of staff specialists are available to him.

5. Location : In the case of geographically scattered operations, span has to be narrow, as the executive cannot manage effectively the distant operations.

6. Clarity of Plan : More clear and understood are the goals and policies and more specific the duties, wider can be the span of control. In the absence of clear plans, span has to be narrow, because the subordinates require much consultation with their superior and his guidance.

7. Communication Techniques : More effective is the communication systems, lesser is the need for personal contact and wider may be the span. Wide established grievances, redressal procedure and suggestion systems widen the executive span.

8. Availability of Time : At higher levels, the managers have less time for supervision. They have to devote the major portion of their time in planning and organising. So, the span has to be narrowed down.

9. Degree of Decentralisation : When a manager clearly delegates authority to the subordinates, they themselves will take many decisions, and the manager can effectively supervise a large number of employees. On the other hand, if the manager does not delegate adequate authority to the subordinates, they require frequent consultation and the manager has to take many decisions himself. As a result, he can supervise few subordinates.

The span of control might be enlarged by—(i) the further development of managerial abilities; (ii) improved training of the senior assistants; (iii) making more use of programmed decisions; (iv) laying down standard procedure; (v) the appointment of personal assistants to managers, etc.

None can deny that there is a limit to the supervisory capacities of individuals but an over emphasis on limiting the span of control can lead to worse results. Narrow spans of control are likely to involve an enterprise in heavy administration cost. The more is the limit of the span of control, the more is lengthened the chain of command and the number of levels of authority is increased. Thus, the administration cost will be heavy. Furthermore, problems of communication and motivation arise. A decision taken at the top level takes a longer period to filter down to the bottom and the chance of distortion increases.

The demand for better co-ordination and greater consistency of decision may make wide span of control desirable. Thus, it may be concluded that the wider span of control may be desirable according to changed circumstances.

8.10 Tools or, Techniques of Control

Different techniques of control are applied to implement the control process. The various tools or techniques of managerial control may be classified into two broad categories : (a) Traditional control techniques, and (b) Modern control techniques.

The important traditional control techniques include—(i) Personal Observation, (ii) Budgetary Control, (iii) Break-even Analysis, (iv) Ratio Analysis, (v) Cost Control, (vi) Internal Audit, (vii) Statistical Report, etc.

Modern control techniques are—(i) Management Audit, (ii) Network Techniques, (iii) Return on Investment, (iv) Responsibility Accouting, (v) Performance Budgeting, (vi) Zero-base Budgeting, (vii) Management Information System, etc.

TECHNIQUES OF CONTROL

Traditional Control Techniques	Modern Control Techniques
• Personal Observation	• Management Audit
• Budgetary Control	• Network Techniques
• Break-even Analysis	• Return on Investment
• Ratio Analysis	• Responsibility Accounting
• Cost Control	• Performance Budgeting
• Internal Audit	• Zero-base Budgeting
• Statistical Report	• Management Information System

Fig. 8.3: Techniques of Control.

The application of these techniques depend on the situations and nature of activities of the organisation.

The important techniques of control are described in sections 8.10.1. to 8.10.14.

8.10.1 Personal Observation

Personal observation of actual performance of the subordinates at the work place is the most effective, direct and oldest method of control. The managers need to hold discussion with the persons whose work is being controlled and they should watch the actual operations. There are certain kinds of information and impression which can be conveyed only through face-to-face contact—personnal observation and conversation. The personal observer exactly knows what is wrong and can take necessary actions rapidly. Personal observation has also a psychological impact on the employees. They try to achieve better performance when they know that they will be observed personally by their superior. Thus, the managers can maintain work discipline among the employees.

The immediate superior managers are given ample power to take necessary measures for controlling the activities of the subordinates as and when required. As the superior managers are aware of the difficulties and problems of their subordinates relating to work environment and other grievances, they can take immediate action to prevent resistance to control measures. However, personal observation may have a negative impact in some cases. The self-motivated employees do not like to be closely supervised. This system of control is also time-consuming. Besides, there may be the influence of personal bias of the observer which may affect the evaluation. The managers have the responsibility of implementing the organisational objectives whatever control techniques they use. Personal observation largely involves the evaluation of human performance. Therefore, the success of personal observation as a tool of control depends upon how much information a manager can collect through this method.

8.10.2 Budgetary Control

(A) Meaning : 'Budgetary Control' is the process of utilising budgets for comparing the actual performance with the corresponding budget performance in order to find out the deviations, and to remove the deviations by either adjusting the budget estimates or correcting the causes of deviations. A budget is a highly useful tool for controlling the day-to-day operations of the enterprise. It provides a standard by which actual performance can be evaluated to find out the deviations from the planned results. This information enables the managers to take corrective action for bringing the actual results in conformity with the plans. Budgetary control is an effective and widely used control technique.

(B) Characteristics : The important features of Budgetary Control are as follows :

1. Budgetary control formulates a plan or fixes a target of performance that becomes the basis of measuring the progress of activities in the organisation.

2. It tries to evaluate the results of the activities in terms of quantity so that the actual result can be compared with the budgeted result.

3. It draws attention of the managers on deviation between what is planned and what is being achieved so that required actions can be taken to remove the deviation and to implement the objectives of the activities. Thus, it does not control the activities directly; but points out where control and corrective measures are necessary.

(C) Benefits : Budgetary control leads to maximum utilisation of resources with a view to ensuring maximum output because it provides aid to managerial planning, co-ordination and control. The various advantages of budgetary control are as follows :

1. Budgetary control compels the managers to plan their activities. As budget allocation is made on the basis of the nature of activities undertaken in a section or depertment, the managers have to define what activities they plan for the future.

2. Budgetary control is fully concerned with concrete numerical goals, it has no ambiguity relating to the targets. Thus, every manager in the organisation is sure about what he is expected to do. It gives the opportunity of objective evaluation of performance and self-examination.

3. Since budgetary control keeps a rigid check over the activities in the organisation, it leads to a cautious utilisation of resources. It arouses efforts to achieve the goals and yet keeps them within the well-defined boundaries.

4. It indirectly assists the managerial planning at higher levels. Budgetary control provides an effective means by which the managers can delegate authority without sacrificing overall control.

5. Budgetary control process promotes co-operation among various sub-units in the organisation. As it is an instrument of planning, it brings the activities of various departments under overall perspective. This inspires team-spirit and helps in co-ordination.

6. It encourages free flow of information among various units of the organisation.

7. It promotes balanced activities in the organisation. The volume of each activity depends on the objectives of the organisation. So, each activity is to be performed in proportion to other activities.

8. Budgetary control, as a control device, is very exact, accurate and precise. A budget provides the standards against which control systems are undertaken. Thus, the managers can keep a watch whether their efforts are proceeding in the right direction.

9. Budgetary control points out any deviation between the actual performance and budgeted performance. This is communicated very quickly and the managers can take remedial actions to overcome the deviations.

10. It can also identify the reasons which are responsible for the deviation between budget and actual. Thus, it provides direction for necessary control actions.

(D) Problems : Although budgetary control is a vital and important tool of planning, co-ordinating and controlling the activities in an organisation, it has some problems. So, the managers should be well aware about these problems in order to take adequate precautions to minimise the impact of these drawbacks.

The problems of budgetary control are described below :

1. Budgetary control faces problems due to uncertainty of future. Budgets are prepared on the assumptions of future happenings in a certain way. But due to change in situations, budgets do not become always meaningful and reliable for achieving control.

2. A budget is just a guesswork. Therefore, question may be raised about its usefulness for being used as standard against which performance is measured and actions are taken.

3. It may work against the morale of the people in the organisation—particulary if the budgetary control system does operate properly.

4. Budgetary control is a complicated process of controlling. It may generate internal pressures and conflict.

5. It is an expensive and time-consuming system of control. It cannot be applied in small enterprises.

6. Budgetary control system needs a lot of paperwork which the technical personnel may resent. Actually, it does not fit with their own areas of specialisation. So, the applicability of budgetary control process may be limited.

8.10.3 Break-even Analysis

(A) Meaning : 'Break-even Analysis' is an important technique of cost control. It is an analysis of the inter-relationships among the cost of production, volume of production and the amount of profits. It is also known as 'Cost-Volume Profit Analysis'. Costs are of two types—fixed and variable. The relationships are shown on a chart called 'Break-even Chart' as given in Fig. 8.4 on next page. In this chart, the X-axis represents the sales volume in thousand units, while the Y-axis represents the cost of production and sales revenue in lakh rupees. The fixed cost line is horizontal to the X-axis and the total cost line is drawn vertically from the intersection of fixed cost line at the Y-axis. The revenue line has been drawn through the zero point on the Y-axis. The point 'B' at which the total revenue line intersects the total cost line is known as 'Break-even Point'(BEP). At this point there is no profit and no loss. The spread to the right of this point represents profit and the spread to the left represents loss. The volume of sales is 50,000 units at which the total cost and total revenue (Rs. 5 lakhs) are equal.

$$\text{BEP} = \frac{\text{Fixed Costs}}{\text{Sale Price per unit} - \text{Variable Cost per unit}}$$

(B) Advantages : The advantages of Break-even Analysis are mentioned below :

1. Break-even chart depicts graphically the total cost and sales revenue at various levels of sale. It helps in determining the minimum volume of sales at which costs are fully recovered and beyond which profit can be earned. It is an useful tool of managerial control.

2. Break-even analysis can be applied to estimate profits at different levels of activity or to estimate the turn-over for desired profits.

3. Through separating fixed costs and variable costs it enables the managers to exercise control over variable expenses.

4. Break-even analysis is useful to the managers for decision-making and the preparation of budgets.

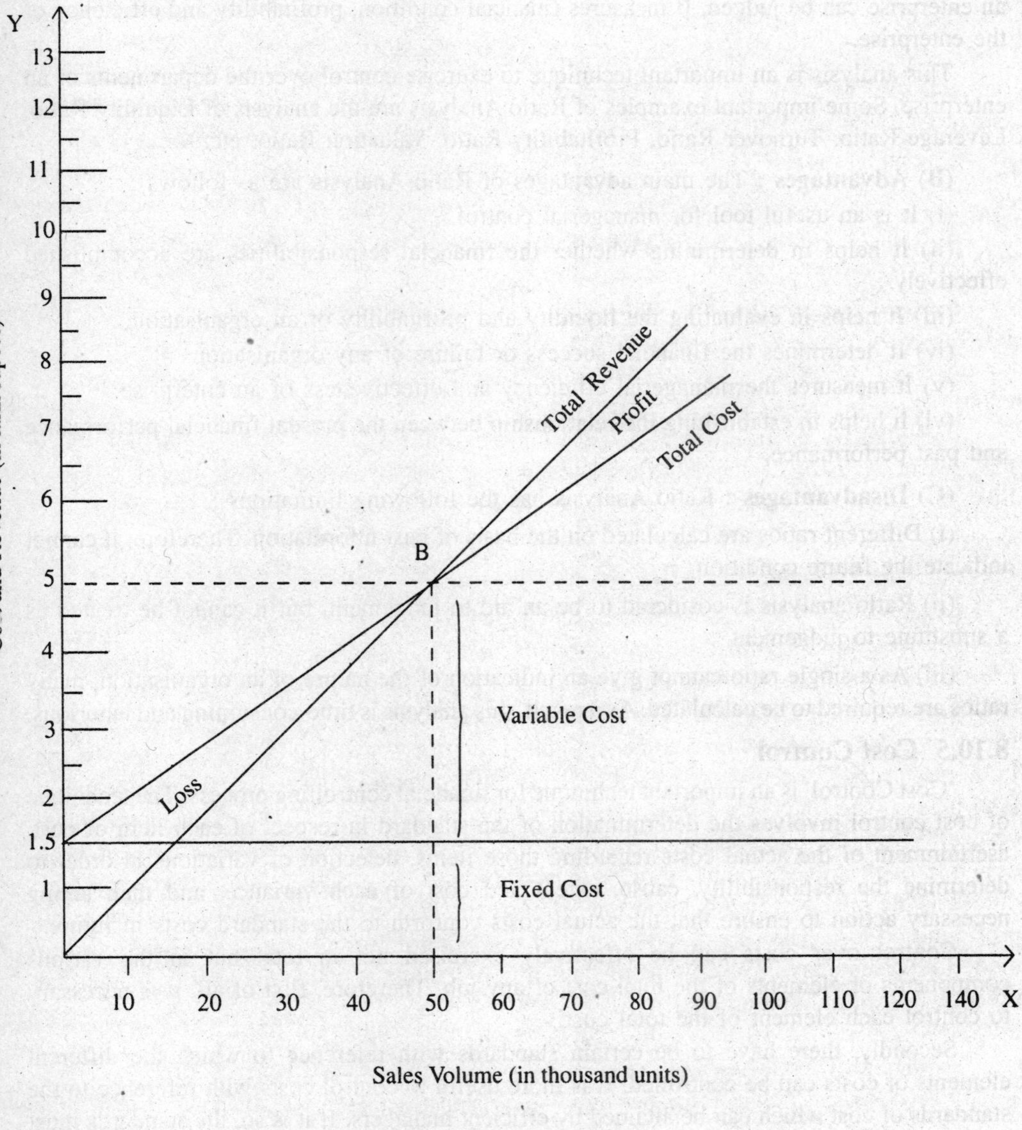

Fig. 8.4: Break-even Analysis.

(C) Disadvantages : Break-even Analysis suffers from some limitations. These are mentioned below :

1. The classification of costs and their relationship which are assumed in this tool is not always possible.

2. In this analysis, it is assumed that factor prices, technology and all other things are constant. But this is not always true. Actually, they are dynamic.

3. Fixed costs remain fixed only up to a certain level of activity, and after this level, they rise considerably.

8.10.4 Ratio Analysis

(A) Meaning : A 'Ratio' is an arithmetical relationship between two figures. 'Ratio Analysis' is a study of ratios between various items or groups in the financial statement of an organisation. With the help of such analysis, the efficiency of financial performance of an enterprise can be judged. It measures financial condition, profitability and efficiency of the enterprise.

This analysis is an important technique to exercise control over the departments of an enterprise. Some important examples of Ratio Analysis are the analysis of Liquidity Ratio, Leverage Ratio, Turnover Ratio, Profitability Ratio, Valuation Ratio, etc.

(B) Advantages : The main advantages of Ratio Analysis are as follows :

(i) It is an useful tool for managerial control.

(ii) It helps in determining whether the financial responsibilities are accomplished effectively.

(iii) It helps in evaluating the liquidity and profitability of an organisation.

(iv) It determines the financial success or failure of any organisation.

(v) It measures the managerial efficiency and effectiveness of an enterprise.

(vi) It helps in establishing the relationship between the present financial performance and past performance.

(C) Disadvantages : Ratio Analysis has the following limitations :

(i) Different ratios are calculated on the basis of past information. Therefore, it cannot indicate the future condition.

(ii) Ratio analysis is cosidered to be an aid to judgement, but it cannot be treated as a substitute to judgement.

(iii) As a single ratio cannot give an indication of the nature of an organisation, many ratios are required to be calculated. As a result, this analysis is time-consuming and laborious.

8.10.5 Cost Control

'Cost Control' is an important technique for financial controlling process. The technique of cost control involves the determination of the standard in respect of each item of cost, asertainment of the actual costs regarding those items, detection of variations in order to determine the responsibility, cause, extent and cost of each variance, and then taking necessary action to ensure that the actual costs conform to the standard costs in future.

Control over costs can be effectively exercised not in total but in the various components or elements of the total cost of any job. Therefore, first of all, it is necessary to control each element of the total cost.

Secondly, there have to be certain standards with reference to which the different elements of costs can be controlled. It is more useful to control costs with reference to the standards of cost which can be attained by efficient managers. If it is so, the standards must be set in regard to all the elements of costs on this basis.

Thirdly, the actual costs have also to be recorded as and when they are incurred. These records are analysed and the costs are charged to different cost centres so that they may be compared with the corresponding standards fixed in advance. Thus, cost control includes some methods of accounting as well.

The next step in the cost control is making of comparison between the standard and actual costs and finding out as to where the costs have deviated from the standard fixed. The causes of the variances are to be identified and necessary step is to be taken in order to see that these variances do not occur in future. This is a very important part of cost control. A suitable reporting system for furnishing prompt reports to different managerial levels has also to be installed.

8.10.6 Internal Audit

(A) Meaning : 'Internal Audit' is an effective technique of financial and managerial control. It means the independent process of verifying and evaluating the accounting, financial and other functions of the business organisation. Internal Audit is carried out by the managers themselves or by the special staff appointed for this purpose. Compared to 'External Audit' that remains unconcerned with the operational aspect of the organisation, internal audit is much broader in scope and concerned with the whole range of activities of the organisation. Thus internal audit, in addition to ensuring that the accounts properly reflect the facts, evaluates the policies, procedures and effectiveness of the methods, the use of authority, special problems and other operations.

Internal audit feeds the managers with a perpetual supply of control information. By measuring the performance and evaluating the results on the basis of the standard, internal audit makes suitable recommendations for managerial actions. It also varifies the relevance and applicability of the policies, procedures and methods. Such a verification helps in selecting a suitable working procedures. The introduction of internal audit arouses morale and working efforts of all members in the organisation, because it involves the risk of being exposed before the managers and they try to avoid the errors of omission and commission.

(B) Advantages : The various advantages of Internal Audit may be stated as follows :

(i) It points out the defects and weaknesses in financial and managerial activities of an enterprise and suggests preventive actions, so that these cannot occur in future.

(ii) It helps in increasing the individual efficiency and organisational effectiveness.

(iii) It acts as the safeguard for maintaining the assets of the enterprise.

(iv) It provides for the overall control on all activities of an enterprise.

(C) Disadvantages : The disadvantages of Internal Audit are as under :

(i) Internal Audit is not applicable to all kinds of enterprises.

(ii) It is an expensive method of controlling. Its installation and operation require extra costs which may be too much for smaller enterprises.

(iii) It creates complications in the functional areas of an enterprise.

(iv) It leads to create confusion among the employees.

(v) It brings monotony to the employees due to its repetitive procedures.

(vi) Sometimes, the report of internal audit team may not be acceptable to the managers because of some deficiency in it.

(vii) The internal audit team has a tendency to scruitinise every aspect of business operations from accounting point of view. This may lead to faulty conclusions.

However, recently the system of internal audit has been developed to a new height by organising a centralised audit unit with a view to supplying greater and wider control information to the managers. In managing such unit, accounting qualifications alone are not sufficient, but greater emphasis is being given to managerial skill and experience. In order to avoid biasness, internal auditors in many organisations are selected from the rank of the line managers.

8.10.7 Statistical Reports

- **Meaning :** The analysis of 'Statistical Reports' is a very important tool of control. Often quantitative control is exercised on the basis of analysis of the statistical reports prepared by different managers or higher authorities of an organisation. In such reports, they provide various information in respect of the accomplishment of work, productivity, effectiveness and efficiency of the subordinates, deviations of performance from the standards, and the possible reasons for the deviations of the work or responsibilities allocated to different employees of the enterprise.

The analysis of statistical data in terms of averages, percentages, ratios, co-relation and so on is very helpful in controlling production, quality, inventory, etc. The statistical reports are analytical documents in the form of tables, charts, graphs, etc. They provide factual data and the trends which are useful for managerial control. These reports reveal whether the prescribed policies are being implemented or not.

On the basis of the statistical reports, the top level managers take decisions with regard to the performance of the subordinate employees and direct corrective measures for immediate implementation. However, this technique of control is time-consuming.

8.10.8 Management Audit

(A) Concept and Meaning : None of the control techniques discussed in the previous sections, evaluates the quality of management. Since the quality of management ultimately brings success or failure of an organisation, this quality should be assessed. 'Management Audit' is an attempt for this purpose.

Management Audit is an overall and scientific evaluation of the quality of management. It is an independent and critical examination of the entire management process. It is a systematic search and appraisal of the efficiency and effectiveness of the managers of an enterprise. It locates the deficiencies in the performance of management functions.

Therefore, **management audit is a comprehensive and constructive review of the performance of the management team of an organisation.**

The scope of management audit is very wide. Some of the areas of management audit are as follows :

(i) Organisation structure;
(ii) Functioning of the management board;
(iii) Executive appraisal;
(iv) Economic functioning;
(v) Research and development;
(vi) Production efficiency;
(vii) Soundness of earnings;
(viii) Sales vigour;
(ix) Service to stockholders; and
(x) Fiscal policy.

(B) Advantages : The Management Audit has several advantages. The main advantages may be stated as follows :

(i) It makes a total and system review of the management process which helps in locating the present and potential deficiencies in management. On the basis of such information major structural improvements can be made.

(ii) Continuous review of all aspects of the organisation helps in improving performance and protecting the organisation from inefficiency.

(iii) It helps in improving communication, co-ordination and control system by keeping the whole organisation under continuous review.

(iv) It helps in evaluating the performance of control mechanism.

(v) It gives opportunities for innovation in the light of the changes in the environment.

(C) Disadvantages : The disadvantages of Management Audit are the following :

(i) There is no standard technique of management audit.

(ii) The scope of management audit is not well-defined.

(iii) The managers may not like the critical evaluation of their policies and actions.

(iv) It may create complication in authority relationship.

(v) It is expensive.

8.10.9 Return on Investment

(A) Meaning : 'Return on Investment' (ROI) is a useful tool of controlling overall performance of an enterprise. It is also called 'Return on Capital Employed' (ROCE). The basic aspect of this technique is that profit is taken not as an absolute figure but is considered in relation to the invested capital. Rate of return is calculated by dividing the net profits by the total amount of investment. It can be computed in respect of historical data so as to reveal the rate of return realised, or it may be applied to budgeted data to give a projected rate of return.

(B) Advantages : As a control technique, ROI provides the following advantages :

1. It places high values on the effective and efficient use of organisational resources.

2. It is a mirror which reflects the entire image of the operating activity. As such, suitable action can be taken for removing inefficiency.

3. It can be treated as a total control system in the sense that rate of return reflects the objectives of the organisation.

4. It indicates how effectively the resources are being used. It makes the managers alert to wastage and inefficiency.

5. It is a useful technique of comparing the performance of the organisation over the years as well as with other enterprises. It also helps in comparing the performance of different departments and divisions of the organisation.

6. It facilitates balanced use of capital resources. It identifies the areas where capital is being effectively utilised so that future operations may be planned accordingly.

(C) Disadvantages : There are some limitations of ROI as a control tool. These are as follows :

(i) It requires too many calculations and continuous recording—which is time-consuming and expensive.

(ii) It gives excessive emphasis on financial factors ignoring other important factors like executive skills, good public relations, sound industrial relations, research and development etc.

(iii) Valuation of assets becomes difficult as prices change over time.

(iv) It is difficult to find out a standard rate of return.

8.10.10 Network Techniques

(A) Concept and Meaning :

'Network Techniques' are being widely utilised as control systems. In such technique a project or programme is broken down into small activities which are arranged in a technological sequence. Various activities should be accomplished according to the sequence. The time limit for each activity is determined. A network diagram is then drawn in order to present the inter-dependence and inter-relationships among all the operations involved in the project.

The drawing of a network diagram needs detailed analysis and evaluation of each component of the total project. The total project is highly time critical and each part of the project is optimally timed. In network analysis, an activity is defined as an operation needed to achieve the goal. It is indicated by an arrow in the diagram. The start and termination of an activity is represented by a circle. The arrows originated at an event indicate the activities that can be started only when all the activities at that event have been completed. For clarity, thick arrows or different coloured arrows are used to show critical path activities after they have been identified through analysis. The events are distinguished by numbers. Each event which indicates the termination of an activity has higher number than the event that denoted the start of the same activity. On the basis of the analysis, critical activities are determined. These are represented by a critical path which shows that if the activities on this path are not completed in time, the entire project will be delayed accordingly. Thus, on the basis of estimates the earliest or latest start time of an activity can be calculated.

There are two popular network techniques—(i) 'Programme Evaluation and Review Technique' (PERT), and (ii) 'Critical Path Method' (CPM).

1. Programme Evaluation and Review Technique : It is a network technique which is appropriate for planning and controlling the complex and unique projects. The steps involved in constructing PERT/CPM diagram are pointed out below :

(i) Breaking down of the whole project into a number of clearly identifiable activities.

(ii) Preparation of a network diagram to show the sequene of the activities which has a starting point and a completion point for the project.

(iii) Estimation of time for each activity.

(iv) Determination of the critical path which is the longest path through the network in terms of time to represent the sequence of the activities that is critical for the completion of the project.

(v) Modification and improvement of the initial plan to control or minimise the time involved in the project.

2. Critical Path Method : The major steps and principles involved in the CPM are the same as those in the PERT. But there are differences between the PERT and CPM, which are stated below :

(i) In the CPM it is considered that the duration of each activity is constant, and so, only one time estimate is made for each activity. But in the PERT, uncertainty in the duration

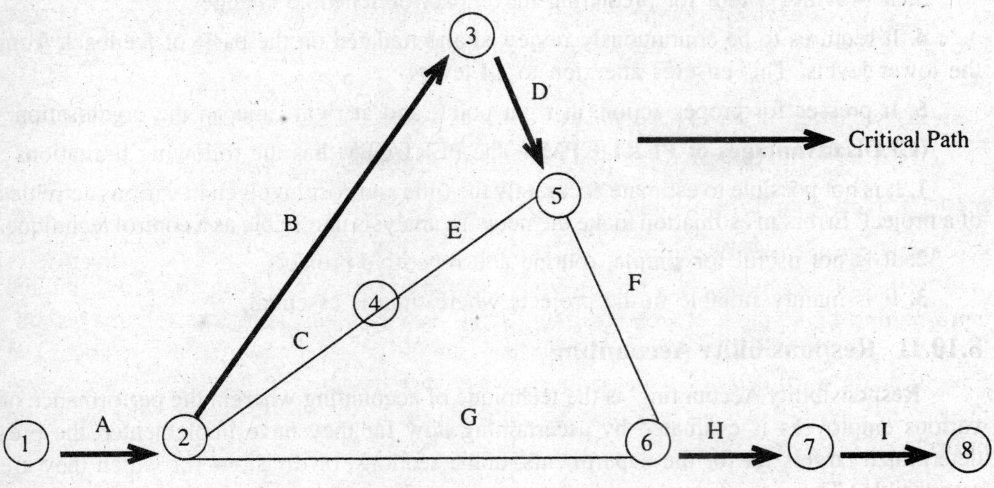

Fig. 8.5: PERT Network.

of the activities are taken into account and estimates are made thrice for every activity—(a) optimistic time showing the shortest time required for an activity, (b) Pessimistic time showing the maximum time required for an activity, and (c) most probable time which lies in between the two.

(ii) In the CPM, main focus is on cost; whereas in the PERT the focus is on time.

(iii) The CPM is more appropriate for the projects with well-known times, while the PERT is more suitable where activity timings are relatively unknown.

• **Applications of the PERT and CPM :** The PERT and CPM are very useful tools for project management. Some of the common uses of these techniques are as follows :

(i) Launching new products;

(ii) Construction of a new plant;

(iii) Installation of a computer system;

(iv) Planning and launching of a new project;

(v) Ship-building;

(vi) Building of Airport facilities;

(vii) Setting up of industry.

(B) Advantages of the PERT/CPM : The PERT/CPM is convenient and useful tool in the hands of particularly the top level manager who has the whole managerial responsibility of a project. It is also helpful in solving the problems of scheduling the activities of one-time projects, that is, the projects which are not formulated on routine basis.

The specific advantages of the PERT/CPM are as follows :

1. It forces the managers to analyse all possiblities, uncertainties and defects. This eliminates wastage. All the factors affecting the successful completion of the project are analysed in advance.

2. It focuses attention on critical activities because delay in their performance will delay the whole project, unless the managers are able to make up the time by shortening some future activities.

3. It provides a tool for predicting the impact of schedule changes.

4. It requires to be continuously reviewed and updated on the basis of feedback from the lower levels. This ensures attention to all levels.

5. It presses for proper action, at right point, and at right time, in the organisation.

(C) Disadvantages of PERT/CPM : The PERT/CPM has the following limitations :

1. It is not possible to estimate accurately the time and cost involved in various activities of a project. Errors in estimation make the network analysis unreliable as a control technique.

2. It is not useful for simple, routine and repetitive projects.

3. It is mainly suitable in the projects where time is essential.

8.10.11 Responsibility Accounting

'Responsibility Accounting' is the technique of accounting wherein the performance of various employees is evaluated by ascertaining how far they have implemented the pre-determined targets set for the departments, units, sections, or divisions for which they are responsible. The use of responsibility accounting focuses attention on management by objective rather than management by domination. Each employee is responsible for his area of operation and for effective control. He must know what his costs should be and what his costs were. Thus, in responsibility accounting, costs are allocated to responsibility centres instead of products. A responsibility centre is an organisational unit such as department, division or section headed by a responsible person. The head is responsible for reaching the target set for his centre. The costs incurred by a responsibility centre are divided into two categories—(i) controlable costs, and (ii) uncontrolable costs. Costs are accumulated and reported according to the classification. The head of a responsibility centre is responsible directly for the controllable costs of his centre.

There are three types of responsibility centres stated as follows :

1. Investment Centre : The head of this centre is responsible not only for costs and profits but also for the effective use of assets. The investment made in each centre is separately calculated and the return on investment is applied as the basis of evaluating the performance of the centre. It is the ultimate extension of responsibility.

2. Cost Centre : Most of the departments and sections are cost centres. In a cost centre the targets are fixed in terms of costs. The performance of cost centres is evaluated by making a comparision between the actual expenses and the budgeted costs. In cost centres, the control system measures only the costs incurred by responsibility centres; no attempt is made to measure the value of their outputs.

3. Profit Centre : In a profit centre the targets are set in terms of profits. The performance of this centre is evaluated by comparing the profits actually earned with the target profit. This is done by preparing departmental profit and loss account.

8.10.12 Zero-Base Budgeting

(A) Concept and Meaning : 'Zero-base Budgeting' (ZBB) is comparatively a newer concept in business and non-business budgeting. It was applied for the first time in the USA in 1971. Since then it has been used by a number of states and business enterprises in the USA and other countries. In India it became the focus of discussion only a few years ago. It has been applied by many departments of the Government of India and also some State Governments. Besides, some public sector enterprises have also adopted it.

ZBB is based on the system in which each function must be justified in its entirety each time a new budget is formulated. Instead of taking the current year's budget as the base as is done in traditional system of budgeting, the budget is prepared from a zero-base. All budget proposals are considered from scratch as if it is the first budget of the enterprise. All proposals are analysed thoroughly to test their validity and effectiveness in the light of actual experience and changed conditions.

ZBB process involves the following four basic steps—

(i) Identification of decision units, that is, the activities or assignments within the jurisdiction of a manager's operations for which he is accountable;

(ii) Analysis of each decision unit in the context of total decision package;

(iii) Evaluation and ranking of all decision units on the basis of benefits to the organisation; and

(iv) Allocation or resources to each unit according to the ranking.

Thus, emphasis is given on resource allocation according to the contributions of each decision unit.

(B) Advantages : ZBB has a number of benefits. These benefits are as follows :

(i) It is an effective means to control costs. It forces the managers to make each programme afresh and to review each expense again.

(ii) It is an innovative and creative approach. It helps in avoiding inefficiencies and mistakes of the past.

(iii) It allows the managers a great deal of freedom and flexibility in allocating resources from year to year.

(iv) It permits greater participation in the budgeting process.

(v) It eliminates unnecessary activities.

(vi) There is clearer and more objective evaluation of budget proposals.

(vii) It saves time of the top managers.

(C) Disadvantages : ZBB has the following disadvantages :

(i) The review process involved in ZBB is very time-consuming.

(ii) Difficulty may arise in identifying decision units.

(iii) It may result into extra paper-work.

8.10.13 Performance Budgeting

(A) Concept and Meaning : According to the tradition, Government Budgeting was made on the basis of the heads of expenses. The budget contained the expenses for each head such as administration, defence, travelling, etc. In modern times, a large part of public administration is engaged in economic activities. It was felt that a new approach was required to prepare plan and to control performance. As a result, a new technique called 'Performance Budgeting' was introduced. A performance budget is an 'input/output' or 'costs/results' budget. It contains the expenses according to the heads of performance. The concept of performance budget originated in the USA during 1960s when defence budgeting led to the thinking of the ways and means of matching outputs to inputs. Afterwards, it became popular in many government departments outside the USA. At present, performance budgeting is being utilised in business and other organisations besides the government departments. In India, although the concept of performance budget was discussed during the debate of Parliament in 1964, it was adopted much later.

Performance budgeting gives emphasis on non-financial measures of performance which can be related to financial measures in explaining the changes and deviations from planned performance. The historical comparisons of non-financial measurements of activity are particuiarly helpful in justifying the budget proposals and in showing how the resources of the organisation are being used. Personal measurements are useful for evaluating the past performance and planning the future activities.

The principal steps in Performance Budgeting are as follows :

(i) Identification of goal, that is, the results or output of a performing department, unit or undertaking;

(ii) Preparation of a schedule of performance leading to the identified goal;

(iii) Linking all expansions to performance heads; and,

(iv) Development of a yardstick or unit of accomplishment that measures performance.

Performance budgeting is being increasingly applied in business, government and other organisations. The commercial banks are applying it for decision-making and evaluation. It highlights the end results instead of money to be spent. It reveals whether the organisation is getting adequate results for the money spent.

(B) Advantages and Limitations : The **benefits** provided by Performance Budgeting may be stated as follows :

(i) to improve budget preparation, review and decision-making at all levels of management;

(ii) to make performance audit more effective;

(iii) to co-relate the physical and financial aspects of every programme or activity;

(iv) to bring the annual budgets and development plans closely together; and

(v) to measure progress towards the long-term objectives determined in the plans.

Performance budgeting leads to higher efficiency as it measures the activities in terms of results or output. However, performance budgeting has the following **limitations** :

(i) To be effective, performance budgeting needs fundamental structural changes in the organisation. Such changes are usually resisted by the people within the organisation.

(ii) It requires a sound system and network of planning. If the goal is not clear, it cannot be applied for controlling performance effectively.

(iii) It is very difficult to determine goals of performance and to measure the actual performance against the goal where the output is intangible such as—research, training, education, etc. Disputes may arise on the criterion and measurement of performance.

8.10.14 Management Information System

(A) Meaning : 'Management Information System' (MIS) is the method of providing the relevant and required information through computer to each manager of an organisation at the proper time and in the right form which aids his understanding and stimulates his action. In other words, it is the system of giving the past, present and projection information regarding internal operations and external intelligence. It supports the planning, control and operational functions of an organisation by providing uniform information in right time and correct form to assist the decision-making process.

With the increasing use of electronic devices, particularly computers, a great deal of attention has been given to the development of information systems which provide relevant information to the managers concerned for decision-making and control. A pre-requisite of effective control is timely and authentic information for the controlling authority. The flow of information is made regular by an information system known as Management Information System or MIS. It is applied as a very important tool of control in large organisations where a huge number of activities take place. It helps to a large extent in quantitative and qualitative controlling of all types of activities of an enterprise. But, the system is expensive and efficient managerial persons are needed for effective operation of the technique.

(B) Role of Management Information System :

The role played by MIS can be evaluated by the quality and quantity of information supplied to the various points in the organisation. The system helps the managers of the organisation to collect relevant information and precise data more quickly. MIS is a refined form of traditional information collection and supply to different organisational points. In large enterprises, there are so many decision points that it is not possible to manage effectively without MIS. The major problems of such enterprises are that data are to be collected from a large number of points. This process takes much time in the absence of MIS. Besides, there are many departments in big organisations and each of them may be storing information and needing data on common points. This puts unnecessary duplication in the efforts. MIS can relieve much pressure by unifying the information storage.

8.11 Essentials of an Effective Control System

The essentials or requirements of an effective and efficient control system are discussed below :

1. Simplicity : A good control system must be simple and easily understandable so that all the managers can apply it effectively. Complicated control techniques fail to communicate the meaning of control data to the managers.

2. Objectivity : The standards of performance should be objective and specific, quantified and verifiable. They should be based on the facts so that control is acceptable and workable.

3. Promptness : The control system should provide information soon enough so that the managers can detect and report the deviations promptly and necessary corrective actions may be taken in proper time. Corrective measures are of no value if those are taken too late.

4. Economy : The control system must justify the expenses involved. In other words, anticipated earnings from it should be greater than the expected costs in its working. A small organisation cannot use the expensive control technique applied in large enterprises.

5. Flexibility : Internal goals and strategies must be responsive to the changes in the environment and the control system should be flexible enough to adapt the changing conditions or unforseen situations. It should be adaptable to the new developments. Flexibility in control system can be introduced by making alternative plans.

6. Accuracy : The control system should encourage accurate information in order to detect deviations. The technique of control used should be appropriate to the work being controlled.

7. Suitablity : Control must reflect the needs and nature of the activities of the organisation. The control system should focus on achieving the organisational goals.

8. Forward-looking Nature : The control system must be directed towards the future. It must pay attention on how the future actions can be conformed with the plans adopted.

9. Focus on Strategic Points : The control system should focus attention on strategic or critical deviations. Only exceptional deviations require the attention of the managers.

10. Motivating : A good control system should pay due attention to the human factor. It should be designed to secure positive action from the workers. Self-control tends to be motivated. Direct contact between the controller and the controlled also helps in making the control system motivational.

11. Reflection of Organisation Pattern : Control must reflect organisation pattern. Since the events are controlled through people, it is essential that controls must conform to the organisation pattern. The control process should be acceptable on the psychological front.

12. Corrective Action : Control system must ensure corrective actions. An adequate control technique should not only detect the deviations and failures, but should also disclose where they are occuring; who is responsible for them; and what should be done to correct them.

EXERCISES

[A] Essay-Type Questions

1. What is meant by control? Discuss the main features of control.
   [**Ans.** Sections 8.1 and 8.3.1]
2. Discuss the importance and limitations of control in a business organisation.
   [**Ans.** Sections 8.4 and 8.6]
3. "Control is a fundamental management function that ensures work accomplishment according to plans."—Analyse the statement and outline the various steps involved in control of process.
   [**Ans.** Sections 8.1 and 8.5]
4. "Planning is the basis, delegation is the key, informaion is the guide, and action is the essence of control."—Discuss.
   [**Ans.** Sections 8.2]
5. In what way are planning and control related to each other? Explain clearly the essential steps in control process.
   [**Ans.** Sections 8.8 and 8.5]
6. (a) What is meant by 'control' in management?
   (b) What are the principal stages of control? [C.U. B.Com. 1983]
   [**Ans.** Section 8.1 and 8.5]
7. Discuss the basic elements of control in management. [C.U. B.Com. 1986]
   [**Ans.** Section 8.5]
8. Define control. Discuss the different stages of control. [C.U. B.Com. 1988]
   [**Ans.** Sections 8.1 and 8.5]
9. What do you understand by control in organisation? Discuss the steps in control.
   [C.U. B.Com. 1990, 1992, 1994]
   [**Ans.** Sections 8.1 and 8.5]
10. What is control? Explain its importance. [C.U. B.Com. 1995]
    [**Ans.** Sections 8.1 and 8.4]
11. Discuss in brief the steps involved in controlling. [C.U. B.Com. 1996]
    [**Ans.** Section 8.5]

12. (a) What is controlling?
(b) What are the steps involved in controlling? [C.U. B.Com. 1998]
[**Ans.** Sections 8.1 and 8.5]

13. Give a brief account of the different types of control.
[**Ans.** Section 8.7]

14. What is meant by 'Span of Control'? Discuss the factors which affect it. How might it be widened?
[**Ans.** Section 8.9]

15. Discuss, in brief, the steps involved in the controlling process [C.U. B.Com. 1999, 2004]
[**Ans.** Section 8.5]

16. Discuss the different stages of control. [C.U. B.Com. 2001]
[**Ans.** Section 8.5]

17. Explain the important features of a sound control system. [C.U. B.Com. 2003]
[**Ans.** Section 8.3]

18. Explain the process of control. [C.U. B.Com. 2006, 2008]
[**Ans.** Section 8.5]

19. State the major features of a good control system. [C.U. B.Com. 2006]
[**Ans.** Section 8.11]

20. Define control. Mention the different techniques of control and state the merits and demerits of Budgetary Control. [C.U. B.Com. 2006]
[**Ans.** Sections 8.1, 8.10 and 8.10.2]

21. State the tools and techniques of an effective control system. [C.U. B.Com. 2007]
[**Ans.** Section 8.10]

22. What are the pre-requisites of effective managerial control? [C.U. B.Com. 2009]
[**Ans.** Section 8.11.]

23. What do you mean by 'Budgetary Control'? Explain its characteristics.
[**Ans.** Sections 8.10.2(A) and 8.10.2(B)]

24. Describe the merits and demerits of Budgetary Control.
[**Ans.** Sections 8.10.2(C) and 8.10.2(D)]

25. What is 'Break-even Analysis'? Discuss its advantages and disadvantages.
[**Ans.** Sections 8.10.3(A), 8.10.3(B) and 8.10.3(C)]

26. What is 'Ratio Analysis'? State its merits and demerits.
[**Ans.** Sections 8.10.4(A), 8.10.4(B) and 8.10.4(C)]

27. What is meant by 'Cost Control'? Describe the process of cost control.
[**Ans.** Section 8.10.5]

28. What is 'Internal Audit'? Explain its merits and demerits.
[**Ans.** Sections 8.10.6(A), 8.10.6(B) and 8.10.6(C)]

29. What do you mean by 'Management Audit'? Explain its advantages and disadvantages.
[**Ans.** Sections 8.10.8(A), 8.10.8(B) and 8.10.8(C)]

30. What do you understand by'Return on Investment'? Discuss its advantages and disadvantages.
[**Ans.** Sections 8.10.9(A), 8.10.9(B) and 8.10.9(C)]

31. What is 'Responsibility Accounting'?—Explain it.
[**Ans.** Section 8.10.11]
32. State the concept of Zero-base Budgeting.
[**Ans.** Section 8.10.12(A)]
33. Describe the merits and demerits of Zero-base Budgeting.
[**Ans.** Sections 8.10.12(B) and 8.10.12(C)]
34. Explain the concept of 'Performance Budgeting'.
[**Ans.** Section 8.10.13]
35. What are the advantages and disadvantages of 'Performance Budgeting'?
[**Ans.** Section 8.10.13(B)]
36. What do you mean by 'Management Information System'. Describe its role.
[**Ans.** Sections 8.10.14(A) and 8.10.14(B)]
37. State the essentials of an effective control process.
[**Ans.** Section 8.11]
38. Discuss, in brief, the steps involved in controlling. [C.U. B.Com. 2011]
[**Ans.** Section 8.5.]
39. What factors should be taken into consideration for determining the 'Span of Management' of an organisation? [C.U. B.Com. 2011 New Syllabus]
[**Ans.** Section 8.9.]
40. Mention the steps in control process with a diagram.
[C.U. B.Com. 2011 New Syllabus]
[**Ans.** Section 8.5]
41. Briefly discuss, 'Budgetary Control'. [C.U. B.Com. 2011 New Syllabus]
[**Ans.** Section 8.10.2.]

[B] Short Answer-Type Questions

1. Write short notes on the following:

(i) Nature of Control.
[**Ans.** Section 8.2]
(ii) Importance of Control.
[**Ans.** Section 8.4]
(iii) Limitations of Control.
[**Ans.** Section 8.6]
(iv) Planning and Control.
[**Ans.** Section 8.8]
(v) Span of Control.
[**Ans.** Section 8.9]

2. Answer in brief the following questions:

(i) Define 'Control'.
[**Ans.** Section 8.1]
(ii) Point out any two characteristics of control.
[**Ans.** Section 8.3]
(iii) Mention any two types of control.
[**Ans.** Section 8.7]

(iv) What are the basic elements of the control process?
[**Ans.** Section 8.5]

(v) What is 'Span of Control'? [C.U. B.Com. 1988, 1993, 1995, 1999]
[**Ans.** Section 8.9]

(vi) What is 'Control'? [C.U. B.Com. 1999]
[**Ans.** Section 8.1]

(vii) Mention any four features of control. [C.U. B.Com. 2000, 2006]
[**Ans.** Section 8.3]

(viii) Mention any two limitations of control. [C.U. B.Com. 2002]
[**Ans.** Section 8.6]

(ix) What do you mean by 'Span of Control'?
[C.U. B.Com. 2003, 2005, 2006, 2008, 2011]
[**Ans.** Section 8.9]

(x) What do you mean by 'Control'? [C.U. B.Com. 2005]
[**Ans.** Section 8.1]

(xi) What is the relationship between planning and control? [C.U. B.Com. 2007]
[**Ans.** Section 8.8]

(xii) What do you mean by 'Budgetary Control'? [C.U. B.Com. 2011]
[**Ans.** Section 8.10. 2(A)]

Module II

BUSINESS COMMUNICATION

CHAPTER 1

Nature of Business Communication

"The most important thing in communication is to hear what isn't being said."

—Peter Drucker

TOPICS

i. Introduction ◆ ii. Business Communication—Definition and Meaning ◆ iii. Elements of Business Communication ◆ iv. Features or Characteristics of Business Communication ◆ v. Objectives of Business Communication ◆ vi. Process or Steps of Business Communication ◆ vii. Channels of Business Communication ◆ viii. Feedback as the Essence of Communication ◆ ix. Levels of Business Communication ◆ x. Effective Communication: (a) Principles, (b) Benefits ◆ xi. Communication Barriers ◆ xii. Methods of Overcoming Communication Barriers ◆ xiii. Communication Models.

Subject-matter of the Chapter : *No one can live without communication. Communication of information, ideas, facts, emotions, feelings, etc. are necessary in our day-to-day life. Today's business world is entirely dependent on communication. It is impossible to go a single step forward without it.*

In this chapter an attempt has been made to define business communication, describe its importance, visualise its objectives, narrate its various channels, analyse the steps and explain the principles of effective communication. The barriers to communication and the methods of overcoming those barriers have been discussed. A brief discussion on communication models has also been included. Thus, this chapter will provide the readers with elementary knowledge regarding business communication.

● **Introduction:** Business Communication is necessary for making contacts, giving orders, issuing instructions, managing work-place, conveying technical know-how, providing feedback, and a series of such other activities. In this age of globalisation, computers and information technology, it is important that the right information is communicated at the right place and in the right time. Failure to communicate properly may result in loss of opportunity, improper planning, wrong decision-making, inefficient management, erosion of competition edge and surrender of pioneering position. The success of a business enterprise depends, to a great extent, on the harnessing of the communication process in the right manner.

1.1 Business Communication—Definition and Meaning

The word "Communication" has come from the Latin word "*communis*", which means common. Thus, communication signifies sharing of ideas in common. The dictionary meaning of communication is to convey or exchange information and share ideas. It is a process through which two or more persons transmit or exchange thoughts and ideas among themselves. According to **W. H. Newman** and **C. F. Summer, "Communication is an exchange of facts, ideas, opinions or emotions by two or more persons."**

Communication is the process of transmitting information and understanding from one person to another or from one unit to other unit with a view to getting the desired response from the receiver. Through this process two or more persons exchange ideas and understanding among themselves to achieve the desired effect in the behaviour of another person. It is a two-way channel for transmitting ideas, feelings, plans, commands, instructions, reports and suggestions that influence the attitude towards an organisation's objectives. The communicator's goal is to convey the meanings or ideas without distortion. Success of the leader and the enterprise depends upon adequacy of communication. It is the responsibility of the managers to establish and maintain the channels whereby they can convey their own thinking and policies to the subordinates, and can receive their reactions and an account of their problems.

Louis A. Allen defines communication in the following manner:

"Communication is the sum total of all the things one person does when he wants to create understanding in the mind of another. It is a bridge of meaning. It involves a systematic and continuous process of telling, listening and understanding."

The definition involves two aspects in communication. *First*, there is something which is transmitted, such as facts, feelings, ideas, etc. It implies that there must be a receiver if communication is to occur. *Second*, the definition emphasises the understanding element in the communication process. Sharing of understanding would be possible only when the person to whom the message is sent, understands in the same sense in which the sender of message wants him to understand. So, communication involves something more than mere transmission of the message or transmission and physical receipt thereof. The correct interpretation and understanding of the message is important from the point of view of organisational efficiency. Effective communication, as such, might be the accurate transmission and receipt thereof, and its correct understanding. In their book "Business Communication Today" **C. L. Bovee, J. V. Thill and B. E. Schatzman write: "Communication is the process of sending and receiving messages. However, communication is effective only when the message is understood and when it stimulates action or encourages the receiver to think in new ways."**

Communication made among persons to convey their personal information, message or thought are personal communication; but exchange of information, facts and ideas relating to business may be termed as **"Business Communication"**. Business Communication refers to the communication relating to business activity which means providing goods and services to the consumers with a view to earning profit. It is a process through which information, facts, ideas, orders, advices, decisions, etc. are conveyed, sent or exchanged between/among the persons associated with business. Thus, **Communication relating to trade, law, finance, administration, management, etc. of a business enterprise may be termed as 'Business Communication'.** The success of a business enterprise depends largely upon good communication. Effective communication wipes out the hindrances in achieving the target of a business enterprise. Ineffective communication or communication failure may cause loss of money, time, energy, opportunity and even goodwill of a business.

In this age of globalisation every business enterprise, big or small, requires proper communication for its existence. The success of any business concern largely depends upon successful communication. In this age of speed, complexity and competition, sending of information regarding the product to the ultimate consumer is very important. Unless they know about the product of the business enterprise, it is not possible for them to make contact and buy the product. Communication plays a vital role in this sphere.

1.2 Elements of Business Communication

Business communication involves *six* basic elements. They are as follows:

1. **Message:** This is the subject-matter which is transmitted or passed by the sender to the other party or group of persons. This might be opinion, order, suggestion, attitude, feeling, view, etc.
2. **Sender:** He/she is the person who intends to make contact for passing information and understanding to other person.
3. **Receiver:** The person to whom the message is meant for is known as receiver or communicatee.
4. **Channels:** Information is transmitted through certain channels (e.g., radio, television, telephone, letter, e-mail, etc.). The media is selected by the sender considering various factors.
5. **Symbols:** These are the words, actions and signs which are passed on by the sender while communicating with the receiver.
6. **Feedback:** When the receiver acknowledges the message of the sender and responds back to him/her, feedback takes place. Without feedback communication is incomplete.

1.3 Features or Characteristics of Business Communication

Business Communication has certain features or characteristics which enable us to distinguish it from other communication. A communication to be business communication must be:

i. Practical,
ii. Factual,
iii. Clear and brief,
iv. Target-oriented,
v. Persuasive.

1. **Practical:** Effective business communication deals with the practical aspect of the information explaining why, how, when and the like queries. It avoids impractical, imaginary, unnecessary or repetitive information to eliminate waste of time. It conveys important information to the receiver.
2. **Factual:** In general a business message contains facts and figures in place of overall idea. Important date, place, time, etc. should be clearly mentioned in a business communication.
3. **Clear and Brief:** The language used in business communication should be simple, clear, brief and without ambiguity. Sometimes charts, photographs, diagrams, etc. are used to condense or clarify the information.
4. **Target-Oriented:** A business communication must have a specific objective and must be planned properly so that the objective can be achieved.
5. **Persuasive:** Business communication often plays a persuasive role. It persuades an employee to perform his/her duties, a customer to buy a product or service etc.

The basic characteristics mentioned above are related to the message or information of the communication. The process of business communication has certain other characteristics. They are:

1. Integral Part of Management Process: Communication encompasses those activities by which the ideas, opinions and decisions of the managers are conveyed to the subordinates of different ranks. It also involves the exchange of facts, feelings, suggestions and responses between the superiors and subordinates. Communication, in this way, puts the people into action, guides and directs their activities, regulates and co-ordinates them for proper work performance. A manager, thus, performs the management functions through communication and managerial positions become the communication centres to receive information from various sources for its transmission to relevant points. So, communication is a part and parcel of management function, and is, thus, an integral part of management process. That is why, **Chester I. Bernard** remarks, "the first executive function is to develop and maintain a system of communication".

2. Two-Way Traffic: Communication does not only mean its downward movement from superior to the subordinates it implies both the transmission and reception. So, when conveying any information, a manager should know its reactions and responses. Otherwise, managerial task of guiding and directing will be ineffective. A man should, thus, not only speak, inform and order, but should also be able to listen, answer and interpret. Communication, therefore, involves two-way traffic from the managers to the employees and from the employees to the managers. It is not complete unless the message has been correctly understood by the receiver and its response becomes known to the sender.

3. Mutual Understanding: The basic purpose of business communication is to bring about understanding between individuals in the organisation. It is an important element for establishing human relationships. A leader can lead and a manager can direct effectively by establishing perfect understanding with the subordinates, peers and superiors in the organisation. The greater the degree of understanding present in the communication the more possibility that human action will proceed in the direction of accomplishing the goals.

4. Pervasive: The subject-matter of business communication covers a wide range and extends to all functions—purchases, production, sales, finance, recruitment, wages, dividends, market standing, innovation, productivity, etc. It also moves through all levels of management—upward, downward and sideways. Business communication is, thus, said to be a pervasive function.

5. Continuity: Communication is an ever-present activity and without it an organisation cannot exist. Communication is as necessary to an organisation as blood circulation in a living body. Therefore, the managers should ensure that adequate and smooth communication flows in all directions. Breakdown of communication results in misunderstanding, creation of unfavourable attitudes, hostility and conflict. So, communication must be a continuous process and move up, down and sideways for active participation of all concerned.

6. Specific: A business communication is generally specific in nature. It means that a particular communication should deal with a single subject at a time. This is necessary for the effectiveness of communication. Multiplicity of subject in a communication has the possibility of creating confusion which is dangerous to sound management. It must be specific with regard to the information intended to be conveyed or received.

7, Result and not Cause: Sound communication is the result of competent management, not the cause of it. Business communication is a means to an end and acts as a tool in the hands of the managers. Successful handling of this tool depends upon the competence of the managers. It is not an independent activity, rather an essential ingredient of managerial function. So, good communication does not produce good manager. But good manager is nearly always a good communicator. Misconception of management process often leads to poor communication.

8. Internal and External: Business communication is primarily internal. It is, thus, a part of administrative function and intended to apply to the members belonging to an organisation. Orders, instructions, suggestions and even public notice announcing the annual general meeting of a company are some of the examples of internal communication. But nowadays, many communications move beyond the organisational horizons and touch the outside population exceeding the organisation's own (e.g., advertisement). Business communication may thus be internal and external.

9. Different Types: Business communication may be of different types—formal, informal, upward, downward, sidewise, written, oral, etc.

10. Feedback: A communication cannot be complete unless and until feedback or response of the recipient is made. Feedback may be written, oral or gestural. Sometimes mere silence may also constitute a feedback.

1.4 Objectives of Business Communication

The main objective of communication is to give information and to persuade different persons. Other objectives include conveying suggestion, opinion, idea, advice, request, etc.; imparting instructions, guidance and counselling; providing training; giving warning; appreciating good work; boosting of morale; etc.

In the case of a business enterprise the main objective of communication is the improvement of its activities, all-round development of the organisation, and ultimate success in its operation.

1. Giving Information: The primary object of communication is to make the members of an organisation aware of its goal and acquaint them with all the relevant information. This helps the business enterprise to achieve success through concerted efforts of all the people concerned. It is a fact that well-informed people can achieve better.

The managers should know in details the social, political, economic and other conditions of the place where the business is situated. Information regarding the employees, consumers and competitors should be at their fingertips. Employees, likewise, should be well-informed about their positions, powers and responsibilities in particular, and the aims and objectives of the organisation in general.

Information regarding demand for a particular product, the taste, liking, etc. of the consumers; availability of raw materials, credit facility, advertising media; latest government rules and regulations, etc. are required for the production and selling of the product.

Information can be obtained from past records, books, journals, newspapers, government publications, seminars, conferences, exhibitions, trade fares, etc. The other sources of information are the chambers of commerce, structured questionnaires, radio, television, internet, etc. Whatever might be the sources, the information must be reliable, accurate, complete and latest.

2. Persuasion: To persuade means to make other people decide to do something, especially by repeatedly asking them or telling them the reasons why they should do it; in other words, influencing other people to believe or to do what one wants. This is one of the important objectives of communication.

The seller often influences the buyer through persuasion to buy his/her products rejecting earlier decision to buy other products. This persuasion should be so planned that the buyer becomes least conscious of being persuaded and even if he/she becomes conscious, he/she should be made to understand that it is for his/her own interest. Actually persuasion is an art which should be suggestive in nature rather than coercive.

3. Conveying Suggestion: Communication helps in conveying suggestions, opinions and ideas. The workers who are actually engaged in the work know better the loopholes in it and can suggest to the managers the ways to plug the loopholes. This is an example of upward communication. In big offices, suggestion boxes are provided and suggestions are received throughout the year. Sometimes further communication is made with the suggestions for clarification. Interaction of suggestions and ideas help the progress of an organisation.

Suggestions are not in the nature of order or advice and are, therefore, never obligatory to follow them. Either acceptance or rejection is possble in the case of a suggestion. Some executives, supervisors or managers who have a false notion of self-dignity, self-respect, higher position, etc. may not accept a suggestion, even though it is good one because it comes from lower level. But dynamic executives welcome constructive suggestions in the interest of the organisation.

4. Advice: One of the objectives of business communication is to advise an individual or a group of people. The manager advises the subordinates about the ways and means of better performance.

Advice involves personal opinion and it influences the opinion and action of the other person(s) to whom advice is being given.

Today's business world is very complex and no one can be an expert in all the spheres of business. So, a businessman has to take advice from experts regarding the matters in which he is not well-informed. For example, he may need advice regarding banking, insurance, stock exchange, tax rules, legal procedures, etc. Within the business the managers, supervisors and executives may advise each other (a case of horizontal communication) and the subordinates (downward communication).

5. Motivation: Communication is made to inspire, to motivate, and to create a sense of loyalty among the employees. Through communication their morale is boosted up and it leads to better performance. Regular communication is necessary for motivating the employees and infusing in them a positive attitude towards work and a healthy relationship with the managers. This, ultimately, increases managerial efficiency.

Motivating someone means inspiring but not forcing him/her to do something. A motivated worker is an asset of any organisation.

The greater the motivation, the lesser is the cost of supervision, because a motivated worker never neglects his duties. Motivating factors include monetary incentives, security of job, job satisfaction, good working environment, participation in decision-making, fixation of target, etc. Money works as a good motivator. A worker works overtime when he/she is allowed extra wages. Security of job motivates an employee to devote himself/herself wholeheartedly to the job. If an employee is satisfied with the job, he/she gets pleasure in doing it. Good working environment attracts him/her to work in co-operation with other members. Workers' participation in decision-making gives them a sense of being part and parcel of the organisation. Fixation of production target, sales target, etc. of an organisation helps the workers to work together to achieve the target. Thus, different factors of motivation contribute to achieve performance excellence of an organisation.

6. Training: To meet the need of an organisation, senior employees may need to be trained to update them about the new technological developments so as to adjust themselves to changing work environment or job demands. The new employees may also require training at the initial stage to cope up with the methods, techniques and systems of work in the organisation. Communication is the key to all these kinds of training. Such communication can be made through classroom teaching, lectures, seminars, short courses, conferences, educational tours, film shows, etc. Not only the ordinary employees, but the managerial staff also need to be trained in the process stated above.

7. Instruction, Guidance and Counselling: One of the objectives of business communication is to manage the employees by means of imparting instruction, providing guidance and arranging for counselling. Legal, vocational and medical guidance and counselling are provided free of cost for the employees in a good business organisation. Doctors, lawyers, coaches, etc. are employed for the purpose. The underlying objective of such assistance is to keep the employees physically fit and mentally alert so that they can work whole-heartedly for the well-being of the organisation.

8. Giving Warning and Appreciating Good Work: It is very much necessary to appreciate a good worker. It will encourage him/her to strive for better performance and greater involvement. It makes the employee conscious about his/her responsibilities.

On the other hand, it is also necessary to give warning to the employees who tend to be indisciplined, non-accountable and unproductive or create disturbance.

The objective of both appreciation and warnings may be accomplished through oral or written communication.

9. Resource Utilisation: Communication checks wastage of the resources of the organisation and helps their better utilisation. Lack of knowledge or lack of proper direction in time may cause the waste or misuse. Communication helps to bridge the gap of knowledge through instruction, advice, etc. and waste or misuse of resource is minimised. Not only material resources, but also the financial resources, human resources and other resources are utilised properly through communication.

10. Management Efficiency: One of the objectives of business communication is to increase efficiency of the management. If there is a good network of communication (formal and informal), the organisation can be managed efficiently and effectively.

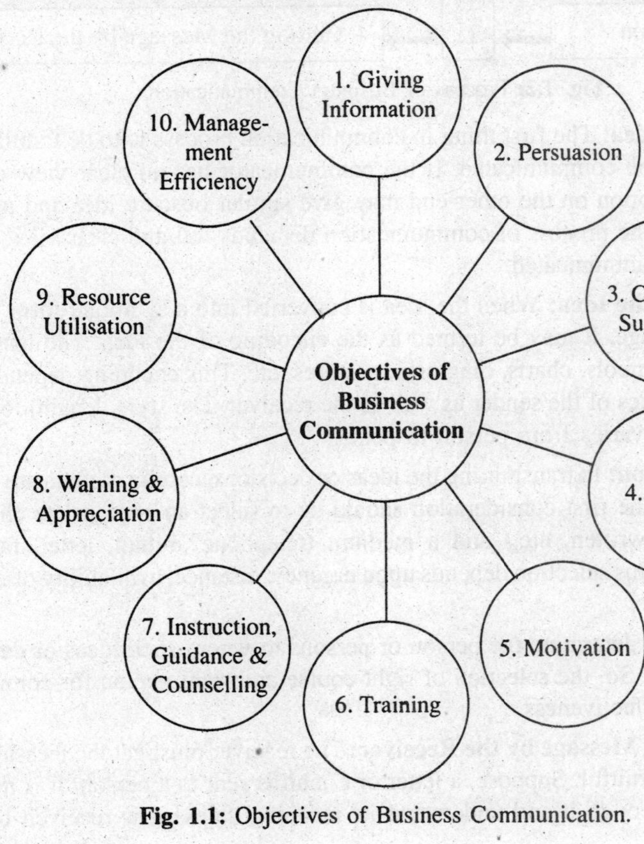

Fig. 1.1: Objectives of Business Communication.

1.5 Process or Steps of Business Communication

The process or steps of communication involves a series of actions and operations undertaken for the fulfilment of a certain end or objective. According to **Lawrence A. Appley,** the basic communication process involves the following steps:

(i) Clarifying the idea or problem, (ii) Getting participation in developing a solution to the problem, (iii) Transmitting the idea or decision, (iv) Motivating others to take action agreed upon, and (v) Measuring the effectiveness of communication.

Charles E. Redfield states that the following elements are involved in the process of communication:

(a) **A communicator** (a speaker, sender, issuer), (b) **transmits** (says, sends, issues), (c) **stimulus** (message, orders, reports) to a (d) **communicatee** (adressee, respondent, audience) to influence his behaviour as seen in his (e) **response** (reply, reaction).

The process of communication can best be expressed by **Laswell's** popular **five 'Whs'**: " 'Who' says 'What' in 'Which Channel' to 'Whom' with 'What effect'?"

In the light of the above, the process or steps of business communication can be described as follows :

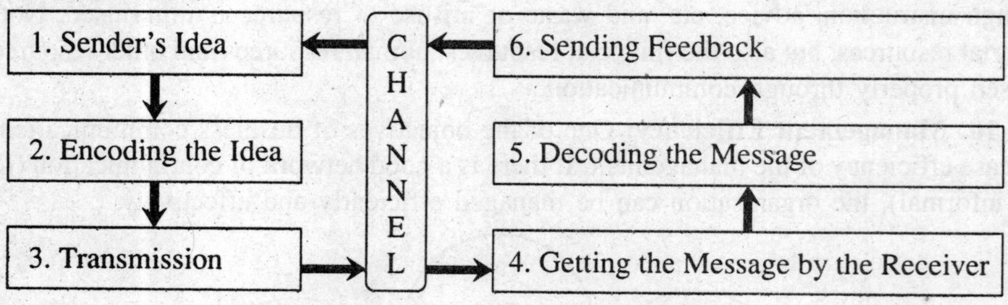

Fig. 1.2: Process of Business Communication.

1. Sender's Idea: The first thing in communication process is to be familiar with the idea or problem to be communicated. If the communicator has no clear view of this idea or problem, its reception on the other end may give similar obscure idea and may thus be misunderstood. So, the process of communication demands full and clear view of the idea or problem to be communicated.

2. Encoding the Idea: When the idea is converted into a symbolic form in terms of some kind of language, it may be termed as the encoding of the idea. The language may consist of words, symbols, charts, diagrams, gestures, etc. This encoding depends upon the personal characteristics of the sender as well as the receiver. The style, length, form, clarity, etc. of the message varies from person to person.

3. Transmission: In transmitting the ideas or decisions, certain matters are to be taken into consideration. The first consideration should be to select an appropriate channel (i.e., verbal, non-verbal, written, etc.) and a medium (telephone, e-mail, letter, face to face conversation, etc.). This selection depends upon urgency, distance, availability of means, cost and time factor, etc.

Next thing is to determine the person or persons to whom such ideas or decisions are to be communicated. So, the selection of right course and right person for communication is essential for its effectiveness.

4. Getting the Message by the Receiver: The receiver must get the message to make the communication fruitful. Suppose, a letter or e-mail is sent to a person. It is not possible for him/her to go through it and understand its meaning unless it is received by him/her.

5. Decoding the Message: Decoding means understanding or bringing out the meaning of the message. It is very vital. If the receiver understands the message in the same sense as the sender intends, the objective of communication is presumed to be fulfilled.

6. Sending Feedback: Feedback is the receiver's response to the message. Having understood the message the receiver reacts to it and responds accordingly. The feedback evaluates the effectiveness of the message. If the sense of the message is realisd properly, the feedback or the response will be desirable and, if it is not, one has to understand that there are some barriers in the process. Steps are required to be taken for the removal of such barriers.

7. Channel: Channels are the routes or paths of the communication. The sender's idea is transmitted to the receiver through this path. Again, the receiver sends feedback to the sender through the channel. Thus, channel is used at least twice in the process of communication. Oral or telephonic message, letter, different audio and video media, computer, e-mail, fax, etc. are the popular channels of communication. Selection of channel depends upon the nature of the message, necessity, urgency and situational conditions.

8. Noise: It is not a separate step in the process. It may be present at every step and make the communication less effective or ineffective. Noise distorts the message and conveys ideas not intended by the sender resulting in chaos, confusion and complexity.

1.6 Channels of Business Communication

Channels are the routes or paths through which messages are sent or received.

- **Examples of Channels:**
  1. Here ABC are the three persons and there are three channels of communication between AB, BC and CA.

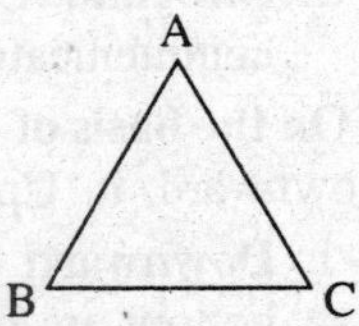

Fig. 1.3: Channels of Communication.

  2. Here, ABCD are the four persons and there are six channels of communication between AB, BD, DC, CA, AD and BC.

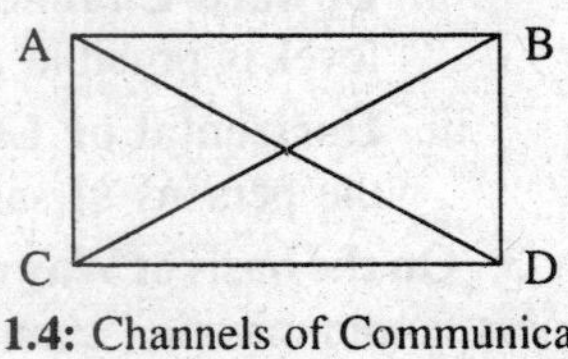

Fig. 1.4: Channels of Communication.

  3. Here the number of persons are five—ABCDE—and ten channels of communication between AB, BC, CD, DE, EA, AC, AD, BD, BE and CE.

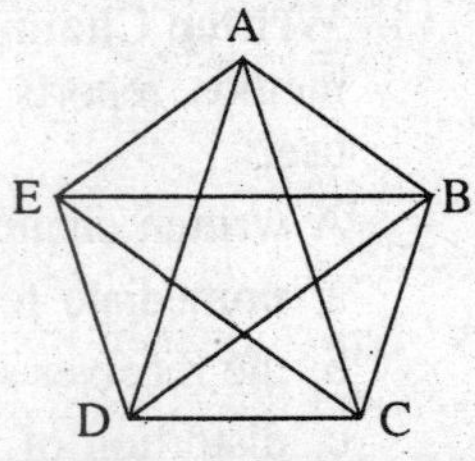

Fig. 1.5: Channels of Communication.

If channels are used for the purpose of communication relating to any business activity, such channels may be called 'the channels of business communication'.

A departmental manager issuing orders to the supervisors in writing is an example of business communication. Its direction is downwards as it is made by a superior to his subordinate. Here a downward channel is used. Again, the communication is expressed in writing. Therefore, a written channel of business communication is in operation. Once again, as the communication is carried on through an official route, it is a formal communication channel also.

1.7 Classification of Channels of Business Communication

Channels of business communication may be classified from different viewpoints as follows:

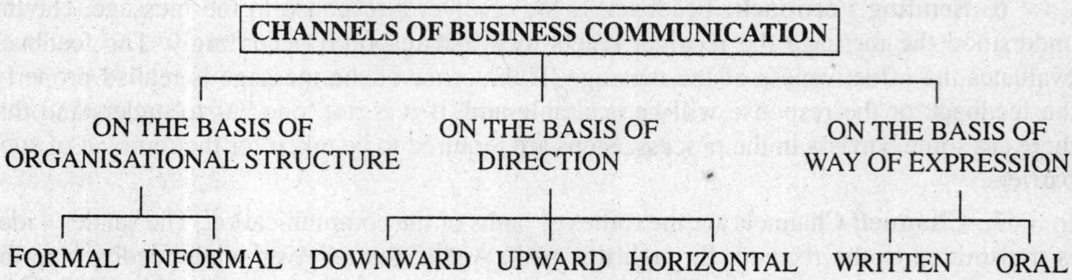

Fig. 1.6: Classification of Channels of Business Communication.

[**N.B.** All these types of communication have been discussed elaborately under the heading 'Types of Communication' in Chapter III of Business Communication. A bare outline of each of the above channels are given below.]

1. On the basis of Organisational Structure: On the basis of organisational structure, the channels of business communication may be divided into: (i) Formal, and (ii) Informal.

i. **Formal Channel:** When communication is carried on through structured, organised or official route, the channel is called 'Formal Channel'.

ii. **Informal Channel:** Non-structured, unofficial and unorganised route of communication is 'Informal Channel'.

2. On the basis of Direction: The direction of business communication channels may be—i. Downward, ii. Upward and iii. Horizontal or Lateral.

i. **Downward Channel:** Channels used for flowing information from top towards bottom are called 'Downward Channel'.

ii. **Upward Channel:** Communication of information from lower level to upper level is possible through 'Upward Channel'.

iii. **Horizontal or Lateral Channel:** When communication takes place between the persons of same rank a 'Horizontal Channel' is said to be formed.

3. On the basis of Way of Expression: On the basis of the ways or means of expression business communication channels are of two types: (i) Written, and (ii) Oral.

i. **Written Channel:** When communication takes place in writing through letters, memos, reports, proposals, e-mail, faxes, etc. 'Written Channel' is said to be in use.

A written channel is often selected in the following cases:

a. immediate feedback is not required;

b. the receiver stays in a far off place and cannot be brought to contact easily;

c. distortion of message is not desirable;

d. detailed, complex and planned messages are required to be sent; and

e. permanent record is necessary for future reference.

ii. **Oral Channel:** 'Oral Channel' includes different media e.g., face-to-face conversations, speeches, meetings, telephone, voice mails, audio and video tape, tele-conference or video conference, etc.

An oral channel is to be selected if:

a. feedback is required immediately.

b. the receiver of message or audience can be brought to contact easily.

c. interaction is necessary.
d. simple messages are communicated.
e. no permanent record is to be kept.

1.8 Feedback as the Essence of Business Communication

[A] Meaning: In the case of inter-personal communication, only sending of message by the sender to the receiver is not enough. He/She must be eager to know the reaction or to get return information. **The message sent by the receiver back to the source is called feedback. It is the response by the recipient.**

[B] Importance of Feedback: Feedback is essential in communication. Actually, communication is a two-way process—(i) sending the message, and (ii) receiving the response or feedback. The sender is interested to know the reaction of the recipient. He/She is also willing to know whether the recipient has understood the message in the same sense as intended. If there is any lapse in it, further negotiation or communication is necessary. On the other hand, the recipient might have understood the meaning and intention of the message, but, due to barrier of some kind, say, language barrier, he/she could not convey his/her reactions properly. In such case also actual picture is to be brought to light by removing the barriers.

In face to face communication feedback is no problem, because the speaker and the listener both are present and can ask and clarify the message instantly if there is any ambiguity. One can ask the other to repeat what has been missed. They can also observe the gestures and facial expression in oral communication. But in the case of written communication the feedback is not instant. It requires some time. Whatever may be the mode or channel (i.e., verbal, non-verbal or written), feedback is very important. It is the key which unlocks the success of communication. The objective of communication is bound to remain unfulfilled unless the process of communication is complete with feedback. It is an inseparable part of successful communication.

[C] Process of Feedback: The process or technique of feedback should include the following steps:

1. Listening and understanding the message properly.
2. Asking question if the message is not understood properly and get it clarified.
3. Understanding the message in the sense originally intended.
4. Conveying the reaction to the sender of the message.

[D] Types of Feedback: Feedback may be positive or negative. Positive feedback is the kind of feedback which is more or less acceptable or satisfactory to the sender. It means that the recipient of the message has responded in the way intended by the sender and taken the intended course of action. It signifies that everything is on the right track and no corrective measure regarding communication is necessary. On the other hand, if the recipient does not understand what the sender wants to convey, the feedback must be poor and further communication becomes necessary to wipe out the misunderstanding. Thus, negative feedback suggests that the communication has not been effective and some correction, adjustment or re-assessment is required in the process.

[E] Requirements of Effective Feedback: Effective feedback needs to be: 1. Clear, 2. Well-timed, 3. Specific, 4. Bearing Right Attitude, 5. Truly Representative, 6. Impersonal, and 7. Informative.

These points are discussed in brief in the following paragraphs :

1. Clear: Effective feedback is possible if the recipient understands the message communicated to him/her properly. It should be clear in two respects: (i) The sender of the message can understand that the feedback is related to the message sent; and (ii) The meaning of the feedback should be clear. The sender of the feedback should take care about it and ensure proper understanding of the feedback by the receiver. Use of simple language for communication is highly necessary.

2. Well-timed: Feedback may not be instant. It may require some time to get feedback. But much delayed feedback may not be worthwhile or even may not serve any purpose at all. It should be made within a reasonable time.

3. Specific: In general, feedback, to be effective, should be particular or specific. A generalised response or an ambiguous reply is of little value. To a specific question, specific answer should be given.

Sometimes general impression of a large section of people is necessary as feedback. In that case, the communication should be designed in such a way that the people are encouraged to give their general impression.

4. Bearing Right Attitude: 'I' attitude should be replaced by 'We' or 'You' attitude to get the co-operation of the person with whom communication is being made. If the sender thinks that he/she is superior to the recipient in every respect, it will be reflected in the message and the recipient will feel embarrassed in giving a feedback. Therefore, such attitude should be avoided.

The recipient should also avoid the fault-finding attitude with the sender. If much of the time is spent in finding fault with the subject-matter, presentation skill and similar matters related to the message, the feedback process is sure to suffer.

Therefore, both undermining attitude of the sender and fault-finding attitude of the receiver should be avoided to make the feedback effective.

5. Truly Representative: Feedback may be positive or negative. One should not hesitate to convey negative feedback. Actual, true and honest reaction should be communicated. We should not hesitate to convey our disagreement. We should also clearly state if we fail to understand the message.

6. Impersonal: Feedback, to be effective, should be free from personal reactions. Let us suppose, Mr. X is depressed due to some personal problems in his life. This state of mind should not be reflected in the feedback process of the official work or business communication. Similarly, any personal rivalry or conflict should not have any influence on official feedback.

7. Informative: The sender of a message expects from the receiver some information in the form of feedback which the sender does not already know. Therefore, feedback, to be effective, should be informative.

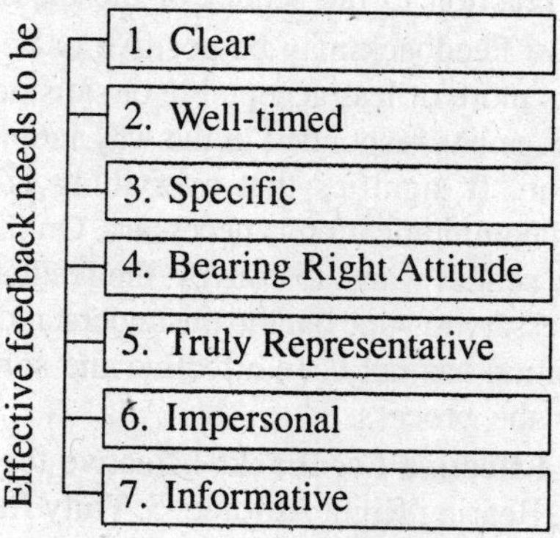

Fig. 1.7: Requirement of Effective feedback.

1.9 Levels of Business Communication

Levels of business communication may be determined on the basis of direction of communication and the ranks or positions of the persons with whom communication is being made. It may be classified as:

1. Lower Level Communication
2. Upper Level Communication
3. Horizontal or Side-wise or Lateral Communication.

1. Lower Level Communication: When information flows from the persons occupying higher positions to those at lower levels, it is called 'Lower Level Communication'. The flow of communication being downward it is also called 'Downward Communication'. It is usually conveyed through oral or written orders, reports, manuals, etc. and is the most common practice in all business organisations.

In an organisation, people at lower levels have a high degree of loyalty, faith, respect and sometimes a mixed feelings of fear and obedience towards the people of higher levels. This leads to high degree of acceptance of the communication.

In the lower level communication there is a possibility of distortion of information through gossip or 'grapevine' communication. In such a case the ultimate objective of communication is lost. So, care should be taken to send the information, message or order and receive feedback without any loss, alteration or distortion of information.

2. Upper Level Communication: When communication moves upward from the subordinates to the superiors, it is called 'Upper Level Communication'. The means of upper level communication includes the submission of reports and suggestion, opinions and attitudes, complaints and grievances, etc. The upper level employees can understand the pulse of the lower level employees through such communication. But, it is less common because it is less favoured by the top managers due to its troublesome and perplexing nature.

The effectiveness of such communication depends upon good superior-subordinate relationship and intention of the superiors to remove the grievances and honour the emotions of the subordinates. The subordinates should also be co-operative and avoid unnecessary criticism, fault-finding attitude, complaining for fake or baseless grievances, etc.

3. Horizontal or Side-wise or Lateral Communication: 'Horizontal or Sidewise or Lateral Communication' takes place between the people of same level in the positional hierarchy of the organisation through oral or written method. Communication between the employees or supervisors or managers of the same department or another department are examples of horizontal or lateral communication. It helps to promote understanding and co-ordination in the organisation. It is especially important in large or decentralised organisation.

1.10 Principles of Effective Business Communication

Business communication is a dynamic and complex process. To make this process effective and achieve the objectives of business, we should take into account the following:

[A] The Views of Chester I. Barnard

According to **Chester I. Barnard,** business communication, in order to be effective, must have a message which is:

i. Understandable to the receiver;
ii. Compatible with the interests of the persons concerned;
iii. Relevant to the objectives of the organisation; and
iv. Physically and psychologically viable.

[B] Ten Commandments of the American Management Association

The American Management Association has prescribed the following ten essentials for effective business communication:

i. Form a clear idea about the information before communication;
ii. Fix the aim, objective or purpose of communication;

iii. Create physical and psychological environment for communication;
iv. Make plan for communication through consultation;
v. Select properly the subject-matter of communication;
vi. Make the receiver realise the value of the message;
vii. Follow-up the communication;
viii. Have a clear idea of the importance of communication;
ix. Act in accordance with communication;
x. Listen properly.

[C] General Principles of Effective Business Communication

The general principles for effective business communication may be outlined as follows:

1. Clarity: The communication process, in order to serve the purpose, must ensure clarity of communication. A business communication possesses clarity when it is expressed in a language and transmitted in a way that will be comprehended by the receiver. The basic objective of communication is to bring two minds together, and this can be possible only when what the sender means is understood by the receiver in the same way. So, the communication should be clear and simple in easy understandable language.

2. Adequacy: The goal in communication is to ensure an optimum flow of information. It should be enough to cover the field. The process of communication must ensure that all those of messages that are needed by the various individuals in the organisation in connection with the effective discharge of their official duties must flow up to them and, further, that this flow in respect of different types of messages must be adequate.

3. Attention: The message, when received, should be properly understood in its meaning and content with full attention. In spite of clarity of expression, the well-composed message may appear to be very difficult and, as such, may not be understood because of our half-hearted attention. So, the receiver's full attention and concentration over the message listening or reading should be considered to be very essential for proper understanding of the message communicated. If the message receives due recognition and understanding at the hands of the recipients, the communicator will feel much encouraged in his efforts.

4. Timing: The utility of any message to the receiver is markedly affected by its timeliness. The process of communication should, therefore, not only ensure that the message reaches the receiver but also that it reaches to him/her when he/she requires it. It is possible that a person may require some time to compile an information having diversified and complex contents. A suitable time span should be allowed for the purpose of considering urgency and time requirement of the information.

5. Integrity: This principle demands that the business communication should support the organisational structure and objectives. A communication is a means and a tool for securing and maintaining co-operation between the superiors and subordinates needed to meet the enterprise objectives. For this purpose, particular attention should also be paid to the position of the subordinate managers who are the centres of communication. They should have support and encouragement to use their positions and status. Top managers often forget this and communicate messages by passing these subordinate managers in an effort to contact directly the employees for whom the communication is meant. This procedure cannot be to the liking of the subordinate managers who occupy important positions with definite status. Therefore, a communication from top to bottom should pass through every stage of line authority.

6. Strategic Use of Informal Organisation: Informal organisation originates from the need for transmitting information. It continues with or without the approval of the managers and may have constructive or destructive ends. So, it should be the duty of a manager to use it constructively as a means of communication. When informal organisation grows spontaneously, it is not advisable to subdue or stamp it out. It should not also be ignored, but should be utilised to transmit and receive communications to supplement those of formal organisation. This will ensure proper co-ordination and enterprising efforts. Moreover, the message that flows formally between the superior and the subordinate may appear to be inadequate and unrealiable in handling them expeditiously with proper understanding. In such a situation, strategic use of informal organisation is conductive to the communication process.

7. Balance between Adaptability and Uniformity: The smooth working of an organisation depends in part upon uniformity. Yet adaptability should be resorted to when different situations and individuals are involved. Orders and reports may be communicated through the systems that provide opportunity for adaptation to specific situations.

8. Interest and Acceptance: The purpose of a business communication is to secure a positive response. The person communicated to should be interested in the message and accept it. Downward communication is more effective if morale is good, and upward communication gets through when the superior is a good listener.

While applying the principles of communication, it should be remembered that they can seldom be enforced. So, voluntary acceptance of these principles by all members of the organisation is to be tried.

9. Courtesy: Courtesy should be maintained at all costs in any communication. In business communication, especially, courtesy is a sign of a good organisation.

Use of polite language, apology for a mistake, thanking for a favour, answering a letter without delay, etc. are some of the examples of courtesy in business communication.

10. Conciseness: Business communication, to be effective, should be concise. Only necessary facts are to be stated avoiding repetitions.

11. Channel: Use of direct and shortest channel saves the subject-matter of the communication from distortion. Care should be taken in this regard.

12. Feedback: A communication is complete when feedback is received from the receipient. The ultimate objective of communication is fulfilled through this principle.

13. Two-way Communication: One-way communication is not desirable. It cannot fulfil the purpose of business communication. Both the sender and the receiver should communicate with each other. It helps the feedback process.

1.10.1 Seven Cs in Effective Communication

A communication to be effective, requires the following seven Cs:

1. Completeness: The first criteria of an effective communication is its completeness. The message or the context of the communication should contain all facts required for proper reaction by the recipient. A complete communication clarifies all possible questions and helps to take proper decision.

2. Conciseness: The subject-matter of the communication should be brief and short in nature. No unnecessary elaboration is to be made in a communication. Words used in a communication should be appropriate and expression should be precise. Repetition should be avoided. Concise message saves time of both the sender and the receiver.

3. Consideration: While making communication the sender should consider the social and cultural background, education, age, emotions, etc. of the recipient and modify language, change attitude and approach accordingly.

4. Concreteness: Concrete communication refers to exchange of specific, definite and exact information instead of vague and general information. It is convincing and acceptable to the recipient as there is no ambiguity in it.

5. Courtesy: A courteous approach should be present in an effective communication. The sender of the message should be alert in respect of dignity, respect and honour of the receiver. Care should be taken so that the communication may not hurt, injure, belittle or irritate the receiver in any way. Sender will also be respected in turn as honour begets honour.

6. Clarity: Clarity must be maintained in communication. The idea contained in the message should be expressed clearly. There will remain no confusion in respect of the meaning of the message. The sender and the receiver of the message will understand it identically.

7. Correctness: Effective communication should be correct in spelling, construction of sentence and use of language. Grammatical mistakes must be avoided. Dictionary, computerised spelling checker, etc. may be used to make the message error free. Revision of the text is needed to avoid any careless omission. A correct message creates good impact on the receiver and enhances prestige of the sender.

1.11 Benefits of Effective Communication

Communication is a process of exchange of information, facts, ideas, thoughts, opinions between two or more persons or group of persons. When the communication is clear, complete, concise, correct and fully understood by the recipient, it is known as 'Effective Communication'. If the communication is vague, incomplete, incorrect and difficult to understand, it may be termed as 'Ineffective Communication'. Ineffective communication produces no good result, on the contrary, it is the breeding ground of misunderstanding, mistrust, animocity, conflict and chaos. In a business organisation effective communication is of utmost importance as it helps in decision-making, speeds up flow of work, increases productivity, makes business relationship strong, increases customers' satisfaction and solves many other problems. The benefits of effective business communications are:

1. Helps in Making Decision: A decision, in order to be correct and appropriate, must be based on adequate and correct information which only effective communication can bring together.

2. Speeds up Flow of Work: Flow of work is not obstructed if orders, instructions, suggestions, etc. are communicated properly and timely.

3. Increases Productivity: Effective communication allows the team of workers to concentrate on their respective jobs removing confusion from their minds. It increases their ability, efficiency and quality of performance which ultimately leads to higher productivity.

4. Improves Job Satisfaction: Effective communication among the employees and the supervisor in a workplace can boost up job satisfaction at both the ends. The employees think that they are essential to the organisation and on the other hand, the supervisor also feels satisfied that his orders are carried out by the employees. When the employees know clearly what to do, when to do and about the reward of their performance they can accomplish their jobs efficiently. They remain satisfied and loyal to their higher authority.

5. Saves Time and Money: If a communication is not understood properly further conversation will be needed for clarity involving extra time and money. Effective communication saves time and money by preventing multiple communication. Selection of appropriate means of communication from among various methods (e.g. telephone, mobile phone, e-mail, fax, letter, face to face conversation, etc.) as per requirement can save both time and money.

6. Boosts up Promotional Activity: Goods and services are brought to the knowledge of the consumers through communication and promotional activities (e.g. advertisement, use of different media, etc.) are made effective through it.

7. Makes Business Relationship Strong: Fruitful communication with outside people and organisations (e.g. creditors, banks, insurance companies, co-business managers, etc.) make a healthy relationship with all concerned.

8. Enhances Professional Image: The way an organisation communicates casts on impression of its efficiency on the communicatee. Good communication signifies good and professionally efficient organisation.

9. Increases Customers' Satisfaction: Customers' satisfaction is a vital aspect of consideration for a business organisation. The existence and growth of a business largely depends upon it. Effective communication is necessary in achieving confidence of the customers. It clarifies all the queries (regarding products, services, availability, prices, quality, variety, etc.) of the customers and makes them happy and satisfied.

10. Solves Various Problems: Innumerable problems (e.g. gossip, rumours, conflict, mistrust among the employees, managers etc.) crop up in a business organisation due to poor communication or no communication. Effective communication can solve the problems easily. It establishes a link between the managers and the employees. The relationship between them are eased and various problems and grievances are removed.

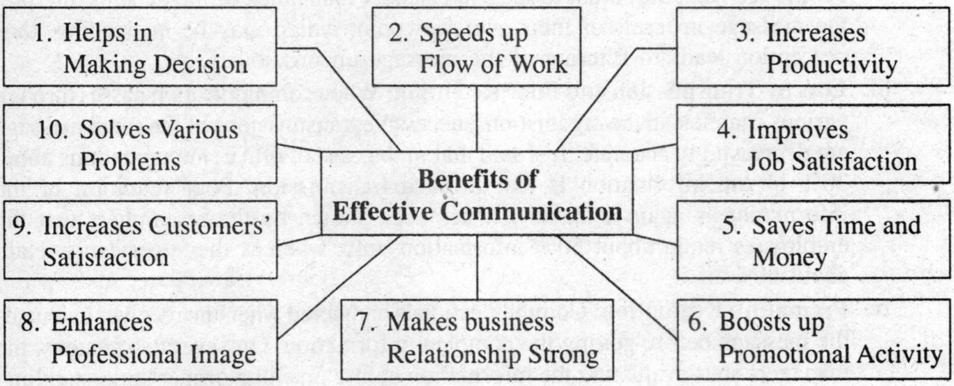

Fig. 1.8: Benefits of Effective Communication.

1.12 Barriers to Business Communication

- **Meaning:** The importance of communication in modern business can hardly be overemphasised. This is why the managers usually spend a considerable portion of their time to communicate with others. But communication is not always as effective as it should be. Research has pointed out that almost 75% of all business communication fails to achieve the desired result. Certain external and internal forces impede the flow of communication. They interrupt or block communication or prevent mutual understanding. Communication may be vague and badly expressed. It may suffer from lack of clarity or poor retention. Barriers between people do not screen out all communications, rather they operate like filter to permit some communications but hold back others, thereby making communication inadequate. Non-listening of the communication is a chronic problem. Many communications do not receive the attention they deserve. These limitations or causes of breakdown of communication channels are called 'Communication Barriers'.

- **Important Barriers to Business Communication:** Communication is impeded by various types of barriers. These may be classified into three categories: (A) External Barriers, (B) Organisational Barriers; and (C) Personal Barriers.

All these types of communication barriers are explained below:

[A] External Barriers: External barriers to business communication may be in the following forms:

1. Semantic Barriers: The words and symbols used to communicate the facts and feelings may have variety of meanings. Different people interpret the same message in different ways depending upon their education, experience, social and cultural backgrounds etc. The language of the sender may be incomprehensible to the receiver. Thus, words and symbols sometimes fail to convey the true meanings.

2. Emotional or Psychological Barriers: Emotional or psychological factors are the prime barriers in inter-personal communication. The following are some of the emotional barriers:

- **i. Inattention:** It is one of the major chronic psychological barriers. When the receiver does not pay complete attention to the message, communication becomes ineffective. A person may be pre-occupied with other important matters, or the message may be uninteresting or contrary to his/her expectations. These may cause lack of attention. It is a common phenomenon that people simply fail to react to bulletins, notices, minutes and reports.
- **ii. Perceptual Barrier:** Every individual has specific areas of interest. So, he/she may hear, read or see that part of the message which is valuable to him/her. People see what they want to see and consider it a reality. Some persons interpret the message in terms of their own viewpoint which may be misleading, thus perception leads to filtering of the message unconsciously.
- **iii. Loss by Transmission and Poor Retention:** When communication passes through various channels in the organistion, successive transmissions of the same message are decreasingly accurate. It is said that in the case of oral communications about 30% of the information is lost in each transmission. Poor retention of the information is again a malady. It has been shown by the researchers that the employees retain about 50% information only, whereas the supervisors retain about 60% of it.
- **iv. Premature Evaluation:** Communication is hampered when the receiver evaluates the message before getting the complete information. On several occasions, the managers start evaluating the information before reaching proper understanding. Decision is taken before knowing the full facts. Such a premature evaluation tends to inhibit the free flow of information and understanding and distorts the communication.
- **v. Undue Reliance on the Written Words:** Written words are no substitute for sound face-to-face relationships. A written communication might fail to explain the purpose of order, procedure or directive. Written communication often tells what is to be done, but not why it should be done, and lacks the persuasive quality. Moreover, a written communication may be above the comprehension level of the reader and failure to ascertain the response to communication is also there. Hence, written media must be considered as supplementary to productive face-to-face relationships.
- **vi. Distrust of Communicator:** It arises out of all ill-considered judgments or illogical decisions by the communicator. Repeated experience of this kind gradually conditions the receiver to delay action or act unenthusiastically, thus, making the communication unsuccessful, though apparently it is complete.
- **vii. Failure to Communicate:** It is quite an accepted fact that the managers often fail to transmit the needed messages. This might be because of laziness on the part of the communicator or his/her false assumption that everybody knows it.

[B] Organisational Barriers: Major organisational barriers may be as follows:

- **i. Organisational Policy:** The general organisational policy regarding communication acts as an overall guideline to everyone in the organisation regarding how he is normally expected to behave in this matter. The policy might be in the form of explicit declaration in writing, or it has to be interpreted from the behaviour of organisation members, particularly people at the top. If this policy is not supportive to the flow of communication in different directions, communication flow would not be smooth and adequate.

ii. **Status Relationship:** In the formal organisation structure, superior-subordinate relationship may cause obstacle to free and frequent communications, more particularly in upward direction. A manager may not communicate to subordinates his/her weaknesses. The subordinates do not feel free to talk to the superiors. They pass on only what the superiors would like to hear and hold back unpleasant facts. They may communicate to their superiors only those things which they expect would be appreciated by the latter. When a subordinate does not have trust in his superior, communication becomes less effective.

iii. **Organisational Rules and Regulations:** Organisational rules and regulations affect the flow of communication by prescribing the subject-matter to be communicated and also the channel for such communication. The rules may restrict the flow of certain messages and may leave many important ones. On the other hand, communication through proper channel in a specified way prescribed by these rules delays it and works against the willingness of the persons to convey the message. This barrier is strongly operative in Indian public sector enterprises where observance of rules and regulations is rigid.

iv. **Complexity in Organisation Structure:** In an organisation, where there are a number of managerial levels, the number of filtering points are many. As a result, the process of communication gets delayed and the chances of communication getting distorted increase. This is more true in the case of upward communication, because the subordinate employees generally do not like to pass up the adverse criticism either of themselves or of their superiors. The more complex the organisation structure is, the more difficult it becomes to ensure that correct information is passed on to the right person at the right time through the right medium.

v. **Organisational Facilities:** Organisational facilities provided for smooth, adequate, clear and timely flow of communication may take a number of forms such as meetings, conferences, complaint box, suggestion box, social and cultural gathering, etc. If these are not properly emphasised, generally people fail to make effective communication.

vi. **Information Overload:** The managers are overloaded with information from various sources. They may not always be able to regulate the flow of information. As a result, the effectiveness of communication is reduced. They may ignore or misinterpret some of the messages. Time pressures may also create communication problem.

[C] Personal Barriers: As communication is basically an inter-personal process, there are also some personal factors which are responsible for blocking communication. Personal barriers may be listed as follows:

1. Barriers in Superiors: The role of the superiors in communication is very vital. Because of their hierarchical relationships with the subordinates, they act as barriers in a number of ways discussed below:

i. **Attitude of Superiors:** The attitudes of the superiors towards communication in general, or in any particular direction, affect the flow of messages in different directions. If this attitude is unfavourable, there is a greater possibility that messages would not flow adequately from and/or to the superiors.

ii. **Fear of Challenge to Authority:** A person in the organisation always tries to get a higher position and prestige. As such, the managers generally try to withhold the information coming down the line or going up—as frequent passing of information may disclose their weakness.

iii. **Lack of Confidence in Subordinates:** The superiors generally perceive (correct or otherwise) that their subordinates are less competent and less capable, they are not able to advise their superiors or they may not have some information to convey.

iv. **Lack of Time:** The superiors feel—whether correct or otherwise—that they are over-burdened with the work and they have little time to talk to their subordinates.

v. **Lack of Awareness:** Sometimes the superiors may lack the awareness about the usefulness and significance of communication in different directions in general or particular subject-matter. In such a case, communication flow is blocked.

vi. **Ignoring Communication:** Sometimes the superiors —consciously and deliberately ignore the communication from their subordinates to maintain their importance. This works against the willingness of the subordinates to communicate.

2. Barriers in Subordinates: Vertical communication in either direction can take place only when the subordinates also actively participate in this process. There are various factors in the subordinates that adversely affect such active participation on their part. Some of these are mentioned below:

i. **Unwillingness to Communicate:** Sometimes, the subordinates do not communicate upwards certain information because they are not willing to do so. If a subordinate feels that he/she is likely to be adversely affected by supplying a particular information to his superior, he/she would not be willing to supply it. Information going up is utilised for control purposes and the subordinates would not be willing to give any information to their superiors about any unfavourable happening. If there is any compulsion to communicate, they would do the same after modifying the information in such a way so as to protect their own interest.

ii. **Lack of Proper Incentive:** Lack of motivation to communicate also refrains the subordinates from communicating upwards. If a novel suggestion by a subordinate does not evoke any attention from the superiors, he/she would not convey it.

Barriers to Business Communication are shown by a chart as follows:

BARRIERS TO BUSINESS COMMUNICATION

A. External Barriers
1. Semantic Barriers
2. Emotional or Psychological Barriers
   i. Inattention
   ii. Perceptual Barriers
   iii. Transmission Loss
   iv. Premature Evaluation
   v. Reliance on Written Words
   vi. Distrust
   vii. Failure to Communicate

B. Organisational Barriers
i. Organisational Policy
ii. Status Relationship
iii. Rules & Regulations
iv. Complexity in Structure
v. Organisational Facilities
vi. Information Overload

C. Personal Barriers
1. Barriers in Superiors
   i. Attitude
   ii. Fear of Challange to Authority
   iii. Lack of Confidence in Subordinates
   iv. Lack of Time
   v. Lack of Awareness
   vi. Ignoring Communication
2. Barriers in Subordinates
   i. Unwillingness
   ii. Lack of Proper Incentive

Fig. 1.9: Barriers to Business Communication.

1.13 Methods of Overcoming Communication Barriers

Considering the importance of effective communication in the successful functioning of business organisations, it is essential on the part of the managers to overcome the different barriers to communication. Though it may not be possible to eliminate the communication barriers altogether, yet suitable managerial actions in this direction can minimise their effect.

The following methods are suggested to avoid the communication barriers:

1. Full Information: To make the communication effective, it is first of all necessary that the communicator should know completely and clearly what he intends to communicate.

2. Mutual Trust: Communication is intended for acceptance and desired action. Such acceptance is, to a great extent, influenced by trust and confidence in the motives and sincerity of the communicator. If trust is lacking, communication will fall short of its expected results. So, it is necessary that an environment of trust and confidence is established within the organisation. This will encourage people to communicate honestly with one another.

3. Appropriate Language: The language used for communication should be such that it can be easily comprehended by the receiver. Most popular symbols, clear and precise language should be used for proper communication.

4. Inter-personal Relationship: Proper inter-personal relationships must be developed between the superiors and the subordinates so that the latter may feel free and frank to transmit complete and correct information to the former. The superiors must appreciate useful criticisms and beneficial suggestions of the subordinates.

5. Selection of Appropriate Channel: The managers must be competent enough to select the most appropriate channel for sending messages. A rich channel such as face-to-face discussion or telephone should be used to send a complicated message. On the other hand, memos, letters or electronic mail may be used to send routine messages, because there is hardly any chance of misunderstanding.

6. Mutual Understanding: It is of considerable importance for both the senders and receivers to make a special effort to understand each other's perspective. By understanding others' perspectives, remarks can be classified, perceptions understood, and objectivity maintained.

7. Empathy in Communication: The way for effective communication is to be sensitive towards the receiver's needs, feelings and perceptions. The communicator should convey the message in such a way that the emotions and sentiments of the receiver are not hurt. When the sender of the message looks at the problems from the receiver's point of view, many of the misunderstandings can be avoided.

8. Two-way Communication: Communication is a two-way process. Two-way communication brings two minds together—which is the basic core of any communication. It involves a continuous dialogue between the sender and receiver of the message. Upward communication can become a reality in the organisation and effective if this fact is recognised.

9. Supporting Words with Actions: The most persuasive kind of communication is not what you say but what you do. The managers must make sure that their actions support the communication process. This will ensure the seriousness in communication.

10. Examples and Visual Aids: To fix the idea of communication in the receiver's mind, appropriate stories and word pictures may be used in appropriate situations to the understanding of the receiver. Further, visual aids through charts and diagrams can be advantageously used to stress particular points or ideas which may be difficult to describe properly by words.

11. Good Listening: Careful listening is essential for effective communication. By this process, one is not only giving chance to others to speak but gathers useful information for further communications. By concentrating on the speaker's explicit and implicit meanings, the manager can obtain a much better understanding of what is being said.

12. Delaying Reaction: It is a good practice for effective communication not to be influenced by immediate reaction of the first impression. Hasty reaction often results in ignoring the real implication of communication and experience shows that the delaying of action by the recipient becomes helpful in understanding the intended meaning of the communication.

13. Strategic Use of Informal Communication (Grapevine): A manager should use the informal channels of communication to supplement the formal communication system. For this purpose, he must understand the informal communication networks and should make their intelligent use to fill up the gaps in formal channels of communication.

14. Evaluation: There should be continuous programme of evaluating the flow of communication in different directions. This would highlight the problems in this area, identify their causes and thereby enable the adoption of suitable corrective action. The superiors should not be quick to evaluate the information before understanding it properly.

1.14 Communication Models

A model is a visual and symbolic representation of the concept or the theory. A communication model presents before us a visual picture of the relationship of various elements of the process of communication.

As a map of the world can illustrate the mountains, rivers, plateaus, seas, oceans, continents, countries, etc. and can create an idea of the actual things, a communication model helps us to conceptualise the relationship of the various elements involved in the process of communication.

Different writers have different models to describe the process of communication. Some of them are described below.

The Greek philosopher **Aristotle** presented a systematic model of communication about 2,300 years ago. It contains five elements—(i) the speaker, (ii) the message, (iii) the audience, (iv) the occasion; and (v) the effect. He advised the speaker to prepare the message keeping in view the audience, the occasion and the effect of it.

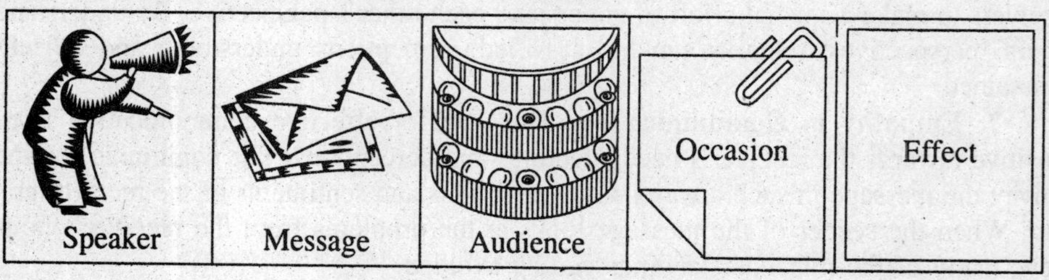

Fig. 1.10: Aristotle's Model of Communication.

In 1948 **Harold Laswell** presented his model of communication in a different way. He asked the following question to describe communication:

Who
Says What
In What Channel
To Whom
With What Effect ?

He has tried to analyse the speaker, the speech, the media, the audience, and the effect.

Claude E. Shannon and **Warren Weaver** made a communication model in 1947. It was published in 1949. They named it 'The Mathematical Theory of Communication'. The Shannon-Weaver model analyses the process of transmission of a message and puts emphasis on the accurate transmission of it. It is the most popular model of communication. It has four elements—(i) Source of information, (ii) Transmitter or Sender who sends a message through a signal, (iii) Receiver who receives and decodes the signal, and (iv) Destination which is the ultimate goal of a message. A new concept, the concept of noise, is introduced in the model. In transmitting message, distortions may take place owing to the interference of noise. The model is presented as under:

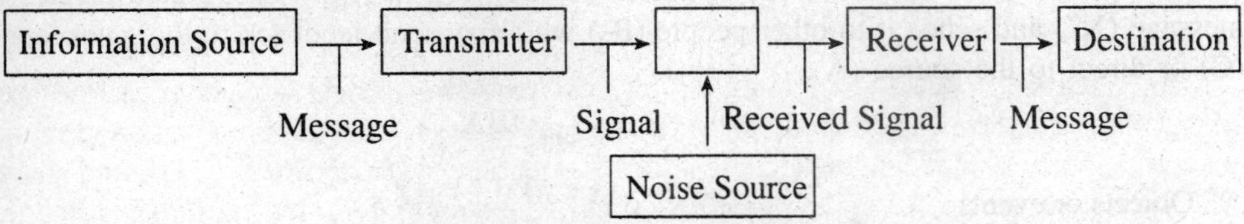

Fig. 1.11: The Shannon-Weaver Model.

Various components in the communication process have got importance in the communication model of **David Berlo**. There are four basic components in the model—(i) Source, (ii) Message, (iii) Channel, and (iv) Receiver **(SMCR)**. Each component has five elements which influence the communication.* Five personal factors (Communication Skills, Attitudes, Knowledge, Social System, and Culture) of the Sender (source) and the Receiver are similar. David Berlo's SMCR model of communication is produced as under:

Source	Message	Channel	Receiver
S	M	C	R
1. Communication Skills	1. Elements	1. Seeing	1. Communication Skills
2. Attitudes	2. Structure	2. Hearing	2. Attitudes
3. Knowledge	3. Content	3. Touching	3. Knowledge
4. Social System	4. Treatment	4. Smelling	4. Social System
5. Culture	5. Code	5. Tasting	5. Culture

Source: David Berlo, The Process of Communication, 1960, P. 72

Fig. 1.12: David Berlo's SMCR model.

The **Westley** and **Maclean's** model of communication is applicable to both inter-personal and mass communication, B. H. Westley and M. S. Maclean wanted to show in their model that—in face-to-face communication between two persons—the feedback is immediate but, in mass communication, the feedback is delayed and reduced to the smallest degree. There are five elements in the model: (i) object or event in the environment (denoted by X), (ii) a message (X′), (iii) a source (A), (iv) a receiver (B), and (v) feedback (f). In mass communication another element, the gatekeeper or opinion leader (denoted by C) is added.

In the case of inter-personal communication the source (A) creates a message (X′) about object or event in his/her environment (X_1, X_2, X_3, . . . X_n). The message is transmitted to the receiver (B) who sends feedback (fBA or feedback by B to A) to the source (A).

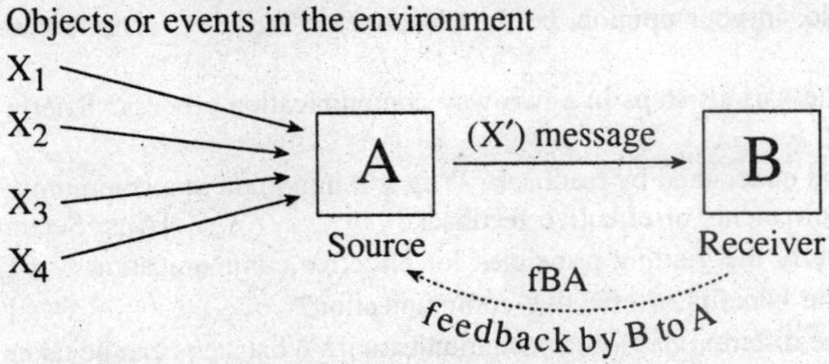

Fig. 1.13: The Westley and Maclean model.†

* David Berlo, The Process of Communication. (New York, Holt, Rinchart and Winston, 1960) Pp. 23-38

† Source: M. Bargoon & M. Ruffner—Human Communication, Halt, Rinchart & Ninston, USA, 1978

In condition of mass communication this model brings the concept of a filter or a gatekeeper or an opinion leader (C) who selects information from many sources of mass media (As) or from objects in his/her environment (X_1, X_2, X_3, ... X_n). He/She then creates a message (X″) and sends it to other people (Bs) who may send feedback to the gatekeeper (C) or direct to the source (A).

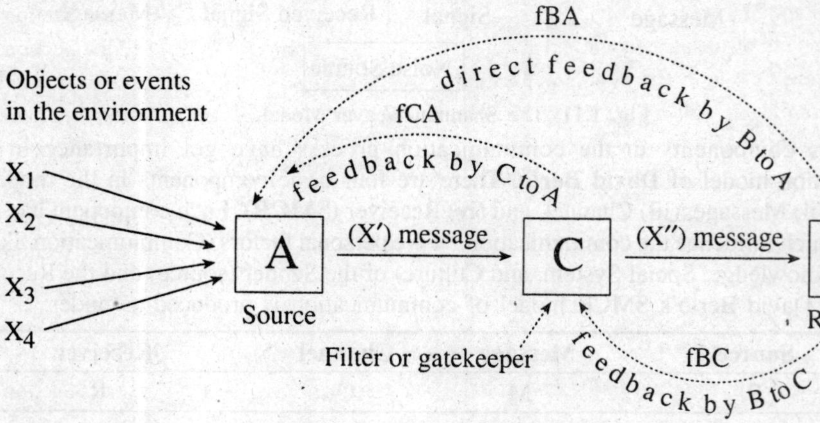

Fig. 1.14: The Westley and Maclean model.*

None of the models described above are absolutely perfect or complete. There are some sort of deficiencies in each model. While one is too simplified to ignore some of the elements, the other lacking feedback process, the third one not applicable to mass communication, and so on. But it has been noticed that a newly introduced model has always tried to eliminate the difficulties in the previous one. In other words, a gradual improvement may be traced in the newer models. In general these models attempt to illustrate the process of communication describing the relation of the elements in the process. The study of these models will help us to understand the communication process more clearly.

EXERCISES

[A] Essay-Type Questions

1. What is meant by communication? When is a communication called a business communication? [**Ans.** Section 1.1]
2. What are the distinguishing features of the message of a business communication? [**Ans.** Section 1.3]
3. What are the features of business communication? [**Ans.** Section 1.3]
4. Discuss the essential characteristics of a business communication system. [**Ans.** Section 1.3]
5. What should, in your opinion, be the objectives of business communication? [**Ans.** Section 1.4]
6. What are the various steps in a two-way communication process? Briefly describe the steps. [**Ans.** Section 1.5]
7. What do you understand by feedback? Why is it important in a communication process? What are the requirements of effective feedback? [**Ans.** Section 1.8(A), (B), (E)]
8. Discuss briefly the guiding principles for effective communication. [**Ans.** Section 1.10]
9. What are the benefits of effective communication? [**Ans.** Section 1.11]
10. What are the different barriers to communication? What steps can be taken to overcome these barriers? [**Ans.** Section 1.12, 1.13]
11. "Most of the barriers to communication are emotional or psychological."—Explain. [**Ans.** Section 1.12]

* Source: M. Bargoon & M. Ruffner—Human Communication, Halt, Rinchart & Ninston, USA, 1978

[B] Short Answer-Type Questions

1. Write short notes on:

i. Semantic barriers. [**Ans.** Section 1.12]
ii. Art of persuasion. [**Ans.** Section 1.4]
iii. Feedback. [**Ans.** Section 1.8(A), (B)]
iv. Communication channel. [**Ans.** Section 1.6]
v. Levels of business communication. [**Ans.** Section 1.9]
vi. Seven Cs in effective communication. [**Ans.** Section 1.10.1]
vii. Harold Laswell model of communication. [**Ans.** Section 1.14]
viii. Shannon and Weaver model. [**Ans.** Section 1.14]

2. Explain the following statements in brief:

i. "Communication is a two-way traffic." [**Ans.** Section 1.3]
ii. "Communication is sharing of understanding." [**Ans.** Section 1.3]
iii. "Feedback is the key which unlocks the success of communication." [**Ans.** Section 1.8(B)]

[C] Very Short Answer-Type Questions

Answer the following questions in brief:

i. Name any four features of communication system. [**Ans.** Section 1.3]
ii. Point out any four barriers of communication. [**Ans.** Section 1.12]
iii. Mention four objectives of business communication. [**Ans.** Section 1.4]
iv. Point out four important principles of business communication. [**Ans.** Section 1.10]

● **Questions of University Examinations:**

(A) Questions of Very Short Answer-Type [Each Question Carries 2 Marks]:

(i) What are the objectives of Business Communication? [C.U. B.Com. 2005]
Ans. Ans. of Short Question No. (6)

(ii) State two objectives of business communication. [C.U. B.Com. Old Syllabus 2006]
Ans. Ans. of Short Question No. (6)

(iii) Mention two principles of effective communication. [C.U. B.Com. Old Syllabus 2006]
Ans. Section 1.10

(iv) Mention four elements of communication. [C.U. B.Com. New Syllabus 2006]
Ans. Section 1.2

(v) What do you mean by 'Feedback'? [C.U. B.Com. New Syllabus 2006]
Ans. Ans. of Short Question No. (16)

(vi) What are the elements of communication? [C.U. B.Com. New Syllabus 2007]
Ans. Section 1.2

(vii) What is feed-back? [C.U. B.Com. New Syllabus 2007, 2009]
Ans. Ans. of Short Question No. (16)

(viii) What is channel of communication? [C.U. B.Com. New Syllabus 2007]
Ans. Section 1.6

(ix) What do you mean by 'Encoding'? [C.U. B.Com. New Syllabus 2008]
Ans. Point No. 2 in Section 1.5

(x) What is Internal Communication? [C.U. B.Com. New Syllabus 2009]
Ans. Point No. 8 in Section 1.3

(xi) What does the term 'Business Communication' imply? [C.U. B.Com. New Syllabus 2011]
Ans. Section 1.1

(xii) Mention any two components of 'Business Communication'.
[C.U. B.Com. New Syllabus 2011]
Ans. Section 1.2

(xiii) What do you mean by 'Feedback' in the process of Communication? [C.U. B.Com. New Syllabus 2011]

Ans. Ans. of Short Question No. 16

(B) Questions of Short Answer-Type [Each Question Carries 4 Marks]:

(i) Explain the major categories of barriers to communication. [C.U. B.Com. New Syllabus 2011]

Ans. Sections 1.12

(ii) Briefly explain the principles of effective communication. [C.U. B.Com. New Syllabus 2011]

Ans. Sections 1.10

(C) Questions of Long Answer-Type [Each Question Carries 10 Marks]:

(i) Define Communication. Discuss the essentials of good communication system. [C.U. B.Com. 2005]

Ans. Sections 1.1 and 1.10(C)

(ii) What are the barriers of communication? [C.U. B.Com. New Syllabus 2006]

Ans. Section 1.12

(iii) Briefly describe the various steps in a two-way communication process. [C.U. B.Com. New Syllabus 2007]

Ans. Section 1.5

(iv) What are the different barriers to communication? What steps can be taken to overcome these barriers? [C.U. B.Com. New Syllabus 2007]

Ans. Section 1.12 and 1.13

(v) What do you mean by process of communication? Discuss the importance of feedback in the process. [C.U. B.Com. New Syllabus 2008]

Ans. Section 1.5 and 1.8(B)

(vi) What is Business Communication? Explain all the elements of Business Communication. [C.U. B.Com. New Syllabus 2009]

Ans. Sections 1.1 and 1.2

(vii) Discuss the essentials or requisites of a good communication system. [C.U. B.Com. New Syllabus 2009]

Ans. Section 1.10(C)

CHAPTER

2 Importance of Business Communication

"Good communication is as stimulating as black coffee, and just as hard to sleep after."

—Anne Morrow Lindbergh

TOPICS

i. Significance or Importance of Business Communication ◆ ii. Conflict—Reasons, Benefits, Cost and Levels of Conflict ◆ iii. Group Conflict—Inter-group and Intra-group Conflict ◆ iv. Conflict Resolution ◆ v. Group Cohesiveness.

Subject-matter of the Chapter : *Efficient work performance in business depends on individual as well as group or team performance. A co-ordination among all of them is necessary to achieve good result. Communication does the task. But working in groups brings conflict as a natural consequence. An attempt has been made to define conflict, to find out its causes and to describe the benefits and cost of it. Attempts have also been made to answer how and why inter-group and intra-group conflicts take place, how a conflict can be resolved and how group cohesiveness can be achieved. After studying the chapter the readers are expected to answer elementary questions relating to importance of communication, conflict, conflict resolution and group cohesiveness.*

2.1 Significance or Importance of Business Communication

The significance or importance of business communication is increasing very rapidly day-by-day. The business world of today cannot move smoothly without the help of communication. It makes a business enterprise dynamic and increases its efficiency. It is regarded as the motivating force that leads to industrial harmony. It can be used as a device for controlling the business activities to ensure the achievement of organisational goals. According to **Keith Davis**, the role of communication in business is as essential as the blood veins or arteries in human body. In its absence, a business organisation would cease to exist.

Business communication has a significant role to play in management whose objective is to direct the individual efforts for securing overall co-ordination of organisational activities. It performs the energising function in the organisation by transmitting information, facts and ideas and thereby making co-ordinated efforts possible. Communication can, as such, be regarded as basic to the functioning of an organisation.

Theo Haimann has rightly said that the success of management activities, to a great extent, depends on good communication system. Communication creates favourable work environment, motivates the workers to work hard and, thus, management activities become easier. Through communication process it is possible to supply all necessary and important messages or information at all levels of the organisation.

Business communication promotes managerial efficiency and induces the human elements in an organisation to develop a spirit of co-operation which finally leads to peak performances. The process of leadership depends on effective communication. Sound communication system is an essential requirement of good labour-management relations. With the help of communication there is better understanding of the objectives and policies which encourage co-ordination. Growing importance of human relations in every business with customers and workers has made communication the life-line of business. Producers are required to make sales appeal to their customers.

The subordinates are required to communicate their grievances and complaints to their superiors, otherwise they may lead to conflicts. Proper communication helps in implementing the decisions effectively and leads to smooth running of the business. It creates mutual trust and confidence and builds up the morale of the employees and, thus, provides job satisfaction to them.

Business communication is all the more important in management because the success of an enterprise depends upon how effectively its employees understand one another. Most of the problems of business can be attributed to poor communication between the managers and workers. So, lack of communication or poor communication will affect a business in different ways. It will greatly affect understanding of the employees, place them in utter confusion, create apathy to their work, hinder their willing co-operation, put co-ordination out of gear and invite dislocation, chaos and conflict in all business affairs and, ultimately, the very survival of the business will be at stake.

The importance of effective communication in management has been widely recognised in recent years. It has become one of the most vital factors in the efficient performance of management. It has an important bearing on management affairs from different points of view.

Above discussion of the significance of business communication may be stated point-wise as follows:

1. Movement of Information: Communication helps to move information from one place to another and from one person to another. It develops a chain of understanding among the workers of different levels in a business enterprise..

2. Efficient and Smooth Running of Enterprise: The smooth and efficient functioning of an enterprise entirely depends upon the effectiveness of the system of communication. It provides the basis of direction and actuates people to action in accordance with the desires of the management authority. According to **G. R. Terry:** "Communication serves as the lubricant fostering the smooth operation of the management process."

3. Promotion of Management Efficiency: Communication encircles all the functions of business management. So, without it, no function of business management can proceed towards its desired goal. It is the tool of managerial efficiency. The managerial efficiency depends upon getting things done through other people by making them know and understand what the manager wants them to do. It is the work of communication to keep the employees informed of everything necessary for smooth work performance.

4. Proper Planning: Communication is very helpful in planning the activities of business. It provides the managers information and ideas necessary for sound planning. According to **Theo Haimann** "Only through good communication can company policies and practices be formulated and administered." Secrecy of information creates suspicion among the workers and separates them. Understanding of the common problems unites them for showing a better record of their performance.

5. Basis of Decision-making: Communication helps the managers to take essential decisions and conduct vital operations. The quality of decisions made in an organisation entirely depends on the volume and quality of information available to the management authority. In the absence of effective communication it may not be possible for top management personnel to come in closer contact with their subordinates.

6. Basis of Co-operation: By promoting mutual understanding and meeting of minds, communication paves the way for co-operation. Communication creates condition for mental acceptance of the work before its actual performance. This mental acceptance is the will-to-do before actually doing it. Communication involves understanding and willing acceptance of orders and instructions and acts as the basis for individual and co-operative efforts.

7. Means of Co-ordination: Co-ordination implies orderly group efforts to provide unity of action. This unity of action is the result of team work which, in turn, depends, to a great extent, upon clear understanding of the organisational goals, the mode of their achievement and situation of the work. The function of the business communication is to get the workers fully informed of everything relating to the work and bring a perfectly tuned harmony in their work.

8. Job Satisfaction: Proper communication system extends mutual trust and faith. It thus creates confidence in the ability of their manager, promotes their loyalty to the enterprise and stimulates their job interest. Proper communication system enables the subordinates to bring to the notice of the managers their viewpoints, grievances and troubles. This facility raises the morale of the workers and, ultimately, leads to job satisfaction for high performance.

9. Establishment of Public Relations: A business enterprise comes into contact with several social groups, e.g., customers, investors, trade unions, government and the local community. It must maintain cordial relations with each of these groups to develop a favourable image. It must continuously strive to convince the public in general that its actions are taken in the interest of the society. No public relation can be established without communication.

10. Establishment of Effective Leadership: Effective leadership is established through communication. The ideas, orders, instructions, direction, etc., of the leader or manager is transmitted to the subordinate employees through communication. The manager can influence them and create a healthy relation by wiping out misunderstanding and distrust between management authority and subordinates through communication.

11. Assisting Motivation: Communication creates motivation. Through it the managers and employees are well-acquainted with the latest information relating to the organisation. This leads to avoidance of hostility, acceptance of reality, change of attitude, consciousness of responsibility and—ultimately—motivation to work.

12. Loyalty: The confidence and loyalty of the lower employees on the management personnel increases as they become aware of the competence of efficiency of their boss through communication. It helps to strengthen mutual trust.

13. Accomplishment of Goals: Communication fulfils the organisational objectives through co-operation and co-ordination among the managerial and working staff. Inter-connections between the managers and subordinate employees are established through effective communication system.

14. Industrial Peace: Workers' unrest is a problem today. It is communication which can establish peace in the industry. Two-way communication helps to develop mutual co-operation and understanding. Through downward communication the management personnel send their orders, instructions, directions, etc. to the subordinates. On the other hand, the upward communication helps the subordinates to convey to their superiors their demands, grievances, complaints, suggestions, etc. Thus, through communication of facts and information between the superiors and subordinates, industrial peace can be established.

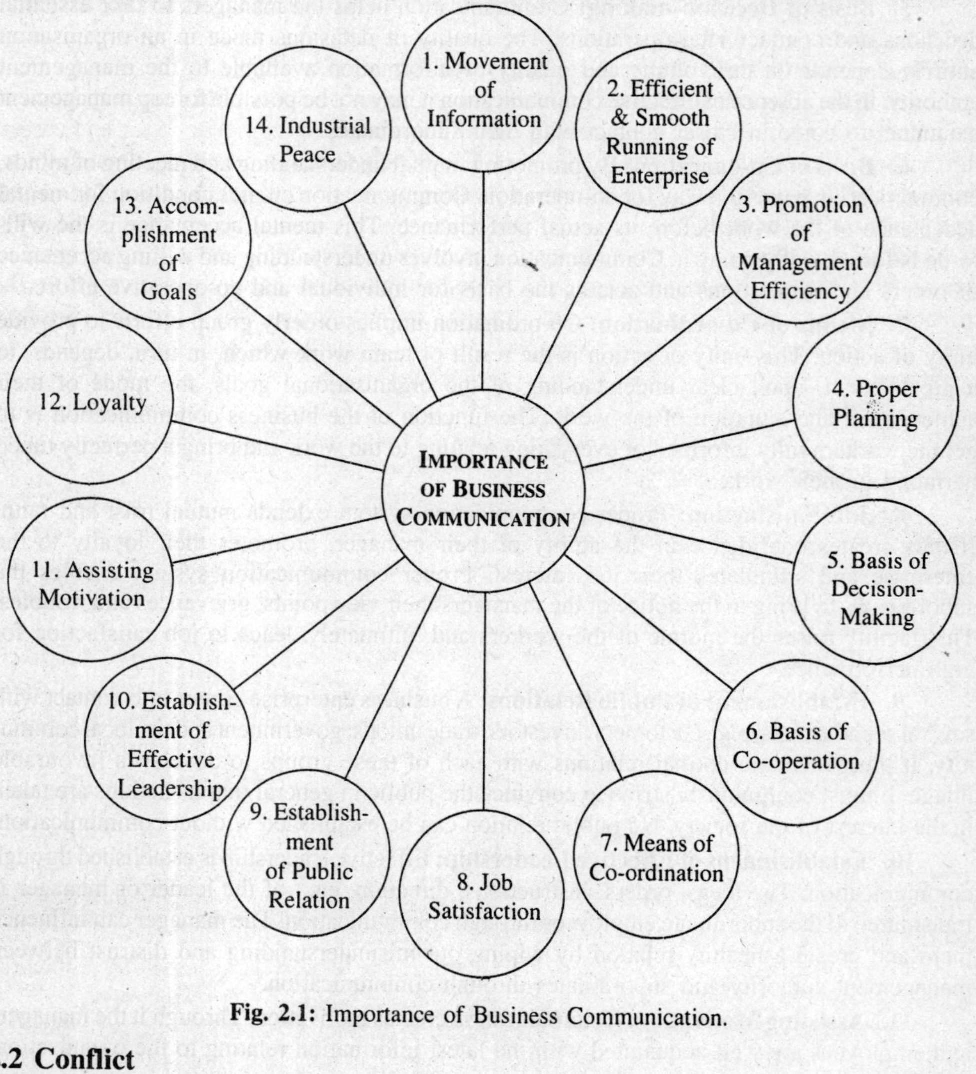

Fig. 2.1: Importance of Business Communication.

2.2 Conflict

[A] Definition: 'Conflict' means disagreement, opposition of any kind, argument, antagonism or hatred between two persons or groups or among many persons or groups. People working in an organisation may have difference of values, ideas, opinions, attitudes, objectives, preferences and personalities. Therefore, conflict becomes natural between/among persons, groups or teams on issues like sharing of resources, responsibilities, authority, accountability, etc. Conflict may arise between individuals, between groups, between individuals and groups, between individuals and the management personnel or between groups and the management personnel, etc.

[B] Examples:

(1) A, an individual, does not perform his duties properly. B, the manager of the department, warns him on the issue. A becomes disgruntled and a conflict arises between A and B.

(2) There are two groups 'X' and 'Y' in a factory where incentive depends on total performance. Given that group Y's performance depends on the performance of group X, or vice versa, the group that has performed well will be at conflict with the other, if the other group has not performed up to the mark.

2.2.1 Reasons for Conflict

The various reasons for conflict are pointed out below:

1. Poor Communication: Conflict generally arises owing to poor communication or communication gap which usually takes place in the absence of complete, clear and correct information or due to language barriers. Poor communication leads to suspicion, misunderstanding, and wrong or partial impression between individuals, groups or teams, and gives rise to conflict.

2. Competition: Competition for monetary incentives (e.g., bonus for individual or group performance), higher position, attainment of benefits, etc. may cause conflict. The problem of competition comes in where resources are limited and only a few are rewarded, and a large section remains deprived. This competition generates dissatisfaction and, ultimately, gives rise to conflict.

3. Individual Differences: There are differences among people in education, culture and upbringing, and differences in values, attitudes and personalities. When people with so many differences work together, there is always a possibility of conflict.

4. More Power: To remain satisfied with a limited power is generally not found in human nature. An individual or a group has a general tendency to become more powerful and more important. From this tendency, an individual or a group may defy or question the authority of the superior. This leads to conflict. A conflict may also arise if a group claims to deserve more power to itself than other group or groups.

5. Difference in Objectives: Individuals or groups with different objectives are likely to oppose each other. They cannot go along the same route for long. The activity of an individual with a strong sense of responsibility and ambition is bound to clash with that of a person having less of those qualities, even though both of them may be the employees of the same rank. Such differences gradually generate dissatisfaction between them, and result in a conflict.

6. Lack of Well-Defined Responsibility: Lack of well-defined responsibility regarding the performance of a work gives ample scope for a conflict. Where no particular person or group is given responsibility for a work, it becomes nobody's job to see it well done. This has an adverse effect on the performance level of all concerned and leads to low productivity for which the individuals or groups may start blaming one another, and constitutes a potential cause for conflict.

7. Retaliation: When an individual or group is threatened or hurt by another individual or group, the former usually threatens or hurt the latter in retaliation. Thus, a conflict is likely to crop up.

8. Difference in Work Environment: If there are differences in work environment among different employees or different groups of employees, conflict may take place. Employees of less convenient environment may feel deprived and can contribute to conflict.

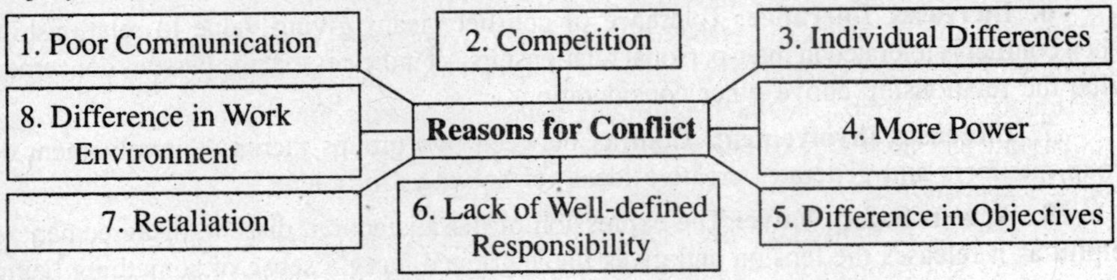

Fig. 2.2: Reasons for Conflict.

Communication and conflict are inter-related. Conflict comes to light through communicative processes. **Burgoon and Ruffner** observe, 'Conflict can be manifested only through some sort of communication behaviour. We can certainly have communication without conflict, but conflict without some type of communication is impossible.' Therefore, conflict does not mean an end or breakdown of communication. Rather, it is a different way of communication.

2.2.2 Benefits of Conflict

Conflict is not necessarily harmful. It has been recognised as an unavoidable and natural phenomenon in human life. It may create misunderstanding, distrust, ill-feeling, real or imaginary differences among people. But conflict has some positive values. It evaluates the existing system, brings social changes, helps to clarify issues, boosts development in the fields of science and technology and promote self-improvement.

The benefits of conflict may be stated as under:

1. Evaluates Existing System: There may be a system in vogue in a particular society. The system may have some weaknesses in it. Criticism of the system may give rise to conflict. This may produce arguments and counter-arguments, actions and reactions. Thus, the system faces the test of its strength and evaluation takes place. We come to know the bright and dark sides of the system.

2. Clarifies Situation and Issues: Different opinions regarding an issue often confuse us, but a confrontation of such opinions with conflicting arguments can clarify the situation and the issue. An individual evaluating the situation from his/her own perspective may think his/her evaluation to be 100% correct—which often may not be the case in reality. Varied and conflicting opinions bring out the actual position and misunderstanding is removed.

3. Brings Out Social Change: No change is possible without conflict. Sometimes a social system requires change. Old values need to be replaced or modified by newer ideas. Out-dated values that prove to be a hindrance to social change are often too deep rooted to be easily dispensed with. Here, a strong conflict between the old and new values brings about social change.

4. Strengthens Relationship: It is better to go in for a conflict rather than suppressing it. Suppression of conflict may create tension, irritation, etc., and a long-drawn suppression may result in irreparable damage to the inter-personal relationship. On the contrary, conflict may make the mind tension-free. Internal anger, irritation, rivalry, etc. cool down after the manifestation of conflict. Thus, though conflict may generate temporary disagreement or ill-feeling, it strengthens relationship in the long run.

5. Develops Science and Technology: New horizon of science and technology may be opened through conflict. Each conflicting party wants to be supreme in power over the others. Thus, the craze for power encourages scientific and technological development. For example, a war between two countries may boost up the technological innovations related to military requirements. These innovations often have non-military applications as well.

6. Increases Tolerance: Tolerance of conflict means giving value to relationship. When conflict is tolerated in inter-personal relationship—it indicates that the persons concerned value the relationship above other considerations.

7. Increases Involvement: Conflict between two groups increases involvement of group members and generates creative ideas for solving a problem.

8. Acts as Safety Valve: The expression of dissatisfaction, dissent, disagreement is helpful as it releases the tension and gives the aggrieved party a sense of something being done and that in itself gives a sense of relief.

2.2.3 Disadvantages (or Costs) of Conflict

The disadvantages of conflict are the following:

1. Causes Less Communication: A conflict creates differences in opinion and distance in relationship. People become less communicative and avoid each other.

2. Enlarges Differences: Conflict magnifies the differences between persons. Imaginary and real differences crop up and the relationship deteriorates.

3. Breeds Distrust and Suspicion: Conflict breeds distrust and suspicion among the conflicting parties. Confidence and reliance diminishes with the increase in the intensity of the conflict.

4. Causes Inefficiency in Performance: As considerable energy is lost in the effort of making and resolving a conflict, efficiency in work performance is bound to be affected. Whether the conflict is between individuals or groups, performance level is likely to fall from the one achieved in a 'no-conflict' situation.

5. Results in Adverse Effect on Self Image: A good and efficient worker or a group of workers cannot do justice to their good image if involved in the conflict. In such a situation, even prudent persons behave in an undesirable manner.

6. Brings in Hostile Attitude: Conflict creates hatred and breeds hostility. Even a gentle and obedient employee may disobey the superior and become hostile in his/her behaviour. The same behaviour can be noticed between co-employees or between groups during conflict.

7. Plays Destructive Role: Conflict may involve the employees in acts that are harmful and destructive for the organisation.

8. Creates Undesirable Situation: Conflict creates undesirable and unpleasant situation in the organisation. Chaos, indiscipline and pandemonium may reign supreme in place of peace, harmony, co-operation and discipline.

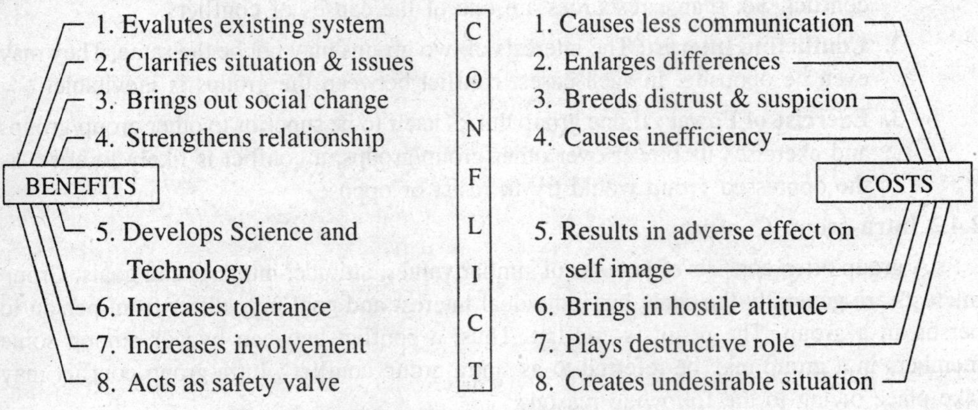

Fig. 2.3: Benefits and Costs of Conflict.

2.3 Levels of Conflict

Conflicts occurring at different levels (e.g., personal, group and institutional) in the hierarchy of inter-personal interaction may be classified* as follows:

i. **Intra-personal Conflict:** It is an internal struggle between perception or choice. We experience an internal struggle between what we think we are and what others think us to be. When self-concept differs from another's perception an intra-personal conflict arises.

* M. Burgoon & M. Ruffner, Human Communication, Holt Rinehart and Winston, USA (1978), PP 484-490

ii. **Inter-personal Conflict:** Inter-personal conflict takes place when two or more individuals compete for a scarce resource such as love, recognition, material goods or application. It depends upon difference in liking, personality, views, attitude, etc.

iii. **Intra-group Conflict:** It refers to a conflict among the members in a group. It is a result of differences in individuals and group goals.

iv. **Inter-group Conflict:** It refers to a conflict between two or more groups, when two or more groups compete for scarce resources.

v. **Institutional Conflict:** In any institution there are individuals, groups, sub-groups, etc. When a conflict is raised by an individual or a group against the established rules and procedures of the institution, it amounts to institutional conflict.

2.4 Group Conflict

A group is a 'combination of two or more persons who interact with each other to accomplish a common purpose'.* Conflict, as defined earlier in this chapter, means disagreement, opposition of any kind, argument, etc. A 'group conflict' refers to a conflict involving a group or groups. It may take place between two or more groups or between/among the members within the group.

2.4.1 Inter-group Conflict

When a conflict takes place between two or more groups it is called 'inter-group conflict'.

- **Causes of Inter-Group Conflict:** The causes of inter-group conflict are as follows:
  1. **Scarce Resources:** When resources are scarce and different groups within the organisation or outside it want to get hold of the same, they may come into conflict. So, scarce resources are one of the causes of conflict.
  2. **Conflicting Interest:** The interests of two groups may not be the same. They may even be opposite. In such cases, conflict between the groups is inevitable.
  3. **Exercise of Power:** If one group thinks itself to be superior to other group/groups and exercises its power over other group/groups, a conflict is likely to arise, as the oppressed group would try to resist or oppose.

2.4.2 Intra-group Conflict

A group often consists of persons of similar values, attitude, interests and goals. Group interests are generally the same but individual interest and goal may differ from person to person in a group. The result is conflict. Thus, a conflict between two or among some members in a group may be referred to as 'intra-group conflict'. Intra-group conflict may take place owing to the following reasons:

1. Difference in Goals: If some members in a group aim at a certain objective and others differ—a conflict is likely to occur. Let us suppose, some members of a production unit of a factory are trying to improve the quality of product and others are interested in increasing the quantity of output. There is a possibility of a conflict between the two sets of members with two different objectives within the group.

2. Denial of Responsibility: Owing to lack of well-defined responsibility, some people in a group may avoid their work and make other members responsibile for non-performance of the same. Thus, conflict among the members of the group emerges.

---

* W. Haynes—Principles and Practice of Management (1991). New Central Book Agency, Kolkata

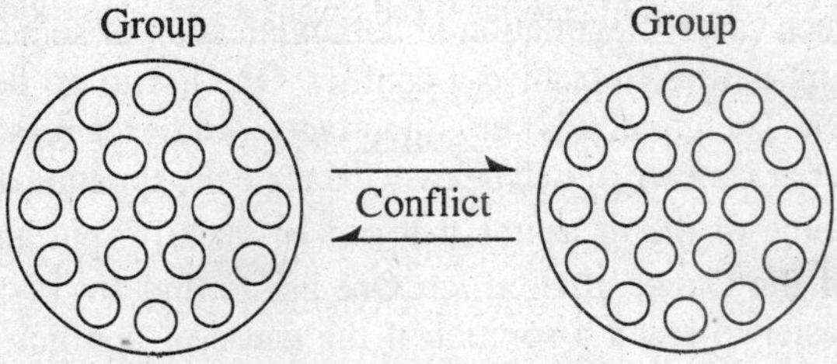

Fig. 2.3: Inter-Group Conflict.

Fig. 2.4: Intra-Group Conflict.

3. Ineffective Control Over the Group: When leadership is weak and there is less control over the members of the group, a conflict on a petty issue may crop up.

4. Ideological Differences: A person's ideology, morality, ethics, etc. may not be in conformity with those of the group to which he/she belongs. A conflict is inevitable in such cases. The person is likely to disassociate himself/herself from the group as a result.

5. High Degree of Competition: High degree of competition for any scarce thing (e.g., money, power, position, supplies, etc.) among the members of a group may lead to conflict, because the scarce thing is not for all—somebody will get and others will be deprived of it.

6. Communication Gap: Poor communication or communication gap may create misunderstanding or partial impression about a person in a group. Such impression creates wrong ideas about the person and conflict may take place.

2.5 Conflict Resolution

● **Meaning:** Conflict Resolution refers to putting an end to the conflict. It is a means of finding a solution to a disagreement, argument and opposition. It is a settlement of dispute through negotiation, persuasion, arbitration or any other action suitable for the settlement.

Fig. 2.5: Conflict Resolution.

Conflict may take place in our personal life, in social sphere or at work place. We try to resolve conflict according to the situation. In any organisation, 'Conflict Resolution' is an important function of the management authority. An early action by the management personnel helps to resolve a conflict in its primary stage. So the managers should not neglect any conflict whether it takes place between two employees, groups or between the employees and the manager himself/herself.

2.5.1 Measures for Conflict Resolution

In a situation where there is a conflict no one can perform to the best of one's capacity, because any decision taken in the workplace is likely to be opposed or criticised. The fear of opposition or criticism has a dampening effect on performance and results in low productivity.

It is easier to resolve a conflict at an early stage. If a conflict is allowed to stand for long and/or intensify, it may turn out to be a very difficult one to be resolved. Communication plays a vital role in such cases. Negotiation or communication of some kind has to be made between the conflicting parties to resolve a conflict. One has to go deep into the problem before trying to solve it. Therefore, it is very important to know the reasons behind a conflict. If the reasons or causes are known, it will be easy to tackle the situation and resolve a conflict.

Following are some of the measures that can be taken to put an end to conflict:

1. **Removal of the Cause of Conflict:** One has to find out first the actual cause for conflict. It will be easier to reach a solution if the cause of conflict is removed.

2. **Early Action:** If a conflict is resolved at an early stage, it does not grow into a big problem. It is also easy to find out the solution in a minor conflict. So, timely action can help to resolve a conflict.

3. **Positive Attitude:** The conflicting parties should come forward to resolve the conflict. If both the parties agree to talk to each other in resolving the conflict, half of the war is won. Negative attitudes of accusing each other, finding fault with one another, criticising others unnecessarily, etc. should be avoided. An intention of keeping the conflict alive on the part of either party may prove detrimental to any possible resolution of the conflict.

4. **Effective Persuasion:** To persuade means to try to bring about changes in the thinking process of an individual or a group. Through the process of persuation newer view-points may emerge and lead the way to a solution.

5. **Flexibility:** To get closer to a solution the parties should give up rigidity and should be flexible in their attitude.

6. **Diversion of Focus to Greater Interest:** Group conflict may be resolved if the conflicting parties are trained to fight jointly with the external enemy forgetting internal conflict and thus channelising their energy and spirit for achieving greater interest.

7. **Leaving the Field:** To avoid a direct conflict one may physically depart from the situation, or may psychologically depart (i.e., remain silent and show a cool attitude), ask the other to change the topic or himself/herself to divert the topic. A Sanskrit proverb is very much applicable here—'One who flees survives.'

8. **Tolerating the Hazards:** If any one bears the trouble of conflict for the time being and ignores it altogether, the conflict will disappear gradually with the passing of time. 'Time is the best healer'—goes the proverb.

9. **Accepting the Truth:** One of the easiest ways of ending a conflict is to accept that one was wrong or made a mistake in involving himself/herself in a conflict.

10. **Re-establishing Mutual Trust:** Trust is the key word in establishing friendship and repairing a relationship. A conflict takes place when mutual trust is lost. Re-establishing mutual trust can wipe out the conflict.

11. **Effective Communication:** Complete, clear and correct information through effective communication can wipe out misunderstanding and suspicion between the managers and employees. Thus, effective communication can resolve conflict.

12. **Arbitration:** Committees, teams, task force, etc. may be formed; an expert co-ordinator or arbitrator may be appointed to resolve a conflict. The appointed committee or the person listens to the problems of the conflicting parties and gives a verdict after considering the practical situation. Generally, both the parties are asked to step down from their stand-point and a compromise is made. It is an age-old and effective method of conflict resolution.

13. **Participation in Management:** If the employees are allowed to participate in various committees and bodies of the management, they feel that they are part and parcel of the management body and have a say in the decision-making. Such feeling can help to avoid conflict with the managers.

2.5.2 Result or Outcome of Conflict Resolution

According to **Keith Davis** the result or outcome of conflict resolution may be: (i) Win-Lose, (ii) Lose-Lose, (iii) Win-Win, or (iv) Lose-Win.

When conflict between two parties is sought to be resolved by winning of one over the other (win-lose policy) it is sure to result in dissatisfaction of one of the two parties. In reality, however, it is often found that neither of the conflicting parties would allow the other to win. Rather, they would both lose (i.e., lose-lose policy). Such attitudes are destructive in nature and often delay the resolution process and may never reach a solution. On the other hand, if the conflicting parties take a positive or constructive outlook and agree to compromise on their demands, nobody loses the battle, rather both win (i.e., win-win policy). This strategy is beneficial for individuals, groups and the organisation as a whole.

Individual x		Individual y: LOSE	Individual y: WIN
	WIN	WIN-LOSE	WIN-WIN
	LOSE	LOSE-LOSE	LOSE-WIN

Fig. 2.6: Result of Conflict Resolution.

2.5.3 Role or Importance of Communication in Conflict Resolution

Conflict is a very common and normal incidence in our daily life. No one can say that he/she never got involved in a conflict. Difference of opinion, disagreement, argument, quarrel, physical clash, etc. are outward expressions of a conflict. Conflict may take place in personal life at home with relatives, outside the home between friends, in the sports ground with the players, in a club with the members, or in any other place even with the strangers. It may also occur at the work-place with the co-workers or with the manager. People working together in a department, team or group are different in nature. They have different habits, religions, customs, culture, political affiliations, etc. So their ideas, attitudes, emotions and values differ from each other. Such differences may contribute to the conflict in some form or other in the work-place. There are certain other factors which may create conflict. When an employee feels that he/she is being exploited and the boss is taking advantage of the situation, a sense of dissatisfaction or deprivation gradually grows and, ultimately, turns into a conflict. When job duties are not explained clearly the employees become confused and cannot distinguish between his/her own duties with those of others. Again, if the employee is over-ambitious which his/her job is unable to provide, job satisfaction may disappear, frustration may grow and conflict may arise.

There is no short-cut or readymade formula for resolving a conflict. One has to find out the causes of conflict first and then try to find a solution. Besides this, early action, positive attitude, intention to resolve, effective communication, persuasion, flexibility of the conflicting members/groups, etc. are useful measures for conflict resolution. Conflict cannot be resolved automatically, some forms of initiative, effort and negotiation are necessary. Communication is the only means to make the conflicting persons understand, initiate changes in their thinking and bring them out of the conflict.

In the case of inter-personal or group conflict the manager, leader or the mediator should meet the conflicting persons together and try to know their views on the conflict. It is important to give a patient hearing of what both the parties are saying. Everyone tries to prove that he/she is right and the other person is wrong. It is vital to analyse both the views impartially. The person who is trying to resolve should ask each of the conflicting party to suggest action, they would like to see, to be taken by the other in resolving conflict. By negotiation and persuasion he/she should try to develop positive thinking among the conflicting persons who should also realise that they might have involved in the conflict in the heat of the moment. If any of them comes forward and says to the other, "I am sorry. I had no intention to hurt your sentiments", half of the conflict is resolved. But it is not easy to do so overcoming their personal ego. To resolve a conflict people should be separated from the problem. The problem or the cause of conflict should be sorted out and given attention to. One has to be careful to the fact that the main objective is to find out a solution to the problem, not to disturb or dissolve the relationship but to restore it. In some extreme cases where all negotiations, suggestions, advice, arbitrations, etc. fail, the management authority takes recourse to punitive measures against the conflicting employees by making demotion, transfer, etc. Sometimes, forgiveness is the only way to resolve a conflict.

Every step in resolving a conflict requires communication. One cannot even think of resolving a conflict without effective communication. Whatever may be the cause and whatever strategy is applied to resolve a conflict, good communication is the key to conflict resolution. Complete, clear and correct information can wipe out misunderstanding and suspicion and can improve relations and create an atmosphere congenial for development and growth. It increases trust, reliance and dependability. On the other hand, poor communication leads to disorder and chaos. It cannot resolve, rather, creates conflict. Therefore, good and effective communication is needed at every level of the organisation. The better the flow of communication, the greater is the possibility of staying away from conflict.

From the above discussion we can summarise the role or importance of communication in conflict resolution as follows:

1. Every step in resolving a conflict requires communication.
2. Communication is the only means to initiate changes in the thinking process of the conflicting persons.
3. Negotiation and persuasion is possible through communication which, ultimately, may resolve a conflict.
4. Communication brings conflicting parties closer. It narrows down the differences between them and they can stay away from conflict in protecting their own interest and the goodwill and interest of the organisation where they work together.
5. Effective communication is the key to conflict resolution. Complete, clear and correct information can wipe out misunderstanding and suspicion. It increases trust, reliance and dependability.
6. Poor communication leads to disorder and chaos. It cannot resolve, rather creates conflict.
7. To avoid a conflict the flow of communication should not be obstructed by any means.

2.6 Group Cohesiveness

While 'conflict' refers to disagreement, argument, disassociation, separateness, hate, animosity, etc., 'cohesiveness', on the other hand, relates to close relation, solidarity, co-operativeness, friendliness and unity.

'Group cohesiveness' signifies the overall attraction of the group members to each other. It is the force which makes the members of a group loyal to the group and attracts them to remain in it.

Group cohesiveness may, therefore, be defined as the result of the forces that hold the group members together. Since several individuals form a group, the level of cohesion of a group is often measured as the average of each individual member's attraction to the group.

2.6.1 Determinants of the Degree of Group Cohesiveness

The degree of cohesiveness in a group is considered to be high if—

i. The members of the group desire to remain in the group.
ii. They are co-operative and friendly with one another.
iii. They follow group norms.

iv. They interact with and influence one another.
v. They promote solidarity among the members.
vi. They feel proud to identify themselves within the group.
vii. They remain associated with the group for a long time.
viii. They belong to a group of manageable size.
ix. They are members of a group having past success.

Group cohesiveness develops slowly. It is a long process of interaction among the members of the group. A person is attracted initially to the members of similar values, culture, age, etc. in the group. Gradually he/she comes closer to other members and interacts with them. Sometimes he/she influences the thinking and activities of others and many a time he/she is influenced by other group members. The process leads to group cohesiveness in the long run. The duration of group membership is a determining factor of cohesiveness. The longer the interaction with the group, the greater is the cohesiveness. Group members with low cohesiveness, on the contrary, have less interest in following group ideology. They are less co-operative and less interactive with other group members. They behave much independently—having little concern for the other co-group members.

EXERCISES

[A] Essay-Type Questions

1. Discuss the significance of business communication. [C.U. B.Com. Old Syllabus, 2006] [**Ans.** Section 2.1]
2. Describe the importance of business communication. [**Ans.** Sec. 2.1]
3. What is conflict? What are the reasons for conflict? [**Ans.** Section 2.2, 2.2.1]
4. Discuss the benefits and costs of conflict. [**Ans.** Section 2.2.2, 2.2.3]
5. What is inter-group conflict? What are its causes? [**Ans.** Section 2.4.1]
6. What is intra-group conflict? Why intra-group conflict takes place? [**Ans.** Section 2.4.2]
7. What do you understand by conflict resolution? What measures can be taken for resolving a conflict? [**Ans.** Section 2.5, 2.5.1]
8. What is meant by group cohesiveness? What are the determinants of the degree of group cohesiveness? [**Ans.** Section 2.6, 2.6.1]
9. Discuss the role of communication in conflict resolution. [**Ans.** Section 2.5.3]

[B] Short Answer-Type Questions

1. **Write short notes on:**
   i. Group conflict. [**Ans.** Section 2.4]
   ii. Levels of conflict. [**Ans.** Section 2.3.4]
   iii. Inter-group conflict. [**Ans.** Section 2.4.1]
   iv. Intra-group conflict. [**Ans.** Section 2.4.2]
2. 'We can certainly have communication without conflict, but conflict without some type of communication is impossible'—Explain. [**Ans.** Section 2.2.1]
3. Mention six reasons for a conflict. [**Ans.** Section 2.2.1]
4. What are the possible outcome of Conflict Resolution? [**Ans.** Section 2.5.2]

[C] Very Short Answer-Type Questions

1. Define conflict. [**Ans.** Section 2.2]
2. Mention four benefits of conflict. [**Ans.** Section 2.2.2]
3. State four disadvantages of conflict. [**Ans.** Section 2.2.3]
4. What is group conflict? [**Ans.** Section 2.4]
5. Mention two causes of inter-group conflict. [**Ans.** Section 2.4.1]
6. Write the causes of intra-group conflict (any four). [**Ans.** Section 2.4.2]
7. State four measures for resolving a conflict. [**Ans.** Section 2.5.1]
8. What is group cohesiveness? [**Ans.** Section 2.6]

- **Questions of University Examinations:**

(A) Questions of Very Short Answer-Type [Each Question Carries 2 Marks]:

(i) What do you understand by Intra-group conflict? [C.U. B.Com. New Syllabus 2005, 2008]

Ans. Section 2.4.2

(ii) What is Group Cohesiveness? [C.U. B.Com. New Syllabus 2005, 2009]

Ans. Section 2.6

(iii) State two causes of conflict? [C.U. B.Com. 2006]

Ans. Section 2.2.1

(iv) What is Inter-group conflict? [C.U. B.Com. New Syllabus 2006, 2010]

Ans. Section 2.4.1

(v) Define Group Cohesiveness? [C.U. B.Com. New Syllabus 2006]

Ans. Section 2.6

(vi) State two methods to resolve conflict. [C.U. B.Com. New Syllabus 2009]

Ans. Section 2.5.1

(vii) What is meant by Conflict Resolution? [C.U. B.Com. New Syllabus 2011]

Ans. Section 2.5

(B) Questions of Long Answer-Type [Each Question Carries 10 Marks]:

(i) What is meant by Group Cohesiveness? What are the determinants of degree of Group Cohesiveness? [C.U. B.Com. New Syllabus 2007]

Ans. Sections 2.6 and 2.6.1

(ii) How can conflicts be resolved? [C.U. B.Com. New Syllabus 2010]

Ans. Section 2.5.1

CHAPTER

3

Types of Communication

"When all other means of communication fail, try words." —Anonymous

TOPICS

i. Different Types of Communication ◆ ii. Selection of the Means of Communication ◆ iii. Corporate Communication—Characteristics—Importance—Guidelines ◆ iv. Business Communication Network—Meaning, Classification ◆ v. Formal Communication—Purpose—Characteristics—Channels Used—Advantages and Disadvantages ◆ vi. Informal Communication—Meaning—Purpose—Channels Used—Types—Characteristics—Advantages and Disadvantages—Effectiveness—Right Mixture of Formal and Informal Communication ◆ vii. Distinction between Formal and Informal Communication ◆ viii. Oral or Verbal Communication—Advantages and Disadvantages ◆ ix. Written Communication—Advantages and Disadvantages ◆ x. Distinction between Verbal (Oral) and Written Communication.

Subject-matter of the Chapter : *Communication may be carried out through various means. The selection of such means is one of the important aspects of communication. An attempt has been made to give an idea of different types of communication used in today's business world in this chapter. The characteristics, media, objectives and essentials of corporate communication have been incorporated to make the readers familiar with the nature of corporate communication. It has been noticed that communication flows not only through structured and official path, but also takes place through informal methods. The discussion on formal and informal communication has been included in view of its importance in modern business world. Oral and written communication being important means of communication have been given due importance and coverage.*

3.1 Different Types of Communication

Exchange of facts, information and ideas may be called 'Communication'. Various means of communication are in use in modern business. The choice depends upon a number of factors like cost, distance, situation, availability, nature of communication, etc. This is why the types of communication differ in different organisations.

Communication may be classified according to different criterion as follows.

(a) **According to area of operation:**

(i) Internal Communication, and (ii) External Communication.

(b) **According to relation involved:**

(i) Formal Communication, and (ii) Informal Communication.

(c) **According to direction:**

(i) Upward Communication, (ii) Downward Communication, (iii) Horizontal Communication, and (iv) Diagonal Communication.

(d) **According to means used:**

(i) Verbal Communication, (ii) Written Communication, and (iii) Gestural Communication.

Different types of communication used in business are shown by a diagram as follows:

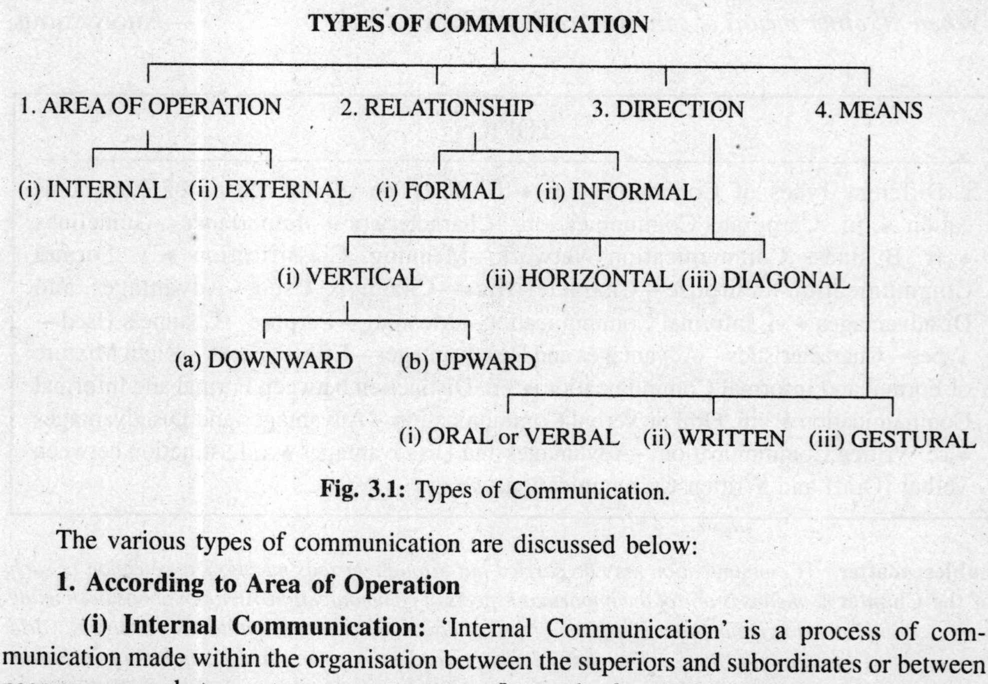

Fig. 3.1: Types of Communication.

The various types of communication are discussed below:

1. According to Area of Operation

(i) Internal Communication: 'Internal Communication' is a process of communication made within the organisation between the superiors and subordinates or between peer persons or between two or more groups. It may be formal or informal, oral or written. It may flow upward, downward or horizontal as per requirement. The oral means of internal communication are face-to-face discussion, verbal instruction, message, telephone, intercom, meeting, conference or seminar, speech, etc. The written methods include notice, circular, memo, report, chart or graph, bulletin, e-mail, fax, etc.

(ii) External Communication: A business organisation needs to communicate with the external agencies like customers, suppliers, investors, other business houses, banks, insurance companies, government offices, etc. Such communication may be called 'External Communication' as its area of operation is with the people outside the organisation. International business organisations need to communicate with foreign individuals, government agencies/organisations, etc. Oral external communication is made through face-to-face discussion, meeting, conference, seminar, telephone, speech, etc. The written process includes notice, letter, telegram, report, e-mail, advertisement, fax, press release, etc.

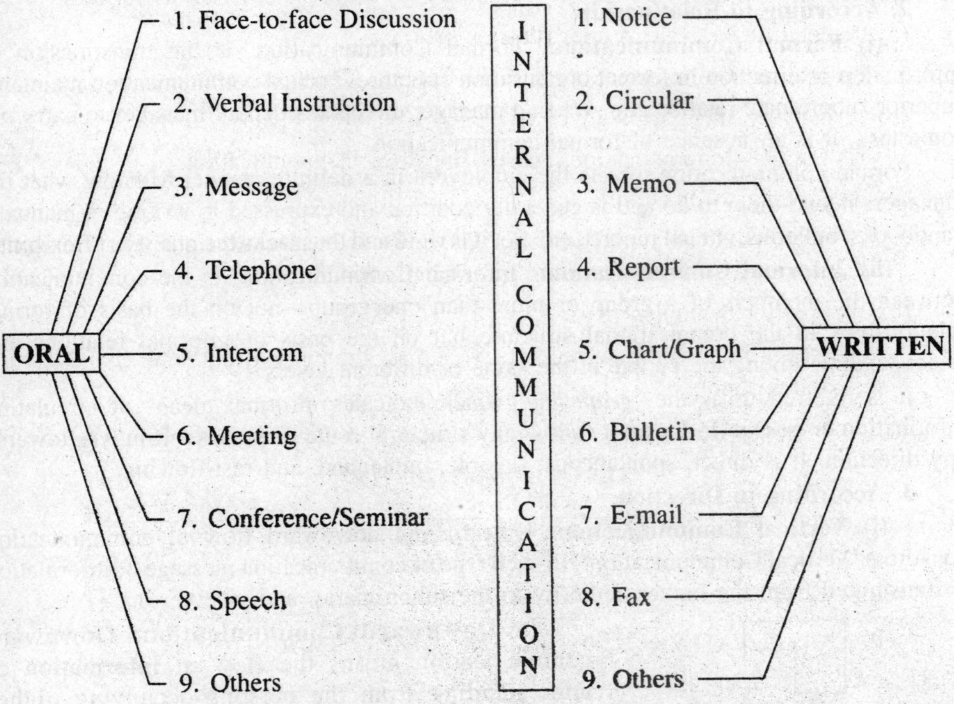

Fig. 3.2: Methods of Internal Communication.

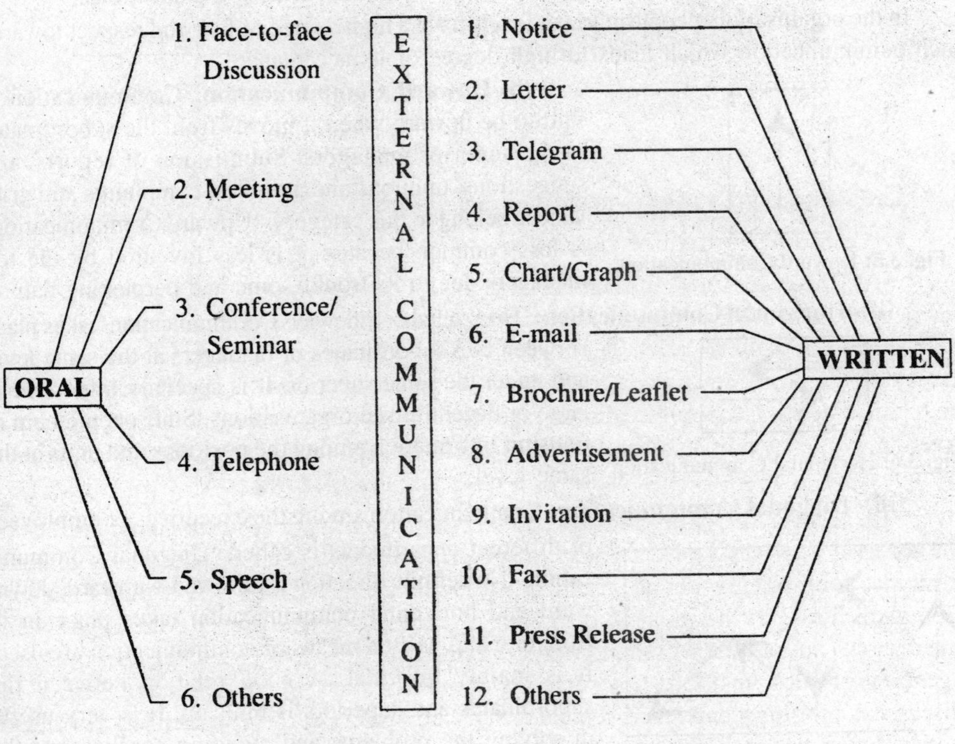

Fig. 3.3: Methods of External Communication.

2. According to Relationship

(i) Formal Communication: 'Formal Communication' is the transmission of information or direction in formal organisation structure. Formal communication maintains superior-subordinate relationship. When a manager directs his deputy manager to carry out some task, it is an instance of formal communication.

Formal communication directs the employees in a definite manner to know what the managers intend them to do and is generally codified and expressed in writing in manuals, handbooks, bulletins, annual reports, etc. So, it is rigid and thus lacks the quality of flexibility.

(ii) Informal Communication: 'Informal Communication' is the communication between the members of a group or more than one group—not on the basis of formal relationships in the organisational structure but on the basis of informal relations and understanding among the people at the same or different levels.

It is referred to as the '*grapevine*' which indicates informal means of circulating information or gossip. It does not follow any structural route or process. It moves towards any direction. It is direct, spontaneous, flexible, unplanned, and fast-flowing.

3. According to Direction

(i) Vertical Communication: Upward and downward flow of communication constitute 'Vertical Communication'. In such type of communication message or information is transmitted from the higher authority to the subordinates, and vice versa.

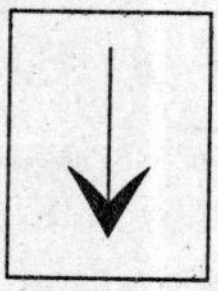

Fig. 3.4: Downward Communication.

(a) Downward Communication: Downward communication means the flow of information or understanding from the persons occupying higher positions to those at lower levels. It usually passes through written orders, reports and manuals and is the most common feature of all business organisations.

In the organisation, people at lower levels have a high degree of fear and respect towards such communication which leads to high degree of its acceptance.

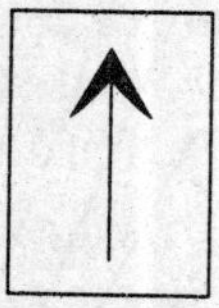

Fig. 3.5: Upward Communication.

(b) Upward Communication: Communication is said to be upward when it moves from the subordinates to the superior managers. Submission of reports and suggestions, opinions and attitudes, complaints and grievances belong to this category. 'Upward Communication' is less common because it is less favoured by the top managers due to its troublesome and perplexing nature.

(ii) Horizontal Communication: 'Horizontal or Sideways Communication' takes place between two subordinates or managers at the same level and under the same superior. It is specially important in large or decentralised organisations. Staff people help to transmit information among the positions and units at the same level.

Fig. 3.6: Horizontal Communication.

(iii) Diagonal Communication: Communication among the executives or employees of different departments is called 'Diagonal Communication.' No definite direction is followed—upward, downward and horizontal communication takes place in it. Both oral and written means of communication are used. It is mainly informal. A good relation between the subordinates and superiors is built up. It is very useful in solving the problems and avoiding conflict, but the chances of spreading rumours are high.

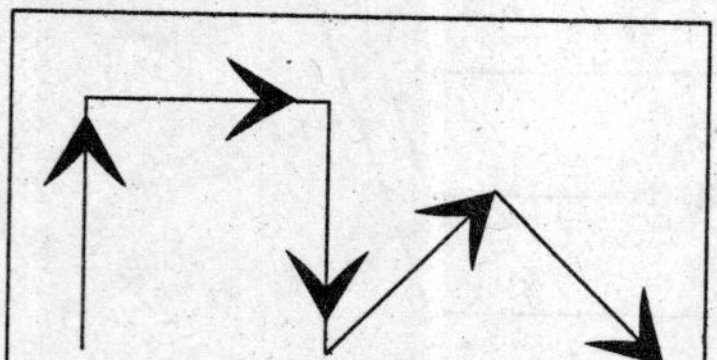

Fig. 3.7: Diagonal Communication.

4. According to Means

(i) Verbal Communication: 'Verbal or Oral Communication' implies the transmission of orders, messages or suggestions through spoken words. It may be face-to-face or through a speaking instrument like telephone.

Fig. 3.8: Verbal Communication.

Verbal communication may pass directly between one person and another or group or indirectly through meetings and conferences. Whatever tool is used, it saves much time and permits personal contact. This fosters a friendly and co-operative spirit, ensures quick understanding and proper explanation, encourages questions and answers, and stimulates interest.

The speaker is also in a position to know the reaction of the listener. Again, it is most suitable for confidential and emergent talks. But it is not suitable if the distance between the speaker and the listener is too long. It is also unsuitable if the matter to be communicated is lengthy and is to reach many persons simultaneously. It also lacks recorded evidence and future reference and does not allow the listener much time to think, act, and react.

(ii) Written Communication: A 'Written Communication' means the sending of message, order or instruction in writing through a letter, circular, manual, report, telegram, office memo, bulletin, etc. It is a formal method of communication and is suitable for long distance communication and repetitive standing orders. It creates the records of evidence and future reference, and can be sent to many persons at a time. It gives the receiver sufficient time

Fig. 3.9: Written Communication.

to think, act, and react. A written communication in order to be effective should be clear, concise and complete. Moreover, it is time-consuming and expensive, and it cannot maintain secrecy, offers difficulty in explaining all matters, has no chance of clarification, is less flexible and not effective in emergency.

(iii) Gestural Communication: Communication can be made through movement of body, facial expression, smile, modulation of voice, sign, handshake, rubbing of hands, eye-to-eye contact, style of walking, etc. As communication is made through bodily gestures it is called 'Gestural Communication.'

Fig. 3.10: Gestural Communication.

It should be kept in mind that, though the methods of communication are different, no one method can be used exclusively. So, different methods may be used in combination to suit the purpose of the communication.

3.2 Factors to be Considered for the Selection of the Means of Communication

Right choice of the means of communication increases its effectiveness. The following factors are to be considered in selecting the means of communication:

1. **Nature of Message:** The means of communication depends upon the nature of the message. Urgent, confidential, private and important messages should be distinguished from ordinary, routine, open and less important messages and the means of communication are to be chosen accordingly.
2. **Cost:** The cost of sending a message is also to be considered while selecting a mode of communication. The result obtained should justify the expenditure.
3. **Record:** If the record of the communication is important it should be written, otherwise oral communication is sufficient.
4. **Distance:** Distance is another factor for consideration. The mode of communication to be chosen depends on whether the message is to be sent to a nearby place or somewhere at a long distance.
5. **Scale of Organisation:** Means of communication in large-scale business is different from that in the small-scale. In small business most communication is oral while in large business it is written.
6. **Supporting Technology:** Both the sender and the receiver must have supporting technological communication tool to make communication through a particular medium. Suppose, A sends an e-mail to B. To get the e-mail B should have a personal computer. Again, to get a fax message one should possess a fax machine.

Therefore, while selecting a means of communication one has to consider whether supporting technological tool is available at the other end.

7. **Urgency:** Selection of the means of communication is to be made keeping in view the urgency of the communication. Time available is the main factor here. Higher cost may be justified for sending the message in time.
8. **Secrecy:** If the message to be communicated is secret or confidential, such means are required to be adopted that can maintain secrecy. A telephone call can be overheard, an e-mail or fax may not be appropriate, and an office memo may be less confidential. In such cases, face-to-face talking may solve the problem.
9. **Safety:** The sender has to be careful about the safety of the message. He/She has to decide whether the message would be sent by ordinary post or by registered post; through courier or messenger, etc.
10. **Relationship:** The relationship between the sender and recipient may be a decisive factor in the choice of the means of communication. Message of private nature may require personal contact whereas formal relationship demands official and conventional mode of communication.

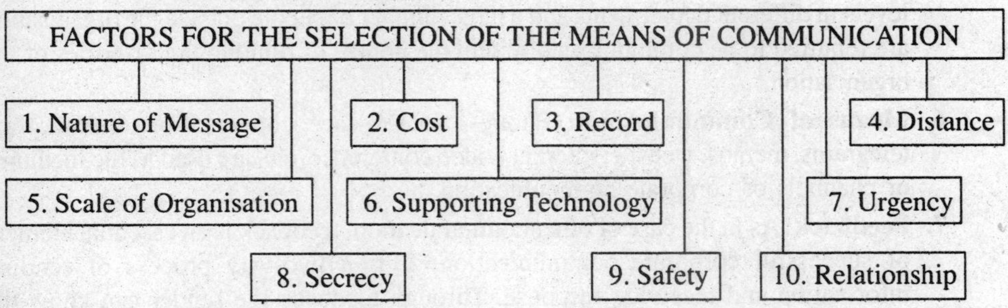

Fig. 3.11: Selection of the Means of Communication.

3.3 Corporate Communication

'Corporate Organisation' means an organisation formed by some people, having a separate entity and perpetual succession. A company, statutory corporation, co-operative ventures, etc. are considered to be corporate organisations because these are registered and have separate legal entity and perpetual existence.

Generally such organisations are not small, they are medium or large in size. Therefore, exchange of information and news with a large number of people within and outside the organisation is required to be made. Various departments and employees of the organisations are connected through communication network by phones, face-to-face discussion, e-mail, fax, memos, etc. to convey orders, instructions and information, to supervise and evaluate performance, to understand and perform individual job, to identify and solve a problem and, ultimately, to fulfil the objectives of the organisation. External communication with the customers, vendors, distributors, competitors, investors, government agencies, etc., through letters, reports, memos, phones, faxes, websites, internet, etc., are made to introduce, negotiate, co-ordinate, explain, interact, discuss and to develop co-operation and understanding.

Therefore, **corporate communication refers to a process of communication through which the managers, supervisors and executives exchange their views, opinions, feelings, etc. with the subordinates and employees in any corporate organisation and negotiate with the outside world with a view to fulfilling the objectives of the organisation.**

3.3.1 Characteristics of Corporate Communication

The various characteristics of corporate communication are mentioned below:

1. **Formal Communication:** Most of the corporate communication are formal in nature. Orders, instructions, information, suggestions, etc. are sent, maintaining formal procedure in a systematic way. It has to pass through several organisational stages.

2. **Informal Communication:** The size and structure of a corporate organisation being large and complex, informal communication or grapevine communication among different groups of employees takes place side by side with formal communication.
3. **Internal and External Communication:** Exchange of information with a large number of people within and outside the business is required in corporate communication. Internal communication with the managers and employees, and external communication with the customers, vendors, distributors, competitors, investors, government offices, etc. are made.
4. **Oral and Written Communication:** While oral communication is used for closer and internal communication with the employees, written communication is made with the outsiders and distant people.
5. **Wide Coverage:** Corporate organisations are large and a wide range of people are required to be covered in communication. People within the organisation at different levels in different departments and a large number of people outside the organisation are required to be communicated within the course of running the activities of the organisation.
6. **Means of Communication:** Phones, face-to-face conversation, e-mail, fax, telegrams, memos, website, internet, video conference, etc. are used as the mediums or channels of corporate communication.
7. **Feedback:** As in the case of other communication, feedback is an essential element of successful corporate communication. It is a two-way process of sending information and receiving response. Through feedback the sender can know the reaction of the recipient and take necessary action.
8. **Long-term System:** Corporate organisation has a perpetual existence. So, corporate communication is not a temporary arrangement. It is a long-term system or process. Communication is carried out continuously through a stable process.

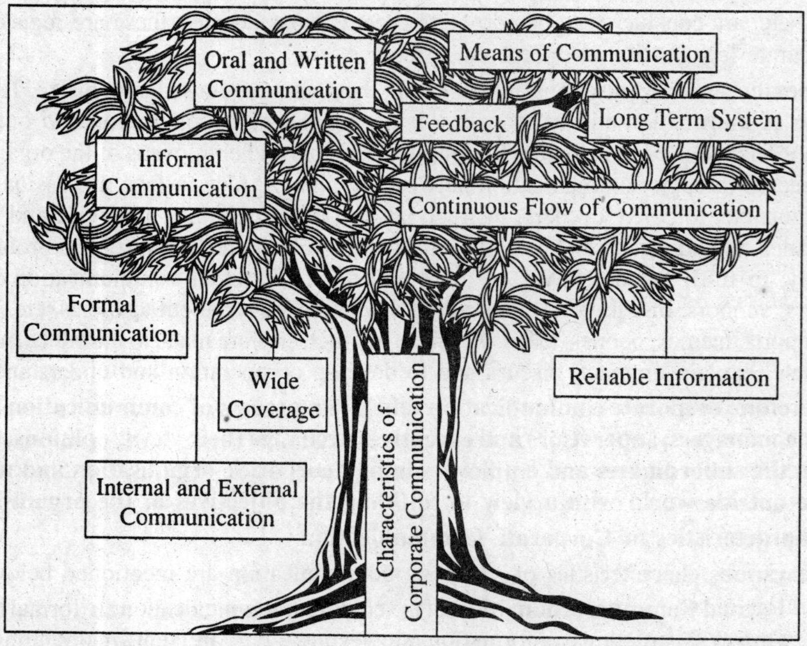

Fig. 3.12: Characteristics of Corporate Communication.

9. **Continuous Flow of Communication:** In a corporate organisation, flow of communication is continuous and uninterrupted; continuous due to the organisation's perpetual existence, and uninterrupted owing to following the formal or official channel.
10. **Reliable Information:** In a corporate organisation, information is collected through various sources and decisions are taken after necessary scanning, scrutinising, etc. to make the information dependable and correct.

3.3.2 Importance of Corporate Communication

Communication has an important role to play in the corporate world. With the increase in the complexities of activities in modern business, its importance is growing day-by-day. To achieve the objectives of the organisation, co-ordination among the persons and departments within the organisation and establishment of connecting link with the outside world are very much necessary. Motivating the employees for better and greater performance, facilitating group performance, controlling their activities, taking corrective measures, wiping out misunderstanding, maintaining peace, establishing discipline, and, above all, ensuring the quality of work within the organisation is possible through effective communication. Establishing link with the outside world—with the customers, vendors, investors, bankers, similar business organisations within and outside the country, various departments of the government, etc. also depends on communication. Corporate business houses are, in most cases, engaged in international business. Excellence in communication in such cases is a basic need. They are required to make corporate presentation of their goods and services, inform and report, explain change, interact with the colleagues, motivate and support the staff, supervise, organise and co-ordinate a course of action, build and maintain relationship with overseas clients, participate in meeting, introduce themselves as business houses, promote a sales drive, make market research, cope with mixed language problem interacting with the foreign colleagues and so on. All these activities require communication skill.

Phone, e-mail, fax, office memos, verbal communication, etc. are the internal means of corporate communication. External communication depends on phones, letters, fax, website, internet, video conferencing, etc.

Modern technologies in communication have made the communication process speedy. It is a boon to corporate communication because a slightest delay in making decision may place one in a difficult position—behind one's competitors.

The importance of corporate communication may be described as follows:

1. **Internal Co-ordination:** To fulfil the objectives of the organisation, co-ordination among the employees is necessary and to co-ordinate various activities communication is essential. Corporate organisation being large in size, division of work and specialisation in activities are the characteristics of such organisation. Communication helps to co-ordinate such activities and to develop co-operation.
2. **Connecting Link with the Outside World:** In a corporate organisation, communication with the external people, such as customers, vendors, investors, competitors, government departments, etc. are essential. Even connecting links with the foreign counterparts and centres are necessary for proper functioning of the organisation.
3. **Motivation:** Communication helps to motivate the employees to obey the orders and directives of the management authority. The feedback of the employees also enlightens the managers. The interaction between the managers and the employees improves the relation between them and encourages all to devote themselves fully to achieve the objectives of the organisation.

4. **Efficient Management:** George Terry's remark that communication works as a lubricant to increase the efficiency of management is applicable to corporate organisations more appropriately. Communication supplies the managers and employees with the information, co-ordinates and motivates the employees. This results in co-operation and better performance, resolves conflicts, builds confidence and ultimately develops efficient management. The managers, supervisors and executives get instructions, orders, messages, etc. from their superiors through communication, become aware of their duties and responsibilities and exact performance from their subordinates. Thus, communication stimulates efficient management.
5. **Decision-making and Implementation:** The success of any corporate organisation depends largely upon decision-making. Right decision-making, again, depends upon correct and timely information which is obtained through communication. Again, implementation of the decision requires proper communication. The managers convey the procedure of implementing the decision through communication channels and evaluate the work of the employees. Thus, corporate communication has a meaningful role in decision-making and its implementation.
6. **Leadership:** The manager communicates orders and instructions to the subordinates, who, in turn, carry out the instructions and sometimes send feedback in the form of suggestions, grievances and complaints. The manager tries to remove the inconvenience as far as possible. The entire process establishes the basis of leadership. Lack of communication creates distrust, doubts and misunderstanding among the subordinates. Proper communication helps to remove them and create an environment of mutual co-operation, trust and dependence and, ultimately, achieve acceptance of the leadership of the official head.
7. **Corrective Measures:** In a corporate organisation the number of employees are large. Everybody's performance may not achieve required standard and some corrective measures may become necessary. Such measures against the employees not performing their duties properly can also be taken through communication. Communication thus protects the interest of the organisation.
8. **Speed:** Speed is the key word of today's corporate world. Modern technologies have made communication faster. Now, no one has to wait for weeks or months for a reply letter. E-mail, fax, internet, etc. have made communication almost instant. Immediate flow of information helps in taking correct decision in time and anticipates solution to a probable problem.
9. **Discipline and Peace:** Maintenance of discipline in large corporate sector is difficult. Control over a large number of managers and employees is not an easy task. But regular communication (Two-way) between the management authority and the workers creates a healthy human relation and sense of co-operation, assistance and unity. Thus, peace is established and discipline is maintained within the organisation.
10. **Training:** Communication is necessary in imparting training to the managers, supervisors, executives and general employees to upgrade their knowledge and skill of performance in order to meet the needs of the changing corporate world. This may include training in the field of science and technology, upgradation of technical know-how, development of management skill, and even a training in learning a language for communication.

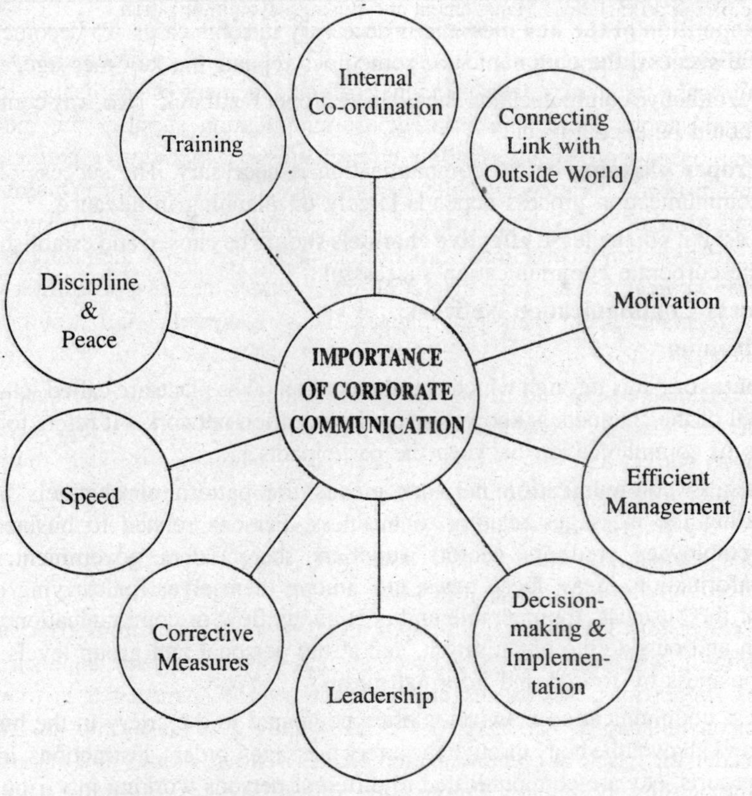

Fig. 3.13: Characteristics of Corporate Communication.

3.3.3 Guidelines for Effective Corporate Communication

Corporate communication to be effective should follow some guidelines stated below:

1. It should be **simple.** Jargon and buzz words create confusion and difficulty in understanding.
2. It should be **concise.** Repetition of words and unnecessary explanation are to be avoided. It should be kept in mind that more communication is not necessarily better communication.
3. It should be **clear** in meaning and free from ambiguity.
4. The message should be **courteous,** no matter whether it is being sent to the subordinates, to the superiors, or to the peer persons. It is to be remembered that courtesy begets courtesy.
5. The communication should give **correct** information in proper time and in right manner.
6. It should be **complete** in all respects. Before communicating one should check whether the following '5 Whs' are answered: Who, What, Where, When and Why.
7. Corporate communication should be **consistent** to the norms of the organisation. It should keep track of the previous communication and maintain a continuity.
8. **Metaphors, analogy or examples** are sometimes necessary to bring out the meaning of communication easily. So, appropriate use of these are recommended for better communication.

9. **Repetition of the key message** is necessary in some cases. To become sure about the success, the communicator sometimes repeats the key message.
10. An effective communication should have proper **feedback**. Two-way communication should be encouraged.
11. **Proper planning** before communication is necessary. The success of the entire communication process depends largely on planning in advance.
12. Last but not the least, **effective channels** should be chosen and established to make the corporate communication successful.

3.3.4 Business Communication Network

[A] Meaning:

The routes or paths through which communication takes place are called 'channels' and the sum total of the channels is known as 'communication network'. It refers to the pattern of channels of communication between the participants.

A business communication network means the pattern of channels built up in communicating the messages relating to business. Persons related to business such as managers, employees, creditors, debtors, suppliers, shareholders, government, and so on exchange information, ideas, facts, news, etc. among themselves for carrying out day-to-day work of the business. Innumerable and continuous flow of communication takes place daily within and outside the organisation, and at the personal and group levels of persons related to business by formal and informal means.

Business communication network is often compared to the artery in the human body. As blood flows all over the body through the artery messages, orders, instructions, information, proposals, reports, etc. are communicated to different persons working in various positions in a business organisation through the communication network. It is very important in as much as the success of an organisation is concerned.

[B] Classification of Business Communication Network:

Business communication network can be divided into the following two parts:

i. Formal network; ii. Informal network.

i. Formal Business Communication Network: Formal business communication network is one which follows recognised official channels in the organisation chart. Orders, instructions, messages, etc. are sent from top to the bottom level following the positional hierarchy. When direction is given by the manager to the deputy manager, the deputy manager to the supervisor, the supervisor to the worker—these are the cases of formal network. Managers of two departments, or supervisors of different departments may need to communicate through horizontal channels as a part of their official duty. Thus, formal network of communication includes the channels of all directions—downward, upward, and horizontal. This network helps to keep control on, allocate specific responsibility to and perform routine work by the employees. The superiors can concentrate on other important work assigning the routine work to the subordinates through this network. Flow of information in this network may be obstructed and interrupted at various centres and the desired result may not be obtained.

ii. Informal Business Communication Network: No structured pattern is followed in such a network. It works side by side with the formal network. While formal network is the artery, informal network is like that of veins in a human body. Informal network is unorganised and complex in nature. A social relationship with a number of people working together develops and a large number of informal communications take place. The subject-matter of such communication includes any topic starting from domestic problem to official scandal. This is why informal communication is called 'grapevine' as it may swiftly spread in any direction like grapevine. The speed of communication in an informal network is very high. Rumours, stories, scoop news, secret and confidential information are spread easily and speedily through this network. Care should be taken to prevent the damaging effect of this network.

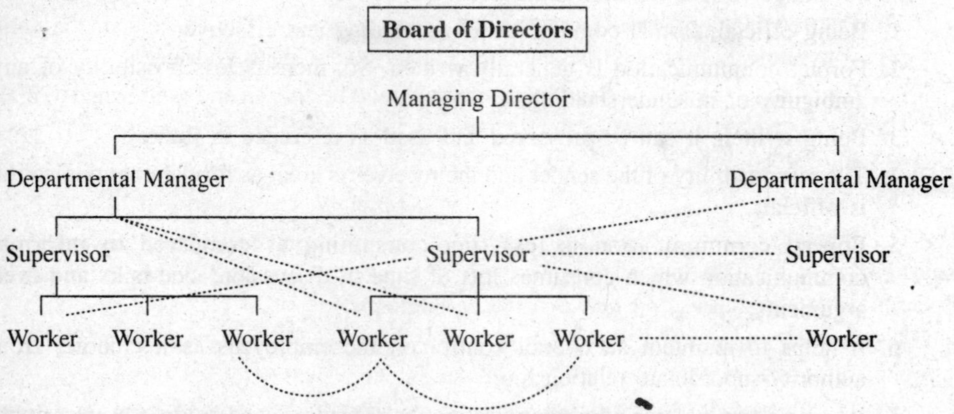

- Straight lines constitute formal business communication network.
- Broken lines form informal business communication network.

Fig. 3.14: Formal and Informal Communication Network.

3.4 Formal Communication

'Formal Communication' refers to the flow of information through a structured path in a formal organisation. It maintains superior-subordinate relationship and follows the chain of command. It is a two-way communication. It is, in general, downwards as the higher authorities send orders, instructions, information, messages, etc., to the subordinate employees following the rules and regulations of the organisation. The subordinate employees may also inform the authority their feedback, grievances, suggestions, demands, etc., through the structured channels. So, it is upward also. Letters, reports, memos, speeches, e-mail, internet, website, etc. are used in formal communication. It is routine type, rigid, official, systematic and reliable.

3.4.1 Purpose of Formal Communication

The purpose of formal communication is to give orders, convey instructions and fulfil the objective of the organisation through some pre-determined rules and regulations.

3.4.2 Characteristics of Formal Communication

The characteristics of formal communication are stated as follows:

1. Formal communication flows through structured path.
2. It is official and formal in nature.
3. It is mainly in writing but sometimes verbal communication is also considered as formal communication.
4. It requires sanction of higher authority.
5. It may be downward, upward or two-way.
6. The rank, position and authority have great significance in such communication.
7. A standard is maintained in such communication.
8. Flexibility is not found in it. It is generally rigid in nature.

3.4.3 Channels Used in Formal Communication

Both verbal and written communication are used in formal communication. The verbal or oral media includes conversation through telephone, mobile, etc., talks/consultation in departmental meeting, group discussion, seminar, video conference, interview, etc. Written communication includes printed statements, new bulletin, journals and periodicals, fax, e-mail, telegram, letter, etc.

3.4.4 Advantages of Formal Communication

The advantages of Formal Communication are as follows:

1. Being official, formal communication is binding and effective;
2. Formal communication is generally written. So, there is less possibility of any ambiguity or misunderstanding;
3. Being written, it can be preserved and used as reference in future;
4. The responsibility of the sender and the receiver is great as formal communication is official;
5. Formal communication is less time-consuming as compared to informal communication which consumes lots of time in discussion, side-talks and even arguments;
6. It helps to maintain an overall control on the employees as it emerges from authority-subordinate relationship;
7. It being a routine type of communication the managers need not take much trouble about the message. It will reach its goal in its formal course;
8. In sensitive situations, formal communication saves the parties from the embarrassment of face-to-face conversation which they may want to avoid.

3.4.5 Disadvantages of Formal Communication

The disadvantages of Formal Communication are mentioned below:

1. The scope of formal communication is limited within the boundaries of the department and the jurisdiction fixed by the authority;
2. Being written, it uses stereotype language in almost all communication which often fails to convey the real meaning intended;
3. Lack of explanation may sometimes lead to confusion;
4. It is less effective where personal guidance and motivation are necessary;
5. Owing to official procedure and formalities it requires much time and money;
6. Formal Communication encourages bureaucracy and authoritarianism because it flows downward in most cases. Upward communication (e.g., reports, information or feedback) are lesser in comparison. That means the employees are to obey what the authority desires;
7. It sometimes emphasises on explaining simple and unimportant matters underestimating the recipients' capacity to comprehend;
8. It may be cut-short or distorted while passing through different points or centres of authority.

3.5 Informal Communication or Grapevine Communication

'Informal Communication' is the communication among the people of an organisation not on the basis of formal relationship in the organisational structure but on the basis of informal relations and understanding. It may overlap routes, levels or positions.

Informal communication creates a situation where the different workers communicate with each other, work side by side, hour after hour and day after day irrespective of their formal positions and relationships. It is referred to as the 'grapevine' which indicates informal means of circulating information or gossip. It is direct, spontaneous and flexible. It is personal, unofficial, and mostly verbal.

The term 'Grapevine Communication' originated during the American Civil War (1861-1865). During the period the communication of intelligence information through telegraph was not effective and reliable because the telegraph system was unorganised. Telegraph lines were strung in a happazard way through the trees like a real grapevine. The messages received or sent through these lines were often incorrect and confusing. Rumours were rampant during the civil war. Thus any rumour, whatever might be the source, was presumed to be originated from the unarranged telegraph lines or grapevine. Later, in course of time, grapevine communication has become synonymous with informal communication.

- **Examples of Informal or Grapevine Communication:**

1. The manager calls an employee to his chamber and talks with him for sometimes relating to official work. Rumour is spread that the employee will be promoted to higher position ignoring the promotion of other employees.
2. The employees of a company have come to know the profit figure for the year from the accounts department. Somebody among the employees within the company puts some imagination to it and tells others that the company is going to offer bonus to the employees on the basis of profit earned.
3. Due to delay in supply and shortage of raw materials the work in a factory has been stopped for a few days. The workers made it a rumour that the management authority is going to retrench a large number of employees soon.

The informal communication is a part and parcel of the organisational process. Proper analysis and suitable clarification of informal communication will be helpful in making its use towards organisational efficiency.

3.5.1 Purpose of Informal or Grapevine Communication

The purpose of informal communication includes sharing of information, establishing personal contacts, making friendship, influencing and motivating others, resolving conflicts, supplementing official channels, getting relaxation, searching escape from monotony of work, etc.

3.5.2 Channels Used in Informal or Grapevine Communication

Informal Communication is conveyed through verbal and gestural means in all directions with the help of the following media :

i. Personal conversation and gossip;
ii. Unofficial discussion;
iii. Spontaneous advice and suggestion;
iv. Facial expression;
v. Body movement;
vi. Silence, etc.

3.5.2.1 Types of Grapevine Communication

Since grapevine works through informal channels, it does not follow any scheduled path or operate by specific rules. Like a grapevine it spreads fast in any direction. Specialists in the field have classified grapevine communication into four types:

1. Single Strand Chain, 2. Gossip Chain, 3. Probability Chain, 4. Cluster Chain.

1. Single Strand Chain: In this type of grapevine communication the information passes through a number of persons like a chain. A tells something to B, who tells it to C, who tells it to D and so on.

(A)→(B)→(C)→(D)→(E)→(F)

Fig. 3.15 : Single Strand Chain.

It is generally a long chain. The longer the chain the greater is the possibility of distortion of the information.

2. Gossip Chain: In Gossip Chain one person actively conveys information to other persons around him. A circle or wheel-like figure is formed in this communication.

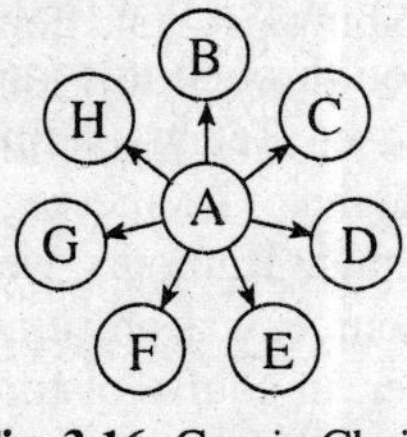

Fig. 3.16: Gossip Chain.

Here, in this picture, A is at the centre and transmits messages to 'B', 'C', 'D', 'E', 'F', 'G', and 'H' around him/her.

Gossip Chain is generally used when information to be communicated is non-job oriented in nature.

3. Probability Chain: It is a random process in which information may move from one person to any other person or persons according to law of probability. Naturally, in this type of communication, some people of the organisation will be informed and some others will remain outside the arena of the communication. Here, in the illustration, E, F, G and K are outside the communication chain. This chain is used when information is interesting but less important.

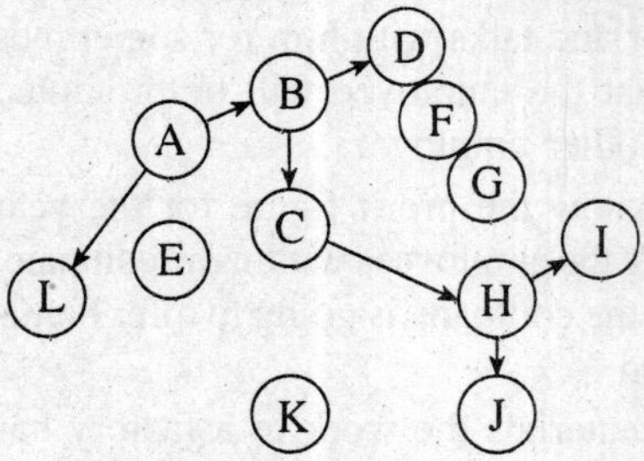

Fig. 3.17: Probability Chain.

4. Cluster Chain: Cluster chain is mostly used and the dominant pattern of grapevine communication. In this type one person tells something to some selected trust worthy persons. Some of these persons may inform a few selected other individuals.

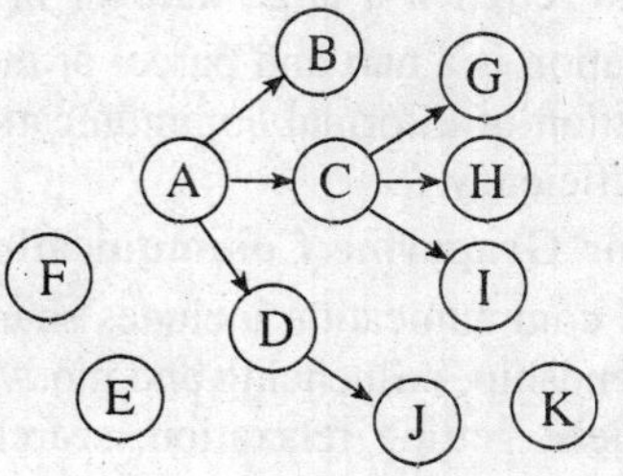

Fig. 3.18: Cluster Chain.

Here in the picture, A tells some selected and trustworthy persons, B, C and D. C again relays it to his selected persons, G, H and I. D tells J, a person of his choice. E and F remain outside The cluster.

3.5.2.2 Importance of Informal or Grapevine Communication

Informal or Grapevine communication is an indispensable part of entire communication system. Formal communication is compared to arteries of a living being, whereas, grapevine or informal communication are like veins. The later is a supplement to the former. Where formal communication fails to operate, grapevine or informal communication is used. Sometimes, grapevine communication is more effective than the formal communication. In fact, it carries more information than formal communication. Not only a large volume of information, important and vital information is also conveyed through it.

In an organisation small groups of people work together. It is quite natural that they will become interested about each other and want to know various information regarding each other's service condition, salary, facilities available, appointment, retirement, transfer, punishment, etc. They will also be interested to know any private, secret and confidential information which includes any romantic affair, family disputes, marriage, birth of a child, examination results of their children, special treatment or favour by boss to any member and so on. The employees generally exchange their views with their peers openly during lunch break or at an interval and get emotional relief from monotony and stress. Thus, the informal or grapevine communication promotes social relationship among the participants. It helps to build up unity, integrity and soliderity among them and boosts up their morale.

Grapevine or informal communication is faster than the formal communication. Being oral in nature, it has little or no cost and can reach maximum number of people irrespective of their positions within a very short time. Since there is no official procedure and formalities it is not binding and compelling, rather it is flexible and spontaneous.

The managers can get feedback from their subordinates quickly on the plan and policies through grapevine. New ideas, suggestions, opinions may come out as people can express their feelings without fear.

3.5.3 Characteristics of Informal Communication

The informal communication has the following characteristics:

i. It is based on informal relationship;
ii. It grows spontaneously;
iii. It takes the form of gossip;
iv. It is conveyed through conversation, facial expression, body movement, silence, etc.;
v. It does not follow any structured route or channel;
vi. Small groups are formed with like-minded people in such communication;
vii. It is direct and fast;
viii. It is flexible and dynamic in nature.

3.5.4 Advantages of Informal or Grapevine Communication

The advantages of informal communication are pointed out below:

i. Informal communication, being unofficial and personal, promotes a social relationship among the participants;
ii. Flow of information is fast and is suitable for emergencies;
iii. New ideas, suggestions, opinions may come out through such communication as people can express their feelings without fear;
iv. It can create an atmosphere congenial for work as the relationship between the managers and the employees improves;
v. The managers can collect information regarding reaction of the workers, attitude of the employees of other departments, intention of peer officers through such communication. It is not possible in the case of formal communication. Thus, informal communication supplements the formal communication to fulfil the objective of the organisation;
vi. Sharing of information in a free atmosphere makes the picture clear, bringing out the hidden dimension of the management, if any. It puts an end to misunderstanding and suspicion;
vii. It is an outlet of expression of complaints, dislikings, grievances, etc.

3.5.5 Disadvantages/Limitations of Informal or Grapevine Communication

Informal Communication has the following disadvantages or limitations:

i. Inaccurate, incomplete and half true informations are spread through informal communication as everybody interprets it in his/her own way;
ii. In most cases it is emotional and full of sentiments which can change its meaning;
iii. No one can be held responsible as it is not possible to find out the supplier of wrong information in the case on an enquiry;
iv. It is not reliable. The managers cannot depend upon such information as it does not follow any norm and is too loose a system. No decision can be taken depending upon such communication;

v. It spreads rumours and endangers consolidation and unity of the organisation;

vi. It creates conflicts between groups by spreading rumours against them and reducing their mental strength.

3.5.6 Effective Use of Informal or Grapevine Communication

Since grapevine communication is an integral part of communication system it works side by side with the formal communication. The nature of grapevine communication can be guessed from its name. Like a grapevine plant it grows fast, spreads to any direction and goes a long way in creating informal relationship.

Here, information spreads very quickly in geometric progression from one to a few and from a few to many persons irrespective of their formal positions. Spread of half true information or rumour is not congenial to the organisational health. It breeds conflict, weakens consolidation and unity, diminishes morale of the workers and creates a chaotic situation within the organisation. It becomes more harmful for an organisation when the managers take decisions depending upon such unreliable, inaccurate and incomplete information.

The efficient managers can make proper use of informal or grapevine communication and apply it for the well-being of the organisation if some general steps like the following are taken.

i. The managers should keep a watchful eye on the leaders who spread rumours and keep them well-informed about the actual situation.

ii. The managers should contradict rumours as soon as possible.

iii. They should involve the employees in decision-making, etc.

The managers, on the other hand, can supplement formal communication with grapevine communication. They can feel the pulse of the organisation through informal communication. They can even use it to convey any official information with a bit of care.

3.5.7 Right Mixture of Formal and Informal Communication

An appropriate mixture of formal and informal communication makes a business communication more effective. There is no golden rule of arriving at the right mixture but the experienced managers and executives who are familiar with the ins and outs of the department and understand the nature of the employees can find out a proper blend for a particular situation. While formal communication will help the execution of official orders, informal communication will assist in improving human relations and work environment.

3.6 Distinction Between Formal and Informal Communication

Formal Communication	Aspects of Distinction	Informal Communication
'Formal Communication' is the transmission of information in formal organisational structure and in specific direction.	1. Meaning	'Informal Communication' is the communication on the basis of informal relations and understanding among the people at the same or different levels.
The purposes of formal communication are to give orders, convey instructions and fulfil the objectives of the organisation through some pre-determined rules and regulations.	2. Purpose	The purposes of informal communication are to build up informal relationship through personal contacts, sharing of information, etc.

Contd.

Formal Communication	Aspects of Distinction	Informal Communication
Letters, reports, memos, speeches, e-mail, internet, website, etc. are used in the case of formal communication.	3. Media or Channel	Usually verbal channels (e.g., face-to-face conversations, telephone calls, gossip, etc.) are used in the case of informal communication.
In the case of formal communication feedback requires some time due to completion of formal procedure.	4. Feedback	In informal communication feedback is immediate.
Formal communication is time-consuming and costly.	5. Time and Money	Informal communication being verbal is less costly and immediate. Of course, gossip may consume productive working hours.
It is official and formal in nature.	6. Nature	It is unofficial and informal in nature.
It requires sanction of the higher authority.	7. Sanction of Higher Authority	No sanction of the higher authority is required.
Flexibility is not found in it. It is generally rigid in nature.	8. Flexibility	It is loose and very much flexible.
Information is reliable, correct, factual and standard in it.	9. Standard	There is every possibility of information being inaccurate and half true in it and hence it is not dependable and trustworthy.
Formal communication is routine type and systematic.	10. Type	Informal communication does not follow any structured route or process.
It is generally written.	11. Written or Oral	It is mostly verbal.
Formal communication being written and structured is transparent. Hence, it is reliable.	12. Transparency	Informal communication is less transparent because gossip generates concocted stories and rumour. It lacks reliability.
Formal communication flows in a systematic manner according to the procedure. It takes its own time.	13. Speed	Informal communication is fast-flowing, specially in the case of rumours.

Contd.

Formal Communication	Aspects of Distinction	Informal Communication
Generally formal communication moves both downward and upward.	14. Direction	Informal communication moves towards any direction —upward, downward, sidewise, parallel, etc.
Personal influence is almost nil in such communication.	15. Personal Influence	Personal influence is the basis of such communication. Personal opinion, suggestion, views, liking, etc. are very important here.
Person giving wrong information can be located and be made responsible for the offence.	16. Responsibility	No one can be made responsible for any distorted information or rumour as the source of information is difficult to locate here.

3.7 Oral or Verbal Communication

Transmission of orders, messages, information or suggestions through spoken words is called 'Oral or Verbal Communication'. It is effective for communication in meetings, conferences, gatherings, group discussions, interviews, face-to-face talks, telephonic talks, etc. It is a direct and informal method of communication. A personal contact is established in such communication. So, it is useful in motivating people. It is very much flexible in nature. It is speedy, economic and suitable for confidential and emergent talks.

3.7.1 Advantages of Oral Communication

The advantages of Oral or Verbal Communication are mentioned below:

1. It **saves time.** Contact can be established quickly. Time spent on preparing draft of letters, circulars, notes, explanation and finalising them in the case of written communication can be saved.
2. **Clarification and feedback is possible immediately.** The listener may ask questions for proper explanation and the speaker is also in a position to know the reaction of the listener immediately.
3. A personal contact between the communicator and the communicatee helps to build up **better relationship** between them.
4. It **fosters a friendly and co-operative spirit** as oral communication is often carried on through informal basis.
5. It is most **suitable for confidential and emergent talks.**
6. Oral communication is **effective for** communication in **meetings, conferences, gatherings, group discussions, interviews,** face-to-face talks, telephonic talks, etc.
7. It is **flexible** and changes can be made easily.
8. It is **economic.** It saves money. Stationery spent in written communication can be saved.
9. While making oral communication the gestures, **body language,** changes in voice, etc. of the participants disclose their intention.
10. Oral communication is effective in **persuading** people. This is why, the managers and supervisors prefer to communicate their ideas, opinion and thinking to their subordinates through this mode.

11. If for some reasons or other cancellation of any communication becomes necessary, **withdrawal** of oral communication **is easier** than written communication.

3.7.2 Limitations or Disadvantages of Oral Communication

The limitations or disadvantages of Oral or Verbal Communication are as follows:

1. It is not suitable if distance between the speaker and the listener is great. Of course, this difficulty may be removed with the help of some mechanical devices like telephone.
2. It is unsuitable if the matter to be communicated is lengthy.
3. Economy in such communication depends on control. Use of telephone may cost a lot if proper control is not exercised.
4. It lacks recorded evidence for future reference.
5. It does not allow the listener much time to think, act and react.
6. It can be easily distorted or changed.
7. As no records of oral communication are generally kept, denial is easy.
8. It has no legal validity unless it is tape-recorded or video-recorded.
9. In the case of a mistake or neglect of duty no one can be specifically held responsible owing to the absence of proof in oral communication.
10. Communication of statistical data is not suitable in oral communication as mistake is likely to occur easily.

3.8 Written Communication

A 'Written Communication' means the sending of messages, orders or instructions in writing through letters, circulars, manuals, reports, telegrams, office memos, bulletins, etc. It is a formal method of communication and is less flexible. A written document preserved properly becomes a permanent record for future reference. It can also be used as legal evidence. It is time-consuming, costly and unsuitable for confidential and emergent communication.

Written communication, to be effective, should be clear, complete, concise, correct, and courteous.

3.8.1 Advantages of Written Communication

The advantages of Written Communication are stated below:

1. It is suitable for **long distance** communication and **repetitive** standing orders.
2. It creates **permanent record** of evidence. It can be used for future reference.
3. It gives the receiver **sufficient time to think,** act and react.
4. It can be used as **legal document**.
5. It can be **sent to many persons** at a time.
6. It is suitable for sending **statistical data, chart, diagram, pictures,** etc.
7. Order, allocation of work, job distribution, etc. in written form **reduce ambiguity** and help in fixation of responsibility.
8. **Uniformity in work** procedure can be maintained through written communication.
9. It is **easy to send unpleasant or bad news** through written communication.
10. A good written communication can **create goodwill** and promote business.

3.8.2 Limitations or Disadvantages of Written Communication

Followings are the limitations or disadvantages of Written Communication:

1. It is **time-consuming.** Composing a message in writing takes much time. Writing letters, typing orders, notices, etc. and sending to appropriate destination require time. Feedback process also is not instant.
2. It is **expensive** not so much due to postal charges but in terms of so many people spending so much of their time.
3. It **cannot maintain strict secrecy** which would have been possible in oral communication.
4. Written communication has **no scope for immediate clarification** if not understood properly.
5. Being written in nature it is **less flexible** and cannot be changed easily.
6. It is **not effective** in the case of **emergency**.

3.9 Distinction Between Verbal (Oral) and Written Communication

Verbal (Oral) Communication	Aspects of Distinction	Written Communication
'Verbal or Oral Communication' implies the transmission of orders, message or suggestions through the spoken words.	1. Meaning	'Written Communication' means transmission of message, order or instruction in writing.
The media of oral communication are face-to-face talk, speech, lecture, interview, meeting, telephonic talk, video conference, etc.	2. Media or Channels	The media of written communication are letter, circular, manual, report, telegram, office memo, bulletin, journal, magazine, e-mail, fax, internet, etc.
It is an informal method of communication.	3. Method	It is a formal method of communication.
In oral communication the contact being direct, feedback is immediate.	4. Feedback	In written communication feedback requires some time.
It saves time and money as communication is direct.	5. Time and Cost	It is time-consuming and costly.
Oral communication is very much flexible.	6. Flexibility	It is less flexible.
Explanation may be sought and misunderstanding may be removed immediately through discussion.	7. Explanation	The chances of misunderstanding remains unless feedback is proper.
If not understood, immediate clarification is possible in oral communication.	8. Immediate Clarification	It has no scope for immediate clarification.

Contd.

Verbal (Oral) Communication	Aspects of Distinction	Written Communication
Secrecy can be maintained.	9. Confidentiality	Secrecy may be endangered.
The employees can be motivated by personal contact.	10. Motivation	Motivation through written words is less effective.
It is expensive to communicate orally with the persons at distant places by telephone.	11. Distance	Communication can be made to the person/persons at distant places at a low cost by post, fax or through internet.
Communication of long message or statistical data is not suitable for it.	12. Long Message and Statistical Data	Sending of long message or statistical data with accuracy is suitable for written communication.
Uniformity of work procedure cannot be maintained in oral communication.	13. Uniformity	Uniformity of work procedure can be maintained here.
No record is kept generally (unless audio or video tape-recording is made).	14. Permanent Record	A written document preserved properly becomes a permanent record of the organisation and can be used as future reference.
Unless recorded in tapes, videos, etc. verbal communication cannot be considered as legal evidence.	15. Legal Evidence	Written communication can easily be used as legal evidence.

EXERCISES

[A] Essay-Type Questions

1. How is communication classified according to different criteria? Give a brief idea of such classification. **[Ans.** Section 3.1]
2. What factors are to be considered in selecting the means of communication? **[Ans.** Section 3.2]
3. What do you understand by Corporate Communication? What are its characteristics? **[Ans.** Sections 3.3, 3.3.1]
4. What is Corporate Communication? Discuss the importance of corporate communication. **[Ans.** Sections 3.3, 3.3.2]
5. Explain the guidelines for effective Corporate Communication. **[Ans.** Section 3.3.3]
6. What is Formal Communication? What are its purposes and characteristics? Discuss the advantages and disadvantages of formal communication. **[Ans.** Sections 3.4, 3.4.1, 3.4.2, 3.4.4, 3.4.5]
7. What is meant by Informal Communication? What are its purposes and characteristics? Discuss the advantages and limitations of Informal Communication. **[Ans.** Sections 3.4.1, 3.4.2, 3.5, 3.5.1, 3.5.3, 3.5.4, 3.5.5]
8. What is Grapevine Communication? How can such communication be made effective? **[Ans.** Sections 3.5, 3.5.6]

9. State the importance of Grapevine Communication. [**Ans.** Section 3.5.2.2]

10. Distinguish between Formal and Informal Communication? [**Ans.** Section 3.6]

11. What do you mean by Oral or Verbal Communication? What are its merits and demerits? [**Ans.** Sections 3.7, 3.7.1, 3.7.2]

12. What is Written Communication? What are its advantages and limitations? [**Ans.** Sections 3.8, 3.8.1, 3.8.2]

13. Distinguish between Verbal and Written Communication. [**Ans.** Section 3.9]

[B] Short Answer-Type Questions

Write short notes on:

i. Internal Communication. [**Ans.** Section 3.1]

ii. External Communication. [**Ans.** Section 3.1]

iii. Gestural Communication. [**Ans.** Section 3.1]

iv. Channels used for Formal Communication. [**Ans.** Section 3.4.3]

v. Channels used for Informal Communication. [**Ans.** Section 3.5.2]

vi. Grapevine Communication. [**Ans.** Section 3.5]

[C] Very Short Answer-Type Questions

Answer the following questions briefly:

i. State two advantages of Formal Communication. [**Ans.** Section 3.4.4]

ii. State two advantages of Informal Communication. [**Ans.** Section 3.5.4]

iii. Mention two characteristics of Informal Communication. [**Ans.** Section 3.5.3]

iv. What is Written Communication? [**Ans.** Section 3.8]

v. What is Oral Communication? [**Ans.** Section 3.7]

vi. What is Business Communication Network? [**Ans.** Appendix, Short Question No. 61]

- **Questions of University Examinations:**

[A] Questions of Very Short Answer-Type [Each Question Carries 2 Marks]:

i. What do you understand by Oral and Written Communication? [C.U. B.Com. 2005]
Ans. Sections 3.7 and 3.8

ii. What is Corporate Communication? [C.U. B.Com. 2005]
Ans. Section 3.3

iii. What is Grapevine Communication? [C.U. B.Com. 2005, New Syllabus 2009]
Ans. Section 3.5

iv. What is Formal Communication? [C.U. B.Com. Old Syllabus 2006]
Ans. Section 3.4

v. What do you mean by Horizontal Communication? [C.U. B.Com. Old Syllabus 2006]
Ans. Point No. 3(iii) in Section 3.1

vi. What is Business Communication? [C.U. B.Com. Old Syllabus 2006, New Syllabus 2008]
Ans. Short Questions No. 8

vii. Define Formal Communication. [C.U. B.Com. New Syllabus 2006]
Ans. Section 3.4

viii. What is Lateral Communication? [C.U. B.Com. New Syllabus 2006, 2010]
Ans. Point No. 3 in Section 1.10

ix. What is Informal Communication? [C.U. B.Com. New Syllabus 2007]
Ans. Section 3.5

x. Mention two points of difference between Verbal Communication and Written Communication. [C.U. B.Com. New Syllabus 2007]
Ans. Section 3.9

xi. What is Horizontal Communication? [C.U. B.Com. New Syllabus 2008]
Ans. Point No. 3(ii) in Section 3.1

xii. State two advantages of Formal Communication. [C.U. B.Com. New Syllabus 2008]
Ans. Section 3.4.4

xiii. What is Internal Communication? [C.U. B.Com. New Syllabus 2009]
Ans. Point No. I(i) in Section 3.1

xiv. State two disadvantages of Oral Communication. [C.U. B.Com. New Syllabus 2010]
Ans. Section 3.7.2

xv. Corporate communication has certain characteristics.—Mention two of these characteristics. [C.U. B.Com. New Syllabus 2011]
Ans. Section 3.3.1

xvi. What is meant by 'Communication Network'? [C.U. B.Com. New Syllabus 2011]
Ans. Section 3.3.4(A)

[B] Questions of Short Answer-Type [Each Question Carries 4 Marks]:

i. Distinguish between 'Formal Communication' and 'Informal Communication'. [C.U. B.Com. New Syllabus 2011]
Ans. Sections 3.6

ii. Do you think the idea of 'grapevine' is positive in nature? Give reasons for your answer. [C.U. B.Com. New Syllabus 2011]
Ans. Sections 3.5.6

iii. Write short notes on 'Horizontal Communication' and 'Vertical Communication'. [C.U. B.Com. New Syllabus 2011]
Ans. Sections 3.1 [Types of communication according to direction—Point Nos. 3(i) and 3(ii)]

[C] Questions of Long Answer-Type [Each Question Carries 10 Marks]:

i. Define Corporate Communication. Discuss the essentials for success of Corporate Communication. [C.U. B.Com. Old Syllabus and New Syllabus 2006]
Ans. Sections 3.3 and 3.3.3

ii. What is Written Communication? State its advantages and disadvantages. [C.U. B.Com. New Syllabus 2008]
Ans. Sections 3.8, 3.8.1 and 3.8.2

iii. What is Corporate Communication? Discuss the importance of Corporate Communication. [C.U. B.Com. New Syllabus 2008]
Ans. Sections 3.3 and 3.3.2

iv. Define Written Communication. Discuss the advantages and disadvantages of Written Communication. [C.U. B.Com. New Syllabus 2010]
Ans. Sections 3.8, 3.8.1 and 3.8.2

CHAPTER 4

Modern Tools of Communication

"While modern technology has given people powerful new communication tools, it apparently can do nothing to alter the fact that many people have nothing useful to say."

—Leo Gomes

TOPICS

i. Emergence of Communication Technology ◆ ii. A Brief History of Development of Communication Technology ◆ iii. Reasons for Emergence of Communication Technology ◆ iv. Objectives of Emergence of Communication Technology in Business ◆ v. Revolution in Communication Technology ◆ vi. Various Communicating Tools Used in Modern Business ◆ vii. Fax—Importance, Advantages and Disadvantages ◆ viii. E-mail—Composing, Advantages and Disadvantages ◆ ix. Video Conferencing—Importance, Advantages and Disadvantages.

Subject-matter of the Chapter : *The conventional method of Communication being unable to meet the growing need of business, modern communication system like e-mail, fax, video-conferencing, etc. has emerged and further developments are taking place in the field of communication. The new tools of communication have increased efficiency, enhanced effectiveness and improved the process of conducting business. Modern technology has increased speed, reduced cost, narrowed distance, ensured preservation, minimised space and saved time, money and labour. This chapter gives a general idea of the emergence of modern technology in communication, its uses in business world and its advantages and disadvantages.*

4.1 Emergence of Communication Technology

In early years business communication was conducted mainly through face-to-face conversation in verbal communication and restricted to the use of pen, pencil, ink, etc. in written communication. After the Industrial Revolution (1760 onwards) the need for technological communication was felt with the spread of trade and commerce. The conventional methods of communication were not enough to meet the growing need of communication. The managers required information support to arrive at a decision to run the business efficiently. Since *necessity is the mother of invention*, a series of inventions took place to gradually replace the old system. Today we have telephone, mobile phone, pager, computer, fax, e-mail, voice mail, website, etc. for business communication.

4.2 A Brief History of Development of Communication Technology

Business Communication was confined to face-to-face conversation or restricted to use of pen, pencil, ink, etc., until about the end of the nineteenth century. Then, three important innovations—the telegraph, the typewriter and the telephone—brought about a major change in communication technology. The telegraph enabled immediate communication between distant places through wires. The typewriter, the most used equipment in an office, improved the material quality and presentability of written communication. The telephone brought about a revolution in oral communication. It is still a very important medium of business communication.

During the 20th century the development in communication technology gained momentum. A series of innovations gave communication processes a quantum leap. In the first phase of the century there was enormous development in electrical and electronic field. The second phase was noted for electronics and telecommunication. Invention of radio, television and computer and development in space research, etc. were some of the important events of the period. Though radio and television used as mass communication had limited significance for business, still their technology helped to develop a number of electronic machines later. From typewriter developed electric typewriter and then electronic one. Improvement in duplicating (letters, reports, messages, etc.) technology took place. From hand-written copies to carbon copy, to mass copy by photocopy machine—the rapid development added speed to business communication. The electronic revolution had made it possible to offer us a series of electronic equipment. The most important of them were electronic typewriter, the word processor and the personal computer.

During 1960-1970 the technology of personal computer underwent a major change. Copper wires were replaced by silicon memory chips which increased the memory capacity of the computer and helped to reduce cost. With the increase in memory capacity more data could be stored in it. From large size first generation computers (1951-1959) we have now highly sophisticated fourth generation computers (1971 onwards) in use.

Gradually development took place in software technology. Newer softwares have been made to be more user friendly. Now almost everybody can use computer without knowing the technical programming. With the development of computers, printers and softwares it is now possible to produce single-handed nice printed business report with various data, charts, graphs, etc. at one's desk. A variety of alphabet (called fonts) sizes, types and designs are available in the software to choose from while preparing the text. Now, with the help of software, computers recognise human voice and answer it. Instead of keyboard command, simple voice command or touch screen command can work.

Development in the field is in progress. Vast potentialities await for development with touch screen and voice activation in the field of business communication.

4.3 Reasons for Emergence of Communication Technology

Following are the reasons for the growth of communication technology:

i. **Speed:** Speedy communication is essential in modern business, otherwise the competitors will get the advantages and capture the market.

ii. **Cost:** Sending of information through modern communication system like e-mail, fax, etc. are less costly than conventional communication like postal or through messenger.

iii. **Neatness:** Information sent through modern communication technology are neat and well-arranged.

iv. **Distance:** Communication to distant places required much time and expenditure. The object of communication sometimes got lost in delay. Therefore, the need for such technology emerged that can eliminate the problem of distant communication.

v. **Mass Communication:** When communication of information is required to be made to a large number of people at the same time, technological tools of communication become necessary.

vi. **Lengthy Messages:** For sending lengthy messages, use of communication technology is helpful.

vii. **Secrecy:** Secrecy can also be maintained by the use of communication technology, for example, communication made through e-mail or pager is known only to the sender and the receiver of the message.

viii. **Assessment of Reaction:** As communication is possible very quickly through new technology, assessment of reaction of the sender and the receiver is possible immediately and appropriate measures can be taken to solve any problem arising out of such communication.

ix. **Selection from a Wide Range of Alternatives:** Modern communication technology provides wide range of oral and written communication tools, e.g., telephone, mobile phones, video and audio tape in oral communication and e-mail, fax, website in written communication. A selection from so many alternatives to suit one's need is possible.

x. **Pictorial Representation:** Pictorial representation of statistical data can be conveyed through newly developed technology of communication. It is now possible to send chart, diagram, picture, etc. through internet to any distant place.

xi. **Preservation of Data:** Preservation of data is possible for future reference in modern technology. Computer, compact disk (CD), digital versatile disk or digital video disk (DVD), tape recorder, video tape, etc. are used to preserve information for future.

xii. **Space:** Space required for preservation of information is minimum as compared to the preservation of papers, files, documents before the innovations of modern technology. Now, computers can store huge information in the hard disk. The contents of hundreds of pages can be stored in one CD or DVD.

4.4 Objectives of Emergence of Communication Technology in Business

Communication always played a pivotal role in the conduct and management of a business enterprise. With the development of Science and Technology communication system has also developed considerably. Previously it was not easy to make contact with a person staying at a distant place. Emergence of improved technology in the field of communication has made communication quicker and easier. Now, with the help of electronic media any person in any part of the world can be contacted within a very short time. In fact, the objectives of emergence of new communication technology are to make communication quick, economic, easy, widespread, effective and helpful to management.

The various objectives of emerging communication technology may be described as follows:

1. **Quick Transmission of Message:** The new technologies of communication ensure quick transmisssion of information and messages in comparison with the old day's communication. The speed is the key factor of today's business. If right information is not conveyed in right time, modern business will lag behind its competitors.

2. **Reduction in Cost:** Use of modern tools of communication reduces cost. Sending of messages through e-mail and fax are less costly than the conventional sending of messages through post or by messengers. Thus economy is achieved in handling communication.

3. Saving of Time and Labour: Since messages are transmitted very quickly by the use of modern communicating tools, there is no delay or waiting for the information. Messenger needs not to be sent even for any personal message. Drafting of letters, typing them, inserting them to envelops, writing addresses on them, posting them in the post box, etc. required enough time and labour. The receiver had to wait for a few days for getting the letter in hand. Now alternative means like, e-mail, fax, telephone, internet facility, etc. are available for instant communication. These tools save both time and labour and justify their emergence.

4. Sending Message to Distant Places: Previously it took much time to send a message to a distant place. Naturally business activities were not widespread throughout the world. Now, with the help of modern technology messages can be sent easily with minimum possible time. Different places of the world have become much closer by the grace of modern communication. The huge world is turned into a global village.

5. Increase in the Effectiveness of Communication: Since feedback is possible within a short time, misunderstanding is minimised and clarity of the message is established. If the message is not understood at the first instance, it can be made clear by query within a short time. Thus, the effectiveness of communication increases. Audio, video and instant reaction facilities in certain tools of modern communication technology add to their effectiveness further.

6. Helping the Managers in Decision-making: The managers of an enterprise can collect information quickly, process them, analyse them, get graphical charts and pictorial representation with the help of the modern communication tools. All these help the management authority in taking right decision.

7. Increase in the Efficiency and Productivity of the Organisation: Right information at the right moment helps to increase the efficiency of any business enterprise. The managers and administrators know—"What is the target?" and the workers know "what is expected from them within what time frame?" Since there is easy flow of information with the help of modern technology the productivity of the workers increases.

8. Maintenance of Secrecy: Secrecy of information in an office of any business enterprise is very important. Modern communication technology is fully equipped to cope with the matter of secrecy of information.

9. Communicating to a Large Number of People: Modern age is an age of mass communication. The business enterprise which can make contact with a large number of people, acquires an edge over its competitors and can widen the area of operation. Today's communication technology is competent enough to fulfil the need of communicating to a large number of people.

10. Preservation of Information for Future Reference: Previously letters, deeds, agreements, legal notices and such other important documents were preserved as hard copies in original paper forms only. They were sometimes eaten by insects, damaged by natural wear and tear and lost due to carelessness. Now with the development of technology photo copies, scanned copies of the original documents can be preserved in computer, CDs, DVDs, etc. without damage for a long period and may be used for reference as and when required.

11. Requirement of Space: Since paper work is minimised with the help of computer, website, internet, etc. the space required for the preservation of files, documents letters etc. are minimised. CDs and DVDs are also used to store various documents. The huge space required earlier for storage of documents has now been reduced to a large extent.

12. Choice from a Large Variety: A large variety of communication tools are made available by the modern technology. People can choose from amongst those as per their requirements.

4.5 Revolution in Communication Technology

Not very long ago it required days and weeks to communicate through postal system. But at present with the help of ISD (International Subscriber Dialling) and STD (Subscriber Trunk Dialling) facilities one can make communication with even overseas people within a few seconds. Unprecedented development in the communication process and innovation of various methods have made communication easy, quick and effective. Communication technology has developed so much in recent years that we can call it a revolution. The emergence of the internet and development in the information technology have brought the world very close and totally wiped out the barriers of time and zone. Each and every place of the world is so close to us that we can say that we are living in a 'global village'.

4.6 Various Communicating Tools Used in Modern Business

Tools of comunication mean the medium or mechanical devices through which information can be sent or received.

There are many communicating tools that are used in modern business. They send and receive information from one person to another and from one place to another place with speed, accuracy and economy. Those variety of tools may be grouped under (i) Oral communication, (ii) Audio-visual communication, and (iii) Written communication. Oral or verbal tools of modern communication include telephone (with cord), cordless telephone, cellular phone, wireless and other electronic machines (e.g., dictaphone, speakophone, isophone). Certain audio-visual tools are also used in modern business, e.g., pager, television, cinema shows, video conferencing etc. Written tools include telewriter, telegram, teleprinter, telefax, e-mail, website..

These tools of communication have increased efficiency, enhanced effectiveness and improved the process of conduct of business. If utilised properly, these tools can create competitive edge over other competitors. They save time and labour, make interaction and feedback possible almost immediately, maintain secrecy and increase the prestige and status of the organisation. But the initial cost and maintenance cost of these tools are high, technical knowledge is required to use them. It is also expensive to repair them.

Following is a diagram which shows the classification of communicating tools used in modern business:

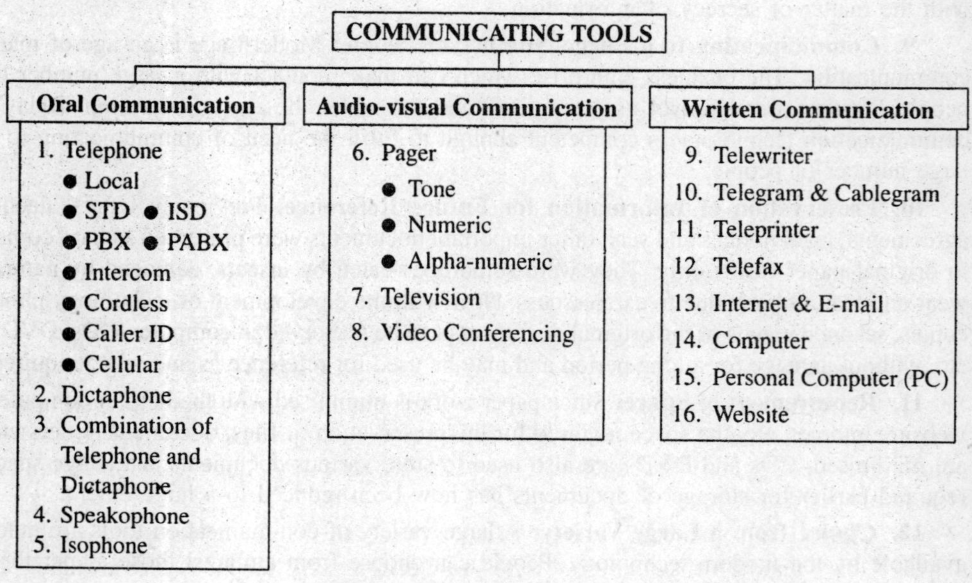

Fig. 4.1: Communicating Tools.

• **Oral Communication:** In oral communication the messages can be sent through words of mouth and can be heard only. Some of the tools used in it are discussed below:

1. Telephone: It is the most widely used communicating machine in an office. This is a mechanism by which two persons sitting in their respective places can speak to each other. It is a very popular device for speedy and direct negotiation.

A telephone which connects the local area only is called local telephone. But if the subscriber wants to make connection with anyone within the country he/she has to arrange for STD (Subscriber Trunk Dialling) facility in his/her telephone. With a special arrangement with the telephone exchange the subscriber can communicate with any other person having a telephone in any corner of the country. The caller should first dial the STD code of the city or town of the person with whom he/she wants to talk and then dial the telephone number of the person. Immediately he/she will be connected with the required number. The charges of STD calls are higher than ordinary local calls and depend upon the distance between the two places and time spent in talking. Recently difference of charges between ordinary and STD calls has been wiped off in certain cases.

If a subscriber wants to make contact with a subscriber residing in a foreign country the telephone is required to be installed with ISD (International Subscriber Dialling). There is no much difference in operation with STD service. The caller has to dial the country code first, then the city or area code and then the telephone number of the receiver. ISD connection from India to any foreign country is made through Inter-Continental Automatic Exchange (ICAX). The charges of ISD calls are higher than the STD calls.

There may be two types of telephones—internal and external. Internal telephones are used by the members of the same office for inter-departmental communication. External telephones are used for talking with the outside people. Now-a-days arrangements are also made for PBX (Private Branch Exchange) or PABX (Private Automatic Branch Exchange) connecting various departments with the outside telephones.

i. PBX (Private Branch Exchange): In almost all big offices, there is an arrangement of Private Branch Exchange. Under this system a private switchboard is maintained to receive external telephone lines directly from the exchange. Extension lines are connected with the departments from the switchboard for inter-departmental communication. It is operated by a trained telephone operator.

ii. PABX (Private Automatic Branch Exchange): Under this system, the private switchboard which is connected with the external telephone line is automatically operated without the help of a telephone operator. It ensures quick connection. It is economical because no operator is needed.

iii. Intercom System: It is an internal telephonic system. The main telephone connection is extended to the different departments to make them inter-connected. As its name signifies it is used for internal communication only, no outside communication is possible through it. The managers, executives or departmental heads can communicate with their superiors, peer persons or subordinates within the organisation sitting in their own seats. Indian Telephone Industries Ltd., Bangalore, is the inventor of this system.

iv. Cordless Telephone: Cordless telephone is one of the latest varieties of telephone. The handset is free of cord and can be taken away for conversation or kept anywhere within a certain distance from the mother set. One need not travel up to the telephone connection point to receive or send messages. It is like a cellular phone but it operates within a limited area from the mother set.

v. Caller ID: Some telephones have in-built mechanism of recording and display of the telephone number of the caller. A separate electronic instrument is also available as attachment to the ordinary telephone. This attachment displays the identity (i.e., telephone number) of the caller. As soon as the bell rings, this mechanism displays the telphone number of the telephone from which the caller is making the call. A good number of telephone numbers (say, 30, 60, 90, etc. according to the capacity of the machine) are recorded and preserved as per calling order even in the absence of the receiver. The receiver may call back afterwards in the required recorded number. Caller ID also helps to trace out any ill-motivated person trying to disturb, harass or threat others.

Fig. 4.2: Caller ID.

vi. Cellular Telephone: Cellular phones, usually known as mobile or cell phones, have become very popular. It is a small, portable and wonderful gadget which can be used anywhere—at home, at the office, away from home or office, in a bus, train, railway station or playground. It is like a cordless telephone but its area of operation is quite larger. It has a very small in-built inside antenna which helps to receive and send messages. It has a screen which displays short messages sent and received and indicates the area through which the owner passes in a vehicle or on foot. Tunes of pupular songs are being used as signals to make the owner of the mobile alert to attend the calls. It is an useful instrument for immediate communication. It has become almost an essential item to a large section of people of the society.

Fig. 4.3: Cellular Telephone.

2. Dictaphone: This is a communicating machine used for recording the dictation of a senior officer at his/her convenient time. The typist can listen to the voice recorded and simultaneously type it out afterwards. It can be listened to by the typist by headphones to avoid noise and disturbance to others. There are also arrangements for playing it back for re-hearing. It saves much time and labour of the stenographer.

3. Combination of Telephone and Dictaphone: This machine is a combination of telephone and dictaphone in the sense that it records telephonic talk between two parties by twin-cylinder system and can be heard afterwards or used for future reference. The speciality of this machine is that it can record the conversation of both the parties over telephone. It is mostly used by the news agencies to record important telephonic conversation.

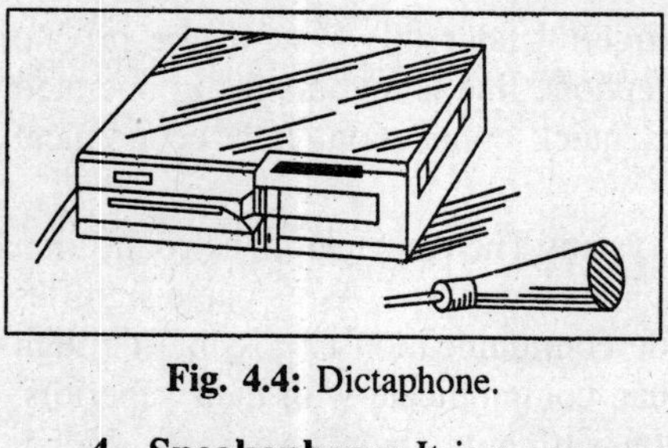

Fig. 4.4: Dictaphone.

4. Speakophone: It is a communicating tool used for internal oral communication of information between the employees of different departments of a large office.

5. Isophone: In the case of a telephone call in the absence of the receiver this machine records the name, address, telephone number and subject-matter of the message by an automatic system. The receiver can make contact with the desired person afterwards listening to the recorded details.

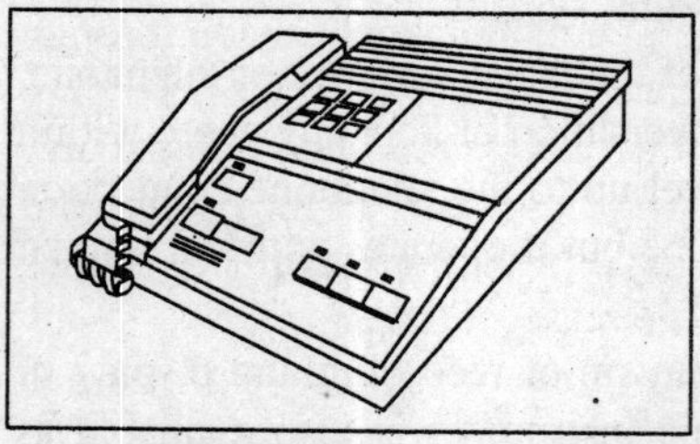

Fig. 4.5: Isophone.

• **Audio-Visual Communication:** In modern offices some audio-visual tools of communication are used. These gadgets provide the advantages of both listening and seeing or visualising the message. Some of them are described below:

6. Pager: The pager is a small and portable communicating instrument of receiving messages. It has an integrated chip which receives messages electronically and sends them to the holder in an audio-visual form.

The pager may be of three types:

i. **Tone Pager:** The holder is informed by a sound through this type of pager that certain person is calling him/her.

ii. **Numeric Pager:** In addition to making alert by sound this pager displays the caller's telephone number on its LCD (Liquid Crystal Display).

iii. **Alpha-numeric Pager:** It is one step ahead of the mechanism of numeric pager. In addition to the facilities provided by a numeric pager it can display the text of the message through its LCD.

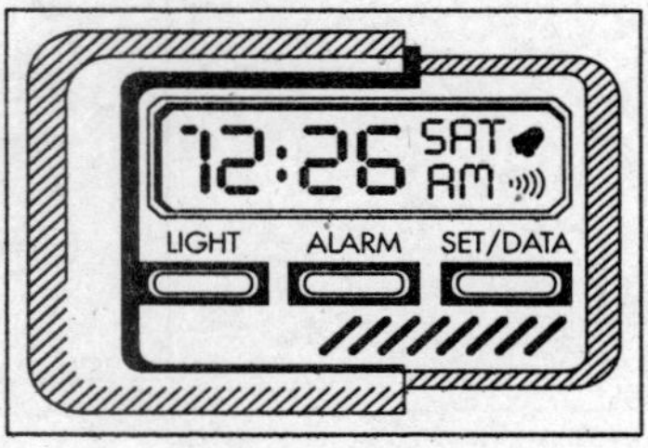

Fig. 4.6: Pager.

The pager is useful in receiving information quickly. The maintenance cost is not also so high but being one-way communication, conversation is not possible through it. It cannot also work beyond its limited area. Besides, no long message can be received through it.

7. Television: It is used for transmitting reports, documents, papers, etc. quickly and easily through camera media. A clear picture of the subject-matter is projected on the screen at the receiving end. This device helps one to inspect records and documents from a distance without the files being removed from the central office. It saves time and labour. This machine has become very popular in business houses in foreign countries.

8. Video Conferencing: Video Conferencing—also known as Teleconferencing—is emerging as an important tool of communication. It is a technology which allows people of two or more distant places to see and talk to each other in real time. The busy executives can save time and money by communicating in an audio-visual manner with the persons of far off places through it. But its components are costly and some technical knowledge is required to use it.

[A detailed discussion on Video conferencing is made later in this chapter]

• **Written Communication:** The tools used in written communication are large in number. Hand-written, typed, faxed or e-mailed communications are the examples of written communication. We give below a brief description of some of the machines used in written communication.

9. Telewriter: This machine is used for sending hand-written messages. Under this system, messages are written by hand on a metal plate which is connected to the sending machine at one end of the telewriter. When the machine is operated, the same hand-written message is reproduced on the receiving machine at the other end. It operates on the same principles of teleprinter machine. It saves time and cost in operation. But it is a costly instrument.

10. Telegram and Cablegram: Telegram is a written communication, made through telegraphic system of the post office. It is used for quick transmission of messages. Sending of messages within the country and outside—it is known as 'Telegram' and 'Cablegram', respectively. The cost of telegram and cablegram is high. Fees are charged for every word and every punctuation used. So, messages are written using minimum words as far as practicable and a telegram or cablegram is sent only in the case of urgency.

11. Teleprinter: This is a communicating machine by which one can send a message from one place to a distant place through electrical circuits over the telegraph wires. The machine has sending operation at one end and receiving device on the other end. Whatever message is typewritten at one end is automatically typed at the other end. It is widely used in newspaper offices. It helps quick despatch of important messages. It saves time, but it is very costly.

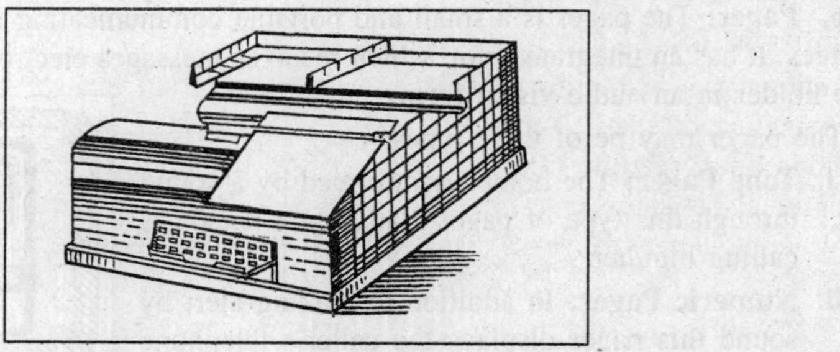

Fig. 4.7: Teleprinter.

12. Telefax or Fax: Through this machine drawings, diagrams, sketches, etc. can be quickly transmitted to a distant place. Under this system, the sketches or the images are wrapped round a cylinder in the machine and they are automatically transmitted and reproduced on a paper by the receiving machine. It helps quick despatch of drawings etc. to distant places. It saves time and labour. [Discussed in greater details in Section 4.7]

Fig. 4.8: Telefax or Fax.

13. Internet and E-mail:

(a) Internet : Internet refers to inter-connected network of communication. The internet is a global system of inter-connected governmental, academic, corporate, public and private computer network. It is an electronic communication system that connects computers and computer networks throughout the world. It is a vast computer network which links commercial, governmental, academic, corporate, public and private smaller computer networks world wide.

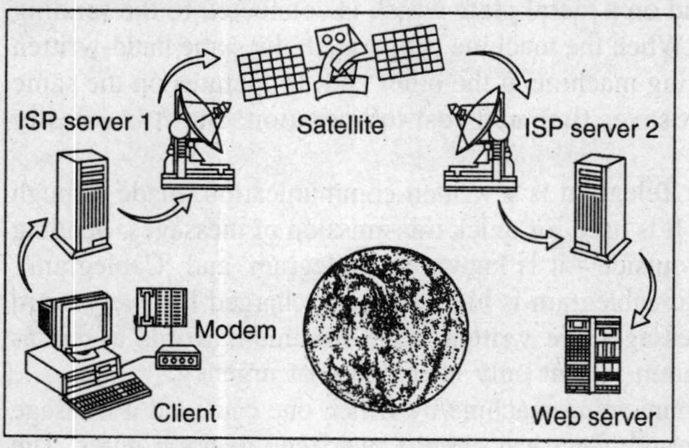

Fig. 4.9: Internet System.

A number of networks are connected to it and is often described as a 'Network of networks'. It provides information relating to education, medicine, employment, accommodation, travel, entertainment, games and sports, and various other subjects at a high speed. Its service is available 24 hours a day.

It provides high speed, accurate information and easy data flow at a very low cost. It is not controlled by any country or government. No individual, institution, government or country can claim ownership over it.

• Utilities of Internet in Modern Business

Internet is a revolutionary means of communication through computer networks. It is a combination of smaller networks and other connected machines done with the help of telephone lines, satellite lines and other media spanning the entire world. It is accessible to individuals, business enterprises, educational institutions, government agencies and other organisations all over the world to provide different types of high level services and resourceful information.

The utilities of internet in modern business may be identified if we point out the following objectives of internet:

(i) To use it as a communication method around the world.

(ii) To use it as a powerful tool for re-engineering business process.

(iii) To exchange electronic mail with others all over the world at a lower cost.

(iv) To find educational tools sharing online information.

(v) To order different products through internet to different commerical electronic stores.

(vi) To get technical support for products.

(vii) To participate in group discussions on topics of interest, etc.

(b) E-mail : E-mail or electronic mail is a service provided by internet. It is an electronic system through which letters, messages or any text-based subject-matter can be sent almost instantly by computers across the geographical boundaries. The text is typed on the screen of the sender's computer and the same is sent to the far-off receiver's address within seconds.

[An elaborate discussion on E-mail is made later in this chapter]

14. Computer: Charles Babbage of England, a professor of mathematics, is known as the 'Father of Computer'. He designed Difference Engine, a working model of mechanical computer, in 1822. After a long journey from his time, computer has entered the fourth generation era. It is a wonderful gift of science and technology. It has changed the world radically by performing various works speedily, neatly, accurately and continuously.

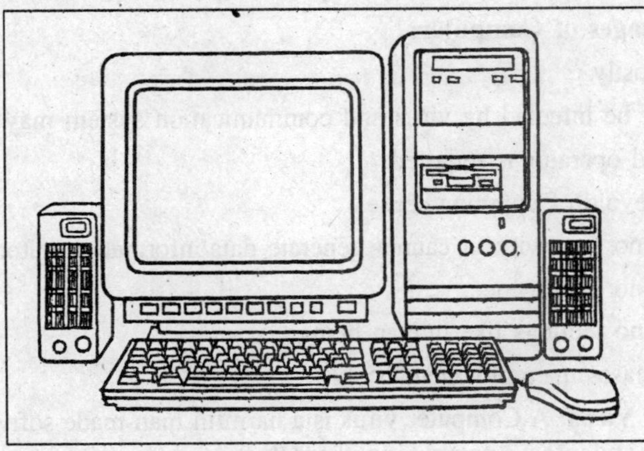

Fig. 4.10: Computer.

Computer is an electronic device which accepts data as input, processes the same through various components and produces the results of processing as output.

The components of a computer are as follows:

i. **CPU or Central Processing Unit:** Its function is to read, interpret and calculate the input data according to programme. It is divided into three units—**Control Unit, Arithmetical Logical Unit (ALU),** and **Memory Unit.** The control unit co-ordinates various operations of the computer and keeps an overall control on them. Arithmetical logical unit has two types of functions: (a) Arithmetical, and (b) Logical. The first part performs the arithmetical calculation (e.g. addition, substraction, multiplication and division) and the second part makes logical processing (e.g. arranging, analysing or comparing data). The memory unit stores up information for future reference and work.

ii. **Input Unit:** Data and instructions are fed to the computer through this unit. The devices used for feeding data and instructions include keyboard, mouse, punch card, magnetic tape, special electronic pen, touch screen, microphone (voice input), floppy disks, etc.

iii. **Output Unit:** It produces the results of processing data. Many output devices such as Visual Display Unit (VDU) or monitor, printer, floppy disks, magnetic disks, etc. are available to produce or display results of processing.

- **Advantages of Computer:**

1. It performs work at a high speed.
2. Complex and large calculations are done within a very short time.
3. It can work continuously without fatigue.
4. It saves time and labour.
5. Its performance is accurate because it can auto check its own performance.
6. Its results or output are reliable.
7. It can store data for future reference.
8. The quality of work being high it increases the prestige of the organisation.
9. It is the gateway to internet, website, e-mail, etc.
10. Personal computers with multimedia system can entertain the user by providing him/her with music, film, video games, etc.

- **Disadvantages of Computer:**

1. It is costly.
2. It may be infected by virus and communication system may be interrupted.
3. Trained operator is required.
4. It is devoid of common sense.
5. It has no creativity; it cannot generate data/information automatically.
6. It has no intelligence.
7. It has no feelings like human being.
8. It increases unemployment.

- **Computer Virus:** A Computer virus is a harmful man-made software program that can replicate itself and infect a computer without the knowledge of the user. It needs another program in order to be able to be activated and infect other computer files. Thus a computer virus has two important characteristics—(i) it can copy itself, (ii) it can attach itself to other computer files.

Computer viruses are most easily spread by attachments in e-mail messages. They can be hidden in pirated softwares and spread while using them. They also spread by downloading files from the Internet. A computer may be infected by virus through removable medium like a floppy disk, CD, DVD or USB drive, etc.

A virus can spread quickly through a network, with effects that range from mildly damaging to highly destructive depending upon the nature of a virus. It may damage, corrupt, change or delete data on a computer, interfere normal operation, degrade the performance of the computer system, reduce memory or disk space, erase the hard drive or cause more severe damage.

The symptoms of virus infection in a computer include :

- Unusual error messages,
- Distorted text and graphics,
- Extensive pop-up ads,
- Inability to open files with existing pass word,
- Vanishing of files or increasing the number of files without deleting the existing files or creating new files,
- Slowing down of system,
- Printing problem,
- Restarting automatically,
- Crashing of the system.

The best defence is to run anti-virus software and update it periodically.

- **Computer Worms:** A computer worm is a self replicating computer programme that uses network to spread from computer to computer without any human action. It is considered to be a sub-class of a virus, but unlike virus it can travel independently. It does not attach itself to other programmes. Since it can replicate itself, it overloads the system memory and slows down the computer operation process. It can send itself through network connection to the Web servers, network servers and individual computers without anybody's help. Using e-mail address book in a computer it can send copies of itself to all addresses causing huge damage to many computers. Malicious users can also take control of anybody's computer remotely using computer worms.

15. Personal Computer (PC):

Personal Computer is a small computer which can be used by one person at a time at home, in an office or at school for daily purpose.

It is a 'general purpose' tool based on microprocessor. General purpose means that one can do different things with a PC. It can be used to type documents, keep financial records, plan daily work, play games, listen to music, view movies and to do many other things. If it is connected to the internet it can be used to browse the web, send and receive e-mails, connect for instant communication, download files, make appointment with a doctor or a hospital, buy rail and air tickets and to do such other things of daily life.

A PC may be a desktop computer, a laptop, a tablet PC or a hand held PC (also called a Palmtop).

System unit (CPU), internal memory consisting of RAM (Random Access Memory) and ROM (Read Only Memory), data storage devices (including a hard disc, a floppy disc or CD ROM), monitor, keyboard, mouse and printer are integral parts of a modern PC. In addition to these an internet connection and provision for connecting plug and play devices (such as, speakers, scanners, digital cameras, external hard drives and other components) can be included as accessories.

PC evolved after the development of microprocessor during late 1970s when some computers were built from components or kits. Prior to invention of PC large expensive mainframe systems were used involving many people at a time for processing large data. In the early 1980s the first low cost, fully assembled units were mass marketed. Individuals began to purchase their own computers for the first time in history.

Its speed, accuracy, reliability, quality of output, etc., have made people dependent on it. Its size, usefulness, affordable price, etc. are attracting more and more people to use it. Now-a-days PC has become an integral part of our lives.

16. Website:

A Website is a place on the World Wide Web that contains information, texts, graphics, audio and visual documents, etc. about an individual, a company or an organisation. Website is the latest technological invention in the field of communication. It provides information on variety of topics. Any organisation or person can prepare a website for giving information

Fig. 4.11: Website.

regarding the organisation or the person to the public. In business world the business houses or the industrial units advertise their products giving details about them through website. The prospective customer can log on the website on a computer through internet and can buy the product giving orders through the internet on the website address. A website address begins with the alphabets www meaning World Wide Web. A website is required to be improved or modified from time to time to incorporate necessary changes. A website may consist of single web-page or comprise of a series of web-pages. The starting page of the website, called home page, contains index with links to other sections of the site.

Among the various communicating tools mentioned above and discussed briefly the following three are very important and require separate discussion:

1. Fax, 2. E-mail, and 3. Video Conferencing.

4.7 Fax

Facsimile (in short fax) is a system of sending and receiving letters, messages, information, etc. electronically. One fax machine each with a connected telephone on both end—at the sender's and at the receiver's end—are required for communication. The fax machine scans the original document electronically and sends signals through telephone system to the receiving end. The other fax machine at the receiving end converts the signal into identical copy of the original document and prints the same on a piece of paper.

4.7.1 Importance of Fax

Fax has become a popular tool of communication in almost all the business houses now. It is a modern and latest technology of communication of written documents. It eliminates time-zone barriers between the sender and receiver and can communicate with telephonic speed. It is useful in sending messages, documents, deeds, certificates, charts, diagram, pictures, data, statistics, etc. with speed and accuracy. Fax helps the business world to plan its activities by sending information to the appropriate persons in right time. News agencies and newspaper offices depend upon fax for collecting news. News can be sent or collected instantly through fax machine. Hospitals, transport companies, educational institutions, etc. take the help of fax machine for communication. Again, there is no possibility of virus attack in a fax machine like that in a computer. Thus, fax has proved itself an important tool in modern communication system.

4.7.2 Advantages of Fax Communication

The advantages of Fax Communication are as follows:

1. **Quick and Time Saving:** Fax can send the photo copy of a document practically within no time, almost immediately. It is one of the speediest methods of modern communication. It works at the speed of telephone call. So, time in communicating can be saved in fax.
2. **Instant Feedback:** Immediate feedback is also possible through it.
3. **Preservation of Documents:** Being a written document on paper, fax communication can be preserved as record for future reference.
4. **Dependable:** Fax communication is flawless and dependable because photocopy of documents sent from one fax machine to the other is a replica of the original one.
5. **Sending of Various Documents:** Various documents including information, messages, pictures, images, graphs, statistics, deeds, agreements, etc. can be sent and received through it.
6. **Less Costly:** Fax is relatively less costly than communication by post or through messenger.
7. **Simple Mechanism:** Its mechanism is not much complex. A simple operational training is required to use it.
8. **No Virus Attack:** Unlike in the case of computer, fax machine is free from virus attack.
9. **Universal Use:** Almost all types of organisations, e.g., business houses, news agencies, transport companies, hospitals, educational institutions can use the fax machine for written communications.
10. **International Business:** It is an indispensable tool for international business. In postal system there is no guarantee of receiving letters timely. Again, in telephonic conversation, there is a difficulty of time-adjustment because the working time in one country may be midnight in a far off country. Fax can overcome both the postal and time-zone barriers in international business.

4.7.3 Disadvantages of Fax Communication

The disadvantages of Fax Communication are stated below:

1. **Costly:** The initial cost of purchasing fax machine is high. Again, the charges of fax communication is higher in comparison to e-mail and other electronic communication. Therefore, selective use of the machine is required.
2. **Not So Clear Image:** Generally, the image of the faxed document is not as clear as the original text.
3. **Rigid Process:** No change in message is possible in the text of fax communication. To make a change one has to send another fax incorporating the change.
4. **Training for Operation:** A fax machine cannot be operated except by trained employees.
5. **Secrecy and Privacy:** No secrecy can be maintained in the process. It lacks privacy.
6. **Loss of Information:** Important news or information may remain out of sight if regular and proper search is not made in fax machine.

4.8 E-mail

The internet—especially its e-mail—has emerged as the most frequently used business tool around the world. In developed countries (like USA, UK, Germany, France, Canada) this means of electronic communication is used in the offices on a large scale, while in developing countries its use is increasing day-by-day.

In spite of its recent origin, e-mail has revolutionised business communication. It has also made its way into the lives of a large number of people who communicate through it to their friends, relatives and colleagues.

What is e-mail?

'E-mail' is the short form of electronic mail. It is an electronic system through which letters, messages, or any type of text can be sent almost instantly by computers across the geographical boundaries. It is a wonderful means of communication for text-based messages. Through e-mail one can also send still pictures, animations, diagrams, musical attachments, etc.

4.8.1 E-mail Address

The internet users are identified by their e-mail addresses. E-mail address consists of the following elements:

1. User's name or identification number;
2. Separator marked by an '@' symbol which separates user's name and domain name;
3. Domain name or the name of the institution providing the internet connection. Here dots (.) are used as separators;
4. Country code—It signifies the name of the country in brief. Generally two letters are used as abbreviation, e.g., in for India, uk for United Kingdom, jp for Japan, ca for Canada, nz for Newzealand. USA is the only country which does not use the country code in e-mail.

It is illustrated by an example as follows:

indranil	@	yahoo.co.	in
1	2	3	4
User's Name	Separator	Domain Name	Country Code

4.8.2 Composing E-mail

While composing e-mails one should keep the following points in mind:

1. **Clarity:** The meaning of the text of the e-mail should be clear. There should be no ambiguity in the text.
2. **Conciseness:** It should be concise. Repetition should be avoided.
3. **Correctness:** Spelling mistakes and grammatical errors should be carefully checked. Word processing programme of the computer can be put to service to do this.
4. **Proper Language:** Proper care should be taken in the use of appropriate language, maintaining etiquette, prestige and goodwill of the person or the organisation on behalf of whom the mail is being sent.

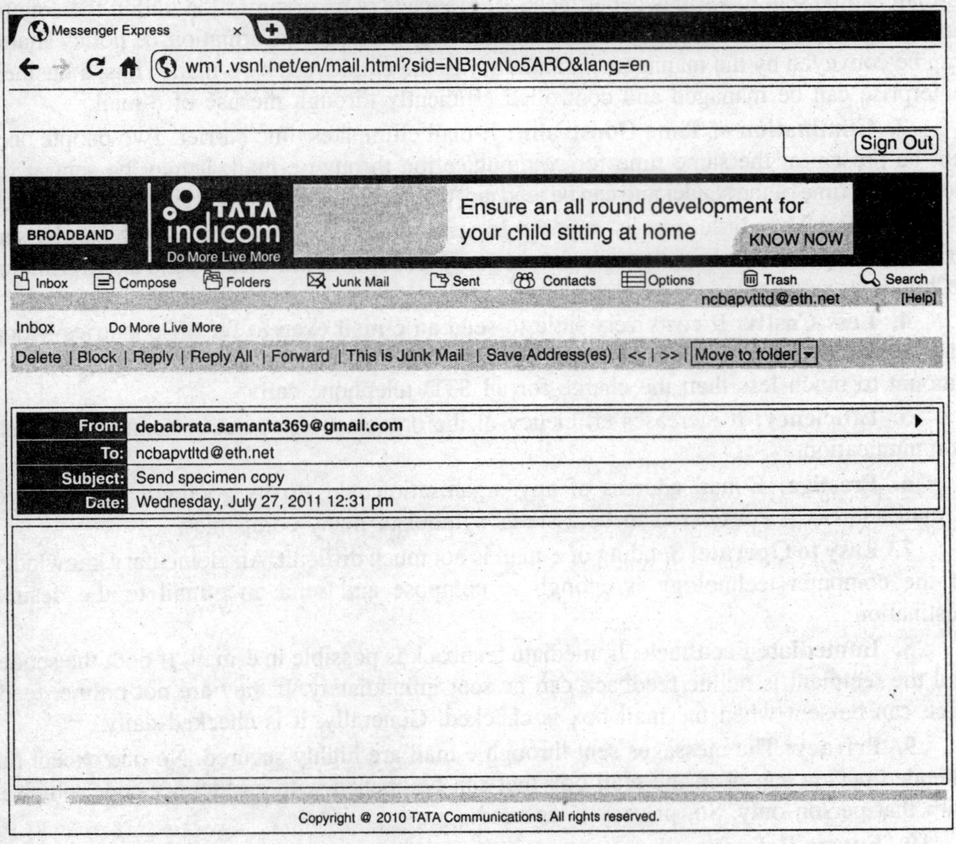

Fig. 4.12: E-mail.

5. **Required Information:** The required information or message must be there in an e-mail.
6. **Title:** A heading or title of the e-mail may be given but that should be specific and not vague.
7. **Writing of the Text:** To economise on mailing time one should prepare the text in the word processing programme of the computer 'offline' and paste it on the message window of the e-mail saving 'online' time thereby.
8. **Correct Address:** Correct address of the recipient should be typed. Slightest variation in the addresses will bounce the e-mail back to the sender. Care should be taken regarding capital and small letters, dots, underscores, gaps, etc. in the address.

9. **Attachment and Decorations:** Photos, graphs, pictures, animations, etc. may be attached with e-mails if necessary. The fonts may also be made colourful, in italics, or in different sizes to make it attractive.

10. **Copy of E-mail:** Copy of e-mail may be sent to different persons by entering multiple addresses but care should be taken to send them only to the desirable and relevant places.

4.8.3 Advantages of E-mail

The advantages of E-mail may be described as follows:

1. **Widespread Communication:** E-mail enables communication across the geographical boundaries which in this context means not only across territorial boundaries of a country but also intra- and inter-organisational communication within the country. E-mail can be sent to various departments or branches of an organisation within the country and also to the addresses in far off countries. Any message, information or policy matter can be conveyed by the management authority to the employees by e-mail. Thus, a business enterprise can be managed and controlled efficiently through the use of e-mail.

2. **Elimination of Time Constraint:** E-mail eliminates time barrier. Two people need not be present at the same time for communication through e-mail. It may be sent at the convenient time of the sender and can be read any time according to the recipient's convenience.

3. **Fast:** Very little time is required to send an e-mail. Thus, a message can be sent very fast to a large number of people. It takes only a couple of minutes to send an information to hundreds of people.

4. **Less Costly:** It costs very little to send an e-mail even to far off countries—local call telephone charges, electricity charges for running a computer and other charges which amount to much less than the charge for an STD telephone call.

5. **Efficiency:** It increases efficiency of the organisation by neat, prompt and timely communication.

6. **Prestige:** E-mail address of any organisation adds to its goodwill and prestige. E-mail address is considered to be a status symbol to many companies.

7. **Easy to Operate:** Sending of e-mail is not much difficult. An elementary knowledge of the computer technology is enough to compose and send an e-mail to the desired destination.

8. **Immediate Feedback:** Immediate feedback is possible in e-mail. If both the sender and the recipient is online feedback can be sent immediately. If they are not online, feed-back can be sent when the mail box is checked. Generally, it is checked daily.

9. **Privacy:** The messages sent through e-mail are highly secured. No one except the intended person can open the mail box that can be opened with an identity code which is with that person only. So, privacy is ensured.

10. **Future Reference:** Important e-mail can be preserved for future reference. It may be stored in a floppy, disk or in the hard disk of the computer. A printout of the e-mail may be taken and be preserved in files also.

4.8.4 Disadvantages of E-mail

E-mail has the following disadvantages:

1. **No Reflection of Feeling and Emotions:** Compared to telephonic or face to face conversation, e-mail is not an effective means of communication. Body language, tone of voice, state of mind of the participant and other environmental effects—which are reflected in face-to-face conversation or telephonic call—are absent in e-mail. Feelings, emotions, personal likes, dislikes and reactions are difficult to convey vividly through written text of e-mail. However, some symbols and signs are used in e-mails to convey the sender's mood, emotions, and state of mind.

2. Control: Once an e-mail is sent, the sender has no control over it. The sender cannot call it back or make necessary changes.

3. Privacy: There is no guarantee of privacy in this system. Hackers (cyber-pirates) can make an access to one's e-mail and read the contents unless it is in a coded form.

4. Loss of Business Hours: It has been observed that surfing of other websites consumes a large portion of business hours. While checking the mail box an employee not only checks it and arranges for reply of enquiries but also switches over to various other websites not connected with the organisational work—thereby uselessly spending hour after hour. Thus, business suffers in terms of cost and efficiency.

5. Personal Work: During office-hours personal e-mails are also sent and received by the employees. This goes against the interest of the organisation by increasing the cost of operation and wasting time.

6. Authenticity: Authenticity of the text of an e-mail may sometimes be put to question. A rival company may send fake e-mail on behalf of a company endangering the prestige and reputation of that company on bahalf of whom it is written. The recipient may take it to be authentic and may get confused.

7. High Initial Cost: The initial cost of purchasing a computer, modem, etc. required for e-mail communication is high.

8. Technical Knowledge: Some technical knowledge of operating a computer and logging in the internet is necessary for using e-mail.

9. Negligence in Checking: Sometimes e-mail box is not checked for a long period. Thus, many important letters may remain unseen and unanswered causing loss and damage to the organisation.

10. Cannot be Connected: It may so happen that in spite of repeated attempts the required e-mail address/site cannot be connected due to busy channel. This generally happens when a large number of people try to establish link through the same channel at a time.

11. Dependent on Telephone Connection: If for some reasons telephone connection is out of order, internet service will not be available and e-mail cannot be sent. It is dependent on telephone connection.

4.9 Video Conferencing

'Video Conferencing' is a newly developed method of communication. It is fast getting popular. It is also called 'Tele-conferencing'. It is a technology which allows people of two or more distant places to see and talk to each other in real time. In a room equipped with audio-video tele-communication system, communication can be made among the persons at different sites in a homely atmosphere as if they are sitting in the same room. Now desk-to-desk video conferencing has made the system more user-friendly. They can see and talk to each other as in a face-to-face meeting. They can not only exchange ideas, facts, information, etc. by conversation but can also view charts, diagrams, deeds, agreements, pictures, maps, etc. on the screen.

Now, for a meeting, seminar, or a conference people need not travel from distant places to assemble together. Participants hundreds and thousands of kilometres apart can now communicate in audio-visual manner—eliminating cost and time of travelling.

4.9.1 Importance of Video Conferencing

Though a newly developed means of communication video conferencing is emerging as an important tool of communication. People at distant places can talk to each other as in face-to-face real conversation. It has already become popular in the field of business and distant education. Business people generally have busy schedules and shortage of time. The

Fig. 4.13: Video Conference.

managers, supervisors, executives, etc., often require communication with their counterparts within and outside the organisation situated within and outside the country. Video conferencing is an effective solution to them. They can discuss any important matter with the persons staying anywhere in the world almost as in a face-to-face interaction. They can also view important documents like deeds, agreements, charts, maps, blueprint of a plan, etc. on the video monitor. Any doubt, misunderstanding or mistake can be resolved immediately by asking questions and explanations.

A record of such conversation may be preserved as document for future reference. Therefore, authenticity of the conference cannot be challenged. In the case of recruitment of persons in a business house, interviews of candidates of distant places can be made through video conferencing and thus a candidate need not travel long distance for an interview. It saves time, money and harassment. It is also useful for distance training of the employees to make them suitable for work.

Video conferencing plays an important role in educating students. In developed countries like USA, UK, Germany, France, Canada video conferencing is used as a tool for distance learning. Students can take the advantage of classes which are not offered in their campus. Teachers also need not travel from distant places to deliver lectures. These lectures can be attended at different campuses at a time by many students. More and more countries are adopting this technology and universities and colleges are being equipped with it to their benefit.

Video conference may be made between two sites, that is, one site with another site or one-to-one basis. It can also be made from one site to many sites, e.g., a telecast of a speech to many sites. Again, when more than two remote persons take part, the communication is being made on many-to-many basis. Whatever may be the basis it is speedy and effective in all cases.

Though the cost of installing a video conference system is quite high the recurring expenses are within the bearable limits. It has great potentialities to be used in a wider range in different fields throughout the world.

Keeping in view the importance and popularity of video conferencing a question may crop up in our mind—"Will face-to-face meeting be gradually replaced by vide conferencing?" The answer is: Of course, not. The importance of face-to-face meeting will never be reduced in the cases where personal involvement are required. Making a compromise, resolving a conflict, explaining a subject, giving solace, etc. require personal interaction. Face-to-face meetings are more suitable than video conferencing in these cases. Moreover, the high initial cost and complex process of the technology are also the factors that limit its wide use. However, gradual development and innovations are making it less costly and user-friendly.

4.9.2 Advantages of Video Conferencing

We get the following advantages from Video Conferencing:

1. Meeting, seminar, conference, symposium, etc. can be conducted through it from far off situations.

2. Interview, training, instruction, consultation, etc. are possible from remote locations.

3. Demonstration of medical or any other process is possible through it from distant places.

4. Not only ideas, facts, information, etc. are exchanged but charts, deeds, agreements, pictures, maps, blue-print of plans, etc. also can be viewed on the screen.

5. Text with supporting diagram, chart and images help to analyse the subject clearly.

6. Video conferencing is helpful in establishing personal relationship as in the case of face-to-face discussion.

7. The reaction of the person receiving the information is known immediately in video conference.

8. As any query can be answered immediately video conferencing eliminates the chances of misunderstanding.

9. The persons who participate in a video conference can influence each other by their way of talking, behaviours, manners, etc. and an informal positive attitude to each other is built up.

10. Organisations having a number of branches within the country or in foreign countries and having relation with distant centres require video conferencing for effective negotiation.

4.9.3 Disadvantages of Video Conferencing

The disadvantages of video conferencing are as follows:

1. It is a costly affair. The installation charges of a video conference system is very high. The telephone charges and other expenditure on various tools in video conferencing are also very high.

2. Persons participating in video conference should have some technical knowledge regarding the equipment and tools in use. Owing to complex mechanism the operators require some training.

3. Only the big business houses can afford to use video conferencing. This device is not affordable by small business or small educational institutions.

4. Making preparation for video conferencing requires some time. Setting of gadgets and preliminary arrangement are a bit time-consuming. It is not immediately accessible like telephone and e-mail.

5. Unknown persons in video conference feel uneasy and cannot talk freely.

6. It being less interactive the students or trainees are not benefited as in direct teaching and learning process.

7. An influential or stronger participant can consume major time-period of discussion in stating his/her viewpoint but the weaker party is deprived of the opportunity.

EXERCISES

[A] Essay-Type Questions

1. Give a brief history of the development of communication technology. [**Ans.** Section 4.2]
2. What are the reasons for emergence of communication technology? [**Ans.** Section 4.3]
3. What do you understand by modern communicating tools? Mention the various communicating tools used in modern business. [**Ans.** Section 4.6]
4. How may communicating tools be classified? [**Ans.** Section 4.6]
5. What is Fax? Discuss its importance. [**Ans.** Sections 4.7, 4.7.1]
6. Discuss the advantages and disadvantages of Fax. [**Ans.** Sections 4.7.2, 4.7.3]
7. What is E-mail? What are the points that should be kept in mind while composing e-mail? [**Ans.** Sections 4.8, 4.8.2]
8. What do you mean by E-mail? Discuss its advantages and disadvantages. [**Ans.** Sections 4.8, 4.8.3, 4.8.4]
9. What is meant by Video Conferencing? Why is it emerging as an important tool of communication? [**Ans.** Sections 4.9, 4.9.1]
10. What are the advantages and disadvantages of Video Conferencing? [**Ans.** Section 4.9.2, 4.9.3]
11. Describe the objectives of emerging Communication Technology. [**Ans.** Section 4.4]

[B] Short Answer-Type Questions

1. **Write short notes:**
   - i. Oral Communication. [**Ans.** Section 4.6]
   - ii. Audio-visual Communication. [**Ans.** Section 4.6]
   - iii. Written Communication. [**Ans.** Section 4.6]
   - iv. Computer. [**Ans.** Section 4.6]
   - v. Website. [**Ans.** Section 4.6]
   - vi. Pager. [**Ans.** Section 4.6]
   - vii. Fax. [**Ans.** Section 4.7]
   - viii. E-mail [**Ans.** Section 4.8]
   - ix. E-mail Address. [**Ans.** Section 4.8.1]
2. What are the advantages and disadvantages of Computer? [**Ans.** Section 4.6]
3. Will face-to-face meeting be gradually replaced by video conferencing? [**Ans.** Section 4.9.1]

[C] Very Short Answer-Type Questions

1. Where is a Fax machine used? [**Ans.** Section 4.7.1]
2. Which country does not use country code in E-mail address? [**Ans.** Section 4.8]
3. Name four written communicating tools. [**Ans.** Section 4.6]

● **Questions of University Examinations:**

[A] Questions of Very Short Answer-Type [Each Question Carries 2 Marks]:

i. What is Internet? [C.U. B.Com. New Syllabus 2006]
Ans. Point No. 13 in Section 4.6]

ii. What is Website? [C.U. B.Com. New Syllabus 2007, 2010]
Ans. Point No. 16 in Section 4.6]

iii. What is Dictaphone? [C.U. B.Com. New Syllabus 2007]

Ans. Point No. 2 in Oral Communication in Section 4.6]

iv. What is Fax? [C.U. B.Com. New Syllabus 2008]

Ans. Section 4.7

v. What is Video Conferencing? [C.U. B.Com. New Syllabus 2009]

Ans. Section 4.9

vi. What is Tele-conferencing? [C.U. B.Com. New Syllabus 2011]

Ans. Section 4.9

vii. Why is FAX essential in modern office? [C.U. B.Com. New Syllabus 2011]

Ans. Section 4.7.1

[B] Questions of Short Answer-Type [Each Question Carries 4 Marks]:

i. Write a short note on emergence of Communication technology. [C.U. B.Com. New Syllabus 2011]

Ans. Section 4.1

ii. Discuss the advantages and disadvantages of E-mail. [C.U. B.Com. New Syllabus 2011]

Ans. Sections 4.8.3 and 4.8.4

iii. Discuss the advantages of Video Conferencing. [C.U. B.Com. New Syllabus 2011]

Ans. Sections 4.9.2

[C] Questions of Long Answer-Type [Each Question Carries 10 Marks]:

i. What is meant by Video Conferencing? Discuss the advantages and disadvantages of Video Conferencing. [C.U. B.Com. New Syllabus 2005]

Ans. Sections 4.9, 4.9.2 and 4.9.3

ii. Define E-mail. State the advantages of E-mail. [C.U. B.Com. 2006]

Ans. Sections 4.8 and 4.8.3

iii. Why are communication tools used in modern day business. [C.U. B.Com. 2006]

Ans. Section 4.4

iv. Discuss the objectives of emergence of Communication Technology in Business. [C.U. B.Com. New Syllabus 2007]

Ans. Section 4.4.7

v. What is Internet? What are its utilities in modern business? [C.U. B.Com. New Syllabus 2008]

Ans. Point No. 13 in section 4.6

CHAPTER

5

Drafting

"The first draft reveals the art, revision reveals the artist." —Michael Lee

TOPICS

i. Planning Business Messages ◆ ii. Rewriting and Editing ◆ iii. First and Final Draft ◆ iv. Drafting ◆ v. Drafting of Notice ◆ vi. Drafting of Circulars ◆ vii. Drafting of Minutes and Resolutions ◆ viii. Drafting of Reports ◆ ix. Letter Writing : Drafting of Business Letters in Matters like (a) Offers, Quotations and Orders; (b) Confirmation, Execution, Refusal and Cancellation of Orders; (c) Status Enquiries; (d) Recommendations and Credit; (e) Collection; (f) Claims ◆ x. Bank Loan ◆ xi. Writing Application, Resume and CV.

Subject-matter of the Chapter : *It is well-known that for a valid meeting, notice must be served by the right person to all the persons entitled to attend the meeting. The notice has a definite form and style of writing. Again, on many occasions it becomes necessary to notify certain things or to convey certain information to the customers and friends of a business firm as well as to the public in general. It may be done by issuing 'circulars' to the interested parties. 'Minutes' are the official records of the proceedings of a meeting and decisions arrived at the meeting. Minutes have to be drafted with utmost care so that nothing untrue is recorded. 'Resolution' is the decision of a meeting. When a motion is adopted or passed by majority votes of the members, it becomes a resolution.*

Various kinds of reports have to be prepared in the office for different purposes. It is a part of secretarial functions. Business letter occupies a very important position in the field of trade and commerce. It is the best and cheapest method of communication all over the world.

In this chapter, some specimens of drafting of notices, circulars, letters, minutes and resolutions suitable for effective business communication are presented. Discussion on the types, style and presentation of reports are made. Some examples of drafting reports are provided. The functions and importance of business letters are explained. In this connection, the style of writing business letters are also considered with some specimens thereof.

The reader will also be made familiar with the art of writing applications for a post of employment, and writing resume and C.V.

5.1 Planning Business Messages

There is no hard and fast rule or ideal method which is universally accepted in writing a business message. Business messages may be written in the form of letters, memorandum, notice, circulars, advertisement etc. Every writer has his/her own style which may not tally with that of the other. Style may differ but a general format is usually followed. A letter is not written in the form of a notice. The skill of writing good business messages does not grow automatically. It is required to be practised with due care and devotion. Planning is necessary before writing.

5.1.1 Object of Planning Business Messages

There are two objects of planning a business message—primary and secondary. The primary object is the immediate object for which the message is being written (e.g., the letter asking due payment, the letter requesting extension of period for delivery of goods etc.). The secondary object is long lasting. It aims at building up goodwill of the business, retaining the existing customers, and attracting additional customers, etc. So, business messages should be properly planned and carefully drafted in order to fulfil both the objectives.

5.1.2 Guidelines for Successful Planning of Business Messages

In addition to keeping in view the primary and secondary objectives stated above, the following guidelines will help in successful planning of business messages:

1. The writer should know about earlier correspondences, if any.
2. He/She should know the situation in full.
3. He/She should know the company's policy.
4. He/She should have clear idea about the person to whom the letter is being written.
5. The language of the message should be simple, courteous, clear and correct.
6. The message should not be too long.
7. 'You' attitude is to be encouraged rather than 'I' or 'We' attitude in writing a letter. For example : (i) It is better to write 'you can avail 5% discount.' than writing 'we allow 5% discount.' (ii) 'Thank you' is preferred to 'I convey my thanks'.
8. The writer should have a clear idea of the layout of a meassage. For example, the address, date, correct salutation, correct reference, enclosures, etc. should be properly written in drafting a letter.
9. The points are to be jotted down on a sheet of paper.
10. The points are to be arranged in logical order.
11. A rough draft is to be prepared.
12. Paragraphs are to be made for different points.
13. Correction, revision and re-draft is necessary till the draft satisfies the writer.
14. After finalising the draft the writer sould ensure visual appeal of the message. Good paper, neat typing, proper margin, etc. give the message a good look which enhances the goodwill of the organisation.
15. A copy should be preserved for future reference.

5.2 Rewriting and Editing

After making the draft of a business message the writer has to examine it carefully. He/She must ensure that—

1. The subject-matter is expressed clearly.
2. All the important facts are included.
3. All unnecessary materials are eliminated.

4. It is not too long.
5. It is courteous and respectful.
6. It generates goodwill.
7. The language is simple and pleasant.
8. It is complete in all respects.
9. There is no spelling mistake and grammatical error.
10. Proper approach ('you' approach) is chosen.
11. Paragraphs are made for different points.
12. Effective beginning and ending are made.

If any defect is found in a draft the writer should re-write the message after correcting the errors and making additions, alterations and modifications; in other words, editing the draft thoroughly. Editing includes replacement, deletion, inclusion or change of words, sentences, paragraphs, style, etc. and making the draft complete in all respects. The process of editing will continue till the writer is satisfied with the draft. Several drafts may have to be prepared before getting the final draft. Each successive draft is an improved and rectified version of the previous one.

5.3 Several Drafts for a Final Draft

As already mentioned several drafts of a business message may be needed to get a final draft. The defects or errors in the first draft may be rectified in the second, third, or even in subsequent drafts.

We give below an example of a letter to show the corrections made in the first and second drafts to arrive at the final draft.

Example : Draft of a letter requesting for substitute product in place on an order.

FIRST DRAFT

NEW PAINT CO. LTD.
46, Canning Street, Kolkata

To
The Manager,
Makhanlal & Co. (2) (3)
Dear Sir, (1) Date

We thank you for your kind order of the 5 February 11 for 'Golden Brand' paint but our stock of this brand of paint is totally exausted. We like to inform you further that we (4)
(5) have decided not to stock this brand at present because its price has gone up very high. Moreover, we had an unpleasant experience of irregular supply of this brand paint by the manufacturer. (6)

Now, if you are not compelled to use the same brand we can supply our 'Diamond Brand' paint which is in no way inferior to the 'Golden Brand' paint, but is comparatively cheaper and better. This new brand has already acquire much popularity in the market within a very short time. (7)

(8) Now, it is up to you to decide whether you will accept the substitute offer or not. We wait for your instruction for immediate supply.

Thanking you,

Yours faithfully,
L. K. Majumder
(Sales Manager)

After going through the first draft various defects and errors have been found. Those errors are numbered from (1) to (8) in the draft. The following table shows the errors. their corrected version and the reasons for their correction.

Nos.	Errors/Defects	Corrections	Reasons for Correction
1.	Date of writing the letter is not given.	To insert the date	A letter without a date is imcomplete.
2.	We thank you	Thank you	Use of 'you' attitude in place of 'we' attitude.
3.	Kind	To delete	Unnecessary
4.	exausted	exhausted	Spelling mistake
5.	We like ... very high.	To make a new paragraph	It tells a different idea.
6.	Moreover ... manufacturer.	To delete	No need of telling internal reason to the outsider.
7.	Acquire	Acquired	Grammatical mistake
8.	Now...or not.	To be replaced by—'we request you to kindly place your order for this new brand instead of 'Golden Brand' paint and we are sure that you will find it satisfactory'.	To make the language polite.

SECOND DRAFT

NEW PAINT CO. LTD.
46, Canning Street, Kolkata

(1)

To
The Manager,
Makhanlal & Co. (2) (3)

Dated : 15 February, 2011 (4)

Dear Sir,

Thank you for your order of 5 February 2011 for 'Golden Brand' paint. But our stock of this brand of paint is totally exhausted.

We like to inform you further that we have decided not to stock this brand at present because its price has gone up very high.

Now, if you are not compelled to use the same brand we can supply our 'Diamond Brand' paint which is in no way inferior to the 'Golden Brand' paint, but is comparatively cheaper and better. This new brand has already acquired much popularity in the market within a very short time.

(5) We request you to kindly place your order for this new brand instead of 'Golden Brand' paint and we are sure that you will find it satisfactory.

We wait for your instruction for immediate supply.

Thanking you,

(6) Yours faithfully.
L. K. Majumder,
(Sales Manager)

(7)

The second draft is an improved version of the first draft. Various modifications are made, grammar and spellings are checked, unnecessary words and sentences are deleted but still it has some defects, The following table shows the errors (indicated by numbers in the second draft), their corrections and reasons for corrections. After correcting the errors in the second draft, the third draft will be the final draft.

Nos.	Errors/Defects	Corrections	Reasons for Correction
1.	Reference, internal telephone no., telegram and e-mail address are not written.	To insert the relevant infomation.	Without these information the letter is incomplete.
2.	Address of Makhanlal and Co. is not there.	To insert the address.	Letter is incomplete.
3.	Subject-matter is not written.	To insert 'Re : Offer for substitute product'.	It helps the reader to understand the subject-matter immediately.
4.	Few words signifying courtesy should be written.	To insert—'We regret to inform you that'.	To maintain courtesy.
5.	We request you	You are requested.	To use 'you attitude'.
6.	Signature is to be made on behalf of the Co.	To insert 'For New Paint Co. Ltd.	Usual format to follow.
7.	Enclosure is not mentioned.	To write—'Enclo.: Price list of Diamond Brand paint'.	Without price list order for substitute product cannot be produced.

THIRD AND FINAL DRAFT

NEW PAINT CO. LTD.
46, Canning Street, Kolkata

Dated : 15th February, 2011

Telephone : 2226-6033
Telegraphic Address : NPL
E-mail Address : NPL@ yahoo.co.in
Ref. No. C/N-59/20I3

To
The Manager,
Makhanlal & Co.
9, Lenin Sarani
Durgapur

Re : Offer for Substitute Product

Dear Sir,

Thank you for your order of 5 February 2011 for 'Golden Brand' paint, but we regret to inform you that our stock of this brand of paint is totally exhausted.

We like to inform you further that we have decided not to stock this brand at present because its price has gone up very high.

Now, if you are not compelled to use the same brand we can supply our 'Diamond Brand' paint which is in no way inferior to the 'Golden Brand' paint. On the other hand, 'Diamond Brand' paint is comparatively cheaper and better. This new brand has already acquired much popularity in the market within a very short time.

You are requested to kindly place your order for this new brand instead of 'Golden Brand' paint and we are sure that you will find it satisfactory.

We wait for your instruction for immediate supply.

Thanking you,

Yours faithfully,
For New Paint Co. Ltd.
L. K. Majumder
(Sales Manager)

Enclo : Price list of Dimaond Brand Paint

5.4 Drafting

'Drafting' means the preparation of any letter or document in writing. It is an important secretarial function. It involves the perparation of notice, agenda, minutes, reports, resolutions, business letters, circulars and many other things.

Several specimen drafts of notices, circulars, minutes, resolutions, reports and business letters are given in this chapter. From these examples, the students will get an idea regarding how to prepare drafts.

5.5 Drafting of Notices

[A] Definition and Meaning of Notice : The word 'Notice' has been derived from the Latin Word, '*Notitia*' which means knowledge. So, notice is a prior intimation or a warning of something. It is a written or printed announcement. A notice is issued to notify some information of general nature to the customers, shareholders, members, office staff and others. The notice, therefore, has two aspects—[i] it may be an intimation or information, and, [ii] it may be a kind of warning. It may be general or confidential. A meeting cannot validly transact its business unless all the persons entitled to attend the meeting are informed beforehand of the date, time and place of the meeting, as well as the business to be transacted therein. All organisations from a club or association to a company or corporation have to issue notices to notify information or instruction under various circumstances.

[B] Form and Style of Writing a Notice : Whatever may be the category of the notice, each has a specific form and style of writing. A notice : [i] Must be written in a language understandable to those for whom it is meant. In some cases there is a statutory direction too. [ii] Must convey the message clearly—what was intended to be conveyed. [iii] Must be brief and avoid unnecessary words. [iv] Must be drafted according to a form. That form may be a statutory form; [v] Normally bears a date. [vi] Must be signed by the authorised person. A confidential or individual notice or any public notice having legal implications must be drafted by a lawyer. A qualified secretary is expected to have the competence for the same.

Notice has to be drafted and issued for every kind of private meeting. There are two distinct kinds of forms for the purpose—[a] **Form No. 1 :** In the case of a notice for the meeting of a committee like an Executive Committee or Managing Committee or the Board of Directors, etc. the notice is in the form of a letter. [b] **Form No. 2 :** In the case of a notice for the meeting of general body of members of an organisation, the notice is in the form of a circular with some special features.

[C] Circumstances of Issuing Notice : Some of the circumstances under which notices are issued are as follows :

[i] Convening of a meeting;

[ii] Notifying a change in internal business or administrative procedure;

[iii] Notifying some administrative order or instruction to the subordinate staff;

[iv] Inviting tenders for the supply of some goods;

[v] Notifying declaration of dividend by the company, etc.

[D] Requisites or Essential Elements of Notice : Generally, the rules of every organisation specify the person who is authorised to convene a meeting. In most cases, the Chairman or the Secretary of the organisation is authorised to convene a meeting. The notice of a meeting is normally drafted and issued by the Secretary with the approval of the Chairman. The mode of issuing notice and the period of notice are usually determined by the rules of the organisation or by custom and convention.

The essential elements of a valid notice are discussed below :

1. The notice must specify the date, time and place of the meeting, all of which must be reasonably convenient to the majority of the persons entitled to attened it.
2. The notice must be served to all the persons who are entitled to receive it. However, a notice need not be issued to a person living abroad or whose address is not known.
3. The notice must be clear, explicit and unconditional.
4. The notice must be served in the manner provided in the rules that is by messenger or mail. Verbal notice may be given if it is customary, but it must be confirmed by a written notice.
5. Proper length of notice should be given as provided by the rules. It means the number of days, specified by the rules, that must elapse from the date of issuing the notice to the date of the meeting. Different lengths of notice are generally prescribed by the rules for different kinds of meetings.
6. The notice must include the 'Agenda' of the meeting. Agenda means the list of business to be transacted at the meeting. It may be given in summarised form or in detail.

[E] Rules for or Principles of Drafting Notice/Factors to be Considered in Drafting a Notice : The following rules or principles should be followed while drafting a notice :

1. The notice should not be lengthy. It should be as brief as possible, avoiding unnecessary words.
2. The language of a notice must be simple, free from ambiguity. so that it can be easily understood by the recipients of the notice.
3. It should always convey the message clearly, without any doubt.
4. It should clearly mention the date, time and place of the meeting.
5. It should be written in an impersonal manner and in an indirect form of speech.
6. It should be preferably printed or type-written.
7. It should clearly and precisely mention the business to be transacted at the meeting.

8. It should be issued to all the persons who are entitled to attend the meeting.
9. It should be written and issued only after getting proper instruction from the proper authority.
10. It should always maintain the provision in respect of the prescribed number of clear days.
11. It should be drafted by a lawyer when there is any legal complication.
12. The explanatory notes, notes of proxy and shareholders' transfer book should be given in it whenever necessary.
13. A notice must be dated and signed by the person authorised to issue it.

[F] Important Points to be Remembered by the Secretary while Drafting a Notice :

Among the duties of a Secrerary of an association, commercial organisation, non-trading concern and a company, drafting of notice of a meeting is very significant. In this matter, the primary requirement is to follow the provisions of the constitution of the respective organisation, standing rules, laws and bye-laws relating to notice and agenda. However, the Secretary should be careful about the following matters of importance :

1. The nature of the meeting should be written in precise manner.
2. The notice should be clear so that the intention can be easily understood.
3. The day, date, time and place of the meeting should be sequentially stated.
4. The time gap between the date of issuing the notice and the date of the holding the meeting should be clear as per provision of the constitution of the organisation or law. It means that the date of serving the notice and the date of holding the meeting should not be counted in considering the 'clear days' notice.
5. The notice should be brief and free from grammatical errors.
6. It must be unconditional and without any ambiguity.
7. It should be served after receiving the order or instruction from the competent authority.
8. Every person entitled to receive the notice of the meeting must get it in due time.
9. A short 'agenda' should point out the business to be taken up for discussion at the meeting.
10. Explanatory notes, proxy form, share-transfer book should be given along with the notice, when these are necessary.
11. The notice must be signed by the Secretary with the date indicated.
12. Above the signature of the Secretary, the words, "By order of the Board" or "By order of the Managing Committee", as applicable to the organisation must be clearly mentioned.

5.5.1 Agenda

[A] Meaning : Literally the word 'Agenda' means 'things to be done'. It is a list of the items of business to be transacted at a meeting. An agenda is generally appended to every notice of a meeting. The systematic discussion of the items of business in their proper order of importance is ensured by it. It may be prepared in a summarised form or in detail. The routine items are usually mentioned first and the controversial items later.

[B] Object of Preparing Agenda : The principal object of preparing an 'Agenda' is to inform the members of an organisation about the items of business to be transacted at the meeting. It enables the members to come prepared for the discussion on these items. An agenda is considered essential for the systematic discussion of the items in their proper order of importance. It also helps in the preparation of the minutes of the meeting.

[C] Method of Preparing Agenda : The agenda of a meeting is generally prepared by the Secretary after consulting with the Chairman or Senior Executives of the organisation. The items of the agenda may be mentioned very briefly or in detail. In some cases, copies of reports and resolution forming the subject-matter of a particular item are also included in the agenda. However, in each case it should be a clear summary of the business to be transacted at the meeting. Normally, the routined items are stated first and the controversial items are given later. Usually, the business of the meeting is transacted in the same order as mentioned in the agenda. But it can be changed with the consent of the members of the meeting. The agenda is generally appended below the notice. Sometimes, it is typed in a separate sheet on the left-hand side, leaving a wide margin on the right-hand side for taking notes on discussions by the Secretary or the Chairman. Again, in some cases, the agenda is entered in a separate Agenda Book. It maintains a permanent record of the agenda. It may also be utilised by the Chairman for keeping notes of discussions at the meetings.

5.5.2 Quorum

[A] Meaning : 'Quorum' means the minimum number of persons required to be present at a meeting for valid transaction of business. Unless a quorum is present at the beginning and throughout the meeting, it cannot be considered to be valid. Generally, the rules of an organisation lay down the quorum for different kinds of meetings. The main object of quorum is to ensure that the decisions at a meeting are not taken by a minority of members, which may not be acceptable to others.

[B] Rules regarding Quorum : Usually, the number constituting quorum for a meeting is laid down in the laws, bye-laws, Articles, Standing Orders etc. of the organisation. If it is not laid down in the rules of an organisation, even two persons can constitute a quorum. The quorum for different types of company meetings are generally laid down in the Articles of Association. When nothing is laid down regarding quorum in the Articles, five members for a public company and two members for a private company can form the quorum according to the provision of the Companies Act.

A quorum of members must be present at the beginning and also throughout the meeting. Any discussion in a meeting without a quorum is invalid. If a quorum is not present at the scheduled starting time, the Chairman will wait for some time and then adjourn the meeting to a subsequent date. Again, if the meeting starts with a quorum but subsequently the number falls below quorum, the Chairman must adjourn the meeting as soon as he notices it or it is pointed out to him. However, when an adjourned meeting is held on a subsequent date, it needs no quorum.

5.5.3 Requisites of a Valid Notice for a General Meeting of a Company

Certain rules for the issue of the notice of the general meeting of companies are laid down in the Companies Act. Generally, the Articles of Association of every company lay down some rules regarding the issue of notices of the company meetings. The requisites of a valid notice for a general meeting of the company may be described as follows :

1. **Proper Authority :** The Board of Directors of a company is the proper authority to convene the general meeting of the company. Notice of such meetings can only be issued by the Board of Directors. The Secretary of the company can issue the notice when he is authorised by the Board to do so.

2. **Length of Notice :** In accordance with the provision of the Companies Act to call a general meeting at least 21 days' notice must be given in writing to all members. However, a general meeting can be called at a shorter notice, if—[a] in the case of an Annual General Meeting, all the members entitled to vote give their consent to it; and [b] in the case of all other general meetings, members holding at least 95% of the share capital having voting rights or representing at least 95% of voting power consent to it.

3. **Contents of Notice :** According to the Companies Act. every notice of a company meeting must specify the place, date and time of the meeting and contain an agenda, that is, a statement of the items of business to be transacted at the meeting. In the case of a Statutory Meeting, the notice must be accompanied by a copy of the Statutory Report. And, in the case of Annual General Meetings, the copies of the audited Accounts and Balance Sheet, Directors Report, proxy form, etc. must also be attached to every notice. Explanatory Statement must be given with the notices of Extra-ordinary General Meetings.

4. **Manner of Services :** Notices of General Meetings of a company must be given to—[a] all members of the company entitled to receive it; [b] the auditors of the company; and [c] the legal representatives of insolvent and deceased members, if any. Notices may be served by messenger or by post to the registered address of each member. In the absence of any address, an advertisement in newspaper in the locality of the registered office of the company will serve the purpose.

Specimens of some notices of company meetings are given below :

[I] Notice for the First Board Meeting of a Public Limited Company Containing Suitable Agenda.

MONDAL TRADING CORPORATION LTD.

Regd. Office : 15, M. G. Road, Kolkata 700 007

Dated : 5th March, 2011

To

Mr. A. K. Saha (Director)
2, Shyambazar Street
Kolkata 700 017

Dear Sir,

I have to inform you that the first meeting of the Board of Directors of Mondal Trading Corporation Ltd. will be held at its Registered Office on Saturday, the 16th April, 2011 at 3 p.m. to consider the following agenda.

Your presence is solicited.

Yours faithfully,
K. P. Roy (Secretary)

Agenda :

1. Election of the Chairman of the meeting.
2. Production of the Certificate of Incorporation, the Memorandum and Articles of Association.
3. Appointment of the first Director of the Corporation.
4. Election of the Chairman of the Board of Directors of the Corporation.
5. Appointment of Managing Director, Secretary, Solicitor, Auditors and Bankers.
6. Adoption of the Corporation's Seal.
7. Fixing the Quorum for the Board Meetings.
8. Adoption of preliminary contracts and preliminary expenses made by the promoters.
9. Approval of the Draft Prospectus.
10. Fixing the date of the next Board Meeting.
11. Any other business with the permission of the Chairman.
12. Vote of thanks to the Chair.

[II] Notice for any Board Meeting of a Public Limited Company other than the First.

BENGAL ELECTRICAL CO. LTD.

Regd. Office : 15, Ballygunge Road, Kolkata 700 019

Dated : 10th March, 2011

To

Mr. S. K. Chakraborty (Director)
20, Park Street, Kolkata 700 015

Dear Sir,

This is to inform you that the 9th meeting of the Board of Directors of Bengal Electrical Co. Ltd. will be held on Thursday, the 24th March, 2011 at 4 p.m. at the Registered Office of the Company to transact the following business.

Your presence is solicited.

Yours faithfully,

S. K. Basu (Secretary)

Agenda :

1. To confirm the minutes of the last Board Meeting.
2. To approve Share Transfer.
3. To consider the proposal of opening a new branch at Mumbai.
4. To produce the financial statements and to declare the interim dividend.
5. To appoint a Personnel Manager.
6. To fix up the date of the next Board Meeting.
7. To deal with any other business with the consent of the Chair.

[III] Notice of the Statutory Meeting of a Public Company.

IDEAL TRADING CO. LTD.

Regd. Office : 17, Chowringhee Road, Kolkata 700 013

Dated : 15th March, 2011

NOTICE

Notice is hereby given in pursuance of Section 165 of the Companies Act, 1956, that the Statutory Meeting of the Company will be held at the Registered Office of the Company on Thursday, the 31st March 2011, at 2 p.m., to consider the Statutory Report and to transact the following business.

A copy of the Statutory Report is attached herewith.

By order of the Board,
D. K. Mukherjee
(Secretary)

Agenda :

1. Consideration and adoption of the Statutory Report.
2. Inspection of the list of members.
3. Discussion on any matter related to the formation of the Company.

Note : A member entitled to attend and vote at the meeting may send a proxy who need not be a member of the Company.

A proxy form is attached herewith.

[IV] Notice for an Annual General Meeting of a Company with Usual Agenda.

ROY AND COMPANY LTD.

Regd. Office : 12, Netaji Subhas Road, Kolkata 700 001

Dated : 15th April, 2011

NOTICE

Notice is hereby given that the 10th Annual General Meeting of the Company will be held on Wednesday, the 18th May, 2011 at 4 p.m. at the Registered Office of the Company to transact the business given below.

By order of the Board,
A. K. Chowdhury
(Secretary)

Agenda :

1. To read out and get confirmed the minutes of the 9th Annual General Meeting.
2. To consider and adopt the Directors' Report and the Auditor's Report for the year ended 31st March, 2010.
3. To consider and adopt the Profit and Loss Account for the year ended 31st March, 2010 and the Balance Sheet as at that date.
4. To declare dividend as recommended by the Board of Directors.
5. To elect a director in place of Mr. A. K. Patra who retires by rotation, but, being eligible, offers himself for re-election.
6. To appoint the Company's auditors for the current year and to fix their remuneration.
7. To transact any other business with the permission of the Chair.

Notes :
1. A member entitled to attend the meeting and to vote may send a proxy who need not be a member. A proxy form is attached herewith.
2. Members' Register and Share Transfer Register will remain closed from 26.4.11 to 20.5.11, both days inclusive.
3. Dividends, if declared, shall be payable from 26.5.11.

[V] Notice of the Extra-ordinary General Meeting of a Public Limited Company.

SEN AND COMPANY LTD.

Regd. Office : 18 B. T. Road, Kolkata 700 056

Dated : 12th March, 2011

NOTICE

Notice is hereby given that an Extra-ordinary General Meeting of the Company will be held at the Registered Office of the Company on Wednesday, the 13th April, 2011 at 2 p.m. to consider and, if thought fit, to pass with or without modification, the following resolution as a special resolution. "That Article 23 of the Articles of Association be, and hereby is modified by increasing the maximum number of Directors of the Company from seven to nine".

By order of the Board,
S. N. Dutta
(Secretary)

Notes : 1. A member entitled to attend and vote at the meeting may send a proxy who need not be a member. A proxy from is attached herewith.

2. A copy of the Articles of Association of the Company is available at the Registered Office of the Company for inspection between 2 p.m. and 4 p.m. on all working days.

3. An Explanatory Statement is annexed to this notice.

Explanatory Statement

As the activities of the Company have been largely increased on account of introducing diversification of products, there is an urgent need for the services of additional executive directors to ensure the efficiency of management. The Board of Directors considers that this new circumstance requires increasing the maximum number of Directors for the Company from seven to nine in the interest of the Company. Hence, Article 23 of the Articles of Association of the company is proposed to be amended.

[VI] Notice for the Annual General Meeting of a Club with Usual Agenda.

BURDWAN SPORTING CLUB

98, R. B. Ghosh Road, Burdwan

Dated : 12th April 2011

NOTICE

Notice is hereby given that the 9th Annual General Meeting of the Club will be held on Wednesday, the 20th April, 2011 at 3 p.m. in the main building of the Club to discuss the following business.

All members are requested to be present and participate in the proceedings.

By order of the
President,
S. Sain
(Secretary)

Agenda :

1. To read the notice convening the meeting.
2. To confirm the minutes of the last Annual General Meeting.
3. To consider and adopt the Report of the Hony. General Secretary.
4. To consider and adopt the audited accounts of the last session.
5. To approve the budget estimates for 2010-2011
6. To appoint auditor for the next year.
7. To elect office bearers and members of the Executive Committee for 2010-2011.
8. To consider the proposal for increasing the rate of subscription fee from Rs. 25 to Rs. 30.
9. Miscellaneous.

[VII] Notice of the Annual General Meeting of a Co-operative Society.

NABAGRAM H.L.P. COLLEGE CO-OPERATIVE CREDIT SOCIETY LIMITED

1. College Road, Nabagram, Hooghly

Dated : 25th April, 2011

NOTICE

Notice is hereby given that the 6th Annual General Meeting of the Society will be held on Tuesday, the 3rd May, 2011 at 2 p.m. at the Registered Office of the Society, to consider the following business.

By order of the Board,

N. C. Pandey

(Secretary)

Agenda :

1. Confirmation of the minutes of the last meeting.
2. Consideration and adoption of the report of the Secretary.
3. Consideration of the audited Accounts, Balance Sheet and the Auditor's Report and declaration of dividends.
4. Consideration of the Annual Budget Estimates for 2010-2011.
5. Election of the Directors.
6. Fixing up the maximum amount of borrowings from the Bank in the ensuing year.
7. Fixing up the credit limit of the borrowers and the rate of interest to be charged.
8. Consideration of any other business with the permission of the Chair.
9. Vote of thanks to the Chair.

[VIII] Notice and Agenda of the Ordinary Meeting of a Local Body.

Meeting Notice

List of business to be brought forward at the Ordinary Meeting of the Commissioners of Burdwan Municipality to be held at the Central Office on Saturday, the 28th May, 2011 at 2 p.m.

1. To confirm the minutes of the last ordinary meeting.
2. To consider the monthly Progress Report of the Health, Food and Public Works Departments for the month of January, 2011.
3. To consider the reports of (a) Finance Standing Committee as per meeting held on 10.3.11, and (b) Health and Sanitation Standing Committee as per meeting held on 5.4.11.
4. To approve the lease of Sadar Ferry Ghat to Sri S. Bhowmik for one year, from 1st January, 2011 at Rs. 30,000 lump sum at a public auction held on 28.11.10.
5. To consider and sanction an Estimate for Rs. 60,000 for repair of a part of the Ramkrishna Road.
6. To consider some petitions for connections of water supply to houses.
7. To consider the steps to be taken in respect of unauthorised construction at 20, Sarbamongala Para Lane.

8. To consider an application from Sri A. Dasgupta, Lighting Inspector, for a loan of Rs. 5,000 from P. F. Account.
9. To consider the report of the Secretary regarding the extension of the office building.

Central Office, J. Bhattacharya
Burdwan Municipality Vice-Chairman
The 20th May, 2011.

5.6 Drafting of Circulars

[A] Meaning of Circular : A 'circular' means the notification of certain information to the customers, employees, public or other interested parties. Any information which must be known to a large number of persons, is circulated. In the business life, circulars have to be sent to the customers, dealers, agents, etc. These are known as trade circulars.

[B] Principles of Drafting Circulars : In drafting circulars the following principles should be followed :

1. Circulars must be simple, precise and concise.
2. The purpose must be clearly stated.
3. Circulars must be drafted carefully. They must be courteous in tone and pleasing in form.
4. They must be free from ambiguity.
5. They must be informative.

[C] Purpose of Circulars : Circular letters are usually issued to convey the following types of information :

1. Announcement of the establishment or transfer of a business.
2. Taking over or closing down of a business.
3. Announcement of opening a new branch or show room.
4. Shifting of a business to a more convenient place.
5. Admission, retirement or death of a partner.
6. Appointment of sole-selling agent.
7. Termination of the service of a salesman.
8. Any change in internal management or business policy etc.

Trade circulars are issued to stimulate sales, to open up new markets, to offer a new product to the customers or to intimate any change in price or quality of a product.

[D] Notice and Circulars : 'Notice' is an invitation or intimation of some meeting in writing to the persons who are entitled to participate in it for discussion and making decision. But 'Circulars' are the letters which are addressed to different persons or firms intimating certain messages or information.

[E] Examples : Some examples of circulars are given below :

SPECIMEN I. Circular announcing the Establishment of New Business.

MUKHERJEE AND CO. LTD.

(Cloth Merchants)

30, Shakespeare Sarani, Kolkata 700 017

Circular No. C/195/11 Dated : 20th January, 2011

Dear Sirs,

We have the pleasure to announce that we have established a wholesale showroom to sell quality garments under the name and style of 'Mukherjee and Co.' Ltd. at the above address.

We have sufficient stocks of large varieties to satisfy the demand of different categories of customers. We assure you of supplying quality clothes at moderately competitive prices. 'Service to Customers' is our motto.

We expect your kind co-operation, patronage and enquiries.

Yours faithfully,
For Mukherjee and Co. Ltd.
T. Mukherjee
(Manager)

SPECIMEN 2. Circular announcing the Opening of a New Branch.

BOSE T. V. CO. PVT. LTD.
62, Rash Behari Aveneue, Kolkata 700 009

Circular No. T/54/11 Dated : April 10, 2011

Dear Sir,

We are glad to announce that owing to the large increase in the volume of our business and increasing demand for our products, we have opened a new branch at 28, College Street, Kolkata-700 012 to meet the increasing demand of our customers in that area. The new branch will start operation from 15.4.11. Mr. A. K. Samanta, who was the Assistant Sales Manager in our Head Office has been appointed the Branch Manager of our new branch. With his long experience he will be able to manage this branch efficiently and supply the requirements of our customers.

We hope you will extend your partronage to our new branch.

Yours faithfully,
P. K. Patra
(General Manager)

SPECIMEN 3. Circular announcing the Shifting of Business to a More Convenient Place.

NEW INDIA ELECTRIC CO. LTD.
18, Strand Road, Kolkata 700 001

Circular No. E/98/11 Dated : June 16, 2011

Dear Sirs,

We are happy to announce that due to large expansion in the volume of our business, we are going to shift our business to 34, Lenin Sarani, Kolkata-700 013 with effect from 1st July, 2011.

The new site of the business would have enough space and comforts for our customers and visitors. We hope they will find it more convenient and pleasant.

Please note that the new telephone numbers of our address are 2624-9266 and 2624-9367.

We eargerly look forward to your visit in our new accommodation. With assurance of our best services,

Yours faithfully,
For New India Electric Co. Ltd.
J. N. Mukherjee
(Manager)

Specimen 4. Circular announcing the Appointment of a Sole Selling Agent.

IDEAL CHEMICAL INDUSTRIES PVT. LTD.

25 Park Street, Kolkata 700 016

Telephone No. 2458-2021

Circular No. C/212/11 Dated : May 25, 2011

Dear Sirs,

We have much pleasure to announce that Messrs. Dhar and Co. Ltd. of 27, Strand Road, Kolkata 700 001 has been appointed our Sole Selling Agent for the sale of our chemical products in West Bengal, Bihar and Orissa.

Sufficient stocks of large varieties are available with the sole-selling agent at catalogue prices.

We would request you to kindly place your orders through M/s Dhar and Co. Ltd.

We hope that our customers of the above States will be benefited by this new arrangment.

Yours faithfully,

For Ideal Chemical Industries Pvt. Ltd.

S. N. Sarkar

(Manager)

Specimen 5. Circular announcing the Admission of a New Partner.

DATTA AND ROY CO.

35 Netaji Subhas Road, Kolkata 700 001

Telephone No. 2486 5551

Circular No. D/R/11 Dated : 18th June, 2011

Dear Sirs,

We feel pleasure to announce that owing to large increase in the volume of our business, Sir P. R. Hazra has been admitted as a third partner in our partnership firm with effect from 1.7.11. Henceforth the name of our firm shall be 'Datta, Roy and Hazra Co.'

There will be no change in the line of business. This is for your information.

We hope that you will extend your co-operation and patronage as before.

Yours faithfully,

For Datta and Roy Co.

A. B. Datta

(Partner)

Specimen 6. Circular announcing the Increase in Listed Prices of the Products.

BENGAL TRADING CO. LTD.

(Manufacturer of Electrical Fixtures)

25, Bidhan Sarani, Kolkata 700 006

Telephone No. 2442 3300

Circular No. B/T/85/11 Dated : 25th January, 2011

Dear Sirs,

We regret to inform you that owing to sharp rise in the prices of imported raw materials, increase in wages and transport cost, the cost of production has gone up by more than ten percent. In the circumstances, we have been constrained to increase the prices of our products by ten percent without lowering the quality of the products.

Our new prices will come into effect from 1st February, 2011.

We hope you will appreciate our difficulties and continue to favour us with your valued support and co-operation as in the past.

Yours faithfully,
For Bengal Trading Co. Ltd.
S. K. Sengupta
(Manager)

SPECIMEN 7. Circular announcing the Termination of the Services of a Salesman and Appointment of a New One in his place.

NEW PHARMACEUTICAL CO. LTD.
15, Canning Street, Kolkata 700 001
Telephone No. 2484 4455

Circular No. P/65/11 Dated : 25th August, 2011

Dear Sir,

We regret to announce that due to some grave irregularities we have been compelled to terminate the services of Sri Banshinath Hati, the authorised salesman of our company, with effect from 20th August, 2011. He has no more any connection with our company. He has also no authority to accept any order and collect bills as a representative of our company.

We have appointed Sri Tapas Sikdar in place of Sri Hati. Sri Sikdar has been authorised to secure orders and collect bills on our behalf. The Identity Card containing his specimen signature issued by our company will prove his genuine identity.

We regret any inconvenience that you may suffer due to this change and hope to get your continued patronage.

Yours faithfully,
For New Pharmaceutical Co. Ltd.
P. N. Das
(Sales Manager)

SPECIMEN 8. Circular announcing the Admission of a New Partner in place of an Old Deceased Partner.

MUKHERJEE, CHATTERJEE AND CO.
3, Old Court House Street, Kolkata 700 001
Telephone No. 2682-3315

Circular No. MC/285/11 Dated : July 15, 2011

Dear Sirs,

We regret to inform you that our senior partner, Sri B. N. Mukherjee died on 30th June, 2011. Sri Mukherjee had been associated with our firm for the last thirty years. His death is a great loss to our firm. To fill in the vacancy caused by the death of Sri Mukherjee, we have agreed to admit his son Sri S. N. Mukherjee into the firm as new partner. Sri Mukherjee has been a Sales Manager of our firm for the last five years. He is young, energetic and fully conversant with the management of this firm. There will be no change in the name of the firm.

We trust that you will favour us with your confirmed support and sympathy as before.

Yours faithfully,

For Mukherjee, Chatterjee and Co.

C. S. Chatterjee

(Partner)

SPECIMEN 9. Circular announcing the Retirement of a Partner.

SEN, ROY AND CO.

24, Lenin Sarani, Kolkata 700 017

Telephone No. 2489-2022

Circular No. 5R/7N/11 Dated : July 30, 2011

Dear Sirs,

We regret to inform you that owing to ill health our senior partner, Sri M. S. Roy, retires from business with effect from today. Hence, we find it necessary to change the name of the firm from 'Sen, Roy and Co.' to 'Sen Brothers and Co.' Sri Roy had been associated with our firm since its inception and we shall no more get his valuable guidance.

The business, however, will be carried on at the same premises and there will be no change in the policy of the business. The capital position of the firm has not changed since the existing partners have introduced further capital into the business to meet the deficiency caused by the withdrawal of capital by Sri Roy.

We take this opportunity of thanking you for your valued patronage in the past and we hope that you will favour us with the same in future also.

Your faithfully,

For Sen, Roy and Co.

P. K. Sen

(Partner)

SPECIMEN 10. Circular announcing the Amalgamation of two Business Firms.

Circular No. 8B/5P/11 Dated : July 5, 2011

Dear Sir,

We have the pleasure to announce that, on and from the 25th July, 2011, our firms named 'Messrs. Basu and Co. Ltd.' and 'Messrs. Das and Co. Ltd.' so long carrying on business at 14, Rash Behari Avenue, Kolkata and at 19, Gariahat Road, Kolkata, respectively, have agreed to amalgamate. The name of the amalgamated frim will be as follows :

BASU AND DAS CO. LTD.

The business of the new firm will be carried on at 12, Shakespeare Sarani, Kolkata 700 030 to which all correspondence and communications after 25th July, 2011, may kindly be sent.

We hope that our customers will get more facilities from the amalgamated firm. We assure you of giving you better services.

Yours faithfully,

Basu and Co. Ltd.

Das and Co. Ltd.

(Now) Basu and Das Co. Ltd.

Specimen 11. Circular announcing the Purchase of a New Business.

49, Nutanganj Road,
Burdwan

Circular No. C/1/11

Dated : 25th July, 2011

Dear Sirs,

I have great pleasure in announcing that I have this day purchased from Sri L. Shaw the stationery business known as 'Modern Stores' and so long carried on by him at the above address. I intend to continue the business at the same address but under the style of :

BENGAL STORES

I woud like to assure you that in our new showroom you will have ample stocks of all varieties of stationery goods, and it will have an attractive new look. I hope the customers would be highly satisfied with the new arrangements. I would also like to assure that there will be no change in the business policy so long followed by Shri Shaw. It will be my earnest effort to render our customers the same satisfaction and quality of service as they enjoyed under the previous management. I hope the business will continue to receive the same support and patronage from you as before.

Please take note of my under mentioned signature which will be used in all future correspondence.

Specimen Signature:

Yours faithfully,
Pranab Bakshi

(*Pranab Bakshi*)

(Proprietor)

Specimen 12. Circular announcing the Death of a Partner.

Circular No. CK/19/11

126/1 B. B. C. Road,
Burdwan

Dated : 15th June, 2011

Dear Sirs,

We regret to announce that our senior parner Sri H. N. Sarkar expired on 14th June, 2011. Sri Sarkar has been associated with the firm since its inception and the loss of his valuable assistance will be felt by us for a long time. Hence, we find it necessary to change the name of the firm from 'Sarkar, Sen and Company' to 'Sen and Company'.

The business, however, will be carried on at the same address and on exactly the same principles as before.

We hope that the confidence you have so long reposed in the firm will be in no way affected by the death of Sri Sarkar.

Yours faithfully,
Sen and Co.
(Formerly Sarkar, Sen and Co.)

Specimen 13. Circular announcing the Conversion of a Partnership Firm into a Private Limited Company.

Circular No. CA/1/11

158, G. T. Road, Burdwan

Dated : 5th July, 2011

This is to announce that our business, so long carried on as a partnership, has been convered into a private limited company. It will now function under the name of—

MODERN CHEMICALS PRIVATE LTD.

This change has been necessitated by our demand for more capital. The increasing opportunities for expansion of our business has forced us to convert our firm into a private limited company so as to enable us to raise additional capital from the outside sources.

This structural change, however, will, in no way, affect our relationship with the old customers. We would like to assure you that there will be no change in our business policy and we shall endeavour to give our customers the same satisfaction and quality of service as before.

Yours faithfully,

Modern Chemicals (Pvt.) Ltd.

5.7 Drafting of Resolutions and Minutes

[A] **Definition of Resolution :** 'Resolution' is a motion which has been voted upon and passed in the meeting with or without amendments. It is the agreed decision of the meeting adopted unanimously or by a majority and recorded in the minutes as such. A resolution is the proposal after it has been voted upon and converted into the decision of the meeting.

[B] **Principles and Procedure of Drafting Resolutions :**

When a proposal is passed in a meeting, it is called a 'Resolution'. Drafting a resolution is an important task.

Some points should be remembered while drafting a resolution. These are mentioned below :

Firstly, the resolution should be such that the correct intention of the proposal is expressed.

Secondly, there should not be any vagueness or ambiguity in the wording of the resolution.

Thirdly, the resolution should be so worded that the meaning and purpose of the resolution should be understood in its true sense by the people concerned.

Fourthly, there should not be any scope for misinterpretation or any lacuna or loophole in the wording of the resolution.

Certain procedure should be followed while drafting a resolution. It is as follows :

In the first place the resolution may include some background on the basis of which the decision is taken.

Secondly, the resolution should be drafted in the past tense and in indirect narration.

Thirdly, all the points should be incorporated in the resolution in a systematic way.

[C] **Definition of Minutes :** 'Minute' is the official record of the proceedings and decisions of a meeting. It is prepared after the meeting from the notes of the proceedings taken during the meeting. It contains the summarised record of discussions at the meeting and the resolutions adopted therein. When it is confimed and signed by the chairman, it becomes the official record of the decisions of that body.

[D] **Importance of Minutes :** The activities of every organisation are guided by the decisions arrived at the meetings of that body. Unless these decisions are properly and completely recorded, it is not possible for the managers to remember the exact decisions taken or to implement them rightly. The main purpose of preparing and maintaining the minutes is to preserve a clear, concise and accurate record of the business transacted at a meeting. They constitute a permanent record of the decisions and actions of an organisation and serve as a reminder of the subjects dealt with and decisions reached on previous occasions.

The minute of one meeting is placed before the next meeting, as the first item of business, for confirmation. After confirmation, it is signed by the Chairman and then it becomes the official record of the proceedings and is acceptable in the Court of Law as legal evidence.

[E] **Principles and Rules of Drafting Minutes :** The minutes are the accurate and condensed official records of what have taken place at a meeting. Minutes should be drafted carefully so that nothing untrue is recorded. The Secretary of the organisation generally prepares a draft copy of the minutes and shows it to the Chairman for his suggestions and corrections. After the approval of him the minutes are finalised for presentation in the meeting for confirmation.

There are two forms in which the minutes can be presented. It can be presented either in the paragraph form or in the tabular form. In the paragraph form the minutes are written in terms of paragraphs. On the other hand, in the tabular form, the minutes are presented in the form of a table having suitable number of rows and columns.

The following rules should be followed while preparing the minutes :

1. There must be a heading which specifies the kind of the meeting with date, time and place.
2. The heading must be followed by the names of persons present in the meeting.
3. The name of the chairman of the meeting should be separately written.
4. The resolutions adopted at the meeting should be recorded serially. The names of the proposers and seconders of different motions should be mentioned. If there is voting on any proposal the nature of voting should be mentioned. If there is any note of dissent it should also be recorded.
5. A serial number and a short title should be attached to each paragraph of the minutes.
6. Whenever any reference is made to any letter or report, its date should be mentioned.
7. There should be space for the Chairman to sign at bottom on the right hand side of the minutes with the word 'confirmed'. The Secretary who prepares the minutes should sign on the left hand side at the bottom.

Below are given certain specimens of minutes of different types of meetings. From these specimens the students will get an idea regarding the drafting of minutes for various kinds of meetings.

1. Minutes of the First Board Meeting of a Public Limited Company.

IDEAL MANUFACTURERS CO. LTD.

Minutes of the First Meeting of the Board of Directors of the Company held at the Registered Office of the Company at 25, Fairlie Place, Kolkata-700 001 on Monday, the 18th April, 2011, at 3 p.m.

Present :

Mr. A. B. Mitra—Chairman
Mr. S. K. Sen—Director
Mr. T. N. Dasgupta—Director
Mr. D. B. Roy—Director
Mr. P. N. Bose—Director
Mr. K. S. Banerjee—Director
Mr. H. D. Singh—Secretary

Sl. No.	Subject	Details
1.	Chairman of the Meeting :	Mr. A. B. Mitra was unanimously elected to the Chair.
2.	Production of Documents :	The Secretary of the Company placed before the meeting, the Memorandum, the Articles of Association and the Certificate of Incorporation which were duly adopted.
3.	Appointment of First Directors :	The Secretary reported that all the directors present (being the persons named in the Articles as the first Directors) have signed the consent form and the agreement to take qualification shares. Their appointment as the first Directors were approved and recorded.
4.	Chairman of the Board :	It was resolved, "that Mr. A. B. Mitra be and is hereby, appointed the Chairman of the Board".
5.	Appointment of the Managing Directors :	Resolved "that Mr. T. N. Dasgupta be appointed the Managing Director of the Company and the necessary approval be obtained from the Central Government".
6.	Appointment of the Secretary :	It was resolved "that Mr. H. D. Singh be and is hereby appointed Secretary of the Company on a monthly salary of Rs. 30,000."
7.	Appointment of the Bankers :	It was resolved "that the State Bank of India, Fairlie Place Branch, be appointed the Bankers of the Company to be operated jointly by any two Directors".
8.	Appointed of the First Auditors :	Resolved "that Messrs. Sen and Roy Co. Chartered Accountants, be and are hereby appointed the first Auditors of the Company at a remuneration of Rs. 15,000 per annum'.
9.	Company's Seal :	The Secretary produced the specimen of the common seal of the Company which was duly adopted.
10.	Approval of the Draft Prospectus	The solicitor placed the Draft Prospectus which was approved.
11.	Quorum :	It was resolved "that the quorum for the Board Meeting be three".
12.	Next Meeting :	The Secretary was instructed to convene the next Board Meeting on 15.7.11
13.	Vote of Thanks :	The meeting ended with a hearty vote of thanks to the Chair.

Sd/ H. D. Singh (Secretary)
08.04.11

Sd/- A. B. Mitra (Chairman)
08.04.11

2. Minutes of the Proceedings of the Meeting of the Board of Directors of a Public Limited Company (Not being its First Board Meeting).

BENGAL ELECTRICAL WORKS LTD.

Minutes of the Tenth Board Meeting held at the Registered Office of the Company at 18, Strand Road, Kolkata-700 001 on Tuesday 19th April 2011 at 2 p.m.

Present :

Sri P. N. Roy—in the Chair

Sri K. P. Sen—Director

Sri M. S. Dutta—Director

Sri S. K. Basu—Director

Sri T. K. Mondal—Director

Sri S. P. Nag—Director

Sri A. K. Ghosh—Secretary

1. **Chairman :** Sri P. N. Roy, the Chairman of the Board took the Chair.
2. **Confirmation of the Minutes :** The minutes of the Ninth Board Meeting held on 20.12.10 were read out, and confirmed.
3. **Transfer of Shares :** Resolved "that the shares numbering 250 to 300 be transferred from Mr. R. S. Ghatak to Mr. A. K. Sengupta on the basis of the Transfer Deed executed by Mr. R. S. Ghatak."
4. **Bills for Payment :** The bills produced by the Secretary were considered and passed for payment.
5. **Dividend :** Resolved "that a dividend @ 15% on Equity Shares be recommended to the Annual General Meeting".
6. **Appointment of Personnel Manager :** It was resolved "that a Personnel Manager be appointed on a salary of Rs. 15,000/- per month as per the company rules".
7. **Annual General Meeting :** Resolved "that the Annual General Meeting of the Company be held on 30th June, 2011 at the Registered Office of the Company at 4 p.m. and that the Secretary be authorised to take necessary action in the matter".
8. **Next Board Meeting :** The date of the next Board Meeting was fixed on 20.8.11 at 3 p.m.
9. **Vote of Thanks :** There being no other business, the meeting ended with a vote of thanks to the Chair.

Sd/- A. K. Ghosh	Sd/- P. N. Roy
(Secretary)	(Secretary)
19.04.11	19.04.11

3. Minutes of the Annual General Meeting of a Public Limited Company

BENGAL TRADING CO. LTD.

Regd. Office : 30, Chowringhee Road, Kolkata 700 013

Minutes of the Tenth Annual General Meeting of the Company held at the Registered Office of the Company on Wednesday, 29th June, 2011 at 3 p.m.

Directors Present :

Mr. A. S. Majumder, the Chairman of the Company

Mr. S. B. Patra

Mr. D. K. Chowdhury

Mr. S. K. Sadhu

Mr. A. P. Mallick and

Mr. P. R. Dey (Managing Director)

Members Present :

45 members whose signatures appear in the Attendance Register were present in the meeting.

Mr. T. S. Panda, the Auditor, and Mr. C. R. Samanta, the Legal Adviser were present on invitation.

1. **Chairman :** Mr. A. S. Majumder, the Chairman of the Board took the Chair.
2. **Notice :** The Secretary read out the notice convening the meeting.
3. **Minutes of the last Meeting :** The minutes of the last Annual General Meeting were read and confirmed.
4. **Chairman's Speech :** The Chairman delivered a speech about the satisfactory achievements of the Company and referred to its good prospects.
5. **Directors' Report :** The Secretary read out the Directors' Report.
6. **Auditor's Report :** Mr. T. S. Pande, the Auditor of the Company read out his report upon the Profit and Loss Accounts and the Balance Sheet of the Company.
7. **Adoption of Directors' Report and Account :** It was resolved "that the Directors' Report together with the audited Profit and Loss Accounts for the year ended 31.03.11 and the Balance Sheet as at that date, the Auditor's Report thereon, now placed before the meeting be and are hereby approved and adopted". It was proposed by Mr. S. K. Sadhu and seconded by Mr. P. R. Dey. The resolution was passed by 35 to 10 votes.
8. **Declaration of Dividend :** Resolved "that as recommended by the Board, a dividend @ 10% on Equity Shares, free of income tax be and are hereby declared for the year ended 31.3.11." It was proposed by Mr. D. K. Chowdhury and seconded by Mr. S. K. Sadhu. The resolution was passed unanimously.
9. **Appointment of Directors :** It was resolved "that Mr. S. B. Patra and Mr. A. P. Mallick retiring by rotation, being eligible for re-election, be and are hereby re-elected the Directors of the Company". Their names were proposed by Mr. A. K. Dhar and seconded by Mr. S. P. Ghosh. The resolution was passed by 40 votes *nem. con.*, i.e., nobody contradicting. Two members abstained from voting.
10. **Appointment of Auditors :** It was resolved "that Mr. T. S. Pande, be and is hereby re-appointed the Auditor of the Company for Rs. 15,000 per annum".
11. **Vote of Thanks :** The meeting concluded with a vote of thanks to the Chairman, Directors, Secretary and the Staff of the Company for their services during the last year.

Sd/- N. K. Dutta	Sd/- A. S. Majumder
(Secretary)	(Chairman)
29.06.11	29.06.11

4. Minutes of the Statutory Meeting of a Public Limited Company.

PHILIPS COMPANY LTD.

Regd. Office : 652, Diamond Harbour Road, Kolkata 700 016

Minutes of the proceedings of the Statutory Meeting of the Company held at its Registered Office on Thursday, 14th July, 2011 at 3 p.m.

Present :

Mr. P. R. Chakraborty—Chairman
Mr. S. K. Biswas—Director
Mr. N. C. Ghosh—Director
Mr. M. L. Sen—Director
Mr. T. S. Mukherjee—Director
Mr. S. D. Sarma—Secretary
and 50 other members whose names appear in the Attendance Register.

1. **Chairman :** Mr. P. R. Chakraborty, the Chairman of the Board, took the Chair.
2. **Notice of the Meeting :** The Secretary read out the notice convening the meeting.
3. **Statutory Report :** The Statutory Report dated 30.6.11, copies of which were circulated to the members showing the general position of the Company, were taken as read. The Chairman dealt with the questions raised by the members. On the motion of the Chairman and seconded by Mr. P. Rakshit, it was resolved, "that the Statutory Report be and is hereby approved and adopted".
4. **Vote of Thanks :** There being no other business, the meeting ended with a vote of thanks to the Chair.

Sd/- S. D. Sarma	Sd/- P. R. Chakraborty
(Secretary)	(Chairman)
14.07.11	14.07.11

5. Minutes of the Extra-ordinary General Meeting of a Public Limited Company.

MARCONI ELECTRICALS LTD.

Regd. Office : 18, Brabourne Road, Kolkata 700 001

Minutes of the proceedings of the Extra-ordinary General Meeting of the Company held at the Registered Office of the Company on Friday, 15th July, 2011 at 3 p.m.

Present :

Mr. R. K. Datta—Chairman
Mr. S. K. Banerjee—Director
Mr. P. K. Sarkar—Director
Mr. T. C. Roy—Director
Mr. B. C. Laha—Director
Mr. D. K. Sengupta—Director
Mr. M. S. Koner—Secretary
and 50 other members whose names appear in the Attendance Book.

1. **Chairman :** Mr. R. K. Datta, the Chairman of the Board took the Chair.
2. **Notice :** The Secretary read out the notice convening the meeting.
3. **Chirman's Speech :** The Chairman addressed the meeting mentioning the purpose of the meeting.

4. **Special Resolution :** On a motion of the Chairman and seconded by Mr. P. K. Sarkar, the following Special Resolution was passed unanimously.

   "That subject to the approval of the Central Government under Section 21 of the Companies Act, 1956, the name of the Company be changed from Marconic Electricals Ltd. To New India Electric Co. Ltd."

5. **Vote of Thanks :** The meeting ended with a vote of thanks to the Chair.

Sd/- M. S. Koner	Sd/- R. K. Datta
(Secretary)	(Chairman)
15.07.11	15.07.11

6. **Minutes of the Annual General Meeting of a Private Limited Company.**

ROY AND DAS COMPANY PVT. LIMITED

S. N. Banerjee Road, Kolkata 700 014

Telephone No. 2350 3416

Fax No. 091 033 2350 3416

Date : 20.05.11

MINUTES

Minutes of the 20th Annual General Meeting of Roy and Das Co. (P) Ltd. held on Saturday, the 18th June, 2011 at 3 p.m. at the Registered Office of the Company.

Members Present :

(i) Shri P. N. Rakshit ......Chairman

(ii) Shri V. K. Samanta ...... Director

(iii) Shri R. S. Chowdhury ...... Director

(iv) Shri S. N. Datta ...... Director

(v) Shri T. K. Barua ...... Director

(vi) Shri M. M. Tiwari ...... Secretary

(vii) Shri B. N. Ghatak ...... Auditor

and 150 other Shareholders whose signatures appear in the Attendance Register, were present in the meeting. Shri P. N. Rakshit took the chair.

1. **Notice of the Meeting :** The Secretary read the notice convening the meeting.
2. **Confirmation of the Minutes of the last Annual General Meeting :** The minutes of the last Annual General Meeting held on 15.05.10 was read out by the Secretary and was confirmed by the meeting and signed by the Chairman.
3. **Presentation of the Audited Accounts for the year 2010-11 :** Resolved that the Directors' Report and Accounts for the year 2010-11 as audited and certified by the Company's, auditor be, and is hereby adopted.
4. **Declaration of Dividend :** On the motion of the Chairman and seconded by Sri S. K. Pandey, it was resolved that 10% dividend on Equity Shares be declared and paid within 42 days from the date of declaration of the dividend to those Shareholders whose names appear in the Register of Members as on 31.03.11.
5. **Re-appointment of a Director Retiring by Rotation :** Resolved that Shri V. K. Samanta, a Director retiring by rotation be, and he is hereby re-elected and re-appointed a Director of the Company.

6. **Appointment of the Auditor :** On the motion moved by Shri M. C. Barman and seconded by Shri T. K. Nandi it was resolved that M/s Majumder, Chatterjee and Co., Chartered Accountants be appointed the Auditors of the Company to hold office till the conclusion of the the next Annual General Meeting. Their remuneration has been fixed for Rs. 15,000.
7. **Issue of Shares :** Resolved that 1,000 Equity Shares of Rs. 100 each be issued at a premium of Rs. 5 per Share to collect fund for the Company.
8. **Vote of Thanks :** The meeting ended at 5·30 p.m. with a hearty vote of thanks to the Chair.

Sd/ M. M. Tiwari (Secretary) | Sd/- P. N. Rakshit (Chairman)

7. Minutes of the Annual General Meeting of a Club

BURDWAN SPORTING CLUB

108, J. N. Roy Road, Burdwan

Minutes of the proceedings of the 15th Annual General Meeting of the Burdwan Sporting Club held on Friday, the 15th January, 2011, at the Club premises at 4 p.m.

Present :

Mr. R. K. Mondal—Chairman

Mr. L. S. Bhandari—
Mr. P. N. Talukdar—
Mr. A. K. Singh
Mr. B. N. Konar
Mr. S. N. Tewari
} Members, Managing Committee

Mr. T. K. Sharma—Honorary General Secretary

and 30 members whose names appear in a separate sheet appended at the end of the minutes.

1. **Chairman :** Mr. R. K. Mondal was in the Chair.
2. **Notice of the Meeting :** The notice convening the meeting was read by the Secretary.
3. **Confirmation of the Minutes :** The minutes of the last Annual General Meeting were read, approved and signed by the Chairman.
4. **Consideration of the Secretary's Report :** The Secretary placed before the meeting the Annual Report of the Club. After discussion, the report was unanimously adopted.
5. **Audited Accounts and the Auditors' Report :** The audited Accounts of the Club for the year ending 31st December 2010 were placed before the meeting and, after consideration, the audited Accounts and the Auditors' Report were adopted.
6. **Annual Budget Estimates :** The Annual Budget Estimates for the year ending 31.12.11 were placed and adopted.
7. **Election of the Executive Committee :** The members of the Executive Committee for 2011 were elected unanimously as follows :
   [i] On the motion of Shri P. N. Dhar and seconded by Shri K. C. Das, Shri M. R. Sethia was elected the President of the Club.
   [ii] Shri T. N. Sardar, Shri R. P. Chowdhury, Shri N. K. Pathak, Shri A. L. Bhandari and Shri R. K. Biswas were the elected members of the Executive Committee of the Club.

8. **Appointment of the Auditors :** On the motion of Shri R. P. Chowdhury and seconded by Shri N. K. Pathak, Messrs Mukherjee, Chatterjee and Co., Chartered Accountants, were re-appointed Auditors of the Club for the year 2010-11 on a remuneration of Rs. 5,000 p.a.
9. **Vote of Thanks :** The meeting terminated with a vote of thanks to the Chair.

Sd/- T. K. Sharma	Sd/- R. K. Mondal
(Hony. Gen Secretary)	(Chairman)
15.01.11	15.01.11

8. **Minutes of the Proceedings of the Annual General Meeting of a Co-operative Society.**

BURDWAN CO-OPERATIVE CREDIT SOCIETY

55, G. R. Road, Burdwan

Minutes of the proceedings of the 10th Annual General Meeting of the Burdwan Co-operative Credit Society held at its Registered Office on Sunday, the 15th May, 2011 at 5 p.m.

Present :

Shri K. P. Singha Roy—Chairman

Shri L. S. Banerjee—Director

Shri M. N. Modak—Director

Shri P. C. Chhetri—Director

Shri G. P. Pande—Director

Shri R. N. Maitra—Director

Shri S. P. Sengupta—Secretary

and 50 other members whose names appear in a separate sheet appended at the end of the minutes.

1. **Chairman :** Shri K. P. Singh Roy presided over the meeting.
2. **Notice of the Meeting :** The Secretary read out the notice convening the meeting.
3. **Confirmation of Minutes :** The minutes of the proceedings of the last Annual General Meeting were read, approved and signed by the Chairman.
4. **Consideration of the Secretary's Report :** The Secretary placed before the meeting the Annual Report of the Society during the year ended 31st March, 2011. After discussion, the report was unanimously adopted.
5. **Annual Accounts and the Auditor's Report :** The Audited Accounts and the Auditor's Report were placed before the meeting and considered. It was resolved that the Audited Accounts and the Auditor's Report be adopted.
6. **Declaration of Dividend :** On the the motion of Shri M. N. Modak and seconded by A. B. Samaddar, it was resolved that a dividend of 10% be declared on the paid-up Shares.
7. **Borrowings :** "Resolved that the Board be and it is hereby authorised to raise a loan not exceeding Rs. 1·50 lakhs from the Central Co-operative Bank to meet the demands for loans and advances from the members."
8. **Annual Budget :** The Annual Budget for the year 2011-12 was placed and adopted.

9. **Election of the Directors :** It was unanimously resolved that the following three members be elected the Directors in place of Shri R. N. Maitra, Shri G. P. Pande and Shri L. S. Banerjee :

[i] Shri T. S. Khanna

[ii] Shri K. N. Majumder

[iii] Shri N. P. Sikdar

10. **Vote of Thanks :** The meeting was terminated with a vote of thanks to the Chair.

Sd/- S. P. Sengupta	Sd/- K. P. Singh Roy
[Secretary]	[Chairman]
15.05.11	15.05.11

5.8 Drafting of Reports

[A] Definition of Report : A 'Report' may be defined as a precise and systematic statement of facts relating to a particular subject, prepared by a person or a group of persons after proper investigation and enquiry, and submitted to the person or body appointing the person or the group of persons with or without recommendations. Various kinds of reports have to be prepared in the office for different purposes. It is a part of secretarial function. A secretary is supposed to be an expert in drafting reports.

[B] Types of Report : Reports may be classified under the following heads :

1. **Formal Report :** This report is to be prepared according to the requirements of a Statute or Order and presented in accordance with the prescribed procedure.
2. **Informal Report :** An informal report, on the other hand, does not follow any prescribed form or procedure. It is usually written in the letter form. This report normally contains the recommendation or opinion of the person preparing the report.
3. **Statutory Report :** Such reports are prepared and presented in accordance with the provisions of some law. The form and procedure of preparation and submission of these reports are laid down in the Statutes. For instance, according to the Indian Companies Act, the Directors and Secretary of a company are required to submit the following reports to the Shareholders at the Statutory Meeting and Annual General Meeting :

   (i) Statutory Report, (ii) Annual Report of the Directors, (iii) the Auditor's Report etc.
4. **Routine Report :** It is prepared only with the facts and statistics relating to various aspects of the business for the information of the management body at regular intervals. Production Report, Report of the Auditor, Reports of the Standing Committees, etc. are some examples of routine reports. This report does not normally bear any opinion or recommendation of the writer. It is prepared as a part of routine work.
5. **Special Report :** Such report is related to some specific matters which demand special investigation on special occasion. A report on an accident is an example of a special report. It is prepared as non-routine matters. A Special or Adhoc Committee or Sub-committee appointed for a particular purpose (e.g., Enquiry Committee) submits a special report.
6. **Privileged Report :** Such reports can claim privilege of law. These are reports which are protected from legal action for defamation provided the reports are fair and accurate. Reports of the proceedings of Parliament are examples of this kind.

[C] Style of Drafing A Report :

There cannot be a definite style of writing a report. The style depends on the nature of the report. The main purpose of a report is to enable the management authority to know the facts and take suitable decision or action based on the conclusions and recommendations. In order to achieve this purpose, the report must be written in correct form and in a clear, concise and logical manner. In fact, there are some general principles or guidelines which are followed in drafting a report so that the characteristics of a good report are maintained.

- **Principal Characteristics of a Good Report :**

The principal characteristics of a good report are discussed below :

1. **Heading or Title :** Every report should contain a heading or title indicating the subject-matter of the report.
2. **Address :** A report must contain the name and designation of the person to whom it is being submitted.
3. **Table of the Contents :** Lengthy reports generally contain a list of topics including the list of enclosures.
4. **Body :** It is the main part of the report. It should be divided into some suitable paragraphs each dealing with a particular section. The body is usually divided into four sections—[i] Introduction, i.e., brief analysis of the subject, [ii] Development or Findings, i.e., presentation of facts and data with comments thereon, [iii] Conclusion drawn by the writer therefrom, and [iv] Recommendations i.e., concrete suggestions made by the writer based on the conclusions.
5. **Language :** The language of the report should be very simple, clear and unambiguous so that it can be easily understood. Use of jargons and technical terms should be avoided as far as possible.
6. **Art :** Report-writing is an art. The points in a report should be written in logical sequence, step by step, and not in a haphazard manner.
7. **Accuracy :** The data presented should be accurate and reliable.
8. **Brevity :** A report shall not be unnecessarily long so that the patience of the reader is lost. But at the same time, a report must be complete. A report is not an essay.
9. **Positivity :** Positive statement should be made instead of negative one as far as possible. For example, it is better to say what should be done and not what should not be done.
10. **Recommendations :** The conclusions and recommendations should be impartial and based on facts.
11. **Form :** A report must be in the proper form. Sometimes there are statutory forms to follow.
12. **Presentation :** A report needs an attractive presentation and a logical order. It depends on the quality of typing or printing and also the quality of paper used. Readability is the key-note of a report.
13. **Salutation :** A complementary term like Dear Sir/Madam etc. should be used.
14. **Complementary Close :** Complementary close like 'Yours faithfully', 'Yours truly' etc. should be mentioned.
15. **Signature :** A report must be dated and signed by the person making the report.

[D] Presentation of a Report :

A report should be properly presented. It means that a report is to be produced in an attractive as well as useful manner. Presentation of a report depends on its nature. An informal report produced by the Secretary can be presented in an ordinary letter-head or memo sheet normally used in the office. The Annual Report of a small private company is generally typed out or cyclostyled. Public companies having a large number of members generally get the reports printed. Big and prestigious companies present the Annual Reports on costly papers using colours with designs and decorations. Government reports are presented in the form of printed books.

[E] Specimen of Drafting of Some Common Type of Reports :

1. Report on standardisation of office furniture, forms and stationery.

Dated : 5th July, 2011

To
The Chairman,
Board of Directors,
The National Electric Co. Ltd.
15, College Street, Kolkata 700 012

Sub : Standardisation of Furniture, Forms and Stationery

Dear Sir,

As directed by you, I have carefully investigated about the desirability of standardisation of furniture, forms and stationery in our office and I beg to submit my report on this issue.

Standardisation of office furniture, if properly planned, can save space to a large extent. Standardisation along with centralised selection and purchase, will mean lower price owing to bulk purchase.

Standardisation of forms such as notice form, invoice form, proxy form, etc. will help the office staff to do their work more quickly and accurately. It will reduce the cost of printing and increase efficiency and output.

Standardisation of stationery such as paper, pen, pencil, pins, ink, carbon paper, clip, envelopes, etc. will bring down the cost, improve efficiency of the staff and eliminate wastage.

Under the circumstances stated above, I would suggest to introduce standardisation in our office and request you to get an early approval of the Board.

Yours faithfully,
For the National Electric Co. Ltd.
P. N. Ganguly
(Secretary)

2. Report on mechanisation of office services.

Dated : 10th November, 2011

To
The Chairman,
Board of Directors,
Kalyani Electrical Works Ltd.
28, Chittaranjan Avenue, Kolkata 700 013

Re : Report on the Mechanisation of Office Services

Dear Sir,

As per your instruction, I have thoroughly investigated into the issue of the proposed mechanisation of our office services and I beg to submit the following report :

As you are aware, there is a tendency in all big concerns to replace manual labour by machine on account of some obvious advantages. Our company, because of the tremendous expansion in recent times, is facing the serious problem of tackling the increasing volume of work in the departments. In some of the departments, particularly in the Accounts and Mailing Departments, the staff are over-worked resulting in errors and omissions. Mechanisation increases the output of the workers and thus it enhances the efficiency of the employees. It relieves them from the monotony of office work. It not only saves labour and time but also results in prompt service. The customers and the public in general may also enjoy the benefits of mechanisation.

There is a great scope for mechnisation of Accounts Department with the introduction of modern machines such as Computer, Billing Machine, Adding Machine, Calculating Machine, etc. Photo copier may be used for making copies of various documents. Letter-opening Machine, Folding and Inserting Machine, Franking Machine, Addressograph and Dictaphone may be profitably employed in our mailing section. Mechanisation will reduce cost, bring accuracy and speed. This will also enhance goodwill and reputation of our company.

Of course, mechanisation is not an unmixed blessing. The main problem that we shall have to face is that a good amount of initial capital will be needed which may not be available from our own resources. Moreover, the introduction of mechanisation will surely make some of our staff surplus resulting in an adverse impact on employees. It may ultimately invite troubles from the Workers' Union. Training to the employees would also be essential.

I believe that my observations expressed above will convince you of the necessity of mechanisation in our office and will help you to arrive at a decision in this regard.

Yours faithfully,
For Kalyani Electrical Works Ltd.
S. C. Dhar (Secretary)

3. Report on the damage caused by fire to the factory.

Dated : 15th July, 2011

To
The Managing Director,
Bengal Chemical Works Ltd.
15, Princep Street, Kolkata 700 013

Sub : Damage caused by Fire to the Factory

Dear Sir,

A serious fire broke out in our factory at 6, Camac Street, Kolkata-700 016 at about 6 p.m. on 13th July, 2011. Immediately all possible and effective measures were adopted to check the fire from further spreading. As soon as the fire was noticed by our Security Officer, he informed the Fire Brigade about the accident. It took two hours to bring the fire completely under control. I rushed to the spot at 8 p.m. and informed the matter to the local police for investigation. I have also sent the message to the Insurance Company in writing for an early inspection.

The fire caused an extensive damage to our finished products and raw materials of about Rs. 2,50,000. Moreover, stocks valued at Rs. 50,000 were completely burnt. Furthermore, some new machineries have been severely damaged in our production department.

In my estimate, the re-building and re-furnishing of the rooms damaged by fire will take about two weeks. Alternative arrangements will have to be made to carry on the business during this period. I would, therefore, suggest that the factory office may be temporarily accommodated in the Time-keeper's room and some office furniture may be loaned from the Head Office to carry on the work. As the tool shed and store room have been partly damaged, production work can go on there in the undamaged portion during the re-building of the other part.

I hope the information and suggestions contained in this report will be found sufficient to enable you to come to a decision in the matter.

Thanking you,

Yours faithfully,
For Bengal Chemical Works Ltd.
D. N. Chatterjee
(Secretary)

4. Report to the Board of Directors about the location of a new showroom proposed to be opened by a company.

Dated : 15th September, 2011

To
The Directors,
National Trading Co. Ltd.
10, Chowranghee Road, Kolkata 700 037

Dear Sirs,

As instructed by you, I have the honour to submit below a report on the selection of a suitable site for the new showroom proposed to be opened by our company.

I visited a number of sites shown by our reputed agents. Of these sites, I found the premises at 25, Lenin Sarani, Kolkata, as the most desirable site of our proposed showroom. Generally several factors; such as situation, accommodation, amenities, transport facilities, rent, etc. should be considered in selecting the location of a showroom. The above-stated premises, in my view, satisfies all the essential conditions of an ideal site.

Firstly, the site for the showroom is excellent as it would be convenient both for the people of North Kolkata, South Kolkata, and Central Kolkata, for it is situated just at the heart of the city. This site is also on the bus and tram routes and the customers need not walk to reach the proposed showroom, the tram-bus stops being near the gate of the proposed site. The neighbourhood is quite free from noise, dust, smoke and other nuisance.

Secondly, the floor-space is quite sufficient for our purpose and for future expansion. There is sufficient arrangement for water, lighting, ventilation, bathroom, lavatory, etc.

Thirdly, the rent (Rs. 15,000/- per month) demanded by the landlord seems to be moderate considering the importance of the locality and the space available.

I would, therefore, recommend that the above-mentioned site for the location of a new showroom should be approved by the Board.

Yours faithfully,
For National Trading Co. Ltd.
R. Goswami
(Secretary)

5. Report to the Directors on the agitation of workers for a higher percentage of bonus and threatened strike by them.

Dated : 15th June, 2011

To

The Board of Directors,
Ideal Engineering Works Ltd.
35, G. T. Road, Howrah

Dear Sirs,

I beg to submit below a report on the agitation by the workers for a higher percentage of bonus and their decision to go on a strike if their demand is not met by the end of this month.

As you are aware, according to the agreement with the Workers' Union signed in May, 2009, we have been paying bonus to the workmen at the rate of 15% during the last two years. The Agreement expired in May, 2011. On 3rd June last, the Workers' Union submitted a Charter of Demands for our consideration, including therein a demand for bonus at the rate of 20% for the year 2010-11.

The leaders of the Workers' Union have argued that since the sales of the company have increased during the current year by more than 25%, the workers are entitled to share the increased profit earned by the company. They have further stated that if the legitimate demand of the workers is not met within 30 days from the date of their submission of Charter of Demands, the workers would be compelled to resort to go on a strike till their demand is fulfilled.

In course of my discussion with the union leaders, I have said that since the company's Profit and Loss Account has not yet been audited, it will not be possible for the company to offer any bonus to the workers at present. However, I have assured them that as soon as the company's Final Accounts are audited, the Directors will definitely consider their demand, as they have done in the previous years.

I shall be obliged if you kindly let me know your opinion on the matter, so that I can have further talks with the Workers' Union to the benefit of the company

Yours faithfully,
For Ideal Engineering Works Ltd.
M. P. Samanta
(Secretary)

6. Reort on the grievances of the employees e.g., lack of accommodation, poor lighting, insufficient ventilation, unhealthy surrounding, canteen problems and recommending measures to be taken to remove the grievances.

Dated : 16th October, 2011

To

The Chairman,
Board of Directors,
Bengal Trading Co. Ltd.
25, Chittaranjan Avenue, Kolkata 700 013

Sub : Report on the Grievances of the Employees

Dear Sir,

As directed by you, I have investigated into the causes of the grievances of our employees and now I submit my report for your kind perusal.

The long-standing grievances of the employees include the following :

[i] **Lack of adequate accommodation :** In fact, there is an acute shortage of accommodation in some of our departments. The Accounts Department and Type Department should be provided with more space. For this purpose, I suggest that these two departments should be shifted to a more spacious room.

[ii] **Poor lighting :** The lighting arrangement of the building is old-fashioned. The employees in the office really feel much difficulty in performing their work. Lighting problem may be solved through the arrangement of more artificial lighting and colour conditioning.

[iii] **Insufficient ventilation :** Ventilation is a common problem. Free movement of fresh air is almost impossible in this crowded area. To solve this problem, air-cooler machines are to be set up.

[iv] **Unhealthy surroundings :** The unhealthy surroundings of the office room are responsible for poor output of office work. Our Care-taker should be advised to take more care on the cleaning of office premises regularly.

[v] **Canteen problems :** The employees have an acute complain about the poor quality of food served by the canteen. To solve this problem, the Staff Welfare Officer may be instructed to look into the matter and to arrange better supply of quality food to the employees at competitive prices.

I hope that the above report will help you to arrive at a decision.

Yours faithfully,
For Bengal Trading Co. Ltd.
K. C. Das
(Secretary)

7. Report on an accident caused by a collapse of a storage-shed in a factory.

Dated 5th June, 2011

To
The Managing Director,
Sen and Roy Co. Ltd.
25, College Street, Kolkata 700 009

Sub : Collapse of a Storage-shed in the Factory

Dear Sir,

As per your assignment, I do hereby submit my report on the accident caused by the collapse of a storage-shed in the factory killing three employees.

On receipt of your instruction on the 25th May, 2011, I personally inspected the spot of the accident which happened exactly at 2 p.m. on the 20th May, 2011. At that time a gale was passing with high speed resulting in throwing down the asbestos sheds of the storage-shed. Two iron beams along with asbestos sheets fell suddenly on the workers who were working just under the shed and they became the victims of the accident. It occurred so suddenly that they did not get any scope to save themselves.

The names of the three workers are Shri Mahesh Das aged 42 years, Shri Pannalal Goswami aged 48 years and Shri Atmaram Sahani aged about 52 years. They were clerical staff of the Stores Department. They were very sincere and experienced employees of our organisation and our company is certainly going to be deprived of their valuable services.

I met the members of the deceased employees who were paid Rs. 1,00,000 each immediately.

I would like to mention here that we cannot avoid our responsibility in the unfortunate accident because of improper maintenance of the roofing for a long period. So, considering the point of safety and security of men and materials, it is necessary to undertake the repairing work of the storage-shed immediately.

Under the circumstances, I would request your kindself to look into the matter sympathetically and to render much needed generous financial help to the ill-fated families of the deceased.

Yours faithfully,
R. B. Poddar
(Secretary)

8. Report on raising additional capital for financing extension and schemes of rationalisation.

Dated : 5th December, 2011

To
The Chairman,
Board of Directors,
Unique Cloth Mills Ltd.
15, Central Avenue, Kolkata 700 013

Dear Sir,

As per your instruction I submit below the report on the necessity as well as the means of raising additional capital for our company.

As you are aware, during the last several years the demand for cloth in our country has been steadily increasing and it will continue further. At the same time, there is a growing foreign market for India-made cloth. It calls for immediate extension of the scale of our production.

Furthermore, most of our machines have become too old and many of them should be replaced by modern machines. Many new cloth mills have been recently established. They use the modern machines and can produce cloth at a cheaper cost than the old mills like ours. Naturally, the market for our commodity has become more complicated and compeitive. Moreover, the new machines can produce in large quantities resulting in reduction in the cost of production.

To implement the proposed schemes of extension and rationalisation, the company would require about Rs. 2,00,000 of additional capital. This capital may be raised by fresh issue of 2,000 Equity Shares of Rs. 100 each.

I trust that my report will help you to arrive at a decision.

Yours faithfully,
T. S. Nandy
(Secretary)

9. Report on the recent trend of sales and immediate need for an advertising campaign.

Dated : 10th July, 2011

To
The Chairman,
Board of Directors,
Chatterjee and Mukherjee Co. Ltd.
27, Sadar Ghat Road, Burdwan

Sub : Advertising Campaign

Dear Sir,

As directed by you, I have thoroughly investigated into the causes of the recent decline in the sales of our products.

The principal reason for their decline is the growing competition from several rival companies. Our products enjoy a good reputation in the market and they are in no way inferior to other rival products. Our prices are also competitive. But we lack in one thing which today is one of the most vital aspects of achieving success in business. That thing is 'publicity'. Constant publicity in favour of our products through advertisement is the only way to attract the customers spread throughout the country. Hence, a network of sales campaign through advertisement is now the need of our products.

I would, therefore, suggest to arrange for an extensive advertising campaign in favour of our products and to contact a reputed Advertising Agency immediately for this purpose.

I trust that this report will convince you about the necessity of undertaking immediately an advertising campaign to boost up the sale of our products.

Thanking you,

Yours faithfully,
For Chatterjee and Mukherjee Co. Ltd.
A. B. Patra
(Secretary)

10. Report on the defects in the routine work of the office of a company.

Dated : 15th July, 2011

To
The Managing Director,
Raniganj Paper Mills Ltd.
85, Raniganj, Burdwan.

Dear Sir,

After joining this office on 01.01.11 I have found some major defects existing in the routine work of the office for a long time. I feel that unless some effective steps are taken immediately to remove these defects, the goodwill of the company will be adversely affected. I, therefore, like to point out some of the defects for your information and necessary action :

[i] **Lack of punctuality :** The majority members of the staff are unpunctual in their attendance and departure. They usually come late and leave the office early. This practice has seriously lowered the efficieny of the staff and the output of work. In order to remove this defect, I suggest that the Attendance Registers should be kept in the room of the responsible officers. The staff should be instructed to sign in their presence at the time of both arrival and departure.

[ii] **Allowing the visitors on working desks :** Often it is found that the visitors. whether they have any business or not, are allowed to stay on the working desks. This practice results in gossiping and interference with the office work. I would suggest that the visitors should stay in the Visitors' Room.

[iii] **Low standard of efficiency :** A good number of members of our staff are ill-trained and inefficient. That is primarily the result of defective mode of recruitment. Secondly, postings and promotions, in most cases, have not been made on the basis of merit and experience. It is very surprising that the supervisor of the Filing Department knows nothing of the modern filing system.

[iv] **Carelessness :** A considerable number of the staff are careless and irresponsible, even in the performance of their allotted duties. The typist, for example, does not even type important letters. So, I suggest that the standard of supervision of the work of the office should be improved.

To conclude, the major defects in the office routine work enumerated above should be carefully considered and adequate measures must be taken to remove them.

Yours faithfully,
For Raniganj Paper Mills Ltd.
M. K. Tarafdar
(Secretary)

11. Report for consideration of the Board to focus on the following : Punctuality and regularity in office work, improving office output, minimum over-time expenses, continuing canteen grievances, recruitment and promotion methods.

Dated : 4th September, 2011

To
The Board of Directors,
Arun and Tarun Co. Ltd.
42, B. T. Road; Kolkata 700 002

Dear Sirs,

With reference to your enquiry vide letter No. EN/217 dated the 10th July, 2011, I beg to submit the following report for your kind consideration :

1. **Punctuality and regularity in attendance :** Due to sincere and constant efforts on the part of the management authority for improvement of the working conditions of the office, the punctuality and regularity of the office staff has been steadily improving. As the employees are getting two days' holiday in a week as against one day previously, they do not feel it desirable to be absent. Apart from that, the imposition of strict rule of making late attendance for 15 minutes for three days in a week amounts to one day's absence has made the employees more punctual.
2. **Improvement of office output :** Because of the punctuality and regularity in attendance of the employees and introduction of bonus plan based on individual efficiency, the office output has rapidly gone up.
3. **Minimum overtime expense :** On account of regularity in the staff's attendance it has now been convenient to allocate their duties beforehand and the employees are, therefore, aware of the work they have to perform within the specified time. Hence, the day-to-day work of the office never remains unfinished. As a result, the overtime has become minimum.
4. **Canteen grievances :** The continuous increase in the prices of foodgrains, vegetables and non-vegetable commodities has made it impossible to supply food of sufficient quantity to the employees at concessional price. So, their grievances regarding canteen are continuing.
5. **Grievances regarding recruitment and promotion :** Though sufficient improvements have been made on different aspects, yet our old method of recruitment and promotion of the staff has remained unchanged. Most of the employees are of the opinion that the promotion must be considered on the basis of efficiency and experiences. So, there is still a discontent among the employees regarding the method of recruitment and promotion.

To conclude, the defects as mentioned in items 4 and 5 should be carefully considered and effective steps must be taken for remedies.

Yours faithfully,
For Arun and Tarun Co. Ltd.
T. P. Neogi
(Secretary)

12. Report to the Directors regarding the causes and implications of dissatisfaction among the workmen of a company.

Dated : 25th August, 2011

To
The Board of Directors,
Bengal Manufacturing Co. Ltd.
20, Lenin Sarani, Kolkata 700 013

Dear Sirs,

As instructed by you, I have made a thorough enquiry into the causes and implications of the recent dissatisfaction among the workmen of our company and would like to submit below my considered opinion in this respect :

Firstly, the Workers' Union demands an immediate upward revision of the existing scale of pay offered by our company. In view of the continuous rise of prices of essential commodities, the demand is not unjustified. The workers in other companies are also raising the same demand. I suggest that, before the situation goes out of our hands, the matter should be discussed with the Union to come to an understanding with them and to give the workers some benefit in the form of increased Dearness Allowance instead of a revision of the existing payscale.

Secondly, the workers have demanded rent-free residential accommodation. We should tell the workers that we are favourably considering the matter. Since, it involves heavy capital outlay, its implementation require a healthy co-operation between the company and the Union. This matter may, therefore, be deferred for the time being.

I am confident that if my suggestions are duly considered, it will go a long way in satisfying the workers. And it is needless to say that the company will also be benefited from the satisfied and contented workers.

Yours faithfully,
P. K. Agarwal
(Secretary)

5.9 Drafting of Business Letters

[A] Definition and Meaning of Business Letters or Commercial Correspondence :

Letters are called the "Silent Ambassadors" of a business. 'Correspondence' means the communication through written media between individuals and institutions. Commercial correspondence means the communication of informaion on matters of 'trade and commerce'. It is the means through which businessmen communicate with each other on business matters.

[B] Functions of Business Letters :

The main functions of business letters are to establish and maintain good relation between two parties and to initiate, conduct and conclude business transactions of all types.

In the field of trade and commerce, it performs the vital function of bringing the buyer and the seller together. It makes demand, maintains demand and expands demand.

[C] Importance of a Business Letter :

Correspondence occupies a very important position in business world. Importance of communication is very great in business life. Business people have to communicate with the customers, suppliers, debtors, creditors, public authorities and public at large as well as among themselves for the purpose of exchanging their views and sending or receiving information. Business letters are the cheapest and the most extensive form of communication. This method had been accepted as the best method of communication all over the world.

Maintenance of personal contact with the customers is a vital necessity for the success of a business. But today the size of most business organisations has grown up so large that it is impossible to maintain such contact through telephone or personal conversation. Commercial letters help to solve these problems by providing an effective means of communication at low cost. Their importance is increasing gradually as industry, trade and commerce are growing more and more in volume and complexity.

Standardisation of the form and the style of business letters has made them more popular and acceptable to all. Day-by-day improvements are being made in the form and style of business letters making them more impressive and meaningful. Indeed, business letters are as vitally important for business as respiration is to human life.

[D] Style of Business Letters :

Every business letter needs a specific style. A business letter should satisfy all the characteristics of this 'Style'.

The **first thing** is the choice of words. Not only the correct words have to be chosen, but they also have to be arranged perfectly—making the meaning clear. The modern style is not to use uncommon words but to make the sentences simple. Flowery language is never appreciated. Technical words and jargons should be avoided as far as possible.

Secondly, it is to be noted that the layout must be proper. The layout of a letter has the following parts—[a] A proper form, [b] Writing the letter leaving margins, and [c] Dividing the body of the letter into paragraphs. Generally, a separate paragraph is allotted to each point.

Thirdly, the points have to be arranged in logical sequence. The approach should be positive and not negative as far as possible.

Fourthly, a letter must satisfy the following characteristics :

[i] simplicity, [ii] clearness, [iii] conciseness, [iv] completeness, [v] courtesy, [iv] well-planned, and [vii] effectiveness.

[a] **Essentials or, Principles of Business Letters :** The essential qualities of a good business letter are the following :

[i] **Simplicity and Clearness :** Business letters must be written in simple language and the subject must be clearly understandable. Sentences should be simple and bombastic words should be avoided as far as possible.

[ii] **Conciseness and Preciseness :** A business letter should be concise and precise. Use of needless words or expressions should be avoided. It should not be unnecessarily long.

[iii] **Unambiguous :** Business letters must be free from ambiguity. There should not be any vagueness about the message or information.

[iv] **Completeness :** A good business letter must be complete in all particulars. It must contain all the points which are necessary and relevant to the subject-matter on which the letter is written. The points must be arranged

systematically and logically and then only a complete and clear picture comes out. An incomplete letter will fail to serve the purpose for which it is written.

[v] **Courtesy :** The language of a business letter must be courteous. It means that there should be a polite attitude. A courteous letter is that which is full of sincerity and free from unwanted pride or self-assertion by the writer. A courteous letter can earn appreciation and favourable action. Even an unpleasant thing may be pesented in a courteous manner. A discourteous letter can never be effective and can even be harmful to a business.

[vi] **Effectiveness :** Effectiveness of a business letter is proved by the prompt and favourable reaction from the recipient. It depends upon all the characteristics taken together. To be effective, a business letter must be well-planned.

[b] Form and Arrangement of a Business Letter :

In order to be effective, a business letter should be arranged according to a recognised form.

The recognised or conventional form of a business letter contains the following :

[i] **The Heading :** Every letter begins with a heading. The name of the firm and nature of the business, its full address and date, telephone number, e-mail and telegraphic address, if any, reference number are printed here. Generally the name, address and nature of the business are printed at the top centre. The telephone number etc., the code and the date should be given on the right hand side.

[ii] **Inside Address :** It includes the name, designation and address of the person to whom the letter is addressed. It is usually written on the left hand top margin just above the 'opening salutation'. Some complimentary titles like Ms., Mr., Mrs. Messrs., Sarbashree etc. are used before the name of the addressee. Mr., Mrs., or Shri, Smt.—these are used before personal names in general. Messrs. is used before the names of firms, companies etc. Usually, a letter is addressed to an important officer of the organisation like the chairman, director, general manager, sales manager, partner, secretary, etc.

[iii] **Opening Salutation or Greeting :** A letter starts with the complimentary term like 'Sir', 'Dear Sir', 'Madam' etc. in the case of individuals. In the case of companies, firms, public association or body etc. the expressions used for such salutation are 'Sirs', 'Dear Sirs', 'Gentlemen' etc. 'My dear Sir' or 'My dear Madam' may be used in D.O. (demi-official) letters when there is a close intimacy between the writer and the addressee. Such greetings are used for the sake of courtesy.

[iv] **Subject-matter :** The subject-matter of the letter is mentioned in brief as Re : ('Re' means 'regarding') or Sub : 'Sub' means 'subject'. This can be written in between the Inside Address and Salutation.

[v] **The Body of the Letter :** Evidently, it is the main part of the letter. It is usually divided into paragraphs, each paragraph dealing with a particular point or topic or aspect of the subject-matter.

The body of the letter includes the following three parts :

[a] Introduction of the subject-matter with or without reference to any previous communication—The introduction draws the attention of the reader. It should be very brief.

[b] Middle Portion—It contains the principal information or message suitably arranged and explained. This should be divided into paragraphs based on the points.

[c] Conclusion—This is the closing portion of the body of the letter, which contains the action desired. The letter ends with 'Thank you', or 'With regards'.

[vi] **The Complimentary Close :** It is the formal leave-taking with some expression of obedience, respect, regard or friendliness towards the addressee, like 'Yours faithfully', 'Yours truly', 'Yours sincerely', etc. It is written just below the body of the letter, on the right hand side. Now-a-days, however, it is being written on the left hand side also.

[vii] **Signature and Date :** Every business letter must be signed by the authorised person with date. The signature should be given just below the complimentary close.

[viii] **Enclosures :** If any paper, cheque, draft etc. is attached to the letter, it has to be mentioned at the left hand side, bottom corner of the letter stating the number and the nature of the enclosure(s). In brief it is written as 'Encl'.

[E] Kinds of Business Letters

There are various kinds of business letters depending upon the subject-matters or purposes for which they are written. The common business letters may be grouped as under :

1. Offers, Enquiries, Quotations and Orders. 2. Confirmation, Execution, Refusal and Cancellation of Orders. 3. Claims, Complaints and Adjustments. 4. Collection of Dues. 5. Agency Letters. 6. Status Enquiries and Recommendation Letters. 7. Banking and Insurance Letters. 8. Advertisement and Application Letters. 9. Company Matters. 10. Representation Letters to Government.

Specimens of some business letters which are included in the syllabus are given below :

(1) ENQUIRIES, OFFERS, QUOTATIONS AND ORDERS

[a] Draft of an enquiry to the supplier for sending quotations.

ROY AND SONS CO. LTD.

12, B. C. Road, Barabazar; P.O. and Dist. Burdwan

(Dealers in all types of readymade garments)

Dated : 15th January, 2011

Telephone : 95342 4359

Telegraphic Address : RSCL

E-mail Address : roysons@rediffmail.com

Ref. No. 28/G/11

To

Messrs. Garments Stores (P) Ltd.

10, Strand Road, Kolkata 700 001

Re. : Enquiry regarding Supply of Readymade Garments

Dear Sirs,

It is a pleasure to inform you that we have opened a readymade garments shop at Burdwan. We require huge garments of different varieties. We would be glad if you would kindly inform us of the terms and conditions on which you are prepared to supply ready-made garments of different kinds made by you. Please quote your minimum price so as to enable us to place a large amount of order with you.

We would ask you to send us your latest price quotations and terms of payment, discount you would allow to us, if garments in bulk are bought. We expect to place a large order if your quotation is really competitive. In view of the above, we hope that you will send us your lowest quotation and best possible terms.

Thanking you,

Yours faithfully,
For Roy and Sons Co. Ltd.
S. K. Jas
(Manager)

[b] Draft a reply to the above enquiry for quotation.

GARMENTS STORES (P) LTD.
10 Strand Road, Kolkata
(Manufacturers of garments of all qualities)

Dated : 25th January, 2011

Telephone : 2721-5748
Telegraphic Address : GST
E-mail address : gsl@gmail.com
Ref. No. 596/G-7/11

To
The Manager,
Roy and Sons Co. Ltd.
12, B. C. Road, Barabazar; Dist. Burdwan

Re : Price-list and Terms of Payment

Dear Sir,

We thank you very much for your kind letter of enquiry No. 28/G/11 of 15th January, 2011 regarding readymade garments of different varieties.

We have much pleasure in sending you our latest price list of different varieties of garments. We would like to inform you that our catalogue prices are subject to 15% reduction, if your monthly order amounts to Rs. 20,000 in value. All details are shown in our enclosed catalogue. Our usual terms of business are that one-fourth of the total value of goods ordered should be paid in advance along with the order and the balance within one month of receipt of the goods. We have quoted you the lowest possible price and look forward to receiving your valued order, which, we assure you, will be executed with utmost care.

Thanking you, we remain,

Yours faithfully,
For Garments Stores (P) Ltd.
P. N. Ganguly
(Sales Manager)

Encl. one catalogue

[c] Draft of an enquiry for the supply of uniforms to peons and bearers of a large commercial concern.

NATIONAL ELECTRONIC (P) LTD.

135, G. T. Road, Asansol, Burdwan

Dated : 25th August, 2011

Telephone : 2228-6782

Telegraphic Address : NEL

E-mail address : nel@yahoo.in

Ref. No. 287/N-6/11

To

Messrs Excellent Dress Co. Ltd.

45 Netaji Subhas Road, Kolkata 700 001

Ref. : Enquiry regarding the Supply of Uniforms

Dear Sir,

We require a large number of uniforms for the peons and bearers of our office. We should be obliged if you would send us your quotations for the following items of ready-made uniforms.

[i] White full bush-shirts (Size No. 20″-30″)

[ii] White drill trousers (Waist Size 30″-42″)

[iii] White half bush-shirts (Size No. 30″-42″)

We hope to place a large order if your quotations are really competitive. In view of the above, we expect that you will send us your lowest quotation and best possible terms.

Thanking you,

Yours faithfully,

For National Electronics (P) Ltd.

T. N. Dostidar

(Manager)

[d] Draft of a quotation for the supply of uniforms to peons and bearers (a reply to the above enquiry).

EXCELLENT DRESS CO. LTD.

45, Netaji Subhas Road, Kolkata 700 001

Dated : 5th September, 2011

Telephone : 2924-3267

Telegraphic Address : EDL

E-mail address : edl@yahoo.in

Ref. No. 523/ED/11

To

The Manager,

National Electronics (P) Ltd

135, G. T. Road, Asansol, Burdwan

Sub : Prices and Terms and Conditions

Dear Sir,

We thank you for your letter of your enquiry dated 25th August, 2011 and have much pleasure in submitting below our quotations for readymade uniforms as requested :

[a] White full bush-shirts (Size No. 20″-30″)—@ Rs. 2,000 per dozen.

[b] White drill trousers (Waist Size No. 30″-42″)—@ Rs. 1,400 per dozen.

[c] White half bush shirts (Size No. 30″-42″)—@ Rs. 1600 per dozen.

The usual terms and conditions of our business are the payment of one-fourth of the total value of goods in advance along with the order, and 15% discount against cash payments within 30 days after executing the order.

We have quoted you the lowest possible price and we hope to receive your valued order which will be executed with utmost care and speed.

Thanking you, we remain,

Yours faithfully,
For Excellent Dress Co. Ltd.
S. N. Bhakat
(Manager)

[e] Draft of an enquiry for the supply of different varieties of stationery articles.

BASU AND MALLICK CO. LTD.
22, Rabindra Road, Paschim Medinipur

Dated : 15th December, 2011

Telephone : 953222 264286
Telegraphic Address : BML
E-mail address : bmcl@rediffmail.com
Mobile No. : 8233001235
Ref. No. 456/G/11

To
Messrs. Modern Stationery Stores
25, M. G. Road, Burrabazar, Kolkata-700 002

Sub : Enquiry regarding Supply of Stationery Articles

Dear Sirs,

We require some stationery articles for use in our office. We would be glad if you please send us, as early as possible, your lowest quotations and best possible terms.

The specification of the articles are given below :

[i] 100 dozen of Ronald Dot Pens

[ii] 50 dozen of Writer Fountain Pens

[iii] 50 dozen of Pilot Fountain Pens

[iv] 30 packets of Pin

If your prices and terms suit us, we shall place you an order.

Thanking you,

Yours faithfully,
For Basu and Mallick Co. Ltd.
B. Mallick

[f] Draft of a quotation for the supply of stationery articles (a reply to the above enquiry).

MODERN STATIONERY STORES

25, M. G. Road, Burrabazar, Kolkata 700 002

Dated : 25th December, 2011

Telephone : 2726-4328
Telegraphic Address : MS
E-mail address : ms@sifi.com
Ref. No. 75/MS-7/11

To
The Manager,
Basu and Mallick Co. Ltd.
22 Rabindra Rd.
Paschim Medinipur

Ref : Price List and Terms of Payment

Dear Sir,

We thank you for your enquiry dated the 15th December, 2011 and have the pleasure to submit below our latest price list as desired :

[a] 100 dozen of Ronald Dot Pens—Rs. 120 per dozen.
[b] 50 dozen of Writer Fountain Pens—Rs. 100 per dozen.
[c] 50 dozen of Pilot Fountain Pens—Rs. 150 per dozen.
[d] 30 packets of Pin Rs. 10 per packet.

We are ready to offer you a discount of 10% on the total price against cash payments within 10 days from the date of executing the order.

Thanking you,

Yours faithfully,
For Modern Stationery Stores.
T. K. Dey
(Sales Manager)

[g] Draft of a quotation for the supply of stationery articles (reply to an enquiry)

KALYANI SOAP WORKS LTD.

18, Central Road, Kalyani, Nadia

Dated : 1st April, 2011

Telephone : 2224-3024
Telegraphic Address : BSWL
E-mail address : kswl@rediffmail.com
Ref. No. 58/S/11

To
Messrs, Jnanada Stores
65, S. P. Mukherjee Road;
Kolkata 700 025

Re : An Offer for Sale

Dear Sirs,

We thank you for your letter of enquiry dated, the 25th March, 2011 and as requested, enclose a sample packet of Diamond Soap Powder which we have just placed in the market.

This product is the result of our long and careful research and we are confident that it is superior to the similar products in the market.

From the catalogue enclosed, you will find that it possesses some special merits. It is highly economical, it dissolves readily in water, leaving no sediment, and cleans all kinds of garments very quickly.

We are receiving enquiries from different parts of the country including your district. We are confident that our soap powder will quickly get a large selling market.

We are now ready to offer you a discount of 20% with 30 days' credit.

We can promise delivery within ten days from receiving the order and expect both sample and price will give you immense satisfaction.

Thanking you,

Yours faithfully,
For Kalyani Soap Works Ltd.
B. K. Mukherjee
(Sales Manager)

Encl. : One catalogue

[h] Draft of a general offer from a manufacturer of goods.

SAMANTA AND SONS TRADING CO.
48, Mahatma Gandhi Road, Kolkata 700 009
(Manufacturer of electric fans)

Dated : August 24, 2011

Telephone : 2826-3025
Telegraphic Address : SSTC
Telex : D/5348
E-mail address : sstc@gmail.com
Ref. No. Cir/EL/F-15/11

To

All the Dealers

Re. : Introducing 'Raju' Electric Fan

Dear Sirs,

We have the pleasure in announcing that we have just placed in the market our 'Raju' brand ceiling and table fans. This model is much improved in quality and design as compared to our previous models.

From the illustrated catalogue enclosed, you will find that this model has some special features compared to other fans in the market. It is highly economical, the power consumption being 10% less than other varieties of fans. Moreover, it is specially designed for a long life. It is spray-painted in several shades of colour and has a pleasing finish.

We have already received many enquiries from different parts of the country. We are offering a special discount of 25% on the list-price to our registered dealers on all orders received by us on or before the 30th September, 2011, other terms remaining the same. We hope, you will not miss the advantage of this excellent offer.

Thanking you,

Yours faithfully,
For Samanta and Sons Trading Co.
T. S. Bhattacharyya
(Marketing Manager)

Encl : One catalogue

[i] Draft of an order for the supply of goods.

SEN AND SONS CO. LTD.

12, N. S. Road, Barabazar; Siliguri, District : Darjeeling
(Dealers in all types of garments)

Dated : 5th February, 2011

Telephone : 2255-4359
Telegraphic Address : SSCL
E-mail address : sensons@yahoo.com
Ref. No. 35/G/11

To
The Sales Manager,
Garments Stores (P) Ltd.
10, Strand Road, Kolkata 700 001

Re. : Order for the Supply of Readymade Garments

Dear Sir,

We thank you for your letter of the 25th January, 2011 and we are pleased to accept your quotation (No. 596/G-7/11 dated 25.1.11) for ready-made garments. We have the pleasure in placing the following order with you as per description and prices of your current catalogue :

[i] Long Cloth Shirts : Size No. 20 : 100 doz @ Rs. 1200 per doz.
[ii] Poplin (White) Shirts : Size No. 22 : 80 doz @ Rs. 1500 per doz.
[iii] Saffron Coloured Khaddar Punjabi : Size No. 24 : 50 doz. Rs. 1400 per doz.
[iv] Addi Punjabi : Size No. 24 : 50 doz @ Rs. 1600 per doz.
[v] Terene Shirts : Size No. 30 : 50 doz @ Rs. 2,000 per doz.
[vi] Terene Trousers : Size No. 30 : 50 doz @ Rs. 2,400 per doz.

We shall be glad if you kindly despatch the above-mentioned articles within 15 days from date by Rail Transport. Please send the invoice showing the net price payable after deducting discount @ 15% as per your quotation.

On receipt of the consignment, we shall immediately arrange for the payment of the amount due as per your terms and conditions.

Please confirm the order.

With thanks,

Yours faithfully,
For Sen and Sons. Co. Ltd.
S. K. Banerjee
(Manager)

[j] Draft of an order for supply of uniforms for the use of office peons and bearers.

NATIONAL ELECTRONICS LTD.

Atul Market, Malda

Dated : 15th September, 2011

Telephone : 2228-6782
Telegraphic Address : NEL
E-mail address : natelec@rediffmail.com
Ref. No. 305/N-8/11

To
Messrs Excellent Dress Co. Ltd.
45, Netaji Subhas Road
Kolkata 700 001

Re : Placement of Order for the Supply of Uniforms

Dear Sirs,

Many thanks for your letter dated, 5th September, 2011. We are glad to accept your quotation for ready-made uniforms and place an order with you of the following uniforms as per your quotation :

[i] White full bush-shirts (Size No. 20″-30″) @ Rs. 2,000 per dozen = 50 dozen.

[ii] White drill trousers (Waist Size No. 30″-42″) @ Rs. 1400 per dozen = 50 dozen.

[iii] White half bush-shirts (Size No. 30"-42") @ Rs. 1600 per dozen = 50 dozen.

We look forward to the delivery within the next few days.

Thanking you,

Yours faithfully,
For National Elecronics Ltd.
T. N. Dostidar
(Manager)

(2) CONFIRMATION, EXECUTION, REFUSAL AND CANCELLATION OF ORDER

[i] Draft of a letter acknowledging and confirming an order.

GARMENTS STORES (P) LTD.
10, Strand Road ; Kolkata 700 001
(Manufacturers of garments of all qualities)

Dated : 15th February, 2011

Telephone : 2621-5748
Telegraphic Address : GST
E-mail : gsl@hotmail.com
Ref. No. 635/G-24/11

To
The Manager,
Roy and Sons Co. Ltd.
12, B. C. Road, Barabazar; Dist. Burdwan

Re. : Confirmation of Order

Dear Sir,

We are glad to acknowledge the receipt of your letter No. 35/G-11 dated, 5th February, 2011 and thank you for your order.

As desired by you we shall despatch the articles by Rail Transport. We have arranged to despatch the materials tomorrow by next available goods train and it is expected that the consignment will reach your destination by the third week of this month.

We enclose our invoice No. 256/Garments/63/11 dated 16.2.11 to the amount of Rs. 38,000/- being the next amount of dues payable, latest by the end of this month.

We hope, you would settle our dues in time and improve our business relations. We shall be happy to receive your further orders.

Thanking you,

Yours faithfully,
For Garments Stores (P) Ltd.
P. N. Ganguly
(Sales Manager)

[ii] Draft of a letter on execution of an order.

GARMENTS STORES (P) LTD.
10, Strand Road, Kolkata 700 001
(Manufacturers of Garments of all qualities)

Dated : February 16, 2011

Telephone : 2621-5748
Telegraphic Address : GST
E-mail : gsl@hotmail.com
Ref. No. 685/G-75/11

To
The Manager,
Roy & Sons Co. Ltd.
12, B. C. Road, Barabazar,
Dist. Burdwan.

Re. : Execution of Order

Dear Sir,

Please note that with reference to your letter No. 55/G 04-11 dated 05.02.11 placing an order for ready-made garments and our reply dated 15.02.11 in confirmation of the order, we have despatched the same today by railway parcel.

The consignment has been booked for despatch by Eastern Railway having R/R No. 6215 dated, 16.02.11 enclosed herewith. We also enclose our invoice No. 256/Garments/63/11 dated 16.02.11 for Rs. 38,000 being the net dues payable by the end of this month.

We trust that you would not hesitate to settle the dues in time and improve our business relations.

We hope to be favoured with your further orders in future. We assure that your orders will always receive our best attention.

With thanks,

Yours faithfully,
For Garments Stores (P) Ltd.
P. N. Ganguly
(Sales Manager)

Encl. : 1. R/R No. 6215
2. Invoice No. 256/Garments//63/11

[iii] Draft of a letter of acknowledgement and confirmation of order.

EXCELLENT DRESS CO. LTD.

45, Netaji Subhas Road, Kolkata

Dated : 25th September, 2011

Telephone : 2924-3267
Telegraphic Address : EDL
E-mail : edcl@indiatimes.com
Ref. No. 600/ED/11

To
The Manager,
National Electronics Ltd.
135, G. T. Raod, Asansol, Burdwan

Re. : Confirmation of Order

Dear Sir,

We acknowledge with thanks the receipt of your letter dated, 15th September, 2011 placing an order for the supply of uniforms.

We have arranged to despatch the uniforms by next available goods train and it is expected that the consignment will reach your destination by the first week of October, 2011. We enclose our invoice No. 150/Uniforms/78/11 dated, 26.09.11 for Rs. 40,000/- being the net amount of dues payable latest by the second week of October, 2011.

We hope you would settle your dues in time and improve our business relations. We shall be happy to receive your further orders.

Thanking you,

Yours faithfully,
For Excellent Dress Co. Ltd.
S. N. Bhakat
(Manager)

[iv] Draft of a letter requesting extension of the period of delivery.

DEY AND DATTA CO. LTD.

172, College Street, Kolkata 700 009

Dated : 5th December, 2011

Telephone : 2728-6248
Telegraphic Address : DDC
E-mail : deydutta@sify.com
Ref. No. 658/G-5/'11

To
The Manager,
Kabiguru Stores
7, Sripally Road, Santiniketan, Birbhum

Re. : Extension of Time for Exceution of Order

Dear Sir,

We thank you for your letter No. Or/57/11 dated, 25.11.11 for supply of 100 bottles Camel Blue Ink, but we regret to inform you that due to frequent and prolonged power cut and acute scarcity of raw materials, we are not in a position to supply the goods immediately. So, we request you to allow us an extension of fifteen days' time for the execution of your order. We shall be ready to despatch the goods positively by 20.12.11.

We hope that you would appreciate our difficulties. Please let us know whether you would be kind enough to wait till the above-mentioned date.

With thanks,

Yours faithfully,
For Dey and Datta Co. Ltd.
R. K. Samanta
(Manager)

[v] Draft of a letter advising delay in the execution of order.

MODERN STATIONERY STORES

25, M. G. Road, Burrabazar, Kolkata 700 002

Dated : 10th January, 2011

Telephone : 2426-4328
Telegraphic Address : MS
E-mail address : mss@yahoo.com
Ref. No. 6/M-27/11

To
The Manager,
Basu and Dhar Co. Ltd.
28, Alamganj Road, Burdwan

Re : Delay in Execution of Order

Dear Sir,

We are obliged by your order dated 5th January 2011 for 200 dozen Fountain Pens to be supplied in accordance with the specification submitted by you. But we regret to inform you that it is not possible for us to deliver the fountain pens you require immediately as they are not in our stock at present.

We shall require at least one month's time to meet your demand.

If you are in a position to extend the time for delivery of the goods by at least one month, we shall complete your order by that time. Please let us know whether you will kindly extend the time for delivery of the goods as mentioned above.

With thanks.

Yours faithfully,
For Modern Stationery Stores
S. P. Guha
(Sales Manager)

[vi] Draft of a letter requesting for substitute product in place of an order.

NEW PAINT CO. LTD.

46, Canning Street, Kolkata

Dated : 15th February, 2011

Telephone : 2926-6033
Telegraphic Address : NPL
E-mail : newpaint@hotmail.com
Ref. No. C/N-59/11

To
The Manager,
Makhanlal and Co.
9, Lenin Sarani, Durgapur.

Re : Offer for Substitute Product

Dear Sir,

Thank you for your kind order of the 5th February, 2011 for 'Golden Brand' paint, but we regret to inform you that our stock of this brand of paint is totally exhausted.

We like to inform you further that we have decided not to stock this brand at present because its price has gone up very high.

Now, if you are not compelled to use the same brand, we can supply our 'Diamond Brand' paint which is, in no way, inferior to the 'Golden Brand' paint. On the other hand, the 'Diamond Brand' paint is comparatively cheaper and better. This new brand has already acquired much propularity in the market in a very short time.

You are requested to kindly place your order for this new brand instead of 'Golden Brand' paint and we are sure that you will find it satisfactory.

We wait for your instruction for immediate supply.

Thanking you,

Yours faithfully,
For New Paint Co. Ltd.
L. K. Majumder
(Sales Manager)

Encl. : Price list of Diamond Brand Paint

[vii] Draft of a letter refusing an order on technical ground

MUKHERJEE AND CO. LTD.

26, Netaji Subhas Road, Kolkata 700 001

Dated : 31st August, 2011

Telephone : 2556-6298
Telegraphic Address : MCL
E-mail : mukco@live.com
Ref. No. T/211/11

To
Messrs. Datta Brothers
53, New Maket; Dhanbad

Re : Sending Order to Authorised Agent

Dear Sir,

We thank you for your order No. MDB/195/2011 dated, the 25th August, 2011. We are, however, extremely sorry to inform you that we are unable to accept the order for direct supply from any retailer from Dhanbad as we have already given exclusive retail selling agency for that area to Messrs Gupta and Sons, 46, Hirapur; Dhanbad.

Hence, we are sending your order to Messrs Gupta and Sons who will surely contact you in the matter shortly.

We are glad for the interest you have in our goods and hope that it will steadily increase to our mutual advantage. For further supplies, please write to our above agent directly.

Thanking you,

Yours faithfully,
For Mukherjee and Co. Ltd.
S. K. Samanta
(Sales Manager)

[viii] Draft of a letter refusing an order on personal ground.

CHAKRABORTY AND CO. LTD.

55, Bidhan Sarani, Kolkata 700 006

Dated : 5th September, 2011

Telephone : 2834-1687
Telegraphic Address : CCL
E-mail : chakra@indiatimes.com
Ref. No. D/25/11

To
The Manager,
Dhar Brothers
79, Station Road, Asansol

Re : Your order No. TLP/45/11 dated, 30.8.11

Dear Sir,

We thank you for your kind order, but we regret to state that we are not in a position to supply the machine owing to the following difficulty.

It is not our principle to allow credit to any of our dealers or customers for a period of two months, which you have asked for in your valued order.

In the circumstances, we are sorry, we cannot oblige you by accepting the terms of your order. We are returning herewith the Bank Draft for Rs. 5,000/- sent by you.

Thanking you and hoping to be of service in future.

Yours faithfully,
For Chakraborty and Co. Ltd.
B. M. Bhadra
(Manager)

Encl. : One Bank Draft for Rs. 5,000/-

[ix] Draft of a letter to the supplier cancelling an order due to failure to deliver the goods within the scheduled time.

SEN BROSS. LTD.

5, B. B. Ghosh Raod, Nutanganj Bazar, Dist. Burdwan.
(Dealers in Cocoanut Oil)

Dated : September 10, 2011

Telephone : 2255-4638
Telegraphic Address : SBL
E-mail : sbl@sifi.com
Ref. No. CO/527/11

To
The Manager,
Mahalakshmi Trading Co. Ltd.
77, Posta Market, Kolkata 700 007

Re. : Cancellation of Order

Dear Sir,

Please refer to our order No. CO/514/11 dated, the 15th August, 2011 for the supply of 500 tins of 'LION-MARK' cocoanut oil to be delivered by the end of August, 2011.

We regret to inform you that you have neither executed the order, nor have acknowledged the receipt of our order. We have lost a good deal of business because of your unusual delay.

We, therefore, have no other alternative but to cancel the above order. Please note that we shall refuse the goods if delivered.

Thanking you,

Yours faitfhfully,
For Sen Bros. Ltd.
N. K. Bhowmik
(Manager)

[x] Draft of a letter to the supplier cancelling an order due to fall in market price.

PIONEER CLOTH MERCHANTS
17, Chandni Chak, Barabazar, Dist. Paschim Medinipur
(Dealers in all types of cloths)

Dated : 25th July, 2011

Telephone : 2256-5368
Telegraphic Address : PCM
E-mail address : pioneer@yahoo.com
Ref. No. CL/82/11

To
The Manager,
Woollen Trading Co. Ltd.
78, Strand Road, Kolkata 700 001

Re. : Cancellation of Order due to Fall in Market Price

Dear Sir,

I placed with you an order for 300 woollen shawls and 200 woollen coats of different varieties and sizes to be delivered by the first week of August, 2011. But we regret sending you a telegram today as under :

"Cancell Order No. CL/65/11 for shawls and coats"

We have been compelled to take this decision because the market prices of woollen shawls and woollen coats have considerably come down in Medinipur market due to the arrival of huge stocks of similar goods from different manufacturing centres. We, therefore, request you to treat this order as cancelled. We are sorry for the inconvenience caused to you.

We, however, assure you that we shall place a similar order with you in near future after the market becomes favourable.

Thanking you,

Yours faithfully,
For Pioneer Cloth Merchants
C. S. Chatterjee
(Manager)

[xi] Draft of a letter to the supplier cancelling an order for unavoidable reason.

BENGAL WOOL HOUSE

78, B. C. Road, Coochbehar

Dated : 5th March, 2011

Telephone : 95245-2629
Telegraphic Address : BWH
E-mail : bengalwool@gmail.com
Ref. No 67/G-28/11

To
The Manager,
Punjab Woollen Germents Co. Ltd.
Ludhiana

Sub : Cancellation of Order for Unavoidable Circumstances

Dear Sir,

We sent you an order on 25th February, 2011, for 600 Woollen Garments of different sizes and varietes, but we are extremely sorry to request you to treat this order as cancelled.

We have been compelled to take this decision due to the circumstances beyond our control. On the 4th March, 2011, our business premises were completely destroyed by fire. Hence, we do not require any more stock until we have found suitable alternative business premises.

We are sorry that it has been necessary to cancel this order, but we shall not fail to place an order with you as soon as we have found suitable premises.

Thanking you,

Yours faithfully,
For Bengal Wool House
D. N. Debnath
(Manager)

[xii] Draft of a letter containing confirmation of a telegraph sent cancelling an order.

BISWAS CO. LTD.

35, B. B. Ghosh Road, Krishnanagar, Nadia

Dated : 25th March, 2011

Telephone : 2252-6234
Telegraphic Address : BL
E-mail : biswas@rediff.com
Ref. No. 78/CK-2/11

To
The Manager,
Ghosh Brothers and Co.
28, Rashbehari Avenue, Kolkata

Re. : Cancellation of Order for Unavoidable Reason

Dear Sir,

We write this letter to you confirming the following telegram today :

"Cancel yesterday's order for T.V. sets."

We have been forced to take this decision because the buyer of these television sets has just cancelled the order.

We, therefore, request you to treat this order as cancelled.

We are extremely sorry that it has been necessary to cancel the order, but we assure you that we shall not fail to send you our further orders as soon as the occasions arise.

With thanks,

Yours faithfully,
For Biswas and Co. Ltd.
A. R. Chattoraj
(Manager)

(3) STATUS ENQUIRIES

[i] Draft of a letter making an enquiry about the financial standing of a firm from a business concern.

SEN AND CO. LTD.

15, Canning Street, Kolkata 700 001

Dated : 15th October, 2011

Telephone : 2835-8324
Talegraphic Address : SCL
E-mail : senco@indiatimes.com
Ref. No. P/18/11

Confidential

To
The Manager,
Chandra Trading Co. Ltd.
54/8, B. C. Roy Road, Asansol

Re : Status Enquiry

Dear Sir,

Recently we have received an order for the supply of electrical goods worth Rs. 30,000 from Messrs. Saha Enterprise of 56, G. T. Road, Asansol, who have desired to buy the goods on credit and mentioned your name as a referee.

We, therefore, request you to kindly inform us at your earliest convenience about their credit-worthiness and goodwill in the market. We shall remain grateful to you if you kindly let us know whether you recommend a credit sale for Rs. 30,000 to the firm.

We assure you that any information given by you in this respect will be kept in strict confidence.

Thanking you,

Yours faithfully,
For Sen and Co. Ltd.
S. P. Neogi
(Manager)

[ii] Draft of a favourable reply to the letter of an enquiry as to the financial status of a firm.

CHANDRA TRADING CO. LTD.

54/8, B. C. Roy Road, Asansol.

Dated : 25th October, 2011

Telephone : 2285-3628
Telegraphic Address : CTL
E-mail address : chandra@gmx.com
Ref. No. C/64/11

Confidential

To
The Manager,
Sen and Co. Ltd.
15, Canning Street, Kolkata 700 001

Re : Financial Status

Dear Sir,

We acknowledge with thanks the receipt of your letter dated 15th October, 2011 and we are glad to advise you that the firm you enquired about enjoys a high business reputation in the local market. We have been dealing with the firm for the last ten years. They are very prompt and punctual in respect of payments. The proprietors have carried out business in the town for many years and they are all men of high business connections and financial standing. We, therefore, feel no hesitation in granting the firm a credit of Rs. 30,000.

We would like to mention here that this information given to you is highly confidential and we do not like to accept any responsibility in this matter.

Thanking you,

Yours faithfully,
For Chandra Trading Co. Ltd.
R. P. Sengupta
(Manager)

[iii] Draft of a letter to a bank enquiring about the financial status and credit-worthiness of a prospective customer.

IDEAL MANUFACTURING CO. LTD.

75/3, G. T. Road, Chinsurah, Hooghly

Dated : 5th November, 2011

Telephone : 2282-2416, 2282-2417, Mobile : 9051122661
Telegraphic Address : IMC
E-mail : idealmanufac@live.com
Ref. No. MC/35/11

Confidential

To
The Branch Manager,
United Bank of India
49, B. C. Road, Burdwan

Re : Status Enquiry

Dear Sir,

We have recently received an order for the supply of electric motors worth Rs. 50,000 on credit from Sarkar and Co. of 38, R. B. Ghosh Road, Burdwan; and the firm has mentioned the name of your Bank as referee. The Firm's Account No. is C/46856.

But we do not have any knowledge about the credit-worthiness and financial condition of the firm. We, therefore, request you to let us know the firm's financial soundness and business reputation.

We shall be glad to learn from you whether the firm may be granted a credit sale of Rs. 50,000.

Any information which would be supplied by you would be kept in strict confidence.

Thanking you,

Yours faithfully,
For Ideal Manufacturing Co. Ltd.
T. N. Dasgupta
(Manager)

[iv] Draft of a favourable reply by a Bank to the letter of enquiry about the financial standing of a firm.

UNITED BANK OF INDIA
49, B. C. Roy Road, Burdwan

Dated : 10th November, 2011

Telephone : 2296-4819
Telegraphic Address : UBI
E-mail : ubiburd@gmail.com
Ref. No. UB/SE/28/09

Confidential

To
The Manager,
Ideal Manufacturing Ltd.
75/3, G. T. Road, Chinsura, Hooghly

Re. : Status Enquiry

Dear Sir,

Thank you for your letter no. MC/35/11 dated, 05.11.11. In reply to your enquiry about the credit-worthiness of Messrs. Sarkar and Co. of 38, R. B. Ghosh Road, Burdwan, we are pleased to inform you that the firm has been maintaining Current Account with us since 2000. They are the traders in machine tools and appliances. Loans and Overdraft facilities are often extended by us to the firm. The firm is very prompt and punctual in making payments. They have high business reputation and sound financial standing. The average credit balance to their Account is Rs. 1,00,000.

Please keep this information in strict confidence. We decline to accept any responsibility in this matter.

Thanking you,

Yours faithfully,
For United Bank of India
N. K. Mukherjee
(Branch Manager)

(4) LETTERS OF RECOMMENDATION AND CREDIT

[i] Write a letter of recommendation for an employee who gives up his post and seeks employment in his home state.

BENGAL MANUFACTURING CO. LTD.

85, Ganesh Chandra Avenue, Kolkata 700 013

Dated : 5th August, 2011

Telephone : 2262-3512
Telegraphic Address : BMC
E-mail : bmcl@sify.com
Ref. No. R/15/11

To

Messrs. Indian Trading Co. Ltd.
8, Sahid Bhagat Singh Road, Mumbai-400 023

Dear Sirs,

It is a pleasure on my part to recommend to you the bearer of this letter, Sri Sanat Chatterjee, who is our Senior Sales Supervisor in West Bengal. Sri Chatterjee, a permanent resident of Mumbai, possesses a good B.Sc. Degree with Honours in Chemistry. He joined us in the Sales Department some five years ago and during his service he has shown great responsibility in the discharge of duties. We were greatly benefited by his expert knowledge in the manufacture of plastic goods. His services were excellent and at present he has to leave Kolkata and settle in his own State due to some serious family problems. Any organisation will be proud of having a trusted and hard-working person like Sri Chatterjee.

I shall appreciate very much if this honest, loyal, energetic and sincere youngman finds an employment in your company.

Yours faithfully,
For Bengal Manufacturing Co. Ltd.
R. K. Bhattacharyya
(Secretary)

[ii] Draft of a letter of recommendation for a business friend who wants to establish new business.

UNIQUE TRADING CO. LTD.

5B, Ashutosh Mukherjee Road, Kolkata 700 020

Dated : 15th July, 2011

Telephone : 2484-3564
Telegrphic Address : UT
E-mail : uniquetrading@rediffmail.com
Ref. No. R/261/11
Messrs. Roy and Co. Ltd.
178, Nariman Avenue, Mumbai 400 005

Re : Letter of Recommendation

Dear Sirs,

I have great pleasure to recommend to you Sri Basudeb Banerjee, the bearer of this letter, who is a business friend of mine. Sri Banerjee, an expert in making handloom shirts, is personally known to me for years. He has a workshop for machine-made handloom shirts. He is leaving for Mumbai to explore possibilities for export orders for his ready-made garments. I shall feel obliged if you render him all possible assistance since you have a good command over the export market.

I am sure that your advice and able guidance will be profitable on the part of Sri Banerjee. Any help extended by you to Sri Banerjee will be treated as a personal favour to me for which I shall remain thankful to you.

Thanking you,

Yours faithfully,
For Unique Trading Co. Ltd.
M. K. Biswas
(Manager)

[iii] Write a letter of credit in favour of an employee requesting to pay him a certain sum of money.

SADHU AND SONS
52, Mahatma Gandhi Road, Kolkata 700 012

Dated : 10th December, 2011

Telephone : 2764-2948
Telegraphic Address : SSC
E-mail : sadhu@rediffmail.com
Ref. No. LC/25/11

To
The Manager,
Datta and Co. Ltd.
5, Chandni Chawk, Delhi

Re : Letter of Credit

Dear Sir,

We have the pleasure to introduce Sri G. K. Sengupta, the bearer of this letter, who is a Sales Representative of our firm. He is leaving Kolkata on the 15th December, 2011 for an extensive tour in Delhi to establish new business connections for our firm.

We shall feel obliged if you kindly supply him any sum of money that he may require but not exceeding Rs. 10,000 (Rupees Ten Thousand) against signed receipt. The specimen signature of Sri G. K. Sengupta is enclosed herewith for your verification. This letter will remain valid till the end of March, 2012.

Any payment made to Sri G. K. Sengupta may be debited to our account.

Please accept our thanks, in advance, for any service rendered.

Yours faithfully,

Specimen Signature of
G. K. Sengupta
(*Gopal Krishna Sengupta*)

For Sadhu and Sons
S. K. Banik
(Manager)

[iv] Draft of a letter on behalf of a businessman, to a Bank requesting to arrange for providing him with a letter of credit.

DATTA AND CO. LTD.

19, Ajoy Mukherjee Avenue, Tamluk, Purba Medinipur

Dated : 25th October, 2011

Telephone : 2263-2817
Telegraphic Address : DCL
E-mail : dattaco@gmail.com
Ref. No. L/C/65/11

To
The Branch Manager,
State Bank of India
Tamluk Branch
Tamluk, Purba Medinipur

Re : Letter of Credit

Dear Sir,

Let me communicate to you that I wish to make an extensive business tour to the prominent industrial zones of Mumbai to establish new business connections for our firm. The trip will start on and from the 1st November, 2011.

I shall be thankful to you if you kindly issue a letter of credit to your Mumbai branch so as to enable to get me an amount of Rs. 15,000/- (Rupees Fifteen Thousand only). This letter will remain in force up to 31st December, 2011.

This amount may kindly be debited to my current account including other usual charges.

Thanking you in anticipation,

Yours faithfully,
For Datta and Co.
P. K. Datta
(Partner)

(5) LETTERS OF COLLECTION

Sample 1. A Series of Sample Letters in connection with the Collection of Outstanding Dues.

[i] First Letter

NEW BENGAL TRADING CO. LTD.

65, Bowbazar Street, Kolkata 700 013

Dated : 5th January, 2011

Telephone : +91-033-2468-7931
Telegram : Bengal
E-mail : nbtco@sify.com
Ref. No. NB/58-D/11
M/s. Kalyani Electricals
92, G. T. Road, Burdwan-4

Sub : Collection of Dues

Dear Sirs,

We draw your attention to our Bill No. 975 for Rs. 8,970 on the 28th October, 2010 representing the supply of electric goods to you as per your Order No. 46-E/11 dated the 20th October 2010. According to the terms of agreement you ought to have cleared off the due amount within one month after the delivery. Two months have already been elapsed but we have received neither the amount due nor any letter from you intimating the reasons for such unusual delay in paying off the due.

We would request you to arrange for payment of the bills at an early date.

Yours faithfully

N. K. Tiwari

(Sales Manager)

Encl. : [i] Statement of Account
[ii] Copy of Invoice

[ii] Second Letter

NEW BENGAL TRADING CO. LTD.

65, Bowbazar Street, Kolkata 700 013

Telephone : +91-033-2468-7931
Telegram : Bengal
E-mail : nbtco@sify.com
Ref. No. NB/82-D/11

Dated : 14th January, 2011

M/s. Kalyani Electricals,
92, G. T. Road, Burdwan-4

Sub : Collection of Dues

Dear Sirs,

We regret to state that we have not yet received any reply to our letter No. NB/58-D/11 dated 05.01.11 in which we asked you to settle your outstanding dues of Rs. 8,970 to us. Your silence has naturally led us to think that you have not received our letter and statement of account.

We, therefore, enclose a duplicate statement of account and hope that you will oblige us by remitting the amount within a week.

Yours faithfully,

N. K. Tiwari

Sales Manager

[iii] Third Letter

NEW BENGAL TRADING CO. LTD.

65, Bowbazar Street, Kolkata 700 013

Telephone : +91-033-2468-7931

Dated : 23rd January, 2011

Telegram : Bengal
E-mail : nbtco@sify.com
Ref. No. NB/90-D/11

M/s. Kalyani Electricals,
92, G. T. Road, Burdwan-4

Sub : Collection of Dues

Dear Sirs,

We regret to point out that our letters of 05.01.11 and 14.01.11 drawing your attention to make the payment of our Bill No. 975 dated, 28.10.10 are still unacknowledged.

You should admit that the amount is overdue and it is not possible for us to wait any longer. It is not our principle to allow such a long credit to our customers.

You are, therefore, requested to give immediate attention to this matter so that we may receive the amount by 30th January, 2011 positively.

Yours faithfully,
N. K. Tiwari
(Sales Manager)

[iv] Fourth Letter

[Registered with A/D]

NEW BENGAL TRADING CO. LTD.

65, Bowbazar Street, Kolkata 700 013

Telephone : +91-033-2468-7931
Telegram : Bengal
E-mail : nbtco@sify.com
Ref. No. NB/105-D/11 Dated : 31st January 2011

M/s Kalyani Electricals,
92, G. T. Road, Burdwan-4

Sub : Collection of Dues

Dear Sirs,

It is a matter of great regret that in spite of our repeated reminders to you for the settlement of your dues to us for Rs. 8970·00, you have not cared to settle the account and have not even acknowledged the letters by way of ordinary business courtesy.

In the circumstances, we have only to inform you that if you do not pay the amount by 5th February, 2011, we shall be compelled—much against our desire—to place the matter in the hands of our lawyers.

We trust that you will realise the situation and do the needful to avoid unpleasantness.

Yours faithfully,
N. K. Tiwari
(Sales Manager)

[v] Final Letter

[Registered with A/D]

NEW BENGAL TRADING CO. LTD.

65, Bowbazar Street, Kolkata 700 013

Telephone : +91-033-2468-7931
Telegram : Bengal
E-mail : nbtco@sify.com
Ref. No. NB/124-D/11 Dated : 6th February, 2011

M/s Kalyani Electricals
92, G. T. Road; Burdwan-4

Sub : Collection of Dues

Dear Sirs,

We have to inform you that as we have not received any reply from you to our letter No. NB/105-D/11 of 31.01.11, as well as to all the previous letters requesting you to settle your account with us, we have, this day, been compelled to hand over the matter to our lawyer for necessary action. You will hear from our lawyer in due course.

Yours faithfully,
N. K.Tiwari
(Sales Manager)

Sample 2. A Sample Letter Requesting the Supplier for Some More Time for Settlement of Bill.

MODERN TRADING CONCERN

48, Ramkrishna Road, Burdwan-2

Telephone : 2257-8439
Telegram : Modern
E-mail : modtrading@hotmail.com
Ref. No. MTC/61-P/11 Dated : 12th June, 2011

Mr. T. S. Barman
Manager,
Universal Trading Co. Ltd.
57/B, Canning Street, Kolkata 700 071

Sub : Request for Extension of Time for Settlement of Account

Dear Sir,

We are in receipt of your letter of the 5th June, 2011 and are extremely sorry for our inability to settle our accounts with you within the scheduled period.

This is due to the slackness of the market in our area during the last season and owing to our ill-luck, our business virtually came to a standstill.

Under the circumstances, we would request you to kindly allow us an extension of time for two months to settle the bill. We are confident that we shall be able to clear our dues by the middle of August, 2011 because of improvement of the market in recent times.

Hoping to be favoured by your kind and sympathetic consideraion.

Yours faithfully,
R. K. Sen Chowdhury
(Sales Manager)

Sample 3. A Sample Letter Allowing the Customer Extension of Time for Settlement of Accounts.

[A Favourable Reply to the above Letter]

UNIVERSAL TRADING CO. LTD.

57/B, Canning Street, Kolkata 700 071

Telephone : 2654-7198
Telegram : Universal
E-mail : unitrading@live.com
Ref. No. UTCL/35-S/11 Dated : 20th June, 2011

M/s Modern Trading Concern,
48, Ramkrishna Road, Burdwan-2

Sub : Extension of Time for Payment

Dear Sirs,

We thank you for your letter of the 12th instant. We have realised the difficulties you have been unfortunately placed in due to the dullness of the market.

We have a long-standing business relation with you and, considering the temporary difficulties, we agree to allow you two months' time for the payment of your dues to us.

As assured by you, we shall expect your remittance by 20th August at the latest and it must be understood that no further extension of time for payment will be allowed in future.

We hope that with the recovery of the market, you will be able to place further orders with us.

Yours faithfully,
T. S. Barman
(Manager)

Sample 4. A Sample Letter from the Customer Making Arrangement for the Payment of Dues to the Supplier.

[A Reply to the the First Reminder of the Supplier for the Settlement of Accounts.]

PIONEER ELECTRONICS

57A/1, City Centre, Durgapur-2

Telephone : 2251-8243 Dated : 25th July, 2011
Telepram: Pioneer
E-mail : pelectro@gmx.com
Ref. PE/97-G/11

M/s Indian Electronic Co. Ltd.
25, Lenin Sarani, Kolkata 700 013

Sub : Payment of Bill

Dear Sirs,

We are in receipt of your letter dated 18th July, 2011 along with a duplicate bill No. 257, dated 5th May, 2011 for Rs. 6,570.

We are sorry to inform you that due to some financial problems we have not been able to pay your above bill in time. However, we are enclosing herewith a cheque (No. 524167) on United Bank of India for Rs. 6,570 for final settlement of your above bill.

Kindly acknowledge receipt of the same and send us your official stamped receipt.

Once again we regret for the delay in payment.

Thanking you,

Yours faithfully,
P. K. Datta
For Pioneer Electronics

Encl. A cheque amounting to Rs. 6,570 on UBI, Durgapur Bazar Branch.

Sample 5. A Sample Letter Acknowledging Receipt of a Payment.

[A Reply to the above Letter]

INDIAN ELECTRONIC CO. PVT. LTD.

25, Lenin Sarani, Kolkata 700 013

Telephone : 2435-9876 Dated : 1st August, 2011
Telegram : Electronics
E-mail : iecpl@hotmail.com
Ref. EL/175-DC/11

M/s Pioneer Electronics
57 A/1, City Centre, Durgapur-2

Sub : Receipt of Payment

Dear Sirs,

We thank you very much for your letter dated, 25th July, 2011 enclosing a cheque for Rs. 6,570 towards full payment of our Bill No. 257 dated, 5th May, 2011.

An official stamped receipt is enclosed herewith.

Thanking you,

Yours faithfully,
D. K. Shethia
(Proprietor)

Encl. A Stamped Receipt.

No. 568 **INDIAN ELECTRONIC CO. PVT. LTD.**

25, Lenin Sarani, Kolkata 700 013

Received with thanks from M/s Pioneer Electronics, 57 A/1, City Centre, Durgapur- 2, the sum of Rupees Six Thousand Five Hundred Seventy only (Rs. 6,570) in payment of our Bill No. 257, dated, 05.05.11

D. K. Shethia
For Indian Electic Co. Pvt. Ltd.

(6) LETTERS OF CLAIMS, COMPLAINTS AND ADJUSTMENTS

[i] A Letter to a Supplier Complaining about Inferior Quality of Goods Supplied and Asking for Suitable Remedy.

IDEAL TEA CENTRE

58, R. B. Ghosh Road, Station Bazar, Burdwan

Telephone No. 2255-7298 Dated : 10th September, 2011
Telegram : IT
E-mail : idealtca@yahoo.com
Ref. No. ITC/68/Com/11
The Sales Manager,
Bengal Tea Suppliers
Rabindra Sarani, Kolkata 700 070

Sub. : Supply of Inferior Quality of Tea
Re. : Our Order No. ITC/ORD/35/11 dated, 16.08.11

Dear Sir,

We thank you for the prompt execution of our order dated, 16th August, 2011. But we regret very much to point out that the quality of tea supplied by you appears to be of second grade whereas the quality ordered for by us was of first grade.

In the circumstances, we have to advise that this quality can be accepted by us provided, of course, you allow us a discount of 25% on the price quoted by you. Alternatively, we would have no option but to return the goods at your cost. In the meantime, we are holding the goods at your risk and responsibility.

If the first option is acceptable to you, we will be pleased to place with you our original order for immediate execution.

We are waiting for your earliest reply regarding the matter.

Yours faithfully,
For Ideal Tea Centre
A. K. Roybarman
(Purchase Manager)

[ii] A Letter to a Supplier Complaining about Shortage in Quantity and Inferior Quality of Goods Supplied and Claiming Suitable Remedy.

MODERN TRADING STORES

67, M. G. Road, Kolkata 700 006

Urgent

Telephone No. 2468-0357
Telegram. MT
E-mail : mts95@rediffmail.com   Dated : 15th Septemeber, 2011
Ref. No. 59/MT/Com/11

The Sales Manager
New India Sugar Co. Ltd.
Kanpur

Sub : Supply of Sugar against Our Order No. 25/MT/ORD/11 dated, 05.08.11 —Shortage in Quantity and Inferior Quality

Dear Sir,

We acknowledge with thanks the receipt of your consignment containing 40 bags of sugar as per our order dated, 5th August, 2011. But we regret to say that the sugar was found to be short by 5 Quintals when proper weight was taken. Moreover, the quality of the sugar also appears to be inferior to the sample forwarded to us along with your quotation. As this consignment was meant for replenishing our stock, which is almost exhausted, we shall be in great difficulty unless these defects are remedied immediately. We are, however, agreeable to accept this consignment, provided you agree to allow suitable adjustments in price. In the alternative, we would request you to replace the entire consignment at an early date.

Please treat the letter as extremely urgent and let us know your decision, pending which the goods are being held by us at your disposal.

Yours faithfully,
For Modern Trading Stores
R. N. Tiwari
(Proprietor)

[iii] A Letter of Complaints Regarding Perishable Goods Received in Damaged Condition and Sold at Considerable Loss.

UNIQUE FRUIT TRADING CO.

45, M. G. Road, Kolkata 700 009

Telephone : 2798-4263
Telegraphic Address : UFT
E-mail : unikfruit@yahoo.com
Ref. No. 32/UF/Comp/11   Dated : 5th October, 2011

Messrs. National Fruit Dealers
Kulu, Himachal Pradesh

Re. : Supply of Apples in Damaged Condition
Our Order No. 12/UF/ORder/11 dated, 15.09.11

Dear Sirs,

We thank you for the supply of 50 boxes of Kulu apples against our order dated, 15th September, 2011; but regret to inform you that out of this consignment 20 boxes were received in a damaged condition.

Due to faulty packing and rough handling during railway transit these boxes were damaged badly spoiling most of the apples. Because of their perishable nature, we had to arrange an immediate sale of the damaged apples at a considerable loss. The sales was conducted by an auction organised by the Auction House. Howrah. The apples were sold for Rs. 10,750 only, resulting in a loss of Rs. 9,250. The relevant bill of sale is attached herewith.

We now submit our claim of Rs. 9,250—the difference between the price paid by us for 20 boxes of apples and the sale proceeds of the auction.

We shall be thankful to you if you kindly arrange for its early payment.

Yours faithfully,
For Unique Fruit Trading Co.
P. N. Sharma (Manager)

[iv] A Letter of Complaint Regarding Shortage of Weight of the Goods Sent.

PIONEER TEA HOUSE

285, B. C. Road, Kalitala, Burdwan-713104

Telephone : 2255-6723 Dated : 25th October, 2011
Telegraphic Address : PTH
E-mail : poineertea@gmail.com
Ref. No. 96/PTH/Comp/11

The Manager,
Himalayan Tea Co. Ltd., Jalpaiguri

Sub : Order No. 54/PTH/Ord/dated 20.09.11

Dear Sir,

We thank you for the prompt despatch of 35 chests of tea ordered by us on the 20th September, 2011, and are glad to note that the quality of the tea is quite satisfactory. But we are really sorry to draw your attention to the fact that when the consignment arrived, it was found short in weight by 100 kilograms. This shortage, you will surely apperciate, is too heavy to ignore.

We shall, therefore, request you to kindly send us a credit note of Rs. 6,000 being the cost of the shortage of the tea.

Yours faithfully,
For Pioneer Tea House
T. N. Bhandari
(Proprietor)

[v] A Letter of Complaint in Respect of Inferior Quality of Goods.

MUKHERJEE AND BROTHERS

12, A. P. C. Road, Kolkata 29

Telephone : 2243-8327 Dated : 25th November, 2011
Telegram : MUB
E-mail : mukbros@hotmail.com
Ref. No. 48/MB/Comp/11
Messrs. Shankaralal and Co., Nagpur

Sub : Order No. 25/MB/ORD/11 dated, 28.10.11

Dear Sirs,

We thank you for the prompt execution of our order placed with you on the 28th October, 2011. But we regret to inform you that the butter supplied to us by you is inferior in quality to the sample you showed to us.

We did not expect that such a thing will come from you. Under the circumstances, we can accept the goods only if you are prepared to allow us a discount of 10% on the invoice price; otherwise, we would have no option but to retain them at the sole risk and responsibility of yours.

We shall be glad to know your decision in this mattter at an early date.

Yours faithfully,
For Mukherjee and Brothers
Monilal Deshmukh
(Manager)

[vi] A Letter of Complaint Regarding the Execution of Order in Part.

SILK EMPORIUM
24, Gariahat Market, Kolkata 29

Telephone : 2256-3947
Telegraphic Address : SILK
E-mail : silkempo@sify.com Dated : 15th November, 2011
Ref. No. 68/SLEM/Com./11

The Manager,
Mysore Silk Mills Ltd., Bangalore-5

Sub : **Order No. 25/SLEM/OR/11 dated, 12.10.11**

Dear Sir,

We are drawing your attention to our order placed with you on the 12th October, 2011 for 200 pieces of quality silk sarees and regret to state that you were very unpunctual and also careless in executing the order.

Firstly, you have so far supplied us only half of the quantity ordered for and we do not yet know when the rest will be despatched. Perhaps you have not forgotten your confirmation to supply the entire quantity within the first week of Novemeber, 2011.

Secondly, the sarees received by us are not in accordance with the quality of the sample supplied by your travelling agent on 5th October last. We have no market for such goods here.

We are extremely sorry to ask you to take back the goods immediately. This deal has adversely affected our market and our reputation. We have, therefore, no other alternative than to cancel our order and claim from you damages to the extent of Rs. 2,000. We hope that you will make an early settlement of our claim to avoid bitterness of our relations in future.

Yours faithfully,
For Silk Emporium
P. K. Srivastav
(Manager)

[vii] A Letter of Adjustment Replying to the Complaint Regarding the Supply of Goods of Inferior Quality.

NAGBAHADUR OIL MILLS LTD.
Chettiar Street, Chennai

Telephone : 2698-7639
Telegraphic Address : NOM
E-mail : nagoil@mail.com
Ref. No. 78/NBM/ADJ/11 Dated : 16th November, 2011

Messrs. Moonlight Oil Merchant
19, S. P. Mukherjee Road, Kolkata 26

Re. : Your Complaint Against the Quality of Coconut Oil

Dear Sir,

We feel embarrassed and regret that you had to take the trouble of sending us your complaint of November 12.

After a careful investigation we have found out that the delivery of the wrong quality was entirely due to wrong labelling of your name by one of our packers. The consignment of inferior quality was meant for another customer. The person concerned has been taken to task.

We, however, take the entire responsibility for this unfortunate mistake and assure you of our best endeavours to prevent such recurrence in future.

Now, we suggest two alternate solutions for your choice. Either you agree to accept the goods on an additional discount of 10% or allow us to replace the goods. In the latter case you have to send the goods back to us in proper packing only. We shall bear the cost of sending the goods.

We are genuinely sorry for the inconvenience caused to you. Kindly let us know your decision at an early date for necessary action.

Yours faithfully,
For Nagbahadur Oil Mills Ltd.
Motilal Desai
(Sales Manager)

[viii] A Letter to a Customer Replying to the Complaint for Wrong Quality of Goods and Offering Suitable Remedy.

INDIAN SILK CO. LTD.

Bangalore-6

Telephone : 2468-49345
Telegram : ISCL
E-mail : indsilk@gmail.com
Ref. 285/IS/AD/11 Dated : 20th November, 2011

The Manager,
Sunlit Silk Cenre,
Ballygunge A.C. Market, Kolkata 19

Sub : Your Complaints Against the Quality of Silk Sarees

Dear Sir,

We are sorry to note from your letter, dated 12th November, 2011, that the silk sarees supplied by us have been found to be of wrong quality.

On receipt of your complaints, we have looked into the matter and have come to learn that this happened due to a mistake in our despatching section. The silk sarees of a different quality, meant for delivery to another customer, were sent to you by mistake.

We sincerely regret for the mistake and we have already despatched to you a fresh consignment of silk sarees of the right quality at our cost. As regards the silk sarees despatched earlier, you may return the same to us at our cost. In the alternative, we may offer you a special discount of 10% to enable you to dispose of the inferior quality sarees locally.

We are extremely sorry for the inconvenience caused to you and assure you that such a mistake shall not recur in future.

Yours faithfully,
For Indian Silk Co. Ltd.
S. K. Rangarajan
(Sales Manager)

[ix] A Reply to the Complaint Regarding Goods Unfit for Consumption

TRUSTFUL BABY FOOD CO. LTD.
48, Chandni Chawk Street, Kolkata 13

Telephone : 2435-6298
Telegram : TBF
E-mail : trustbfood@rediffmail.com Dated : 18th November, 2011
Ref. No. 86/TBFC/ADJ/11

The Manager,
Parijat Stores,
98, G. T. Road, Burdwan-4

Re. : Your Complaint Against Defective Goods

Dear Sir,

We regret to learn from you that 10 tins of our baby food supplied to you have been found unfit for consumption.

On receipt of your complaint, we have investigated the matter and found that 10 tins from the old stock were despatched to you by mistake due to the fault of one of our packers. Those tins were already kept separately, but somehow they got mixed up with your consignment.

We, however, take full responsibility of this unfortunate affair. We are despatching at our cost a fresh consignment of 10 tins of baby food to replace the defective ones.

We sincerely regret for the inconvenience caused to you for our negligence and assure you to execute your future orders with utmost care.

Yours faithfully,
For Trustful Baby Food Co. Ltd.
Gangadhar Kapuria
(Sales Manager)

[x] A Reply to the Complaint Regarding Defective Conditions of the Goods on Arrival.

NEW BENGAL TRADING CO. LTD.
21B, Ashutosh Mukherjee Road, Kolkata 20

Telephone : 2465-7839
Telegraphic Address : NBT
E-mail : nbtrading@yahoo.com Dated : 16th November, 2011
Ref. No. 69/NBTC/AD/11

The Manager,
Excellent Trading Stores
47, Nutangunge Market, Burdwan 2

Sub. : Your Complain Against Defective Condition of Goods

Dear Sir,

We come to know with regret from your letter that the goods supplied to you by us have been found defective on arrival. As this may cause serious inconvenience to you, we have sent today a separate parcel of goods and hope they will give you full satisfaction.

It is our usual practice to examine the goods before they are despatched and we have not failed to do so in your case also. We believe that the defect has been caused in course of transit.

Now the goods under complaint may be sent back to us at our cost, if they do not serve your purpose. If, however, you are ready to retain them, by some adjustments, we can allow you a special discount of 5%.

We shall be glad to be informed of your decision regarding the former parcel at an early date.

Yours faithfully,
For New Bengal Trading Co. Ltd.
Ram Rudra Bhaduri
(Sales Manager)

[xi] Draft a Letter to the Insurance Company intimating the destruction of insured goods by a fire at your business premises and requesting to arrange for an early survey and settlement of the claim.

EXCELLENT PAPER TRADING CO. LTD.

82, Old China Bazar Street, Kolkata 700 001

Dated : 12th November, 2011

Telephone : 2226-8375
Telegraphic Address : EPTC
E-mail : info@eptcl.in
Website : www.eptcl.in
Ref. No. INS/1/2011

To
The General Manager,
National Insurance Co. Ltd.
15, Chittaranjan Avenue, Kolkata 26

Re. : Inspection of Premises Damaged by Fire, Fire Policy No. 65819

Dear Sir,

We regret to inform you that a fire broke out in our godown on Tuesday night, the 11th November, 2011 at about 9 p.m. As soon as the fire was detected by our night watchman, all possible steps were taken by our staff to put down the fire. The Fire Brigade was also contacted immediately and information was sent to the local police station.

But due to the inflammable nature of the store, a severe damage was caused before the Fire Brigade could extinguish the fire. The damage is estimated to be valued at Rs. 3,00,000.

Our security staff have investigated into the causes of the fire and found out that the fire broke out due to a short circuit in the electric wiring of the godown.

Please arrange for an early inspection of the damage by your representative to enable us to put things right without delay and to submit our claim for damages.

Thanking you,

Yours faithfully,
For Excellent Paper Trading Co. Ltd.
M. K. Chowdhury
(Manager)

[xii] Draft a Letter from the Fire Insurance Company stating that they are sending representative to inspect the damage caused by fire for proper assessment of the party's claim and enclosing the forms for submission of the claim.

NATIONAL INSURANCE CO. LTD.

15, Chittaranjan Avenue, Kolkata 700 026

Ref. No. F/INS/25/2011 Dated : 20th November, 2011
Tel. No. : +91-033-2262-5282
E-mail : enquiry@nationalinsurance.in
Website : www.nationalinsurance.net

To
The Manager,
Excellent Paper Trading Co. Ltd.
82, Old China Bazar Street, Kolkata 1

Re. : Inspection of Your Premises Damaged by Fire.

Dear Sir,

We have received your letter dated the 12th November, 2011. Please note that our inspector, Sri N. K. Bardhan will inspect your premises on the 25th November, 2011 at about 11 a.m. to assess the extent of damage and loss caused by fire. So, we are requesting you to keep the premises under lock and key till the completion of the inspection.

Please make out your claim on the form enclosed herewith and return it to us for an early settlement of your claim.

Thanking you,

Yours faithfully,
For National Insurance Co. Ltd.
M. K. Mahato
(Fire Manager)

[xiii] Draft a Letter of advice to an Insurance Company about the damage caused to an incoming consignment covered by a Marine Policy issued by them, requesting early settlement of the claim.

THE ORIENTAL CO. LTD.

32, R. N. Mukherjee Road, Kolkata 700 001

Telephone : 2248-5287 Dated : 9th September, 2011
Telegraphic Address : OCL
E-mail : contact@orientalco.in
Website : www.orientalcokol.in
Ref. No. 9/MP/CL/2011

To
The Manager,
Marine Insurance Co. Ltd.
7, Lyons Range, Kolkata 1

Re. : Claim against Marine Insurance Policy No. MIP/36805

Dear Sir,

We learn with regret from our London Agent that S. S. Mahalakshmi, carrying the consignment of cotton goods insured under your above policy, met with an accident on its way to Liverpool. This has caused major damage to the ship and the cargo meant for us has been reported to be totally destroyed.

We have got the report on damage surveyed by your authorised surveyor, whose report is enclosed herewith. It will be seen that the estimated value of the damage suffered by us amounts to Rs. 1,73,500.

We would request you to arrange for an early settlement of our claim as stated below :

[i]	Cost of 100 bales of cotton goods totally damaged ...	Rs. 1,50,000·00
[ii]	5% Insurance charge	Rs. 7,500·00
[iii]	Surveyor's fees	Rs. 1,000·00
[iv]	Expected profit (10%)	Rs. 15,000·00
	Total	Rs. 1,73,500·00

The original policy and the supplier's invoice are enclosed herewith.

Yours faithfully,
For The Oriental Co. Ltd.
L. K. Bhandari
(Manager)

Enclo. 3

(7) LETTERS ON BANK LOAN

1. A Letter to The Manager of a Bank Requesting for a Bank Loan.

M/s PAN, KARMAKAR AND CO.
88, Bidhan Sarani, Kolkata 700 006

Telephone : 2663-6525
E-mail : pkc@vsnl.com
Ref. No. Req./1/11 Dated the 8th March, 2011

To
The Manager
State Bank of India
105, Bidhan Sarani Branch, Kolkata 700 006

Re. : Prayer for Granting Loan

Dear Sir,

We are plased to inform you that our company is maintaining a Current Deposit Account (No. 556789) with your bank since its establishment in January 2008. We are also pleased to inform you that our business has made a steady progress within a short period of time. The sales tournover has increased to a great extent due to increase in the demand of our products both within and outside the country. To keep pace with the increased demand we are required to buy raw materials for production in huge quantities. Moreover, the suppliers, now-a-days, are not granting credit for more than one month. Therefore, we are facing acute shortage of working capital.

To cope with the situation our company has decided to make an approach to your bank for a loan of Rs. 1,00,000/- (Rupees One Lakh only) for a period of one year.

For this loan we are ready to hypothecate the Plant and Machinery of our Factory valuing Rs. 2,00,000 (as per audited accounts of our company for the year ended 31.12.10), as security.

Please let us know whether your bank can grant the above-mentioned loan against the hypothecation of the said assets and if you can at what rate of interest.

An early reply will be highly appreciated.

Yours faithfully,
S. Kundu
(Secretary)

2. A Favourable Reply from The Banker

STATE BANK OF INDIA

105, Bidhan Sarani Branch, Kolkata 700 006

Telphone : 2350-6002 Dated : 12th March, 2011
E-mail : sbikol@vsnl.com
Website : www.sbi.net
Ref. No. : Loan/115/11

To
The Secretary,
M/s Pan, Karmakar and Co.
88, Bidhan Sarani, Kolkata 700 006

Re. : Your Application for Bank Loan against Hypothecation of Plant and Machinery.

Dear Sir,

In response to your letter dated 8th March, 2011, we convey our hearty congratulations and good wishes for a steady progress of your company within a short period of time.

We have the pleasure to inform you that our bank agrees to your company's proposal for a loan of Rs. 1,00,000/- (Rupees one lakh only) for which your company is ready to hypothecate the Plant and Machinery worth Rs. 2,00,000/- (Rupees Two lakhs only). The rate of interest will be charged @ 10% p.a.

We attach herewith a blank application form for loan. Please fill in the form, bring a copy of your last audited accounts, and contact our office for further formalities.

Thank you,

Yours faithfully,
P. Datta
(Branch Manager)

Encl. Application form for loan.

3. A Letter by a Bank Refusing Further Loan

ALLHABAD BANK

Bally, Howrah

Telephone : 2654-7700, 7701
Website : www.allhabadbank.net
Ref. No. Refuse/25/11 Dated : 25 May, 2011

To
The Manager,
M/s Mukherjee and Co.
15, Goswami Para Rd., Bally, Howrah

Re. : Refusal of Further Loan

Dear Sir,

We have received your letter dated the 20th May, 2011, requesting to allow your company a further loan for Rs. 50,000/-.

It may kindly be noted that your company have already taken a loan of Rs. 2,00,000 (Rupees Two Lakhs only) six months ago. While we feel the urgency of a further loan we are not in a position to provide your company with the same as the value of securities furnished by your company in the case of former loan account do not cover for additional loan of Rs. 50,000 (Rupees Fifty Thousand only).

In the circumstanes, we can consider your request for further loan only if your company is ready to furnish the required security for it.

Thanking you,

Yours faithfully,
S. P. Dey
(Branch Manager)

4. A Letter from The Customer to a Bank Requesting Overdraft Facilities

VISWAKARMA ENGINEERING WORKS LTD.
148/2, Rashbehari Avenue, Kolkata 700 026

Telephone : 2086-9756 Dated : 5th January, 2011
Telegraphic Address : VEW
E-mail : vewl@yahoo.com
Ref. No. MGC/36/11

To
The Branch Manager,
United Commercial Bank,
12, Gariahat Road, Kolkata 700 031

Re. : Requesting Overdraft Facilites

Dear Sir,

We are very glad to inform you that we have undertaken a contract for the South-Eastern Railway and the amount of investment has already exceeded our original estimates. So, we are in need of further investment to meet our current requirements. However, we shall be able to overcome this difficulty, when a large sum of money due to us by several reliable customers, will be realised by the end of the next month.

In the circumstances, we would request you to kindly grant us an overdraft facility up to Rs. 3,00,000 for a period of two months only for which we are ready to deposit with you sufficient securities.

We shall be glad to receive a favourable reply from your end at an early date.

Thanking you in anticipation,

Yours faithfully,
S. P. Samanta
Managing Director,
Viswakarma Engineering Works Ltd.

5. A letter to a Company from Bank Manager Requesting not to Overdraw without Prior Arrangement

UNITED COMMERCIAL BANK
140, B. B. Ganguli Street Branch, Kolkata 700 012

Telephone : 2204-5678
E-mail : ucobank@unitedcommercialbank.com
Website : www.unitedcommercialbank.com Dated : 10th March, 2011
Ref: No. OD/102/11

To
The Manager,
Ghosh and Co. Ltd.
121/2, B. B. Ganguly Street, Kolkata 700 012

Re : Requesting not to overdraw without Prior Arrangement

Dear Sir,

In spite of repeated request not to overdraw any amount without prior arrangement, your company has issued a cheque of Rs. 60,000 dated the 8th March, 2011 in favour of M/s Das and Co. resulting in an unfavourable balance of the Current Account (No. 057892202) of your company to the extent of Rs. 5,500.

Considering our long-standing relation with your company we did not hesitate to honour your company's cheque. But in future we may be compelled to dishonour cheques on the ground of insufficient balance causing damage to the reputation of your company.

In this connection, we like to remind you that your company overdrew the current account on two previous occasions without making arrangement with the bank in advance and that on both the occasions we duly made payments of the cheques. In both the occasions we requested your company not to violate the banking rules in future..

Therefore, we like to request you to take proper care for not issuing cheques without considering the available balance.

We further request you to deposit the overdrawn amount immediately in your company's Current Account.

Thank you,

Yours faithfully,
R. K. Chatterjee
(Branch Manager)

6. A Letter from The Manager of The Bank to The Customer asking for Further Particulars for granting Overdraft Facilities

UNITED COMMERCIAL BANK

12, Gariahat Road, Kolkata 700 031

Telephone 2423-5198
Telegraphic Address : UCB
E-mail : ucobank@unitedcommercialbank.com
Website : www.unitedcommercialbank.com
Ref. No. OD/56/11 Dated : 10th January, 2011

To
The Manager,
Viswakarma Engineering Works Ltd.
148/2, Rashbehari Avenue, Kolkata 700 026

Re. : Your Application Regarding Overdraft Facilities

Dear Sir,

We are in receipt of your letter of the 5th January, 2011, requesting us to grant overdraft facilities to your company to the extent of Rs. 3,00,000/- for two months only.

As you are one of our valued customers, we are willing to consider your application for granting overdraft facilities. But, in accordance with our usual practice we cannot let you know our decision without knowing the exact value of securities you are going to hypothecate with us.

So, I would request you to call on me within a week to discuss the matter fully. It would be helpful to decide the matter, if you bring with you a copy of your audited Balance Sheet and a detailed statement of your securities.

Thank you,

Your faithfully,

P. R. Mukherjee

(Branch Manager)

5.10 Writing Application

In this age of severe competition, writing a good application letter for a job is of utmost importance. A large number of people apply but only a few get the interview. It means that in spite of possessing minimum qualifications a good number of applications are rejected. The causes of rejection, among other reasons, include bad or illegible handwriting, inadequate information, insufficient address, haphazard arrangement of data, spelling and grammatical mistakes, etc. Only writing down the qualifications and experience on a sheet of paper is not enough for a good application. The presentation of the personal data and information in a systematic and elegant manner constitute a good application and is often rewarded by selection for an interview.

An application is a kind of sales letter. As a sales letter is meant for selling a product, an application is written with the object of selling the services of the applicant. The applicant tries to sell his/her services by stating how his/her skills and experiences would prove valuable to the organisation.

Drafting an application for a job requires skill which again depends upon practice.

Following are the guiding points in writing a good application :

1. Source of information with date should be mentioned (It may be newspaper, notice board, reliable source, etc.).
2. Advertisement should be read thoroughly to know the requirements.
3. Writing of full address of the sender and of the receiver is very important.
4. 'Sir' or 'Madam', as the case may be, is suitable salutation for an application.
5. Clear mention should be made about the post for which the application is being sent.
6. Qualification and experience should be stated in details. Academic and professional qualifications should be mentioned with grades, classes, etc.
7. The application should emphasise on the special ability in any field which may help the present job.
8. Details regarding age, date of birth, height, weight, eyesight, passport, etc. should be written as per requirement.
9. Separate paragraphs should be made for different types of information.
10. Language of the application should be pleasant and dignified.
11. It is preferable to write the names and addresses of at least two eminent persons as referees from whom the prospective employer can enquire about the applicant.
12. Minimum salary expected to be stated where it is specifically asked for.
13. The applicant should mention the time required for joining the post.
14. The applicant should conclude by seeking an interview with the prospective employer.
15. The writer should end with an assurance of satisfying the employer by his/her services.

16. Complimentary close should be made by the words 'Yours faithfully'.
17. After that signature of the applicant is to be made. In the case of a lady applicant 'Ms', or 'Mrs' is to be prefixed as the case may be.
18. Photocopies of the certificates and testimonials are generally attached with the application. Number of copies and the type of documents attached with the application should be mentioned at the left hand corner of the end of the application.
19. The application should be brief and the handwriting should be legible.
20. Quality paper, proper margin and right arrangement give the application a smart look.

• SOME DON'TS IN AN APPLICATION •

1. Do not write boasting and exaggerative expressions.
2. Do not beg sympathy.
3. Do not flatter.
4. Do not say that you are not satisfied with the present job.
5. Do not use the letter-head of the present organisation for the application.
6. Do not write adverse remark in respect of the present employer.
7. Do not write irrelevant matter.
8. Do not use unpleasant and undignified words.
9. Do not make the application too long but do not forget to include the important information.
10. Do not make spelling and grammatical mistakes.

• STRUCTURE OF AN APPLICATION LETTER •

1. **Address of the applicant and Date**

2. **Name, Designation and Address** of the person/organisation to whom the application is addressed.

3. **Opening Salutation or Greeting.**

4. **Subject-matter** in brief

5. **The Body of the Letter** to be divided into different paragraphs, each paragraph dealing with a particular point or topic or aspect of the subject-matter.
   - [i] **Introductory Para** should contain the source of information (e.g., newspaper, notice board, etc. with date) and the post for which the application is being made.
   - [ii] **Middle Portion**—It contains the principal information e.g., academic and professional qualifications, experience, special abilities, age, habits, information relating to health, etc. This should be divided into paragraphs based on points.
   - [iii] **Conclusion** to be drawn by seeking an interview and with an assurance of satisfying the employer.

6. **Complimentary Close** should be made by 'Yours faithfully'

7. **Full Signature** by the applicant.

8. **Enclosures** Papers attached with the application to be mentioned here.

Example 1 : **• An Application for the Post of an Account •**

To
The Secretary
Sunrise and Co.
M. G. Road, Kolkata 700 007

25/2 C. S. Street,
Konnagar, Hooghly
Mob. : 9831305062
E-mail : manna_P20@rediffmail.com
14th August, 2011

Sir,

Ref. : Application for the Post of an Accountant

In response to your advertisement in The Statesman dated the 12th August, 2011 for the post of an Accountant in your office, I would like to apply for the same.

I passed the B.Com. (Honours) Examination of the University of Calcutta in 2008. I have a typing speed of 40 w.p.m. I have also working knowledge of maintaining accounts in Computers.

I have one year's experience of working as an Accountant in a temporary vacancy in Star Brothers and Co., Kolkata. I can prepare final accounts independently.

I am a young man of 23 years having sound health and active habits.

I am a good football player and represented the college team in inter-college competition.

I enclose the photo-copies of the certificates of my qualifications and experience for your ready reference. The originals will be produced at the time of interview or any other time as and when required.

If I am appointed I shall leave no stone unturned in discharging my duties to the entire satisfaction to my superiors.

With thanks,

Yours faithfully,
Partha Manna

Example 2 : **• An Application for the Post of an Assistant Secretary •**

To
The Advertiser,
Box No. 5678
The Statesman, Kolkata

Dear Sir,

In response to your advertisement in The Statesman dated 4th January, 2011 for the post of an Assistant Secretary for your Company, I would like to offer myself as a candidate for the same. I furnish below my qualifications, experience and other details for your favourable consideration :

1. **Name** : ARINDAM RAY
2. **Address** : 259, J. K. Street, Uttarpara, Hooghly
3. **Telephone No.** : 2663-6525/**Mob.** : 12345 67890
4. **E-mail address** : ray_a84@gmail.com
4. **Age** : 27 years
5. **Educational Qualification** : M.Com. L.L.B

Year of Passing	Exam.	Institution	Board/University	% of Marks Obtained
[i] 2004	B.Com. (Hons.)	Goenka College of Commerce and Business Administration	University of Calcutta	65
[ii] 2006	M.Com.	University of Calcutta	University of Calcutta	62
[iii] 2009	L.L.B.	Surendranath Law College	University of Calcutta	58

7. **Professional Qualification** : I am a member of the Institute of Company Secretaries of India.
8. **Experience** : Working as a clerk in XYZ Co. Ltd. 202, M. G. Road Kolkata-7 for last one year.

I shall be highly obliged if you kindly allow me an opportunity to call on you for an interview when I shall be able to supply you with further information that you may require.

Thank you,

Dated the 6th January, 2011
Uttarpara, Hooghly.

Yours faithfully,
Arindam Ray

Example 3 : • **An Application for the Post of a Personal Assistant** •

To
The Personnel Officer,
Modern Computers Pvt. Ltd.
18, B. B. D. Bag, Kolkata

Dear Sir,

Re. : Application for the Post of a Personal Assistant

I would like to apply for the post advertised in The Telegraph on 15th March, 2011 for a Personal Assistant to the Marketing Manager in your Company.

I am at present working as a Junior Secretary in Basak and Co., Kolkata. I have to deal with the routine work of a Secretary including typing, copying reports, taking dictation, drafting letters, etc. I have a working knowledge of using personal computer and I do all official work on computer. I have to make official tour with my superiors several times in a year.

I am a young man of 26 years with active habits and sound health.

I am good in outdoor games and Cricket is my favourite game.

I enclose my Bio-Data for detailed information and your kind consideration.

I attach herewith the photocopies of my certificates and testimonials for your kind perusal.

I shall be glad if you call me for an interview when I shall be able to supply any further information that you may require.

Thanking you in anticipation,

The 18th March, 2011
Janai, Hooghly

Yours faithfully,
Dibakar Dutta

BIO-DATA

1. **Name** : DIBAKAR DUTTA
2. **Date of Birth** : 4th January, 1985
3. **Father's Name** : Late N. K. Dutta
4. **Address for Communication** : Janai Simlai Para, P.O.-Janai, Dist.-Hooghly, West Bengal, 712 304
5. **Telephone No.** : (3212)237626/Mobile : 9007010203
6. **E-mail** : ddutta@sify.com
7. **Marital Status** : Single
8. **Physique** : Height 5′8″, Weight 60 kgs.

9. [a] **Educational Qualifications :**

Examination	Year	School/College	Boad/University	% of Marks
[i] ICSE	2002	Assembly of God Church, Kolkata	Delhi Board	94
[ii] ISC	2004	St. James School, Kolkata	Delhi Board	93
[iii] B.Sc. (Hons.)	2007	Vidyasagar College, Kolkata	C.U.	80

[b] **Other Qualification** : I have completed a certificate course for six months in Secretarial Practice and Office Procedure.

9. **Extra-Curricular Activities** : I can play all outdoor games but Football is my favourite game.

10. **Work Experience** : I am working for more than two years as Jr. Secretary in Basak and Co. 33, J. N. Road, Kolkata-1.

11. **Other Information** : I have a special interest for sales promotion activity. I took part voluntarily in market survey for a product in the present Co. in 2005.

12. **Testimonials** :
[i] Photocopy of Certificate for ICSC Examination.
[ii] Photocopy of Certificate for ISC Examination.
[iii] Photocopy of Marksheet for B.Sc.(H) Exam.
[iv] Photocopy of Experience Certificate from the present employer.

13. **References** :
[i] Mr. S. K. Basak, Basak and Co., 33, J. N. Rd., Kolkata-1; Telephone 2220 0630
[ii] Mr. P. K. Pal, Manager, Joy Industries, Serampore, Hooghly, Telephone : 2652 5833

14. **Language Known** : Bengali (Mother Tongue), English, and Hindi.

15. **Current Salary** : I am drawing Rs. 9,000/- p.m.

Dibakar Dutta

5.11 Resumé

A 'Resume' is a brief statement of a candidate's personal, educational and other qualifications, experiences, achievements, etc. used as an attachment with the application for a job. It is a list of personal information of an applicant willing to get an appointment. Bovee, Thill and Schatzman in their book 'Business Communication Today' write : "A resumé is a structured, written summary of a person's education, employment background and qualifications."

5.11.1 Purpose of Resumé

The purpose of a resume is to kindle interest of the employer to call the candidate at the interview where he/she will be able to say more about himself/herself. It is not a place to say all about oneself. Only some hints are enough. Giving elaborate information is considered to be disqualification in a resume. The brief hints in a resume arouse willingness in the mind of the employer to know more about the candidate. It is a form of self-advertising for a candidate willing to get an interview. It can bring a candidate up to the interview board. It reflects the communication skill of a person. It refers to the capacity of a person to project himself/herself as a suitable candidate for a job.

5.11.2 Features of Resumé

An analysis of the above discussion reveals that a resume has the following characteristics :

1. It is in writing.
2. It is a structured statement.
3. It is brief in nature.
4. It highlights a person's educational and other qualifications and also employment background.
5. Its object is to get a call for an interview.

5.11.3 Writing a Resumé

All necessary personal information is to be collected in details e.g., years of examinations passed, awards won, experience gathered, achievements made, etc. before preparing a resume. With all the information in hand resume is to be prepared to suit a situation. Only those information relevant to the job should be written, e.g., if the post is for a Mathematics teacher the mention of experience as a football coach is of no use. The candidate has to adjust with the requirements of the employer and his/her intention, interest and ability.

Instead of using complete sentences, short and lively phrases should be used in a resume. It should not be too long or too short—a balance should be maintained. It should not be difficult to read. The print of the resume should be vivid. Neatness should be maintained. Sufficient margin and space should be provided to make it visually appealing. Language should be simple and lucid. No high sounding promises, gimmick or dishonest statement should be used in a resume. The total approach should be professional. Preparing resume in an amateurish style may dampen the purpose of resume.

A resume should include the name, address, academic and other qualifications, experience, skill, prizes won, excellence achieved and other relevant information. Emphasis should be given on the strong points. Weakness of the candidate should not be highlighted. If the candidate's education is the strong point, focus should be made on it; but if the work experience is the main consideration the resume should highlight this. Other positive aspects such as languages known, knowledge about computers, etc. should be clearly noted. Any social service work undertaken or participation in any community development programme should also find place in a resume. The candidate should be careful not to exaggerate or fabricate these information.

In short, a good resume should be neat, simple, accurate, honest, informative, well-written and visually appealing.

Now, resume may be produced with the help of a computer where the total subject-matter can be scanned. Spelling and grammar may be corrected, format may be designed according to choice, different pattern of fonts, bullets or numbers may be used.

Resume may be of three types—(i) chronologocial, (ii) functional, and (iii) hybrid or combination resume. In a chronological resume work experience gets the prominence. Beginning with the recent job previous work experience is written in a reverse order. This type of resume is helpful to an experienced person seeking a job opporunity. The functional resume, on the other hand. emphasises on the qualities and abilities of the candidate. New and less experienced persons generally take the help of functional resume. A hybrid resume is a combination of chronological and functional resume. It assimilates the advantages of both the types. The suitable type of resume should be selected according to need.

Following are the examples of the different types of resume :

Example 1 **: Chronological Resume**

Name : Soumya Kundu

Address : 12, M. K. Patil Marg, Deonar, Mumbai-400 008

Telephone No. : (022) 2566 9135

E-mail : Soumya30@rediffmail.com

Objective : Looking for a challenging career where my experience and specialised knowledge in the field of financial management may be utilised.

Employment Experience : 10 years of experience in Accounting and financial field.

March 2005 to present date : Senior Accountant, Grasim Co. Ltd. Mumbai :

- Super-vision of Accounting Process
- Preparation of Financial Reports
- Checking of Bank Reconciliation Statement
- Solving problems relating to computerisation of accounts
- Assisting the auditors of the company by supplying information and documents and explaining the justification of the expenditure, if required.

June 2002 to February 2005 : Accountant, L and T Co. Chennai :

- Preparation of Annual Budget
- Preparation of Cash Flow Statement
- Analysis of Statistical Data, e.g., Ratio Analysis
- Preparation of Financial Accounts
- Checking of daily transactions.

Feb. 2001 to May 2002 : Accounts Clerk, BK and Co., Mumbai

- Assisting the Senior Accountant in all accounting work.
- Writing Cash Book
- Light typing and other office activities

Education : 2002 C.A. from The Institute of Chartered Accountants of India.
2000 M.Com. (Accountancy Group), Bombay University, 1st class
1998 B.Com. Bombay University, 1st class.

Computer Training : Completed Computer Course on keeping of Accounts from R. B. Institute, Mumbai.

Special Interest : Football, Music and Travelling.

Reference : To be furnished if required.

Example 2 **: Functional Resume**

Contact Information :

Name : Ratan Mukherjee

Address : 17 Girish Chandra Ghosh Road, Dakshineswar, Kolkata

Tel. No. : (033) 2572 6660

Mobile No. : 09433 5555

E-mail : rm1980@gmail.com

Objective : Management Trainee in a reputed concern to build up a Management-based career.

Education : [i] Passed B.Com. (Hons.) in 1998 from the University of Calcutta with 62% marks.
[ii] Passed M. Com. (Business Management) in 2000 from C.U. with 61% marks.
[iii] Passed LL.B in 2003 from C.U. with 55% marks.
[iv] Passed MBA from the University of Calcutta in 2006 with 73% marks.

Computer Course : Completed 3 months' Course on Computerised Accounting System in 2004.

Languages Read, Write and Speak : Bengali, English, Hindi and German

Special Interests : Reading, Painting and Travelling

Co-Curricular Activities : [i] Cultural Secretary, Students' Union, City College, Kolkata, in 1997.
[ii] Participated in many Drawing and Painting Contests and won prizes.

Work Experience : Working as an Assistant Teacher in Commerce in Vivekananda Higher Secondary School, Dakshineswar, from October, 2007 to date.

Example 3 **: Combination Resume or Hybrid Resume**

Tamal Datta
Pleasant Park II, House No. A/11, Flat No. 4
Fatima Nagar, Solapur Rd., Pune-411 013
Telephone No. : (020) 6871431, **Mobile :** 09822347312
E-mail Address : tdutta@rediffmail.co.in

Objectives :
- To obtain a position as a Teacher in a college that will utilise my skills and experience.

Education :
- Graduated in 1st class from B.M. College of Commerce, Pune, in 2000
- M.Com. (1st class) from the University of Poona in 2002
- Ph.D.—thesis submitted in June, 2005

Languages Known :
- Bengali (mother tongue), English, Marathi, and Hindi.

Extra-Curricular Activities :
- Represented the College as captain of the Cricket Team.
- Played in the University Cricket Team.
- Participated in inter-college debate competition and won prizes.
- Organised exhibition on Commerce.

Other Abilities :
- Co-author of a book on Accountancy in English for B.Com. students.
- Working knowledge of using a Computer.

Work Experience :
- Worked as a part-time lecturer in commerce for one year in B.M. College of Commerce, Pune.
- Working as a guest lecturer in Poona College for the last two years.
- Coaching B.Com., M.Com., Costing and Chartered students at home.

5.12 Curriculum Vitae [CV]

The term "Curriculum Vitae" (in short CV) comes from the Latin words—'*curriculum*' and '*vitae*'. '*Curriculum*' means 'course' and '*Vitae*' means 'life'. Thus, the term "Curriculum Vitae" signifies 'the course of one's life'. It provides an overview of a person's life and qualifications. It is an arranged list of information regarding a job seeker's qualifications, experience, skills and achievements prepared with the objective of giving an overview of professional accomplishments to the prospective employer.

In addition to the name, address, contact information, education and work experience a Curriculum Vitae should contain research and teaching experience, publications, grants and fellowships, professional associations, licences, awards, and other information suitable for the position.

There is no need for adding a photograph (unless requested by the employer), previous salary record, reason for leaving the previous job or references in a C.V. References should be given on request.

CVs are frequently longer than resumes because they emphasise on clarity and completeness rather than brevity. In general, a resume is limited to one or two pages (of A-4 size paper) whereas a CV may exceed two pages in length. In the United States and Canada a CV is specifically used at the time of applying for international, academic, educational, scientific or research positions or when applying for fellowship or grants and elaborates on education, professional history, contribution and achievement. A British CV is short and limited to two pages. It contains only a summary of qualification, work experience and personal information of the job-seeker. In other countries of Europe, the Middle East, Africa and Asia, the employers prefer elaborate information from the job-seekers and like to receive a CV rather than a resume.

5.12.1 Distinction between a Curriculum Vitae [CV] and a Resume

A Curriculum Vitae and a Resume are similar in many ways. Sometimes these two terms are also used inter-changeably as both are used in job applications with the intention of conveying the facts about the applicant's qualifications, experience, achievements, etc. There is similarity in format of both of them but some important differences between them are as follows :

1. **Length :** A resume is brief and concise. On the other hand, a CV is longer in length. While a resume is accommodated within one or two pages, a CV may be more than two pages of A-4 size paper.
2. **Nature of Information :** A resume contains general information whereas a CV contains personal information in addition to general information of the job-seeker.
3. **Focussed on :** A CV focusses more on education, research and professional accomplishment whereas a resume highlights the experience, specialisation and work history.
4. **Purpose :** Generally CV is used for the purpose of applying for academic, education, scientific or research positions. It may also be used for applying for fellowship or grants. A resume, on the other hand, is generally used for application for non-academic jobs.
5. **Projection of Identity :** A resume projects a professsional identity whereas a CV reflects a scholarly identity of a job seeker.

5.12.2 Format of a CV

A CV is a living document which requires frequent updates with the obtaining of new qualification, acquiring of new experience and achieving new success. The format of a CV should be changed as per requirement. Some information may be required to be omitted and some others to be included depending upon the position for which the application is being made. No single format of CV is applicable for all the positions. A CV for the post of a commerce lecturer must be different from that of a swimming trainer in respect of their contents. However, the types of information that are included in a CV may be arranged as follows :

FORMAT OF A CV

● **Contact Information :**	Full Name : Address : Telephone and Mobile No. : E-mail Address :
● **Objective**	: [Short and specific statement referring to the position, skill, etc.]
● **Employment History**	: [For the new applicants having no work experience this section is to be omitted. Emphasis should be given more on recent job. Therefore, it is required to state the carreer history in reverse order starting with the recent job. Responsibilities, achievements, awards, promotions, etc. are to be mentioned against each position.]
● **Specialisation and Interest**	: [To be mentioned in short]
● **Research Experience**	: [Name and address of the institution and year to be mentioned]
● **Dissertation**	: [Topic and area of dissertation is to be mentioned. A separate synopsis of one or two page(s) may be attached]
● **Publication**	: [A list of publications with date and the name of Journals, Books and Publishers is to be furnished]
● **Seminar and Presentation**	: [With data, place and topic]
● **Community and Social Service**	: [e.g., participation in Banamohotsava, Malaria eradication programme, etc.]
● **Organisation and Leadership**	: [e.g., Organised Seminar, Blood Donation Camp, etc.]
● **Education**	: [Care should be taken to include the years and names of the institutions attended in a reverse order, i.e. University level education should be stated before the school-level.]
● **Personal Information**	: [Sex and Marital Status Date of Birth Nationality Passport No. .... Expiry date .... Willingness to serve—within and/or outside the country.]
● **Reference**	: [To be furnished upon request]

5.13 Cover Letter

A cover letter is necessary both for a Resume and for a Curriculum Vitae. Without a cover letter the application is incomplete. A resume or a CV is an attachment to the cover letter. While a cover letter introduces the applicant to the employer, the resume or the CV tells in detail about the applicant's ability to serve the institution or work in the position. Care should be taken to write a cover letter as it creates the first impression of the applicant.

A cover letter may be divided into three parts. In the first part or paragraph, the applicant introduces himself/herself to the employer and tries to create favourable impression. Here the applicant states the position for which the application is being made and how he/she came to know about the organisation.

The second part of the cover letter will describe very briefly the justification for applying for the post and how the applicant's qualifications and experience will be suitable for the post and beneficial for the organisation. In other words, the second part states why the employer should select the applicant for an interview.

The third part will state for specific action. The applicant will request for an interview, an appointment, or for such other specific action. To facilitate such follow up action, contact number, e-mail address, etc. are to be provided. This paragraph is to be concluded showing interest to join the post.

If computer is used in preparing a cover letter, the basic common fonts like Arial, Times New Roman, Courier New, Dejavu etc. are to be used and 12 point font size is to be utilised. No stylish font should be applied with an intention to make it attractive. The fonts used in a cover letter should match the resume or the CV.

Cover Letter Format

Contact Information	: Name of the Applicant Address Phone No. E-mail Address Date
Employer's Contact Information	: Name/Title of the Employer (If known) Name of the Company Address
Salutation	: Dear Mr./Ms Last name (If known, otherwise use Sir/ Madam as applicable)
Body of Cover Letter	: **First Paragraph :** It should include information on why the application is being made, for what position it is being made and from where the applicant got the information regarding the post. **Middle Paragraph(s) :** This part of the cover letter should describe how the applicant's qualifications match the requirements of the job and the employer should select the applicant for an interview. **Final Paragraph :** The cover letter should be concluded by thanking the employer and giving contact information for follow up.

Complimentary Close : Words like Sincerely yours, Yours faithfully or Respectfully Yours, etc. may be used.

Signature of the Applicant : Full Signature

Encloser : Resume, CV or Certificates, etc.

Example 1 : An application for the post of a clerical job for data entry with cover letter and Resume.

COVER LETTER

Applicant's Contact Information :

Rakesh Sharma
15, M. G. Road, Kolkata-700 007
Phone No. (033) 2222 1000
Mobile No. 98765 43210
E-mail address : rsharma@yahoo.com Date 16.08.2011

To
Mr. B. K. Godrej
Alpha Consultancy Services,
Salt Lake, Sector V, Kolkata

Dear Mr. Godrej

Please consider my resume for the post of a clerical job for data entry in your company.

I am at present working as a Data Entry Operator in PQR System Company, Kolkata. My present position is almost similar to the position you have advertised in The Statesman on 12.08.2011. I am sure that my work experience, skill and education will be most suitable for this position. The Key Strength that will help me to achieve success in the position includes :

- My ability to make data entry for long hours at a stretch.
- Almost error-less input at a reasonable speed.
- Expertise in computer operation for the job.

Being a commerce graduate I have an overall knowledge of the commercial organisations and their workings. The course from Career Institute, Kolkata, on data processing has enabled me to acquire knowledge for systematic work.

Please have a glance on my resume for my humble skills in computer and other abilities.

I look forward for an interview at an early date.

Thank you,

Respectfully yours,
Rakesh Sharma

Enclo : Resume

RESUME

Rakesh Sharma
15, M. G. Road, Kolkata-700 007

Objective

To obtain a clerical job for data entry in a well-known company

Work Experience

From April, 2005 to present date :
PQR System Co., 48/1 Bidhan Sarani, Kolkata

Data Entry Operator

- Data entry from daily records
- Compilation of spread sheets from various systems
- Verification of accuracy of data

From June, 2004 to March, 2005 : XYZ Electronics, N. S. Road, Howrah

Assistant Clerk

- Preparation of bills on computers
- Filing of records
- Deposit of cash and cheques into bank.

Skills

Software : 1. Windows
2. Microsoft Excel
3. Microsoft Word
4. Oracle-DBMS

Programming Languages : HTML coding for designing Web pages

Languages : Read, Write and Speak : Hindi, Bengali, English.

Education

2001-2004—RAC College of Commerce, Kolkata—B.Com. (University of Calcutta)

2004—Completed a course for three months in data processing from Career Institute, Kolkata.

Example 2 : An application for the post of a Company Secretary with cover letter and CV.

[**COVER LETTER**]

Kamal Mahindra
52, Russel Street, Kolkata 71
Mobile No. : 12345 67890
E-mail : kmahindra22@rediffmail.com
Date : 14.07.2011

The Managing Director,
Rolta Industries Ltd.
158, J. N. Road, Kolkata 700 001

Dear Sir,

I am writing to apply for the post of a Company Secretary in your company advertised in the Times of India dated 12th July 2011.

I am currently employed in XYZ Co. Ltd., Medinipur, as a Company Secretary. The scope and responsibility is almost similar to the position advertised. I hope my competence, education and experience will make me a competitive candidate for the post. During my tenure of 3 years in XYZ Co. Ltd. I have made lots of changes in the activities and management of the company. The company was running at a loss prior to my appointment. I suggested certain changes (e.g., closure of a loss-making unit, introduction of technical training of the employes, opening of Labour Welfare Unit, etc.) at the Board Meeting and those were approved. Now it is a good profit-earning company with happy employees.

I hope you will be able to assess my ability from the above description in combination with my attached CV.

I look forward for an interview when I shall be able to supply any further information that you may require. Thanking you in anticipation,

Yours faithfully,

Encl. CV.

Kamal Mahindra

CURRICULUM VITAE

- **Contact Information** : Kamal Mahindra
  52 Russel Street, Kolkata
  Mobine No. : 12345 67890
  E-mail : kmahindra22@rediffmail.com
- **Objective** : Seeking an appointment in secretarial position where my experience and competence can be utilised.
- **Employment History** :
  - ❑ Have been working in XYZ Co. Ltd., Chota Bazar, Paschim Medinipur, from June, 2007 to present date as a Company Secretary. My duties include :
    - — All day-to-day secretarial work of the company.
    - — Preparation of development and growth oriented plans for the company.
    - — Watching carefully proper execution of plans.
    - — Making communication with all the officers of the company for due discharge of their duties and removal of difficulties.
    - — Coping with the internal and external problems including legal and tax oriented problems.
    - — Arranging meeting whenever necessary, etc.
  - ❑ Worked in PQR Co. Ltd., Duragapur from March, 2005 to May, 2007 as an Accountant.
    My performance included :
    - — Preparation of Annual Budget
    - — Working out Cash Flow Statement
    - — Preparation of Final Accounts of the company
- **Specialisation and Interest** : I have a special aptitude for Secretarial and Administrative Work. By doing those works for not less than 3-4 years mentioned in employment history I have become specialised in the field.
- **Writing and Publication** : Published Articles :
  - [i] in "Contemporary Commerce" magazine in March, 2007 issue : Relevance of E-Commerce in the changing modern world.
  - [ii] in "Economic Review" magazine in May 2008 issue : The Investor and the Stock Exchange.
  - [iii] in "Indian Management" in August, 2009 issue : Workers' Participation in Management—a new dimension.

- **Seminar and Presentation** : ❑ Made a presentation in a seminar in MNOP College in December, 2007 : Employment Opportunites of Commerce Graduates.
  ❑ Made a presentation with projector and slide in a seminar in UVWX College in January, 2009 : How to face a job interview?
- **Community and Social Service** : ❑ Participated in illiteracy removal programme organised by the Government of West Bengal in March, 2009.
  ❑ Participated in Awareness Programme of Environmental Pollution organised by a local club.
- **Organisation and Leadership** : ❑ Organised Blood Donation Camp on behalf of a local club.
  ❑ Organised Trekking with few friends several times.
- **Educational Qualifications** : 2001 Passed the M. Com. Examination (Business Management), C.U., with 63% marks
  1999 B. Com. (Hons.), C.U. with 68% marks.
- **Professional Qualifications** : 2006 Passed the Company Secretaryship Examination from the Institute of Company Secretaries of India and obtained the membership of the institute.
  2004 LL.B, Calcutta University with 60% marks.
  2003 Computer Course for one year on Computerised Accounting System.
- **Personal Information** : *Sex and Marital Status* : Male, Married
  Date of Birth : 14th September, 1978.
  Naionality : Indian
  Passport No. : G1234567, Expiry Date 31/06/2021
  Willing to Serve : Within and outside the country
- **Joining Ability** : One month's notice required.
- **Reference** : Not Wanted.

EXERCISES

[A] Essay Type Questions

1. Why is planning of business messages necessary? Give the guidelines for successful planning of business messages. [**Ans.** Secs. 5.1, 5.1.1, 5.1.2]
2. Why are editing and re-writing of a business message required? Explain with examples how several drafts are prepared to get a final draft of a business message. [**Ans.** Secs. 5.2, 5.3]

NOTICE

3. [i] What is a notice? Describe the form and style of a notice. [**Ans.** Sec. 5.5 (A) and (B)]
   [ii] Mention the circumstances of issuing notice. [**Ans.** Sec. 5.5(C)]
   [iii] State the essential elements of a notice [**Ans.** Sec. 5.5(D)]
   [iv] Describe the rules for drafting a notice. [**Ans.** Sec. 5.5(E)]
   [v] Point out the principles to be followed while drafting a notice. [**Ans.** Sec. 5.5(E)]
   [vi] Discuss the factors to be considered for drafting a notice. [**Ans.** Sec. 5.5(E)]

[vii] What points should be kept in mind by the secretary of an organisation while drafting the notice of a meeting? [**Ans.** Sec. 5.5(F)]

[viii] What is an Agenda? State the purpose of preparing an agenda. [**Ans.** Secs. 5.5.1(A) and (B)]

[ix] State the method of preparing an agenda. [**Ans.** Sec. 5.5.1(C)]

[x] What is 'Quorum'? Mention the rules regarding quorum of a meeting. [**Ans.** Secs. 5.5.2(A) and (B)]

4. Describe the requisites of a valid notice for a general meeting of a company. [**Ans.** Sec. 5.5.3]
5. Draft the notices with suitable agenda of the following meetings :

[i] First Board Meeting of a Public Limited Company. [**Ans.** Sec. 5.5(I)]

[ii] 9th Meeting of the Board of Directors. [**Ans.** Sec. 5.6(II)]

[iii] Statutory Meeting of a Public Company. [**Ans.** Sec. 5.5(III)]

[iv] Annual General Meeting of a Company. [**Ans.** Sec. 5.5(IV)]

[v] Extra-Ordinary General Meeting of a Public Limited Company [**Ans.** Sec. 5.5(V)]

6. Draft a notice of the Annual General Meeting of a club or association with usual agenda. [**Ans.** Sec. 5.5(VI)]
7. Draft an appropriate notice convening the Annual General Meeting of a Co-operative Society stating the usual items of business to be transacted. [**Ans.** Sec. 5.5(VII)]
8. Draft a suitable notice with agenda of the ordinary meeting of a local body. [**Ans.** Sec. 5.5(VIII)]

CIRCULAR

9. [i] What is a circular? [**Ans.** Sec. 5.6(A)]

[ii] State the principles of drafting a circular. [**Ans.** Sec. 5.6(B)]

[iii] What is the purpose of drafting a circular? [**Ans.** Sec. 5.6(C)]

[iv] Distinguish between a circular and a notice. [**Ans.** Sec. 5.6(D)]

10. Draft a circular announcing the establishment of a new business. [**Ans.** Sec. 5.6, Specimen 1]
11. Draft a circular addressing to your customers and dealers announcing the opening of a showroom or branch. [**Ans.** Sec. 5.6, Specimen 2]
12. Draft a circular about the appointment of a sole-selling agent for a company's products covering a particular territory. [**Ans.** Sec. 5.6, Specimen 4]
13. Draft a circular informing the customers and others of the admission of a new partner in place of an old partner who has died and that the firm is continuing business with great vigour and expecting large business. [**Ans.** Sec. 5.6, Specimen 8]
14. Draft a circular informing the customers of the death of the senior partner and that the firm is continuing business with the same policy. [**Ans.** Sec. 5.7, Specimen 12]
15. Draft a circular to all customers of the firm advising them the termination of the services of a travelling salesman and appointment of a new representative in his place. [**Ans.** Sec. 5.6, Specimen 7]
16. Draft a circular letter to all customers announcing the purchase of a new business and expressing the hope that the firm will receive the patronage of the customers as before. [**Ans.** Sec. 5.6, Specimen 11]
17. Draft a circular to your customers informing them that your company has been forced to increase the prices of its products due to rise of prices of imported raw materials, increase in labour cost, and increase in the cost of transport and seeking their co-operation as before. [**Ans.** Sec. 5.6, Specimen 6]
18. Draft a circular announcing the conversion of a partnership business into a private limited company and explaining that the change has been made to facilitate the raising of capital for expansion of the business. [**Ans.** Sec. 5.6, Specimen 13]

MINUTES

19. [i] What is meant by 'Resolution'? [Ans. Sec. 5.7(A)]
    [ii] State the principles of drafting the resolution of a meeting. [Ans. See. 5.7(B)]
    [iii] What do you mean by 'Minutes'? [Ans. Sec. 5.7(C)]
    [iv] Describe the importance of the Minutes of a meeting. [Ans. See. 5.7(D)]
    [v] What are the rules of drafting the Minutes of a meeting? [Ans. Sec. 5.7(E)]
20. Draft the minutes of the First Board Meeting of a Public Limited Company. [Ans. Sec. 5.7(1)]
21. Draft the minutes of any Board Meeting other than the First Board Meeting of the Alpha Company Limited of Kolkata. Use relevant particulars wherever necessary. [Ans. Sec. 5.7(2)]
22. Draft the minutes of proceedings of the 8th Annual General Meeting of the Shareholders of Associated Iron and Steel Company Limited in which the items of ordinary business were transacted. [Ans. Sec. 5.7(3)]
23. Prepare the draft minutes of the Statutory Meeting of a company. [Ans. Sec. 5.7(4)]
24. Draft the minutes of an Extra-ordinary General Meeting of a company. [Ans. Sec. 5.7(5)]
25. Draft the minutes of the proceedings of the Annual General Meeting of a club. [Ans. Sec. 5.7(7)]
26. Draft the minutes of the Annual General Meeting of a co-operative society. [Ans. Sec. 5.7(8)]

REPORTS

27. [i] What is a 'Report'? [Ans. Sec. 5.8(A)]
    [ii] Mention the different types of Report. [Ans. Sec. 5.8(B)]
    [iii] State the characteristics of a good report. [Ans. Sec. 5.8(C)]
    [iv] Describe the style of drafting a report. [Ans. Sec. 5.8(C)]
28. Draft a report for submission to the Board of Directors of a company about the desirability or otherwise of standardisation of office furniture, forms and stationeries. [Ans. Sec. 5.8(1)]
29. Outline the broad principles governing the preparation of reports. [Ans. See. 5.8(c)]
30. Prepare a draft report for the consideration of the Board of Directors on the proposal for mechanisation of the office referring to its advantages from the point of view of the company and its employees. [C.U. B.Com 1965, '80, '82]

    Or,

    The Managing Director of your company has sought your advice on the desirability of installing a mechanised acounting system in your office. As the Secretary of the company draft a suitable report giving your advice. [C.U. B.Com. 1986]

    Or,

    As the Secretary of a large company draft a report for consideration of the Board of Directors proposing mechanisation of the Accounting Department indicating expected benefits, cost involved, problems of personnel training, etc. [C.U. B.Com. 1972] [Ans. Sec. 5.8E(2)]
31. Draft a report to the Managing Director on the nature and extent of damages caused by fire to the factory and indicate the means of carrying on the business during rebuilding of the factory. [C.U. B.Com 1970] [Ans. Sec. 5.8E(3)]
32. Draft a report to be submitted to the Board of Directors on an accident caused by a collapse of storage shed in the factory killing two employees. The report is prepared on the Managing Director's assignment. [C.U. B.Com. 1974] [Ans. Sec. 5.8E(7)]
33. Draft a report to be submitted to the Board of Directors about the location of a new showroom proposed to be opened by the company. [C.U. B.Com. 1992, 1967] [Ans. Sec. 5.8E(4)]
34. Draft a secretarial report for raising fresh additional capital to undertake new extensions and schemes of rationalisation. [Ans. Sec. 5.8E(8)]

35. Draft a report to the Board of Directors on the recent trend of sales and immediate need for advertising campaign. [**Ans.** Sec. 5.8E(9)]
36. Draft a report to the Managing Director of a Company on the defects in the routine work of the company's office. [**Ans.** Sec. 5.8E(10)]
37. As an Office Manager draw a report for consideration of the Board of Directors indicating [i] punctuality in office work, [ii] minimum overtime expenses, [iii] improving clerical output, [iv] continuing canteen grievances, and [v] recruitment and promotion methods. [**Ans.** Sec. 5.8E(11)]
38. Draft a suitable report on the grave dissatisfaction of the workers of a company containing your recommendations. [**Ans.** Sec. 5.8E(12)]

BUSINESS LETTERS

39. [i] What do you mean by Business Letter? [**Ans.** Sec. 5.9(A)]
 [ii] State the main function of a business letter. [**Ans.** Sec. 5.9(B)]
 [iii] Point out the importance of a business letter. [**Ans.** Sec. 5.9(C)]
 [iv] Describe the essentials of a good business letter. [**Ans.** Sec. 5.9D(a)]
 [v] Discuss the form of a business letter. [**Ans.** Sec. 5.9D(b)]
 [vi] Describe the style or characteristics of a business letter. [**Ans.** Sec. 5.9(D)]
40. [a] What are the essential qualities of a good business letter? [b] Enumerate the principal features and outline the broad principles governing the preparation of a commercial letter. [**Ans.** Sec. 5.9
41. Draft an enquiry for the supply of uniforms to the peons and bearers of a large commercial establishment. [**Ans.** Sec. 5.9E(I)(c)]
42. A firm of stationery supplier submits quotation for stationery articles in reply to an enquiry from a large office. Draft the letter of quotation. [**Ans.** Sec 5.9(I)(f)]
43. Draft an order for the supply of uniforms for the use of office peons and bearers. [**Ans.** Sec. 5.9(I)(j)]
44. Thank your customer for giving orders. State when and how the goods are being sent, enclose the invoice, mention the total figure and tactfully ask for an early payment. Endeavour to make your letter a means of encouraging business. [**Ans.** Sec. 5.9(2) iii]
45. An ink-supplier of Kolkata informs his customer at Burdwan that his order of ink is accepted, but it will take nearly a week to get ready for the delivery. Draft the letter. [**Ans.** Sec. 5.9(2) iv]
46. You have received an order. Draft a letter informing your customer that there will be delay in execution of the order because the articles are no longer in the stock at present. Assure your customer that the delivery would be made within a week. [**Ans.** Sec. 5.9(2)v]
47. Draft a letter to your customer requesting for substitute product in place of an order. [**Ans.** Sec. 5.9(2) vi]
48. Sen Bros., Kolkata writes a letter to the Ganesh Mark Oil Co. Ltd. of Mumbai, confirming a telegram in which they have cancelled their order for 1,000 tins of Mustard Oil due to fall in market price of the oil. Draft the letter. [**Ans.** Sec. 5.9(2)x]
49. [a] M/s Black and White Co., P-3, Chowringhee Road, Kolkata, placed an order for 200 'unique' Multi-colour Dot pens on M/s Office Equipment Supply Co., B.B.D. Bag, Kolkata, about a month back. But the suppliers did not supply them in the time nor did they request for extension of time. Now M/s Black and White wants to cancel the order. Draft a suitable letter. [**Ans.** Sec. 5.9(2)ix]
50. Draft a letter to your customer requesting him to extend time for execution of order stating suitable reasons. [**Ans.** Sec. 5.9(2)iv]
51. Draft a letter to a supplier cancelling an order due to failure to supply goods within a specified period. [**Ans.** Sec. 5.9(2)ix]
52. Draft a letter making an enquiry about the financial standing of a firm from a business concern. [**Ans.** Sec. 5.9(3)i]

53. Draft a favourable reply by a Bank to a letter of enquiry about the financial standing of a firm. [**Ans.** Sec. 5.9(3)iv]
54. Draft a letter of recommendation for a business friend who wants to establish new business. [**Ans.** Sec. 5.9(4)iii]
55. Write a letter of credit in favour of an employee requesting to pay him a certain sum of money. [**Ans.** Sec. 5.9(4)iii]
56. Draft a letter requesting the supplier for extension of time for settlement of accounts. [**Ans.** Sec. 5.9(5) Sample 2]
57. Write a leter to a supplier complaining about shortage in quantity and inferior quality of goods supplied, claiming suitable remedy. [**Ans.** Sec. 5.9(6)ii]
58. Draft a reply to a complaint against the goods unfit for consumption. [**Ans.** Sec. 5.9(6)ix]
59. Draft a letter to the insurance company intimating the destruction of insured goods by a fire at your business premises and requesting to arrange for an early survey and settlement of the claim. [**Ans.** Sec. 5.9(6)xi]
60. What is meant by 'Resume'? State its features. [**Ans.** Secs. 5.11 and 5.11.2]
61. What is the purpose of a 'Resume'? Describe the style of writing a resume. [**Ans.** Secs. 5.11.1 and 5.11.2]
62. What points should be kept in mind for writing a good application letter for a job. [**Ans.** Sec. 5.10]

[B] Short Answer-Type Questions

1. What are the objects of planning a business message? [**Ans.** Sec. 5.1]
2. What is drafting? [**Ans.** Sec. 5.4]
3. When is a letter called a circular? [**Ans.** Sec. 5.6]
4. Distinguish between a circular and a notice. [**Ans.** Sec. 5.6D]
5. State the rules to be followed while preparing the minutes of a meeting? [**Ans.** Sec. 5.7B]
6. What is a report? When can a report claim 'Privilege'? [**Ans.** Sec. 5.8 A, B]
7. What are the characteristics of a good report? [**Ans.** Sec. 5.8 C]
8. What is the importance of a business letter? [**Ans.** Sec. 5.9C]
9. **Write Short Notes on the following :**
   [a] Statutory Report [**Ans.** Sec. 5.8B]
   [b] Routine Report [**Ans.** Sec. 5.8B]
   [c] Special Report [**Ans.** Sec. 5.8B]
   [d] Business Letters [**Ans.** Sec. 5.9A]
   [e] Cover Letter [**Ans.** Sec. 5.13]
   [f] Resume [**Ans.** Sec. 5.11]

[C] Questions of the University Examinations

1. Draft the notice of the 12th Annual General Meeting of Ruma Industries Limited with usual agenda. [C.U. B.Com 1995]
2. As the Secretary of a Company draft a report for submission to the Board of Directors on irregularity in attendance by some of the members of the staff and suggesting suitable measures for stopping this undersirable practice. [C.U. B.Com. 1995]
3. Draft a letter to your customer requesting him to extend time for execution of order stating suitable reasons. [C.U. B.Com. 1995]
4. Draft the minutes of the 10th Annual General Meeting of Roy Industries Ltd. B. B. D. Bag, Kolkata-700 001 held on 12.10.95 with usual items of busines transacted at the meeting. [C.U. B.Com. 1996]
5. You have been asked by the Board of Directors of the company where you are working as the Secretary to enquiry into the causes of the steep fall in production of the company and to suggest remedial measures. [C.U. B.Com. 1996]

6. Draft a letter from Messrs. Ghosh Brothers, Calcutta to the Sales Manager, Silk Mills, Bombay, requesting the latter to appoint them sole-selling agent for their silk goods in the state of West Bengal. [C.U. B.Com. 1996]
7. Write a letter to a supplier cancelling an order due to failure to supply within a specified period and reserving the right to claim payment of difference in price, if any, arising out of purchase from other sources. [C.U. B.Com. 1996]
8. Draft the notice convening the 2nd Annual General Meeting of 'Zenith Industries Ltd.' 4, Sarat Bose Road, Calcutta-700 020, with usual agenda. [C.U. B.Com. 1997]
9. 'XY Printers' of Calcutta has received a bulk supply of papers from 'R. Paper Syndicate' of Madhya Pradesh. The paper is of inferior quality. Write a letter of complaint to the supplier and ask them to settle the deal by offering 10% discount on the price charged or make arrangement for taking back the papers supplied at their own cost. [C.U. B.Com. 1997]
10. Draft a circular letter notifying increase in selling prices of 'tea' due to rise in cost and seeking continued patronage of the customers. [C.U. B.Com. 1997]
11. Draft a report to be submitted to the Board of Directors about the location of a new showroom proposed to be opened by the company. [C.U. B.Com. 1997]
12. Draft the notice along with the agenda of the first meeting of the Board of the Directors of a Public Limited Company. [C.U. B.Com. 1998]
13. Draft the minutes of the tenth Annual General Meeting of a Public Limited Company. [C.U. B.Com. 1998]
14. Draft a circular letter to the Shareholders of a Public Limited Company informing them that the company will issue Bonus Shares in the ratio of 2 : 1 and that the Shares will be sent to them in due course. [C.U. B.Com 1998]
15. As the Secretary of a developing business, draft a report addressed to its Chief Manager stating the advantages of installation of computerised accounting system in the firm. [C.U. B.Com. 1998]
16. Draft a business letter to your customer drawing his/her attention to the expiry of the period of credit granted to him/her, and requesting him/her to settle the overdue account at an early date. [C.U. B.Com. 1998]
17. Draft the minutes of the 1st Annual General Meeting of J. P. Bagri Industries Ltd., 38, Ezra Street, Calcutta-700 001 held on 12.10.98 with usual items of business transacted at the meeting. [C.U. B.Com. 1999]
18. Draft a letter to the company's bankers asking them to make enquiries as to the financial standing of a firm with which the company wishes to enter into a business contract. [C.U. B.Com. 1999]
19. A firm of stationery suppliers submits quotation for stationery articles in reply to an enquiry from a large office. Draft the letter of quotation. [C.U. B.Com.1999]
20. Draft the notice along with the agenda of the first Board Meeting of a Limited Company. [C.U. B.Com. 2000]
21. Draft the minutes of the 6th Annual General Meeting of the Asim Skyshop Ltd., Marine Drive, Bombay. [C.U. B.Com. 2000]
22. Draft a letter to Citi Bank Corporation enquiring about the financial status of Alpha Company Limited, London, to whom a big consignment is to be sent by your company shortly. [C.U. B.Com. 2001]
23. Draft a notice of the 20th Annual General Meeting of Zee Network with usual agenda. [C.U. B.Com, 2001]
24. Coca Cola purchases the business of Thumps Up and intends to continue it in the name of Thumps Up. No change will be made in the existing policy. Draft a circular letter embodying these facts and expressing the hope that it will receive the patronage of the customers and well-wishers as before. [C.U. B.Com. 2001]

25. Draft a notice of the Statutory Meeting of a company with usual agenda. [C.U. B.Com. 2002]
26. Draft the minutes of the Annual General Meeting of a Co-operative Society. [C.U. B.Com. 2002]
27. Write a letter complaining to your supplier about the shortage in quantity and inferior quality of materials supplied, claiming suitable remedy for the same. [C.U. B.Com. 2002]
28. Draft the notice with agenda of the Tenth Annual General Meeting of a a Public Limited Company. [C.U. B.Com. 2003]
29. Draft the minutes of the first meeting of the Board of Directors of a Public Limited Company. [C.U. B.Com. 2003]
30. Draft a circular letter notifying increase in selling prices of products and seeking continued patronage of customers. [C.U. B.Com. 2003]
31. Draft the notice along with agenda of the First Annual General Meeting of a Public Limited Company. [C.U. B.Com. 2005, New Syl.]
32. Draft a circular announcing the opening of a new Showroom of your product in a village area. [C.U. B.Com. 2005, New Syl.]
33. Draft the Minutes of the Annual General Meeting of a Private Limited Company. [C.U. B.Com. 2005, New Syl.]
34. Draft a letter inviting quotation for purchasing computer in designing your New Computer Centre of the College. [C.U. B.Com. 2005, New Syl.]
35. Draft a letter to your Bank requesting them to grant Overdraft facilities for your business. [C.U. B.Com. 2005, New Syl.]
36. Draft a notice including agenda convening the 15th Annual General Meeting of a Public Limited Company. [C.U. B.Com. 2006, New Syl.]
37. Draft the minutes of the proceedings of the First Board Meeting of XYZ Ltd. where ordinary businesses were transacted. [C.U. B.Com. 2006, New Syl.]
38. As a Secretary of a Public Company draft a report for submission to the Board of Directors regarding the need for introducing Computer in the Accounts Department. [C.U. B.Com. 2006, New Syl.]
39. Draft a letter to the supplier complaining about the inferior quality of goods delivered and asking him for suitable remedy. [C.U. B.Com. 2006, New Syl.]
40. Mr. X has applied for a dealership from a reputed company. But Mr. X is quite unknown to the company. As a Secretary of the company draft a suitable letter of Status enquiry to the Banker of Mr. X regarding his credit-worthiness. [C.U. B.Com. 2006, New Syl.]
41. Draft the notice along with agenda of the First Meeting of the Board of Directors of a Public Limited Company. [C.U. B.Com. 2006, Old Syl.]
42. Draft a circular letter to your customers informing them that your Company has been forced to increase the price of the products due to rise in prices of raw materials, increase in labour and transport cost and seeking their co-operation as before. [C.U. B.Com. 2006, Old Syl.]
43. Draft the minutes of the proceedings of the Annual General Meeting of a Public Limited Company. [C.U. B.Com. 2006, Old Syl.]
44. Draft a report for submission to the Directors of your company on the agitation of the workmen for a higher percentage of bonus and threat for strike by workmen. [C.U. B.Com. 2006, Old Syl.]
45. Write a letter to your supplier complaining about inferior quality of goods supplied and claiming suitable remedy for the same. [C.U. B.Com. 2006, Old Syl.]
46. Draft a letter to your supplier complaining against supply of inferior quality of goods and requesting him to take back the consignment at his own cost. [C.U. B.Com. 2007, New Syl.]
47. Draft a Report on the charter of demand submitted by the Workers' Union of your company. [C.U. B.Com. 2007, New Syl.]

48. Draft the notice along with agenda of the Annual General Meeting of a co-operative society. [C.U. B.Com. 2007, New Syl.]
49. Draft the minutes of the proceedings of the Board Meeting of a Public Limited Company. [C.U. B.Com. 2007, New Syl.]
50. Write a letter requesting for extension of time of supply of goods to your customer. [C.U. B.Com. 2007, New Syl.]
51. Draft a circular addressing to your customers and dealers announcing opening of a showroom. [C.U. B.Com. 2008, New Syl.]
52. Draft a report to the Board of Directors on the recent trend of sales and immediate need for advertising campaign. [C.U. B.Com. 2008, New Syl.]
53. Draft a notice of the Annual General Meeting of a club with usual agenda. [C.U. B.Com. 2008, New Syl.]
54. Draft the minutes of the Annual General Meeting of a public limited company. [C.U. B.Com. 2008, New Syl.]
55. Draft a letter to the Insurance Company stating the loss of goods by fire and requesting immediate action for the settlement of the claim. [C.U. B.Com. 2008, New Syl.]
56. Draft the notice of the 20th Annual General Meeting of a Public Limited Company with usual agenda. [C.U. B.Com. 2009, New Syl.]
57. Write a letter to your Banker complaining delay in preparing Bank Statement and excess debit of Bank Charges. [C.U. B.Com. 2009, New Syl.]
58. Draft a letter to your customer requesting him to extend time for execution of order stating suitable reasons. [C.U. B.Com. 2009, New Syl.]
59. Draft a letter to your customer reminding him about a debt still remaining unpaid. [C.U. B.Com. 2009, New Syl.]
60. Draft the notice along with agenda of the First Meeting of the Board of Directors of a Public Limited Company. [C.U. B.Com. 2010, New Syl.]
61. As the Secretary of a developing business, draft a report to the Chief Manager stating the advantages of installation of a computerised accounting system in the firm. [C.U. B.Com.2010, New Syl.]
62. Draft a letter to your Bank requesting them to grant overdraft facilties for your business. [C.U. B.Com. 2010, New Syl.]
63. Draft a notice along with agenda of an Annual General Meeting of a Public Limited Company. [C.U. B.Com. 2011, New Syl.]
64. Write a letter to the manager of a nationalised bank seeking a loan for a small-scale enterprise. [C.U. B.Com. 2011, New Syl.]
65. Write a letter, seeking quotation of stationery items, to suppliers. [C.U. B.Com. 2011, New Syl.]

APPENDIX I

SELECTED IMPORTANT SHORT QUESTIONS AND ANSWERS

MODULE I

PRINCIPLES AND PRACTICE OF MANAGEMENT

Chapter 1

Introduction to Management

Q. 1. What do you mean by 'Management'?

[C.U. B.Com. 1988, 1996, 1997, 2010, 2011 (Old and New Syllabus)]

Ans. : 'Management' is the sum total of various activities of determining objectives, formulating policies, and selecting procedures, making programmes; securing men, machine, money, materials etc. required for the realisation of the objectives; putting them into operation; co-ordinating various actions; supervising and checking the performance of the employees of an enterprise; and providing them with financial and mental satisfaction.

Q. 2. Mention the functions of Management. [C.U. B.Com. 2001, 2006]

Ans. : The various functions of management are stated as follows :

(i) Planning, (ii) Organising, (iii) Command, (iv) Directing, (v) Motivating, (vi) Co-ordinating, (vii) Control, (viii) Innovation, (ix) Communicating, (x) Representation etc.

Q. 3. Is Management an Art or a Science? [C.U. B.Com. 2001, 2005]

Ans. : Management is a combination of art and science. Management is an 'art' because it is a process or technique which can be acquired by learning, and which are applied to manage the affairs of an enterprise. Management is also a 'science' as it is a particular knowledge based on research and experiment which are applicable to manage the activities of all enterprises.

Q. 4. Is Management a Profession? [C.U. B.Com. 1995, 1998, 2008]

Ans. : Management cannot termed as true profession, though it is emerging as profession. Management may not be a profession—similar to the medical or legal profession, but it possesses some basic elements of a profession.

Q. 5. What do you mean by Universality of Management?

[C.U. B.Com. 1996, 2002, 2004, 2006, 2008, 2010]

Ans. : Universality of Management means that the basic principles and techniques of management are applicable not only to business concern, but also to non-business institutions like social, political, cultural, religious etc. situated in any country.

Q. 6. What do you mean by 'PODSCORB'? [C.U. B.Com. 2002, 2005]

Ans. : Luther Gullick made a list of the functions of management and formed an abbreviated term to indicate them. This term is PODSCORB.

P = Planning, O = Organising, D = Directing, S = Staffing, Co = Co-ordinating, B = Budgeting.

Q. 7. Mention the different levels of Management.

[C.U. B.Com. 1987, 2011 (New Syllabus)]

Ans. : There are generally three levels of management in big enterprises. They are as follows :

(i) Top level of Management;

(ii) Middle level of Management; and

(iii) Lower level of Management.

Q. 8. Define 'Authority'. [C.U. B.Com. 2010]

Ans. : 'Authority' is the right to give orders and the power to exact obedience. Whenever a manager is allocated tasks, he should be given requisite authority so that he can exercise his own skill and initiative for performing the tasks.

Q. 9. State any four of Fayol's 'Principles of Management'.

[C.U. B.Com. 2011]

Ans. : (i) The whole work of each department, section or unit of an enterprise should be divided among the workers.

(ii) There should be a parity between authority and responsibility.

(iii) An employee should receive orders from one superior only.

(iv) The remuneration payable to the employees must be fair and reasonable.

Q. 10. State two managerial tasks. [C.U. B.Com. 2011 (New Syllabus)]

Ans. : Two managerial tasks or roles are mentioned below :

(i) Inter-personal Roles as 'Figurehead', 'Liaison-maker', and 'Leader'.

(ii) Decisional Roles as 'Entrepreneur', 'Disturbance-handler', 'Allocator of Resources', and 'Negotiator'.

Q. 11. Mention any four skills of a Manager.

Ans. : Four skills of a successful manager are as follows :

(i) Organisational skill;

(ii) Technical skill;

(iii) Decision-making skill; and

(iv) Leadership skill.

Q. 12. Distinguish between 'Administration' and 'Management'.

Ans. : 'Administration' is the process of determining the objectives and policies of an enterprise and formulating rules and regulations for the execution of those objectives. It is the task of the top level managers.

On the other hand, 'Management' is the process of implementing the objectives and policies of the enterprise. The managers of the middle level and lower level perform the management functions.

Q. 13. Point out the difference between 'Organisation' and 'Management'.

Ans. : The differences between 'Organisation' and 'Management' are pointed out below :

'Organisation' is the structure by which a harmonious inter-relation is established between the workers and their work. It is one of the various functions of Management.

On the other hand, 'Management' is the executive process of getting works performed by the subordinate employees. It includes the tasks of planning, setting up organisation, giving command and direction, motivating the employees, co-ordinating and controlling the various activities of the enterprise.

Chapter 2

Different Schools of Management Thought

Q. 1. What is 'Scientific Management'?

[C.U. B.Com. 1984, 2000, 2003, 2005, 2007, 2009, 2010]

Ans. : 'Scientific Management' is the art or technique based on clearly defined laws and principle which are applicable to all forms of human activity. The objective of scientific management is to develop each man to his greatest efficiency and to maximise prosperity for both the employer and the employee.

Q. 2. What do you mean by 'Time Study'? [C.U. B.Com. 1987, 1990, 1993]

Ans. : 'Time Study' is a tool of Scientific Management. It involves the careful measurement of the time required to do each part of an industrial operation. The basic purpose of time study is to determine the proper time for performing the operation.

Q. 3. What is 'Motion Study'? [C.U. B.Com. 1994]

Ans. : 'Motion Study' is a study of the movements of an operator in performing an operation for eliminating useless motions. The purpose of such a study is to find out the one best method of job performance which every worker will be expected to follow.

Q. 4. What is meant by 'Fatigue Study'?

Ans. : 'Fatigue Study' is the study the purpose of which is to provide for measures to eliminate or minimise fatigue of the workers at jobs. Its objectives are to regulate the working hours and provide for rest to the workers at scientifically determined intervals so that the workers get opportunity to restore the energy lost in continuous work.

Q. 5. Write any four features of Scientific Management. [C.U. B.Com. 2002]

Ans. : Four features of Scientific Management are mentioned below :

(i) Development of Science for each element of a man's work.

(ii) Scientific Selection and Training of workmen.

(iii) Financial Incentives for the workers.

(iv) Maximum output.

Q. 6. State two benefits of Scientific Management.

Ans. : The following are the two benefits of Scientific Management :

(i) In scientific management process, the employees are selected, trained and employed on the basis of scientific principles. As a result, efficiency of the employees is increased.

(ii) By avoiding guesswork and encouraging scientific analysis and observations for plans and procedures, scientific management increases productivity and eliminates wastage and losses.

Q. 7. Mention any two criticisms against Scientific Management.

Ans. : Two criticisms against Scientific Management are stated as follows :

(i) The introduction of scientific management involves huge expenditure.

(ii) It is a mechanical approach to the workers undermining the human element in industry.

Q. 8. Write any two criticisms against Henry Fayol's approach to Management.

Ans. : Two criticism against Henry Fayol's approach to management are the following:

(i) Fayol has analysed management theory mainly from the view point of the top level managers. He has not considered the importance of the lower level managers of the organisation.

(ii) Fayol's concept of universality of management is controversial.

Q. 9. What is meant by 'Bureaucratic Management'?

Ans. : 'Bureaucratic Management' means the system of management, the functioning of which is bound by rules. The Bureaucratic Managers set norms, frame specific rules and regulations which must be enforced for the smooth operation of the organisation. It is applicable to all types of large and complex organisations.

Q. 10. Mention any two points of criticism against Max Weber's Theory of Bureaucratic Management.

Ans. : Max Weber's theory of Bureaucratic Management may be criticised from the following two aspects :

(i) Bureaucratic management theory is a non-human thought; it is a mechanical system.

(ii) This type of management process is not flexible to adapt readily to the changing nature of modern system.

Chapter 3

Planning

Q. 1. What is meant by 'Planning' in Management?

[C.U. B.Com. 1989, 1995, 1997, 1999, 2005, 2006, 2007, 2009, 2011, 2011 (supplementary)].

Ans. : 'Planning' is the process through which the managers of an organisation set objectives and policies, determine procedures, make programmes and budgets in order to achieve the organisational goals.

Q. 2. Point out any four principles of Planning. [C.U. B.Com. 1998, 2002]

Ans. : Four principles of Planning are pointed out below :

(i) Principle of Efficiency;
(ii) Principle of Flexibility;
(iii) Principle of Pervasiveness; and
(iv) Principle of Selection of Alternative Courses of Action.

Q. 3. Name the elements of Planning. [C.U. B.Com. 2004]

Ans. : The elements of Planning are the following : (i) Purpose, (ii) Policies, (iii) Forecasting, (iv) Procedures, (v) Programmes, (vi) Rules, (vii) Budget, (viii) Project, and (ix) Strategies.

Q. 4. What is 'Decision-making'? [C.U. B.Com. 1997, 2006]

Ans. : 'Decision-making' is the managerial process of selecting a right and effective course of action from the alternatives for the purpose of achieving a desired result.

Q. 5. What do you mean 'Planning Premises'? [C.U. B.Com. 2011 (New Syllabus)]

Ans. : 'Planning Premises' are planning assumptions relating to the expected environmental and internal conditions. This involves collection of facts and information necessary for planning the future course of action of the enterprise.

Q. 6. Mention the characteristics of Decision-making. [C.U. B.Com. 2005]

Ans. : The characteristics of Decision-making are as follows :

(i) Decision-making is a process of evaluating the alternative courses of action; (ii) It is a process of selecting the best alternative; (iii) It is an objective-oriented process; (iv) It is a thinking process; (v) It is a rational process; (vi) It is a continuous process; (vii) It is a managerial function, etc.

Q. 7. Define 'Forecasting'. [C.U. B.Com. 2007, 2010, 2011 (New Syllabus)]

Ans. : 'Forecasting' is the process of assessing the future using calculations and projections that take account of past performance, current trends, and anticipated changes in the foreseeable period ahead.

Q. 8. Mention two features of Forecasting. [C.U. B.Com. 2008]

Ans. : Two features of forecasting are stated below :

(i) Forecasting relates to future. (ii) Forecasting is made by analysing the past and present factors relevant for the functioning of an organisation.

Q. 9. What is Derivative Plan? [C.U. B.Com. 2008]

Ans. : The plan which is prepared for implementing the various parts of the basic plan is known as 'Derivative Plan'. The departmental plans are the examples of derivative plans.

Q. 10. Mention two techniqus of Forecasting.

Ans. : The following are the two techniques of forecasting :

(i) Survey Method; and (ii) Statistical Method.

Q. 11. What is Master Planning? [C.U. B.Com. 2011]

Ans. : 'Master Planning' means the preparation of the plan for the accomplishment of activities of the enterprise as a whole. This plan includes the objectives, policies, procedures, programmes, budget, time-schedule, strategies, etc.

Q. 12. Give an idea of 'Policy' as a plan. [C.U. B.Com. 2011 (New Syllabus)]

Ans. : Policies are the statements or principles that guide and direct the different managers of an enterprise in making decisions. Policies set overall boundaries within which they are expected to operate for arriving at decisions.

Q. 13. Briefly explain the importance of 'Planning'.

[C.U. B.Com. 2011 (New Syllabus)]

Ans. : Planning is a very important managerial function because of the following reasons :

(i) Planning provides the basis of decision.
(ii) It focuses attention on the objectives of the enterprise.
(iii) It minimises risks and uncertainties.
(iv) It helps the enterprise in adapting with the changes.
(v) It secures economy.
(vi) It assists in maintaining co-ordination of various activities of the enterprise.
(vii) It makes controlling process effective.
(viii) It increases organisational effectiveness.

Q. 14. State four characteristics of a Plan.

Ans. : Four characteristics of a plan are stated below :

(i) A plan helps in the fulfilment of objectives of an enterprise.
(ii) It is creative in nature.
(iii) It is necessary to make plans in all levels of the organisation.
(iv) A plan is the result of deep and efficient thinking.

Q. 15. Point out the benefits of Planning.

Ans. : The important benefits obtained from effective planning are as follows :

(i) Planning gives certainty in work performance.
(ii) It helps in reduction of cost.
(iii) It determines specific goals of an enterprise.
(iv) With the help of planning an organisation becomes strong and effective.
(v) It provides assistance in controlling process.
(vi) It helps in coping up with the changed situation.
(vii) It facilitates to maintain co-ordination.
(viii) It provides for optimum utilisation of resources.
(ix) A sound plan improves the competitive power of an enterprise.

Q. 16. Give an idea of 'Strategic Planning'.

Ans. : 'Strategic Planning' is the process of determining the objectives of an enterprise, the resources that are to be used to attain these objectives and the policies to govern the acquisition, utilisation and disposition of those resources. Such planning is made for achieving the long-term objectives of the enterprise. Duration of a strategic plan is three to five years. The main function of strategic planning is to decide the various steps for fulfilling the objectives. Making of such planning is a very difficult and complicated job. The managers are required to consider the internal and external situation and environment very carefully for the preparation of a strategic plan. The planning in respect of diversification of business into new lines, use of new and advanced technology etc. are the examples of Strategic Planning.

Q. 17. State briefly the importance of Forecasting.

Ans. : Forecasting is essential for making plan of an enterprise. Planning is not possible without forcasting. To determine the future course of action, it is necessary to forecast the future demands for commodities, sales, market condition, wages of the workers, government policies, technological trends, political environment and so on.

Forecasting provides the basis for planning. The success of planning depends to a great extent upon correct forecasting. It is forecasting that helps the planners in selecting the sources of finance, establising the target of production, fixing the sales target, and determining the strategy for reaching this target. A good plan is the outcome of right forecasting.

Q. 18. Describe the importance of Decision-making.

Ans. : The task of decision-making is very much significant in management process. The managers perform their all works through making decisions. They cannot go a step without decision. Planning, organising, directing, motivating, co-ordinating, controlling—all the functions of management are determined by decisions. The planner has to choose a course of future action from some alternative courses and then it becomes necessary to take the valuable decision. In fact, decision-making is an inevitable part of management. For that very reason a considerable number of management experts opines that, "Management is actually a decision-making process." George Terry views that, if a manager has one quality or symptom, then it is the task of decision-making. Decisions pervade all levels of management, and each aspect of the organisation. The success and progress of an enterprise depends largely on the proper decisions taken by the efficient managers.

Q. 19. Mention any four principles of Decision-making.

Ans. : For principles of Decision-making are given below :

(i) Decision is to be taken on the basis of the analysis of the objectives and policies of the enterprise.

(ii) Decision-making depends on the organisation structure of the enterprise.

(iii) For taking correct and effective decisions, all necessary facts and information are to be collected in proper manner.

(iv) The decision-maker should also participate in the implementation of his decision.

Q. 20. State the relation between Planning and Decision-making.

Ans. : There is a very close relationship between 'Planning' and 'Decision-making'. Firstly, both are intellectual process including judgement and reasoning. Secondly, both are continuous processes. Thirdly, both are objective-oriented. Fourthly, both involve making choice from alternative courses of action. Lastly, both of the processes need information about the internal and external environment of the organisation.

Planning and decision-making are not considered separately. Both are complimentary to each other. They depend on each other. Decision-making process determines the correct means and procedure of the functions of planning process. Actually, decision-making is a particular type of planning and it is based upon forecasts and assumptions about the future.

Q. 21. Mention two limitations of Forecasting. [C.U. B.Com. 2011, (supplementary)]

Ans. : Two limitations of Forecasting is mentioned below :

(i) Forecasting is a very time-consuming and expensive process. (ii) Forecasting cannot be accurate, because forecasting depends on some assumptions.

Chapter 4

Organising

Q. 1. What is 'Organisation'?

[C.U. B.Com. 1983, 1986, 1991, 1997, 1998, 2005, 2011 (supplementary)]

Ans. : 'Organisation' is the structural framework of duties and responsibilities to be performed by a group of people for the attainment of the objectives of a business enterprise. It is the process of identifying and grouping the work to be done, defining and delegating responsibility and authority and establishing relationship for the purpose of enabling the employees to work effectively together for achieving the common objectives.

Q. 2. What is meant by 'Organisation Structure'?

[C.U. B.Com. 1989, 2000, 2009, 2010, 2011 (supplementary)]

Ans. : 'Organisation Structure' is the frame work that provides a set of relationships among various activities and group of people in the enterprise.

Q. 3. What is 'Delegation of Authority'?

[C.U. B.Com. 1985, 1987, 1988, 1993, 1996, 1997, 1999, 2001, 2003, 2006, 2011 (supplementary)]

Ans. : 'Delegation of Authority' is the process of entrusting some part of the work of operations or management to others and thus sharing one's responsibilities with others.

Q. 4. What do you mean by 'Decentralisation'?

[C.U. B.Com. 2003, 2005, 2008, 2010]

Ans. : 'Decentralisation' means dispersal of authority for decision-making in various levels of organisational operations throughout the organisation. Decentralisation is actually an extension of the process of delegation of authority.

Q. 5. Mention the elements of Delegation of Authority. [C.U. B.Com. 2004, 2009]

Ans. : The elements of delegation of authority are stated below :

(i) Assignment of Duties;

(ii) Granting of Authority; and
(iii) Creation of Accountability for Performance.

Q. 6. Define 'Organising'. [C.U. B.Com. 1996, 2008]

Ans. : 'Organising' is the process of creation of a structure of relationship among the employees and jobs for the realisation of the goals of the enterprise.

Q. 7. What do you mean by 'Line Organisation'? [C.U. B.Com. 2001, 2003, 2005, 2011]

Ans. : 'Line Organisation' is the oldest form of organisation structure. In such type of organisation structure, authority flows from the person at the top level to the man of the lowest level vertically. In line organisation command is given from top to the bottom through a straight line.

Q. 8. What is 'Line and Staff Organisation'?

Ans. : 'Line and Staff Organisation' is a combination of line organisation and staff organisation structure. In such organisation structure, line authority flows in a vertical line; and the staff specialists are employed to advise the line managers for efficient performance of the special functions.

Q. 9. What is an 'Organisation Chart'? [C.U. B.Com. 2005]

Ans. : 'Organisation Chart' is a diagrammatical representation of the various positions in an enterprise and the formal relationships among them. It gives a picture of the relationships between different departments or divisions of the enterprise and the relationships between the employees of various levels.

Q. 10. What is meant by 'Staff Organisation'?

Ans. : 'Staff Organisation' is that type of organisation structure in which some experts are employed to execute the advisory functions of an enterprise. The staff persons have no authority to command and provide direction. They only give advice to the line manager in various organisational aspects.

Q. 11. Distinguish between 'Delegation of Authority' and 'Decentralisation of Authority'. [C.U. B.Com. 2004]

Ans. : 'Delegation of Authority' means transfer of authority from one individual to another; whereas 'Decentralisation of Authority' implies dispersal of decesion-making authority throughout the organisation. Decentralisation is much more comprehensive than delegation. Delegation of authority can take place without decentralisation; but decentralisation without delegation is not possible.

Q. 12. Distinguish between 'Centralisation' and 'Decentralisation'? [C.U. B.Com. 2011 (New Syllabus)]

Ans. : 'Centralisation of Authority' means concentration or reservation of authority at the top level of an organisation. On the other hand, 'Decentralisation of Authority' refers to systematic dispersal or delegation of authority in the organisation. Decentralisation of authority is actually an extension of the concept of delegation of authority. Delegation can take place from one superior to one subordinate and be a complete process; but decentralisation takes place only when the fullest possible delegation or distribution of authority is made to all, or most of the people in the organisation.

Q. 13. What are the basic elements of Delegation?

Ans. : The basic elements of Delegation are the following :

(i) Allocation of Duties;
(ii) Granting of Authority; and
(iii) Creation of Accountability for Performance.

Q. 14. What is meant by 'Departmentation'?

Ans. : 'Departmentation' means the process of grouping the activities of an enterprise into some units for the purpose of administration at all levels. The administrative units so created may be 'departments', 'divisions', 'branches', 'sections', etc.

Q. 15. Mention the various bases of Departmentation.

Ans. : The following are the different bases of Departmentation :

(i) Function; (ii) Product; (iii) Territory; (iv) Process; (v) Customer; (vi) Time, etc.

Q. 16. Explain in brief the role or importance of Organisation.

Ans. : All trading and non-trading enterprises require sound organisation for their smooth, efficient and economical operation to achieve maximum results with minimum of efforts and cost. When two or more persons are engaged in an enterprise, the task of each person is required to be fixed through division of total activities among them and they should have a concerted action. It is the process of organisation that distributes the works among a number of persons on the basis of their knowledge, capacity and experience. As a result, the speed of performance is ensured and the standard of works performed is improved. Organisation is a tool of efficient management. It provides a means by which human efforts are properly directed to more productive, effective and fruitful results. In fact, the success and progress of any enterprise depend to a large extent on efficient organisation process.

Q. 17. Mention any four benefits of Organisation.

Ans. : The following are the four benefits that are obtained through sound organisation:

(i) Efficient Management;
(ii) Prompt Accomplishment of Activities;
(iii) Optimum Utilisation of Resources and Advanced Technology; and
(iv) Growth of Business and Diversification of Production Process.

Q. 18. Point out any four features of a good Organisation Structure.

Ans. : Four important features or characteristics of a good organisation structure are pointed out below :

(i) Simplicity;
(ii) Flexibility and Continuity;
(iii) Proper Delegation of Authority; and
(iv) Unity of Command and Direction.

Q. 19. State any four types of Organisation Structure.

Ans. : Four types of organisation structure are stated as follows :

(i) Line Organisation Structure;
(ii) Staff Organisation Structure;
(iii) Functional Organisation Structure; and
(iv) Line and Staff Organisation Structure.

Q. 20. Describe briefly the need for Departmentation.

Ans. : The basic need for or importance of 'Departmentation' is to make the size of each departmental unit manageable effectively and to secure the benefits of specialisation. Grouping of activities and personnel into departments makes it possible to expand an enterprise to any extent. In short, departmentation is necessary for—(i) Availing of the merits of specialisation; (ii) Enjoying autonomy and freedom in action and decision-making; (iii) Expansion of the enterprise; (iv) Fixation of responsibility; (v) Development of managerial skill; (vi) Administrative control; etc.

Q. 21. Write any four principles or factors to be considered in Departmentation.

Ans. : Four principles or factors which are to be taken into account are the following :

(i) Adequate attentions should be given to all the activities.
(ii) Maximum possible economy should be achieved in the utilisation of existing resources, facilities and personnel.
(iii) Human aspect in the organisation should be considered.
(iv) The activities of the enterprise should be grouped in such a way that it leads to obtain the benefits of specialisation.

Q. 22. Mention any four features of Delegation.

Ans. : The following are the four features of Delegation :

(i) Delegation is authorisation to a subordinate manager to perform certain responsibility.
(ii) A top manager delegates authority out of the authority vested in him.
(iii) Authority once delegated can be enhanced, reduced or withdrawn depending on situation and requirement.
(iv) Delegation of authority may be specific or general.

Q. 23. Explain briefly the need for Delegation of Authority.

Ans. : Delegation of authority is a very essential requirement for effective and efficient management. In large enterprises due to its complexities, delegation of authority is a must. It is not possible for a chief executive to manage and control everything. Delegation arises from the natural limitations of the human being.

Besides physical limitation the need for delegation arises in a big and complex organisation for securing expert's services. Delegation of authority also ensures continuity in business activities.

Q. 24. What are the important benefits of Delegation of Authority?

Ans. : The important benefits that are obtained through Delegation of Authority are as follows :

(i) Delegation of authority reduces the work-burden of the chief executive.

(ii) It enables the manager to utilise the specialised knowledge and experience of the persons at lower levels.

(iii) It encourages expansion and diversification of business activities.

(iv) It provides the key to smooth and efficient running of the various departments, divisions or branches, etc.

Q. 25. Indicate any four basic principles to be followed in Delegation of Authority.

Ans. : Four basic principles which are to be followed for Delegation of Authority are indicated below :

(i) Before delegating authority, a manager should define clearly the functions to be performed by the subordinates.

(ii) Authority should be delegated to a position according to the results expected from that position.

(iii) The lines of authority should be clearly defined.

(iv) A subordinate should be given necessary authority to perform his assigned duties.

Q. 26. State the importance of Decentralisation in brief.

Ans. : Decentralisation of authority is basically useful to large organisations with multiple products or operating in different geographical locations. Its importance may be stated as follows :

(i) Decentralisation of authority provides relief to the top executives.

(ii) It motivates the lower level managers.

(iii) It improves the work performance.

(iv) It promotes the subordinate's morale.

(v) It increases flexibility in the operations of the enterprise.

Q. 27. What are the merits of Decentralisation of Authority?

Ans. : The important merits or advantages of Decentralisation of Authority may be stated as follows :

(i) Decentralisation of Authority increases managerial efficiency.

(ii) It facilitates diversification of activities.

(iii) It helps in minimisation of risk or possibility of loss.

(iv) It ensures quick performance of activities.

(v) It provides a better means of developing future managers and executives.

(vi) It motivates the subordinates for better performance of duties.

(vii) It improves morale of the subordinates etc.

Q. 28. Mention any four principles of Decentralisation of Authority.

Ans. : Four basic principles to be followed for Decentralisation of Authority are as follows :

(i) There should be real and full delegation of Authority.

(ii) The superiors must have full confidence in the abilities of the subordinates.

(iii) The subordinate should be given requisite authority so that he can shoulder responsibility.

(iv) Result-oriented Personnel Policies should be formulated.

Q. 29. Point out any four factors determining the Degree of Decentralisation.

Ans. : Four factors determining the Degree of Decentralisation are as follows :

(i) Decentralisation depends on size of the organisation.

(ii) Availability of qualified managers directly influences the degree of decentralisation.

(iii) Effective control techniques enable greater decentralisation.

(iv) Authority tends to be decentralised when the operations of the organisations are dispersed over different territories.

Q. 30. What is meant by 'Span of Management'?

Ans. : 'Span of Management' means the number of subordinate employees that a manager can effectively supervise. The span of management is a very important concept in every organisation. It is vital to determine how many subordinates can be managed by a superior. But its determination is a very controversial matter. However, usually it is considered that a manager of top level may be able to supervise the tasks of four subordinates and at the lowest level of the organisation the number of subordinates may be eight to twelve.

Q. 31. What factors should be taken into consideration for determining the 'Span of Management' in an organisation. [C.U. B.Com. 2011 (New Syllabus)]

Ans. : The following factors should be taken into consideration for determining the 'Span of Management' in an organisation :

(i) Capacity of the superiors;

(ii) Variety and importance of the works to be supervised;

(iii) Time devoted for supervising the activities;

(iv) Nature of the organisation;

(v) Ability of the subordinates;

(vi) Degree of decentralisation of authority;

(vii) Facilities of communication;

(viii) Use of staff assistance; etc.

Chapter 5

Motivation

Q. 1. What do you mean by 'Motivation'?

[C.U. B.Com. 1986, 1989, 2004, 2009, 2011 (supplementary)]

Ans. : 'Motivation' is the managerial process of inspiring the subordinate employees in order to intensify their desire to execute their duties and to co-operate for achieving the common objectives of the enterprise. It is the actuating force that stimulates a man to put his best in the accomplishment of a task.

Q. 2. Name the five human needs as suggested by Abraham Maslow.

[C.U. B.Com. 1984, 1990, 2001, 2010]

Ans. : The five human needs mentioned by A. Maslow are as follows :

(i) Physiological Needs; (ii) Safety Needs; (iii) Social Needs; (iv) Esteem Needs; and (v) Self-actualisation Needs.

Q. 3. Mention four features of Motivation. [C.U. B.Com. 2008]

Ans. : Four features of Motivation are mentioned below :

(i) Motivation is a psychological concept.

(ii) Motivation is related to satisfying human needs.

(iii) Motivation is classified into two aspects—financial and non-financial.

(iv) Motivation is a continuous process.

Q. 4. State two factors of Motivation. [C.U. B.Com. 2002, 2007, 2011]

Ans. : Two factors of Motivation are stated below :

(i) Adequate Financial Incentive; and (ii) Security of Job.

Q. 5. Mention any four important roles of Motivation.

Ans. : Four important roles of Motivation are as follows :

(i) Motivation secures full support and energy of the workers.

(ii) It helps in maximum utilisation of the resources of the enterprise.

(iii) It increases efficiency of the employees and output of the organisation.

(iv) It facilitates other functions of management.

Q. 6. Point out any two assumptions of Mc Gregor's Theory 'X'.

Ans. : Two assumptions of McGregor's Theory 'X' are pointed out below :

(i) The average people dislike to do work. They will avoid it if they can.

(ii) Most of the persons prefer to be led, and wish to avoid responsibility.

Q. 7. State any two assumptions of Theory 'Y' as propounded by Mc Gregor.

Ans. : Two assumptions of Theory 'Y' as propounded by McGregor, are as follows :

(i) People like to work naturally as taking rest or playing.

(ii) External control or threat of punishment is not the only means of motivating people to work and achieve organisational goals.

Q. 8. State the role or importance Motivation in brief.

Ans. : Motivation plays a vital role in management. It is the essence of management. It has direct impact on productivity and profitability of an enterprise. It provides incentives to the employees and increases their ability of performance. Thus, it fulfils the individual objectives of the employees in one hand, and the objectives of the organisation on the other. Proper motivating process increases individual and organisational efficiency. It enhances the effectiveness of management and ensures the success of managerial performance. Motivation increases the morale of the employees, makes them conscious of their responsibilities, and establishes an appropriate work environment in the organisation. In fact, the achievement of organisational goals of an enterprise depends largely on effective motivation process.

Chapter 6

Leadership

Q. 1. What is meant by 'Leadership' in Management? [C.U. B.Com. 1992, 2006]

Or, Define 'Leading'. [C.U. B.Com. 2011, 2011 (supplementary)]

Ans. : 'Leadership' in management is the ability of influencing the behaviour of the subordinates so that they strive willingly towards the achievement of group goals with zeal and confidence. It is the process by which a manager of an organisation directs, guides and influences the work of the subordinate employees for attaining the specified objectives.

Q. 2. Mention any four qualities of a good Leadership. [C.U. B.Com. 2009]

Ans. : Four qualities of a good Leadership is pointed out below :

(i) Motivating Skill;
(ii) Technical Competence;
(iii) Physical and Mental Strength; and
(iv) Sense of Judgement.

Q. 3. State the various styles of Leadership. [C.U. B.Com. 1994, 2011]

Ans. : The various styles or types of Leadership are as follows :

(i) Autocratic or Authoritarian Leadership;
(ii) Bureaucratic Leadership;
(iii) Democratic or Participative Leadership; and
(iv) Free-rein or, Laissez-faire Leadership.

Q. 4. What are the elements of Leadership? [C.U. B.Com. 2007]

Ans. : The elements of Leadership are stated below :

(i) Personal qualities of the Leader such as—

(a) Intelligence, (b) Sense of judgement, (c) Emotional stability, (d) Knowledge of human relations, (e) Ability to inspire, (f) Technical competence, (g) Social skills, (h) Attractive personality etc.

(ii) Followers; and (iii) The Situation.

Q. 5. What is meant by 'Democratic or Participative Leadership'? [C.U. B.Com. 2008]

Ans. : 'Democratic or Participative Leadership' is that type of leadership in which the leader takes decisions in consultation and participation with his subordinates or followers. A democratic leader provides freedom of thinking and expression to his subordinates. He listens to their suggestions, grievances, and opinions.

Q. 6. What is 'Bureaucratic Leadership'? [C.U. B.Com. 2011 (supplementary)]

Ans. : 'Bureaucratic Leadership' is the leadership style which depends on the rules specifying the responsibilities and duties of the subordinates. These rules direct them to perform particular tasks in definite ways and provide a specification of a minimum level of acceptable performance by the subordinates. Such type of leadership is usually followed in government organisations.

Q. 7. What do you mean by 'Autocratic Leadership'?

Ans. : 'Autocratic or Authoritarian Leadership' refers to the leadership style in which the leader centralises authority in himself and takes all decisions without consulting with the subordinates. He exercises full control over the subordinates, dominates, and drives them through issuing orders.

Q. 8. What is 'Free-rein or, Laissez-faire Leadership'?

Ans. : 'Free-rein or Laissez-faire Leadership' means giving complete freedom to the subordinates in decision-making. There is full delegation of authority in such type of leadership. Here the leader serves only as an advisor.

Q. 9. State the importance of Leadership.

Ans. : Effective leadership is an essential element for a successful organisation. Providing proper leadership to his subordinates is an important responsibility of a manager or supervisor. In fact, wherever a group of people work for achieving a common purpose, they are required to be directed and guided, and motivated with the will force to perform the works. And, it is leadership that shows the way the group should follow by providing it with necessary guidance, direction, and motivation. So, effective leadership has a significant role in business management. It produce a good business by creating a vital, dynamic and life-giving force in the organisation. The success and development of a business enterprise largely depends on the good and efficient leadership of the managers.

Q. 10. Point out any four characteristics of Leadership.

Ans. : The following are the four characteristics of Leadership :

(i) Existence of followers;
(ii) Process of influencing the behaviour of the followers;
(iii) Assumption of responsibility;
(iv) Clear understanding of the feelings and problems of the followers.

Q. 11. Mention any four functions of Leadership.

Ans. : Four important functions of Leadership are pointed out below :

(i) Initiating action and fostering conviction;
(ii) Providing direction and maintaining discipline;
(iii) Giving inspiration to the subordinates and motivating them; and
(iv) Creating confidence in the subordinates and building their morale.

Q. 12. Distinguish between 'Leadership' and 'Management'.

Ans. : 'Leadership' is the process of directing, guiding and influencing the followers and establishing inter-personal relationship for implementation of the objectives of an organisation.

On the other hand, 'Management' is the process by means of which some pre-determined goals are achieved securing maximum output with minimum efforts and cost through planning, organising, directing, motivating, co-ordinating and controlling. The managers determines the common goals of the enterprise, and formulate broad policies to guide the operations of the enterprise. And leadership initiates the actions for implementation of the common goals. All managers should possess the quality of leadership; but leadership may exist without being a manager.

Q. 13. What are the advantages of Democratic Leadership?

Ans. : The advantages of Democratic Leadership are as follows :

(i) Democratic leadership provides job satisfaction to the subordinate employees.

(ii) It improves the morale of the subordinates.

(iii) It ensures organisational stability.

(iv) The opinions and suggestions of the subordinates are received for making decisions.

(v) The subordinates share the responsibility of work performance with the leader.

(vi) No external control is imposed on the subordinates.

(vii) This leadership style develops positive attitude of the subordinates and reduces resistance to change.

(viii) Creative leadership is evolved in democratic leadership.

Q. 14. What are the features of Autocratic Leadership?

Ans. : The features or characteristics of Autocratic Leadership are mentioned below :

(i) An autocratic leader never delegates authority to his subordinates.

(ii) The subordinates cannot express their opinions.

(iii) They are to obey the orders of the leader.

(iv) The leader takes all decisions.

(v) Full control over the subordinates is exercised by the leader.

(vi) Downward communication is followed in this type of leadership.

Q. 15. State the advantages of Autocratic Leadership.

Ans. : The following are the advantages of Autocratic Leadership :

(i) In such leadership style, quick decision is possible.

(ii) Effective control is possible in this type of leadership.

(iii) Unity of command is maintained in this leadership.

(iv) Autocratic leadership provides strong motivation to the leader.

(v) Such type of leadership is suitable where the subordinates are less educated and unskilled.

Q. 16. What are the disadvantages of Autocratic Leadership?

Ans. : The disadvantages of Autocratic Leadership are pointed out below :

(i) In Autocratic Leadership the subordinates are not motivated to perform their duties and responsibilities.

(ii) It leads to low morale and creation of conflict among the subordinates.

(iii) Due to strict control they do not like this leadership style.

(iv) The creative ideas of the subordinates are not utilised.

(v) The subordinates get no opportunity for their own development.

(vi) The benefits of delegation of authority cannot be enjoyed.

(vii) There is every possibility of wrong decision.

Q. 17. State the disadvantages of Democratic Leadership.

Ans. : The disadvantages of Democratic Leadership may be stated as follows :

(i) Democratic Leadership Style is time-consuming. So, it may result in delays in making decisions.

(ii) Such type of leadership cannot be applied in a complex organisation structure.

(iii) A considerable number of employees are unwilling to participate in the process of leadership.

(iv) Some subordinates may have the mentality only to work under others.

(v) As specific responsibility is not given, the subordinates may try to avoid responsibility.

(vi) Consultation with the subordinates may indicate incompetence of the leader to deal with the problems.

Q. 18. What are the disadvantages of Bureaucratic Leadership?

Ans. : The following are the disadvantages of Bureaucratic Leadership :

(i) The subordinates have no right of participating in decision-making in bureaucratic leadership.

(ii) Such type of leadership leads to workers' apathy.

(iii) The subordinates may remain indifferent to the work, as they know just how minimum work they have to perform.

(iv) This leadership style leads to red tapeism and too much paper work.

(v) The process of management is reduced by the rules to a series of routine mechanical actions.

Q. 19. Write a short note on Free-rein or, Laissez-faire Leadership.

Ans. : Under Free-rein or Laissez-fair Style or Leadership, the subordinates take most of the decisions. There is complete delegation of authority in this leadership style. Controlling process in this type of leadership is not strict. The subordinate can express their views and suggestions freely. The leader does not give direction to his followers; he plays the role of an advisor. Open communication system is followed in this style of leadership. Such type of leadership can produce effective results, if the subordinates are highly educated and experienced persons having sincere efforts to work with responsibility.

Q. 20. Indicate the merits of Free-rein or Laissez-faire Leadership.

Ans. : The merits or advantages of Free-rein or, Laissez-faire Leadership Style are as follows :

(i) A good relationship is established between the subordinates and leader in such type of leadership.

(ii) There is a positive effect on morale and job satisfaction of the subordinates in this leadership style.

(iii) Full utilisation of production capacity of the subordinates is possible in this case, and as a result, productivity of the enterprise increases.

(iv) There is a possibility of maximum development of the subordinate employees.

Q. 21. Point out the problems or limitations of Free-rein or, Laissez-faire Leadership.

Ans. : The problems or limitations of Free-rein or Laissez-faire Leadership may be stated as follows :

(i) In this leadership style, the leader has no significant role to play.

(ii) The subordinates do not get the direction and guidance of the leader.

(iii) There may be lack of co-ordination in such type of leadership.

(iv) As the subordinates enjoy more freedom, proper management may not be possible in this case.

(v) The subordinates may move in different direction and may work at cross-purposes.

(vi) In such style, the unity among the subordinates cannot be established in all cases.

(vii) For effectiveness of such leadership style, the subordinate employees are required to be highly educated, self-motivated, well-trained and ready to perform the work with responsibility.

Chapter 7
Co-ordination

Q. 1. What is meant by Co-ordination in Management?

[C.U. B.Com. 1990, 1992, 2005, 2008, 2011]

Ans. : 'Co-ordination' is the managerial function of integrating or unifying all the group actions in an enterprise to achieve its goals. It is the process through which an executive develops an orderly pattern of group efforts among his subordinates and secures unity of action in the pursuit of a common purpose.

Q. 2. Mention any four principles of Co-ordination. [C.U. B.Com. 2007, 2009]

Ans. : Four principles of co-ordination are stated as follows :

(i) Co-ordination should be attained by direct contact with the parties concerned.

(ii) Co-ordination must be maintained as a continuous process.

(iii) All activities, decisions and opinions are to be integrated to achieve the enterprise objectives.

(iv) All functions in the enterprise are to be done at the same time and at the same speed.

Q. 3. Point out any four techniques of Co-ordination. [C.U. B.Com. 2006]

Ans. : Four techniques of co-ordination are the following :

(i) Harmonised programmes and policies.

(ii) Well-designed methods of communication.

(iii) Appointment of special co-ordinator.

(iv) Co-ordination by committees through meetings and conferences.

Q. 4. Distinguish between Co-ordination and Co-operation.

[C.U. B.Com. 2001, 2004, 2006]

Ans. : 'Co-operation' is the collective efforts directed towards the accomplishment of some work when some persons are engaged voluntarily to do that work. On the other hand, 'Co-ordination' means putting together all the group efforts of the enterprise, carefully unified and harmonised so as to give them a commonness of purpose. However, co-operation and co-ordination are inter-related and inter-dependent.

Q. 5. Why is Co-ordination treated as essence of Management?

[C.U. B.Com. 2011 (New Syllabus)]

Ans. : Co-ordination is very essential in management. It is a process by which the manager achieves harmonious group efforts and unity of actions through integrating the activities of different individuals and groups for the attainment of common goals. Without proper co-ordination among all the members of group, the managers cannot bring together the diverse elements into one harmonious whole. Co-ordination is required in all the activities at every level of organisation. It is to be exercised both within and outside the organisation. It makes planning more purposeful, organisation more well-knit, and control more regulated. The effectiveness of other functions of management depends to a large extent upon proper co-ordination. Co-ordination is so important that instead of considering it to be a separate function of management, now-a-days, it is regarded as the essence of management.

Q. 6. State the principles of Co-ordination. [C.U. B.Com. 2011 (New Syllabus)]

Ans. : The various principles of effective co-ordination are as follows :

(i) Direct contact with the persons or groups concerned; (ii) Early beginning; (iii) Maintaining continuity; (iv) Pervasiveness; (v) Good leadership; (vi) Timely performance of all functions of the enterprise; (vii) Balancing all works; (viii) Integrating all activities, decisions and opinions, etc.

Chapter 8

Control

Q. 1. What is Control? [C.U. B.Com. 1999, 2005]

Ans. : 'Control' is the managerial process of verifying whether the results of the operations of an organisation are in conformity with the plan adopted, pointing out the reasons if any gap is seen between the target and actual result, and taking corrective actions immediately. Proper control ensures efficiency and effectiveness of the organisation.

Q. 2. What do you mean by 'Span of Control'?

[C.U. B.Com. 1988, 1993, 1995, 1999, 2003, 2005, 2006, 2008, 2011 (supplementary)]

Ans. : 'Span of Control' means the number of subordinate employees that a manager can supervise and control effectively. Normally the ideal number of the subordinates may be four at higher levels and eight to twelve at lower levels.

Q. 3. Point out any four features of Control.

[C.U. B.Com. 2000, 2006, 2011 (supplementary)]

Ans. : Four features of Control are mentioned below :

(i) Control is a continuous process.

(ii) Control has a forward-looking character.

(iii) Control involves measurement of performance.

(iv) Control process is flexible and dynamic.

Q. 4. Mention any four limitations of Control System. [C.U. B.Com. 2002]

Ans. : The following are the four limitations of Control System :

(i) It is very difficult to control the external factors.

(ii) Control system loses its effectiveness when the standard of performance cannot be defined in quantitative terms.

(iii) There is difficulty in fixation of individual responsibility of an employee.

(iv) Control process is expensive.

Q. 5. Briefly discuss 'Budgetary Control'? [C.U. B.Com. 2011 (New Syllabus)]

Ans. : 'Budgetary Control' is an useful control technique. It is the process of utilising budgets for comparison of the actual performance with the corresponding budget performance in order to find out the deviations, and to remove the deviations by either adjusting the budget estimate or correcting the causes of deviations. A budget is an important tool for controlling the day-to-day operations of an enterprise. It provides a standard by which actual performance can be evaluated to find out the deviations from the planned results. This information enables the managers to take corrective action for bringing the actual results in conformity with the expected results according to the plan. Budgetary control is an effective and widely used control technique. It leads to maximum utilisation of resources in order to ensure maximum output.

Q. 6. Briefly describe the importance of Control.

Ans. : Control is a very important function of management. The managers of an enterprise cannot complete their tasks without control. The control process ensures that the planned performance is achieved with minimum of deviations. It assures that the plans are carried out and the objectives are reached. Control is the ultimate weapon at the hands of the management authority to remove mistakes, to modify defective plans, to check misdirection, and to effect co-ordination of diverse elements where it is lacking. A combination of well-planned objectives, strongly built organisation, proper direction and effective motivation have little possibility of success unless there exists an adequate system of control. Like a traffic signal control guides the organisation and keeps it on the right track. Control process puts a mental pressure on the employees for better performance. Proper control technique ensures efficiency of the organisation. Since it focuses on the achievement of organisational objectives, it necessarily leads to organisational effectiveness. In fact, control is an indispensable function of management.

Q. 7. Mention the steps in Control Process with a diagram.

[C.U. B.Com. 2011 (New Syllabus)]

Ans. : The Control Process involves the following steps :

(i) Establishment of the Standards;

(ii) Measurement of the Performance;

(iii) Comparison of the Actual Performance with the Standard;

(iv) Identification of Deviations;

(v) Analysis of the Causes of Deviations;

(vi) Correction of the Deviations by Remedial Measures;

[For diagram see Fig. 8.1 : The Process of Control (Page No. 176)]

Q. 8. Explain the relation between Planning and Controlling.

Ans. : Controlling is closely related with Planning. It is a basic management function that ensures work performance according to plans. In planning, the managers determine how the resources of the enterprise would be utilised to attain the objectives; and in controlling they verify whether the resources are utilised in the same way as planned. Controlling is concerned with checking the actual performance against the agreed standards of plans in order to ensure adequate progress of desired performances. The desired performance is indicated through planning in the shape of standards or targets; and controlling is to see that the performances tally with the plans. Actually, planning and controlling go hand in hand. Without planning there can be no controlling, and without controlling the planned target cannot be achieved. Planning is the basis of controlling; and controlling is the result of particular plans. So, planning and controlling are the inseparable functions of management. Planning is meaningless without controlling; and controlling is aimless without planning.

Q. 9. What are the different Tools of Control?

Ans. : The different Tools or Techniques of Control are as follows :

(a) Traditional Tools of Control :

(i) Personal Observation, (ii) Budgetary Control, (iii) Break-even Analysis, (iv) Ratio Analysis, (v) Cost Control, (vi) Internal Audit, and (vii) Statistical Report.

(b) Modern Tools of Control :

(i) Management Audit, (ii) Network Techniques, (iii) Return on Investment, (iv) Responsibility Accounting, (v) Performance Budgeting, (vi) Zero-base Budgeting, and (vii) Management Information System.

Q. 10. State the advantages of Budgetary Control.

Ans. : The various advantages of Budgetary Control may be stated as follows :

(i) Budgetary control compels the managers to plan their activities.

(ii) Since budgetary control is fully concerned with concrete numercial goals, every manager beomes sure about what he is expected to do.

(iii) As it keeps a rigid check over the activities in the organisation, it leads to cautious utilisation of resources.

(iv) It promotes co-operation among various sub-units in the organisation.

(v) It encourages free flow of information among various sub-units.

(vi) It promotes balanced activities in the organisation.

(vii) It points out any deviation between the actual performance and budgeted performance.

(viii) It can also identify the causes of deviation between actual and budget.

Q. 11. What are the problems of Budgetary Control?

Ans. : Budgetary Control has some problems. Its problems are as under :

(i) Budgets are prepared on the assumptions of future happenings in a certain way. But due to change in situation, budgets do not become always meaningful for achieving control.

(ii) Budgeting is just a guesswork. So, question may be raised about its utility for being used as standard against which performance is measured.

(iii) Budgetary control is a complicated process of controlling.

(iv) It is an expensive and time-consuming system of control.

(v) Budgetary control system needs a lot of paperwork which the technical personnel may not like.

Q. 12. What do you mean by 'Budgetary Control'? [C.U. B.Com. 2011]

Ans. : 'Budgetary Control' means the method of using budgets for comparing the actual performance with the corresponding budget performance in order to find out the deviations and to remove them by either adjusting the budget estimates or correcting the causes of deviations.

Q. 13. What is 'Break-even Analysis'?

Ans. : 'Break-even Analysis' is a technique of cost control. It is an analysis of the inter-relationships among the cost of production, volume of production, and the amount of profits with the help of break-event point, cost-volume-profit is analysed. Break-even analysis helps to determine the increase in profit with respect to increase in sales and vice-versa. So, it assists in implementing the corrective measures by analysing the causes. Break-even analysis is also known as 'Cost-Volume-Profit Analysis'.

Q. 14. What is meant by 'Ratio Analysis'?

Ans. : 'Ratio Analysis' is a study of ratios between various items or groups in the financial statement of a business enterprise. With the help of such analysis, the financial efficiency of an enterprise can be evaluated.

Q. 15. What is 'Cost Control'?

Ans. : 'Cost Control' means the determination of the standard relating to each item of cost, ascertaining the actual costs regarding those items, identifying the variations with a view to determining the responsibility, cause and cost of each variance, and then taking necessary action to ensure that the actual costs conform to the standard costs in future.

Q. 16. What is 'Internal Audit'?

Ans. : 'Internal Audit' means the technique of verifying and evaluating the accounting, financial and other functions of a business enterprise. It is carried out by the managers of the enterprise or by the special staff employed for this purpose.

Q. 17. What is meant by 'Management Aduit'?

Ans. : 'Management Audit' is an overall evaluation of the quality of management. It is a critical examination of the entire management process. It is a systematic appraisal of the efficiency and effectiveness of the managers of an enterprise.

Q. 18. What is 'Return on Investment'?

Ans. : 'Return on Invetment' is an important tool of controlling overall performance of a business enterprise. It is calculated by dividing the net profits with the total amount of investment.

Q. 19. What do you understand by 'Responsibility Accounting'?

Ans. : 'Responsibility Accounting' is the process of accounting in which the performance of various employees are evaluated as to how far they have implemented the pre-determined targets set for the departments, sections, units, or divisions for which they are responsible.

Q. 20. What does Zero-base Budgeting mean?

Ans. : 'Zero-base Budgeting' means the system in which each function must be justified entirely as if each time a new budget is formulated. Instead of taking the current year's budget as the base, the budget is prepared from a zero-base.

Q. 21. What is 'Performance Budgeting'?

Ans. : 'Performance Budgeting' is an input/output or, costs/results budgeting. It contains the expenses according to the heads of performance.

Q. 22. What do you understand by 'Management Information System'?

Ans. : 'Management Information System' is the process of supplying the required information through computer to each manager of an organisation at the proper time, in the right form and relevent one which helps his understanding and stimulates his action.

Q. 23. Mention the requisites of effective Control Measures.

Ans. : The requisites of effective Control Measures are pointed out below :

(i) Simplicity, (ii) Objectivity, (iii) Economy, (iv) Flexibility, (v) Forward-looking Nature, (vi) Accuracy, (vii) Suitability, (viii) Focus on Strategic Points, (ix) Corrective Action, (x) Motivating etc.

MODULE II

BUSINESS COMMUNICATION

Group—A

Answers to the Very Short Questions Carrying 2 [Two] Marks Each

Chapter 1

Q. 1. What is 'Communication'?

Ans. 'Communication' is the process of transmitting information and understanding from one unit to other unit with a view to getting the desired response from the receiver.

Q. 2. What is meant by 'Business Communication'? [C.U. B.Com. 2011 (New Syl.)]

Ans. Exchange of information, facts and ideas relating to business may be termed as 'Business Communication'. It refers to communication relating to business activity which means providing goods and services to consumers with a view to earning profit. It is a process through which information, facts, ideas, orders, advices, decisions, etc. are conveyed, sent or exchanged between/among the persons associated with the business.

Q. 3. What are the elements of Business Communication? [C.U. B.Com. 2006, '07, '11]

Ans. Business communication involves six basic elements such as : [i] Message, [ii] Sender, [iii] Receiver, [iv] Channel, [v] Symbol, and [vi] Feedback.

Q. 4. State the Steps of Business Communication.

Ans. The Steps of Business Communication are mentioned below :

[i] The sender is to be familiar with the idea to be communicated.

[ii] The idea is to be converted into a symbolic form.

[iii] The idea is to be transmitted through a channel.

[iv] The receiver must get the message.

[v] The receiver is to decode the message to understand it.

[vi] The receiver has to send feedback to the message through a channel.

Q. 5. Mention five characteristics which distinguish a business communication with the other type of communication.

Ans. Business communication has certain features or characteristics which enable us to distinguish it from other communications. A communication, to be business communication, must be : [i] Practical, [ii] Factual, [iii] Clear and Brief, [iv] Target-oriented, [v] Persuasive and [vi] related to Business Activity.

Q. 6. Mention four objectives of Business Communication.

Ans. Four objectives of business communication are—[i] Giving Information, [ii] Helping Persuasion, [iii] Conveying Suggestion, and [iv] Providing Motivation.

Q. 7. What is meant by Business Communication Channel? [C.U. B.Com. 2007, 2010]

Ans. Communication Channels are the routes or paths through which messages are sent or received. If channels are used for the purpose of communication relating to any business activity, such channels are called channels of business communication.

Q. 8. How are the Channels of Business Communication divided on the basis of Direction?

Ans. On the basis of direction, the channels of business communication are divided into—[i] Downward, [ii] Upward, and [iii] Horizontal Channels.

Q. 9. How are the Channels of Business Communication classified on the basis of the way of expression?

Ans. On the basis of the way of expression, the channels of business communication are classified into—[i] Written, and [ii] Oral Channels.

Q. 10. What is Written Channel of Business Communication?

Ans. When business communication takes place in writing through letters, memos, reports, e-mails, faxes, etc. written channel is said to be in use.

Q. 11. When is a Written Channel of Business Communication selected?

Ans. A written channel is often selected in the following cases:

[i] Immediate feedback is not required.

[ii] The receiver stays in a far off place and cannot be brought to contact easily.

[iii] Distortion of message is not desirable.

[iv] Detailed, complex and planned messages are required to be sent, and

[v] Permanent record of communication is necessary for future reference.

Q. 12. When is an Oral Channel selected?

Ans. An oral channel is to be selected if:

[i] feedback is required immediately, [ii] the receiver of message or audience can be brought to contact easily, [iii] interaction is necessary, [iv] simple messages are communicated, and [v] no permanent record of communication is to be kept.

Q. 13. What do you mean by Feedback? [C.U. B.Com. 2006, '07, '09, '11 (New Syl.)]

Ans. The message sent by the receiver back to the source is called feedback. It is the response by the recipient.

Q. 14. What is the importance of feedback?

Ans. The sender is interested to know the reaction of the recipient and also willing to know whether the recipient has understood the message in the same sense as intended. A feedback by the recipient satisfies the sender's intention and establishes a mental link between them.

Q. 15. What types of feedback are there?

Ans. There are two types of feedback—[i] Positive, and [ii] Negative. Positive feedback means that the recipient of the message has responded in the way intended by the sender. On the other hand, negative feedback suggests that the communication has not been effective and some corrections, adjustments or re-assessments are required in the process.

Q. 16. What are the steps in the process of feedback?

Ans. The steps in the process of feedback are the following :

[i] Listening and understanding the message properly.

[ii] Asking questions if the message is not understood properly and get it clarified.

[iii] Understanding the message in the sense originally intended.

[iv] Conveying the reaction to the sender of the message.

Q. 17. What are the requirements of effective feedback?

Ans. Effective feedback needs to be: [i] clear, [ii] well-timed, [iii] specific, [iv] bearing right attitude, [v] truly representative, [vi] impersonal, and [vii] informative.

Q. 18. What are the levels of Business Communication?

Ans. Levels of business communication may be determined on the basis of ranks or positions of the persons with whom communications are being made. It may be classified as:

[i] Lower Level Communication, [ii] Upper Level Communication, and (iii) Horizontal or Side-wise Communication.

Q. 19. State briefly the views of Chester I. Barnard regarding the principles of effective Business Communication.

Ans. According to Chester I. Barnard, business communication—in order to be effective—must have a message which is—

[i] understandable to the receiver, [ii] compatible with the interests of the persons concerned, [iii] relevant to the objectives of the organisation, and [iv] physically and psychologically viable.

Q. 20. What are the Ten Commandments of American Management Association for effective Business Communication?

Ans. American Management Association has prescribed the following ten essentials for effective business communication:

[i] Form a clear idea about the information before communication.

[ii] Fix the aim, objectives or purpose of communication.

[iii] Create physical and psychological environment for communication.

[iv] Make plan for communication through consultation.

[v] Select properly the subject-matter of communication.

[vi] Make the receiver realise the value of the message.

[vii] Follow up the communication.

[viii] Have a clear idea of the importance of the communication.

[ix] Act in accordance with the communication.

[x] Listen properly.

Q. 21. Name four general principles of effective Business Communication.

Ans. Four general principles of an effective business communication are—[i] Clarity, [ii] Adequacy, [iii] Timing, and [iv] Courtesy.

Q. 22. State four benefits of effective communication.

Ans. Four benefits of effective communication are—[i] Problems are solved quickly and easily, [ii] Decision-making is stronger, [iii] Productivity is increased, [iv] The flow of work is steady.

Q. 23. What are the Seven Cs in Effective Communication?

Ans. A communication, to be effective, requires : [i] completeness, [ii] conciseness, [iii] consideration, [iv] concreteness, [v] courtesy, [vi] clarity, and [vii] correctness. These are the Seven Cs in effective communication.

Q. 24. In how many categories can barriers to Business Communication be classified?

Ans. Barriers to business communication may be classified into three categories, such as—[i] External Barriers which is again divided into [a] Semantic barrier, and [b] Emotional or Psychological Barriers, [ii] Organisational Barriers, and [iii] Personal Barriers.

Q. 25. Name four psychological barriers in Communication.

Ans. Four psychological barriers in Communication are : [i] Inattention, [ii] Perceptual barrier, [iii] Pre-mature evaluation, [iv] Undue reliance on the written words.

Q. 26. What are the personal barriers to Communication?

Ans. Personal barriers to communication are divided into:

[i] **Barriers in Superiors:** [a] Unfavourable attitude of the superiors towards communication, [b] Fear of challenge to the authority, [c] Lack of confidence in the subordinates, [d] Lack of time, [e] Lack of awareness, [f] Deliberate ignoring of communication.

[ii] **Barriers in Subordinates:** [a] Unwillingness to communicate with the superiors, [b] Lack of motivation to communicate.

Q. 27. Mention six methods of overcoming communication barriers.

Ans. Six methods of overcoming communication barriers are mentioned below : [i] Full information about the subject-matter of communication is necessary, [ii] Environment of mutual trust and confidence is to be established, [iii] Easy and simple language should be used, [iv] Proper inter-personal relationship must be developed between the superior and the subordinates, [v] Appropriate channel should be selected, [vi] Two-way communication should be encouraged.

Q. 28. What is a Communication Model?

Ans. A model is a visual and symbolic representation of the concept or the theory. A communication model presents before us a visual picture of the relationship of various elements of the process of communication.

Q. 29. How does a Communication Model help us to understand the process of Communication?

Ans. As a map of the world can illustrate the mountains, rivers, plateaus, seas, oceans, continent, countries, etc. and can create an idea of the actual things, a communication model helps us to conceptualise the relationship of the various elements involved in the process of communication.

Q. 30. Name four models of Communication.

Ans. Four models of Communication are as follows :

[i] Aristotle's Model of Communication.

[ii] Harold Laswell's Model of Communication.

[iii] Shannon-Weaver Model of Communication.

[iv] David Berlo's SMCR Model of Communication.

Chapter 2

Q. 31. Define 'Conflict'.

Ans. 'Conflict' means disagreement, opposition of any kind, argument, antagonism or hatred between two persons or groups or among more than two persons or groups. People working in an organisation may have difference of values, ideas, opinions, attitudes, objectives, preferences and personalities. Therefore, conflict becomes natural between/among persons, groups or teams on the issues like sharing of resources, responsibilities, authority, accountability, etc.

Q. 32. Mention six reasons for Conflict.

Ans. The reasons for conflict are: [i] Poor communication, [ii] Competition for monetary incentives and other benefits, [iii] Individual differences, [iv] Tendency to become more powerful, [v] Difference in objectives of individuals and groups, and [vi] Lack of well-defined responsibility.

Q. 33. Is there any benefit of Conflict? Mention any four of them.

Ans. Conflict is not necessarily harmful. The benefits of conflict are: [i] It evaluates the existing system, [ii] It clarifies situation and issue, [iii] It brings out social change, and [iv] It acts as safety valve by releasing tension.

Q. 34. Mention four disadvantages of Conflict.

Ans. The disadvantages (or cost) of conflict are as follows :

[i] It magnifies the differences between persons.

[ii] It breeds distrust and suspicion among the conflicting parties.

[iii] People become less communicative and avoid each other.

[iv] It creates hatred and hostility.

Q. 35. What is a 'Group Conflict'?

Ans. A 'Group Conflict' refers to a conflict involving a group or groups. It may take place between two or more groups or between/among the members within the group.

Q. 36. What are the causes of 'Inter-group Conflict'? Mention any two causes.

Ans. The causes of inter-group conflict are: [i] Competition for scarce resources, and [ii] Conflicting interests of different groups.

Q. 37. What is meant by Intra-group Conflict?

[C.U. B.Com. 2005, 2008, 2011 (supplementary)]

Ans. A conflict between two or among some members in a group may be referred to as 'Intra-group Conflict'.

Q. 38. What are the causes of Intra-group Conflict?

Ans. Intra-group conflict may take place owing to the following:

[i] Differences in goals, [ii] Denial of responsibility, [iii] Ineffective control over the group, [iv] Ideological difference among the members, [v] High degree of competition, and [vi] Communication gap.

Q. 39. What measures may be taken to resolve a Conflict? Mention any four measures.

[C.U. B.Com. 2009]

Ans. The measures to resolve a conflict include:

[i] finding out the actual cause of conflict,

[ii] early action,

[iii] effective persuasion, and

[iv] arbitration.

Q. 40. What is understood by 'Group Cohesiveness'? [C.U. B.Com. 2005, 2009, 2011]

Ans. 'Group Cohesiveness' signifies the overall attraction of the group members to each other. It is a force which makes the members of a group loyal to the group and attracts them to remain in it. It may be defined as the result of the forces that hold the group members together.

Q. 41. When is the degree of cohesiveness in a group considered to be high? Mention any four points.

Ans. The degree of cohesiveness in a group is considered to be high if:

[i] The members of the group desire to remain in the group;
[ii] They are co-operative and friendly with one another;
[iii] They follow group norms;
[iv] They interact with and influence one another.

Chapter 3

Q. 42. Classify Communication according to the area of operation.

Ans. According to the area of operation, communication is classified into—[i] Internal communication, and [ii] External communication. Internal communication is made within the organisation whereas external communication is made with the external agencies.

Q. 43. Name the factors that are to be considered in selecting the Means of Communication. Mention any four factors.

Ans. The factors that are to be considered in selecting the means of communication are: [i] Nature of Message, [ii] Cost of Communication, [iii] Distance, and [iv] Availability of supporting Technology.

Q. 44. What do you understand by 'Corporate Communication'? [C.U. B.Com. 2005]

Ans. 'Corporate Communication' refers to a process of communication through which the managers, supervisors and executives exchange their views, opinions, feelings, etc. with the peers, the subordinates and employees in any corporate organisation and negotiate with the outside world with a view to fulfilling the objectives of the organisation.

Q. 45. State four characteristics of Corporate Communication.

[C.U. B.Com. 2011 (New Syl.)]

Ans. Four characteristics of Corporate Communication are:

1. Most of the corporate communication are formal in nature.
2. Informal or grapevine communication among different group of employees takes place side by side with formal communication.
3. Corporate communication covers a wide range of people—both inside and outside the organisation.
4. Corporate communication is a long-term system as a corporate organisation has a pepetual existence.

Q. 46. Write a few lines on the importance of Corporate Communication.

Ans. Corporate communication co-ordinates internal activities of the organisation and establishes the connecting link with the outside world. It helps to motivate the employees to obey the orders and directives of the management authority. It ensures efficient management and plays meaningful role in decision making and its implementation by supplying the right information at the right time. Regular communication between the managers and employees create a healthy human relation and sense of co-operation, assistance and unity.

Q. 47. Give four guidelines for making Corporate Communication effective.

Ans. The following are the four guidelines for making Corporate Communications effective:

[i] Corporate communication should be simple and clear in meaning.
[ii] It should be concise but complete in all respects.

[iii] Effective channels should be chosen for communication.

[iv] Proper planning before communication is necessary.

Q. 48. What is the purpose of Formal Communication?

Ans. The purpose of formal communication is to give orders, convey instructions and fulfil the objectives of the organisation through some pre-determined rules and regulations.

Q. 49. Write four characteristics of Formal Communication.

Ans. Four characteristics of Formal Communication are as follows:

[i] Formal communication flows through structured path.

[ii] It is official and formal in nature.

[iii] It is mainly in writing.

[iv] It requires sanction of the higher authority.

Q. 50. State two advantages and two limitations of Formal Communication.

[C.U. B.Com. 2008]

Ans. The following are the advantages and limitations of Formal Communications: *Advantages* : [i] Being official, formal communication is binding and effective. [ii] Being written, it can be preserved and used as future reference.

Limitations : [i] The scope of formal communication is limited within the boundaries of the department and the jurisdiction fixed by the authority. [ii] It is less effective where personal guidance and motivation are necessary.

Q. 51. What is 'Informal Communication'? [C.U. B.Com. 2005, '07, '11]

Ans. 'Informal Communication' is the communication among the people of an organisation on the basis of informal relations and understanding. It may overlap the ranks, levels or positions. It is referred to as the "grapevine". It is spontaneous, unofficial and mostly verbal.

Q. 52. What are the purposes of Informal Communication?

Ans. The purposes of informal communication include—sharing of information, establishing personal contacts, making friendship, influencing and motivating others, resolving conflicts, supplementing official channels, getting relaxation, searching escape from monotony of work, etc.

Q. 53. Mention four characteristics of Informal Communication.

Ans. Four characteristics of Informal Communications are mentioned below:

[i] Informal communication is based on informal relationship.

[ii] It grows spontaneously.

[iii] It takes the form of gossip.

[iv] It does not follow any structured route or channel.

Q. 54. State two advantages of Informal Communication.

Ans. Two advantages of Informal Communication are:

[i] Informal communication, being unofficial and personal, promotes a social relationship among the participants, [ii] Flow of information is fast and suitable for the emergencies.

Q. 55. State two disadvantages of Informal Communication.

Ans. Two disadvantages of Informal Communication are:

[i] Inaccurate, incomplete and half true information is spread through informal communication as everybody interprets it in his/her own way, [ii] No decision can be taken depending upon such communication.

Q. 56. What is 'Oral Communication'? [C.U. B.Com 2005]

Ans. Transmission of orders, messages, information or suggestions through spoken word is called 'Oral or Verbal Communication'. It is effective for communication in meetings, conferences, gathering, group discussions, interviews, face-to-face talks, telephonic talks, etc.

Q. 57. Write four advantages of Oral Communication.

Ans. Four advantages of oral communication are as follows :

[i] Contact can be established quickly.
[ii] Clarification and feedback is possible immediately.
[iii] It fosters a friendly and co-operative spirit.
[iv] It is most suitable for confidential and emergent talks.

Q. 58. Mention four limitations of Oral Communication. [C.U. B.Com 2010]

Ans. Limitations of Oral Communication are :

[i] Oral communication lacks recorded evidence for future reference.
[ii] It does not allow the listener much time to think, act and react.
[iii] It can be easily distorted or changed.
[iv] It has no legal validity unless it is recorded.

Q. 59. What is meant by Written Communication? [C.U. B.Com 2005, 2011 (Supp.)]

Ans. A written communication means the sending of messages, orders or instructions in writing through letters, circulars, manuals, reports, telegrams, office memos, bulletins, etc. It is a formal method of communication and is less flexible.

Q. 60. State four advantages of Written Communication.

Ans. Four advantages of Written Communication are the following:

[i] Written communication creates permanent record of evidence. It can be used for future reference.
[ii] It gives the receiver sufficient time to think, act, and react.
[iii] It can be used as legal document.
[iv] It can be sent to many persons at a time.

Q. 61. Write four disadvantages of Written Communication.

Ans. Four disadvantages of Written Communication are pointed out below:

[i] Written communication is time consuming.
[ii] It cannot maintain strict secrecy.
[iii] It has no scope for immediate clarification.
[iv] It is not effective in the case of emergency.

Q. 62. What is 'Business Communication Network'?

[C.U. B.Com 2008, 2010, 2011 (New Syl.)]

Ans. A 'Business Communication Network' means the pattern of channels built up in communicating messages relating to business. Through such network innumerable and continuous flow of communication takes place daily within and outside the business and at personal and group levels of persons related to business by formal and informal means.

Q. 63. Why is Business Communication Network often compared to the artery in human body?

Ans. As blood flows all over the human body through the artery, messages, orders, instructions, information, proposals, reports, etc., are communicated to different persons working in various positions in a business organisation through the communication network. That is why Business Communication network is often compared to the artery in human body.

Q. 64. Classify the Business Communication Network.

Ans. Business communication network is divided into two parts, such as:

[i] Formal Network, and [ii] Informal Network.

Q. 65. What is 'Vertical Communication'? [C.U. B.Com. 2011]

Ans. Upward and downward flow of communication constitute 'Vertical Communications'. In such type of communication, message or information is transmitted from the higher authority to the subordinates, and vice versa.

Q. 66. Write short notes on: [a] Two-way Communication, [b] One-way Communication.

Ans. [a] **Two-way Communication:** Two-way communication means the process in which there is direct interaction between the sender and the receiver about the information or message. The sender transmits information to the receiver and the receiver responds to it. This process of communication is the combination of upward and downward communication system. In two-way method of communication, the top level management gives instructions to the lower level employees and the lower level employees can convey information or message about their demands and grievances to the upper levels. Hence, there is less possibility of misunderstanding between the two parties of communication.

[b] **One-way communication:** When communication is made by one person to another in one-way direction only, it is called one-way communication. It can be made through face-to-face verbal order, instruction, message, information, etc. or by telephone, or in written form like letter, notice, circular, etc. Since one-way communication has no feedback system, errors and flaws in the communication cannot be corrected and misunderstanding may crop up easily. But information passes through it very fast.

Q. 67. What are the Advantages of Upward Communication?

Ans. The main advantage of upward communication is that it is summarised and condensed as it passes through various levels of the organisation. It gives feedback on the effectiveness of downward communication. This feedback is essential for the improvement of effectiveness of communication. Secondly, this type of communication helps the managers to know about the views, reactions, feelings and attitudes of the subordinate employees. Thirdly, it provides the basis of control. Lastly, it supplies data and information for decision-making. Upward communication provides these benefits.

Q. 68. What do you mean by 'Non-verbal Communication'?

Ans. Non-verbal communication is the method of communication without words. In this method messages are sent through facial expressions, tone of voice, posture, body movements, etc. These are used to express superiority, respect, dependence, love, dislike, and other feelings. Non-verbal communication helps in judging the capabilities of an individual. The forms of non-verbal communication are: [i] signs and symbols, [ii] smile, [iii] cry, [iv] body language, [v] gesture, [vi] simple glance and others.

Q. 69. Write short note on the types of Informal Communication.

Ans. Informal communication may be internal and external. Internal informal communication is the casual communication among the employees of an organisation in the form of face-to-face conversation, telephone calls, and E-mails. External informal communication is a casual communication with the suppliers, investors, customers and other outsiders in the form of telephone calls, E-mails and face-to-face conversation.

Q. 70. What do you mean by Body Language in Communication?

Ans. Body Language is a form of Non-verbal communication. It consists of some body, eye, or facial movements or actions which are not specifically intended to replace words but transmit meaning.

Q. 71. What is 'Pictorial Communication'?

Ans. 'Pictorial Communication' is the process of transmitting information and message from one person to another in any distant place through chart, diagram, statistical data, picture, etc. by means of newly developed communication technologies like E-mail, Fax, Internet, etc.

Q. 72. How did the term 'Grapevine Communication' originate?

Ans. The term 'Grapevine Communication' originated during the American Civil War (1861-1865). During the period the communication of intelligence information through telegraph was not effective and reliable because the telegraph system was unorganised. Telegraph lines were strung in a haphazard way through trees like a real grapevine. The messages received or sent through these lines were often incorrect and confusing. Rumours were rampant during the Civil War. Thus any rumour, whatever might be the source, was presumed to be originated from the unarranged telegraph lines or grapevine. Later, in course of time, grapevine communication has become synonymous with informal communication.

Chapter 4

Q. 73. Write four reasons for the growth of communication technology.

Ans. The reasons for growth of modern communication technology are: [i] It is speedy, [ii] It is less costly, [iii] It can eliminate the problem of distance communication, [iv] Secrecy can be maintained.

Q. 74. Name the Oral or Verbal tools of modern communication.

Ans. Oral or verbal tools of modern communication include telephone (with cord), cordless telephone, mobile phone, wireless, voice mail and other electronic machines (e.g., dictaphone, isophone, speak phone).

Q. 75. What is Fax? [C.U. B.Com. 2008]

Ans. Facsimile (in short—'fax') is a system of sending and receiving letters, message, information, etc. electronically.

Q. 76. How does a Fax-system work?

Ans. A fax machine each with a connected telephone on both ends—at the sender's and at the receiver's end—are required for communication. The fax machine scans the original documents and sends signals through telephone system to the receiving end. The other fax machine at the receiving end converts the signal into identical copy of the original document and prints the same on a piece of paper.

Q. 77. State four advantages of Fax Communication.

Ans. Four advantages of Fax Communication are:

[i] It is quick and time-saving. [ii] Immediate feedback is possible through it. [iii] Fax communication can be preserved. [iv] It is simple to operate.

Q. 78. What is meant by 'Video Conferencing'? [C.U. B.Com. 2005, '09, '11 (New Syl.)]

Ans. 'Video Conferencing' is a newly developed method of communication. It is fast getting popular. It is also called tele-conferencing. It is a technology which allows the people of two or more distant places to see and talk to each other in real time.

Q. 79. Will face-to-face meeting be gradually replaced by video conferencing?

Ans. The importance of face-to-face meeting will never be reduced in the cases where personal involvement are required—making a compromise, resolving a conflict, explaining a subject, giving solace, etc. require personal interactions. Face-to-face meetings are more suitable than video conferencing in these cases.

Q. 80. Point out four advantages of Video Conferencing. [C.U. B.Com. 2005]

Ans. Four advantages of Video Conferencing are as follows :

[i] Meeting, seminar, conference, etc. can be conducted through it from far off situations.

[ii] Interview, training, instruction, consultation, etc. can be made from remote locations.

[iii] Demonstration of medical or any other process is possible through it from distant places.

[iv] The feedback is immediate in video conferencing.

Q. 81. Write two disadvantages of Video Conferencing.

Ans. Disadvantages of Video Conferencing:

[i] It is a costly affair. The installation charges of a video conference system is very high. The telephone charges and other expenditure on various tools in video conferencing are also very high.

[ii] The persons participating in video conference should have some technical knowledge regarding the equipment and tools in use. Owing to complex mechanism, the operators require some training.

Q. 82. What is E-mail? [C.U. B.Com. 2011]

Ans. E-mail is the short form of Electronic Mail. It is an electronic system through which letters, messages or any type of text can be sent almost instantly by computers across geographical boundaries. It is a wonderful means of communication for text-based messages. Through E-mail one can also send still pictures, animation, diagrams, musical attachments, etc.

Q. 83. Mention four advantages of E-mail.

Ans. Four advantages of E-mail are:

[i] It provides widespread communication.

[ii] It eliminates time barrier. Two persons need not to be present at the same time for communication through E-mail.

[iii] It is very fast. Very little time is required to send an E-mail.

[iv] It costs very little to send an E-mail—even to far off countries.

Q. 84. State four disadvantages of E-mail.

Ans. Four disadvantages of E-mail are stated below:

[i] **High initial cost:** The initial cost of purchasing a computer, modem, etc. required for E-mail communication is high.

[ii] **Technical knowledge:** Some technical knowledge of operating a computer and logging in the internet is necessary for using E-mail.

[iii] **Control:** Once an E-mail is sent, the sender has no control over it. The sender cannot call it back or make necessary changes.

[iv] **Dependent on telephone connection:** If, for some reasons, telephone connection is out of order, internet service will not be available and E-mail cannot be sent. It is dependent on telephone connection.

Q. 85. What is a Website? [C.U. B.Com. 2007, 2010]

Ans. A Website is a place on the World Wide Web that contains information, texts, graphics, audio and visual documents, etc., about an individual, a company or an organisation. It is the recent technological invention in the field of communication. It provides information on variety of topics. Any organisation or person can prepare a website for giving information regarding the organisation or the person to the public. In business world the business houses or the industrial units advertise their products giving details about them through website. The prospective customer can log on the website on a computer through internet and can buy the products giving orders through the internet on the website address. A website address begins with the alphabets 'www' meaning World Wide Web. A website may consist of a single web-page or comprise of a series of web-pages. The starting page of the website, called home page, contains index with links to other sections of the site. It is required to be improved or modified from time to time to incorporate necessary changes.

Q. 86. What is Internet? [C.U. B.Com. 2006]

Ans. Internet refers to inter-connected network of communication. It is an electronic communication system that connects computers and computer networks throughout the world. It is a vast computer network which links commercial, governmental, academic, corporate, public and private smaller computer networks world wide. Since a number of networks are connected to it, it is often described as a 'Network of networks'. It provides information relating to goods and services, medicine, education, employment, accommodation, travelling, entertainment, games and sports and various other subjects at a high speed. Its service is available 24 hours in a day. It is not controlled by any country or government. No individual, institution, government or country can claim ownership over it.

Q. 87. What is a Computer Virus?

Ans. A Computer Virus is a malicious, man-made software programme that can copy itself and infect a computer without the knowledge of the user. A computer virus needs another programme in order to be able to be activated and infect other computer files. Computer viruses are most easily spread by attachments in E-mail messages. The viruses can be hidden in pirated softwares. They also spread by using downloads on the internet or through removable medium like a floppy disk, CD, DVD, USB drive, etc. They can spread quickly through a network with effects that range from mildly damage to highly destructive depending upon the nature of viruses.

A computer virus may damage, change or delete data on a computer, interfere normal operation, degrade the performance of the computer system, reduce memory or diskspace, erase the hard drive or cause more severe damage. The best defence is to run anti-virus software and update it periodically.

Chapter 5

Q. 88. In what form may business messages be written?

Ans. Business messages may be written in the form of letters, memoranda, notices, circulars, advertisement, etc.

Q. 89. What are the objectives of planning a business message?

Ans. There are two objects of planning a business message—primary and secondary. The primary object is the immediate object for which the message is being written (e.g., letter asking due payment, letter requesting extension of the period of delivery). The secondary object is long lasting. It aims at building up goodwill of the business, retaining the existing customers and attracting additional customers, etc.

Q. 90. What is a 'Notice'? [C.U. B.Com. 2011 (supplementary)]

Ans. Notice is an instrument or device of giving information to all persons who are entitled to attend a meeting regarding time, date, place and purpose of the meeting.

Q. 91. Define 'Agenda'. [C.U. B.Com. 2010, 2011 (supplementary)]

Ans. The word 'Agenda' literally means "things to be done". Agenda may be defined as the list of businesses to be transacted at a meeting.

Q. 92. What is 'Clear days' Notice?

Ans. It means the number of days between the date of serving the notice and the date of holding the meeting—excluding both the days. A company is required to give at least 21 clear days' notice for holding a general meeting. This means that there should be an interval of 21 days between the date of issuing the notice and the date of holding the meeting.

Q. 93. The notice of an Annual General meeting of a Public Limited Company is dated 5th April 2011, while the date of the meeting is 30th April 2011. Comment on the validity of the notice.

Ans. Since there are more than 21 days' gap in between the date of notice and the date of holding the meeting, the notice of the meeting is valid.

Q. 94. The Annual General Meeting of a Company was to be held on 31 July 2011. The notice convening the meeting was dated 12th July 2011. Is the notice valid?

Ans. As there are only 18 days' clear gap in between the date of notice and the date of holding the meeting, the notice is not valid. According to the Companies Act, clear 21 days' notice is required to be served.

Q. 95. What is 'Quorum'?

Ans. A 'Quorum' may be defined as the minimum number of persons who must be present at a meeting for the valid transaction of its business.

Q. 96. What do you mean by a Circular?

Ans. A 'Circular' means the notification of certain information to the customers, employees, public or other interested parties. Any information which must be known to a large number of persons is circulated. In the business life, circulars have to be sent to the customers, dealers, agents, etc. These are known as trade circulars.

Q. 97. Distinguish between a 'Circular' and a 'Notice'.

Ans. A 'Circular' conveys some general information like the change of address, opening of showroom or branch, change of policy, etc. But a 'Notice' is issued to the members entitled to attend the meeting as regards the date, time, place and agenda of the meeting. A circular may be sent at any time whereas a notice is sent at a specified time. There is a period of notice but there is no period of circulars.

Q. 98. What is a 'Resolution'? [C.U. B.Com. 2007, 2009, 2011]

Ans. When a proposal is passed in a meeting, it is called a 'Resolution'. It is the final decision adopted at a meeting with or without amendment of the proposal.

Q. 99. What do you mean by 'Minutes' of a meeting?

Ans. The 'Minutes' of a meeting are the official records of the proceedings of the meeting and decision arrived at the meeting. It contains the summarised record of discussions held during the meeting as well as the resolutions adopted therein.

Q. 100. Distinguish between 'Minutes' and 'Proceedings' of a meeting.

Ans. 'Minutes' are the official records of the proceedings of a meeting in a summarised form, whereas 'Proceedings' are the detailed recordings of the discussions in the meeting.

Q. 101. Define a 'Report'.

Ans. A 'Report' may be defined as a precise and systematic statement of facts relating to a particular subject, prepared by a person or a group of persons after proper investigation and enquiry, and submitted to the person or body appointing it—with or without recommendations.

Q. 102. What is a 'Statutory Report' of a company?

Ans. A statutory report is a formal report which must be prepared and submitted by a public company at least 21 days before the statutory meeting to the members and filed with the Registrar of Companies. This report contains the description of shares allotted, receipts and payments account audited by the auditor of the company, preliminary expenses, etc.

Q. 103. What is a 'Quotation'?

Ans. A 'Quotation' is a statement of price, terms and condition of delivery and mode of payment sent by the seller to the prospective buyer on request.

Q. 104. What is a 'Letter of Credit'?

Ans. A letter written to introduce a person and to request the addressee to pay a certain sum of money to the person introduced is called a 'Letter of Credit'.

Q. 105. What is a 'Trade Enquiry'?

Ans. 'Trade Enquiry' is a business letter addressed to any prospective supplier stating therein the nature and quality of products to be purchased and asking the supplier to give quotation and other terms of delivery and payment.

Q. 106. What do you mean by 'Status Enquiry'?

Ans. 'Status Enquiry' is an enquiry made by any businessman to bank or another businessman about the financial standing, reputation, credit-worthiness and honesty of any prospective customer.

Q. 107. What is a 'Complimentary Close'?

Ans. A 'Complimentary Close' is the formal leave taking with some expression of obedience, respect, regard or friendliness towards the addressee, like 'Yours faithfully', 'Yours truly', 'Yours sincerely' etc. It is written just below the body of the letter, generally on the right hand side.

Q. 108. What are the chief characteristics of a good business letter?

Ans. The chief characteristics of a good business letter are—simplicity, conciseness, preciseness, completeness, courtesy, etc.

Q. 109. What is a Resumé?

Ans. A Resumé is a brief statement of a candidate's personal education and other qualifications, experiences, achievements, etc. used as an attachment with the application for a job. It is a list of personal information of an applicant willing to get an appointment.

Q. 110. 'An application is a kind of Sales Letter.'—Why?

Ans. As a Sales Letter is meant for selling a product, an application is written with the object of selling the services of the applicant. The applicant tries to sell his/her services by stating how his/her skills and experiences would prove valuable to the organisation. Therefore, an application is a kind of Sales Letter.

Group—B

Answers to the Short Questions Carrying 4 [Four] Marks Each

Chapter 1

Q. 1. What are the characteristics of Business Communication?

Ans. The characteristics of Business Communication are :

[a] **Practical :** Effective business communication deals with the practical aspect of the information explaining why, how, when and the like queries. It avoids impractical, imaginary, unnecessary or repetitive information to eliminate waste of time.

[b] **Factual :** In general a business message contains facts and figures in place of overall idea. Important date, place, time, etc. should be clearly mentioned in a business communication.

[c] **Clear and brief :** The language used in business communication should be simple, clear, brief and without ambiguity. Sometimes charts, photographs, diagrams, etc. are used to condense or clarify the information.

[d] **Target-oriented :** A business communication must have a specific objective and must be planned properly so that the objective can be achieved.

[e] **Persuasive :** Business communication often plays a persuasive role. It persuades an employee to perform his/her duties, a customer to buy a product or service, etc.

[f] **Pervasive :** The subject-matter of business communication covers a wide range and extends to all functions—purchases, production, sales, finance, recruitment, wages, dividends, market standing, innovation, productivity etc. It also moves through all levels of management, upward, downward and sideways. Business Communication is thus said to be a pervasive function.

[g] **Continuity :** Communication is an ever present activity and without it an organisation cannot exist. Communication is as necessary to an organisation as blood circulation in a living body.

[h] **Two-way Traffic :** Business Communication does not only mean its downward movement from superior to the subordinates it implies both transmission and reception. It involves two-way traffic from management body to employees and from employees to management body.

Q. 2. Write briefly the objectives of Business Communication. [C.U. B.Com. 2005]

Ans. The objectives of Business Communication are briefly outlined as follows :

[a] **Giving information :** The primary object of communication is to make the members of an organisation aware of its goal and acquaint them with all relevant information.

[b] **Persuasion :** To persuade means to make other people decide to do something, especially by repeatedly asking them or telling them reasons why they should do it, in other words, influencing other people to believe or to do what one wants. This is one of the important objectives of communication.

[c] **Conveying Suggestion :** Communication helps in conveying suggestions, opinions and ideas. The workers who are actually engaged in the work know better the loopholes in it and can suggest to the management authority the ways to plug the loopholes. This is an example of upward communication. In big offices suggestion boxes are provided and suggestions are received throughout the year.

[d] **Advice :** One of the objectives of communication is to advise an individual or a group of people. Today's business world is very complex and no one can be an expert in all the spheres of business. So a businessman has to take advice from the experts regarding matters in which he is not well-informed.

[e] **Motivation :** Communication is made to inspire, to motivate and to create a sense of loyalty among the employees. Through communication their morale is boosted up and it leads to better performance.

[f] **Instruction, guidance and counselling :** One of the objectives of communication is to manage the employees by means of imparting instruction, providing guidance and arranging for counselling.

[g] **Giving warning and appreciating good work :** The objective of both appreciation and warnings may be accomplished through oral or written communication.

[h] **Management efficiency :** One of the objectives of communication is to increase efficiency of management. If there is a good network of communication (formal and informal), the organisation can be managed efficiently and effectively.

Q. 3. "Feedback is the key which unlocks the success of communication."—Discuss briefly.

Ans. In the case of inter-personal communication only sending of message by the sender to the receiver is not enough. He/She must be eager to know the reaction or to get return information. The message sent by the receiver back to the source is called feedback. It is the response by the recipient.

Feedback is essential in communication. Actually communication is a two-way process—[i] sending the message, and [ii] receiving the response or feedback. The sender is interested to know the reaction of the recipient. He/She is also willing to know whether the recipient has understood the message in the same sense as intended. If there is any lapse in it further negotiation or communication is necessary. On the other hand, the recipient might have understood the meaning and intention of the message but due to barrier of some kind, say, language barrier, he/she could not convey his/her reactions properly. In such case also actual picture is to be brought to light removing barriers.

In face-to-face communication feedback is no problem, because the speaker and the listener both are present and can ask and clarify message instantly, if there is any ambiguity. One can ask the other to repeat what has been missed. They can also observe gestures and facial expression in oral communication. But in the case of non-verbal and written communication the feedback is not instant. It requires some time. Whatever may be the mode or channel (i.e., verbal or non-verbal), feedback is very important. It is the key which unlocks the success of communication. The objective of communication is bound to remain unfulfilled unless the process of communication is complete with feedback. It is an inseparable part of successful communication.

Q. 4. What are the benefits of Effective Communication?

Ans. The benefits of effective communication are discussed below :

[a] **Problems are solved quickly and easily :** Innumerable problems crop up in a business organisation due to poor communication or no communication. Effective communication can solve the problems easily.

[b] **Stronger decision making :** A decision, in order to be correct and appropriate, must be based on adequate and correct information which only communication can bring together.

[c] **Productivity is increased :** Effective communication establishes a link between the managers and employees. The relationship between them are eased and various problems and grievances are removed. Communication thus increases ability, efficiency, and quality of performance of the employees which ultimately leads to higher productivity. Communication with the outside world increases demand for the goods and/or services supplied by the organisation and helps to increase productivity indirectly.

[d] **Steadier work flow :** Flow of work is not obstructed if orders, instructions, suggestions etc. are communicated properly and timely.

[e] **Good business relationship :** Fruitful communication with the outside people and organisations (e.g., creditors, banks, insurance companies co-business manages, etc.) make a healthy relationship with them.

[f] **Clearer promotional materials :** Goods and services can be brought to the knowledge of the customers and promotional activity (e.g. advertisement, use of different media, etc.) can be made more effective through communication.

[g] **Enhanced professional image :** The way an organisation communicates casts an impression of its efficiency on the communicatee. Good communication signifies good and professionally efficient organisation.

[h] **Improved stakeholders' response :** The stakeholders (i.e., the various groups with whom interaction is made) in a business enterprise are likely to respond better if communication is proper and effective.

Q. 5. Discuss briefly the guiding Principles of Effective Communication.

[C.U. B.Com. 2011 (New Syl.)]

Ans. The principles for effective business communication may be outlined as follows :

[a] **Clarity :** The communication process, in order to serve the purpose, must ensure clarity of communication. A communication possesses clarity when it is expressed in a language and transmitted in a way that will be comprehended by the receiver.

[b] **Adequacy :** The goal in communication is to ensure an optimum flow of information. It should be enough to cover the field.

[c] **Attention :** The receiver's full attention and concentration over the message listening or reading should be considered as very essential for proper understanding of the messages communicated.

[d] **Timing :** The utility of any message to the receiver is markedly affected by its timeliness.

[e] **Interest and Acceptance :** The purpose of communication is to secure a positive response. The person communicated to should be interested in the message and accept it. Downward communication is more effective if morale is good, and upward communication gets through when the superior is a good listener.

[f] **Courtesy :** Courtesy should be maintained at all costs in any communication. In business communication, especially, courtesy is a sign of good organisation.

[g] **Conciseness :** Communication to be effective should be concise. Only necessary facts are to be stated avoiding repetitions.

[h] **Channel :** Use of direct and shortest channel saves the subject-matter of the communication from distortion. Care should be taken in this regard.

[i] **Feedback :** A communication is complete when feedback is received from the recipient. The ultimate objective of communication is fulfilled through this principle.

[j] **Completeness :** It should be complete in all respects. Before communicating one should check whether the following '5 whs' are answered : who, what, where, when and why.

Q. 6. Write a short note on Barriers to Business Communication.

[C.U. B.Com. 2006, 2011 (New Syl.), 2011 (supplementary)]

Ans. Certain external and internal forces impede the flow of communication. They interrupt or block communication or prevent mutual understanding. Communication may be vague and badly expressed. It may suffer from lack of clarity or poor retention. Barriers between people do not screen out all communications, rather they operate like filter to permit some communications but hold back others, thereby making communication inadequate. Non-listening of the communication is a chronic problem. Many communications do not receive the attention they deserve. These limitations or causes of breakdown of communication channels are called 'Communication barriers'.

Communication is impeded by various types of barriers. These may be classified into three categories : [i] External barriers, [ii] Organisational barriers, and [iii] Personal barriers.

Barriers to Business Communication are shown by a chart as follows :

Barriers to Business Communication

[A] External Barriers

1. Semantic Barriers
2. Emotional or Psychological Barriers
   - [i] Inattention
   - [ii] Perceptual Barriers
   - [iii] Transmission Loss
   - [iv] Premature Evaluation
   - [v] Reliance on Written Words
   - [vi] Distrust
   - [vii] Failure to Communicate

[B] Organisatinal Barriers

- [i] Organisational Policy
- [ii] Status Relationship
- [iii] Rules and Regulations
- [iv] Complexity in Structure
- [v] Organisational Facilities
- [vi] Information Overload

[C] Personal Barriers

1. Barriers in Superiors
   - [i] Attitude
   - [ii] Fear of Challange of Authority
   - [iii] Lack of Confidence in Subordinates
   - [iv] Lack of Time
   - [v] Lack of Awareness
   - [vi] Ignoring Communication
2. Barriers in Subordinates
   - [i] Unwillingness
   - [ii] Lack of Proper Incentive

Chapter 2

Q. 7. What are the reasons for Conflict?

Ans. The reasons for conflict are stated below :

[a] **Poor Communication :** Conflict generally arises owing to poor communication or communication gap which usually takes place in the absence of complete, clear and correct information or due to language barriers.

[b] **Competition :** The problem of competition comes in where resources are limited and only a few are rewarded and a large section remains deprived. This competition generates dissatisfaction and ultimately gives rise to conflict.

[c] **Individual Differences :** There are differences among people in education, culture and upbringing and differences in values, attitudes and personalities. When people with so many differences work together, there is always a possibility of conflict.

[d] **More Power :** An individual or a group has a general tendency to become more powerful and more important. From this tendency an individual or a group may defy or questions the authority of superior. This leads to conflict.

[e] **Difference in Objective :** Individuals or groups with different objectives are likely to oppose each other. They cannot go along the same route for long. Such differences gradually generate dissatisfaction between them and result in conflicts.

[f] **Lack of Well Defined Responsibility :** Lack of well-defined responsibility regarding the performances of a work gives ample scope for a conflict. Where no particular person or group is given responsibility for a work; it becomes nobody's job to see it well done. Individuals or groups may start blaming one another and this may give rise to conflict.

[g] **Retaliation :** When an individual or group is threatened or hurt by another individual or group, the former usually threatens or hurts the later in retaliation. Thus, a conflict is likely to crop up.

[h] **Difference in Work Environment :** If there are differences in work environment among the different employees or different groups of employees, conflict may take place. Employees of less convenient environment may feel deprived and can contribute to conflict.

Q. 8. Mention the Advantages and Disadvantages of Conflict.

Ans. [A] Advantages : The advantages of conflict are stated below :

[a] **Clarifies Situation and Issues :** Different opinions regarding an issue often confuse us, but a confrontation of such opinions with conflicting arguments can clarify the situation and the issue.

[b] **Brings out Social Change :** No change is possible without conflict. A strong conflict between the old and new values brings about social change.

[c] **Strengthens Relationship :** It is better to go in for a conflict rather than suppressing it. Though conflict may generate temporary disagreement or ill-feeling, it strengthens relationship in the long run.

[d] **Develops Science and Technology :** New horizon of science and technology may be opened through conflict. Each conflicting party wants to be supreme in power over the others. Thus, the craze for power encourages scientific and technological development.

[e] **Acts as Safety Valve :** The expression of dissatisfaction, dissent, disagreement is helpful as it releases the tension and gives the aggrieved party a sense of something being done and that in itself gives a sense of relief.

[B] Disadvantages : The disadvantages of conflict are as follows :

[a] **Enlarges Differences :** Conflict magnifies the differences between the persons. Imaginary and real differences crop up and relationship deteriorates.

[b] **Breeds Distrust and Suspicion :** Conflict breeds distrust and suspicion among the conflicting parties. Confidence and reliance diminish with the increase in the intensity of the conflict.

[c] **Causes Inefficiency in Performance :** As considerable energy is lost in the effort of making and resolving a conflict, efficiency in work performance is bound to be affected.

[d] **Brings in Hostile Attitude :** Conflict creates hatred and breeds hostility. Even a gentle and obedient employee may disobey the superior and become hostile in his/her behaviour. The same behaviour can be noticed between the co-employees or between the groups during conflict.

[e] **Plays Destructive Role :** Conflict may involve employees in acts that are harmful and destructive for the organisation.

Q. 9. What Measures may be taken for Resolving a Conflict? [C.U. B.Com. 2010]

Ans. Following are some of the measures that can be taken to put an end to conflict :

[a] **Removing the Cause of Conflict :** One has to find out first the actual cause of conflict. It will be easier to reach a solution if the cause of conflict is removed.

[b] **Early Action :** If a conflict is resolved at an early stage, it does not grow into a big problem.

[c] **Positive Attitude :** The conflicting parties should come forward to resolve the conflict. If both the parties agree to talk to each other in resolving the conflict, half the war is won.

[d] **Effective Persuasion :** Through the process of persuasion newer view points may emerge and lead the way to a solution.

[e] **Flexibility :** To get closer to a solution the parties should give up rigidity and should be flexible in their attitude.

[f] **Diversion of Focus to Greater Interest :** Group conflict may be resolved if the conflicting parties are trained to fight jointly with the external enemy forgetting internal conflict and thus channelising their energy and spirit for achieving greater interest.

[g] **Accepting the Truth :** One of the easiest ways of ending a conflict is to realise that one was wrong or made a mistake in involving himself/herself in a conflict and accepts the truth.

[h] **Effective Communication :** Complete, clear and correct information through effective communication can wipe out misunderstanding and suspicion between the management authority and employees. Thus, effective communication can resolve conflict.

[i] **Arbitration :** Committees, teams, taskforce, etc. may be formed, and an expert co-ordinator or arbitrator may be appointed to resolve a conflict.

[j] **Participation in Management :** If the employees are allowed to participate in various committees and bodies of management, they feel that they are part and parcel of management and have a say in the decision making. Such feeling can help to avoid conflict.

Chapter 3

Q. 10. Point out the characteristics of Corporate Communication.

Ans. The characteristics of corporate communication are pointed out briefly as follows:

[a] **Formal Communication :** Most of the corporate communication are formal in nature. Orders, instructions, information, suggestions etc. are sent, maintaining formal procedure in a systematic way. It has to pass through several organisational stages.

[b] **Internal and External :** Exchange of information with a large number of people within and outside the business enterprise is required in corporate communication.

[c] **Oral and Written :** Corporate communication consists of both Oral and Written. While oral communication is used for closer and internal communication with the employees, written communication is made with the outsiders and distant people.

[d] **Wide Coverage :** Corporate organisations are large and a wide range of people are required to be covered in communication.

[e] **Means of Communication :** Phones, face-to-face conversation, E-mail, Fax, telegrams, memos, website, internet, video conference etc. are used as mediums or channels of corporate communication.

[f] **Feedback :** As in the case of other communication, feedback is an essential element of successful corporate communication.

[g] **Long-term System :** Corporate organisation has a perpetual existence. So, corporate communication is not a temporary arrangement. It is a long-term system or process.

[h] **Continuous Flow of Communication :** In a corporate organisation flow of communication is continuous and uninterrupted; continuous due to the organisation's perpetual existence and uninterrupted owing to following the formal or official channel.

Q. 11. Distinguish between Formal and Informal Communication.

[C.U. B.Com. 2011 (New Syl.)]

Ans. Distinction between Formal and Informal Communication :

Formal Communication	Aspects of Distinction	Informal Communication
Formal communication is the transmission of information in formal organisational structure and in specific direction.	1. Meaning	Informal communication is the communication on the basis of infomal relations and understanding among the people at the same or different levels.
The purposes of formal communication are to give orders, convey instructions and fulfil the objective of the organisation through some pre-determined rules and regulations.	2. Purpose	The purposes of informal communication are to build up informal relationship through personal contacts, sharing of information etc.
Formal communication flows in a systematic manner according to procedure. It takes its own time.	3. Speed	Informal communication is fast-flowing, specially in the case of rumours.
In the case of formal communication feedback requires some time due to completion of formal procedure.	4. Feedback	In informal communication feedback is immediate.

Contd.

Formal Communication	Aspects of Distinction	Informal Communication
Formal communication is time-consuming and costly.	5. Time and Money	Informal communication being verbal is less costly and immediate. Of course, gossip may consume productive working hours.
It is official and formal in nature.	6. Nature	It is unofficial and infomal in nature.
It requires sanction of higher authority.	7. Sanction of Higher Authority	No sanction of higher authority is required.
Flexibility is not found in it. It is generally rigid in nature.	8. Flexibility	It is loose and very much flexible.

Q. 12. What are the advantages and disadvantages of Written Communication?

[C.U. B.Com. 2010]

Ans. Advantages of Written Communication :

[1] It is suitable for long distance communication and repetitive standing orders.

[2] It creates permanent record of evidence. It can be used for future reference.

[3] It gives the receiver sufficient time to think, act and react.

[4] It can be used as legal document.

[5] It can be sent to many persons at a time.

[6] It is suitable for sending statistical data, chart, diagram, pictures etc.

Limitations or Disadvantages of Written Communication :

[1] It is time-consuming. Composing a message in writing takes much time. Writing letters, typing orders, notices, etc. and sending to appropriate destination requires time. Feedback process also is not instant.

[2] It is expensive not so much due to postal charges but in terms of so many people spending so much of their time.

[3] It cannot maintain strict secrecy which would have been possible in oral communication.

[4] Written communication has no scope for immediate clarification if not understood properly.

[5] Being written in nature it is less flexible and cannot be changed easily.

[6] It is not effective in the case of emergency.

Q. 13. Distinguish between Verbal and Written Communication.

Ans. Distinction between Verbal (Oral) and Written Communication :

Verbal (Oral) Communication	Aspects of Distinction	Written Communication
Verbal or Oral communication implies the transmission of orders, messages or suggestions through the spoken words.	1. Meaning	Written Communication means transmission of messages, orders or instructions in writting.

Contd.

Verbal (Oral) Communication	Aspects of Distinction	Written Communication
The media of oral communication are face-to-face talk, speech, lecture, interview, meeting, telephonic talk, video conference, etc.	2. Media or Channel	The media of written communication are letter, circular, manual, report, telegram, office memo, bulletin, journal, magazine, e-mail, fax, internet, etc.
It is an informal method of communication.	3. Method	It is a formal method of communication.
In oral communication the contact being direct feedback is immediate.	4. Feedback	In written communication feedback requires some time.
It saves time and money as communication is direct.	5. Time and cost	It is time-consuming and costly.
Oral communication is very much flexible.	6. Flexibility	It is less flexible.
Secrecy can be maintained.	7. Secrecy	Secrecy may be endangered.
If not understood immediate clarification is possible in oral communication.	8. Immediate Clarification	It has no scope for immediate clarification.
No record is kept generally (unless audio or video tape-recording is made).	9. Permanent Record	A written document preserved properly becomes a permanent record of the organisation and can be used as future reference.

Q 14. Write short notes on : [a] Vertical Communication, [b] Horizontal Communication.

[C.U. B.Com. 2008, 2011 (New Syl.)]

Ans. [a] **Vertical Communication :** It refers to the flow of information both downward and upward through the organisational chain of command. ↓↑ In such communications superiors send message, orders, directions, etc. to the subordinates and the subordinates also convey information, reactions, grievances and suggestions to the superiors. Vertical communication is formal in nature.

It forms a good manager-employee relationship. It helps the managers to control, supervise, and take decisions properly knowing the view point of the subordinates. On the other hand, the subordinates can also express their feelings to the managers and consider that they are also important in the organisational activities.

[b] **Horizontal Communication :** Horizontal communication is a communication process that is used to communicate with the people working on the same level or similar rank in an organisation. If the managers of the same level consult each other and share ideas, suggestions and solutions for the upliftment of the organisation, it is a case of Horizontal Communication, e.g. the production manager consults the purchase manager to buy better raw materials to improve the quality of production. It is also called Sideways Communation or Lateral Communication. ⇆

The main objectives of Horizonatal Communication are solving problems, developing team-work, improving performance and boosting efficiency. It helps to establish co-operation and co-ordination among the peer persons. It is less formal and structured than the Vertical Communication.

Q. 15. Write a short note on Grapevine Communication.

[C.U. B.Com. 2005, 2009, 2011 (New Syl.)]

Ans. Since grapevine communication is an integral part of communication system, it works side by side with the formal communication. The nature of grapevine communication can be guessed from its name. Like a grapevine plant it grows fast, spreads to any direction and goes a long way in creating informal relationship.

In an organisation small groups of people work together. It is quite natural that they will become interested about each other and want to know various information regarding each other's service condition, salary, facilities available, appointment, retirement, transfer, punishment, etc. They will also be interested to know private, secret and confidential information which include any romantic affair, family disputes, marriage, birth of a child, examination results of their children, special treatment or favour by boss to any member and so on. These information spread very quickly in geometric progression from one to a few and from a few to many persons irrespective of their formal positions. Spread of half true information or rumours is not congenial to the organisation health. It breeds conflict, weakens consolidation and unity, diminishes morale of the workers and creates a chaotic situation within the organisation. It becomes more harmful for an organisation when the managers take decisions depending upon such unreliable, inaccurate and incomplete information.

The efficient managers can make proper use of informal or grapevine communication and apply it for the well-being of the organisation if some general steps like the following are taken.

[i] The managers should keep a watchful eye on the leaders who spread rumours and keep them well-informed about the actual situation.

[ii] The managers should contradict rumours as soon as possible.

[iii] They should involve the employees in decision-making.

The managers, on the other hand, can supplement formal communication with grapevine communication. They can feel the pulse of the organisation through informal communication. They can even use it to convey any official information with a bit of care.

Chapter 4

Q. 16. Write short note on : Emergence of Communication Technology.

[C.U. B.Com. 2011 (New Syl.)]

Ans. In early years business communication was conducted mainly through face-to-face conversation in verbal communication and restricted to the use of pen, pencil, ink, etc. in written communication. After the industrial revolution the need for technological communication was felt with the spread of trade and commerce. The conventional methods of communication were not enough to meet the growing need of communication. The managers required information support to arrive at a decision to run the business efficiently. Since necessity is the mother of invention, a series of inventions took place to gradually replace the old system. Today we have telephone, mobile phone, pager, computer, fax, e-mail, voice mail, website, etc. for business communication. Modern communication technology provides speed, economy, elemination of barriers of distance, maintenance of secrecy, easy and compact preservation of data, smart and neat presentation and such other facilities which the age old technology could not provide.

Not very long ago it required days and weeks to communicate through postal system. But at present with the help of ISD (International Subscriber Dialling) and STD (Subscriber Trunk Dialling) facilities one can make communication with even overseas people within a few seconds. Unprecedented development in the communication process and innovation of various methods have made communication easy, quick and effective. Information and communication technology has developed so much is recent years that we can call it a revolution. The emergence of the internet and development in the information technology have brought the world very close and totally wiped out the barriers of time and zone. Each and every place of the world is so close to us that we can say that we are living in a 'global village'.

Q. 17. What are the advantages and disadvantages of Fax communication.

Ans. Advantages of Fax Communication :

[1] **Quick and Time-saving :** Fax can send the photocopy of a document practically within no time, almost immediately. It is one of the speediest methods of modern communication system. It works at the speed of telephone call. So time in communicating can be saved in fax.

[2] **Feedback :** Immediate feed back is also possible through it.

[3] **Preservation of Documents :** Being a written document on paper fax communication can be preserved as record for future reference.

[4] **Dependable :** Fax communication is flawless and dependable, because photocopy of documents sent from one fax machine to the other is a replica of the original one.

[5] **Sending and Receiving Various Documents :** Various documents including information, messages, pictures, images, graphs, statistics, deeds, agreements, etc. can be sent and received through it.

[6] **Less Costly :** Fax is relatively less costly.

Disadvantages of Fax Communication :

[1] **Costly :** The initial cost of purchasing fax machine is high. Again the charges of fax communication is higher in comparison to e-mail and other electronic communication. Therefore, selective use of the machine is required.

[2] **Not so clear image :** Generally the image of the faxed documents is not as clear as the original text.

[3] **Rigid process :** No change in message is possible in the text of fax communication. To make a change one has to send another fax incorporating the change.

[4] **Training for operation :** A fax macine cannot be operated except by a trained person.

[5] **Secrecy and privacy :** No secrecy can be maintained in the process. It lacks privacy.

[6] **Loss of infomation :** Important news or infomation may remain out of sight, if regular and proper search is not made in the fax machine.

Q. 18. Discuss briefly the advantages and disadvantages of E-mail.
[C.U. B.Com. 2011 (New Syl.)]

Ans. Advantages of E-mail :

[1] **Widespread communication :** E-mail can be sent to various departments or branches of an organisation within the country and also to the addresses in far off countries.

[2] **Elimination of time constraint :** E-mail eliminates time barrier. Two people need not be present at the same time for communication through e-mail. It may be sent at the convenient time of the sender and can be read any time according to the recipient's convenience.

[3] **Fast :** Very little time is required to send an e-mail.

[4] **Less costly :** It costs very little to send an e-mail even to far off countries.

[5] **Efficiency :** It increases efficiency of the organisation by neat, prompt and timely communication.

[6] **Easy to operate :** Sending of e-mail is not much difficult. An elimentary knowledge of the computer technology is enough to compose and send an e-mail to the desired destination.

[7] **Privacy :** The messages sent through e-mail are highly secured. No one except the intended person can open the mail box that can be opened with an identity code which is with the person only. So privacy is ensured.

[8] **Future reference :** Important e-mail can be preserved for future reference. It may be stored in a floppy disk or in the hard disk of the computer. A printout of the e-mail may be taken and be preserved in files also.

Disadvantages of e-mail :

[1] **Control :** Once an e-mail is sent, the sender has no control over it. The sender cannot call it back or make necessary changes.

[2] **Privacy :** There is no guarantee of privacy in this system. Hackers (cyber pirates) can make an access to one's e-mail and read the contents unless it is in a coded form.

[3] **Loss of business hours :** While checking the mail box an employee not only checks it and arranges for reply of enquiries but also switches over to various other websites not connected with organisational work thereby uselessly spending hour after hour.

[4] **High initial cost :** The initial cost of purchasing a computer, modem etc. required for e-mail communication is high.

[5] **Cannot connect :** It may so happen that inspite of repeated attempt the required e-mail address/site cannot be connected due to busy channel. This generally happens when a large number of people try to establish link through the same channel at a time.

Q. 19. What are the advantages of Video Conferencing? [C.U. B.Com. 2011 (New Syl.)]

Ans. Advantages of video conferencing :

[i] Meeting, seminar, conference, symposium, etc. can be conducted through it from far off situations.

[ii] Interview, training, instruction, consultation etc. can be made from remote locations.

[iii] Demonstration of medical or any other process is possible through it from distant places.

[iv] Not only ideas, facts, information, etc. are exchanged but charts, deeds, agreements, pictures, maps, blue-print of plans, etc. also can be viewed on the screen.

[v] Video conferencing is helpful in establishing personal relationship as in the case of face-to-face discussion.

[vi] The reaction of the person receiving the information is known immediately in video conference.

[vii] As any query can be answered immediately, video conferencing eleminates the chances of misunderstading.

[viii] Organisations having a number of branches within the country or in foreign countries and having relation with distant centres require video conferencing for effective negotiation.

Group—C

[For Answers to Questions Carrying 10 [Ten] Marks Each in Business Communication refer to Chapter 5 (Drafting)]

APPENDIX II

MODEL QUESTIONS OF THE NEW SYLLABUS

MODEL QUESTIONS OF THE NEW SYLLABUS

PRINCIPLES AND PRACTICE OF MANAGEMENT

50 Marks

Group—A

[Each Question Carries 2 Marks]

1. Define 'Management'.
2. What do you mean by 'Universality of Management'?
3. Is Management an 'Art' or a 'Science'?
4. Is Management a 'Profession'?
5. What is meant by 'Scientific Management'?
6. Mention any four characteristics of Scientific Management.
7. What do you understand by 'Time Study'?
8. What is 'Motion Study'?
9. What is meant by 'Fatigue Study'?
10. Give the definition of 'Planning'.
11. What are the elements of Planning?
12. What do you mean by 'Forecasting'?
13. Point out the various techniques of Forecasting.
14. What is the meaning of 'Decision-making'?
15. Mention any four features of Decision-making.
16. What do you mean by 'Organisation Structure'?
17. Define 'Line Organisation'?
18. What do you understand by 'Delegation of Authority'?
19. What is 'Decentralisation'?
20. What is meant by 'Motivation'?
21. What are the human needs indicated by Abraham Maslow?
22. What is meant by 'Leadership' in Management?
23. What do you mean by 'Co-ordination' in Management Process?
24. What is the difference between 'Co-ordination' and 'Co-operation'?
25. What is understood by 'Control' in Management?
26. What is the meaning of 'Span of Control'?
27. Mention any four qualities of good Leadership.
28. Point out any four Managerial Skills.
29. State the various roles which a Manager has to play.
30. What is 'Departmentation'?

31. Mention the different bases of Departmentation.
32. What do you mean by 'Planning Premises'?
33. State any four features of a good Plan.
34. State any four aids to Motivation.
35. Point out any four characteristics of a Sound Organisation.
36. What is 'Organisation Chart'?
37. What is meant by 'Line and Staff Organisation'?
38. Mention any four techniques of Co-ordination.
39. What do you mean by 'Budgetary Control'?
40. State any four requisites of a good Control System.

Group—B

[Each Question Carries 4 Marks]

1. State briefly the importance of Management.
2. Give a short description of the Principles of Management indicated by Henry Faol.
3. State briefly the basic principles of Scientific Management.
4. Distinguish between 'Organisation' and 'Management'.
5. "Planning and Forecasting are not synonyms"—Explain the statement.
6. State briefly the importance of Planning in modern business world.
7. Point out briefly the relation between 'Planning' and 'Controlling'.
8. Write a short note on 'Bureaucratic Management'.
9. Describe in brief the principles of Human Relation Approach to Management.
10. Write a short note on 'Hawthorne Experiment'.
11. Give a short description of Human Behavioural Approach to Management.
12. Explain the meaning of 'Organisation'.
13. Point out the features of 'Formal Organisation'.
14. What are the advantages and disadvantages of 'Line Organisation'?
15. What do you mean by 'Staff Organisation'? Point out its merits and demerits.
16. What are the advantages and disadvantages of 'Functional Organisation'?
17. Write a short note on the necessity of 'Delegation of Authority'.
18. What are the features of Delegation of Authority.
19. Point out the merits of Delegation of Authority.
20. What are the limitations or disadvantages of Delegation of Authority?
21. What is meant by 'Centralisation of Authority'? Mention its reasons.
22. Explain the need for Decentralisation of Authority.
23. Distinguish between Delegation and Decentralisation.
24. State the importance of Departmentation briefly.

25. Analyse the role of Motivation in Management.
26. What are the limitations of Motivation?
27. Write a short note on 'Theory X' of Mc Gregor.
28. What are the assumptions of 'Theory Y' indicated by Mc Gregor?
29. Explain the significance of Leadership in brief.
30. Point out the advantages of 'Democratic Leadership'.1
31. What are the demerits of 'Autocratic Leadership'?
32. State the meaning of Co-ordination as the essence of Management.
33. "Co-ordination and Co-operation are inter-dependent."—Explain the statement.
34. Describe in brief the features of control.
35. State the importance of Control in Management in short.
36. Point out the limitations of Controlling Process.
37. Describe in short the various steps in Controlling.
38. Explain the characteristics of Budgetary Control.
39. State the advantages of Budgetary Control.
40. Describe in brief the Principles of Control System.

Group—C

[Each Question Carries 8 Marks]

1. Discuss the contribution of F.W. Taylor to the introduction of Management Theory.
2. Narrate the contribution of Henry Fayol in the history of Management Thought.
3. Describe the various criticisms against Scientific Management.
4. Explain the contribution of Elton Mayo to Management Thought.
5. Discuss the contribution of Mary Parker Follet in Management.
6. Discuss the steps involved in Planning.
7. Explain the characteristics of a Sound Plan.
8. Discuss the various steps in Decision-making.
9. Describe the steps involved in Organising Process.
10. Discuss the relation between Planning and Decision-making.
11. Narrate the features of a strong Organisation.
12. State the importance of Organisation in Management.
13. Give a description of the Process of Delegation of Authority.
14. Describe the advantages and disadvantages of Decentralisation of Authority.
15. Explain the characteristics of Leadership.
16. Give a short description of the various functions of Leadership.
17. Describe the features of Motivation.
18. Explain the benefits of Motivation.

19. Discuss the different Aids to Motivation.
20. Analyse the essential qualities of good Leadership.
21. Analyse the Motivation Theory introduced by Abraham Maslow.
22. Critically describe the Motivation Theory of Herzberg.
23. Discuss Mc Gregor's Theory X and Theory Y with criticism.
24. Give an account of Tannenbaum and Schmidt's Model of Leadership.
25. Distinguish between Leadership and Management.

BUSINESS COMMUNICATION

50 Marks

Group—A

[Each Question Carries 2 Marks]

1. What is Communication?
2. What do you mean by Business Communication?
3. What are the elements of Business Communication?
4. What is Business Communication Channel?
5. Give two examples of Written Channels?
6. State two means of Oral Communication.
7. What is Feedback in Communication?
8. What is a Communication Model?
9. Name four general principles of effective Business Communication.
10. Define Conflict.
11. What is a Group Conflict?
12. What do you mean by Inter-group Conflict?
13. What is Intra-group Conflict?
14. What is Group Cohesiveness?
15. What is meant by Formal Communication?
16. What is Informal Communication?
17. State two advantages of Formal Communication.
18. State two advantages of Informal Communication.
19. What is Corporate Communication?
20. Write short note : Grapevine.
21. Name four verbal tools of Modern Communication.
22. What is Fax?
23. What is Video Conferencing?
24. What is E-mail?
25. What is Website?
26. What is Internet?
27. What is meant by Communication Network?
28. What is Notice?
29. Define Agenda?
30. What is Quorum?
31. What do you mean by a Circular?
32. What is a Resolution?
33. Define a Report?
34. What is a 'Statutory Report' of a company?
35. What is a Quotation?
36. What do you mean by Status Enquiry?

37. What is a Resume?
38. What do you mean by CV?

Group—B

[Each Question Carries 4 Marks]

1. State briefly the objectives of Business Communication.
2. State the steps of Business Communication.
3. When is a Written Channel of Business Communication selected?
4. When is an Oral Channel selected?
5. State briefly the importance of Feedback in Communication.
6. What are the Ten Commandments of American Management Association for effective Business Communication.
7. What are the Seven Cs in effective Communication?
8. State briefly the barriers to Business Communication.
9. Mention four methods of overcoming Communication Barriers.
10. How does a Communication Model help us to understand the process of Communication?
11. Mention four reasons for Conflict.
12. Mention four disadvantages of Conflict.
13. What measures may be taken to resolve a Conflict? Mention any four measures.
14. When is the degree of cohesiveness in a group considered to be high?
15. State four characteristics of Corporate Communication.
16. Write a short note on the importance of Corporate Communication.
17. What is Formal Communication? Write three characteristics of Formal Communication?
18. What is Informal Communication? What are its purposes?
19. Write four characteristics of Informal Communication?
20. State briefly two advantages and two disadvantages of Formal Communication.
21. State briefly two advantages and two disadvantages of Informal Communication.
22. State four advantages of Written Communication.
23. What do you mean by Oral Communication? What are its merits?
24. How did the term 'Grapevine Communication' originate?
25. What do you mean by Non-verbal Communication?
26. What is Business Communication Network? Why is Business Communication Network often compared to the artery in human body?
27. What is Fax? How does a fax system work?
28. Point out four advantages of Vedio Conferencing.
29. Mention the advantages and disadvantages of E-mail?
30. Distinguish between a Circular and a Notice?
31. Distinguish between Minutes and Proceedings of a meeting.
32. What is 'Clear Days' notice?

Group—C

[Each Question Carries 10 Marks]

1. Draft a notice with suitable agenda of the First Board Meeting of a Public Limited Company.
2. Draft a notice of the Annual General Meeting of a Company.
3. Draft a notice of the Extra-ordinary General Meeting of a Public Limited Company.
4. Draft a notice of the Annual General Meeting of a Club with usual agenda.
5. Draft an appropriate notice convening the Annual General Meeting of a Co-operative Society stating the usual items of business to be transacted.
6. Draft a suitable notice with agenda of the ordinary meeting of a local body.
7. Draft a circular announcing the establishment of new business.
8. Draft a circular addressing your customers and dealers announcing the opening of a branch or a showroom.
9. Draft a circular letter to the shareholders of a Public Limited Company informing them that the company will issue Bonus Shares in the ratio of 2 : 1 and that the shares will be sent to them in due course.
10. Draft a circular letter notifying increase in selling prices of products and seeking continued patronage of the customers.
11. Draft a circular to all customers of the firm informing them of the termination of the services of a travelling salesman and appointment of a new representative in his place.
12. Draft a report to be submitted to the Board of Directors about the location of a new showroom proposed to be opened by the company.
13. Draft a report on the charter of demand submitted by the workers' union of your company.
14. Draft a report for submission to the Directors of your company on the agitation of the workmen for a higher percentage of bonus and threat for strike by workmen.
15. Draft a report to the Board of Directors on the recent trend of sales and immediate need for advertising compaign.
16. Draft a report to the Managing Director on the nature and extent of damages caused by fire to the factory and indicate the means for carrying on business during re-building of the factory.
17. Draft the minutes of the First Board Meeting of a Public Limited Company.
18. Draft the minutes of proceedings of the 10th Annual General Meeting of the shareholders of ABC Co. Ltd.
19. Prepare a draft minutes of the Statutory Meeting of a Company.
20. Draft the minutes of an Extra-ordinary General Meeting of a Company.
21. Draft the minutes of the Annual General Meeting of a Co-operative Society.
22. Draft a general offer on behalf of the manufacturer of Raju Electric Fan announcing the introduction of a new model.
23. Draft an enquiry for the supply of uniforms to the peons and bearers of a large commercial establishment.
24. A firm of stationery supplier submits quotation for stationery articles in reply to an enquiry from a large office. Draft the letter of quotation.

25. Draft a letter inviting quotation for purchasing computer in designing your New Computer Centre of a college.
26. Draft an order for supply of computers as per quotation.
27. You have received an order for supply of computers. Draft a letter informing your customer that there will be delay in execution of the order as the brands asked for supply are no longer in the stock at present. Assure your customer that the delivery would be made within a week.
28. Draft a letter to your customer requesting him to extend time for execution of order stating suitable reasons.
29. Draft a letter to the supplier cancelling an order due to failure to supply goods within a specified period.
30. Draft a letter to your supplier complaining against the supply of inferior quality of goods and requesting him to take back the consignment at his own cost.
31. Draft a letter making an enquiry about the financial standing of a firm from a business concern.
32. Draft a favourable reply by a bank to a letter of enquiry about the financial standing of a firm.
33. Write a letter of recommendation for a business friend who wants to establish new business.
34. Draft a letter to the Insurance Company intimating the destruction of insured goods by fire at your business premises and requesting to arrange for an early survey and settlement of the claim.
35. Write a letter to the Manager of a Bank requesting for a Bank Loan.
36. Draft a letter to your bank requesting them to grant overdraft facilities for your business.
37. Draft a letter to your customer reminding him about a debt still remaining unpaid.
38. Write a letter to your banker complaining against delay in preparing Bank Satement and excess debit of Bank charges.
39. Draft a letter to a company on behalf of a Bank Manager requesting not to overdraw without prior arrangement.
40. Write an application for the post of a personal assistant.
41. Draft an application for the post of a clerical job for data entry with cover letter and resume.
42. Draft an application for the post of a Company Secretary with cover letter and curriculum vitae.

QUESTIONS OF THE EXAMINATIONS OF CALCUTTA UNIVERSITY

2005

Business Management—General

First Paper

[Group-I]

Full Marks : 100

Group—A

1. Answer any **five** questions : 2×5

   (a) Mention four principles of Management as prescribed by Fayol.

   (b) What is 'Organising'?

   (c) What do you mean by 'Scientific Management'?

   (d) What is Line Organisation?

   (e) Draw a diagram showing Maslow's Need Hierarchy theory.

   (f) What do you mean by the Grape-vine as a communication system?

   (g) What is meant by Control?

   (h) Mention four techniques of financial control.

2. Answer any **three** questions :

   (a) Explain the process of delegation of authority. 8

   (b) "Planning and forecasting are not synonymous."—Discuss. 8

   (c) Write a note on Max Weber's theory of management. 8

   (d) "Co-ordination is the essence of management."—Discuss. 8

   (e) Compare between oral communication and written communication. 8

3. Answer any **one** question :

   (a) Explain briefly the concept of leadership. Describe the style of leadership introduced by Tannenbaun and Schmidt. 6+10

   (b) (i) Explain the process of communication with a diagram. 6+10

   (ii) Analyse four barriers to effective communication.

Group—B

4. Answer any **five** questions : 2×5

   (a) Define Marketing Management.

   (b) Mention the major elements of Marketing mix.

   (c) What is Branding?

   (d) Explain the concept of skim the cream pricing.

   (e) What is window-display?

   (f) What do you mean by Salesmanship?

   (g) What are the evils of Private Distribution System in India.

   (h) What is Online-marketing?

5. Answer any **one** question :

(a) Compare between the Customer-oriented marketing and the Sales-oriented marketing. 5

(b) "Packaging is an aid to advertising."—Discuss. 5

6. Answer any **one** question :

(a) Discuss the functions and responsibilities of a marketing manager. 10

(b) What is product life cycle? Explain the different stages of product life cycle with the help of a diagram. 10

Group—C

7. Answer any **five** questions : 2×5

(a) Define Human Resource Management.

(b) What is Recruitment?

(c) What do you mean by 'Placement' of an employee?

(d) State the advantages of merit-basis promotion?

(e) What is Job-evaluation?

(f) Define Industrial Relation.

(g) Explain the importance of Labour Welfare.

(h) Mention the weaknesses of Trade Unions in India.

8. Answer any **one** question :

(a) Distinguish between performance appraisal and job-evaluation. 5

(b) "Industrial discipline is an effective tool for personnel motivation and morale."—Discuss. 5

9. Answer any **one** question :

(a) "Of all the tasks of management, managing the human element is the central and most important task."—Examine the statement. 10

(b) What is man-power planning? Discuss the different methods of man-power planning. 2+8

2006

Group—A

1. Answer any **ten** questions : 2×10

(a) Define the term 'Management'.

(b) Is management universal? Comment.

(c) What is 'Hawthorne Effect'?

(d) What are the limitations of Max Weber's theory?

(e) Write two differences between the theories propounded by Taylor and Fayol.

(f) What is 'Theory Y'?

(g) Is a manager always a leader? Justify your answer.

(h) What do you mean by 'Span of Management'?

(i) What is 'Feedforward' Control?

(j) Draw a diagram showing 'Line and Staff' relationship in an organisation.

(k) Can an organisation work without delegation of authority? Give reasons for your answer.

(l) Mention the basic Marketing functions.

(m) Discuss, in brief, the nature of Human Resource Management.

(n) State the main objectives of Finance Management.

(o) Why 'Operations Management' is important?

Group—B

Answer any **six** questions 6×8

2. Explain the basic Principles of Scientific Management.
3. Discuss different types of plans.
4. Explain the process of control.
5. Discuss the basic principles for effective co-ordination in an organisation.
6. Between formal and informal communication, which one is more important? Explain why?
7. What is marketing mix? Explain its components.
8. Discuss the functions of a human resource manager.
9. Explain the main barriers to communication.
10. Discuss, in brief, the different forms of organisation structure.
11. Discuss the nature of Operations Management.

Group—C

Answer any **two** questions

12. (a) Discuss the need for forecasting in planning. 6+10

(b) Discuss the major techniques of forecasting.

13. Explain Maslow's theory of motivation with criticism. 16

14. (a) What do you mean by 'Leadership Style'? 6+10

(b) Discuss the theory of 'Managerial Grid' as propounded by Blake and Mouton with suitable diagram.

2007

Group—A

1. Answer any **ten** questions : 2×10

(a) When is 'Scientific Management'?

(b) Why management is important to an organisation?

(c) What do you mean by Planning?

(d) Define forecasting.

(e) What are the main features of a sound organisation?

(f) What is meant by delegation of authority?

(g) Mention two features of motivation.

(h) What are the elements of leadership?

(i) Mention the advantages of formal communication.

(j) What is relationship between planning and control?

(k) What do you mean by control?

(l) Mention four principles of co-ordination.

(m) What is marketing?

(n) What is the objective of human resource management?

(o) How many types of capital are there in a business? What are those capital?

Group—B

Answer any **six** questions 8×6

2. Distinguish between planning, organising and control.
3. State planning process.
4. Explain Herzberg's Two-factor theory of motivation.
5. "First task of management is to establish an effective communication system."—Explain.
6. State the importance of co-ordination.
7. Expalin the social significance of management.
8. State the features of operations management.
9. Discuss the importance of financial management.
10. "Objective of human resource management is to ensure maximum return on human capital investment."—Explain.
11. Discuss the importance of modern marketing.

Group—C

Answer any **two** questions

12. Make a comparative study on the management theories of F.W. Taylor and Henri Fayol. 16
13. (a) "Organising is a process."—Disucss. 6

    (b) State the advantages and limitations of line and staff organisation. 10
14. State the tools and techniques of an effective control system. 16

2008

Group—A

1. Answer any **ten** questions : 2×10

(a) Is management profession?

(b) Mention two features of forecasting.

(c) Why management is universal?

(d) Define organising.

(e) What is decentralisation?

(f) Mention two factors of motivation.

(g) What are the reasons for developing informal organisation?

(h) What is communication?

(i) What are the characteristics of democratic or participative leadership?

(j) Define co-ordination.

(k) What do you mean by span of control?

(l) What is the difference between sales and marketing?

(m) Define operations management.

(n) What is derivative plan?

(o) What do you mean by human resource management?

Group—B

Answer any **six** questions 8×6

2. Explain the major principles of scientific management.
3. State the advantages and disadvantages of functional organisation structure.
4. "Just as authority is the key to the manager's job, delegation is the key to organisation."—Explain.
5. Discuss different types of communication.
6. Discuss the process of control.
7. Enumerate the features of line and staff organisation structure.
8. Discuss the principles of co-ordination.
9. State the nature of human resource management.
10. State the importance of operations management.
11. "Functions of financial management are raising of fund, investment planning of fund and control for maximisation of wealth of an organisation."—Discuss.

Group—C

Answer any **two** questions 16×2

12. Briefly discuss different types of plan. 16
13. What do you mean by qualities of leadership? Discuss different styles of leadership. 4+12
14. State McGregor's theory of motivation. What are the limitations of this theory? 12+4

2009

Group—A

1. Answer any **ten** questions : 2×10

(a) What is Scientific Management?

(b) What do you mean by Planning in Management?

(c) Explain the term 'organisational structure'.

(d) Mention the elements in the process of delegation of authority.

(e) What is motivation?

(f) Mention any four qualities of a good leadership.

(g) What do you mean by Control in Management?

(h) Mention any four functions of financial management.

(i) What is decoding in communication process?

(j) Define Grape-vine.

(k) What is break-even analysis?

(l) What do you mean by production planning?

(m) Mention four principles of co-ordination.

(n) Show two differences between Human Resource Management and Personnel Management.

(o) Explain dividend decision as financial function.

Group—B

Answer any **six** questions 8×6

2. Explain why management has become so important for modern business.
3. Discuss the importance of planning in the modern business world.
4. Explain the importance of leadership in management.
5. Make a comparison of the theories of motivation of Maslow and Herzberg.
6. What are the pre-requisites of effective managerial control?
7. Explain, in brief, the various techniques of co-ordination.
8. Narrate the importance of human resource management.
9. Make a brief discussion on the functions of financial Management.
10. State, in brief, the functions of marketing management.
11. Explain the features of operations management.

Group—C

Answer any **two** questions

12. Discuss the general principles of management according to Henry Fayol. 6+10
13. Define forecasting. Explain the importance of forecasting. Write a note on the relation between planning and forecasting. 2+10+4
14. Mention the different barriers of communication. What steps can be taken to overcome these barriers? 6+10

2010

Group—A

1. Answer any **ten** questions : 2×10

(a) What is 'universality of management'?
(b) What is scientific management?
(c) What is 'man-power planning'?
(d) Define 'Forecasting'.
(e) Define 'authority'.
(f) What do you mean by 'decentralisation'?
(g) Mention the external environmental factors of a business.
(h) Mention the levels of the Hierarchy of Needs Theory of Maslow.
(i) What do you mean by 'societal marketing'?
(j) What is 'over-capitalisation'?
(k) What is 'branding'?
(l) Define 'staffing'.
(m) What do you mean by 'placement' of an employee?
(n) What is 'sales promotion'?
(o) What is 'professional management'?

Group—B

Answer any **six** questions

2. Define 'management'. Explain the main features of management. 2+6
3. Who are the top-level managerial people in a large size company? Using a diagram discuss the main functions of the top-level management. 3+5
4. What do you mean by the Human Relations Approach to management? Explain the principles of the Human Relations Approach. 3+5
5. Discuss the importance of decision-making in management. 8
6. Explain the features of a healthy organisation. 8
7. "Motivation plays a positive role in management."—Discuss. 8
8. "Human Resource Management is the most important function of management."—Explain. 8
9. "Marketing goes beyond selling."—Discuss. 8
10. Explain the concepts of 'maximisation of profit' and 'maximisation of wealth'. 8
11. Write a note on the basic principles of Operations Management. 8

Group—C

Answer any **two** questions

12. Define organisation. What do you mean by 'organisation structures'? Discuss the importance of organisation structure. 2+6+8
13. Narrate the differences between 'management' and 'leadership'. Write a note on leadership styles. 6+10
14. "Co-ordination is the essence of management."—Discuss. Discuss the principles of effective co-ordination. 8+8

2011

Group—A

1. Answer any **ten** Questions : 2×10

(a) Define 'Management'.

(b) State any four of Fayol's 'Principles of Management'.

(c) What is 'Master Planning'?

(d) What do you mean by 'Line Organisation'?

(e) State two factors of motivation.

(f) Define 'Leading'.

(g) What is 'Formal Communication'?

(h) What do you mean by 'Budgetary Control'?

(i) Define 'Co-ordination'.

(j) Define 'Financial Management'.

(k) Define 'Human Resource Management'.

(l) State four importance of Marketing.

(m) Define 'Operations Management'.

(n) Give the idea of Communication.

(o) What do you mean by 'Span of Control'?

Group—B

Answer any **six** questions 8×6

2. Discuss the contribution of Follett in the field of management.
3. Explain the importance of planning in modern business world.
4. Discuss the features of a sound organisation.
5. Explain the assumptions of theory X and theory Y as propounded by McGregor.
6. Explain the Leadership model of Tannenbaum and Schmidt.
7. Discuss the importance of communication in business.
8. Discuss, in brief, the steps involved in controlling.
9. Discuss the nature and importance of Financial Management.
10. Discuss the features of marketing.
11. "Human resource is the most valuable resource in an organisation."—Explain.

Group—C

Answer any **two** Questions

12. Briefly discuss the principles of management of Taylor. 16
13. What do you mean by planning in management? Discuss the universal steps involved in a planning process. 2+14
14. How many types of Leadership may be there? Discuss the advantages and disadvantages of various types of Leadership. 4+12

2011

(New Syllabus)

Principles and Practice of Management and Business Communication—General

Third Paper

[C—13-G]

Full Marks : 100

MODULE I

Principles and Practice of Management

Group—A

1. Answer the following questions : **2×5**

(a) Define 'Management'.

(b) Mention levels of management with a diagram.

Or,

State two managerial tasks.

(c) Briefly explain the importance of 'planning'.

(d) Give an idea of 'policy' as a plan.

Or,

Define 'forecasting'.

(e) Why is co-ordination treated as essence of management?

Or,

State the principles of 'Co-ordination'.

Group—B

2. Answer the following questions : **4×4**

(a) Give an idea of the 'Planning Premises'.

(b) Draw the relationship between 'line' and 'staff' with a diagram and examples.

(c) Distinguish between 'Centralisation' and 'Decentralisation'.

Or,

What factors should be taken into consideration for determining the 'Span of Management' of an organisation?

(d) Mention the steps in control process with a diagram.

Or,

Briefly discuss 'budgetary control'.

Group—C

3. Answer the following questions : **8×3**

(a) Discuss, in brief, fourteen principles of management as propounded by Henri Fayol.

Or,

Highlight the different aspects of the Behavioural Science Approach.

(b) Elaborate the needs in Maslow's Hierarchy of Needs theory.

Or,

Explain 'Dissatisfiers' and 'Motivators' in Herzberg's theory of Motivation.

(c) Narrate, in detail, the importance and types of leadership.

MODULE II

Business Communication

Group—A

4. Answer the following questions : 2×5

(a) What does the term 'Business Communication' imply?

Or,

Mention any two components of 'Business Communication'.

(b) What do you mean by 'Feedback' in the process of communication?

(c) What is 'Tele-conferencing'?

Or,

Why is FAX essential in modern office?

(d) Corporate Communication has certain characteristics.—Mention two of these characteristics.

Or,

What is meant by 'Communication Network'?

(e) What is meant by 'Conflict Resolution'?

Group—B

5. Answer the following questions : 4×5

(a) Explain the major categories of barriers to communication.

Or,

Briefly expalin the principles of effective communication.

(b) Distinguish between 'formal communication' and 'informal communication'.

Or,

Do you think the idea of 'grapevine' is positive in nature? Give reasons for your answer.

(c) Write a short note on emergence of communication technology.

Or,

Discuss the advantages and disadvantages of e-mail.

(d) Discuss the advantages of video-conferencing.

(e) Write short notes on 'horizontal communication' and 'vertical communication'.

Group—C

6. Answer the following questions : 10×2

(a) Draft a notice alongwith agenda of an Annual General meeting of a Public Limited Company.

(b) Write a letter to the manager of a nationalised bank seeking a loan for a small-scale enterprise.

Or,

Write a letter, seeking quotation of stationery items, to suppliers.

Business Communication—General

2005

Group—A

1. Answer any **five** questions : 2×5

(a) What do you understand by Oral and Written Communication?

(b) What are the objectives of Business Communication?

(c) What do you understand by Intra-group conflict?

(d) What is Group Cohesiveness?

(e) What is Corporate Communication?

(f) What is Grape-vine Communication?

(g) What is Productivity?

Group—B

2. Answer any **two** questions : 10×2

(a) Define Communication. Discuss the essentials of good communication system. 3+7

(b) What do you understand by Tools of communication? Discuss the means or tools of increasing Business Productivity through communication. 3+7

(c) What are the objects of emergence of Communication Technology in business? 10

Or,

What is meant by Video-Conferencing? Discuss the advantages and disadvantages of Video-Conferencing. 10

Group—C

3. Answer any **two** questions : 10×2

(a) Draft the Notice along with agenda of the First Annual General Meeting of a Public Limited Company.

Or,

Draft a circular announcing the opening of a new showroom of your product in a village area.

(b) Draft the Minutes of the Annual General Meeting of a Private Limited Company.

(c) Draft a letter inviting Quotation for purchasing computer in designing your New Computer Centre of the college.

Or,

Draft a letter to your Bank requesting them to grant overdraft facilities for your business.

2006

Group—A

1. Answer any **five** questions : 2×5

(a) Mention four elements of Communication?

(b) What do you mean by 'Feedback'?

(c) Define Formal Communication.

(d) What is Lateral Communication?

(e) What is Inter-group Conflict?

(f) What is Internet?

(g) Give two essential elements of a notice.

(h) State four features of a good business letter.

Group—B

2. Answer any **two** questions : 10×2

(a) What are the barriers to Communication?

(b) Define Corporate Communication. What are the essentials of its success?

(c) What do you mean by the 'Process of Communication'? State the importance of feedback in the Communication Process.

Or,

Define group cohesiveness. State how the communication helps in developing the group cohesiveness.

Group—C

3. Answer any **two** questions : 10×2

(a) Draft a notice including agenda convening the 15th Annual General Meeting of a Public Limited Company.

Or,

Draft the minutes of the proceedings of the First Board Meeting of XYZ Ltd. where ordinary businesses were transacted.

(b) As a Secretary of a Public Company draft a report for submission to the Board of Directors regarding the need for introducing Computer in the Accounts Department.

(c) Draft a letter to the supplier complaining about the inferior quality of goods delivered and asking him for suitable remedy.

Or,

Mr. X has applied for a dealership from a reputed Company. But Mr. X is quite unknown to the Company. As a Secretary of the Company draft a suitable letter of status enquiry to the Banker of Mr. X regarding his credit-worthiness.

2007

Group—A

1. Answer any **five** questions : 2×5

(a) What are the elements of Communication?

(b) What is Informal Communication?

(c) What is Feedback?

(d) What is Website?

(e) What is Dictaphone?

(f) What is Channel of Communication?

(g) Mention two points of difference between Verbal Communication and Written Communication.

(h) Define Resolution.

Group—B

2. Answer any **two** questions : 10×2

(a) Describe briefly the various steps in a two-way communication process. 10

(b) Discuss the objectives of emergence of Communication Technology in business. 10

(c) What are the different barriers to communication? What steps can be taken to overcome these barriers? 5+5

Or,

What is meant by group cohesiveness? What are the determinants of the degree of group cohesiveness? 10

Group—C

3. Answer any **two** questions : 10×2

(a) Draft a letter to your supplier complaining against supply of inferior quality of goods and requesting him to take back the consignment at his own cost.

Or,

Draft a report on the charter of demands submitted by the Workers' Union of your company.

(b) Draft the notice along with agenda of the Annual General Meeting of a Co-operative Society.

(c) Draft the minutes of the proceedings of the Board Meeting of a Public Limited Company.

Or,

Write a letter requesting for extension of time for supply of goods to your customer.

2008

Group—A

1. Answer any **five** questions : 2×5

(a) What is 'horizontal communication'?

(b) What do you mean by 'encoding'?

(c) What is communication network?

(d) Define minutes.

(e) What is business productivity?

(f) What is intra-group conflict?

(g) State two advantages of formal communication.

(h) What is 'Fax'?

Group—B

2. Answer any **two** questions : 10×2

(a) What is written communication? State its advantages and disadvantages. 2+4+4

(b) What do you understand by the process of communication? Discuss the importance of feedback in the process. 4+6

(c) What is internet? What are its utilities in modern business? 2+8

Or,

What is corporate communication? Discuss the importance of corporate communication. 4+6

Group—C

3. Answer any **two** questions : 10×2

(a) Draft a circular addressing to your customers and dealers announcing the opening of a showroom.

Or,

Draft a report to the Board of Directors on the recent trend of sales and immediate need for advertising campaign.

(b) Draft a notice of the Annual General Meeting of a Club with usual agenda.

(c) Draft the minutes of the Annual General Meeting of a Public Limited Company.

Or,

Draft a letter to the Insurance Company stating the loss of goods by fire and requesting immediate action for the settlement of the claim.

2009

Group—A

1. Answer any **five** questions : 2×5
   (a) What is 'Internal Communication'?
   (b) What is 'Group Cohesiveness'?
   (c) What is 'Grape-vine'?
   (d) Define Resolution.
   (e) State two methods to resolve Conflict.
   (f) What are the factors to be considered in drafting a notice?
   (g) What is Video Conferencing?
   (h) What is Feedback?

Group—B

2. Answer any **two** questions : 10×2
   (a) Discuss the essentials or requisites of a good communication system. 10
   (b) Discuss the means for increasing Business Productivity through communication process. 10
   (c) What is Business Communication? Explain all the elements of Business Communication. 2+8

Group—C

3. Answer any **two** questions : 10×2
   (a) Draft the notice of the 20th Annual General Meeting of a Public Limited Company with usual agenda.
   (b) Write a letter to your Banker complaining against delay in preparing Bank Statement and excess debit of Bank charges.
   (c) Draft a letter to your customer requesting him to extend the time for execution of order stating suitable reasons.

Or,

Draft a letter to your customer reminding him about a debt still remaining unpaid.

2010

Group—A

1. Answer any **five** questions : 2×5
   (a) What is Channel of Communication?
   (b) What is Communication Network?
   (c) What is Business Productivity?

(d) Define Agenda.

(e) What is Inter-group Conflict?

(f) State two disadvantages of Oral Communication.

(g) What is Lateral Communication?

(h) What is Website?

Group—B

2. Answer any **two** questions : 2×10

(a) What are the barriers to communication?

(b) Define Written Communication. Discuss the advantages and disadvantages of Written Communication.

(c) How conflicts can be resolved?

Group—C

3. Answer any **two** questions : 2×10

(a) Draft the notice along with agenda of the First Meeting of the Board of Directors of a Public Limited Company.

(b) As the Secretary of a developing business, draft a report to the Chief Manager stating the advantages of installation of a computerised accounting system in the firm.

(c) Draft a letter to your Bank requesting them to grant overdraft facilities for your business.

2011

Group—A

1. Answer any **five** questions : 2×5

(a) State two objectives of Business Communication.

(b) What is Informal Communication?

(c) What do you mean by Vertical Communication?

(d) What is E-mail?

(e) What is Group Cohesiveness?

(f) What do you mean by 'Video Conferencing'?

(g) Define Resolution.

(h) What are the elements of Communication?

Group—B

2. Answer any **two** questions : 10×2

(a) Discuss the significance of Business Communication.

(b) What is Information Technology? Describe the necessity and importance of Information Technology?

(c) Define Corporate Communication. Discuss the essentials for success of Corporate Communication.

Group—C

3. Answer any **two** questions : 10×2

(a) Draft a notice along with agenda of the 10th Annual General Meeting of a Co-operative Credit Society.

(b) Write a letter to your supplier complaining about inferior quality of goods supplied and claiming suitable remedy for the same.

(c) Draft a report to the Board of Directors as to computerisation of the office works.

2011

(New Syllabus)

Business Communication—General

MODULE II

Group—A

1. Answer the following questions : 2×5

(a) What does the term 'Business Communication' imply?

Or,

Mention any two components of 'Business Communication'.

(b) What do you mean by 'Feedback' in the process of communication?

(c) What is 'Tele-conferencing'?

Or,

Why is FAX essential in modern office?

(d) Corporate Communication has certain characteristics.—Mention two of these characteristics.

Or,

What is meant by 'Communication Network'?

(e) What is meant by 'Conflict Resolution'?

Group—B

2. Answer the following questions : 4×5

(a) Explain the major categories of barriers to communication.
Briefly explain the principles of effective communication.

Or,

(b) Distinguish between 'formal communication' and 'informal communication'.

Or,

Do you think that the idea of 'grapevine' is positive in nature? Give reasons for your answer.

(c) Write a short note on emergence of communication technology.

Or,

Discuss the advantages and disadvantages of e-mail.

(d) Discuss the advantages of video-conferencing.

(e) Write short notes on 'horizontal communication' and 'vertical communication'.

Group—C

3. Answer the following questions : 10×2

(a) Draft a notice along with agenda of an Annual General meeting of a Public Limited Company.

(b) Write a letter to the manager of a nationalised bank seeking a loan for a small-scale enterprise.

Or,

Write a letter seeking quotation of stationery items to suppliers.

2011

(Supplementary)

Business Communication—General

Group—A

1. Answer any **five** questions : 2×5

(a) Mention any two principles of effective communication.

(b) What is grape-vine communication?

(c) What is productivity?

(d) What is intra-group conflict?

(e) Define a 'Notice'.

(f) What is formal communication?

(g) What is an 'Agenda'?

(h) What are the mediums of written communication?

Group—B

2. Answer any **two** questions :

(a) What are the different barriers to communication? What steps can be taken to overcome these barriers? 4+6

(b) Define group cohesiveness. State how the communication help in developing the group cohesiveness? 4+6

(c) What do you understand by verbal communication and written communication? State their features, advantages and disadvantages. 2+2+6

Group—C

3. Answer any **two** questions : 10×2

(a) Draft a notice along with the agenda of the first meeting of the Board of Directors of a Public Limited Company.

(b) Draft the minutes of the proceedings of the Annual General Meeting of a Public Limited Company.

(c) Write a letter requesting for extension of time for supply of goods to your customers.